CLARENDON LAW SERIES

D0238708

CLARENDON LAW SERIES

ATIYAH'S INTRODUCTION TO THE LAW OF CONTRACT

P. S. ATIYAH

*Formerly Professor of English Law in the
University of Oxford*

STEPHEN A. SMITH

*Professor and William Dawson Scholar
McGill University, Canada*

SIXTH EDITION

CLARENDON PRESS · OXFORD
2005

OXFORD
UNIVERSITY PRESS

Great Clarendon Street, Oxford OX2 6DP

Oxford University Press is a department of the University of Oxford.
It furthers the University's objective of excellence in research, scholarship,
and education by publishing worldwide in

Oxford New York

Auckland Cape Town Dar es Salaam Hong Kong Karachi
Kuala Lumpur Madrid Melbourne Mexico City Nairobi
New Delhi Shanghai Taipei Toronto

With offices in

Argentina Austria Brazil Chile Czech Republic France Greece
Guatemala Hungary Italy Japan Poland Portugal Singapore
South Korea Switzerland Thailand Turkey Ukraine Vietnam

Oxford is a registered trade mark of Oxford University Press
in the UK and in certain other countries

Published in the United States
by Oxford University Press Inc., New York

British Library Cataloguing in Publication Data
Data available

Library of Congress Cataloging in Publication Data
Data available

Typeset by RefineCatch Limited, Bungay, Suffolk
Printed in Great Britain
on acid-free paper by
Antony Rowe Ltd, Chippenham, Wiltshire

ISBN 0–19–924941–5 978–0–19–924941–1

1 3 5 7 9 10 8 6 4 2

Prefaces to the sixth edition

Successful law books often change a good deal over their lives. The first edition of this book was published in 1961 and the fifth edition in 1995. Anyone who cares to compare these editions will see major differences between the two, much of which has nothing to do with actual changes in the law. Many of the changes in the book were the result of increasing sophistication in the law courses which university students were expected to master, of an increasing emphasis on policies and reasons underlying the law, and of my own desire to relate the teaching of law to business and consumer realities on the ground.

When I invited Professor Stephen Smith to assume responsibility for the sixth edition he told me that he would like to develop future editions along new lines, some of which I had already initiated, such as in particular, a greater emphasis on the underlying theory of contract law. Although I saw and commented extensively on the first draft which Professor Smith produced, this edition is in the result his responsibility, and it naturally reflects his own interests and wishes as to the way contract law should be taught. Law teachers and students familiar with the fifth edition may at first sight find this edition differs more from that one than they might have expected. But this is only partly due to the change in editorial responsibility: it is also obviously partly due to the long gap between the fifth and sixth editions, partly to some re-arrangement of the material, and partly to the way in which the subject itself has tended to change in academic thinking and writing. The outcome of Professor Smith's labours is now presented to university teachers and students in the hope that this book can continue to do service for many years to come.

P.S. ATIYAH

29 June 2005

Patrick Atiyah's *Introduction to the Law of Contract* is rightly regarded as a landmark in English legal scholarship. The first five editions of this book not only introduced countless students to the law of contract; they also changed the way that lawyers, judges, and academics thought about the law. It is a testament to the book's influence that many of the arguments and ideas found in earlier editions are now considered commonplace, even traditional, although they were anything but commonplace at the time. The same is true of the book's general approach to legal knowledge: in the *Introduction*, as in all of his writings, Patrick Atiyah stressed the importance of questioning orthodox dogmas, of looking past what judges and legislators said they were doing to what they were *actually* doing. Again, this methodology is now well accepted; much of the credit must go to Atiyah.

It was with some trepidation that I agreed to prepare a new edition of the *Introduction*. This was not merely from fear of tampering with a classic; Patrick Atiyah's intimate and expansive familiarity with English law, his broad historical knowledge, his readiness to debunk traditional dogma, his skill in drawing connections among apparently unrelated parts of the law, and his ability to bring all this together in a fluid, accessible writing style are matched by few legal academics, and certainly not by the present author.

In preparing the sixth edition, I have, of course, incorporated the changes in contract law that have taken place since the previous edition in 1994. There have been many, particularly in the legislative field, most notably the Unfair Terms in Consumer Contracts Regulations 1999 and the Contracts (Rights of Third Parties) Act 1999. But as has already been suggested, the *Introduction* has never been a mere description of contract law rules and decisions. Past editions of the book are remarkable for their critical and argumentative approach, for engaging readers in debates about the meaning and value of the law. Alongside descriptions of how the law *is* explained by judges, by lawyers, and in other textbooks, Atiyah presented arguments as to how the law *should be* explained, often suggesting radical reinterpretations of current orthodoxies. Significant space was also devoted to discussing *why* contract law is the way it is, whether it can be justified, and, if not, what should be done to improve it. I have attempted to follow in this tradition. Alongside the discussion of recent cases and legislation, new arguments dealing with the explanation, justification, and reform of the law have been introduced. Inevitably, some of Patrick Atiyah's own arguments have been revised, either in substance or in language, tone, or emphasis. The changes introduced by a new editor are never completely neutral, but this is especially true in the case of a text like the *Introduction*. In making these changes, I have taken reassurance in the fact that Atiyah himself was never afraid to revise the book's theoretical arguments. More generally, Patrick Atiyah was always ready to challenge the received or orthodox position—even in cases where that position was one that he had introduced himself.

The most visible changes to the 6th edition concern the arrangements and headings of chapters and sub-chapters. These changes no doubt reflect, at least in part, the present editor's interests (some might say obsession) with classificatory issues, but the intent was also to reflect various changes in contract law teaching and scholarship that have taken place in recent years. Of particular importance were developments in unjust enrichment law and scholarship and, related to this, general developments in the law and scholarship concerning the relations between contractual and (to adopt a useful civilian term) extra-contractual obligations. Incorporating these developments led to significant re-arrangements, especially as regards the materials discussed in Chapters 2 and 3. I took solace, however, in the fact that the changes reinforced the emphasis in this section of the book on the significance of non-voluntary obligations in contractual settings and the inadequacy of traditional law and theory in dealing with such obligations. Indeed, many of the recent developments in tort and unjust enrichment law originated in the need to provide a better explanation for just such obligations. This is one of many instances in which the success of previous editions of the *Introduction* may be said to have led to changes in the current edition.

In preparing this edition, I have been assisted by a number of student researchers at McGill University: Jacob Adamski, Laura Buckingham, Reuben Kobulnik, Adam Kramer, Jason MacLean, and Bryan Thomas. Special thanks go to Toby Moneit, Joshua Parr, and Jeff Roberts. My colleague William Foster read and offered helpful comments on six of the book's chapters. Financial assistance was provided by a grant from the Social Science and Humanities Research Council of Canada.

STEPHEN A. SMITH

Outline Contents

Detailed Contents

Table of Cases

Table of Statutes

This Table includes UK legislation, followed by European legislation and Treaties and then Foreign legislation

European legislation

United States

Table of Statutory Instruments

This Table consists of UK Regulations followed by European

European Regulations

I

Introduction

I. THE CLASSIFICATION OF CONTRACT LAW

THE law of contract is part of the law of obligations, that is to say, it is concerned with obligations that people owe to others as a result of the relations and transactions in which they become involved. Broadly, this is a part of private law, in the sense that obligations of a public character, such as constitutional or political obligations, are neither treated by the law nor thought of by lawyers as part of the law of obligations. Public bodies are, it is true, subject to the law of obligations; for example they can enter into contracts and thus submit themselves to the ordinary law of contract. But the broader duties of such bodies fall outside the scope of the law of obligations as commonly understood. Nor is the criminal law conceived by lawyers as part of the law of obligations. The criminal law imposes legal duties on citizens that are obligations in a sense. But they are not owed to anyone in particular, and their enforcement normally rests with the police and other public bodies. By contrast the law of obligations deals primarily with duties owed by individuals to other individuals, and these duties are generally enforceable only by the persons to whom they are owed. A victim of a crime can complain to the police, who may prosecute the offender. But victims of a breach of a private obligation, such as a breach of contract, must enforce their rights in the courts without the assistance of any public authority.

Obligations arise from a variety of sources and can be classified in various ways. For example, they can be classified according to the social relationships from which they arise. Thus one can distinguish between obligations owed to members of one's family, obligations between neighbours, obligations arising from an employment relationship, and so on. But the law has traditionally treated the basic distinction as that between obligations that are self-imposed, that is to say, obligations arising from an agreement, promise, or other undertaking, and obligations that are externally imposed. Broadly speaking, the law of contract is understood as that part of the law that deals with obligations that are self-imposed. The main parts of the law dealing with externally imposed or 'extra-contractual' obligations are the law of torts (which deals with obligations not to interfere with another's person, property, or liberty) and the law of unjust enrichment (which deals with obligations to restore money or to pay for non-contracted-for benefits).

While the above distinctions play an important role in how lawyers think about the law, they are not clear-cut. Indeed, one of the central questions when thinking about the law of obligations is whether the distinction just drawn between contractual obligations and extra-contractual obligations should be used at all. For example, a *breach* of contract (as opposed to the events that give rise to a contract) is normally regarded as a legal wrong, and so may plausibly be described as a tort ('tort' being another word for 'wrong'). More importantly, many of the obligations recognized by the law of contract cannot be realistically thought of as self-imposed (equally, matters of consent or agreement are by no means irrelevant in the law of tort or unjust enrichment). In a typical consumer sale, for example, the vendor is subject to a wide range of legislatively imposed obligations concerning the quality of the goods, guarantees, and so on. Some scholars have gone so far as to suggest that even in its core applications the law of contract is similar to the law of tort in being fundamentally concerned with externally imposed obligations. In particular, it is sometimes argued that contractual obligations are best understood not as self-imposed obligations, but as obligations to ensure that those whom we induce to rely upon us (by a promise or otherwise) are not left worse-off. And even scholars who do not explain contractual obligations generally on this basis often adopt a reliance-based explanation of particular contract law rules. For example, the rule that the meaning of a contractual statement is established on the basis of how a reasonable listener would understand it rather than according to the meaning the speaker intended to convey is often explained in this way.

Two other classificatory matters should be mentioned at this point. First, even if it is accepted that there is an important difference between contractual duties and extra-contractual duties, it is clear that a single set of facts can sometimes give rise to both contractual and extra-contractual liability. For example, if a vendor fails without good reason to deliver contracted-for goods, the purchaser can normally go to court and obtain an order that the vendor pay compensation equal to the financial value of the vendor's promise to deliver. This is a contractual claim. In addition, if the purchaser has paid in advance for the goods, an alternative claim for restitution of that payment, that is to say, to get back one's money, is usually available. This is a claim in unjust enrichment. Similarly, a negligent failure to provide a contracted-for service (e.g. financial advice) will sometimes give claimants the choice of a claim in contract (for compensation for failure to obtain the promised level of service) or a claim in tort (for losses caused by the negligent provision of services).

Secondly, the generally accepted idea that there exists an English law of *contract*, as opposed to a law of *contracts*, must be treated carefully. Admittedly, the common law, unlike the civil law, does not formally recognize different categories of contracts. In principle, all contracts are subject to the same set of rules. But in practice the common law's approach is not that different from the civil law. Contracts of sale, employment, insurance, agency, partnership, security, and many others have long been subject to special category-specific rules. Indeed, the general rules now constitute a relatively small part of the law of contract. Few contracts are not subject to same category-based special rules, and some contracts (e.g. employment contracts) are almost entirely governed by such rules. Furthermore, it is clear that other, less formal distinctions play an important role in practice. In particular (as we shall see in more detail in subsequent chapters), the distinctions between executory (unperformed) and executed (performed) contracts, commercial and non-commercial contracts, and one-off or 'discrete' contracts (e.g. the typical sale) and long-term or 'relational' contracts (e.g. a franchise contract or a contract of employment) are highly significant in some areas of contract law.

2. THE JUSTIFICATION FOR CONTRACT LAW

Alongside the classificatory questions just considered, a second set of questions about contract law focuses on justificatory ('normative') issues. The most basic question of this kind is the following: what, if anything, is the justification for contract law? Assuming that contracts are voluntary undertakings, why should the law enforce such undertakings? Stated differently, on what basis is it legitimate for the state, acting through the courts, to sanction individuals for breaking contracts? Why lend the state's support to what is an essentially private complaint?

Virtually all societies have evolved laws for the enforcement of contracts, so it is no surprise that most commentators believe that, while certain aspects of the law may pose difficulties, in broad terms the law of contract is justifiable. More specifically, two kinds of justifications are typically given for the law of contract. The first, which is associated with 'economic' and other broadly 'utilitarian' approaches to law, justifies contract law on the basis that it facilitates mutually beneficial exchanges, and so promotes overall social welfare or social 'wealth' (broadly defined). The underlying idea is that where two parties freely agree on a contract involving, say, a simple exchange of money for goods, the seller does so because he thinks he will be better off with the money than with the goods, and the buyer does so because she prefers the goods to the money. Both parties thus emerge from the exchange 'better off' (in one sense) than they were before, and since society's wealth is made up of the total wealth of its members, even a simple exchange of this kind can improve social wealth. In short, contract law (and the officials needed to enforce the law) is a justified use of the state's resources because it helps everyone to become better off.

Exchanges, of course, need not involve contracts—at least if by contracts we mean arrangements in which one or more persons promise or agree to do something in the future. A simple barter or other simultaneous exchange, such as takes place at a supermarket checkout, where the customers unload their trolleys and hand over their money, typically does not involve a promise or agreement. In principle, such exchanges might therefore be regulated entirely by property law rules (specifying when the transfer is consensual, and thus valid), tort law rules (specifying when a transferor is liable for providing a defective good or making a false representation), and unjust enrichment law rules (specifying when a transferred benefit must be returned to the transferor). From an economic perspective, the primary reason a law of contract is needed is that most exchanges of any complexity cannot be performed simultaneously. One or both parties will have to perform in the future, which means that the other party has to have confidence that she will perform. Suppose that I want a special machine made to order for my factory. A manufacturer could make the machine, and then sell the finished product to me in a simultaneous exchange of machine for cash. But the manufacturer is likely to be worried that I might change my mind at the last minute, leaving him with a machine that is difficult to sell. I might also worry that the manufacturer will change his mind, and decide not to make the machine. Admittedly, there are many reasons aside from the law that each of us might keep to our agreement, such as our interests in our reputation or simply our sense of morality. Nonetheless, it is clear that the risk of non-performance will sometimes dissuade people from entering otherwise beneficial deferred exchanges. It is because of this risk that a law of contract is needed. The fundamental role of contract law, in the economic theory now being considered, is to facilitate the making and performing of deferred exchanges. The law fulfils this role in many ways, but the most fundamental is by providing remedies for breaches of contract, either in the form of orders that breaching parties perform or orders that they pay damages.

Thus interpreted, contract law's essential purpose is to secure cooperation in human behaviour, and particularly in exchange. In sophisticated modern societies this cooperation has led to a massive and elaborate system of credit—and 'credit' is simply another word for 'trust' or 'reliance'. In the simplest sort of case, where businesses provide goods or services on credit to consumers, they trust or rely on the consumer to pay, and in the meantime they allow the consumers to have the goods. Generally, the consumers will ultimately pay, but if they fail to do so some sanction is needed: the law of contract provides that sanction. So contract law ultimately provides the backing needed to support the whole institution of credit. A moment's reflection is enough to show to what extent this is true not only in commercial matters, but in all walks of life. The value of consumers' bank accounts, their right to occupy their houses if rented or mortgaged, their employment, their insurance, their shareholdings, and many other matters of vital importance to them, all depend on the fact that the law of contract will enable them to realise their rights. In the striking phrase of Roscoe Pound, 'Wealth, in a commercial age, is made up largely of promises.'[1]

The second general justification that is commonly given for the law of contract can be described more quickly. The individualist or 'moral' justification focuses not on the social benefits of contracting, but on the rights and duties of individual contracting parties. According to this view, when courts order that contracts be performed, the reason is that the defendants have duties, *owed to the claimants* (not society), to do what they contracted to do. And when courts order that damages be paid, the reason is not merely to encourage future contracting or to bring about any other social benefit, but to remedy the injustice caused by the defendant having infringed the claimant's rights. In this view, the payment of damages reflects the idea that the defendant has *wronged* the claimant, and so must repair the harmful consequences of that wrong. Damages correct the injustice *to the individual claimant* caused by the breach. Of course, the defenders of this view do not deny that contracts are socially beneficial, and that contract law facilitates the making of contracts. But they regard these advantages merely as side-effects of an institution whose primary purpose is to ensure that justice is done between individuals.

The economic and moral justifications each provide a plausible justification for the general institution of contract law and, as we shall see in later chapters, for many specific contract law rules. It seems plausible to suppose, therefore, that the best overall justification for the law of contract combines each of these accounts. The idea that contract law is justified on two grounds—an economic ground and a moral ground—is indeed a common conclusion. And as a matter of history, it is clear that lawmakers have been influenced by both grounds (and many others as well). But it is worth noting that many contract scholars are uncomfortable defending a 'mixed' justification of this kind. The reason is straightforward: the two justifications have opposite starting points. The economic view supposes that society's interests take precedence over those of the individual, while the moral view supposes the opposite. A justification for contract law that simultaneously adopts both justifications thus might be thought to raise as many questions as it answers.

3. THE LIMITS OF CONTRACT LAW

The moral and economic theories just described suggest answers to the most fundamental justificatory or normative question about contract law: why give legal enforcement to private agreements?[2] But there is another normative

---

[1] *Introduction to the Philosophy of Law* (reprinted New Haven, 1961), 236.

[2] The distinction between an agreement and a promise (which is discussed in Chapter 3) is not important for present purposes; in this chapter, contracts are generally described as 'agreements'.

question about contract law that is almost as important: Why are certain kinds of agreements *not* enforced? Why, in other words, are there limits to freedom of contract?

It has never been doubted, of course, that there are certain categories of agreements that should not be enforced. In particular, it has never been doubted that courts should refuse to enforce agreements that involve illegal acts (e.g. agreements to sell prohibited drugs), agreements procured by unlawful means (e.g. agreements procured by fraud or a threat to commit a criminal act), agreements involving minors or the mentally incapacitated, and agreements made in social or domestic settings. This debate about the proper limits of freedom of contract is about whether it is proper for the law to refuse to enforce agreements for *other* kinds of reasons. More specifically, the question is whether courts should take into account factors such as: the perceived moral or social value of a contracted-for activity (e.g. paid-for surrogacy); the alternatives available to the contracting parties (e.g. where one party is a monopolist); the intelligence, sophistication, and independence of the contracting parties (e.g. where the contract arises from a door-to-door sale to an unsophisticated consumer); the fact that circumstances have changed since the contract was made (e.g. the cost of a manufacturer's raw materials have tripled); and, perhaps most importantly, the basic fairness of contractual terms.[3] Under a strict application of the classical notion of freedom of contract none of these factors should matter—but the courts and legislature have never adopted this position.

There are three main techniques that courts and legislatures have used to limit freedom of contract. The first, which focuses on the *procedures* for making contracts, is to expand the excuses available to defendants beyond the traditional (and relatively narrow) excuses of duress, misrepresentation, and incapacity. A recent example is the rule that guarantors are not liable on their guarantees if they were given as a result of the principle debtor's wrongdoing (e.g. undue influence) in circumstances in which the creditor should have been aware that this might happen and where the creditor failed to take reasonable steps to prevent it happening.[4] This rule effectively places creditors under positive duties to assist certain classes of guarantors. A second recent example is section 4 of the Consumer Protection (Cancellation of Contracts away from Business Premises) Regulations 1987, which gives consumers in cases of 'doorstep sales' a seven-day 'cooling off' period in which to change their minds. Overall, this first technique has been used relatively little in English law. In particular, and despite the efforts of Lord Denning,[5] English

---

[3] The excuse of 'mistake' is deliberately left out of this list—and the previous list—because its relation to freedom of contract is highly controversial: below, 175–178.

[4] *Barclays Bank plc v. O'Brien* [1994] 1 AC 180.

[5] *Lloyds Bank v. Bundy* [1975] 1 QB 326.

law has never recognized a general principle holding that contracts procured by exploitative or 'unconscionable' behaviour are unenforceable.

The second, more important technique by which freedom of contract has been limited is through rules that regulate the *content* of contracts. Broadly speaking, such rules operate by implying terms into specific categories of contracts or by prohibiting certain kinds of terms. An important distinction must be drawn in this regard between rules that imply mandatory or 'non-waivable' terms and rules that imply non-mandatory or 'default' terms. The latter, which are now found primarily in legislation, apply only insofar as the parties do not stipulate otherwise. For example, Article IV of the Carriage of Goods By Sea Act 1971 describes a long list of situations in which carriers are not responsible for the loss or damage of goods, while Article VI of the same Act makes explicit that shippers and carriers may waive Article IV's exclusionary rule. Rules stipulating default terms are extremely common, but they represent a relatively minor inroad on freedom of contract. By definition, contracting parties can override default terms, at least if they are aware of them. Moreover, in many cases default terms give effect to understandings that are a real, if implicit, part of the parties' actual agreement. In other words, default terms often merely confirm terms that 'go without saying' in an agreement. An example is section 27 of the Sale of Goods Act 1979: 'the duty of the seller [is to] to deliver the goods, and of the buyer to accept and pay for them.'

More important in debates about freedom of contract are rules that imply mandatory terms into contracts or that prohibit certain kinds of terms or even entire contracts. English law has always contained such rules. Agreements not to marry and agreements to pay for sex, for instance, have long been unenforceable—though neither of the activities contemplated by such contracts are themselves illegal. So too, a substantively unfair contract has long been liable to be set aside if the disadvantaged party is 'poor and ignorant' (e.g. illiterate). But the number of such rules has increased dramatically over the past hundred or so years. Most of the increase is in the form of legislation designed to protect persons the law perceives to be vulnerable (e.g. consumers, employees). Such legislation is discussed in more detail later in this chapter. For the moment, two observations suffice. First, the amount and significance of protective legislation can easily be underestimated if one's familiarity with contract law is limited to that learned in an introductory course on contract law. The most heavily regulated contracts, such as employment contracts, are usually discussed in detail only in advanced courses. Secondly, English law has been reluctant to impose or prohibit terms across the board, that is to say, for all categories of contracts. For example, a duty to act in good faith, which civil law jurisdictions imply into all contracts, is implied by English law only into certain categories of contracts (e.g. insurance contracts). Similarly, there is no general rule prohibiting unfair terms; nor (as was noted a moment ago) is there even a general rule prohibiting unfair terms that are obtained by exploiting a disadvantaged person's vulnerability.

The third and potentially most powerful technique for limiting freedom of contract is to impose not just a particular term into a contract, but to impose an entire 'contract'. A long-standing example is the rule that common carriers (e.g. the post office) must accept goods tendered for transport. Admittedly, a common carrier's obligation is not usually regarded as contractual. But rules of this kind are important when thinking about freedom of contract since their effect is to remove whole categories of trans-actions from the reach of contract law principles. Indeed, the reason such transactions are not regarded as contractual (or as only quasi-contractual) is that freedom of contract has been largely or entirely supplanted by other values. A large number of ordinary transactions are of this kind. For example, citizens are required to pay taxes whether or not they want to. The state, for its part, provides services such as education, hospitals, and garbage pick-up to everyone, even to those who would rather obtain such service by private contracts. Such transactions are outside the scope of this book. But they must be kept in mind when thinking about the impor-tance and value our society accords to contract law and contract law principles.

With these observations in mind, we can return to the question that was raised at the beginning of this section: why are certain kinds of agreements not enforced? One possible answer is that agreements are not enforced when the economic and moral (or 'individualist') reasons for enforcement (that were described in the previous section) do not apply. For example, it is some-times argued that the primary aim of consumer protection legislation is the essentially economic aim of facilitating contracting. Consumers will be more willing to enter contracts, it is argued, if they can be confident that their contracts will not contain unreasonable terms. Likewise, individualist theories of contract sometimes explain the unenforceability of contracts to sell human organs on the basis that physical integrity is an 'inalienable' right, the kind of thing that cannot, or at least should not, be sold or exchanged. These explanations cannot be dismissed out of hand. But in most cases they are not the most obvious explanations for the kinds of rules we have been discussing. With respect to protective rules, the more obvious explanation is that such rules reflect basic notions of fairness. More specifically, they reflect, on the one hand, the idea that it is wrong to take advantage of another's vulnerability, and, on the other hand, the idea that a person who has been taken advantage of deserves redress. As for rules that focus on the type of activity contemplated by an agreement (e.g. selling human organs, prosti-tution), the obvious explanation is that the law should not promote this activity. Thus, a common explanation for the prohibition on the sale of human organs is that the intangible value of life will be diminished if such sales become an ordinary practice.

It should be apparent now why rules that limit freedom of contract are often controversial. On the one hand, the economic and moral arguments that justify enforcing contracts in the first place apply to agreements generally, including agreements that may be unfair or that may involve undesirable activities. The economic and moral arguments are closely linked, in other words, to the classical notion of freedom of contract. On the other hand, unrestrained freedom of contract appears inconsistent with basic notions of fairness and (for want of a better phrase) basic social values.

4. THE CONTESTED IDEAL OF FREEDOM OF CONTRACT

Given what has been said above, it should not be surprising to learn that freedom of contract has enjoyed changing levels of support from courts and legislatures over the years.[6] A brief history of these changes provides a convenient framework for describing in more detail some of the arguments for and against limiting freedom of contract, together with the legal changes that accompanied those arguments. The history of freedom of contract is important both for understanding why we have the laws we have and for understanding why we explain those laws the ways we do.

The classical period: 1770–1870

The English law of contract has roots going back to the Middle Ages, but most of the general principles that underpin the modern law were developed in the eighteenth and nineteenth centuries. These principles and, perhaps even more, the general approach of the courts to contractual questions may be referred to as the traditional or classical theory of contract law.

The eighteenth and nineteenth centuries, in particular the period from about 1770 to 1870, were the heyday of theories of natural law and the philosophy of *laissez-faire*, and many of the judges, who were largely responsible for the creation of the law of contract during this period, were considerably influenced by current thought. To the judges of this period, theories of natural law meant that individuals had inalienable rights to own property, and therefore to make their own arrangements to deal with that property, and hence to make contracts for themselves. The philosophy of *laissez-faire*, for its part, was understood to mean that the state, and thus the law, should interfere with people as little as possible.

The function of the private law, in this view, was understood to be that of enforcing whatever private arrangements contracting parties had agreed

---

[6] The subject is dealt with in detail in P.S. Atiyah, *The Rise and Fall of Freedom of Contract* (Oxford, 1979).

upon. In general, the law was not concerned with the fairness or justice of the outcome, and the paternalistic ideas that were more common in earlier centuries came to be thought of as old-fashioned. In particular, many rules designed to protect those who entered into foolish and improvident bargains were whittled away by the judges. The judges were not even greatly concerned with the possibility that a contract might not be in the public interest (say because it restricted competition). The role of contract law was merely to assist one of the contracting parties when the other broke the rules of the game and defaulted in performing a contractual obligation. This is not to say the judges of this period were uninterested in justice: they thought that it *was* just to enforce contractual duties strictly. In this regard, the judges were part of a reform movement that was closely allied to the political movement towards democracy. The reformers of the 1830s proclaimed their belief that people could be trusted to look after their own interests, whether in the marketplace or at the hustings. It would thus be a mistake to think that the judges were indifferent to the public interest. They simply thought that, in nearly all cases, it *was* in the public interest to enforce private contracts. Indeed, it was widely thought that this was proved by fundamental economic principles.[7]

So great was the emphasis on agreement and the intention of the parties that the judges of the nineteenth century tended to elevate the law of contract into the central position in the law of obligations as a whole. This led to two related developments. First, there was a reluctance to impose obligations on those who had not voluntarily assumed them. The law of torts and the law of unjust enrichment remained relatively undeveloped during this period. And secondly, where obligations *were* imposed, there was a tendency to assume that they must be voluntarily imposed. So, for example, the judges denied that they had any power to make a contract for the parties. Courts were loath to fix sloppily drafted contracts, even if one party suffered greatly as a result. Similarly, they attempted to express the great bulk of the actual rules of contract law as depending on the parties' intention. For instance, the rules according to which a contract might be set aside because the parties were mistaken or performance had become impossible were explained as doing no more than giving effect to the implied, but real, intentions of the parties. Thus, in the same way that John Locke had argued that political obligations derived their legitimacy from the social contract to which the people gave an 'implied assent', judges argued that private obligations mostly depended on private contracts to which they could find a real or 'implied' assent.

The picture just described is, of course, an over-simplification. Courts in this period retained the power in certain types of cases to declare contracts to

---

[7] For a famous dictum to this effect, see *Printing and Numerical Registering Co. v. Sampson* (1875) LR 19 Eq. at 465.

be ineffective because they were against the public interest—'public policy' as it is called in the law of contract. As well, from a comparatively early date, legislative interference with freedom of contract began to play an important role. For instance, as early as 1831 the first of the modern Truck Acts was passed to protect employees from the practice of being paid in kind instead of in cash, and in 1845 the Gaming Act enacted that wagers should no longer be capable of enforcement as contracts. Overall, however, the amount of such legislation passed in the period from 1780 to 1870 was minimal in comparison with that passed in the subsequent hundred or so years.

The period from 1870 to 1980

During the period from about 1870 to 1980 this picture changed. Specifically, there was a gradual decline in belief in freedom of contract and a reversion to paternalist and regulatory traditions that were in many respects closer to those of the seventeenth and early eighteenth centuries than that of the nineteenth century. Two main factors underlay this change. First, the idea that free and voluntary exchange was the secret to economic prosperity and, more generally, to a freer and more contented society, went into steep decline. In particular, the problem of 'externalities' was recognized. An externality is, roughly, a side effect of a free exchange that affects third parties. Nineteenth-century England saw massive externality problems arising from the industrial revolution—dirty towns, unsanitary accommodation, disease, pollution, and the like—all of which could be seen as external costs imposed by industry on third parties, that is, the public. Often these externalities were the result of private contracts, for example, for the rent of undrained lodgings into which the parties freely entered, and which they no doubt wanted to make. One kind of negative externality that was (and still is) of particular interest to contract lawyers is the reduction or prevention of competition in the market that can arise from an agreement to form a cartel or to engage in other restrictive trade practices. The parties to such a cartel might well benefit from such arrangement, but the general public rarely does.

Secondly, the idea that 'free and voluntary' contracts lead to desirable or just results for the parties who choose to enter—or not enter—them was also challenged. Stated differently, it was argued that the classical contract law rules provided no guarantee that contracts were free and voluntary in any meaningful sense. On the one hand, it was pointed out that the ideal of freedom of contract means little to someone who lacks the means or talents to make contracts for food, clothing, shelter, or employment. To say that such a person *chose* not to make such contracts would be true only in a restricted sense. On the other hand, it was thought that the legal meaning of 'free and voluntary' provided no guarantee that the contracts that were made were fair or just. The main reason was that in many cases an individual or business had no real choice as to whom to contract with. This phenomenon was first observed with respect to the great railways and public utilities, which provided services that were increasingly regarded as essential, but over which there was little, if any, choice. But more generally, and as we shall see in greater detail in Chapter 8, between about 1870 and 1950 the British economy became a network of restrictive practices (i.e. cartels and monopolies). The result was that in respect of vast areas of life neither the individual nor the small business had much real contractual choice.

Associated with this concern over lack of choice was the emergence and widespread use of the standard-form contract. Industrialization and the emergence of mass commercial market activity meant that most contracts ceased to consist of individually negotiated or custom-made terms. They came to be made on standard printed terms offered by large organizations, often on a take-it-or-leave-it basis. Thus, although nobody could compel passengers to travel by train, anyone wanting to do so had to accept the terms and conditions imposed by the railway companies. Similarly, if householders wished to obtain supplies of gas or electricity for their houses, they had to enter into contracts on terms laid down by the suppliers. And even when the goods or services in question were not controlled by a monopoly, the terms and conditions offered to the public were largely, if not exactly, identical. This was also true in many business dealings. Commercial agreements for the sale of goods would normally be recorded in 'order forms' or 'acknowledgements' with printed clauses; contracts for the carriage of goods by sea would usually be recorded in a printed 'bill of lading'; insurance contracts were nearly always recorded in printed policies, and so on. Quite often, these forms were standard throughout an entire industry, thus depriving the consumer of the benefits of competition. For instance, standard building and engineering con- tract forms were (and are) drafted by the Royal Institute of British Architects and the Institute of Civil Engineers. For many lawyers, standard-form contracts, and in particular the exemption of liability clauses they normally contained, were clear proof that freedom of contract was a chimera.

But lack of real choice was not the only reason for believing that many contracts were not free and voluntary. Even where a degree of choice existed, many contracting parties were unable to exercise that choice effectively because they did not understand the legal implications of their agreements. In this regard, standard-form contracts, in particular standard-form exemption (and limitation) clauses, were again identified as a major problem. Standard- form contracts typically contain long lists of clauses and conditions, often in small uniform type. Exemption clauses, which protect contracting parties from legal liabilities, are difficult for legally unsophisticated individuals to understand; individuals must know the law to understand their effect. Furthermore, it is often difficult to evaluate the practical significance of such clauses, even if one knows the law, since it is difficult to know how likely it is that the contract in question will be breached.

A final point is that both of these problems—lack of choice and lack of understanding—are most likely to be significant in contracts made with consumers. Thus, another reason for the declining belief in freedom of contract during the 1870–1980 period was the emergence of the consumer as a contracting party. Of course, consumers had always made contracts. But the number and magnitude of such contracts, and the likelihood of them being litigated, increased dramatically over the twentieth century.

The changes in attitudes and beliefs just described led to political and legal changes. The concern for the third party effects of contracts, that is, for externalities, led to changes that took place primarily outside the law of contract, strictly defined. In particular, it led to a significant expansion of the law of tort. The landmark case of *Donoghue v. Stevenson*,[8] for example, held that manufacturers could be held liable to anyone injured by a defective product. Previously, such claims were governed purely by contractual rules, with the result that claimants could only succeed if they had purchased the product from the manufacturer. Accompanying these judicial developments was the heavy regulation, sometimes combined with outright state ownership, of those industries that most affected third parties, such as those involved in supplying water or electricity.

Within the law of contract, the most important consequence of this concern for the potentially detrimental effects of private arrangements on third parties was that courts and tribunals became increasingly active in striking down anti-competitive practices, such as cartels and exclusive trading arrangements. This was accomplished in part by a dramatic development of the formerly moribund common law doctrine of restraint of trade, but of greater significance in the long-term was the introduction of statutory 'competition' laws and tribunals to enforce those laws.[9] There were also many other more specific instances of interferences with freedom of contract that were designed to further public policy objectives. For many years, for example, it was the policy of successive British governments to encourage the development of agriculture in order that the nation should not be so dependent upon the importation of food—something that made the country particularly vulnerable in wartime. In *Johnson v. Moreton*,[10] the House of Lords relied upon this public policy in holding that agricultural tenants could not contract out of the protections conferred upon them by the Agricultural Holdings Act 1948.

The concern for fairness and justice, that is to say, for the extent to which individuals are free in a meaningful sense to enter (or not enter) contracts, and to do so on terms of their choosing, had even more significant legal

---

[8] [1932] AC 562.
[9] Restrictive Trade Practices Act 1956, repealed by the Competition Act 1998.
[10] [1980] AC 37.

effects. Again, many of these effects took place outside of contract law. The expansion of tort law was part of this trend. For instance, the creation of the tort of negligent misrepresentation in the 1964 case of *Hedley Byrne v. Heller*[11] meant that parties induced to enter contracts by negligent misrepresentations were able not only to avoid the contract (if the misrepresentation came from the other party), but in addition could recover damages from the misrepresentor. Significantly, damages could be obtained even if the misrepresentor was a third party, such as a manufacturer. In this way, the expansion of non-contractual remedies available in situations formerly governed by contractual principles, which began in *Donoghue v. Stevenson*, was taken one step further. At the same time, the ability of individuals to recover the value of benefits conferred either in anticipation of a contract that failed to materialize or on the basis of a contract that was breached was placed on firmer footing through the development of the law of unjust enrichment. Like the law of misrepresentation, this branch of the law is not usually raised when dis-cussing freedom of contract. Viewed broadly, however, both misrepresenta-tion and unjust enrichment are part of a general movement away from the idea that our duties to others are strictly limited except insofar as we have contracted to undertake such duties.

Moving outside private law entirely (at least as it was traditionally under-stood), the most important consequence of changing views about freedom of contract in the period 1870–1980 was the rise of the various institutions associated with the 'welfare state'. The introduction of institutions such as state-funded education and medical care, not to mention unemployment insurance and welfare, can be understood in large part as premised on the belief that freedom of contract is an empty ideal for those lacking the means to enter the market. Specifically, defenders of the welfare state rejected the idea that all social relations should be governed by market, that is to say, classical contractual principles. A similar idea inspired various forms of 'compulsory contracts' that were introduced in this period. For example, individuals might be compelled to join a trade union (and thus enter into a 'contract' with the union) in order to exercise their trade and earn a livelihood. In the 1950s, tenants of business premises were given, subject to certain conditions, a statutory right to a new lease on the expiry of their old one. The landlord was (and indeed remains today) *legally obliged* to grant the new lease. Though classified as 'contracts', the element of consent in such arrangements is very limited.

Within the law of contract proper, concerns for fairness and justice led to three related developments. First, the substance of the parties' obligations in many categories of contracts came to be specified to a significant extent by legislation. The avowed aim of much of this legislation was to protect a

---

[11] [1964] AC 465.

perceived weaker party. Thus, nearly all the terms in a standard employment contract, save the salary and basic job description, were set out in legislation.[12] In a similar vein, hire-purchase legislation was passed to protect hirers against unfair treatment by finance companies, landlord and tenant legislation was enacted to give better rights to tenants, and a combination of statutes (the Unfair Contract Terms Act 1977 and the Misrepresentation Act 1967) had the effect of precluding attempts by business parties to exclude or limit liabilities to consumers, even if the consumer consented. The full extent of this kind of legislation is not always appreciated because it is studied primarily in courses on employment law, consumer law, the law of sale, insurance law, agency law, banking law, secured transactions law, health law, and the like. Courses in 'contract law' usually focus on the general rules that are applicable to all contracts. This narrowing of focus is unavoidable in an introductory course (or textbook). But it cannot be stressed too strongly that the scope and importance of the general rules of contract law have been diminished greatly by the number of legislated contract terms now in existence.

A second development inspired by the concern for fairness and justice was a move towards providing protection not just for specified categories of contracting parties (e.g. employees), but for all contracting parties. There was an attempt, in other words, to modify the *general* rules of contract law to reflect the new view of freedom of contract. Perhaps the most conspicuous success of this movement was the Unfair Contract Terms Act 1977, which, in addition to the special protection that it gave consumers (as just described), also gave judges a general authority to strike down unreasonable exemption clauses, regardless of the category of contract. This period also saw the expansion of the defences of duress, undue influence, and mistake. For instance, the concept of 'economic duress' was recognized, as was the defence of 'mistake at equity' (which expanded the possibilities of relief for mistake). These changes to the general law were significant. But it should be kept in mind that the general law was changed far less during this period than many reformers would have liked. In particular, English law did not introduce anything similar to the civilian notion that contracting parties have a general duty to act in good faith; nor (despite Lord Denning's efforts)[13] did it follow American (and now Australian) law in introducing a general defence of unconscionability.

---

[12] See, e.g., Employment Rights Act 1966.

[13] In *Lloyd's Bank*, above n. 5, Lord Denning famously argued that English law contained a general principle of 'inequality of bargaining power', according to which the law gives relief to a party who 'enters into a contract upon terms which are very unfair . . ., when his bargaining power is grievously impaired by reason of his own needs or desires, or by his own ignorance or infirmity'. Denning's version of an unconscionability doctrine was rejected by the House of Lords in *National Westminster Bank plc v. Morgan* [1985] AC 686.

The third and final development during the period from 1870 to 1980 was a change in the way the existing law was understood. Specifically, many rules that were previously explained as simply giving effect to the intentions of contracting parties were now explained on the basis that they were imposed by the law in order to advance a policy—in particular the policy that contracts should reflect the interests of *both* parties. Thus, while the guarantees of quality and so forth found in the Sale of Goods Act might previously have been understood as giving content to what the parties had impliedly or tacitly consented, they were now generally understood as being designed to ensure the fairness of the parties' bargain. This change in thinking was even more pronounced with respect to precedent-based rules, such as those providing relief for mistake or frustration. Whereas in the eighteenth and nineteenth centuries, relief for frustration was often explained as resting on an implied-in-fact term (i.e. a term the parties actually, albeit not explicitly, agreed to), by the middle of the twentieth century most commentators regarded this as a polite fiction. The real purpose of such rules, it was said, was to give effect to a sense of justice or fairness.[14] This change in understanding then led to changes in how the rules were actually applied; the courts felt freer to apply the rules in a way that directly gave effect to notions of justice and fairness.

The contemporary period: 1980 to the present

During the contemporary period we have had in effect two massive trends running in opposing directions. The first is a new trend towards a revival of early nineteenth century freedom of contract principles. Since 1980, England, like most Western democracies, has seen a resurgence of support for markets and for the traditional notion of freedom of contract. At the political level, the weakening and eventual dissolution of the former Soviet empire was undoubtedly a major factor in this shift. But at the level of contract law, the most important factor was probably the influence of a new generation of pro-market economists and economist-lawyers. Focusing on the relationship between legal rules and their economic effects, the argument of this group, in broad terms, was that the problems associated with markets were the result of too little, not too much, freedom of contract. More specifically, the main problem was identified as the anti-competitive practices that were rife throughout the British economy in the period around 1900–50. Thus, while it was acknowledged that unfair contracts might be concluded on the basis of standard-form contracts, it was argued that the underlying source of the unfairness was not the use of standard-forms, but, in most cases, the monopoly power enjoyed by the advantaged party. Standard-form contracts and take-it-or-leave-it offers generally are used for the simple reason that it is

---

[14] See in particular the decision of Lord Radcliffe in *Davis Contractors v. Fareham UDC* [1956] AC 696, at 728.

too costly to negotiate individualized terms in an age of mass contracting. The corner store operates on the same principle. If you do not like the terms, you simply go elsewhere. It is only when the potential purchaser cannot go elsewhere that a problem arises.

Using similar logic, it was pointed out that exemption clauses serve a useful economic purpose. In a complex economy, one of the main purposes of a contract is to allocate risks—which is what exemption clauses do. In effect, such clauses specify which of the parties should obtain insurance for the relevant risk. Prima facie, there is no reason that the carrier in a delivery contract should always have the responsibility of obtaining the necessary insurance. The owner has better knowledge of what the goods are worth and may, in any event, already have insurance for other reasons.[15] Thus, if the parties decide to allocate the risk of loss or damage to the owner (by an exemption clause) the courts should respect this choice.

Competition has even been given as the solution to the problem that contracting parties often do not understand or even read exemption clauses and other complex contractual terms. The argument is that because profit margins in competitive markets are narrow, the vendors in such markets worry about losing even a small percentage of their customers and, more generally, worry about their reputations. Thus, vendors will hesitate to impose unfair terms because of the fear of losing even the small percentage of customers who do read and understand the terms. And even where such terms are imposed, vendors will hesitate to enforce them for fear of damaging their reputations.

One criticism of the classical notion of freedom of contract that the economists did not attempt to refute was that many of the opportunities in the market are available only to a wealthy minority. Most economists were not strictly concerned with this problem or regarded it as a necessary evil. But even those who did worry about inequality of resources generally took the view that this problem was better addressed by tax or subsidy programs, rather than by changing the rules of contract law. Prohibiting perceived unfair terms was said to do little to help the less well-off, since the 'stronger' party could always change other terms (in particular the price), or simply move into a different line of business. Thus, the effect of rent control, the economists argued, is that flats are allowed to become run-down or are just taken off the rental market. By distorting the market, everyone is left worse off in the long run. The overall conclusion to this line of argument was that contract law should focus on increasing the size of the pie available for

---

[15] Admittedly, it is often the case that every seller in a particular industry demands a similar exemption clause. But, assuming that the seller is operating in a competitive market, the explanation (according to economic theory) may simply be that the clause is a reasonable one. If it were possible to make a normal profit without such a clause, then we would expect to see one or more sellers doing just this in order to obtain more customers.

redistribution, and that this is best done by enforcing agreements on the terms on which they are made.

Of course, the claim that competition is the cure for all (or nearly all) problems is of little comfort if the economy is not actually competitive. It was thus crucial to the success of the economic argument described above that the English economy became immeasurably more competitive over the last half-century. Part of the reason for this change was the success of the competition and restraint of trade laws that were mentioned earlier and that have continued to receive strong support. But more important were structural changes that took place in the English and international economies. Local monopolies and cartels have been challenged by international competitors. Consumers, for their part, have become increasingly sophisticated, and consumer advocates, whether official bodies or simply the media, have become increasingly stronger. One consequence is that rather than trying to take away a consumer's legal rights, many businesses freely expand those rights.

The second, and opposite trend evident in the contemporary period is a continuation of the older movement, deriving from the late nineteenth century, away from freedom of contract and in favour of regulating the market. But it is noteworthy that the arguments usually now given in defence of intervention are different from those made in the earlier period. Rather than defending intervention on the grounds that consumers and small businesses are inevitably at a disadvantage when contracting with large commercial parties, and that standard-form contracts in particular are indicative of disparities in bargaining power, two other ideas have been put forward. Each has been influenced by the economic arguments described above (and each has been accepted by at least some economists).

The first idea underlying the contemporary defence of intervention is that even if is true that markets have become more competitive, few if any markets are, or ever will be, *perfectly* competitive. Indeed, perfect competition is regarded more as a theoretical or abstract ideal than a real-world phenomenon. Even the smallest vendor usually possesses a degree of monopoly power. The corner store, for instance, has an effective monopoly over milk and eggs to the extent that local consumers find it too expensive or time-consuming to travel to the next nearest store. A related point is that no amount of competition can prevent what economists call 'situational monopolies'. An example is the monopoly over 'rescue services' enjoyed by a ship on the high seas that chances upon another ship that is in danger of sinking and that has no alternative rescuers. More generally, some markets are too small or dispersed to ever be truly competitive; in such cases the benefits to be realized by imposing unfair terms might well outweigh any negative publicity. A final reason that perfect competition is often a chimera is that people rarely act as rationally as classical economic theory appears to assume. Thus, while it might be irrational to include harsh exemption clauses in a contract (say because of the negative reputational effects of enforcing such clauses), it seems clear that some contracting parties continue to do just this. Similarly, empirical evidence suggests that consumers will often discount the significance of such clauses, because they irrationally discount the likelihood of low-probability events occurring (e.g. a breach that causes them injury).

The other idea that is frequently introduced in support of interventionist policies is that regulation is needed not so much to protect weaker parties as to *facilitate* contracting. In other words, regulation can be used to increase the size of the pie. More specifically, the argument is that the law provides useful 'default' terms that make it easier for people to make contracts. Such terms, which are analogized to default settings in computer software, in effect create a standard form contract that is available to all contracting parties. Using this logic, terms implied into particular categories of contracts by legislation such as the Sale of Goods Act 1979 are defended not on the ground that they ensure fair bargains, but on the ground that they save parties the time and expense of writing lengthy contracts. A similar explanation is often given for the rules that stipulate when a contract may be set aside because of a mistake, a change in circumstances, or breach by the other party. Most strikingly, this explanation is even applied to the rules governing 'market failures' of the kind discussed earlier. Thus, the rule of admiralty law that a rescuer at sea cannot charge more than a reasonable price is defended on the ground that this rule will discourage potential rescuers and rescuees from engaging in wasteful and potentially dangerous negotiations over price. Similarly, it has been argued that the ultimate aim of modern legislation prohibiting unfair terms in consumer contracts is not to protect consumers, but to facilitate contracting. If consumers can be confident that contracts will not contain unwelcome surprises, they will be more likely to enter into them.

The legal consequences of the above trends are not easily summarized. On the one hand, the enthusiasm, in England at least, for large-scale protective legislation and doctrines has largely subsided. For instance, the movement towards introducing a general defence of 'inequality of bargaining power' or towards introducing a general duty to act in good faith has stalled. On the other hand, and consistent with the second trend described above, the various regimes of legislatively implied terms have been left intact, and in some cases extended. For instance, the Supply of Goods and Services Act 1982 implies into supply contracts the kinds of terms found in the Sale of Goods Act 1979. Moreover, the assumption from the previous period that the terms in such legislation are based on the law's view of what is appropriate, as opposed to merely giving effect to the parties' implicit intentions, has been sustained. The main difference in this regard, which has already been noted, is that 'appropriate' is now often understood to mean 'facilitating contracting' as opposed to 'protecting the weak'.

The most significant instances of regulatory legislation introduced since 1980 have originated not from England, but the European Community (EC). Much of this legislation deals with consumer contracts, a notable example being the Unfair Terms in Consumer Contracts Regulations 1999, which gives courts wide discretion to strike down abusive terms in consumer contracts. At first glance, the Regulations appear to flow from the kind of paternalist and protective mentality that, in England anyway, was more associated with the period ending around 1980. But as we have seen, it is also possible to view such legislation as aimed primarily at facilitating transactions. This would explain, for example, why the Regulations exclude from scrutiny terms that specify that the price of a contract—a consumer will always be aware of, and understand the meaning of, the price.[16]

A further consequence of EU initiatives in private law and, more generally, of England's increasingly close ties to the continent is that certain civilian notions, most notably the principle that contracting parties must act in good faith, are gaining new supporters. A principle of good faith is incorporated explicitly into the Unfair Terms Regulations, and as such will need to be applied by English judges. As familiarity with this concept grows, it can be expected to take on new roles. For example, rather than explaining banks' duties to ensure that guarantors act independently using the ill-fitting concept of 'constructive notice',[17] the notion of good faith could be employed. Such an explanation would make it clearer that these duties are a departure from traditional English notions of freedom of contract. The good faith principle may also be used to explain certain developments in consumer protection law (itself the subject of various EU initiatives), such as the important role of Ombudsman in regulating insurance and financial contracts, especially as regards the duties of insurers, banks, and other financial institutions to disclose information to consumers (see Chapter 9).

To conclude, it is clear that however much the principles of freedom of contract have been revitalized since 1980, there is no going back to the simplistic pre-1870 belief that all relations should ideally be governed by voluntary obligations. The concept of 'externalities' is firmly entrenched, indeed growing, and the same is true of the body of tort law and general regulatory law designed to deal with them. Similarly, the scope and significance of the law of unjust enrichment has continued to grow unabated. Indeed, it is not possible now, if it ever was, to understand the law of contract properly without also understanding its relationship both to tort law and unjust enrichment law.

---

[16] Except, of course, if the price is stated by means of a complex formula—but this is caught by the obligation to use 'plain, intelligible language': 7(1).

[17] *Barclays Bank*, above n. 4; discussed below, p. 286.

5. THE HISTORICAL DEVELOPMENT OF CONTRACT LAW

In addition to the substantive developments just described, two general features of the historical development of contract law are important for understanding the modern law. The first is the organic development of the law. The common law of contract is not the product of any plan or conscious design. The cases on which the core of the law is based were decided one at a time by countless judges acting over an unbroken period stretching back nearly 800 years. These judges made their rulings in response to whatever cases were brought before them. Moreover, they were rarely concerned with the general structure or organization of the law. Unlike in civil law countries, common law judges traditionally received little in the way of formal training. They were (and still are) picked directly from the ranks of successful lawyers. Indeed, until relatively recently, judges (and lawyers generally) received no academic training in law at all; nor did they have the benefit of a body of scholarly legal literature. It was only late in the nineteenth century that the common law was first taught and studied in universities, and even today it is possible to become a lawyer in England (and in time a judge) without a law degree.

The second important feature of the common law's historical development is the commercial setting in which it took place. Litigation has always been expensive. It is also frequently accompanied by intangible costs, especially for parties who have social or personal ties with one another. The consequence is that most of the cases before the courts, both today and in the past, deal with commercial matters and usually involve medium to large companies. In addition, the judges who decide these cases are themselves typically from a commercial law background. This is in part because of specialization among judges, but it is also because a large percentage of English judges come from the ranks of the commercial bar.

These two features of the common law's history—the organic development and the commercial setting—have had significant effects on the substantive law of contract. The organic development has led to a law that is poorly structured, at least in relative terms. Admittedly, great progress has been made in classifying and 'mapping' the private law over the last 150 years. It is also true that contract law is the best structured of the main areas of private law. But as we shall see, there is much that remains to be done. To give just one example, the 'contract law' rules governing issues such as capacity, duress, mistake, and remedies for breach are often treated as separate from functionally similar rules in the law of tort and unjust enrichment. The various sets of rules are presented as *sui generis*, rather than as instances of a general principle. The result is confusion, if not inconsistency in treatment. It also bears mentioning that the organizational structure of the modern law of contract was largely borrowed, in the nineteenth century, from civilian scholarship. Given the attention paid to classificatory issues in civilian traditions, this was both understandable and useful. But the resulting structure, which remains largely intact today, never fit the common law perfectly. More importantly, the attempt, characteristic of the age, to explain contractual formation as a logical series of discrete moves (offer, counter-offer, revocation, acceptance, etc.), arguably never fit the reality of how more than a few types of contracts are actually made.

The second feature, the commercial setting in which contract law developed, has led to a set of rules that are to a significant extent designed for commercial parties. It is often remarked that English contract law assumes that everyone is able to look after themselves. Thus, contracts are traditionally interpreted narrowly and strictly, while excuses such as mistake or frustration are rarely accepted. So too, the idea that contracting parties are under duties to assist one another (duties of good faith) or at least under duties not to exploit one another (the defence of unconscionability) has never been favourably received. This approach is not surprising when one considers the kinds of commercial cases that have made up the bulk of litigation. Commercial parties usually *are* able to look after themselves. In general, such parties therefore prefer that judges simply give effect to what is written in contracts, rather than decide for themselves what the parties' obligations should be. Consumers, of course, often take a different attitude. But as was noted above, it is only in the last 50 or so years that lawmakers have worried much about consumers.

6. THE PRACTICAL IMPORTANCE OF CONTRACT LAW

As we have seen, contracts are of almost incalculable practical importance in helping individuals to obtain the goods and services necessary to live their lives. So too, from a political perspective, contracts are of fundamental importance. The idea that economic relations should be governed by voluntary contracts is another way of saying that the market, not the state, should be the primary means of organizing economic life. Our ideas about contracts cannot be separated, in other words, from our ideas about the state's role in organizing social relations. Finally, from a moral perspective, the significance of promises, agreements, and voluntary undertakings generally cannot be overestimated. The concept of a promissory obligation is one of humanity's greatest moral inventions. The idea that merely by uttering some words—'I promise'—individuals can put themselves under obligations to do things for other individuals represents the triumph of trust and cooperation over greed and self-interest.

Yet notwithstanding the importance of *contracts*, it is easy to overestimate the practical significance of contract *law*. Contracts are regularly made (or not made) and performed (or not performed) without much concern for the law of contract. And when contracts are broken, parties rarely stand on the rights that contract law says they have, much less do they seek or even threaten redress in the courts. Part of the explanation for this behaviour is that using lawyers, drawing up formal contracts, and going to court are expensive and time-consuming. But just as important in explaining the relative unimportance of law is the relative importance of a myriad of extra-legal factors that influence how parties behave in contractual settings. One obvious extra-legal factor is a concern for reputation. Parties who breach contracts may find that no one wants to deal with them in future. A second extra-legal factor is morality. Despite what economic theory sometimes appears to suggest, it is clear that many people perform their contracts not because they are worried about the negative consequences, legal or otherwise, of breach, but because they believe they have a moral obligation to perform. In a similar way, parties often agree not to enforce their legal rights because they feel it would be unfair, in the circumstances, to do so.

Of course, concerns about one's reputation and moral considerations are not always sufficient to ensure proper behaviour. But in many situations contracting parties do not need to go to the courts to obtain further protection. The simplest, but often the most effective, sanction for a breach is simply refusing to deal further with the breaching party. Consider, for instance, how rarely governments, who borrow enormous sums of money in the world's financial markets, default on their obligations, even though there is no real way of forcing them to observe their contracts. They pay because they know that if they do not they may never be able to borrow again.[18] Other techniques include demanding guarantees from reputable third parties, asking for deposits, refusing to perform without payment, structuring exchanges so they are simultaneous, or simply joining forces through a merger or joint-venture.

In general, extra-legal factors of the kind just mentioned are strongest in situations where the parties are closely bound together, whether by virtue of shared morals, customs, and conventions or because their commercial or social relations are heavily intertwined. For example, in domestic relations, such as between spouses, extra-legal factors will normally dominate almost entirely. They are also important in what were described earlier as relational contracts, involving long-term engagements between repeat players. But where the parties are weakly connected, contract law may have an important role to play. If a purchaser does not trust a vendor (say because they have no previous dealings) and if the same purchaser cannot use extra-legal sanctions against the vendor (say because they are geographically and otherwise unconnected), then contract law may be important in structuring their

---

[18] A recent counter-example is Argentina (which succeeded in forcing its international creditors to accept lower value bonds in exchange for existing bonds), though it remains to be seen what effect this will have on Argentina's ability to borrow again.

relations. This is no doubt part of the reason that cases involving international shipping contracts have played such a large role in the development
of English contract law.

The importance of extra-legal factors in influencing contracting parties'
behaviour raises the question whether such factors should be taken into
account when courts *are* called upon to establish the existence and content of
a contract. Many commentators have criticised English courts for failing to
do just this, arguing, in effect, that such factors are not really *extra*-legal. In
particular, it is often argued that the rules of offer and acceptance are rigid
and mechanical, with the result that arrangements that business parties
regard as perfectly acceptable for 'extra-legal' reasons are denied legal status.
Similarly, it is said that the rules on modification and performance of contracts are based on an unrealistically narrow view of the kinds of excuses that
commercial parties regularly accept. We will consider such criticisms at various points in the book. At this stage, it is sufficient to note briefly why they
raise difficult issues. On the one hand, it is clear that contracts can only be
understood in their context, and that this context will often include shared
conventions, practices, and understandings. Extra-legal factors, in other
words, form part of the background against which the contract must be
interpreted. On the other hand, it is also clear that many of the factors that
influence contracting parties are rightly considered irrelevant by the courts.
A vendor who had previously assisted a purchaser when the purchaser was in
financial difficulties might well be surprised and dismayed if the purchaser
in a later dealing insisted on contractual performance to the letter. Other
participants in the industry might well share this view. But it is not obvious
that courts should take the vendor's past generosity into account when
determining if its present acts constitute a breach of contract. Similarly, the
fact that vendors in a particular industry typically accept late payments
without complaint does not establish that if such a complaint is made it is
improper. A wrong does not cease to be a wrong simply because the victim
did not complain in the past.

7. THE SOURCES OF CONTRACT LAW

The core principles of the English law of contract are almost entirely the
product of judicial decisions.[19] But in other parts of the law of contract the
role played by legislation is large and growing. We have already seen
that, while the common law has not formally adopted the civilian concept

---

[19] The primary exceptions are the rules on the validity of exemption and limitation clauses,
which were modified significantly by the Unfair Contract Terms Act 1977, and the rules stipulating when third parties may enforce contracts, which were completely rewritten by the Contract
(Rights of Third Parties) Act 1999.

of nominate or special contracts, most of the same categories of contracts (e.g. sale, employment, partnership, insurance, etc.) are subject to various category-specific rules, the vast majority of which are now found in legislation. In some categories (e.g. employment and company law), legislation constitutes the principle source of law for practising lawyers. The increasingly important role of EU Directives in generating legislation must also be recognised. Thus far, most Directives in the field of contract law have focused on narrow topics, such as holiday travel packages[20] and late payments of commercial debts.[21] But the Directive on Unfair Terms in Consumer Contracts (implemented by the Unfair Terms in Consumer Contracts Regulations 1999), which gives courts wide-ranging powers to strike down unfair terms in consumer contracts, illustrates the potential of such directives to significantly alter English law.

EC Directives are important, moreover, as part of a broader movement in which ideas drawn from the civil law are influencing how English lawyers think about their law (and vice versa). Of course, the common law has always been influenced by civilian thinking. The classical nineteenth-century model of contract law that was described earlier, and that is still largely intact, was based largely on the writings of Pothier, a French jurist. But the influence of civilian thinking is particularly strong today for a number of reasons. First, the EU Directives themselves are influenced by, and in some cases make explicit reference to, civilian legal concepts. A clear example is the good faith standard adopted in the Directive on Unfair Terms in Consumer Contracts. The same is true of various international initiatives, such as the United Nations (Vienna) Convention on Contracts for the International Sale of Goods, which is familiar to many English lawyers even though it is not yet ratified by the United Kingdom.[22] Secondly, familiarity with civilian ideas is on the rise because of the increasing popularity of university courses in comparative law, not to mention the many university law programmes that involve a year studying abroad. Legal academics, for their part, are increasingly involved in pan-European legal projects (often supported by the EU), for example, the production of 'European' casebooks on contract law. As part of this trend, it is increasingly common for scholars to use civilian concepts when explaining the common law[23] (as is sometimes done in this book). Thirdly, and finally, because most major commercial transactions have international elements, practicing lawyers today regularly deal with documents, clients, and lawyers from civilian jurisdictions. The practicing lawyer is also

---

[20] Package Travel, Package Holidays and Package Tour Regulations 1998.

[21] Late Payments of Commercial Debts Regulations 2002.

[22] The Department of Trade and Industry is currently considering whether it should recommend that the UK adopt the Convention.

[23] Two notable examples are P. Birks (ed.), *English Private Law* (Oxford, 2000), and id *Unjust Enrichment* (Oxford, 2003).

affected by the reality that most large law firms in England are now international firms, in which a large number of the partners, and sometimes the
majority, are from civilian traditions.

These and other factors are already having an influence on how English
lawyers think about the law, and on the content of the law itself. The civilian
experience with contracts for the benefit of third parties, for example, was
cited in the debates predating the passing of the Contract (Rights of Third
Parties) Act 1999 (which statute moved the United Kingdom law into line
with civil law). It seems clear this trend will continue.

Of potentially greater significance than any of the factors just discussed is
the movement now in progress towards the introduction of a European Civil
Code. It is not yet clear if this movement—which has received some support
from the European Commission though for the moment is largely driven
by academics and other private actors—will achieve success, much less if
England (which has shown little support for this movement) would sign on to
any European code. But if these things were to happen, the effects on English
law would be significant. To be sure, any European code would almost
certainly attempt to find common ground between the civil and common law
or at least to combine elements from both traditions. Draft proposals of a
possible code have followed this approach.[24] But the basic method of forming
and developing the law on the basis of a comprehensive code is civilian. The
point bears repeating because most of the unique features of English law—
both good and bad—can be traced to the precedent-based system in which
they developed.

Finally, a few words need to be said about customs, trade practices, conventions, informal rules, and other social 'norms' as possible sources of law.
We have seen that some scholars regard social norms as possible sources of
law—as something that courts draw upon in the same way they draw upon
past precedents, though not always as openly. For others, social norms have
legal significance only insofar as they have been explicitly or implicitly
incorporated into a contractual agreement. Both sides in this debate agree,
however, that social norms can be important in resolving particular disputes.
Neither side would deny, for example, that English judges have long looked to
commercial practice to determine what counts as satisfactory quality in sale
of goods cases or as reasonable mitigation in a claim for damages for breach.
It follows that changes in social norms can affect, if not legal rules themselves, at least the way the rules are applied. Consider, for example, the
common law's traditional narrow and technical approach to contract interpretation. This approach is not inappropriate in a legal culture in which
lawyers have traditionally written legal documents in a narrow and technical

---

[24] O. Lando and H. Beale, (eds), *The Principles of European Contract Law Parts I & II*
(Dordrecht, 2000).

fashion. The industry custom, as it were, is to adopt a narrow and technical style of writing. Today there is a movement (inspired by the same internationalization of legal practice that was discussed above) to draft in plain English, in a style that, ideally, can be understood by both common law and civilian lawyers. To the extent this movement succeeds, that is to say, to the extent that the customs regarding document drafting actually change, judges will almost certainly adopt a less technical approach to interpreting contractual documents. There is evidence that this is already happening.[25]

---

[25] *Investors Compensation Scheme Ltd v. West Bromwich BS* [1998] 1 WLR 898.

2

Definition and Classification

IN the previous chapter, it was explained that the law of contract is usually described as the law dealing with self-imposed obligations, that is to say, promises and agreements. This has been the orthodox view since at least the emergence of the modern law of contract in the nineteenth century.[1] But it was also noted that this view has not gone unchallenged. It may be useful, therefore, to spend a few moments considering why this definition has been adopted and its main implications for a book on the law of contract. The latter discussion also provides a brief outline of this book's general structure.

I. DEFINITION

There are two main reasons that contract law is associated with self-imposed obligations. The first, and most obvious, is that the definition fits reasonably well with how the concept is actually used and applied by lawyers. Most of the arrangements that lawyers describe as contracts are essentially promises or agreements.[2] To be sure, not all contracts (as the term is currently used) involve promises or agreements, and—more importantly—not all promises and agreements are contracts. This point (which is a central theme of the next chapter) cannot be stressed too strongly.[3] Nonetheless, the fit between contract law and self-imposed obligations is reasonably close.

Of course, there are other ways of defining the law of contract that also fit how lawyers use the term reasonably well. For instance, the law of contract might plausibly be defined as the law of 'exchange' or the law of 'market transactions'. In principle, there is nothing wrong with such definitions. Indeed, from certain perspectives—for example the perspective of an economist or a sociologist—they are preferable to the traditional legal definition, as they focus on features of contractual transactions that may be of special importance from that perspective. But from the perspective of lawyers (and

---

[1] B. Simpson, 'Innovation in 19th Century Contract Law' (1975) 19 Law Quarterly Rev 247.
[2] While paper documents or oral communications are often described as 'contracts', in law the term refers to a state of affairs arising from a particular kind of event. This is the primary reason that debates about the meaning of 'contract law' are so difficult to resolve: in order to identify the kind of event that gives rise to a contract it is necessary to apply the rules of contract law.
[3] It should also be kept in mind that there are many rules (e.g., the rules on revoking rewards) and even large groups of rules (e.g., the rules on trusts or and bailment) whose classification remains the subject of strong debate. The boundaries of contract have never been clear or fixed.

law students), such definitions seem less useful or interesting than one focusing on self-imposed obligations. The most important general question about any area of the law, including the law of contract, would appear to be an essentially moral one: is the law justified? The final outcome of a contractual dispute may be a court order that an individual's property be seized or even, in an extreme case, that the individual be placed in prison (which may happen if an earlier order is disobeyed). Clearly, it matters very much whether such orders are justified.

This is the second reason why a definition of contract law that centres on the category of promises and agreements is appropriate: the category is itself morally significant. When individuals promise or agree to do something, they place themselves under duties that previously did not exist, and they do this simply by speaking or writing some words—in a sense, they are their own private legislators. Moreover, in contrast to the vast majority of obligations that morality (and the private law) recognises, self-imposed obligations are typically obligations to assist or benefit others. The fact that you own a bicycle that you would like to sell puts me under no obligation (in morality or in law) to purchase your bicycle. This is true even if you need the money more than I do and I need the bicycle more than you. But if I promise to purchase your bicycle, I will have placed myself under a new obligation (morally and, in most cases, legally) to pay you the price. When the law enforces obligations of this sort it is therefore doing something that is both morally distinctive and morally significant. Indeed, the concept of a promise may be regarded as one of humanity's greatest moral inventions. Thus, in addition to fitting well with current usage, a definition focused on promises and agreements captures something that is (or at least should be) of fundamental concern to anyone with a general interest in the law.

2. CLASSIFICATION

As already noted, the definition of contract law in terms of promises and agreements is not a recent invention. But if this definition is taken seriously, it appears to have far-reaching, even radical, implications for how contract law is presented and understood. Significant parts of what is currently regarded as contract law are arguably not about promises or agreements, or at least not exclusively. Indeed, much of what is found in a standard contracts textbook falls outside this category.

There is no universally accepted way of dividing up the law of contract—different contract textbooks are arranged differently—but the rules discussed in most textbooks (including this text) appear to fall into four broad categories: (1) formation of contracts; (2) content of contracts; (3) excuses for non-performance; and (4) enforcement of contracts (remedies for breach). The definition of contract law in terms of promises and agreements, if adopted strictly, suggests that only the rules in the first two categories are specifically *contract law* rules. The rules in categories three and four clearly *apply* to contractual obligations, but they also apply to other categories of obligations. For example, the category three rules on duress describe a range of situations in which a prima facie valid contract may be set aside at one party's choice. But they also describe, in broad terms, a range of situations in which non-contractual transactions may be set aside or undone. If I am forced at gunpoint to put my signature to an offer to purchase, the normal contractual implications of this action do not follow: I have the option of setting aside the apparent contract. But the same reasoning applies if, rather than being forced to make a promise or agreement (and so a contract), I am forced to physically hand over property, for instance my watch. I have the option of asking that the transaction (which is not a legal contract) be undone, either by returning my watch or its value. The idea that duress may nullify what would otherwise be the normal legal significance of an action therefore applies to both contractual and non-contractual transactions. The same observation can be made about the remedial rules in category four. Refusing to perform a contract may lead, like other legal wrongs, either to an order to perform one's duty (specific performance, injunction) or to an order to pay compensation (damages). The basis on which such orders are made is broadly similar whether the wrong is a breach of contract or a non-contractual wrong, such as trespass over land. In each case, the order to perform is an order to perform the primary duty (in contract, to do what was promised; in the tort of trespass, not to trespass) and the order to compensate is an order to compensate for the losses suffered as a result of not performing that duty. The rules in categories three and four might therefore be considered similar to the rules of, say, evidence: although they may be raised in contractual disputes, they are not uniquely about contracts.

Of course, even if this radical view is accepted, it is clearly important for anyone learning the law of contract to know something about the rules in categories three and four. Aside from their practical importance for lawyers dealing with contract disputes, these rules often tell us important things about contract law. Remedial rules, for instance, are broadly designed either to give direct effect to, or to provide compensation for the breach of, a legal obligation. Thus, remedial rules often tell us something about the nature and content of the underlying legal obligation to whose breach they are a response.

The rules falling under the first two headings mentioned above—formation of contracts and content of contracts—are, of course, squarely contractual, even under a very narrow definition of contract. But as has already been noted, it would be a fundamental mistake to assume that all the transactions and duties currently regarded as contractual arise from promises or agreements. Many clearly do not. The question then arises whether such transactions and duties should be, in effect, moved out of contract law. In principle, an affirmative answer seems appropriate, but in practice this response is vulnerable to the objection that some useful transactions and duties may end up with no home at all. It is clear, historically, that one reason many liabilities were described by courts as contractual despite not arising from a promise or agreement is that the judges could not find any other legal category in which to place them. This appears to have been the case for much of what is now called unjust enrichment law. A more pragmatic approach therefore seems appropriate, which is essentially the approach the courts themselves have followed. A great many kinds of liabilities have in fact been reclassified as non-contractual over the last hundred or so years, but this has generally only happened when developments in *other* areas of the law reached the point where the liabilities in question could be moved to safe homes.

As a final matter, it may be asked what real importance these classificatory issues can have, other than to contract scholars who need to decide what to include in their books; the substance of the rules must surely matter more than whether they are classified as contract rules or tort rules or any other kind of rule. Three brief responses to this difficult question may be mentioned here. First, classification is practically important. Without a good classification scheme, trying to find the law on a particular topic is like looking for books in an unsorted library. Second, and a related point, classification is intimately connected to knowledge. Learning the law, like learning biology or chemistry, is in large part a matter of learning classificatory schemes. By placing a particular rule, animal, or substance into a particular category we are saying what is important or distinctive about that rule or animal or substance. And when we have difficulty doing this, we are saying that the rule, animal, or substance merits further study. Third, and of greatest significance, classificatory questions are morally important. It was noted earlier that perhaps the most important question to ask of the law is an essentially moral question: is law justified? In the case of law, classification and morality are closely linked, because the most basic principle of justice is that like cases should be treated alike. Of course, no classification scheme that is applied to a human endeavour such as the law will fit all the data perfectly. But to the extent that a classification scheme is accurate, it can help courts and other lawmakers to know which cases are alike and which are different.

Part I

Formation of Contracts

3

Offer and Acceptance

THIS and the next chapter examine the requirements for creating a valid contract. The focus of this chapter is the basic requirement that there be an 'offer' by one party which is then 'accepted' by the other; Chapter 4 then examines additional requirements, such as that the offer and acceptance be in a particular form, that they provide for an exchange (the 'consideration' requirement), or that they be made in a 'commercial' setting (the 'intent to create legal relations' requirement).

In the previous chapter it was noted that most contracts are created by promises and agreements, so it should be no surprise to learn that, notwithstanding the sometimes technical language in which they are couched, the rules for establishing an offer and an acceptance are for the most part consistent with the ordinary understanding of what is required to make a promise or agreement. But there are clear exceptions. As we shall see, the offer and acceptance rules are better adapted to establishing the existence of arrangements involving mutual undertakings, that is to say, agreements, than to establishing the existence of arrangements involving a (mere) unilateral undertaking, that is to say, a (single) promise.[1] Because of this difference, the application of the offer and acceptance rules to unilateral undertakings is discussed separately in this chapter. In addition, there are various arrangements that lawyers describe as contractual but that involve neither an agreement nor a promise; equally, there are legal obligations that arise from an agreement or a promise that are not labelled as contractual. Such arrangements and obligations are best examined separately from the main body of offer and acceptance law; they are the focus of the third, fourth, and fifth sections of this chapter.

The concluding section of this chapter briefly describes the main forms of 'extra'-contractual liability that may be relevant in situations in which the legal requirements for a contract, in particular the rules of offer and acceptance, are not satisfied. Though not strictly about contract law, this discussion is important lest it be assumed that the only kinds of obligations potential contracting parties need be concerned about are contractual obligations. As we shall see, there are in fact many kinds of extra-contractual

---

[1] The present editor has argued elsewhere that an agreement is different from a (mere) pair of promises (*Contract Theory*: Oxford, 1999 at 56–7, 180–1), but for present purposes it is sufficient to acknowledge that there is a difference between arrangements that involve mutual undertakings ('agreements') and those that involve unilateral undertakings ('a promise').

obligations that may be relevant in a contractual or pre-contractual setting. We shall also see that the failure to recognize such obligations has sometimes caused problems in the law of contract.

I. AGREEMENTS

We begin with contracts that arise from agreement. In these cases, it is necessary that two or more persons agree to mutual undertakings to do or not do certain things—for example, to deliver goods, on the one hand, and to pay for them, on the other. For this purpose it has become traditional to look for a proposal, or an offer as it is more usually called, and an acceptance. In the words of Pollock:

One party proposes his terms; the other accepts, rejects or meets them with a counter-proposal: and thus they go on till there is a final refusal and breaking-off or till one of them names terms which the other can accept as they stand.[2]

Clearly, not all contracts that arise from agreements are created this way. Frequently, two persons will sign a document that they drew up together or that was written by a third party. The document records an agreement, but it does not arise from what an ordinary observer would describe as a process of offer and acceptance. Another example is a multi-party agreement, as between the members of an association or a partnership. But Pollock's description is a realistic picture of many business transactions, and even where this sort of bargaining does not actually take place, it is often convenient to analyse the negotiations in this way in order to determine precisely when an agreement is reached. This applies in particular where the contract is alleged to have been entered into by correspondence, for it is here possible to examine a sequence of communications (letters, faxes, emails, etc.) to see whether any of them contains a definite offer accepted by a subsequent communication.

The first requirement, therefore, is an offer. In the type of case we are now considering—where the offer contemplates an eventual agreement—the offer is a proposal by the offeror to undertake to do or abstain from doing something provided that the offeree will also undertake to do or abstain from doing something. The offer thus contains two ideas: (1) an expression of a willingness to be bound; (2) a statement of what each party to the proposed agreement must do or not do.

Consistent with the ordinary understanding of agreement, the courts have not demanded that these requirements be satisfied using a particular form of words, or even that they be satisfied using words at all. An offer may be inferred from conduct, such as boarding a bus. On the other hand, the courts

---

[2] *Principles of Contract*, 13th edn (London, 1950) at 4–5.

have generally applied the substantive elements of these requirements strictly. They have required, for instance, proof that the relevant communication express a genuine willingness to be bound. Whether the courts have been too strict in this regard (as some commentators have argued) cannot be addressed without considering (in the last section of this chapter) the various forms of extra-contractual protection available in situations in which no contract is formed. But it should be kept in mind that, while both parties to a contract typically benefit from the arrangement, each party's individual obligations are effectively obligations to benefit or assist the other party, and, moreover, these obligations are created by ordinary citizens rather than the state. These features of contractual liability go some way to explaining why courts approach its preconditions so seriously.

The offer must express a willingness to be bound

The requirement that there be a 'willingness to be bound' is relevant in three main categories of cases. One category consists of cases where it is alleged that the relevant statement was not meant to be taken seriously. Suppose that during a party, I announce that I will give £1,000 to the first person who sings 'God Save the Queen' backwards. It is highly unlikely the courts would enforce this 'offer'. The reason is straightforward: my statement could not reasonably have been understood to be serious. Admittedly, the literal meaning of my words suggested I was willing to be bound—but words must be understood in context, and the context in which my words were made suggest that I was making a joke. Confusingly, the courts sometimes explain the results in such cases on the basis that the speaker did not 'intend to create legal relations'.[3] In my example, it is true that I did not intend to create *legal* relations, but the more fundamental reason no contract could be formed is that I did not express an intention to create *any* relations, legal or otherwise. My statement did not express a willingness to be bound even in purely moral terms. In short, I did not actually make an offer.

A second category of cases in which the requirement of a willingness to be bound is relevant is where it is alleged that the relevant statement, though made seriously, does not propose an undertaking. In principle, the relevant distinction is straightforward, but it can be difficult to apply in a number of common situations. One instance is where it is unclear if the relevant statement expresses an intention to undertake an obligation to do something as opposed to merely an *intention* (or plan) to do that thing. Suppose that I say 'I *will* give you £500 next week'. Depending on the context, the word 'will' might reasonably be understood as expressing either an undertaking (i.e. an agreement or a promise) to transfer the money *or* merely an intention or plan

---

[3] See *Carlill v. Carbolic Smoke Ball Co.* [1893] 1 QB 256, where this argument was made but rejected on the facts. Intent to create legal relations is discussed further in Chapter 4.

to do this. This was essentially the issue in *Kleinwort Benson v. Malaysia Mining Corporation Berhad*.[4] The defendants, in response to the claimants' request to guarantee the debts of one of the defendants' subsidiary companies, stated in a 'comfort letter' that 'it is our policy to ensure that the business of [the subsidiary company] is at all times in a position to meet its liabilities to you under the above arrangements'.[5] When the defendants subsequently allowed the subsidiary to become insolvent, the question arose whether they had thereby breached a contractual undertaking. The court's decision that no undertaking was made seems correct. Assuming the defendants' words were used in their ordinary sense, and taking into account that sophisticated commercial parties are expected to be careful when making and reading documents,[6] to say 'it is our policy to' merely expresses an intention to do something rather than the undertaking of an obligation. Indeed, the very reason for saying 'it is our policy' rather than 'we undertake/promise/agree' is to indicate that one reserves the right to change one's mind or to not follow through on the policy in all circumstances. This is why government ministers typically say 'We plan to do X or Y' rather than 'We promise to do X or Y': they want to reserve the right to change their minds (though such statements are in any event not legally binding because, *inter alia*, there is no intent to create legal relations: see Chapter 4).

Another situation in which it can be difficult to determine if a statement expresses an intention to undertake an obligation is where it is alleged that the statement was a mere 'invitation to treat', that is, an invitation to make an offer. The difference is often obvious. If I say, 'Make me an offer,' or, 'I am open to offers above £100', it is clear that I am asking for offers rather than making one. But in many everyday situations this distinction can be difficult to draw. Advertisements provide a good example. As a matter of ordinary interpretation, it is often unclear whether an advertisement is an offer to sell or an invitation to make an offer. Despite this uncertainty (or perhaps because of it—see below), the common law rule is that advertisements, circulars, catalogues, etc. are presumed not to be offers, even if a price list is attached.[7] The Court of Appeal has even applied this presumption to the display of goods in a shop. In *Pharmaceutical Society v. Boots*,[8] it was held

---

[4] [1989] 1 WLR 379

[5] Ibid at 381.

[6] A different result might be appropriate were the document addressed to a consumer. Thus, in *Bowerman v. Association of British Travel Agents Ltd* [1996] 1 QB 256, a notice issued by the defendant Association informing consumers of the Association's insurance scheme was held to be contractually binding.

[7] *Partridge v. Crittenden* [1968] 1 WLR 1204. The presumption may be rebutted by a categorically worded advertisement, such as 'Special Bargain Offer'.

[8] [1953] 1 QB 401.

that the customer makes an offer by picking up an article and taking it to the cash register, which the cashier then accepts or rejects.[9] A misleading advertisement (or display of goods) is therefore dealt with not by holding the advertiser bound to sell the goods, but by holding the advertiser liable for the tort of misrepresentation and possibly also in violation of consumer protection legislation.[10]

The common law presumption about advertisements is sometimes defended on the ground that the contrary rule could lead to an advertiser being bound to sell advertised items to anyone who accepts the offer, regardless of the number of items available. But as civilian systems have shown, this result is not inevitable: the offer in the advertisement can legitimately be interpreted as subject to an implied term that the offer expires after supplies run out. No one reading an advertisement for a used car can realistically believe that the advertiser intends to sell the same car to more than one buyer.[11] A better explanation, therefore, is that the presumption is a response to what is basically a coordination problem—a situation in which it is important to have *a* solution, though it does not matter which of two or more solutions is adopted, such as which side of the road to drive on. Advertisements raise coordination problems because of the difficulty of determining whether any particular advertisement amounts to an offer as opposed to an invitation to treat. Absent a presumption, advertisers and customers—and their lawyers—would need to make difficult judgments about the meaning of the relevant advertisement. Adopting a presumption avoids this problem, and thus helps such parties to plan their affairs with reasonable certainty; in other words, to co-ordinate their actions. Adopting either the current rule or the contrary rule achieves this end.

A third category of cases in which the requirement of a willingness to be bound is significant involves parties who clearly intend to enter a binding agreement, but who break off negotiations before having firmly committed themselves. This often happens when negotiations inch forward by a series of small steps, making it hard to determine at which point, if any, a party has expressed a definite commitment. The parties themselves often exacerbate the difficulty by attaching ambiguous titles such as 'Heads of Agreement', 'Letter of Intent', or 'Agreement in Principle' to preliminary documents. In many such cases, although there may be an 'expression of willingness' in a broad

---

[9] Later in this chapter, it will be suggested that the customer in cases like *Boots* cannot realistically be said to have agreed or promised to do anything. The customer just does or does not do something—in this case, hand over money. Whether the store has agreed or promised to do anything will also be questioned.

[10] See, e.g., Trade Descriptions Act 1968, s. 14(1)(b).

[11] But not all advertisements can be interpreted as subject to an implied term of this kind: a counter-example might be a travel agent's advertisement for 'Tickets to the USA for only £100 if you book before 31 March'.

sense, this may be nothing more than a preliminary step in the formation of the contract.

This third category is well illustrated by two cases relating to the sale of council houses by the Manchester City Council. In both cases, sales were in the process of being made when a local election resulted in the sale of council houses being immediately stopped. The question was whether the process had gone so far that a legally binding contract had been made. In *Gibson v. Manchester City Council*,[12] the defendants had sent the claimant a brochure explaining the scheme for the sale of council houses, together with a form by which he could apply to the council for information as to the prices. The claimant filled in the form and sent it to the Council, which replied by letter stating the price at which they 'may be prepared to sell', and also giving details of their mortgage proposals. The letter went on to say that it was not to be regarded as a firm offer of a mortgage; a further form was sent to the claimant which he was instructed to complete if he wanted 'to make formal application' to buy the house. The claimant duly filled in this form and returned it. The Council never replied to this application, though it took the house off the list of council houses under the control of its maintenance department. It was held by the House of Lords that there was no concluded contract, but, at most, an offer by the claimant that had never been accepted.

In the earlier case of *Storer v. Manchester City Council*,[13] the procedure had reached a more advanced stage. Here the claimant had received a reply to his formal application to purchase. The reply was a letter from the town clerk forwarding a formal 'Agreement for Sale' for the tenant to sign, and stating that on receipt of that Agreement the town clerk would send a copy of it, signed on behalf of the Council, in exchange. The Agreement contained all the essential terms for the sale of the house. It was signed by the tenant and sent to the Council, but they failed to sign and return their copy in exchange. It was held by the Court of Appeal that there was a binding contract. The town clerk's letter forwarding the formal 'Agreement for Sale' was a clear offer, containing all the essential terms, and the tenant had accepted this offer by signing and returning the 'Agreement'. The Council's failure to return a copy in exchange was immaterial.

Conceptual reasoning in the law of offer and acceptance

As should be evident already, the reasoning in many of the cases discussed in this chapter has an air of unreality to it. In order to explain how this has come about, it is useful to make a short digression to discuss the nature of

[12] [1979] 1 WLR 294.
[13] [1974] 1 WLR 1403. The precise result may well be different today as a result of changes made by the Law of Property (Miscellaneous Provisions) Act 1989 with regard to the requirements of writing contracts for the sale of land.

'conceptual' reasoning in the law. This is not an easy process to explain or to understand, but a correct understanding of the nature of conceptual reasoning is an important part of a lawyer's equipment.

Put very briefly, conceptual reasoning usually takes the form of reasoning *forwards* from legal concepts to the solution of a particular dispute. For instance, if a claimant claims that the defendant has broken a contract and the defendant denies that there was any contract, the court may approach the case by asking whether the defendant's words or conduct amounted to an offer or an acceptance. If this question is answered in the negative, the court then *deduces* that no contract was made.

But this is not the only way in which such questions can be approached; an alternative—and less conceptual—method of approach is to reason *backwards,* For instance, if the court thinks that the claimant ought to have a legal remedy against the defendant for what happened, the court may reason thus: if the claimant is to be given a legal remedy, we must hold that there was a contract; but in order to hold that there was a contract, we must first hold that the defendant's conduct amounted to an offer (or an acceptance). *Therefore* we hold that the defendant's conduct did amount to an offer (or an acceptance). This kind of reasoning is sometimes said to be 'result-oriented', meaning that the reasoning process is determined by the desired result, rather than the result genuinely following from the reasoning.

In practice courts in this country have, in theory at least, traditionally adopted the first approach in preference to the second, but there is no doubt that this has some disadvantages. It tends to lend an air of inevitability to the decisions of the courts which is most misleading. The decision only appears to be inevitable because most of the real issues are not discussed at all; though they may weigh with the courts in arriving at their decisions, their reasoning is not openly and consciously displayed. Instead, a number of other reasons which may be more or less convincing are offered for the decision.

Many of the offer and acceptance cases are good illustrations of this process. For example, the question whether a display of goods in a self-service store amounts to an offer is itself a 'conceptual' question. The answer can have no meaning except in some legal context. The most usual context would be that in which a shopkeeper refused to serve a customer (or perhaps refused to sell the goods at the price indicated) and the real question would be whether he was *entitled* to do this. The conceptual method of answering this is to rephrase the issue in terms of concepts. Instead of asking if the shopkeeper is entitled to refuse to serve a customer, or to refuse to sell at a marked price, the courts ask whether the shopkeeper has made or accepted an offer. And this question is answered with little reference to the consequences. One result is that an important social or moral question is never openly discussed by the courts, namely, should a shopkeeper be allowed to refuse to serve a member of the public or should he be allowed to refuse to sell goods at a marked price?

Another result is that the decisions of the courts often rest on demonstratively faulty reasoning. In this particular area many of the courts' reasons are shown to be unconvincing by other legal decisions dealing with a situation in which the right to refuse to serve a member of the public is *denied*, that is, in the case of 'common inns' or hotels. We have already seen, for example, that much has been made of the difficulties which a shopkeeper may encounter if he receives more acceptances than he has goods to sell. If he is deemed to 'offer' his goods for sale, is he then to be liable to all those customers who 'accept' his offer even though he cannot supply them? But this is an unreal difficulty, as is shown by the law relating to hotel-keepers. If a hotel proprietor is asked for a room when he has no room vacant the courts have had no difficulty in adopting the common sense view that he is not liable.

It will be seen that, if it had been desired to impose liability on a shopkeeper who refused to serve a customer, the relevant legal concepts would not have stood in the way of achieving this result. The courts could have said that a shopkeeper 'impliedly' offers to do business with any member of the public, and therefore that a contract is concluded when a customer 'accepts' the offer by intimating that he wishes to buy something in the shop.

Thus in strict logic the way in which a fact or a particular piece of conduct should be conceptualized by having a legal label attached to it should depend on the result which it is desired to achieve. But it must be recognized that lawyers and courts often reason in a way which suggests that they do not accept the strictly logical position. They frequently attach the label first, and give every appearance of thinking that the selection of the correct label is something which must be done without reference to the result.

In the particular case of self-service shops, legal methods of reasoning probably mean that the law is today out of touch with modern social conditions, and also with public attitudes. Most people would probably be surprised to discover that a shopkeeper is not obliged to sell an article at the price indicated if a customer offers to pay for it, and this public attitude is confirmed by the fact that such behaviour by a shopkeeper would today probably constitute an offence under the Consumer Protection Act 1987 or other consumer protection legislation.[14]

The offer must be certain

In addition to expressing a willingness to be bound, an offer must also describe what the parties to the agreement are meant to do or not do: an agreement is an agreement about *something*. This requirement comes into

---

[14] See *R v. Warwicks CC, ex parte Johnson* [1993] 2 WLR 1.

sharper focus when we consider the situation of a court trying to enforce a contract, either by an order of specific performance or an order to pay damages: before it can make such an order, the court must be able to determine what it is that the defendant agreed to do. Lawyers usually describe this requirement as one of 'certainty'. In theory, certainty and willingness to be bound are distinct, but in practice these requirements often overlap, since a failure to agree on terms is often evidence that the parties were not yet ready to be bound.

Uncertainty may take the form of ambiguity, vagueness, or incompleteness. One famous instance of uncertainty due to ambiguity is provided by the case of *Raffles v. Wichelhaus*.[15] The claimant had agreed to sell goods that were being shipped from Bombay on a ship called the *Peerless*, but he complained that the buyer refused to accept the goods when they were tendered to him. The defendant buyer claimed that there were two ships, both called *Peerless*, one leaving Bombay in October and the other in December. While the goods offered for delivery came from the later ship, the buyer had thought that the contract referred to the earlier one. The court held there was no contract. The case is often treated as an illustration of an operative mistake, and no doubt the parties were mistaken in a sense. But as will be explained in more detail later in this chapter, this sort of mistake does not normally nullify a contract. In the usual case of conflicting intentions as to the meaning of a term, the ambiguity is resolved by giving the term the meaning that a reasonable person would have assumed it to have. This is why pleas of ambiguity are rarely successful. What made the ambiguity in *Raffles* unusual is that it could not be resolved by asking how the reasonable person would have understood the contract. On the facts each understanding of 'Peerless' appeared equally plausible.

Instances of uncertainty due to vagueness and incompleteness are more common. These two types of uncertainty tend to blend into each other, for if the contract's words are so vague as to lack a definite meaning the contract becomes, in effect, incomplete. But a contract may be incomplete without any question of vagueness arising. For instance, the absence of agreement on a vital term may be good evidence that no contract has yet been concluded, and that the parties are still negotiating. A simple illustration of vagueness is provided by a 1941 House of Lords' decision.[16] In this case, it was held that an agreement for the sale of a van, subject to hire-purchase terms being available, was not sufficiently certain to create a valid contract. There are a large number of possible variations in hire-purchase contracts, and it was not possible to say on which terms the parties were agreed.

---

[15] (1864) 2 H & C 906.
[16] *Scammell & Nephew Ltd v. Ouston* [1941] AC 251.

A concern for vagueness also underlies the long-standing rule that an 'agreement to agree' or an 'agreement to negotiate' cannot be a valid contract.[17] Of course, an 'agreement to agree' is enforceable if the parties agree to enter into a contract on terms which themselves are sufficiently definite. Thus, an agreement to enter into a lease is normally perfectly valid because the terms of the intended lease will be set out in the first agreement. Equally, an agreement to terms that, though not fixed at the time of agreement, can later be ascertained with reasonable certainty is enforceable. For example, an agreement to sell at a price specified as a function of a certain price index or to be established by an independent valuer will be valid.[18] The same is true of an agreement *not* to agree with anyone else. For instance, if a party is negotiating for the purchase of a house, but is fearful that the seller will continue to deal with other buyers in the absence of a binding contract, the buyer may seek to persuade the seller to agree not to negotiate with anyone else for a specified period. This is known as a 'lock-out' agreement, and is legally binding because there is nothing uncertain about it:[19] the time-span is clear and the duties of the parties are clear. What the parties cannot do is bind themselves to negotiate and reach agreement, because the negotiations may quite genuinely fail to lead to an agreement. Thus, an agreement under which a builder was to construct a building for a developer was held not to be binding because no price was fixed, it being simply agreed that fair and reasonable sums would be negotiated.[20]

The conclusion that a bare agreement to agree cannot be enforced as a contract does not mean that the parties to such an arrangement could not be bound by other duties, in particular a duty to negotiate in good faith. This duty could hypothetically be founded on an agreement (and so be contractual), as where the parties had agreed to negotiate in good faith, or it might be imposed as a matter of law (in which case it would lead to compensatory, not contractual, remedies). But in a recent ruling[21] the House of Lords reiterated the traditional common law position that negotiating parties are not under duties to negotiate in good faith, even if they have explicitly agreed to such a duty. The court said such a duty is inherently repugnant to the adversarial position of the parties when involved in negotiations, and they noted that in the business world, parties often make statements in the course

---

[17] *Walford v. Miles* [1992] 2 AC 128, a decision much criticized by commentators.

[18] *Sudbrook Trading Estates Ltd v. Eggleton* [1983] 1 AC 444. Note that in some cases the courts will simply impose a reasonable price if the contract is silent.

[19] *Pitt v. PHH Asset Management Ltd* [1993] 4 All ER 961.

[20] *Courtney & Fairbairn v. Toulaini Bros (Hotels) Ltd* [1975] 1 WLR 297. Note that while an agreement that 'a reasonable price will be negotiated' cannot bind the parties, the willingness on the part of modern courts to fill gaps in contracts would allow an agreement that a reasonable price will be *paid* (with no mention of negotiation) to be found binding in some circumstances; see Ch. 6.

[21] *Walford v. Miles*, above n. 17.

of negotiations that are not strictly true (e.g. 'that is my last offer') but are not regarded as commercially improper. It is not clear, however, that this description of negotiating practices is inconsistent with a duty of good faith that (merely) requires negotiating parties to make reasonable efforts. This duty would be breached, for instance, in a case where one of the parties simply refused to negotiate at all. Given that courts appear willing to enforce obligations of this kind when they are explicitly agreed upon by the parties, it is not clear why such obligations could not also be enforced under the heading of good faith.[22]

Not all instances of vagueness or incompleteness are sufficient to render a contract invalid. Indeed, if this were the case, no contract could ever be formed since it is impossible for contracting parties to provide for every possibility in their contracts—our imaginations and our language are too limited. The general rule, therefore, is that so long as there is agreement on the essential terms (or on a mechanism for establishing those terms) the courts are willing to fill gaps in the secondary terms. It is not easy to define in advance what qualifies as a secondary term, and the decisions in this area are inconsistent,[23] but overall the modern trend has been to define the concept broadly. Thus, the willingness to fill gaps has extended into what might be thought relatively important matters, such as the price, date of delivery of goods, date of payment, and so forth.[24] This is especially true in commercial contracts negotiated between experienced parties because in such cases the courts usually have a good idea, based on past dealings, commercial custom, and usage, about how the gaps should be filled in.[25] These gap-fillers, which are discussed in more detail in Chapter 6, can usually be defended as being just and reasonable; they can also often be defended on the ground that the parties implicitly assumed that they would apply. It is not uncommon to order goods without stipulating the price, at least if prices are relatively stable; in such situations the unstated assumption is that the purchaser is agreeing to pay the standard price.

There are two other situations in which courts are more willing than usual to complete apparently incomplete contracts. The first is where the alleged contract is partly or wholly performed. In such cases, the courts are generally (and not merely with respect to claims of uncertainty) more willing to find a valid contract because of the difficulty involved in returning the parties to the

---

[22] See the comments of Lord Ackner in *Walford*, ibid at 138.

[23] *Contrast May and Butcher Ltd v. The King* [1934] 2 KB 17 and *Hillas & Co. Ltd v. Arcos Ltd* (1932) 147 LT 503.

[24] It is now specified by statute that a failure to state the price in a contract for the sale of goods or for the supply of goods or services does not render the contract incomplete. The price will be assumed to be a 'reasonable' price: Sale of Goods Act 1979, s. 8(2), Sale of Goods & Services Act 1982, s. 15(1).

[25] See Viscount Maugham in *Scammell and Nephew Ltd v. Ouston*, above n. 16.

positions they were in prior to the contract. Admittedly, the law of unjust enrichment, which has in recent years been placed on a much more secure footing, can usually ensure that any benefits transferred in reliance on the supposed agreement are returned. But such relief provides little comfort to a party whose basic complaint is that the other party failed to abide by the terms of their agreement (such as it was), for example a purchaser whose complaint is that the goods did not meet the vendor's description. The vendor is not interested in simply getting his money back (and if the goods have been used it may be too late to undo the transaction in any event). In addition, it is much more difficult to obtain compensation for reliance that does not benefit the other party. In cases of this kind, therefore, the courts are often more willing to find that there was a binding contract.[26]

The other situation in which courts are often willing to ignore gaps is where the gap relates to an obligation that is to be performed at a distant date in the future. It is common in such arrangements for the parties to leave unspecified important matters of the kind mentioned above. The reason is obvious: it is difficult to predict the future with precision. Normally these matters will be settled by agreement between the parties when the time comes, but that does not mean that the earlier agreement is of no effect. The earlier agreement may well be a good contract in itself when one includes the terms that may be read into the agreement. These principles were discussed and applied by the House of Lords in *Hillas & Co. v. Arcos Ltd*[27] The Court emphasized that the problem 'must always be to so balance matters that, without violation of essential principle, the dealings of men may as far as possible be treated as effective, and that the law may not incur the reproach of being the destroyer of bargains'.[28] Lord Wright held that:

It is clear that the parties both intended to make a contract and thought they had done so. Business men often record the most important agreements in crude and summary fashion; modes of expression sufficient and clear to them in the course of their business may appear to those unfamiliar with the business far from complete or precise. It is accordingly, the duty of the court to construe such documents fairly and broadly, without being too astute or subtle in finding defects; but, on the contrary, the court should seek to apply the old maxim of English law *verba ita sunt intelligenda Ut res magis valeat quam pereat*. That maxim, however, does not mean that the court is to make a contract for the parties, or to go outside the words they have used, except in so far as there are appropriate implications of law, as, for instance, the implication of what is just and reasonable to be ascertained by the court as matter of machinery where the contractual intention is clear but the contract is silent in some detail. Thus in contracts for future performance over a period the parties may not be able nor may

---

[26] As regards reliance losses, this is expressly stated by Lord Denning in *F. & G. Sykes (Wessex) Ltd v. Fine Fare* [1962] 2 Lloyd's Rep. 52 at 57–8.

[27] [1932] All ER 494.

[28] Ibid, per Lord Tomlin at 499.

they desire to specify many matters of detail, but leave them to be adjusted in the working out of the contract. Save for the legal implications I have mentioned, such contracts might well be incomplete or uncertain; with that implication in reserve they are neither incomplete nor uncertain. As obvious illustrations I may refer to such matters as prices or times of delivery in contracts for the sale of goods or times of loading or discharging in a contract of sea carriage.[29]

A final point is that one area in which the requirements both of certainty and willingness to be bound give rise to constant difficulties concerns the sale of houses and other buildings. Because the sale procedure is so protracted in English practice even a clear 'agreement' is not usually a binding legal contract and sales often fall through because buyers or sellers simply change their minds. To avoid this risk one party sometimes attempts to tie the other party down with a binding contract at an earlier stage. For example, a buyer who is concerned that she may be unable to obtain a mortgage on the property and so find herself bound to buy without having the means to pay may attempt to make a binding contract that is conditional on her being able to obtain a satisfactory mortgage. The effect of such a clause is uncertain in the present state of the law. On the one hand, it has been held that an agreement for the sale of a house may be too uncertain to be a contract if it is made 'subject to [the buyer] obtaining a satisfactory mortgage'[30] because there are no standards by which a court can say what constitutes a satisfactory mortgage; on the other hand, there are dicta of high authority suggesting that a condition of this kind can be waived by the buyer, so that the seller cannot renege on the whole deal.[31]

Termination of the offer

If an offer does not first become a contract by being accepted, it may be 'terminated', that is, it may lose its ability to be converted into a contract. This typically happens in one of three ways. In considering these, it should be kept in mind that we are limiting our attention at this point to offers that propose mutual undertakings, that is, agreements. As will be explained later, special rules often apply to offers that propose a unilateral undertaking, that is, a single promise, such as an offer of a reward.

The most straightforward way that an offer may be terminated is by expiry. Thus, an offer may expire in accordance with its own terms, for example, if it is made subject to a condition and the condition fails. Alternatively, it may expire by lapse of time, either because an expiry date was explicitly stated or, if no date was stated, because a 'reasonable' period of time has passed. In the latter case, the assumption is that it goes without saying that an offer is

---

[29] Ibid at 503–4.
[30] *Lee-Parker v. Izzet* [1972] 1 WLR 775.
[31] *Graham v. Pitkin* [1992] 5 WLR 403 (PC), per Lord Templeman at 405.

intended to lapse after a reasonable time. What is reasonable depends on the circumstances, such as the usual practices in the relevant industry. In the case of perishable goods, for instance, the time period is normally very short. Significantly, this period may be lengthened if the offeror does anything that would lead the offeree to believe the offer had not lapsed.[32] In such a case, the offeror is effectively extending or renewing the original offer.

Secondly, an offer may be rejected by the offeree. This destroys its efficacy insofar as the particular offeree is concerned, unless the offeror renews the offer. The main reason that the offeree is not able to change his mind and have a second bite at the cherry would appear to be that, in most cases, offerees have indicated by their rejection that they are no longer interested in the offer, and thus that an offer may be made to another party. In some cases, this assumption may be incorrect, but here as elsewhere in the law there is a value in adopting a general presumption about intent. The current presumption allows offerors to act on the rejection immediately by making an offer to a new party.[33] If offerees wish to have further time to think, they can simply ask offerors to keep their offers open.

A corollary of this rule is that a counter-offer is equivalent to rejection. The classic illustration is *Hyde v. Wrench*,[34] where an offer to sell an estate for £1,000 was met by a counter-offer to buy for £950. The counter-offer was rejected, and the buyer then wrote to say that he was prepared to pay £1,000 after all. But the seller now refused to sell to the offeree even at this price. Had this case arisen today, it could have been quickly disposed of on the ground that (as is discussed in the next chapter) the necessary formalities for a sale of land were not satisfied. But in the nineteenth century, the informality of such a transaction was not a barrier to its enforcement. Instead, the court held that there was no contract for a different reason: although the offer to sell at the original price had not been withdrawn, the counter-offer had amounted to a rejection of the original offer. It may be questioned whether, as a matter of ordinary interpretation, counter-offers always convey the message that the original offeree is no longer interested in the original offer. But this may be another situation where it is important for practical reasons to have a clear presumption as to meaning. Moreover, the rule can be defended on the ground that the contrary rule would give offerees an unfair advantage in the bargaining process, since they could pitch their first counter-offer at a low level, and then gradually edge upwards, all the while keeping in reserve the

---

[32] *Manchester Diocesan Council v. Commercial & General Investments Ltd* [1970] 1 WLR 141.

[33] But it does not appear that the courts' concern is over possible unfairness to the offeree. In *Marseille Fret SA v. D Oltman Schiffarts* (1981) Com LR 277, it was held that a rejection is binding even where it was made by mistake and retracted before the offeror had a chance to act upon it.

[34] (1840) 3 Beav 334.

original figure. Of course, in practice this often happens, and the offeror is perfectly happy to accept the bargain once the original figure is reached—but, on the legal analysis, at that stage the offeree is counter-offering and the offeror has the right to accept or to decline the new counter-offer even though it is on the same terms as the first offer. It should also be noted that it is sometimes difficult to say whether a reply to an offer amounts to a rejection as opposed to merely an inquiry as to whether the offeror might be willing to revise the offer. In principle, the latter is not a revocation.

The third way in which an offer may be terminated is through revocation by the offeror. Consistent with the idea that an offer does not itself bind the offeror but only expresses a willingness to be bound, an offer may be withdrawn at any time before it is accepted. But the common law (unlike the civil law) goes further, and holds that offers may be withdrawn even if the offeror has promised to keep the offer open for a specified time. The explanation for this result lies not in offer-and-acceptance law, but in the 'consideration' rule that gratuitous promises are not binding unless made under seal. The consideration rule is discussed in the next chapter; here it is sufficient to make two observations. First, the rule has many critics, and those critics often point to the unenforceability of these 'firm offers' as an example of the problems the rule causes. Secondly, it is not difficult to avoid this inconvenient rule if one has taken legal advice. An offer with a fixed term is enforceable if it is made under seal or if it is given in exchange for a sum of money or other consideration, even if only of nominal value (e.g. £1). The resulting contract is usually called an 'option' or an 'option contract'.

Notice of revocation must reach the offeree; otherwise, the offer may be treated as continuing and capable of acceptance. This rule is consistent with the ordinary understanding of an agreement, since it is part of that understanding that agreements are formed by a process of communication between the parties to the agreement. But the notice requirement bears highlighting because it makes clear that agreements—and so contracts—can be formed without there ever being a 'meeting of the minds', understood here as a point in time when both of the parties wish to enter into the contract. It is possible, in other words, to *make* an agreement without actually being *in* agreement.

A final point is that although a revocation must reach the offeree to be valid, it has been held that it is not essential that the information be provided by the offeror or even by anyone acting for the offeror. Provided that the offeree is aware of facts that should have made it clear to a reasonable person that the offeror was no longer interested in keeping the offer open, for example if the offeree hears that goods offered for sale have been sold to a third party, the offer will be considered revoked.[35] No doubt this rule works

---

[35] *Dickinson v. Dodds* (1876) 2 Ch D 463.

well enough in most cases. But it appears inconsistent with the basic idea that agreements (and contracts) are created by a process of communication between the parties to the agreement (or their designated agents). It is also open to the objection that it could lead to unfairness in cases where it is not clear that the information can be trusted or where the information, though false, appears trustworthy.

Acceptance

An offer that meets the conditions described above will lead to a valid contract only if it has been 'accepted' by the person(s) to whom it was directed, that is, the 'offeree'. This requirement appears to be the legal expression of the ordinary idea that it takes two people to make an agreement. The agreement is created by the offeree accepting the offeror's offer to enter into a mutual undertaking. It further follows that two offers, even if identical, cannot form a contract. For instance, if A and B have been negotiating for the purchase and sale of a car, and by chance they sit down and write identical offers to each other, these offers do not create a contract.[36] The two offers are isolated, independent acts, and one is not given in return for the other. This is a case, therefore, where although the parties are in agreement, they have not actually made an agreement.

Acceptance must be absolute and unconditional, and must indicate a willingness to contract on the exact terms of the offeror. A purported acceptance that seeks to add to or vary a term of the offer is no acceptance at all, although it will be treated as a counter-offer, itself capable of acceptance. Moreover, as we have already seen, a counter-offer amounts to a rejection of the original offer, which then ceases to be capable of acceptance. These rules may be too rigid in certain circumstances. It often happens that a person intends to accept an offer, and writes a letter stating that he does accept it, but then adds some further remarks, or some question (e.g. 'I presume payment by cheque will be acceptable'). Though they may be relatively unimportant or trivial, these further remarks or questions may be held to qualify the purported acceptance to such a degree that they prevent it from having the legal character of an acceptance. The offeror may then be free to withdraw at the last minute.

It follows from what has been said above that a conditional acceptance will also fail to count as an acceptance.[37] Where the acceptance is conditional on the offeror agreeing to a further term, this is clear enough. However, one

---

[36] *Tinn v. Hoffman & Co.* (1873) 29 LT 271.

[37] A conditional acceptance must not be confused with a conditional contract. If an offer to do something should a certain condition be satisfied is made and accepted, condition and all, then the result may be a binding contract. Such a contract will, however, only become operative if the condition is fulfilled.

particular class of cases in which parties wish to have an agreement recorded in proper legal form raises difficulties. When A makes a definite offer to B, and B accepts, subject to a formal contract being drawn up by a solicitor (as, for example, when an agreement for the sale of land is made 'subject to contract'), the question may arise whether this acceptance is binding before the document is drawn up. On the one hand, the mere fact that the parties intend to have their contract drawn up in solemn form does not prevent their earlier agreement from being binding; on the other hand, if the parties have intended to reserve their freedom of action until such a contract is drawn up (which is the generally accepted meaning of 'subject to contract'), then the earlier agreement is not binding. The principle is clear enough but its application is frequently troublesome.

Communication of the acceptance

Consistent with the idea that an agreement is formed by a process of mutual communications, the general rule is that a legal contract is not formed until the acceptance is communicated to the offeror.[38] A bare mental intention to accept is certainly unavailing: 'it is axiomatic that acceptance of an offer cannot be inferred from silence save in the most exceptional circumstances.'[39] The explanation for this is that silence or inaction is rarely unequivocal in its meaning. There are many reasons a person may fail to respond to an offer without intending to accept it.

Furthermore, although offerors may prescribe a particular mode of acceptance, it appears that they may not waive the requirement of communication altogether.[40] It would obviously be unreasonable to hold that a person is deemed to have accepted an offer merely because the offer was not explicitly rejected, even where the original offer has stated that acceptance will be presumed unless the offeror hears to the contrary. Any other rule would enable a stranger to thrust an unsolicited offer on an offeree and impose on the offeree the onus of refusing. But it does not follow that offerors should not be bound by their waivers of the need for a reply. If the offeree intends to accept the offer and acts accordingly, it is hard to see why the offeror should be able to plead that there has been no communication of the acceptance if communication was expressly stated to be unnecessary. In

---

[38] See *Brinkibon Ltd v. Stahag Stahl und Stahlwarenhondelsgesellschaft mb H* [1983] 2 AC 34. The rule does not apply where the lack of communication is the fault of the offeror, as where the offeror's fax machine runs out of paper: *Entores Ltd v. Far East Corporation* [1955] 2 QB 327.

[39] *The Leonidas D* [1985] 1 WLR 925, per Goff LJ at 937. Despite the emphatic nature of this dictum, there are cases where it is confidently suggested that the courts would treat a contract as accepted by silence, as recognised by Lord Steyn in *Vitol SA v. Norelf Ltd* [1996] AC 800 at 811; see also dicta in *Re Selectmove Ltd* [1995] 1 WLR 474.

[40] *Carlill v. Carbolic Smoke Ball Co*, above n. 3, is sometimes cited for the contrary proposition, but as will be explained below, this case dealt with a conditional promise, to which different considerations should and do apply.

America, it appears that such a contract would be treated as complete, but the only English decision on point, although not quite conclusive, is usually interpreted as laying down the contrary rule. In *Felthouse v. Bindley*,[41] the claimant wrote to his nephew offering to buy his horse at a certain price, and added that if he heard no more from him he would consider the horse his. The nephew did not reply, but told the defendant, an auctioneer who was selling his stock, that the horse was not to be sold. The defendant sold the horse, and was sued by the claimant who claimed that the horse was his. It was held that the horse did not belong to the uncle as the nephew had never communicated his acceptance of the offer. It is not certain, however, that the decision would have been the same if the action had been brought by the nephew against the uncle, had the latter refused to pay. Admittedly, the explanation for holding the uncle liable in such a case could not be that there was an *agreement* between the parties: a single communication cannot create an agreement. The explanation would instead be that the uncle had effectively promised the nephew that he would purchase the horse at the nephew's request. As we shall see in the next chapter, the common law places severe restrictions on the enforceability of bare unilateral undertakings of this kind. But we shall also see that these restrictions are often difficult to justify and, moreover, are sometimes relaxed (or ignored) where they would cause real injustices.

There is one important exception to the requirement that the acceptance must actually reach the offeror, and that is when the acceptance is dispatched by post (or telegram). In this case, the rule is that the acceptance is deemed to be complete from the moment that it is posted, even if the letter remains unread upon delivery, or is delivered late, or even if it never reaches its destination. The 'postal' or 'mailbox' rule was first propounded in 1818, and, after much fluctuation of opinion, was finally confirmed by the Court of Appeal in 1879. A convincing justification for this rule has yet to be given. Clearly, it cannot be said that the parties have reached a true agreement at the moment of posting, as agreement requires communication. One possible explanation of the postal rule is similar to the explanation above of why the uncle in *Felthouse v. Bindley* should be bound to the nephew: the offeror made a promise to treat the offeree *as if* acceptance were communicated at the moment of posting. Of course, offers do not usually contain express stipulations of this kind, so the promise must be implied. But it is not implausible to suppose that in many cases just such a promise can realistically be implied on the basis that it goes without saying. The offeror controls the mode of acceptance and so can specify that acceptance occurs upon receipt or that the post may not be used at all. If the offeror fails to specify otherwise, it is therefore often plausible to assume that the offeror is implicitly authorising the use of the post; indeed, it could well be that the offeror is requiring it, as

[41] (1862) 11 CBNS 869.

the use of an alternative means may render an acceptance a counter-offer, even if the offer is silent as to the means of acceptance. The more difficult question is whether it follows that the offeror thereby accepts the consequences of the delay or loss of a postal communication. This may be a fair result, since the offeror has effectively chosen the means of communication, but basing it on the idea of an implied term stretches this concept very far. In any event, it is clear that such an implication cannot be drawn every time an offer is sent by post. Thus, even if this explanation is accepted, it must be acknowledged that part of the justification for the postal rule is that it is a presumptive rule of evidence, introduced to resolve uncertainty as to whether or not the offeror has actually promised to accept the consequences of delay or loss.

The courts appear to have realized that the postal rule fits uneasily with the general principles of contract law and they have refused to extend it to telephone communications, telexes, and other instantaneous modes of communication.[42] There does not appear to be any clear law for faxes or emails, but it can be expected that the postal rule will not apply in these cases. The courts have also held[43] that the postal rule may be inapplicable wherever it would lead to manifest inconvenience or absurdity, as for instance where the acceptance was of an option. The acceptance of an option may come quite out of the blue, while an ordinary acceptance is usually the last of a series of communications. This means that the failure of an ordinary acceptance to arrive when expected may lead to inquiry while this would not necessarily be so where an option is accepted.

Agreement inferred from conduct and the 'battle of the forms'

We have already noted that both the offer and the acceptance of a proposal to enter an agreement need not be communicated orally or in writing, but may instead be inferred from conduct. A person who gets into a taxi and gives an address, for instance, is undertaking to pay for the ride, while the driver is undertaking to deliver the passenger to the address—though neither have actually said either of these things. The courts recognize such possibilities. At the same time, certain conduct which has been characterized as acceptance, and so as forming an agreement, is nothing of the kind. Examples include placing money in a vending machine and returning a lost dog for which a reward has been offered. In neither case has the actor agreed to a proposal to undertake mutual obligations. Rather, the actor has simply acted on a promise. This is clear from the fact that once the relevant actions are done,

---

[42] *Entores v. Miles Far Eastern Corp*, above n. 38. Special considerations apply to non-instantaneous telex communications (e.g. telex messages received outside working hours when the office is vacant). See *Brinkibon*, above n. 38. These considerations must also apply to fax messages.

[43] *Holwell Securities v. Hughes* [1974] 1 WLR 155.

there is nothing for the actor to do but await the promised reward, be it candy or money. Contracts of this kind are therefore discussed in more detail when we look at unilateral undertakings (promises) in the next section.

The idea of communication by conduct is not problematic in principle, but it is sometimes difficult to determine if the alleged implication can actually be drawn. This is illustrated by cases involving what has been described as the 'battle of the forms'. Suppose that a vendor makes an offer to sell goods on a form that contains her standard terms and conditions. The purchaser then purports to accept the goods for the price stated in the vendor's document, but on a form that contains the purchaser's own, slightly different, standard terms and conditions. As we have seen, in strict law, the purchaser's form is a counter-offer, which can be either rejected or accepted by the vendor. And if the vendor communicates such rejection or acceptance in a timely fashion, the strict rule applies without difficulty. But what often happens in practice is that no further communication happens (or the communications continue in the same fashion, that is, purporting to agree while insisting on different terms) and instead the vendor delivers the goods and the purchaser pays the price. Subsequently, the parties get into a dispute where the resolution depends on which, if either, of the parties' documents is held binding. For instance, the vendor's form may contain an exclusion of liability clause not found in the purchaser's form. There is only one full appeal court decision on this question and it is complicated by the fact that the vendor, before delivery, returned to the purchaser a 'tear-off' clause from the purchaser's form that purported to accept the purchaser's conditions and also a letter which stated that delivery would be in accordance with the vendor's own conditions.[44] In any event, the general rule appears to be that a contract is created on the terms set out in the last document that was received prior to an act of performance by the other party—the so-called 'last shot rule'. The rationale behind the rule is that if the vendor delivers following receipt of the purchaser's form, the vendor's act of delivery shows the vendor has accepted that form. Equally, if the purchaser accepts delivery after receiving the vendor's documents, the purchaser can be assumed to have accepted the vendor's terms.

No doubt this is a realistic description of the meaning of delivery or acceptance of delivery in some cases. But in other cases, it will be clear that the parties did not in fact reach any agreement on the disputed terms and, furthermore, that this was apparent to both of them. The finding of agreement is a fiction. It might seem that the proper result in such a case is to hold that there is no contract and leave the parties to such relief as other parts of the law, in particular the law of unjust enrichment, affords them.[45] This is not

---

[44] *Butler v. Ex-Cell-O Corporation (England) Ltd* [1979] 1 WLR 401.
[45] As was done in *British Steel Corp. v. Cleveland Bridge & Engineering Co. Ltd* [1984] 1 All ER 504.

always as harsh a consequence as may appear, since under the latter an award of restitution would effectively guarantee the return of any benefit transferred or the payment of a reasonable sum, which is typically similar to the contractual sum. But as was noted earlier, restitutionary awards may be inadequate in cases where the transaction was completed and the only substantive complaint is that the goods (or whatever) provided by one of parties did not satisfy the contract's terms, express or implied.

Thus, a better solution in many cases is to hold the parties to a contract on the basis of those terms that their documents have in common, and to treat the areas of disagreement as simple gaps in the contract. As we have seen, an offer is complete if it specifies with reasonable precision the main or essential elements of the proposed transactions; details that are left out will be filled in on the basis of usage, custom, etc. Of course, this rule does not override the mirror image rule: where an offer includes non-essential terms, the offeree must still accept those terms as well as the essential ones. At first blush, it would appear this requirement is not met in 'battle of the forms' cases—neither party has actually accepted the other's secondary terms—but it can be argued that where the parties have gone ahead and performed despite this non-agreement, they are effectively communicating that they do not actually require agreement on the secondary terms. In other words, what can be inferred from their conduct is that they had agreed not to sort out the subject matter of the conflicting terms. This is a perfectly sensible attitude for the parties to take, since the conflicting terms are either unimportant or, often, unlikely to matter at all except if something goes wrong. In such a case, then, the court should treat the agreement as if it were blank as regards the conflicting terms. Support for this approach can be found in the following statement of Staughton J:

When two businessmen wish to conclude a bargain but find that on some particular aspect of it they cannot agree, I believe that it is not uncommon for them to adopt language of deliberate equivocation, so that the contract may be signed and their main objective achieved. No doubt they console themselves with the thought that all will go well, and that the term in question will never come into operation or encounter scrutiny; but if all does not go well, it will be for the courts or arbitrators to decide what those terms mean. In such a case it is more than somewhat artificial for a judge to go through the process, prescribed by law, of ascertaining the common intention of the parties from the terms of the document and the surrounding circumstances; the common intention was in reality that the terms should mean what a judge or arbitrator should decide that they mean.[46]

There is one kind of case where the approach advocated here is actually followed as a matter of course. Where parties are negotiating for a lease over

---

[46] *Chemco Leasing SpA v. Redifusion PLC* [1987] FTLR 201.

a particular property it is common practice for the landlord to allow the tenant to enter into possession, and for the tenant to start paying rent before the terms of the lease have all been finalized. If the parties then find it impossible to agree on the terms, the law does not declare the contract void. On the contrary, 'the law, where appropriate, has to step in and fill the gaps in a way which is sensible and reasonable.'[47]

The foregoing approach to 'battle of the forms' cases seems intuitively fair and consistent with general contractual principles. But it must be acknowledged that in practice it is often difficult to distinguish between cases where the parties' behaviour shows them to have agreed only to those terms found in both forms, cases where one party has actually agreed to accept the others' terms, and cases where no agreement was reached at all. None of these possibilities can be ruled out in advance.

Finally, one situation where it is standard practice to regard the parties as having contracted on terms drawn up by just one of the parties is that of insurance. Insurance cover is sometimes urgently required—for example, when a new car is bought and cannot be legally driven until insured—and yet there may be no time to issue a complete policy. In such a case, temporary cover is often agreed, sometimes even by telephone, pending the making of a proper contract in the usual way. If no contract is ever made, the temporary cover will come to an end, but it is not retrospectively invalidated; if the insured event occurs during the period of temporary cover, the company will be liable. There is clearly a temporary contract of some kind, but there are no general implied terms that a court can read into such a contract. Each insurance company has its own set of terms, so there is simply no alternative but to treat the temporary contract as being on the insurance company's terms, to which the insured party is taken to have agreed. This is a good example of the kind of case where a lawyer finds it very easy to say that the insured 'must be taken to have agreed' to a set of terms about which the insured knows nothing, and to which (he might later protest) he certainly never would have agreed had he known what they were.

2. PROMISES (UNILATERAL UNDERTAKINGS)

Thus far, we have been examining contracts that are created by mutual undertakings, that is to say, by agreements. But as we shall see now, the law of contract is sometimes willing to enforce unilateral undertakings, that is to say, mere (single) promises. This should not be surprising. Agreements are closely related to promises. Leaving aside cases where 'agreement' means being *in* agreement about the truth of a proposition (e.g. 'I agree that Renoir

---

[47] *Javad v. Aqil* [1991] 1 All ER 243 at 247, per Nicholls LJ.

was a great painter'), which do not concern us, both agreements and promises are created by communicating intentions to undertake obligations, and both have the effect of doing just this—creating obligations. Indeed, an agreement is often described as nothing more than a pair of (conditional) promises.[48]

From the perspective of offer and acceptance law, the important difference between an agreement and a (single) promise is that a promise is an essentially unitary act. It is true that a promise must be made to a promisee, but the promisee is essentially passive in this process. Agreements, on the other hand, require the active participation of two or more persons; each of the parties to an agreement undertakes obligations. If it turns out that only one party to an 'agreement' is actually under an obligation, the agreement is actually a (single) promise.[49] This difference turns out to be important for understanding contract formation rules for two reasons. First, while it is clear (as we shall see) that the law is sometimes willing to enforce unilateral undertakings, that is, mere (single) promises, such undertakings usually do not satisfy the additional requirements for a valid contract (beyond offer and acceptance) that are discussed in the next chapter. In particular, a unilateral undertaking typically does not satisfy the requirement (given effect by the consideration doctrine) that a party to a valid contract must agree to do something in exchange for the other party agreeing to do something.

The second reason the distinction between an agreement and a promise is important relates to the topic of this chapter: the rules on offer and acceptance are essentially tests for an agreement. A person making a promise does not make an offer—she just makes a promise. Nor do promisees 'accept' promises. A promise must be communicated to the promisee and a promisee may no doubt reject a promised benefit. But there is nothing for a promisee to accept. The typical and appropriate response to a promise is not 'I accept' or 'I agree', but 'thank you'. The traditional offer and acceptance tests for establishing the existence of a contract therefore apply awkwardly to contracts created by unilateral undertakings. This can be illustrated by examining how these tests are applied—or not applied—to the four main categories of situations in which the courts have been willing to enforce such undertakings.[50]

---

[48] But see above n. 1.

[49] This distinction is often obscured by the habit of referring to the parties to an agreement as 'promisors' and by referring to their individual undertakings as 'promises'.

[50] It may be useful to mention here that the reason common law courts are unwilling to give legal force to mere promises more generally does not appear to be that such undertakings fit awkwardly with the offer and acceptance rules, but rather that enforcement is often inconsistent with the consideration, formalities, and intent-to-create-legal-relations doctrines that are discussed in the next chapter.

Deeds

A straightforward example of a court enforcing a mere promise occurs when a court enforces a promise made in the form of a 'deed' (or 'under seal').[51] A mere promise, for example a promise to donate £100 to a charity, is clearly enforceable if it is made by deed. It is impossible to explain this kind of contract in terms of offer and acceptance; no offer is made and no acceptance is required or even possible. The beneficiary of the promise is not involved at all in the making of the deed; indeed the beneficiary does not even need to be aware of the deed when it is made. All that has happened is that one person has made an undertaking—a promise—to perform an act.

Courts have never attempted to analyse deeds in terms of offer and acceptance and most contract textbooks ignore deeds when discussing offer and acceptance. This is sometimes explained on the ground that deeds are not actually contracts (though they are typically discussed elsewhere in contract texts). In historical terms, it is true that the rules on deeds developed from a different body of law—the law of 'covenant'—than that from which the core of the modern law of contract developed (the law of 'trespass'),[52] but it is not clear why this should matter today. In substance, a promise or agreement (deeds are also used for certain types of agreements) made as a deed is plainly a contract. An agreement for the sale of land does not cease to be a contractual agreement just because a seal is stamped on the document recording the agreement.[53]

Conditional promises

Perhaps the most common type of unilateral undertaking that is regularly enforced as a contract is a conditional promise. In the sense intended here, a conditional promise is a promise to do something, typically to pay money or transfer a physical object, on the *condition* (not promise) that a certain act is performed. For example, my promise to pay an antiques dealer a £500 commission *if* the dealer obtains for me a rare Ming vase is a conditional promise. So too is a promise of a reward, for instance a promise to pay £100 to anyone who returns my lost dog. The typical vending machine sale also involves a conditional promise. The owners of the machine promise, albeit not always explicitly, that they will provide the advertised goods if the customer inserts the necessary coins. In each of these cases, only one of the parties—the promisor—has undertaken to do something.

---

[51] Below, 98, 114.

[52] D. Ibbetson, *A Historical Introduction to the Law of Obligations* (Oxford, 1999) at 24–8, 126–30.

[53] The actual requirements for a deed, which are minimal, are discussed later at 95.

Orthodox doctrine analyses each of these situations using the rules of offer and acceptance. More specifically, in each of these cases the promise—to pay the commission, pay the reward, or provide a product—is said to be an 'offer', while the performance of the specified act—finding the vase, returning the dog, inserting the money—is the 'acceptance' of the offer.[54] These are typically described as examples of 'acceptance by conduct'. This is obviously strained. There is no sense in which the antiques dealer, the finder of the dog, or the customer 'accepts' the promisor's promise. To accept is to agree—yet there is nothing for the dealer to agree to, since at no point is the dealer bound to do anything.[55] The dealer in the example above does not agree to find me a vase or even to try to find me a vase, the dealer simply does (or does not) find one. To be sure, the dealer may have relied on the promise, and may have legitimate expectations of payment, but neither the act of reliance nor the fact of expecting payment is acceptance: the dealer's act is no more than what it appears to be—the satisfaction of the condition stipulated in the promise. The alternative label sometimes given to such contracts—'unilateral contracts'—is therefore more accurate, and ideally would be applied to all cases in which a contract arises from a unilateral undertaking.

Not surprisingly, the application of the offer-and-acceptance model to conditional promises has made various issues raised by such arrangements more complex than they would otherwise be. One issue is whether and when a conditional promise may be revoked. Consistent with the offer-and-acceptance approach, the orthodox answer is that the promise may be withdrawn until it is accepted.[56] Since acceptance is interpreted as performance, it follows that the promise may be withdrawn until the specified condition is fully satisfied. This rule leads to acceptable results in cases in which performance is a discrete act for which little or no preparation is required, such as putting a coin into a machine, but it can cause problems if performance involves a protracted act or requires significant preparation. Consider a promise to pay a reward of £1,000 to the first person to swim the English Channel: it would clearly be unjust if such a promise could be withdrawn

---

[54] Thus, in *Re Charge Card Services* [1989] Ch 417 a motorist was held to have accepted an offer to provide petrol from a self-service machine by putting petrol in his tank.

[55] Of course, the dealer might have agreed to do something, for instance to use best efforts in looking for the vase, but an agreement of this kind is not required in such arrangements and is typically not made.

[56] Indeed, Lord Diplock once suggested that the very concept of an offer connotes the absence of any obligation until the offer is accepted: *Varty (Inspector of Taxes) v. British South Africa Co* [1965] Ch. 508 at 523. But cf. Hoffmann J in *Spiro v. Glencrown Properties* [1991] Ch. 537 for a more sophisticated and satisfactory approach. It will be seen that this is another instance of dubious legal reasoning. It is first assumed that completion of the act required 'concludes' the contract; and secondly, that it is a universal rule that an offer can be revoked before the contract is concluded. If these assumptions are correct, the conclusion follows inexorably. But of course the whole question is whether the assumptions *are* correct.

when a swimmer was nine-tenths of the way across. Courts have attempted to respond to this kind of problem in various ways. A common approach is to say that in some (but not all) cases, the 'offer' of a conditional promise carries with it a subsidiary implied promise not to revoke the first offer once performance has begun. Thus, the offer of the above reward would likely be interpreted as containing a subsidiary promise, which is itself conditional, to the effect that 'once the swimmer begins an attempt to swim the channel, the offer will not be revoked.'[57] This subsidiary promise is then said to be 'accepted' by beginning the swim. In many cases, this produces a satisfactory result; but it is again a clear fiction to say that to begin to swim the channel is to accept an offer not to revoke another offer. Moreover, this approach does not address the issue of pre-performance preparation, as in the case of someone who spends months training for a channel swim only to be told just before diving in that the promise has been withdrawn.[58]

There is no easy answer to this question, but it is suggested that the solution does not lie in the further manipulation of the rules of offer and acceptance. What must be squarely addressed is whether and when promises of this kind should become binding, and the answer to this question turns not on when an offer is accepted, but on the kinds of issues discussed in the next chapter (i.e. consideration, estoppel, etc.).

A second issue raised by conditional promises is whether the person who performs the specified act should be able to enforce the promise if he was unaware of the promise at the time he acted. Is knowledge of the promise necessary? Consistent with the agreement-based model of offer and acceptance, the usual answer is no,[59] although there are cases that go the other way.[60] The usual answer makes perfect sense if the issue is whether an agreement has been made: it is not possible to make an agreement without knowing that one is making an agreement. But the answer is less obvious once it is recognised that the claimant in such cases is not attempting to enforce an agreement. An offer of reward is a unilateral undertaking. To be sure, an ordinary promise must normally be *communicated* to be valid; if I write on a piece of paper that I promise to give you £100 on your birthday, and then put that paper away in a drawer, it would be strange of you to accuse me of breaking my promise if you found the paper years later. But while that is the general rule, it is not clear that it should apply to the special case of rewards and other 'promises to the world'. A promise to the world seems more akin to a vow or a declaration

---

[57] *Daulia Ltd v. Four Millbank Nominees Ltd* [1978] Ch 231.

[58] The distinction made in American jurisprudence between preparations for performance and commencing performance is a recognition of, but not a solution to, this problem.

[59] *Taylor v. Allon* [1966] 1 QB 304.

[60] *Gibbons v. Proctor* (1891) 64 LT 594. Civilian systems typically adopt the contrary rule. See s. 257 BGB (Germany); Art. 1395, Civil Code of Quebec.

(as in a will or a declaration of adoption) than a standard promise.[61] If this is correct, it helps to explain why the knowledge requirement is often thought to be inappropriate in cases of rewards: it is not part of the meaning of a vow or a declaration that it must be communicated to a particular person in order to bind the speaker. There are, of course, difficult questions as to when vows or declarations should be given legal force, but the examples of wills and declarations of adoption shows that the law is sometimes willing to give effect to such statements. In short, offers of rewards made to the world seem closer to what civilians sometimes refer to as 'unilateral juridical acts' than to contracts.

In theory (though not yet in practice), a third issue raised by conditional promises concerns communication of acceptance. In the case of contracts created by agreements, the requirement that an acceptance be communicated is uncontroversial: a purported acceptance that is filed away in a drawer is not an acceptance. It is part of the meaning of 'acceptance' that it must be communicated. But if we apply this rule to contracts created by conditional promises, it makes little sense. Performance of an act and communication of the performance of an act are very different notions, and unless the promisor specifically required communication, it is not clear on what basis such a requirement could be implied. Moreover, imposing a communication requirement could lead to unjust results. Promisors would be able to withdraw their promises after the relevant act had been performed so long as they had not yet become aware of the performance. This could happen in a situation like that described in the famous case of *Carlill v. Carbolic Smoke Ball Co.*[62] The defendants were the manufacturers of a contraption known as a Carbolic Smoke Ball, which was claimed to be capable of preventing influenza, as well as a variety of other ailments. By way of an advertising stunt the defendants offered to pay £100 to any person who used the smoke ball according to the instructions and nevertheless caught influenza. The claimant caught influenza despite following the directions; the court upheld her claim, dismissing the defendant's argument that the advertisement was not meant seriously, and finding that she accepted the defendant's offer in their advertisement by fulfilling the conditions.[63] It is unrealistic to suppose that

---

[61] Philosophical accounts of the nature of a promise support this point. It has been argued that the distinctive feature of a promise is that it creates a kind of special relationship between the promisor and the promisee, in particular, the promisor is meant to treat the promisee's interests as more important than those of everyone else with respect to the subject matter of the promise. This kind of relationship is obviously not possible in the case of an undertaking that is made to the entire world. See J. Raz, 'Promises and Obligations,' in P. M. S. Hacker and J. Raz (eds), *Law, Morality, and Society* (Oxford, 1977).

[62] Above n. 2. For a modern American case, equally unique and entertaining, see *Jennings v. Radio Station KSCS* 708 SW 2d (1986).

[63] The problems of imposing liability for statements addressed to the public have their parallel in tort where they have generally been found insuperable; see below, 86, 262.

Mrs Carlill's falling sick, or even her decision to use the smoke ball, were in any sense an 'acceptance' of the offer in the defendant's advertisement, but the significance of the case for present purposes is that, were the communication requirement to be taken seriously, the company could have revoked their offer after she had fallen sick but before they had learnt of this fact. No such revocation was made in *Carlill*, but Bowen L.J., apparently assuming that a performing party must normally notify the promisor personally (and immediately upon performance), held that this requirement could be, and was, waived by the Carbolic Smoke Ball Company. The final result makes perfect sense in that the court enforced a serious promise, but the reasoning is clearly strained and could cause problems if it were applied to bilateral agreements. As was noted earlier, a true agreement cannot be created without the participation of both agreeing parties.

Promises to pay for requested acts

In the seventeenth-century case of *Lampleigh v. Brathwait*,[64] the defendant, who had killed a man, asked the claimant to ride to the king to ask for a pardon. The claimant did as he was asked, and on his return was promised a reward by the defendant. In a claim brought for failing to perform this promise, the court held that the defendant was bound to pay the money because, though the promise was strictly speaking gratuitous (and so apparently unenforceable on the basis of the consideration doctrine mentioned earlier), it was made 'in consideration' of the fulfilment of an earlier request. As is discussed in the next chapter, the ruling remains good law, though in *Pao On v. Yiu Long*[65] it was held that such a promise is enforceable only if it was understood at the time of the original request that the requested act would be remunerated.

The qualification introduced in *Pao On* makes it possible to explain such cases on the basis that the original request was a conditional promise to remunerate *if* the specified act was done, albeit with no price specified, and that it is this promise—not the subsequent one—that the court is enforcing. As we have seen, the failure to stipulate a price does not necessarily render a promise incomplete; in a contract for sale, for example, the court will simply imply a reasonable price if no price is mentioned. The difficulty with this interpretation is that if the courts were really enforcing the earlier conditional promise, then in the absence of a price term it would seem that they should simply award the claimant a reasonable sum; instead, the claimant is awarded the precise sum specified in the later promise. This might perhaps be defended on the basis that the later promise provides good evidence of a 'reasonable price', but the more straightforward interpretation of cases like *Lampleigh*

---

[64] (1615) 80 ER 255.   [65] [1980] AC 614.

and *Pao On* is that the court is simply enforcing the later promise. Support for this interpretation can be found in the fact that (as will be explained in more detail in the next chapter) there are good reasons that a court might want to enforce a promise that, while gratuitous (and thus unenforceable under the consideration rule), is made with the intention of compensating for a past service. If this interpretation is correct, then the (so-called) 'past consideration' cases are another example of the courts enforcing a unilateral undertaking and as such constitute another area where the offer and acceptance model appears to make little sense. Unsurprisingly, these cases are omitted in most discussions of offer and acceptance.

Announcements of auctions and calls for tenders

Announcements of auctions and calls for tenders are generally regarded as invitations to treat. The actual offer in such cases is said to be made by putting up one's hand at the auction or by sending in a tender (e.g. a tender to supply goods for a certain price). It follows that the auctioneer or person calling for tenders (hereafter 'auctioneer') is under no contractual obligation unless and until the offer is accepted (which in the case of an auction happens by the falling of the hammer).

But it has also been held that an auctioneer may be bound by conditions advertised in the announcement of an auction. For instance, if an auctioneer advertises that an auction is 'without reserve', it has been held that the auctioneer cannot refuse to sell to the highest bidder.[66] Similarly, if an auctioneer specifies that shares will be sold for the highest bid or that all bids received before a certain date will be considered, the auctioneer will then be obliged to, respectively, sell to the highest bidder[67] or consider all timely bids.[68] The usual explanation for these results is that the auctioneer is bound by a preliminary contract, constituted by the invitation for bids (the offer) and the making of a bid (the acceptance).

Thus analysed, the announcement of an auction without reserve appears to be another example of the courts enforcing a conditional promise. The auctioneer has made a conditional promise to do certain things (e.g. to enter a future contract with the highest bidder) in the case that a condition (making a bid) is satisfied. But the difficulty with this interpretation is that unlike in the usual cases involving conditional promises, the auctioneer is not actually promising to pay or reward a person for performing a requested act; the entering of the subsequent contract of sale is not given as a payment or reward for making an earlier bid. Only one of the bidders will be the highest

---

[66] *Warlow v. Harrison* (1858–9) 1 E & E 295; confirmed in *Barry v. Davies* [2000] 1 WLR 1962.
[67] *Harvela Investment Trust Ltd v. Royal Trust of Canada* [1986] AC 207.
[68] *Blackpool and Fyde Aero Club Ltd v. Blackpool B.C.* [1990] 1 WLR 25.

bidder. Moreover, the *making* of a bid is in itself of no interest to the auction-eer. What the auctioneer wants is simply to sell at the highest price possible. For this reason, it is suggested that an announcement of an auction on terms should be understood as any non-lawyer would understand it, namely as a simple (non-conditional) promise to behave in a certain way when conducting the auction.

This interpretation is supported by the difficulty of applying the traditional analysis of 'without reserve' clauses to cases in which other conditions are specified for an auction. In *Blackpool and Fyde Aero Club Ltd v. Blackpool BC*[69] the claimants had for eight years held a concession from the Borough Council to operate pleasure flights from Blackpool airport. The Council invited a small identified group of interested parties, including the claimants, to tender for a new concession. They insisted that tenders must be delivered before noon on 17 March. The claimants delivered their tender in time, but the defendants mistakenly thought it was late and refused to consider it, and the concession was awarded to another concern. It was held that there was a preliminary contract between the parties: the Council's invitation included an implied promise to consider all tenders submitted in time and this was an offer which was accepted by the claimants. To suppose that the claimants were accepting an offer by submitting a tender is, of course, unrealistic. But it is also unrealistic to treat the Council as having made a conditional promise to reward or compensate the claimant if the claimant performed a requested act. What the Council did was to make a simple promise to behave in a certain way, which it then broke.

The obligations that arise from attaching conditions to announcements of auctions and calls for tenders are therefore best interpreted as straight-forward (that is to say, non-conditional) promissory obligations. But even if the conditional promise interpretation of such contracts is preferred, the point remains that these are another example of contractual obligations that are based on unilateral undertakings—not agreements—and which therefore cannot be understood using the traditional offer-and-acceptance model. Persons who bid at auctions or send in tenders are not 'accepting' a promise; they are acting on one.

Concluding remarks

It is not entirely clear why courts first accepted, and then maintained, the idea that all contracts must be created by a process of offer and acceptance.[70] Part of the explanation is no doubt that most commercial contracts are bona

---

[69] [1990] 1 WLR 25.

[70] The first clear instance of the offer and acceptance model being applied to a mere unilateral undertaking appears to have been in *Williams v. Carwardine* (1833) 4 B & Ad 621; see A. W. B. Simpson, 'Innovation in 19th Century Contract Law' (1975) 91 LQR 247 at 257.

fide agreements, and thus fit reasonably well within the orthodox model, but this is clearly not the whole story.[71] Whatever the explanation, the important point for present purposes is that the inconsistency between what courts say and what they actually do has had predictable consequences. On the one hand, we have seen that courts often ignore the offer and acceptance rules or pay them mere lip service in cases involving contracts that arise from unilateral undertakings. On the other hand, courts sometimes force such contracts into an offer-and-acceptance straitjacket. The end result is a set of rules and decisions that, as any law student will confirm, are at once extremely technical and highly artificial. The orthodox rules simply cannot be applied in any straightforward way to cases involving mere promises, or at least they cannot be so applied by a court that wants to do justice. It would be better, it is suggested, if it were openly recognised that the offer-and-acceptance model is inappropriate for such cases. Instead of asking the meaningless question of whether an offer and an acceptance were made, the courts should ask whether a promise was made and then whether that promise is of the kind that (for reasons discussed in Chapter 4) should be enforced.

3. PROMISSORY AND AGREEMENT-BASED LIABILITY OUTSIDE OF CONTRACT LAW

We noted earlier that the law relating to deeds developed separately from the main body of contract law. One consequence of this division was that such arrangements were traditionally not regarded as contracts, but as 'covenants'. Courts today still apply special rules to promises and agreements made as deeds, but it is widely, and rightly, accepted that these rules are a part of the law of contract and, more generally, that covenants are contracts. The integration of covenant into the main body of contract law is now of primarily historical interest, but it raises the question of whether other legal liabilities not currently described as contractual ought to be so described. Is the law dealing with promissory and agreement-based obligations found entirely within the law of contract as currently understood?

The answer, which is predictable given the untidy history of the common law, is almost certainly 'no'. At the same time, it must be acknowledged that it is not easy to point to uncontroversial examples of promissory or agreement-based liability outside of contract law. One reason for this is that it is often difficult to say conclusively whether a particular obligation is in fact currently understood as contractual or extra-contractual. Common law lawyers have traditionally had little interest in classification. As a consequence, there are a number of large and long-established areas of law for which there is

---

[71] Ibbetson, above n. 52 at 221–3.

little consensus, or even interest, as to their juridical classification. A second reason is that (as we shall see below) the most significant potential examples involve large and complex bodies of law. Without an in-depth examination, it is impossible to say definitively whether they involve promissory or agreement-based obligations.

With these provisos in mind, it is possible to identify four significant bodies of law that are regarded by many lawyers as non-contractual *and* that appear to involve (no stronger term is possible) promissory or agreement-based obligations.

The law of companies

The internal arrangements within partnerships, clubs, and other unincorporated associations are usually discussed only in passing in contract textbooks. Nevertheless, these arrangements are generally assumed to be contractual, even if the process of creating them bears little resemblance to Pollock's marketplace model of offer and acceptance: the 'offer', such as it is, is typically found in the rules of the association. But membership is by agreement and the obligations of the members are fundamentally (though by no means exclusively) determined by that agreement.

By contrast, the law pertaining to incorporated associations is usually regarded as non-contractual. The orthodox view is that a registered company is a creation of the state, not of the registering parties, and thus that the rules setting out the requirements to form a company and those describing the company's obligations are set by the state. This orthodox view is clearly correct in that it is impossible to form a registered company by purely private actions, and in that certain statutory requirements, for example the requirement to file annual reports, are clearly established by the state. In addition, the fact that it is possible to form a company with only one shareholder cannot be explained in contractual terms. Nonetheless, contract law principles clearly play an important role in company law. Companies are traditionally formed by two or more persons agreeing to commit certain resources to a joint endeavour. Those persons must go through a public registration process to form a registered company, but the process begins with an agreement. Consistent with this origin, the relationship between and among directors and shareholders can be analysed in largely contractual terms: their rights and duties, though in part a creation of statute, are fundamentally governed by the agreements under which they obtain their shares or positions. The contractual nature of these rights and duties is reflected in section 14 of the Companies Act 1985, which holds that the articles of association that govern the members' relations with one another must be understood as a contract. In short, while it cannot be maintained that a company is merely a complex contract, it is true that the relations between members of a company are often contractual in substance, if not always in law.

The law of trusts

In broad terms, a trust is created when property is transferred from one person to another with the understanding that the transferee is not to treat the property as her own, but instead to manage it for the benefit of a third party. Thus, if I give money to my lawyer to pay for the purchase of a house, the lawyer will hold that money in trust for the vendor (and as a consequence should keep the money in a separate bank account). The proper legal classification of the trust is a matter of long-standing controversy. Insofar as a majority view can be identified, it is that the trust is *sui generis*, not fitting into any of the traditional private law categories of contract, tort, unjust enrichment, or property. The next most common view is that the trust is a property-law institution. This view identifies the distinctive element of the trust as the proprietary rights enjoyed by the beneficiary, rather than the merely personal rights.

But it can and has been argued that the standard trust is essentially a contract. The steps necessary to create a typical trust look like a straightforward agreement: the transferor agrees to transfer property (e.g. money for a house purchase) and the transferee agrees to deal with the property in a certain way (e.g. pay it to the house vendor on the transfer of title). Admittedly, trusts (unlike contracts) are not subject to the consideration requirement, and (unlike contracts) create rights for third parties, but as we shall see in Chapters 4 and 13, neither the consideration requirement nor the third-party rule appear to be fundamental to the law of contract. More difficult to explain from a contractual perspective are the proprietary rights enjoyed by trust beneficiaries: consistent with the personal nature of promises and agreements, contracts have always been understood to create only personal rights. But a contractual view of trusts need not explain every aspect of the trust in contractual terms. The proprietary aspects, in particular, might be explained as flowing from aspects of the law of property or the law of remedies. Thus a 'trust contract' might be understood as similar to other contracts that have proprietary implications, like a sale contract, which normally transfers ownership in the goods at the moment of contracting.[72] Of course, this cannot be said of all trusts—for example, it is not true of a trust in which the transferor and the transferee are the same person (which is possible). But the point is that many trusts are created by ordinary agreements and, moreover, that the obligations of the respective parties are set by those agreements.

Brief mention should also be made of the 'constructive trust', which is a trust that is imposed on parties despite them not having intended to create a trust. Constructive trusts are essentially fictions, adopted in order to give

---

[72] Sale of Goods Act 1979, s. 18.

certain categories of persons the same proprietary rights they would have had had a true trust been created. Thus, a third party who acquires property from a thief or from an ordinary trustee in breach of trust may be deemed to hold that property on constructive trust for the true owner or beneficiary—meaning that the original owner has a claim to the goods prior to the third party's creditors. Clearly, a constructive trust need not involve a promise or agreement: an owner's rights against a third party 'transferee' are not based on a voluntary obligation. But in certain instances, the courts have used constructive trusts to effectively enforce a promise or agreement that cannot be enforced by the law of contract for some (usually technical) reason. These cases take a variety of forms, but a typical case involves the purchase of a house by an unmarried couple that is followed after some years by the couple splitting up. The question then arises as to the parties' rights in the house.[73] In many of these cases, the parties had an agreement as to how the property was to be divided, but that agreement was unenforceable as a contract because it was not in writing (as is required for contracts involving land).[74] In such cases, courts have sometimes used the concept of a constructive trust to force the parties to divide the property as they had agreed.[75] In finding that one partner holds the property (or a share in the property) on constructive trust for both partners, the court is effectively enforcing the parties' agreement.

The law of estoppel

The law of estoppel generally deals with situations in which a person who has made a representation that is relied upon by another person is not allowed to deny the truth of that representation. For example, if I announce that you may cross my land and you then do so, I will be 'estopped' from suing you in trespass. Similarly, if I tell a builder whom I have hired that it is unnecessary to comply with a particular stipulation of our contract, and the builder then relies by not complying, I will be estopped from bringing an action against the builder for breach of that stipulation.

Estoppel is discussed in contract textbooks, usually (as in this book) following the topic of consideration, but the dominant view is that estoppel is not part of the law of contract. Rather than giving effect to promises or agreements, estoppel is thought to aim primarily at protecting individuals who have been induced to detrimentally rely on another's representation. Such inducement may arise from a promise (or an agreement), but in the

---

[73] In the past, the question arose most frequently following the divorce of married couples, but these cases are now largely remedied through the use of statutory powers that give the courts discretion to make property adjustment and other appropriate orders. These powers make it unnecessary for the courts to invoke contract, trust, or any other legitimating device in dealing with married couples.

[74] See below, p. 95.

[75] *Gissing v. Gissing* [1971] AC 886.

dominant view what matters is not that a promise was made but that reliance was induced. In support of this interpretation, it is pointed out that, in the orthodox account, an estoppel may arise from a mere representation (of intention or fact) as opposed to a promise. Consistent with this view, the formation requirements found in the rules on offer and acceptance, formalities, and consideration are not applied to estoppel.

But as we shall see in the next chapter, a strong argument can be made that in many cases where estoppel is invoked the courts are just enforcing ordinary promises or agreements. This is particularly true in cases of 'proprietary estoppel' since this doctrine (unlike ordinary estoppel) can be used to ground a cause of action. Cases dealing with the rights of parties to a home in which they have been living provide a good illustration. The modern approach[76] involves the court first deciding whether there is anything amounting to an agreement between the parties as to how the property is to be divided in the event that occurred. If this is the case, the claimant must show that he or she has detrimentally relied on that agreement or understanding. This then enables the court to intervene on the ground of proprietary estoppel (or constructive trust, as discussed above) to enforce the agreement. The courts do not, however, treat these cases as involving contracts; aside from the difficulty of finding anything resembling a clear offer and acceptance, the usual formalities required for dealings in land (see Chapter 4) are typically not satisfied. Nonetheless, it seems fairly clear that the courts are effectively enforcing the relevant agreements, much as if they were contracts. This is an illustration of a curious (but very common) tendency in the law: if the rules relating to the kinds of promises or agreements that the courts can enforce lead to injustice, the courts tend to invent new doctrines to fill the gap rather than modify the old ones. Here, while they may refuse to enforce an agreement as a contract, they will enforce it provided the claimant chooses to base his claim on a different legal category.

The law of collective agreements

We noted in Chapter 1 that although ordinary employment contracts are subject to extensive regulation, they are still considered contracts, and so are subjected to the ordinary formation requirements. But collective agreements made between unions and employers are not treated in this way. In determining if a valid collective agreement has been made, it is not asked whether there was an offer and an acceptance or whether the parties provided mutual consideration. It is clear, nonetheless, that collective agreements are essentially contracts. Like employment contracts, they are heavily regulated,

---

[76] See, e.g., *Hammond v. Mitchell* [1992] 2 All ER 109; *Lloyds Bank v. Rosset* [1991] 1 AC 107.

but as their name suggests, they are created by agreements and the obligations they give rise to are, for the most part, grounded in those agreements.

4. CONTRACTUAL LIABILITIES NOT BASED ON PROMISES OR AGREEMENTS: CONTRACTS MADE BY THE STATE

Until relatively recently claims to recover money from a person to whom it had been paid by mistake were said to be based on an implied contract. The defendant was held to have implicitly promised to repay the money, and so had a contractual obligation to do so. It is now widely accepted that this explanation was a fiction. The true explanation for the duty to make restitution is not that the recipients promised to repay the money, but that they received a benefit in circumstances in which it would be unjust to retain that benefit.[77] Accordingly, the topic of mistaken payment has been moved from contract law to unjust enrichment law textbooks. A similar development occurred in the law dealing with the division of matrimonial property: cases in which the courts had previously implied contracts despite the absence of agreement or understanding are now explained on the basis of proprietary estoppel or constructive trust, as was discussed earlier.

The question raised by these examples is whether there are other instances of liability that are said to be contractual, but that do not involve promissory or agreement-based obligations. Again, the answer is almost certainly 'yes'. As illustrated by the examples just given, judges have rarely hesitated to use whatever instruments available in order to achieve a just result in a particular case, and the law of contract is one of those instruments. This practice has its justifications. The usual reason for adopting a fiction is to reach a result that, while in principle better explained on other grounds, cannot as easily be reached on those grounds given the existing law. The fictional classification is made, in other words, because other areas of the law are underdeveloped or deficient. For example, the law of unjust enrichment, which is now recognized as underlying the mistaken payment cases, was for years undeveloped in English law. For judges in earlier periods, the easiest way to reach the correct result in mistaken payment cases was not to appeal directly to an unrecognised principle against unjust enrichment, but to rely on the well-accepted idea that individuals ought to keep their promises. The history of the common law is to a significant extent a history of fictions of this kind.

But while fictions may be inevitable, and in many cases a useful step in the law's evolution, they are usually accompanied by undesirable side-effects. An undesirable consequence of the implied contract theory of unjust enrichment

---

[77] A. Burrows, *The Law of Restitution* (London, 1993), 95–119.

was that minors and others who lacked contractual capacity were sometimes said to be under no duty to repay.[78] More generally, the objection to fictions is that they stand in the way of the proper organization, understanding, and application of the law. A fiction hides the truth, which is always a dangerous thing. It is therefore important that fictions be identified as such and, where possible, discarded.

The category of 'fictional' contracts is, however, not easy to describe. As we have already noted, there is no canonical statement of which arrangements are and are not regarded as contracts under English law. In addition, with respect to certain cases and even whole categories of arrangements, it is often difficult, as a purely factual matter, to say if they are based on a promise or an agreement, or on something else: the parties' intentions just are not clear enough. The result is that for most of the examples described below, all that can be said is that *sometimes* they appear not to involve promises or agreements.

Rather than attempt to provide an exhaustive account of (allegedly) fictional contracts,[79] we will focus on two kinds of arrangements that are practically important and that illustrate the range of issues involved.[80]

Collateral contracts

The term 'collateral contract' does not have a precise meaning, but, as the name implies, it is generally used to describe contracts that are collateral to, or by the side of, another contract. There is nothing unusual in principle about the idea of a collateral contract, and most such contracts are based on promises or agreements. But a significant number are properly regarded as fictional contracts.

One example is the contract allegedly founded on an agent's 'implied warranty of authority'. A person who professes to act as agent of a principal is taken to imply a contractual promise or 'warrant' that he has the principal's authority to act on his behalf. If it turns out that the agent has no such authority, and the other party suffers a loss in consequence, the agent is liable in contract on this implied warranty. This principle was established in the famous decision of *Collen v. Wright*,[81] where the defendant acted as the agent of a third party in negotiating a lease of the third party's property to the claimant. The terms were agreed, and the claimant went into occupation of

---

[78] *Sinclair v. Brougham* [1914] AC 398.

[79] One group of (allegedly) fictional contracts that are not examined here (but that are examined in the discussion of formation mistakes that follows) are those in which the parties appear to make an agreement or a promise without actually intending to do so, as, for example, where I think I am signing a birthday greeting, but I am actually signing an offer to purchase.

[80] The discussion that follows does not examine implied *terms*, even though many such terms can also be properly described as 'fictional'. The question addressed in this chapter is not whether the parties agreed to this or that term, but whether they made any agreement at all.

[81] (1857) 8 E & B 647.

the property. The third party then claimed that the agent had exceeded his authority and that the lease was not binding on him. The result was that the claimant was (after a law suit) turned off the land. He then sued the agent, claiming reimbursement for his losses including the costs of the law suit. It was held that he was entitled to recover these losses against the agent, who must be taken to have warranted that he had the principal's authority to grant the lease. It is important to observe that there was *no other* contractual relation between the claimant and the defendant. The lease itself (apart from the fact that it was not valid) was not a contract to which the agent was himself a party, so the whole content of the contract between the claimant and the defendant was the implied warranty. In theory such a warranty rests on the intention of the party giving it, but in this and most other cases in which implied warranty is argued, it seems clear that the agent never promised or agreed to the guarantee in question. Rather, the warranty— indeed, the whole contract—was created by the court in order to recompense the claimant.

The responsibility arising from the fictional implied warranty seems better understood as an extra-contractual liability arising from the claimant's reasonable reliance on the agent's conduct and the resulting loss. It is worth noting that the present practice of classifying this liability as contractual is practically significant in that the agent becomes liable whether or not he has been careless. For a liability in tort, negligence might have to be proved. The current classification also means that the agent is liable, not only for the claimant's wasted costs, but also for damages representing the loss of his bargain or expectations. Neither of these consequences is easy to justify.

The principle of *Collen v. Wright* has been extended to other cases that do not appear to involve either promises or agreements. For example, in one case[82] the directors of a company appointed a manager and wrote to tell their bankers that he had authority to sign cheques on the company's account. He overdrew the account, which he had no authority to do without the approval of the shareholders, according to the company's regulations. The bank was thus unable to claim the repayment of the overdraft from the company, so they claimed it from the directors personally. The directors were held liable in contract, on the ground that they had warranted that the manager had authority to draw cheques on the company's account even where the account was overdrawn. The defendants argued, not implausibly, that they had never intended to make any sort of a contract with the bank; only the company had entered an agreement with the bank. The directors were nevertheless held liable in contract.

A second well-known group of cases concerns goods that are sold (or let

---

[82] *Cherry and McDougal v. Colonial Bank of Australasia* (1869) LR 3 PC 24.

on hire-purchase) by A to B, and in which a third party, C (perhaps the manufacturer or the hire-purchase dealer), gives B an assurance about the quality of the goods. Here, B intends to make a contract with A, and that is indeed the main contract entered into. But if B wants legal redress he may find that he cannot get it against A (say because A is insolvent or did not give clear assurances about the quality of the goods) and so may wish to sue C. The courts have in a number of cases been willing to allow B to sue C in such circumstances on a collateral contract:[83] C's assurances are treated as warranties which B 'accepts' by entering into the main contract. The courts have sometimes insisted that this device is only permissible where there is a clear intention to make the collateral contract,[84] but there are many decisions that appear to be irreconcilable with this requirement. In reality, liability in such cases is more readily explained on the basis that C was at fault in making a misrepresentation. But as the tort of negligent misstatement was not introduced until 1964, the courts needed another basis on which to ground liability—and decided on the collateral contract.

The collateral contract device has also been imposed in contracts for services. In *Charnock v. Liverpool Corp.*,[85] the claimant's insured car was damaged in an accident and the insurance company arranged for it to be repaired by the defendants; that is to say, they contracted for it to be so repaired. When the defendants were inordinately slow in making the repairs it was held that the claimant, the owner of the car, could sue the defendants on an implied contract to do the work in a reasonable time. It is difficult to believe that the garage really intended to make two agreements in this case, one with the insurance company for payment, and one with the claimant under which they guaranteed to do the work within a reasonable time; it is equally difficult to believe that the claimant thought he was entering into an agreement with the garage when he knew that the insurance company was going to pay the bill. The reality is surely simpler: the court thought the claimant had a (moral) right to have his work done within a reasonable time, and in order to make that right legally enforceable, the court implied a contract between the claimant and the defendant.

A more difficult and controversial decision is *The Eurymedon.*[86] The case concerned goods sold by an English exporter to a New Zealand buyer, and shipped by the exporter to New Zealand. The goods were damaged while being unloaded through the negligence of the stevedores. The claimant was the New Zealand buyer, and the defendants were the stevedores; the action

[83] See, e.g., *Shanklin Pier Ltd v. Detel Products Ltd* [1951] 2 KB 854.
[84] See, e.g., *Heilbut Symons & Co. v. Buckleton* [1913] AC 30; *Lambert v. Lewis* [1980] 2 WLR 289, reversed on different grounds [1982] AC 225.
[85] [1968] 1 WLR 1498.
[86] Also known as *New Zealand Shipping Co. Ltd v. A. M. Satterthwaite & Co. Ltd* [1975] AC 154.

was brought in tort for negligent damage to the goods. The defendants argued that they were not liable because they were entitled to rely on a clause in the bill of lading that exempted them from liability. The bill of lading was the document containing the shipping contract which was, in the first instance, entered into between the exporter and the shipping company (the carriers). Neither the claimant nor the defendant was, in any obvious sense, a party to that contract. Nevertheless, by a somewhat tortuous process of reasoning, the Privy Council held that the exemption clause in the bill of lading governed the relationship between the claimant and the defendant, because it formed the subject matter of a separate contract between them, one that barred the ordinary remedy in tort for negligence. Lord Wilberforce effectively admitted that the courts' reasoning was artificial:

It is only the precise analysis of this complex of relations into the classical offer and acceptance, with identifiable consideration, that seems to present difficulty, but this same difficulty exists in many situations of daily life, e.g., sales at auction; super-market purchases; boarding an omnibus; purchasing a train ticket; tenders for the supply of goods; manufacturers' guarantees; gratuitous bailments; bankers' commercial credits. These are all examples which show that English law, having committed itself to a rather technical and schematic doctrine of contract, in application takes a practical approach, often at the cost of forcing the facts to fit uneasily into the marked slots of offer, acceptance and consideration.[87]

The same result could have been reached more simply, and more consistently with general principles, by holding that the claimant was precluded from suing the stevedores in tort not because of any contract he had with the stevedores, but because he had voluntarily accepted the risk in question. By assenting to the terms of the bill of lading, including the exemption clause, the claimant buyer made clear that he agreed to accept liability for damage to the goods. This is, or should be, a perfectly good defence to a claim in tort but for reasons that are not entirely clear it has never been wholly accepted by English courts.[88] The consequence is that the court in the *Eurymedon* case felt constrained to make a different argument, and, as is often the case, adopted the collateral contract route.

Simultaneous exchanges

Another category of transaction to which the label 'contract' is arguably misapplied is the simultaneous exchange, such as an ordinary purchase of goods in a shop or at a market stall. In many such transactions it would appear that the parties do not promise or agree to do anything. In the typical purchase at a store, for instance, the purchaser hands over money and the

[87] Ibid. 167.
[88] *Scruttons Ltd v. Midland Silicones Ltd* [1962] AC 446; cf. *Norwich City Council v. Harvey* [1989] 1 WLR 828.

vendor hands over the goods or simply allows the purchaser to leave with the goods. Up to the actual moment of handing over the money, the customer appears to be free not to make a purchase. Likewise, the shopkeeper can refuse to make a sale at any point prior to handing over the goods. Admittedly, the shopkeeper might be liable under anti-discrimination legislation for refusing to serve a customer, or for contravening false advertising legislation, or for the tort of misrepresentation, but none of these obligations are based on the existence of a promise or an agreement. This is not to deny that many shopkeepers do promise, implicitly or explicitly, to sell to particular customers or to sell to anyone who comes into their store; in such cases, enforcing a contractual obligation to sell might well be appropriate. But there is no reason to assume that all shopkeepers make such promises. This reality is recognised in the Sale of Goods Act 1979, which defines a contract of sale as a contract 'in which the seller transfers *or* agrees to transfer the property in goods to the buyer for a money consideration.'

One explanation for why such exchanges are classified as contractual is that this allows courts to cure deficiencies in other areas of the law. Liability in tort law for making a defective product and also for making a negligent misstatement about a product is of relatively recent origin. Prior to these innovations, the only way a vendor might be liable where a product was defective or not as advertised was to find that the vendor had breached one of the contractual obligations implied by the Sale of Goods Act (and, previously, by precedent). In particular, the vendor could be found liable for breaching the obligation to provide goods of satisfactory quality. Even today, the Sale of Goods Act gives purchasers greater rights than do the laws of tort and unjust enrichment. For those who believe that purchasers should enjoy such rights, these advantages provide a practical argument for continuing to classify all simultaneous exchanges as contracts. But it should be kept in mind that it is not strictly necessary to declare such exchanges as contracts in order that purchasers enjoy the kinds of legal rights accorded by the Sale of Goods Act; the same result could be reached by amending the Act so that it applies not just to '*contracts* of sale' but to the broader category of 'sales'.

It is arguable, therefore, that many ordinary consumer sales would be better described not as contracts, but as (mere) conditional transfers. The customer hands over his money on the condition that the shopkeeper hand over the goods (or vice versa). If the shopkeeper refuses to hand over the goods, she must return the money; otherwise, she will be unjustly enriched— just like the person who has been paid by mistake. Any other obligations imposed on the parties may be understood as being derived from the general law of tort or supplementary product liability legislation.

5. MISTAKES IN THE FORMATION PROCESS

In the previous sections, we examined a variety of arrangements that appear to fit uneasily with the conventional view of contractual liabilities. Thus, we examined arrangements that are classified as contractual despite the apparent absence of a promise or agreement, as well as arrangements that are classified as non-contractual despite the fact that they involve promises or agreements. Left to the side for separate treatment were various situations that involve 'mistakes' in the formation process. These situations present a unique challenge for students of contract law as they appear to involve both self-imposed (that is to say promissory or agreement-based) liabilities and externally imposed liabilities. Coupled with the traditional hesitancy of English law to accept 'mistake' as a defence to contractual liability, this fact probably also explains why the category of 'formation mistakes' is without a comfortable home in the common law. While it will be argued later that the doctrine is in fact largely superfluous, the puzzle of identifying which of its elements are concerned with identifying the existence of a promise or an agreement (and which are not) remains for the present.

There are innumerable ways in which a person entering into a contract may be mistaken, of which at least five need to be distinguished. First, a person may make a mistake in communicating the terms to which she intends to bind herself, as where I intend to write '£10,000' in a document of sale but actually write '£1,000'. Secondly, a person may mistakenly convey the impression that he wishes to make a promise or an agreement (on whatever terms) when he has no such intention, as, for instance, where an individual thinks he is making an invitation to treat, but the document that he signs expresses an offer to purchase. A third kind of mistake may occur as to the person with whom one is contracting, for example, where I exchange documents by post with a person whom I believe to be John Jones, the banker, but who is actually a rogue impersonating John Jones. In yet a fourth group of cases, one may be mistaken as to circumstances that affect one's purpose in contracting but have no other connection with the contract or with the other party, as where I agree to buy something under a mistaken impression as to the size of my bank balance. Finally, one may be mistaken as to the quality or nature of the object of a contract, as where I buy a painting wrongly believing it to be a valuable old master.

At first sight these various possibilities may appear to raise similar questions, but the law draws a basic distinction in the way it approaches cases involving either of the first three kinds of mistakes and cases involving the fourth or fifth kind: in the former, the focus is on whether the require-ments of offer and acceptance were satisfied, such that a prime facie valid contract was created, while in the latter, the law shifts the focus to whether or not an arrangement that satisfies these requirements ought nevertheless be set aside for other reasons. This distinction shows one way in which the doctrine of mistake is made less important in common law regimes than in civilian regimes: even at the level of orthodox doctrine, cases involving what may be called formation mistakes are treated not as part of an independent doctrine of 'mistake', but as part of the law of offer and acceptance.

The distinction between formation mistakes and other mistakes is also followed in this book, and thus formation mistakes are considered in this chapter, while other kinds of mistakes are dealt with in Chapter 7 (when we examine problems that arise after a prima facie valid contract has been found to exist). But it should be kept in mind that, in principle, formation mistakes could be considered both from the perspective of offer and acceptance rules and from the perspective of a distinct doctrine of mistake. It might thus be argued (though this is not the position adopted by the common law) that regardless of the effect of a formation mistake on offer and acceptance, such a mistake should justify setting aside an otherwise valid contract. This possibility is discussed in Chapter 7.

A final preliminary observation is that although we are focusing here on formation issues, mistakes raise a host of other legal issues. In particular, a mistake in the formation process is often the result of a fraud or misrepresentation. In such a case, the question of whether a contract has been formed is often immaterial, since it is clear that any contract may be set aside on the basis of the fraud or misrepresentation; it is typically only when the rights of an innocent third party are at issue, as when a third party claims title to goods innocently purchased from a fraudster, that it matters whether the original contract by which the fraudster obtained the goods was formed. This is discussed in more detail below.

We are now ready to focus directly on mistakes in the formation process. For this purpose, it is useful to treat each of the three types of formation mistake described above separately.

Mistake as to terms

The first kind of formation mistake concerns the meaning of the terms in a purported contract as, for instance, when an offeror writes '£10,000' when she means to write '£1,000' or when she offers for sale 'X' property when she means to offer 'Y' property. The common law's approach to such cases is to ask what the offeree could reasonably have understood the offeror to be offering:[89] thus where A sells a yacht to B, and B reasonably understands that A is guaranteeing the condition of the yacht, it is immaterial that A had not intended to include any guarantee in the sale. A's mistake as to B's understanding is irrelevant; he is liable just as if he had intended to give a

---

[89] *Investors Compensation Scheme v. West Bromwich Building Society* [1998] 1 ALL ER 94, 114.

guarantee.[90] Similarly, in a well-known case[91] where the defendant was the highest bidder at an auction sale of a public house, it was held that the contract was valid and binding on him, despite his objection that he had mistakenly thought a certain field was included in the land being sold. Had the defendant examined the particulars of sale, as a reasonable person would have assumed he had done, he would have seen that the field was not included in the sale. Again, it has recently been held that an offer by a landlord's agent to fix the rent of commercial premises at a level lower than he intended was binding: even though the agent had made a mistake (which was at once pointed out on receipt of the acceptance), the tenant's acceptance bound the landlord to the offer.[92] More generally, it seems now an established principle that, when the court is construing a written document the actual intentions of the parties as to the meaning of that document are irrelevant and perhaps even inadmissible in evidence.[93]

The courts' approach in these cases is often described as one of ascertaining the parties' intentions from an 'objective' or 'external' perspective. These labels are acceptable so long as it is remembered that they refer to the perspective of a reasonable listener in the shoes of the offeree and not to a mythical 'objective' person or meaning. As will be discussed in more detail in Chapter 5, words take on different 'objective' meanings depending on the context in which they are used. Thus, if both parties agree to a particular set of definitions for a document or if particular words are always given a specific meaning in the industry in which both parties are working the court will adopt that meaning. The importance of the reasonable offeree's perspective also explains why courts will not enforce a term or not enforce the apparent or literal meaning of a term if the offeree knew or should have known that the offeror did not intend to use that term or to give the term its usual meaning. So, where the defendant had offered to sell hare skins to the claimant at so much per *pound*, but it was clear that the claimant knew that the defendant had meant this to be the price per *piece*, it was held that the claimant's purported acceptance did not create a contract at the price actually stated by the seller.[94]

---

[90] *Sullivan v. Constable* (1932) 49 TLR 369.

[91] *Tamplin v. James* (1880) 15 Ch D 215.

[92] *Centrovincial Estates PLC v. Merchant Investors Assurance Co. Ltd* (1983) Com LR 158, an unfortunately inadequate report of this important case.

[93] *Prenn v. Simonds* [1971] 1 WLR 1381.

[94] *Hartog v. Colin & Shields* [1939] 3 All ER 566. The question did not arise whether a contract was created at the price really intended by the seller but it is suggested the answer should be no. Although the claimant was aware of the mistake, he thought the defendant would be bound to the price stated, and thus his acceptance was of an offer at the stated price. It cannot be assumed that the claimant would have been willing to contract on the terms the defendant had intended to offer.

Contract interpretation is discussed in more detail in Chapter 5. At this stage, it is sufficient to observe that the objective approach to interpreting contract terms is not inconsistent with the idea that contracts are essentially promises or agreements. The *meaning* of a promise or agreement, like the meaning of any communication, is established by its public or 'objective' meaning rather than the meaning the speaker intended the communication to convey: words always *mean* what they reasonably appear to the listener to mean. This does not mean, of course, that a mistake as to the meaning of a contract's terms should never give rise to relief. As was noted earlier, there may well be other reasons, aside from a plea that no promise or agreement was ever made, for refusing to enforce a contract. In particular, it may simply be unfair to hold individuals to contracts on terms to which they never intended to agree (although the common law is loath to openly admit such a plea: see Chapters 7 and 12). In the above mentioned case involving the agent's mistake in fixing the rent, for example, it is not obvious why the tenant should receive an immense windfall as a result of the mistake, which was immediately pointed out before any costs had been incurred in reliance upon it. If misleading another party in this way were instead treated as a tort, liability could be limited to any losses that were incurred in reliance on the mistake. At the time the current contractual rules were adopted, the law of tort and of damages were not sufficiently developed to allow for such a possibility. But today such an argument is easier to make.

Mistake as to the existence of a promise or agreement

A second kind of formation mistake concerns the very *existence* of a promise or agreement. In these cases, defendants mistakenly communicate an intention to make a promise or enter an agreement when in reality they have no such intention. For example, I might think I am signing a birthday greeting when I am actually signing an offer to sell you goods. In contrast to a mistake about terms, where the existence of *some* promise or agreement (however malformed) is acknowledged, a mistake of this kind would appear to show that the defendant did not actually make a promise or an agreement. Although it is possible to make a mistake about the *terms* of a valid promise or agreement, it does not seem possible to actually make an entire promise or agreement by mistake. It is part of the everyday understanding of promise and agreement that they can only be created intentionally. If this right, it is arguable that a mistake of this kind should also prevent a contract from being created. Of course, it may well be appropriate to hold a person responsible for misleading another into believing that a promise was made, but as such responsibility is not based on the existence of a promise, it would appear best explained as a species of extra-contractual liability.

Turning to the law, we find that, in principle, courts and commentators rarely distinguish this second kind of mistake from a mistake about terms. At the same time, courts often treat these two kinds of mistakes differently in practice. More specifically, while the orthodox position appears to be that the objective approach described above is applied in both categories,[95] it is difficult to find cases involving existence mistakes in which courts have clearly applied the objective approach. The decisions cited as evidence for the objective approach invariably involve mistakes about the terms of a promise or agreement or mistakes as to the legal enforceability of a promise or agreement.[96] There are a number of cases dealing with documents *signed* by mistake, but here, interestingly, an objective approach is not consistently applied. The general rule is that one is bound by one's signature regardless of whether one is aware of the contents of a document,[97] but a person who is under a fundamental misapprehension about the nature or effect of a document can sometimes invoke the ancient doctrine of *non est factum* to deny the document. This doctrine, which originally was used primarily in cases involving illiterate persons, is restricted in various ways, but the main restriction is the tort-like requirement that the mistaken party must not have been careless or otherwise at fault for the mistake.[98] It is also noteworthy that, while the doctrine is no longer limited to mistakes about the character of a document (which fits closely the category of mistake now under consideration), the requirement that the mistake be fundamental applies most naturally to a mistake of this kind.

The excuse of *non est factum* is thus at least partly explicable as a recognition that there is something unusual about holding individuals contractually bound when they did not intend to make a promise or agreement. But there remains the question of why common law doctrine formally refuses to distinguish between existence mistakes and other kinds of mistakes (even if in practice the courts often do just this). The most plausible explanation lies, again, in the historical relationship between contractual and extra-contractual forms of liability. Individuals who carelessly mislead others into thinking they are making promises or agreements clearly should be responsible for losses that arise from such misrepresentations. But it was only in 1964, with the introduction of the tort of negligent misstatement,[99] that such liability was a possibility in English law. And even today, non-contractual solutions provide imperfect relief because the significant reliance is often by an innocent third party. For example, if the document that I think is a

---

[95] *Shogun Finance Ltd v. Hudson* [1992] 2 WLR 867; below, 83ff.

[96] An example of the latter would be a case in which a party thought an agreement was binding in honour only, but in fact it was legally binding. This special type of mistake is examined when we consider the intent to create legal relations doctrine in Ch. 4.

[97] *L'Estrange v. F Graucob Ltd* [1934] 2 KB 394.

[98] *Saunders v. Anglia Building Society* (also known as *Gallie v. Lee*) [1971] AC 1004.

[99] *Hedley Byrne v. Heller* [1964] AC 465.

birthday greeting purports to convey property to you, you might then use that property as security for a loan with a third party, such as a bank. Because I never communicated with the bank, my signing the document could not support a claim by the bank in negligent misstatement. But given my carelessness it seems clear that the bank should have a better claim to the relevant property than I do. Applying the objective test—the contractual solution—gives this result.

The courts could develop ways of protecting third parties such as the bank in this example that do not involve enforcing unintended contracts. Perhaps the simplest would be to determine the third party's claim to the property entirely on the basis of property law considerations and to treat the validity of the contract as irrelevant. This approach recognises that it is both artificial and unfair to make a third party's property rights depend on the nature of a mistake that was made by someone with whom the third party had no dealings and in respect of which it had no knowledge. Another possibility would be to hold the misrepresentor liable in tort for any losses the third party incurred in reliance on the belief that the secured party had good title to the property. This could not be a claim for negligent misstatement (because the relevant statement was not made to the third party), but would instead need to be framed as a claim in ordinary negligence for the reasonably foreseeable consequences of a negligent action. Such claims have not yet been made successfully in English law (and do not need to be made so long as the objective approach is applied), but in principle there seems no reason they should not be available.

Mistake as to identity

The third and final kind of mistake that might be made in the formation process concerns the identity of the other contracting party. In the famous case of *Cundy v. Lindsay*,[100] a swindler, by name Blenkarn, wrote to the claimants ordering goods from them, and signed his name as though the letter came from Blenkiron & Co., a company known to the claimants. The claimants sent the goods to Blenkarn, who then sold them to the defendants who were innocent of the fraud. When the fraud was discovered the claimants sued the defendants, claiming that the goods still belonged to them when the defendants had bought them, and that the defendants had therefore 'converted' them and were liable in tort. According to orthodox doctrine, no contract is formed in such a case if the mistake concerns the *identity*, as opposed to the *attributes*, of the other party. In *Cundy*, the court held that the defendant's mistake concerned identity, because the claimants had intended to contract with Blenkiron, not Blenkarn, and so no contract was formed. As a result, Cundy obtained damages equal to the value of their goods.

[100] (1878) 3 App. Cas. 459.

As a general proposition, the idea that a mistake as to identity precludes the formation of a contract seems consistent with the basic idea that contracts are created by promises or agreements. Unlike, say, vows and declarations, promises and agreements are made by undertaking obligations to particular persons or classes of persons. Agreements are made between the parties to the agreement, and promises are made to promisees. The agreeing party and the promisee is, in each case, a person with a specific identity. Thus, if I offer to sell my car to Jane, the reason it is not open to John to accept this offer, is simply that the offer was not made to him. By contrast, if I offer to sell my car to Jane and Jane accepts my offer, we have an agreement, and so a contract, even if it turns out that I was mistaken in believing that Jane was, for example, creditworthy. Admittedly, in such a case, the law might conceivably want to relieve me of the normal consequences of my offer (though for good reasons the common law does not do this),[101] but the explanation for such relief would not be that we had no agreement.

In practice, however, the identity/attribute distinction raises two problems. The first arises from the fact that in nearly all mistaken identity cases the real dispute is between the mistaken party and an innocent third party. In *Cundy v. Lindsay*, for example, there was no question that any contract formed between Cundy and the rogue Blenkarn could be set aside for fraud, and that the goods, if still in Blenkarn's possession, would have to be returned. A contract procured by fraud or misrepresentation may be set aside at the option of the party who was misled. But, as is usual in mistaken identity cases, the rogue in *Cundy v. Lindsay* had disappeared, and so the dispute was between Cundy, the innocent vendor, and Lindsay, the innocent third party purchaser. English law resolves such disputes by asking whether the property in the goods had passed to the third party, which in turn is determined by asking if there was a contract between the original owner and the rogue. On this approach, it follows that if the mistake is about identity, the third party loses the goods (because there was no contract), while if the mistake is about attributes, the third party keeps the goods (because there was a contract). In technical terms, the first kind of mistake leads to a *void* contract (i.e. a contract that never existed), while the second leads to a *voidable* contract (i.e. a contract that may be set aside but that is valid—and therefore capable of transferring title in goods—until this is done).

The first problem raised by the identity/attributes distinction, therefore, is that it is used to determine not just the rights of the parties to the alleged contract, but also the rights of third parties. This is a problem because it means that the third party's rights are determined by the classification of a mistake that happened as part of a transaction of which he had no knowledge. The question that would seem to be the most important, namely

---

[101] See Ch. 7.

which of the two parties was more at fault in not preventing the fraud is not even raised. Nor is there any reason for supposing that where a mistake is made as to identity, rather than attributes, that it is the third party who is more likely to be at fault. To the contrary, in most cases it is the vendor who is in a better position to uncover the fraud, since it is the vendor (not the third party purchaser) who actually cares about the fraudster's identity. Often, the vendor can uncover the fraud by making a simple phone call. By contrast, there is usually little that the third party can do to uncover the fraud.[102] Potential purchasers cannot be expected to call the police every time they wish to purchase goods. In any event, the vendor usually does not discover the fraud, and so alert the police, until long after the sale to the third party. The courts are not, of course, entirely blind to considerations this kind; in many cases, the identity/attributes distinction seems to have been applied with an eye to the respective fault of the parties.[103] But it would be better if the Law Reform Committee's recommendation[104] that third parties' rights in such cases be decided separately from the identity/attributes question were openly adopted. Unfortunately, the House of Lords' latest pronouncement on this issue (discussed below)[105] suggests this is unlikely to happen in the near future.

The second difficulty with the idea that a mistake as to identity precludes a contract being formed is that it is difficult to define 'identity'. In *Cundy v. Lindsay*, for example, did Cundy intend to contract with Blenkiron (as the court concluded)? Or did Cundy intend to contract with the person with whom he was communicating, namely the rogue Blenkarn? The older cases do not consistently follow *Cundy v. Lindsay*, but in *Shogun Finance v. Hudson*,[106] the House of Lords affirmed the approach in *Cundy*, albeit by a narrow three-to-two majority. More specifically, the House of Lords held that where the contract is recorded in writing, the intended parties to the contract are the persons identified in the written documents. Thus in *Shogun*, where a rogue operating under the alias of 'D. Patel' obtained a car on credit in a written hire-purchase agreement that identified him by that name, the court held that no contract had been concluded (and therefore, that the third party who had innocently purchased the car from the rogue had to give it back to the original owner—a finance company). But where the contract is oral and is made face-to-face, the court confirmed certain earlier cases that held there was a presumption that the intended party is the person who is making the

---

[102] The situation is different, of course, if the third party purchases the goods in a back alley or for a greatly reduced price; in these circumstances the third party has effectively been warned that there may be a problem with the goods.

[103] *Lewis v. Averay* [1972] 1 QB 198; compare *Ingram v. Little* [1961] 1 QB 31.

[104] Law Reform Committee (Cmd. 2598, 1966), 15.

[105] *Shogun Finance Ltd v. Hudson*, above n. 95.

[106] [1992] 2 WLR 867.

communications (the rogue) and not the person the rogue is representing himself to be. Thus, in face-to-face situations, a contract is formed and the third party is able to keep the property.

There is no suggestion that the third party purchaser in *Shogun* was careless in not knowing that he was buying a car from a fraudster; on the other hand, the original owner—the finance company—could easily have made further inquiries as to the rogue's true identity (or could have instructed the dealer, who acted as its agent and from whom it purchased the car as part of a financing arrangement, to do this). The result of the court's reasoning, therefore, is that, as in *Cundy v. Lindsay*, the goods appear to have ended up with the party who was more at fault in permitting the rogue to operate the fraud. But even apart from this objection, it may be questioned whether, purely as a matter of offer-and-acceptance law, the majority reached the correct result. The minority's view was that no sensible distinction could be drawn between cases in which the parties' dealings are entirely oral and those in which the parties' interactions are wholly or partly in writing, and furthermore, that in each case the presumption should be that the intended co-contractor is the person with whom one is communicating. On the first point, the minority's argument is compelling: why should it make a difference whether the parties are together in a room when they make the agreement or in adjoining rooms communicating by email? The second point—that in each case the intended co-contractor should be presumed to be the person with whom one is communicating—is more difficult, but here again the minority view seems preferable. In nearly all mistaken identity cases, the rogue's alias is important to the claimant not because of identity per se, but because of the creditworthiness attached to that identity; the claimant is generally indifferent as to whether the rogue is some particular person on the planet. This is true regardless of whether the transaction is made face-to-face or by correspondence. In *Shogun*, as in *Cundy*, it was not critical to the claimant finance company's decision to contract that the rogue was the specific individual identified by the name he had given; the claimant would have made the identical contract with other persons, so long as their credit was good. The operative mistake, in other words, was about an attribute.

If the minority's view from *Shogun* had prevailed, successful claims as to mistaken identity would be difficult to make, but they would not be impossible. Suppose I am interested in purchasing the car in the driveway of 150 Ferry Lane. I write a letter to 'the owner' offering to purchase 'your car' for a specific price, but then accidentally address the letter to 160 Ferry Lane. The owner of 160 Ferry Lane, believing this to be a genuine offer, then purports to accept my offer. In this case there is only one person to whom I would be willing to make my offer—the owner of the car at 150 Ferry Lane. This person's ownership of this car is no mere attribute, a trait that she might or might not share with others: it is something that uniquely identifies this individual. It follows that (if the minority view in *Shogun* was adopted) no offer was actually made to the owner of 160 Ferry Lane, and so no contract could be formed even if that person owner reasonably believed me to be making a genuine offer. The result should be the same, of course, if I mistook the physical bodies of the owners of 150 and 160 Ferry Lane and so made an offer face-to-face to the owner of 160. There do not appear to be any reported cases of this kind, but it is suggested the courts would not be likely to find a contract on a similar set of facts.

Cases such as *Cundy* and *Shogun* thus appear to be counter-examples to the many instances in which courts are willing to invent contracts to do justice in an individual case: in these cases, the courts have failed to recognize prima facie valid contracts and in doing so have reached unjust results.

6. NON-CONTRACTUAL LIABILITY IN CONTRACTUAL SETTINGS

As traditionally understood, the principle of freedom of contract requires not just that parties be free to specify the content of their contractual obligations, but that they be free to enter or not enter contracts. Thus, the offer and acceptance rules discussed in this chapter describe the pre-conditions for the creation of a contract; they do not describe duties. Anti-discrimination laws and the like aside,[107] there is in general no obligation to make or accept an offer.

But as has already been mentioned on several occasions, parties who do not succeed in making a contract may sometimes be liable for breach of an extra-contractual obligation. In the classical period (1780–1870), when judges were reluctant to enforce obligations other than those the parties imposed on themselves, the number of such obligations was relatively small. This is part of the reason contract law was often called upon to assist claimants in claims that, to contemporary eyes, appear non-contractual. Today, the number of extra-contractual obligations is much larger, but their potential breadth and significance is not always fully appreciated. Courses on the law of unjust enrichment are a recent addition to the law curriculum and are often not mandatory. Moreover, many of the extra-contractual obligations that are relevant in contractual settings fit awkwardly within the standard accounts of tort and unjust enrichment law and so their importance tends to be downplayed. As a consequence, even today there is pressure to expand the law of contract beyond what might be thought its natural borders. This chapter concludes, therefore, with a brief survey of the main categories of extra-contractual obligations that may be relevant in contractual settings.

---

[107] See below, 87.

Negative duties

'Negative duties' are duties not to harm another's person, property, or liberty. The courts have always enforced such duties, but the meaning given to 'person, property, or liberty' has greatly expanded over the last half-century. In contract formation settings, the most important negative duty is undoubtedly the duty not to tell falsehoods. Until 1964, this duty was limited to a duty not to tell a deliberate falsehood, that is to say a fraud, but since *Hedley Byrne v. Heller*[108] it encompasses duties not to carelessly tell falsehoods. The introduction of the tort of negligent misstatement has dramatically reduced the pressure that previously existed to expand the boundaries of contract law. It has also given rise to the opportunity, which is perhaps not yet fully realized, to narrow the existing boundaries.

For a successful claim in negligent misstatement, the claimant must show that the relevant statement represented a fact, not an opinion, and that the parties were in a 'close' or 'special' relationship, such that (broadly speaking) the defendant assumed responsibility for the claimant's reliance. These requirements are typically satisfied where the parties were negotiating or contemplating a possible contract. Thus, in one case a bank was held liable for a customer's loss where an employee had carelessly encouraged the customer to believe his application for a loan would be approved.[109] The court rejected the argument that, since there was no duty to enter the contract, there could be no liability for a statement concerning the likelihood of entering the contract. They also quickly dismissed the argument that the relevant statements were merely opinions. Strictly applied, the decision in this case would make a tort of the common negotiating stance of deliberately misleading someone into believing you are interested in entering a contract.

Another example of a recently developed negative duty that may arise between negotiating parties is the tort of 'breach of confidence'. If information is divulged in confidence between negotiating parties, and negotiations break down so that no contract is made, the party obtaining the information may be prevented by injunction from using it or, if he does use it, be made to pay for it. For instance, in *Seager v. Copydex Ltd*,[110] the claimant had patented a new type of carpet grip, and he tried to interest the defendants in manufacturing it. There were prolonged negotiations, but nothing came of them. Later, the defendants started manufacturing a carpet grip that the court held was an unintentional copy of the claimant's invention, though not within the patent. Although the defendants had not realised they were making use of the confidential information they had obtained from the claimant, it was held that the defendants had acted in breach of confidence—

---

[108] [1964] AC 465.
[109] *Box v. Midland Bank* [1979] 2 Lloyd's Rep. 391.
[110] [1967] 1 WLR 923, and see also the sequel in [1969] 1 WLR 809.

a sort of equitable tort, if such a term is permissible. The striking feature of this tort is that it imposes an obligation not to use information that the defendant had obtained innocently and with respect to which no promise or agreement was made. The requirement from this and subsequent cases[111] that an 'implied obligation' of confidence be established for an action for breach of confidence makes the liability in such cases very close to contractual.

It is not customary to discuss in detail anti-discrimination legislation in books on contract law, but these statutory (and in the case of sex discrimination, European) rights may also be highly relevant to the position of negotiating parties in particular circumstances. An employer, for example, who refuses to treat an applicant for a job as required by this legislation cannot be sued for breach of contract if no contract is made, but the employer may be made liable (by an industrial tribunal) to pay damages for breach of the legislation and, exceptionally, to hire the applicant.[112] The same is true of commercial organizations that discriminate illegally in the provision of services by not entering contracts.

Finally, legislation implementing European Community Directives on public sector contracts has significantly limited the freedom of public authorities in the awarding of public contracts. The Directives go beyond anti-discrimination legislation in disallowing, for example, refusals that are unfair in view of the private party's 'legitimate expectations'.[113]

Positive duties

'Positive duties' are duties to assist or benefit another person. It is sometimes wrongly supposed that private law recognizes such duties only when a promise or agreement has been made. The most obvious counter-example, though it is rarely described in these terms, is the duty to reverse an unjust enrichment: a person who has been paid money by mistake has a positive duty to return the money or its equivalent. Such duties are enormously important for understanding contracting parties' obligations, both when the parties do and (as is our present concern) when they do not make a contract. In the latter case, they provide the main relief for parties who have relied on an erroneous belief that they already had, or would soon have, a valid contract.[114] Thus, if one party renders services or supplies goods to the other while the negotiations are in process, the recipient may have to pay for those goods or services if no contract ensues if he cannot return them. The recipient is obliged to pay a reasonable price (not necessarily the 'contract' price—in the

---

[111] See, e.g., *Coco v. A. N. Clarke (Engineering) Ltd* [1969] RPC 41.

[112] Race Relations Act 1976, ss. (4)1(c), 56; Sex Discrimination Act 1975, s. 6(1)(c), 65(1)(c); Disability Discrimination Act 1995, ss. 4, 5, 8(2)(c),12, 19.

[113] Local Government Act 1999, s. 3(1).

[114] See, e.g., *British Steel Corp. v. Cleveland Bridge and Engineering Co. Ltd*, above n. 45; *Rover International v. Cannon Film Sales* [1989] 1 WLR 912.

absence of a contract there is, strictly speaking, no contract price) and his obligation arises not because he has agreed, but because he has received a benefit from the other party. The duty to make restitution in such circumstances has always been recognised by English law, but as was discussed earlier in this chapter, it has only recently been given a firm legal foundation. Specifically, it was only in 1991 that the House of Lords recognized unjust enrichment as a distinct cause of action, separate from tort and contract.[115]

If no benefit has been conferred, it will be rare that a negotiating party will be held to a duty to assist the other party. The long-standing English principle that contracting parties are under no obligation to act in good faith towards one another, and in particular, under no obligation to negotiate in good faith, has been consistently affirmed by the higher courts.[116] But there are important exceptions.[117] Anti-discrimination legislation and rules regulating public sector contracts can, as we have seen, remove a negotiating party's normal rights to withdraw or decline an offer, thereby effectively forcing that party to enter a contract. A larger group of counter-examples is found in the statutory obligations imposed on various regulated industries, such as those providing water or electricity. These industries are generally obliged to enter contracts with anyone who wishes to do so and on terms that are partly or wholly set by regulations. Of similar effect are the long-standing obligations of 'common carriers', such as the post office or ferry operators, to contract with anyone seeking their services. Significantly, there are also isolated instances in which affirmative duties have been imposed on professionals who provide what might loosely be described as a quasi-public service. For instance, a solicitor was found liable in tort for negligently failing to advise a possible client that his insurance company would probably pay his legal costs, in the absence of which information the client decided not to instruct the solicitor at all.[118] The decision is striking because the solicitor was found liable despite never having promised or agreed to advise the claimant and despite not having made any statement that could ground an action in misstatement. Liability was grounded directly on a failure to assist the claimant during negotiations about a possible contract.

There is also an altogether different kind of case in which courts, though not strictly enforcing a positive obligation to enter a contract, reach a result that is similar in effect. Suppose that A wants to make a contract with B but B

---

[115] *Lipkin Gorman v. Karpnale Ltd* [1991] 2 AC 548.

[116] *Walford v. Miles*, above n. 17; *Banque Financière de la Cité SA v. Westgate Insurance Co. Ltd* [1990] QB 665, affirmed on narrower grounds, [1991] 2 AC 249.

[117] The duty to disclose information that English courts will enforce in certain circumstances (e.g. insurance contracts) is not discussed here, as it is relevant only when a contract is concluded: see Ch. 9.

[118] *Crossan v. Ward Bracewell* (1986) 136 New LJ 849.

refuses all offers. This may be because he is unwilling to deal at all or because he regards A's offer as unacceptable, for instance because the price is too low. Suppose now that A just proceeds to 'help himself' to what he has tried to buy. Obviously, in most circumstances this is quite unacceptable behaviour and may need to be stopped or deterred by severe sanctions. It may be plain theft. But there are some circumstances where things are not quite as simple as that.

For example, suppose that A has just been trying to 'buy' a temporary right of entry into B's land to carry out necessary repairs to A's building, which abuts B's land and is not otherwise accessible. Or suppose A is a builder who wants to site his crane so that it swings over B's land and so intrudes on his air space, even though it does not actually threaten any harm to B. In cases of this kind it is legally possible for the courts to prevent A from intruding on B's land or air space by granting B an injunction; but it is also possible to refuse to grant an injunction and instead to award B damages. If damages are awarded in such a case then the court is fixing the price to be paid for the right—something that looks very much like the making of a contract over the protest of one of the 'contracting' parties. For this very reason, courts are reluctant to exercise this power.[119] But there are situations in which they will intervene. For example, in one case,[120] the defendant's garage wall encroached on the claimant's land by some four-and-a-half inches and, following a neighbours' squabble, the claimant sought an injunction ordering the defendant to remove his wall. The injunction was refused and damages were offered instead. Similarly, where a new building interferes with an adjoining owner's right to light, courts are often willing to award damages rather than grant injunctions. By doing this they effectively make the contract and fix the price for the interference, rather than leaving the claimant to fix his own, possibly exorbitant, price. There are also some cases, such as patent infringement cases, where the courts are often (in effect) called upon to award damages as a form of fixing a price. A patent owner who is willing to allow manufacturers to exploit his patent rights on payment of an appropriate charge (called a royalty) may be awarded damages, rather than an injunction, against someone who has infringed his patent rights, and such damages represent a sort of price or royalty fixed by the court. There are still other cases (known as 'way-leave' cases) where a defendant has, often unwittingly, infringed the claimant's land-ownership rights by using a right of way to which he had no right. In such a case, the courts may be called upon to award damages, and they are then fixing an appropriate price for the grant of a right

---

[119] See *Shelfer v. City of London Electric Lighting Co. Ltd* [1895] 1 Ch. 287; *John Ternberth v. National Westminster Bank* (1979) 39 P & CR 104.

[120] See *Burton v. Winters* [1993] 3 All ER 847, a report of the subsequent proceedings between the parties. The original case concerning the encroaching wall does not seem to have been reported.

of way (though in this case, the price is only fixed after the event).[121] One case where the courts traditionally refused to intervene was that of the totally unreasonable neighbour who simply refuses access to his land to enable necessary repairs to be carried out. In some legal systems this would be regarded as an 'abuse of right'; the common law has never adopted this idea, but as so often happens, the legislature intervened. Under the Access to Neighbouring Land Act 1992, the court is given explicit power to authorize a person to enter upon another's land where this is necessary to do works of maintenance or repair to a building, and the court may order payment for these rights of access (except where the work is to be done to a residential building).

Reliance-based duties

The extra-contractual obligations discussed above provide a satisfactory response to most situations in which one party has suffered a loss but a contractual action is not possible because there was no offer or acceptance.[122] But there is one major category of loss for which such obligations provide no relief. This is the loss suffered by someone who detrimentally relies on the belief that a contract will soon be created (or has already been created) *and* where (a) the belief or assumption was not induced by a misstatement and (b) the reliance did not benefit the other party. For example, suppose that a manufacturer begins production of goods in reliance on a customer's statement that the customer is intending to make an order in the near future. If the customer then changes her mind and does not make the order, the manufacturer may be left with unwanted goods. In a case of this kind, an action in contract is not possible in principle because the customer never promised to make an order; a statement of intention is not an offer. A claim in fraud or negligent misstatement is also unavailable because there was no misstatement: the customer had actually *intended* to make an order, she just changed her mind. Finally, an action in unjust enrichment is not possible because the customer did not benefit by the manufacturer commencing production.

According to orthodox law, then, no relief is available for the relying party in a case of this kind. The justification usually given for this result is that if the potential customer did not actually make a promise, the manufacturer should have known that he was relying at his own risk. The very point of making a mere statement of intention rather than a promise, it is said, is to make clear that the speaker is reserving the right to change his mind; if the

---

[121] See the note by Waddams and Sharpe in (1982) 2 Ox. J. Leg. St. 290, though the main point made in this note is rejected by the Court of Appeal in *Surrey CC v. Bredero Homes Ltd* [1993] 3 All ER 705.

[122] Situations in which there has been an offer and acceptance but for other reasons (such as the absence of consideration or the failure to satisfy a formality) no contract is created are examined in the next chapter.

manufacturer was uncomfortable about commencing production on such a basis, he should have asked for a promise. On the other hand, critics of the orthodox view argue that the customer should be held responsible on the basis that she induced the manufacturer to rely. This argument is strengthened if, as is often the case, the potential customer was aware that her statement would have this effect. It is strengthened further if the potential customer waited a period of time after changing her mind before alerting the manufacturer of this fact.

Critics who adopt the latter position have also argued that, despite the orthodox statement of the law, in practice parties who have suffered 'pure' reliance losses often obtain legal relief. A variety of legal decisions and rules support this argument. It is reasonably clear, for instance, that courts are more likely to find a promise, misstatement, or benefit in cases in which there has been reliance. We have seen instances of this already in this chapter: an agent's implied warranty of authority is in many cases better explained not as arising from a promise or a misstatement, but as implied by the court because of the claimant's reliance. A second set of cases discussed earlier are the shipping cases, such as *The Eurymedon*, in which the courts said that a collateral contract was created between the owners of the goods and the stevedores who unload the goods. It was suggested above that no promise was actually made to the stevedores and that the result in that case could be explained on the basis that the owner had voluntarily assumed the risk in question. But it seems clear that one reason the court found a contract was that the stevedores had relied on the claimant's representation (not promise) that they were exempt from liability.[123]

Arguably another instance of reliance-based liability arises when parties are made to pay the value of services that they requested despite never having promised to pay. The striking feature of this liability, and the reason it cannot easily be explained on orthodox unjust enrichment grounds, is that in some cases the service is of no apparent value to the defendant. In *Brewer Street Investments v. Barclays Woollen Co. Ltd*,[124] the defendants were prospective tenants of a property owned by the claimants. In anticipation of leasing the property, they requested various alterations, which were carried out by the owners. Negotiations then broke down and no lease was entered. The non-tenants were required to compensate the owners for the cost of the alterations.

Finally, but potentially of greatest significance, negotiating parties who make representations as to their future conduct may be held liable under the doctrine of promissory estoppel if the representations are detrimentally

---

[123] This is related to the larger point that protection for third parties (which is now extensive as a result of the Contracts (Rights of Third Parties) Act) is often best explained as a species of reliance-based liability. Third-party rights are discussed in Ch. 13.
[124] [1954] QB 428.

relied upon by the other negotiating parties. Estoppel is discussed in the next chapter, but two observations should be made at this point. The first is that according to the orthodox view, estoppel can be used to enforce only a waiver of existing rights as opposed to a promise of new rights. In principle, therefore, it would not apply to the earlier example involving the manufacturer and the potential customer. But there are important exceptions to this rule. In particular, an estoppel that involves property may be used to support a cause of action. The case of *Brewer Street Investments*, discussed a moment ago, is sometimes explained as an example of proprietary estoppel—though the court itself did not adopt this reasoning. It should also be noted that other common law jurisdictions have abandoned this limitation on the use of estoppel. A famous American decision holds that a negotiating party who strings another party along with prolonged negotiations, constantly changing his terms, may be held liable to the other party for actual loss suffered in reliance on the other party, even if no contract is eventually agreed.[125] A similar result was also reached in Australia in a case in which a prospective tenant withdrew from negotiations for a lease.[126]

The second and probably more important point is that it is not entirely clear that the law of estoppel is actually about enforcing *representations* that are relied upon so much as *promises* that are relied upon. If the latter is the case, then (as was noted earlier in this chapter) the law of estoppel should probably be understood as part of the ordinary law of contract. To be sure, estoppel is not generally regarded as part of contract law, but the main reason for this is not because of the absence of a promise or agreement, but because other (arguably non-essential) requirements of contractual validity, such as the requirement of consideration or that a contract involving land be made in writing, are not required. Thus, it can and has been argued that the 'representations' that are the focus of the law of estoppel are essentially promises or agreements, and that when courts apply the estoppel doctrine they are therefore doing the same thing they do when they enforce contracts, namely enforcing voluntary obligations. This view is reflected in the name many give to this area of law: promissory estoppel.

---

[125] *Hoffman v. Red Owl Stores* 133 NW 2d 267 (1965).
[126] *Walton Stores (Interstate) Ltd v. Maher* (1988) 164 CLR 387.

4

Beyond Offer and Acceptance: Formalities, Intent to Create Legal Relations, and Consideration

WHILE we saw in the last chapter that most contracts are created by promises or agreements, making a promise or agreement (or any other arrangement that satisfies the offer and acceptance requirements) is not generally sufficient to create a contract under English law. According to the orthodox understanding, three further requirements must be satisfied: (1) the parties must intend to create legal relations, (2) the arrangement must be supported by consideration, and (3) any stipulated formalities must be fulfilled.

This chapter examines the above requirements. What we will find, broadly speaking, is that it is not easy to explain why these requirements (in particular the 'intent' and 'consideration' requirements) are a part of English law. On the one hand, none of the requirements are practically very important. Particularly in commercial contexts, the intent, consideration, and formal requirements are typically satisfied automatically, as a natural consequence of the ordinary features of the parties' arrangement. On the other hand, in those rare cases where these requirements are significant, the decision not to enforce the arrangement often appears unjust. The decision often appears, at first sight anyway, to be based on a mere technicality—a rule with no apparent connection to whatever substantive issues may be at stake. Exploring the various explanations for this state of affairs will occupy much of this chapter, but it may be useful to mention here that most of them are linked to the fact that the concepts of promise and agreement appear to be complete in themselves. In ordinary morality, a promise or agreement is usually considered binding simply by virtue of being a promise or an agreement; nothing further is needed. Of course, if a promise or agreement is made under duress or induced by fraud or if its object is an unlawful act, then morally (and legally) it is not binding. But matters of this kind are not, on the surface anyway, the concern of the requirements discussed in this chapter. The rules in question are presented as positive requirements that any binding contract must fulfil, not as tools for identifying particular arrangements that should *not* be enforced. In short, the requirements examined below appear to conflict with the ideal of freedom of contract. They appear, in other words, to be paternalistic limits on an individual's ability to make binding contracts. Determining whether this is in fact the case is a central concern of this chapter.

I. FORMALITIES

As a general rule, no formalities are required for the creation of a contract in English law. A contract may be created through writing, verbally, through conduct, via electronic communication,[1] or by a combination of these. The exceptional cases where a formality is required are now few and (with one exception) relatively unimportant, and can be dealt with briefly. But it was not always so; for nearly three centuries the famous Statute of Frauds 1677 required various types of contracts to be evidenced in writing and it was only in 1954 that most of these requirements were finally repealed.

Non-lawyers are often surprised that so many legal actions do not have to be in any specified form, but insistence on form is widely thought by lawyers to be characteristic of primitive and less well-developed legal systems. Form requirements are seen to reflect a lack of confidence in the ability of the courts to discover the truth about a case without the trappings of formalities or other rituals. In the particular case of contracts, the absence of formal requirements also reflects the emphasis of classical contract theory on the central role of intention. If individuals are liable on contracts because of what they promised or agreed to do, then an insistence on writing or other formalities seems anomalous inasmuch as it prevents giving effect to a genuine promise or agreement. A requirement of writing therefore often appears to be (and is often clearly intended to be) a paternalistic device, designed to protect people from the consequences of hasty or ill-considered actions.

The Statute of Frauds, insofar as it required writing for certain classes of contracts, may have been inspired partly by these paternalistic ideals, but it was more likely the outcome of weaknesses in legal procedure and, as the name suggests, the prevalence of frauds. Sections 4 and 17 of the Act provided that certain contracts (and a somewhat curious list it was) were to be unenforceable in a court should they not satisfy the writing requirement. Today, all that is left of these provisions is the part of section 4 that requires contracts of guarantee to be evidenced in writing. Until 1989, another part of section 4 survived in a more modern form in section 40 of the Law of Property Act 1925, which dealt with contracts for the sale of interests in land.

---

[1] In principle, electronic communications are as valid as any other type of communication. This was confirmed by the EU Directive on Electronic Commerce, which requires Member States to allow contracts to be made by electronic means and which was implemented in the UK by the Electronic Communications Act 2000 (see also the Electronic Signatures Regulation 2002). It seems likely that courts will interpret requirements that a contract be in writing as satisfied by electronic communications and also that, subject to difficult questions of proof, an electronic signature will have the same status as a written signature. This was the suggestion of the Law Commission (Electronic Commerce: Formal Requirements in Commercial Transactions, 2001), though there are not yet any cases on these issues and it may be questioned if the purposes served by writing requirements are satisfied by electronic communications.

This section has now been replaced by section 2 of the Law of Property (Miscellaneous Provisions) Act 1989, which requires that not just sales but any 'disposition of an interest in land' (a much wider category) be made in writing, incorporating all the terms of the contract and signed by both parties.[2] The same Act stipulates that in the case of a conveyance of land (a sale) the contract must, in addition, be made in a deed. The latter requirement is not onerous; it is sufficient that the document make 'clear on its face that it is intended to be a deed'.

During the nineteenth century, when classical theory was at its height, the Statute of Frauds came to seem anomalous and demands for repeal were frequently made. It is slightly curious that the demands were only successful in 1954 when classical theory had already given way to a different approach, which laid less stress on promissory liability and more on paternalistic devices. At any rate, sections 4 and 17 of the Statute of Frauds were repealed in 1954, except for the two particular cases just mentioned. The contract of guarantee was excluded from the repeal primarily because a contract of this kind is liable to be made between persons of unequal bargaining strength, sophistication, or independence, and the requirement of writing was thought to give some, if meagre, protection to guarantors. In fact this may have been a mistake, because written contracts of guarantee almost invariably strip guarantors of their common law protective rights, leaving them worse off than if the contracts had been oral. The main concern with contracts involving land, the second type of contract to which the Statute of Frauds still applies, appears to have been the risk of fraud.

The Statute of Frauds was passed at a time when English law had just recognised that mutual undertakings could create contractual liability; the procedure of the courts and the rules of evidence were still not sufficiently developed to handle this novelty. This helps to explain why several of the most important provisions of the statute applied only to executory contracts, that is to say, contracts that had been made but not yet performed. In cases where performance had begun, to whatever degree—where there was, for instance, 'part performance' of a contract for the sale of land—the need for writing was dispensed with. In such circumstances, liability was not solely based on the agreement but arose partly from the very fact of part-performance. The 1989 Act has done away with the doctrine of part-performance, although the doctrine of estoppel (discussed later in this chapter) will sometimes allow courts to achieve similar results in cases of this

---

[2] This Act also does away with the effect of the older legislation, which only rendered contracts without writing *unenforceable* (or 'voidable') and not void (on the distinction between void and voidable see above, 82). Under the new Act a contract not in writing is void.

kind.[3] It should also be kept in mind that in this and other cases a party who transfers a benefit under an unenforceable agreement will normally be able to reclaim that benefit (though not necessarily at the contract price) on the basis of unjust enrichment law.[4]

The modern disdain for formalities may not always be soundly based. As noted above, one purpose of formal requirements is to reduce the risk of hasty or ill-conceived decisions. Tele-marketing, electronic contracts that can be formed by the click of a mouse, and other contemporary methods of mass contracting magnify these kinds of risks. A measure of paternalism may be useful in such contexts. A second purpose of formalities, in particular writing requirements, is to assist courts in discovering the truth. It is true, as Jeremy Bentham first noted, that writing requirements have the effect of preventing genuine claims from being enforced where they were not put into writing. In one recent case,[5] an employer's oral promise to pay sub-contractors if the main contractor failed to do so was unenforceable because it was found to be a guarantee. The sub-contractors were left with a worthless claim of £1.3 million against the insolvent contractor. It is also true that since procedural reforms were introduced in the nineteenth century (also under Benthamite influence), courts have been much better equipped to ascertain if parties are telling the truth. But it remains the case that courts cannot always discover the truth, or cannot do so except at disproportionate cost. One purpose of requiring written formalities is therefore to reduce cost. This purpose may be outweighed by other considerations, primarily the risk of excluding an otherwise valid oral contract, but in some cases this risk is worth the price.

It should also be remembered that there are other reasons, aside from the necessity of complying with a legal formality, that contracting parties may wish to record their arrangement in writing. One obvious advantage is that the contract will be easier to prove in court. Another, perhaps more significant reason arises from the fact that courts are not the only institutions called upon to determine the existence and content of contracts. Contracts are often entered into by large organizations or bureaucracies, and in practice it will be for the members of these organizations (in the first instance and subject to appeal to the courts) to give effect to the contracts. These bodies may have fewer facilities than the courts for discovering the truth about oral dealings, and therefore typically insist on recording everything in writing. Indeed, in

---

[3] In *Actionstrength Ltd v. International Glass Engineering* [2003] 2 WLR 1060, the House of Lords refused to allow a plea of estoppel, holding—not entirely happily—that 'something more' than reliance on the unenforceable promise was necessary for estoppel. Lord Bingham, in particular, noted that the writing requirement seemed inappropriate in cases involving experienced commercial parties. This case is discussed further at 96.

[4] Restitution is not possible where the statute imposing the formal requirement expressly or implicitly precludes recovery, as has been held to be the case with respect to the Consumer Credit Act: *Wilson v. First County Trust Ltd* [2004] 1 AC 816.

[5] *Actionstrength Ltd v. International Glass Engineering*, above n. 3.

practice, not only writing, but *signatures* are commonly demanded as a kind of formal requirement for all sorts of contracts. A signature is, and is widely recognised even by the general public as, a formal device which indicates that important consequences may follow from a document. As noted in the previous chapter, the law today gives some recognition to this modern practice because it is very difficult for a person to deny the validity of a signed contractual document. But the law of contract, as opposed to business custom, rarely requires a signature.

The policies underlying those few modern formal requirements that remain are variable. In some cases the policy is probably that of minimizing the risks of error in important transactions. In other cases, especially consumer contracts (such as those falling under the Consumer Credit Act 1974, which provides that certain consumer credit agreements comply with prescribed forms and be signed by the consumer), the policy may be based on an attempt to ensure that consumers fully understand the terms of the transaction. This policy is reflected in the fact that the consumer (not the business) is given the option of enforcing the agreement despite the lack of compliance with the formality. Of course, the protective aims of such Acts are not always achieved: consumers may not read or understand the documents placed in front of them for signature, except in the most general sense. On the other hand, the protection afforded by such Acts may be excessive in some instances. In one recent case,[6] the House of Lords held that a creditor's mistake in including a 'document fee' of £250 in the amount specified as 'credit' in a consumer loan agreement contravened the requirement in the Consumer Credit Act that the total amount of credit in such agreements be specified correctly. The court further interpreted the Act as precluding the creditor from claiming restitution of the money advanced; the end result was that the debtor was excused entirely from her obligation to repay a loan of £5,250. This seems difficult to justify, and, indeed, the Court of Appeal held that the Act's provisions contravened the European Convention on Human Rights, although this potentially far-reaching ruling was later overturned by the House of Lords.

Another group of modern statutes requires certain contracts to be accompanied by the provision of written information by one party to the other. The policy behind these statutes is partly the minimizing of the risks of error, and partly, once again, that of trying to ensure that there is genuine consent to the contractual terms. Thus, employers are required under the Employment Protection (Consolidation) Act 1978 (as amended by the Trade Union Reform and Employment Rights Act 1993) to provide a written document to their employees setting out a number of details concerning the terms of the

---

[6] *Wilson v. First County Trust Ltd*, above n. 4.

employment; landlords under 'secure tenancies' (that is to say, local councils) have to supply tenants with a written statement as to the terms of the tenancy under the Housing Act 1985; other landlords have to supply a rent book containing the information specified in section 5 of the Landlord and Tenant Act 1985. There are also statutes requiring the sellers of certain commodities, for example artificial fertilizers, to provide the buyers with written information so that the latter know precisely what it is they are buying.[7] In all these statutes the principal legal sanction is provided by the criminal law rather than contract law, so a failure to comply with these statutory provisions is an offence that renders the seller liable to penalties. Although this may be a more efficient way of ensuring compliance with the law, it is apt to create difficulties in the law of contract, because the criminality of a failure to comply with the statutory provisions may render performance of the contract illegal, and this, as we shall see later, may involve drastic consequences.[8]

A final point is that there is a connection between the matters discussed above and the doctrine of consideration. As we will see, the most important consequence of the consideration requirement is that gift (or 'donative') promises, such as promises to give money to a relative or to a charity, are in principle unenforceable. These are, of course, exactly the kinds of promises for which formal requirements of validity would seem to be appropriate. It is interesting, therefore, that such promises are indeed enforceable if they are made in a deed or supported by 'nominal' consideration (e.g. £1). The possibility of using a deed or a nominal sum to avoid the normal effect of the consideration doctrine suggests that in such cases the doctrine may effectively function as a formal requirement of validity. The doctrine does not so much invalidate such promises as force promisors (who want to create a legally binding arrangement) to use a deed or nominal consideration. This suggestion is examined in more detail below.

2. INTENTION TO CREATE LEGAL RELATIONS

It is orthodox law that an intention to enter into legal relations must exist before a valid contract can be found, or in other words, that a promise or an agreement will not be legally binding unless it is intended to have this effect. In fact, this proposition cannot easily be supported except by attributing a fictitious intention to the parties. It is more realistic to say that no positive intention to enter into legal relations needs to be shown, and that a deliberate promise seriously made is enforced irrespective of the promisor's views

---

[7] Agriculture Act 1970; other examples are found in the Plant Varieties and Seeds Act 1964 and the Weights and Measures Act 1985.

[8] See Ch. 8. In some acts it is expressly provided that the illegality is not to affect contractual rights.

regarding his legal liability.[9] As we shall see, the cases that are said to be decided on this basis are nearly all more easily explained on other grounds.

Mere puffs and joking statements

It was noted in the previous chapter that the intent requirement is sometimes used to explain why an apparent promise or agreement that could not reasonably have been understood to be serious is denied contractual effect. An example sometimes given is the old case in which a court refused to enforce the defendant's promise that he 'would give £100 to him that should marry his daughter with his consent'.[10] It was on this basis as well that the defendants in *Carlill v. Carbolic Smoke Ball Co.*[11] famously argued that an advertising stunt whereby they had offered to pay £100 to any person who used their 'smoke ball' according to the instructions and nevertheless caught influenza was not intended to create legal relations. The court agreed that an issue of intent was raised, but held that on the facts it was reasonable to regard the advert as a binding promise.

The conclusion that a mere puff, joke, or other such statement does not give rise to a contractual obligation is uncontroversial, but it can be explained without the requirement of intent to create legal relations. Words must be understood in context, and the context in which a mere puff or joke is made makes clear to the reasonable listener that despite the actual words used, no promise or offer to enter an agreement was intended, and no willingness to be bound was expressed, even in purely moral terms. The ordinary rules of offer and acceptance would appear to provide a complete explanation for why such statements are not contractual.

Agreements not to be bound

A second category of cases in which the intent requirement is used to explain the non-enforcement of an apparent promise or agreement is where the parties have specifically declared that their arrangement is not intended to be legally binding. Thus in the well-known case of *Rose & Frank v. Crompton & Bros Ltd*,[12] where two business firms had made an agreement for the supply of goods that was expressly declared not to be a legal contract, but binding in honour alone, the House of Lords held that the agreement was not a legal contract because the intent requirement was not satisfied.

There is no serious objection to the results in such cases, particularly when the relevant clause is agreed upon by business parties dealing on equal terms

---

[9] *Williston on Contracts*, (3rd edn Mount Kisco, New York, 1957), I, 39.
[10] *Weeks v. Tybold* (1605) Noy 11; G. H. Treitel, *The Law of Contract* (11th edn, Oxford, 2003), 162.
[11] [1893] 1 QB 256.
[12] [1925] AC 445.

with one another and fully aware of what they are doing. But, again, it seems unnecessary to invoke the intent to create legal relations requirement to explain why such agreements should not be enforced. The result can be explained on the basis that, although the agreement is a valid contract, one of its terms stipulates that the parties will not seek legal enforcement of the contract's substantive obligations. On this interpretation, the clause disclaiming legal intent is a kind of exemption of liability clause, which the court is asked to enforce, like any other contractual clause.

This interpretation of the second category of intent cases helps to explain why, despite the fact it is orthodox law that an intent to create legal relations is required for a valid contract, courts do not typically require positive evidence of such an intent. The intent requirement is in fact almost never discussed. The usual explanation for this is that in typical cases it is 'presumed' that the parties intend to create legal relations. But with the exception of cases involving domestic and social arrangements (discussed in the next section), it is almost impossible to find a case in which this presumption is rebutted other than where the parties specifically state, as in *Rose & Frank*, that the agreement is not legally binding. Indeed, there are many cases where, if the intent requirement were taken seriously, one might expect the presumption to be rebutted. For instance, in *Simpkin v. Pays*,[13] where the claimant, a lodger in the defendant's house, assisted the defendant in winning a competition organized by a Sunday newspaper, it was held that an agreement that the claimant should have a share of any winnings was a legal contract. One might also have thought that an ordinary wager or bet would be a typical example of an agreement in honour alone, but until 1845, these too could be sued on as valid contracts.

If courts were willing to interpret disclaimer-of-intent clauses as (mere) terms in contracts, this would also have substantive benefits; in particular, if such clauses were understood in this way they could then be regulated by the courts. Disclaimer-of-legal-intent clauses are effectively a type of exemption of liability clause; as such, while they are usually unobjectionable, they are sometimes—like exemption clauses—entirely one-sided in their effect. But unlike in the case of unreasonable exemption clauses, which courts can regulate using, *inter alia*, the Unfair Contract Terms Act 1977 and the Unfair Terms in Consumer Contracts Regulations 1999 (as discussed in Chapter 12), disclaimer-of-intent clauses are not subject to review. According to the current view, such clauses prevent a contract from being created at all, and as such cannot be subject to rules (such as the above legislation) that regulate contract *terms*. This is why the Court of Appeal rejected an argument that a clause in a football pool coupon ousting the jurisdiction of the courts was

---

[13] [1955] 1 WLR 975.

contrary to public policy.[14] The discrepancy between this result and results in cases dealing with unfair exemption clauses is striking, especially since it is a general principle of the law of contract that an agreement to oust the juris- diction of the courts is void on the ground that it offends public policy.[15] In the coupon case, this principle was distinguished on the basis that it only applies where the parties intended to create a legal relationship in the first place. The distinction seems highly artificial, since the object of an 'honour clause' is identical to that of a simple clause purporting to oust the jurisdiction of the court.

In view of the serious effects that disclaimer-of-intent clauses may have, it is not surprising to learn that courts have sometimes regulated them indirectly, by interpreting such clauses as not actually succeeding in their apparent purpose. For instance, in one case[16] where there was an agreement to pay compensation on an 'ex gratia basis' it was held that these words did not prevent the agreement from having legal effect. In addition, courts often give legal effect to 'letters of intent' and other such documents that ostensibly restrain themselves to recording the parties' intentions to enter into a formal agreement, and that invite the addressee to take necessary preliminary steps towards the performance of that agreement.[17]

While parties may preclude enforcement of their bare agreement, it is a more serious matter to prevent actual transactions from having their normal legal significance. Thus, in the *Rose & Frank* case, where it was held that an agreement for the supply of goods was not a binding contract, it was also said that if goods had actually been supplied under the agreement, the nor- mal legal remedies would have operated, including the seller's right to sue for the price of the goods and the buyer's right to complain if the goods had not been of the agreed quality. While it may have been possible for the parties to have excluded even such consequences, very deliberate and clear wording would have been needed. Again, in *British Steel Corp. v. Cleveland Bridge & Engineering Co. Ltd*,[18] where no contract was found because the parties were still negotiating, and yet the goods were manufactured and delivered, it was not seriously disputed that the sellers had a restitutionary remedy for the reasonable value of the goods.

One of the most important practical applications of the principle that parties can exclude the intent to create legal relations by express wording is to

[14] *Appleson v. H. Littlewood Ltd* [1939] 1 All ER 464.
[15] See below, 216.
[16] *Edwards v. Skyways Ltd* [1964] 1 WLR 349.
[17] *British Steel Corp. v. Cleveland Bridge & Engineering Co. Ltd* [1984] All ER 504. See also *Kleinwort Benson Ltd v. Malaysia Mining Corp.* [1988] 1 All ER 714 (discussed above, 38) where a 'letter of comfort' was held a binding contract after it was relied on by making a loan of £10 million. This decision was reversed on the facts: [1989] 1 All ER 785.
[18] Ibid.

be found in the common custom of making agreements for the sale of houses and land 'subject to contract'. This formula is taken to mean that the parties intend their agreement to be recorded eventually in a formal written contract and do not intend it to be binding in the meantime. The words 'subject to contract' are therefore treated by the courts in almost all cases as excluding legal effectiveness.[19] The present practice has its root in the procedures normally used by estate agents in England, who always advise buyers and sellers to make their initial agreements 'subject to contract' in order to avoid legal liability. Very often, these buyers will themselves reach agreements to sell their houses 'subject to contract', so that a whole chain develops in which A is selling to B, who is selling to C, and so on.

This procedure means that there is often a considerable lapse of time, usually several months, between the date when the parties first agree on the sale of a house and the date when they become legally bound. The result is that either party is legally free to change his mind in this interim period, with great disappointment and possible expense to the other party. When a long chain has developed, the withdrawal of one party may cause the collapse of the whole chain, with none of the costs legally recoverable from the party responsible, as that party has not benefited from the expenditures.

Although the present procedures may have worked well at one time, they do not appear to work well today; indeed, the system appears on the verge of total breakdown. Yet it is perfectly easy to have a completely different system. In most countries buyers and sellers enter into binding contracts at an earlier stage than they do in England. Some element of risk may be involved, but if some people are able and willing to take these risks, there does not seem to be any reason to prevent their doing so. Indeed, the present system also involves risks—that everything will fall through—so it is not clear that the risks would be worse if the present procedures were changed.

The problem of the buyer who needs to be assured of a mortgage, prior to committing himself to a purchase, can be, and in some countries is, dealt with in a different way. It is, for instance, possible for a contract to be binding at the outset, but expressly made conditional. For instance, the buyer could be given the right not to complete the purchase after the contract has been made if he fails to obtain a mortgage. Unfortunately, difficulties have occurred in dealing with conditional clauses concerning such matters as the obtaining of a mortgage. As we have seen, an agreement 'subject to the buyer obtaining a mortgage' may be held too uncertain to be enforceable as a contract, though there should be no difficulty in drafting a clause which is less uncertain (e.g. specifying the amount to be raised and the name of the proposed lender). The latest authority on the topic looks more favourably

---

[19] *Cohen v. Neasdale Ltd* [1982] 2 All ER 97.

on such a conditional clause,[20] but there are still many complications involved.

Social, family, and collective bargaining agreements

While an intent to create legal relations is normally presumed where a serious agreement or promise is made, there are situations in which the opposite presumption is drawn. The results in these situations differ from those in the cases discussed above in that they cannot easily be explained on an alternative legal ground, such as offer and acceptance or interpretation. But it is just as unlikely that the true reason for non-enforcement is that the parties did not intend to create legal relations. In most of the cases in this category the parties had no intention one way or the other as regards creating legal relations, and the presumption is better explained on the basis of broader policy concerns.

The simplest illustration is the case of a social engagement, for example an invitation to go to a restaurant for dinner, where all the other ingredients of a contract may be present and yet the agreement will almost certainly not be enforceable. Only one step further removed are cases involving family arrangements, which again the courts will normally refuse to enforce. In the nineteenth century, such cases would have been dealt with by asking if there was 'good consideration' for the promise, but the modern approach has been to inquire whether the parties intended to create legal relations. The classic case is *Balfour v. Balfour*,[21] where the Court of Appeal refused to enforce a promise by a husband to allow his wife £30 a month maintenance on his departure for Ceylon on the basis that the necessary intent was missing.

It is no doubt possible to explain some of the decisions in this category on the same basis as the decisions in the previous category of cases, namely, that the parties did not in fact intend their agreement to be enforceable. This sub-category of cases differ only in the respect that the disclaimer is implicit, not explicit. But it seems evident that in the majority of cases involving social and family arrangements, the real reason the parties' agreement is unenforceable is a policy decision that the courts should not get involved in these sorts of arrangements. Atkin LJ admitted as much in *Balfour v. Balfour*, when he said that domestic agreements 'are outside the realm of contracts altogether. . . . In respect of these promises each house is a domain into which the King's writ does not seek to run, and to which his officers do not seek to be admitted.'[22] The underlying idea appears to be that the special nature of family and social relations would be harmed by the threat of legal enforcement. Of course, once the parties are in court it is unlikely that enforcement will cause further harm to whatever relationship they may still have, but the presumption must apply at the time the agreement is made, since it is the

[20] *Graham v. Pitkin* [1992] 1 WLR 403.   [21] [1919] 2 KB 571.   [22] Ibid. at 578.

threat of enforcement that is thought to be harmful. In this view, the rule is designed to protect family and social relationships generally rather than the specific relationship of the parties who are in court. Consistent with this explanation, it is precisely in cases where the threat of enforcement will not harm the parties' relationship that the presumption is most often rebutted. An example is *Merritt v. Merritt*,[23] where an agreement between a husband and wife who had separated was enforced.

The idea that domestic arrangements should generally not be enforced seems appropriate in principle, but it may be queried whether it should always be applied with full force and effect. In particular, where one of the parties has detrimentally relied on the agreement it would seem appropriate in some case to allow a claim for reliance expenses even if full-blown enforcement of the contract (in the form of specific performance or contractual damages) is refused. At present, there is no general basis on which such reliance-based losses can be claimed in English law, but the courts have other tools that they can—and often do—use to protect reliance. In cases involving domestic agreements, the simplest technique is to find that, on the facts, the presumption of the absence of intent is rebutted. In *Jones v. Padavatton*,[24] for example, the Court of Appeal was divided on the enforceability of a promise by a mother to pay an allowance to her daughter while she studied for the Bar. Careful study of the judgments suggests that the court was less concerned with the real intention of the parties than with the fact that the daughter gave up a well-paid position and a comfortable home overseas in order to move to England and study for the Bar. This fact was dispositive for the minority, but the majority seems to have thought the need for flexibility in family arrangements was so great that it was undesirable to regard them as binding contracts. No doubt this is an appropriate course where the arrangement is wholly executory but perhaps not where parties have actually acted on the arrangement.

In any event, there are many other types of domestic arrangements that will be recognized as creating legal rights after they have been acted upon. A common type of case arises when an elderly widow sells her home and moves in with an adult child, sometimes contributing substantial sums of money for the purchase or extension of the child's house. Such arrangements are unlikely to be regarded as enforceable legal contracts while they are still executory, but once they have been acted upon, the courts are loath to allow the widow to be driven from her child's home as a result of a family quarrel. Sometimes the court will find a contract;[25] other times they will invoke estop-

---

[23] [1970] 1 WLR 1211.   [24] [1969] 1 WLR 328.

[25] See, e.g., *Parker v. Clark* [1960] 1 All ER 93, where an agreement between friends to share a house was held a valid contract after one couple had sold their own house and moved in with the other couple.

pel, in particular, proprietary estoppel.[26] There is another line of cases in which a parent invites a child to build a house on land belonging to the parent[27] or perhaps to move into a cottage already in existence, which may involve giving up an existing home.[28] Here also the courts are hesitant to refuse all legal remedy solely on the ground that the parties did not intend to create legal relations. A remedy must therefore be found, though choosing one that is appropriate is often a matter of great difficulty: in some cases monetary compensation is awarded, sometimes an equitable decree is made, which gives rights akin to ownership, and sometimes a sort of possessory right (for instance to live in a home for life) is recognized.

Then again, there are a large number of cases (dealt with briefly in the previous chapter) in which cohabitants separate and disputes arise concerning the ownership of the house. The fact that cohabitants have deliberately chosen to live together without getting married might suggest that they are agreed in not wanting their relationship to have any legal effect, but to deny all rights on such a ground is clearly unacceptable. Some redress is usually devised by the courts for a partner in such a relationship, even where the house in question is registered in the sole name of the other, subject to proof of detrimental reliance or other justificatory factors (such as that money was contributed for the purchase of the house).

Detrimental reliance is thus often sufficient to persuade the courts to ignore the policy reasons for not getting involved in domestic agreements and to recognize that legal rights have been created. Even a purely social engagement could, surely, suffice in this event, as, for instance, if one person invited another to dinner at the Ritz and pressed him to partake lavishly in the belief that his meal was to be paid for, only to refuse to pay the bill at the end of the meal. It is hardly likely that after such behaviour a court would listen to a plea from the host that the invitation was not intended to create legal relations. Conversely, cases in which, after the agreement was acted upon, it has been held that there was an intention to create legal relations, are not good guides to the likely effect of a wholly executory arrangement.

The application of the intent requirement to collective bargaining agreements raises issues similar to those involved in social and domestic agreements. In *Ford Motor Co. v. A.E.U.*,[29] it was held that a collective bargaining agreement between an employer and a trade union was not enforceable as a legally binding contract. Again, it seems doubtful that this was really the 'intention' of the parties; indeed, there seems to be some circularity in the reasoning in this case. The lack of the necessary intent was at least partly deduced from the fact that the Ford Motor Company's officials

---

[26] See, e.g., *Hussey v. Palmer* [1972] 1 WLR 1286, and below, 125.
[27] As in *Inwards v. Baker* [1965] 2 QB 29.
[28] As in *Williams v. Staite* [1979] Ch 291.   [29] [1969] 2 QB 303.

may have *thought* that the agreement was not a legal contract, but this was likely the case because that is what their lawyers had told them. The truth is that there are some good reasons for *not* treating collective bargaining agreements as binding contracts (though, as was true of domestic agreements, there are also arguments to the contrary). Many clauses in such agreements are couched in language more suited to vague aspiration than binding commitment (e.g. that the parties will cooperate amicably in the settlement of disputes, etc.). In addition, it is generally recognized that litigation is not the best way of promoting good industrial relations; it has been very rare for any party to a collective bargaining agreement to attempt to enforce it in the courts (at any rate in England), and this is one of the main factors that have led commentators to suppose that they are not intended to be legally enforceable contracts. On the other hand, arguments could also be put forward for saying that such agreements should be enforceable: some parts of them, such as clauses agreeing to submit disputes to arbitration, are sufficiently clear and precise to be legally enforced, and the unwillingness of employers to attempt legal enforcement is attributable to the threat of industrial action rather than to any belief that they ought not to have binding legal force. There are many countries (such as the United States and Canada) in which some parts of collective bargaining agreements are regularly enforced by courts without apparent difficulty.[30]

In conclusion, it appears that a (controversial) policy decision that the courts should not become involved in the kinds of relationships that give rise to social, domestic, and collective bargaining agreements plays a larger role in the decision not to enforce such agreements than does the question of whether the parties actually intended to create legal relations. If this is correct, then the legal treatment of such agreements is closely related to the treatment of agreements that are explicitly held to be contrary to public policy, such as agreements to sell human organs or to pay for sex. The main difference, of course, is that in the case of social, domestic, and collective bargaining agreements, the policy aims to support, not discourage, the activity or relationship in question.

3. CONSIDERATION

The doctrine of consideration is generally seen by lawyers as a set of rules that limit individuals' freedom to make binding legal contracts. Only those

---

[30] The Conservative Government's Industrial Relations Act 1971 provided that such agreements should be legally binding in the absence of agreement to the contrary, but this act was repealed by the Labour Government's Trade Union and Labour Relations Act 1974, which provides that collective bargaining agreements are *not* to be treated as binding contracts unless they so provide. This provision of the 1974 act has survived the legislation of subsequent Conservative governments, so it may be assumed that it is likely now to remain the law.

undertakings that are supported by legal consideration are legally binding; other undertakings are not binding, even if the speaker *intends* to bind himself by his undertaking. More specifically, the consideration doctrine is understood to limit individuals' freedom to make binding contracts to two broad categories of arrangements: (1) those involving mutual undertakings to do or not do things, where each undertaking is given in exchange for the other ('executory' consideration); and (2) those involving undertakings that are conditional on the performance of an act, where the act has been performed ('executed' consideration). An example of the first category (where consideration resides in an undertaking) is an ordinary service contract: the service provider's undertaking to perform the service is consideration for the consumer's undertaking to pay for the service, and vice versa. An example of the second category (where consideration consists in a performed act) is where a reward has been promised for the return of a lost dog, and the dog is returned: the consideration for the promise of reward is finding the dog. In the language of the previous chapter, then, the consideration doctrine dictates that contracts are formed either by a mutual undertaking, that is to say by an agreement, or by a (unilateral) conditional promise where the condition is satisfied.[31]

This account of consideration must be qualified in many ways, not least by the fact that the entire doctrine can be circumvented by the use of a deed. But even without these qualifications, the doctrine—which is unique to common law legal systems—presents an evident puzzle. What purpose is served by limiting enforcement to transactions that are supported by consideration? It is sometimes said that the doctrine's aim is to identify those arrangements that involve exchanges or 'bargains'. This explanation falls short on a number of counts: aside from not indicating why bargains are more deserving of enforcement than non-bargains, it fails to account for the fact that a token benefit—traditionally, a peppercorn—is sufficient to satisfy the requirement, even where there is obviously no real bargain.[32] It also fails to account for those cases in which consideration consists in the performance of an act. The

---

[31] Conditional promises must not be confused with promises and agreements that contain conditional undertakings, as where an insurance company promises to pay the value of a house if it is destroyed by fire during a certain year. In the case of a reward, the contract is formed (and consideration exists) only when and if the condition is fulfilled, such as when the dog is returned; in the case of an insurance contract, the contract is formed from the moment the undertaking to pay the insurance premium is exchanged for the undertaking to compensate for loss due to fire. Even if the house is not destroyed, and the insurance company never has to pay, this agreement satisfies the consideration requirement because the insurance company has undertaken to do something in return for the insured's promise to pay, albeit only if a certain event happens. A more difficult modern case is the credit card company that promises to supply a credit card for life without charging an annual fee. This may seem a gratuitous offer but it is not: customers who accept this offer are agreeing to pay their credit card debts if they incur any.

[32] See below, 114.

person who finds a lost dog and claims the reward is not involved in a bargain or exchange with the promisor. By definition, conditional promises are not made *in exchange for* the specified act because that act happens later, if at all; in an exchange, the exchanged things must be exchanged at the same moment. For the same reason, the act is not given in exchange (or in 'return') for the promise.

An alternative suggestion is that the consideration doctrine identifies those arrangements in which the party against whom enforcement is sought (the 'defendant') has received a benefit or the party seeking enforcement (the 'claimant') has detrimentally relied or both. In principle, this idea is more appealing than the (so-called) bargain theory of consideration: the argument for enforcement is intuitively stronger where the defendant has received a benefit from the claimant or where the claimant has detrimentally relied on the defendant. But this explanation cannot account for the enforceability of a standard executory contract, where consideration consists in a mere under-taking to do or not do something. Such contracts are binding at formation, before any performance or reliance has taken place. Admittedly, if the under-taking in question is legally binding then, in most cases anyway, it will be a benefit to the defendant and a detriment to the claimant. But as the legal enforceability of a promise or agreement is determined (at least in part) by the consideration doctrine, this fact cannot be used to explain the doctrine without begging the question.

As we shall see, the reality appears to be that no unitary explanation can explain every aspect of the consideration doctrine. This conclusion is not surprising in light of the doctrine's history. In early medieval times, many actions that would now be described as contractual were classified as actions in debt. Regarded as part of the law of property, these actions were based not on a promise or an agreement, but on the existence of a debt—an obligation to pay for a thing received or a service rendered. This idea was expressed in the rule that a debt required reciprocity, a *quid pro quo*. Eventually, what we would now call contractual claims moved from debt to the law of *assumpsit* (originally a part of tort law), from which the modern law of con-tract eventually developed. As frequently happens in the common law, the new action incorporated features of the old one, in particular the idea of reciprocity. But while the concept maintained the same formal shell and, in some cases, served the same purpose (as where a claim was made on a conditional promise), over time it was put to new uses. Consideration, as the concept came to be called, was understood to be equivalent to a good reason (*'causa'* in Roman law) for enforcing a promise or agreement. Thus, domestic agreements and agreements to pay officials to perform their public duties, to mention just two examples, were said to lack consideration. In the nineteenth century, when freedom of contract was championed, the paternalist aspects of the doctrine began to look anomalous: the courts had no business, it was said, conducting wholesale investigations into contracting parties' motives. At the same time, doctrines like 'duress' and 'intent to create legal relations' were introduced or further developed, providing judges with more narrowly circumscribed tools to invalidate agreements made under duress, domestic agreements, and so on. It was in this period that the modern and relatively technical notion of consideration was developed. That the doctrine, thus understood, did not serve any obvious purpose was perhaps mildly embarrassing, but not practically important since it was easily satisfied if one knew what one was doing (and as we saw in Chapter 1, the courts in this period were not particularly concerned with non-commercial parties). But, again, while lawyers talked about consideration in a very different way, the substance of the old law was not completely discarded. In part this was because change happens slowly in precedent-based systems, but it was also because some of the doctrine's functions could not otherwise be fulfilled.

As this historical overview suggests, the key to understanding consideration is to recognize that it has served a variety of functions. Some of these functions (as we shall see) are essentially negative, in the sense that the consideration doctrine has been used to identify particular types of arrangements for which enforcement is thought inappropriate, such as promises (or agreements) made under duress, social and domestic promises, promises that are contrary to public policy, and promises for which a formal requirement of validity is appropriate. Other functions of the doctrine are essentially positive, in the sense that it identifies certain types of arrangements as particularly deserving of legal enforcement. The common feature of most of these arrangements is that the defendant has received a benefit or the claimant has detrimentally relied, or both. When it fulfils this positive function, the consideration doctrine appears to be closely related to other parts of the law of obligations that are concerned with benefits and reliance, in particular estoppel, unjust enrichment law, and the tort of misrepresentation.

Described in this way, it is evident that the consideration doctrine serves a number of different roles, that these roles are sometimes in tension (as, for example, in the case of a relied-on domestic agreement), and, finally, that the doctrine is not transparent, in the sense that its purpose is not obvious. Perhaps not surprisingly, many commentators have called for the outright abolition of consideration. The criticism is not that courts should be unconcerned about duress, public policy, reliance, and so on; rather, it is that insofar as such factors are taken into account, this should be done openly, and therefore by legal doctrines other than consideration. The criticism, in short, is that whatever values are served by consideration could be better served by other legal doctrines.

*Consideration as a reason not to enforce certain kinds of agreements
and promises*

There are arrangements that appear to satisfy the consideration doctrine, as described above, but in respect of which the courts have nonetheless concluded that consideration is missing, and thus that the arrangement is not legally binding. In attempts to rationalize these cases it is sometimes said that consideration consists not merely in an undertaking or an act, but in an undertaking or act that involves a particular type of benefit or detriment, for instance a 'legal' or 'economic' one. But an examination of these cases suggests that what counts as consideration varies from situation to situation, and that the true explanation for the decisions has little to do with benefit or detriment, however defined.[33] This can be demonstrated by examining four situations in which the doctrine is or has been given as the reason for refusing to enforce particular kinds of promises or agreements.[34]

(1) Domestic and social arrangements

The requirement of intent to create legal relations, discussed earlier in this chapter, was only introduced in 1893, in the famous case of *Carlill v. Carbolic Smoke Ball Co.*[35] Before that date, courts that wished to deny legal enforcement to domestic or social arrangements would typically do this on the basis that the promise or agreement was not supported by consideration.[36] Admittedly, it is possible to explain some of these cases on the basis that the relevant undertakings were not given *in return* for each other. But many of the cases involve arrangements that clearly satisfy the orthodox consideration test; in these cases, it seems evident that the decision not to enforce was reached on the basis of public policy (as described earlier). In some of the cases in this group, the parties made a clear exchange of undertakings. In the famous nineteenth-century case of *White v. Bluett*,[37] for example, a father promised to pay his son's debts if the son stopped complaining. Pollock CB stated that the father's promise was not given in consideration, as the son 'had no right to complain'. Read literally, this cannot be correct: individuals have a perfect right, and sometimes even an obligation, to complain. The arrangement was a bargain, if an unusual one. The better explanation is that, despite satisfying the modern definition of consideration, the agreement was

---

[33] This explains why judges deciding cases in this category frequently say not that the arrangement lacked consideration *simpliciter*, but that it lacked 'good' or 'valuable' consideration. The use of these adjectives is an acknowledgment that consideration exists in the literal sense.

[34] This discussion is not exhaustive; for example, we will not consider the cases in which the consideration rule has been used to invalidate agreements that are too vague or where the doctrine has been used to prevent third parties from enforcing agreements.

[35] Above n.11.

[36] See, e.g., *Shadwell v. Shadwell* (1860) 9 CBNS 159.

[37] (1853) 23 LJ Ex 36.

not enforced because it was made in a domestic setting (or, alternatively, because it was made under duress). In other cases involving domestic and social arrangements there was no bargain, but there was consideration (in the strict sense) in the form of performance of an act. An example is the case in which a court refused a contractual claim to a prize that had been offered for the winner of a competition organized by a golf club.[38] Other cases of this kind involve promises to subsidize a child's education; if the doctrine were applied strictly in such cases, consideration would be found in the child's act of entering the school or university. Contemporary courts appear to support this interpretation of cases such as *White v. Bluett*. The consideration doctrine is now rarely used to invalidate domestic or social arrangements; instead, the courts directly apply the intent to create legal relations requirement.

(2) Promises and agreements to perform pre-existing duties

A second situation in which the consideration doctrine has been used to invalidate certain types of promises or agreements involves cases where no contract is said to be formed because one party merely did or undertook to do what she was already legally bound to do. The duty might have been in the nature of a public duty, not enforceable by any individual, or a private duty, such as a duty arising from an existing contractual relation with the promisee or a third party. Each possibility is examined below.

It is orthodox law that, in most cases anyway, doing or undertaking to do something that is required by the general law cannot qualify as good consideration. Thus, in an old case, an undertaking to pay the claimant six guineas for answering a subpoena and giving evidence was held to be unenforceable, because the claimant only did what he was legally obliged to do anyhow. Similarly, it is settled law that police officers cannot enforce undertakings given in consideration of their performing their duties as police officers (though the police can contract to render services that go beyond the strict call of duty, such as might be requested in connection with large public meetings).

The orthodox explanation of these cases is that consideration is lacking because the act or undertaking was neither a benefit to the claimant nor a detriment to the defendant: the defendant was merely doing or undertaking to do what she was required to do anyway. But in most of these cases, the persons subject to the public duties have (in practice if not in law) discretion as to how and when the duty is performed. This is why such agreements are made in the first place: the payor believed the payment would make a difference as to how the duty would be performed. Given that the law of

---

[38] *Lens v. Devonshire Social Club*, The Times, 4 Dec. 1914.

contract generally treats questions of value from the perspective of the individual involved, it is artificial to say that these arrangements are not supported by consideration, strictly defined. A promise to perform a public duty is a genuine promise. The more plausible explanation why such arrangements are not enforceable is that it is contrary to public policy for a person to demand or sue for remuneration for the performance of certain public duties.[39] A contract of this kind is too close to a bribe.

Understanding the public duty cases in this way helps to explain why exceptions have been made for public duties of a different character from those considered above. For instance, the mother of an illegitimate child is under a statutory obligation to maintain the child. As a matter of 'legal' benefits or detriments, the mother's undertaking to maintain her child is thus similar to a police officer's undertaking to uphold the law. But from a public policy perspective, the case for enforcement is very different. The mother's duty is meant to regulate the relations between her and the state, not between her and the father, who may also be under a duty to maintain the child. So if she agrees to look after the child in return for an agreement by the father to pay maintenance there seems no reason of public policy why the father should not be liable on that agreement. It is no surprise, then, that in a case with these facts the court held the mother's undertaking to be good consideration.[40]

As for pre-existing *private* duties, in particular contractual duties, the general rule until recently was similarly that the performance of, or the undertaking to perform, such a duty was not good consideration. Thus, in the old case of *Stilk v. Myrick*,[41] an arrangement whereby a ship's captain agreed to pay his sailors extra wages after two of the crew had deserted was held invalid for lack of consideration, the crew already being 'bound by the terms of their original contract to exert themselves to the utmost to bring the ship in safety to her desired port'. Again, however, it seems a fiction to explain this result on the basis that the sailors had not agreed to do anything of value. The captain clearly thought he was getting something of benefit, and he was no doubt correct; whatever the terms of their contracts, sailors may desert a ship or work less diligently if they feel they are being underpaid. The better explanation of the result in this and other similar cases is therefore not that there was no bargain or exchange, but that the court was worried the agreement might have been extorted by undesirable or illegitimate forms of pressure.[42] Once a ship has left its home port, the crew effectively have a monopoly vis-à-vis the provision of sailors. There is clearly a risk that they

---

[39] On public policy, see Ch. 8.   [40] *Ward v. Byham* [1956] 1 WLR 496.

[41] (1809) 2 Camp 317.

[42] An alternative report of the decision explains the result on the basis of public policy: 6 Esp 129.

may exploit this monopoly by refusing to perform their contractual duties unless they are paid more. Moreover, this same risk arises in many ordinary cases involving contractual modifications: once a contract has been made, one party (or both parties) will often have little choice but to continue dealing with the other party. For example, a contractor may obtain a contract by putting in a low tender and then demand a higher price when the work is partly done. Theoretically, the employer could refuse and sue for damages should the contractor breach the contract, but in practice the employer will be reluctant to do this if he needs the work completed as soon as possible and it is not feasible to replace the contractor on short notice.

To contemporary eyes, it may seem strange that such cases were not decided under the law of duress. But it must be remembered that until quite recently the defence of duress was undeveloped in English law; in particular, the notion of economic duress (under which heading threats to breaks contracts are analysed) has been recognized only since 1976.[43] Moreover, consideration formerly had a broader meaning than it does today. Thus, it may have seemed both natural and necessary for courts in an earlier age to invoke consideration to deal with these cases. At the same time, it seems clear that the consideration doctrine, as currently understood, is not sufficiently flexible to deal with the issues raised by such cases. The rule that an undertaking to perform a pre-existing contractual duty is not consideration, if applied strictly, invalidates many promises and agreements not made under duress. Agreements to pay more or to give up an existing right are often made in response to the reality that the other party will not be able to perform, or perform adequately, without extra compensation. A contractor who truthfully explains that he is about to go bankrupt is not threatening, but warning. In such cases, an undertaking to pay more, if it is credible, will typically lead to very real practical benefits; for example, it may allow the contractor to obtain further credit, and so complete the work. A rule that such undertakings are unenforceable may thus harm both contracting parties. As well, even where it is possible to perform the contract on the original terms, one party may offer more because he wants to maintain good relations with the other party or because he is worried about his reputation within an industry. Such undertakings are often made in situations where, through no one's fault, one party's costs have increased significantly. There seems no good reason not to enforce such arrangements.

As might be expected, the consideration doctrine is in practice not as significant a barrier to modifying contracts as the above examples suggest. It is not difficult for well-advised parties to make an apparently one-sided modification (or discharge of an entire contract) legally binding. As

---

[43] *Occidental Worldwide Investment Corp. v. Skibs A/S Avanti (The Siboen and The Sibotre)* [1976] 1 Lloyd's Rep 293.

already noted, contracts made in deeds do not require consideration. An even simpler method is to make the relevant undertaking in ostensible exchange for 'nominal' consideration, such as £1 or a mere 'peppercorn': it has long been a principle of contract law that the *real* value of the consideration is immaterial. In the classic words of Lord Blackburn: 'The adequacy of the consideration is for the parties to consider at the time of making the agreement, not for the Court when it is sought to be enforced.'[44] So eagerly have the courts applied this dictum, that in one case it was held that the surrender of a document that turned out to be legally invalid and of no inherent value was good consideration for an undertaking to pay £9,600,[45] even though in terms of its 'legal' value, the surrender was indistinguishable from an undertaking to perform a pre-existing contractual duty. The only qualification to this subjective approach to assessing value, aside from the pre-existing duty cases just described, is where the new undertaking is to pay a smaller amount of the same fungible commodity that was owed under a previous contract. Thus, an agreement to accept partial payment of a debt is not consideration for an undertaking to abstain from demanding full repayment.[46] At the same time, any variation in the mode, time, or place of payment may be a good consideration for the waiver of the rest of the debt, as may be accepting something other than money. An agreement to accept £999,000 in satisfaction of a debt of £1,000,000 is not binding, but an agreement to accept £1,000 plus a peppercorn is.

Even if the parties do not use a deed or nominal consideration, there are other ways that a determined court may enforce a one-sided modification (or any other undertaking apparently unsupported by consideration). Suppose an employee is employed for a fixed period (say under a five-year contract) at a fixed salary, say £20,000 per annum, and that, after a year, the employer agrees to increase the salary to £22,000 per annum. Here, the original contract has been varied, and though the variation may have been agreed upon by both parties, there is, on the face of it, no new consideration. The employee has simply agreed to go on doing what she is already legally bound to do, while the employer has agreed to pay extra money for this, with no apparent benefit to him. It might seem that this salary increase could not be legally enforced. But that result would not generally be found acceptable today, especially where the increase is mere inflation-proofing, and ways of escape are available.

First, it may be suggested that the original contract should be construed as providing for 'a salary of £20,000 or such other amount as might be agreed'. In this case, while the duties of the parties to the contract are being varied,

---

[44] *Bolton v. Madden* (1873) LR 9 QB 55 at 57.
[45] *Haigh v. Brooks* (1839) 10 Ad & E 309.
[46] *Pinnel's case* (1602) 5 Co Rep 117a, discussed below, 117.

the contract itself is not being varied, and so there is no need for fresh consideration. The arrangement would then be similar to a building society mortgage that provides that the borrower pay interest at 10 per cent 'or such other rate as may be specified from time to time by the lender'. The lender may change the rate from time to time (subject to whatever restrictions the contract imposes), but this change is not a variation of the contract itself, and so no new consideration needs to be provided by the building society.[47]

Alternatively, it might be argued that the employee did, in fact, agree to do something beyond her duties imposed by the original contract. As was noted earlier, this may be an undertaking to do something that is of trivial benefit to the other party. But in employment cases even a trivial benefit may be hard to prove because of the open-ended nature of most employees' duties. It is therefore more common to argue that fresh consideration is provided not by an undertaking to do something, but by an undertaking *not* to do something—what lawyers call a 'forbearance'. This argument will often be accepted. For example, if the employee is not bound to work for a fixed period but, as is more usually the case, is free to give notice, it may be argued that by forbearing from giving notice and continuing in her work, she has in law provided consideration for the increased salary. This argument may seem stretched, but as a matter of law it is clear that forbearing from something one has a right to do, however slight the practical benefit, may count as good consideration. So also the temporary suspension of a legal right is a forbearance that may be good consideration: where a debtor whose account was overdrawn undertook to deposit certain deeds with the bank as a security for his overdraft, it was held that the fact that the bank forbore to press the debtor for payment for a certain time was good consideration for the undertaking. It is not necessary in these cases to show that legal proceedings are threatened or even contemplated; it is enough that the creditor has, at the request of the debtor, shown an indulgence that he was not bound to show.

A third possibility is to argue that the parties have implicitly 'rescinded' the old employment contract and made a new one. The new arrangement would be binding because rescission of a continuing contract is possible by agreement. So long as duties remain outstanding on both sides, there will be consideration on both sides. The courts will not examine the circumstances to see if, in reality, this is improbable; the bare possibility that both sides will benefit is enough. Of course, if it were assumed that every time parties appeared to agree to vary an existing contract they were also implicitly agreeing to rescind that contract, the pre-existing duty rule would be meaningless.

---

[47] The Unfair Terms in Consumer Contracts Regulations 1999, Sch. 2, para. 2(a) requires that a 'valid reason' should exist for such unilateral variations, and that the borrower should be informed of the variation; otherwise the contract may be unfair. See further, below, 317ff.

Perhaps for this reason, the courts have been cautious about implying an agreement to rescind.

Finally, if the above arguments fail to show that there was new consideration, the variation may sometimes be enforced under the doctrine of estoppel, if it has been relied upon. This doctrine is treated more fully below.

The techniques described above mitigate the rigours of the rule that performing or undertaking to perform a pre-existing contractual duty is not consideration. But they depend for their success in each case on the court's willingness to take a liberal approach to interpreting the parties' past or present agreement. In addition, the doctrine of estoppel can generally only be used to enforce a waiver of an existing contractual right. It could not be applied, therefore, to the example of the employer's undertaking to pay a higher salary. For these reasons, it is not surprising to learn that in recent years English courts have mounted a more direct attack on the rule barring pre-existing legal duties as consideration. The first move was to hold that the pre-existing duty rule does not apply where the duty is owed to a third party.[48] For instance, if A promises something to B, and then makes a promise to C to do the same thing, in return for some counter-promise from C, C will be allowed to sue A if A fails to perform. A's second, identical promise qualifies as good consideration. It may be said, of course, that C has in fact received a benefit from A's second promise, since this will provide C with a personal right of action against A, but this is true only if A's promise is enforceable, which is the question at issue. Moreover, it was precisely this kind of legally superfluous right that, under the traditional understanding of the rule, was not regarded as good consideration.

Secondly, and more important, the traditional notion that consideration must consist in a 'legal' benefit or burden has recently been replaced by a test of 'practical' benefit or burden, at least in cases involving variations. In *Williams v. Roffey Bros & Nicholls (Contractors) Ltd*,[49] the claimant was a carpenter who had agreed to do work in some houses that the defendants had contracted to refurbish. The claimant was to get £20,000 from the defendants, but after the claimant had done part of the work he found himself in financial difficulty, partly because he had offered too low a price. The defendants were anxious to avoid incurring penalties for lateness under the main contract and their surveyor persuaded them to promise the claimant an additional £10,300. Later they denied liability for this sum, but it was held by the Court of Appeal that there was good consideration for their undertaking. The court held that they had received practical benefits from the undertaking in that it helped avoid delay and saved them the trouble of finding another carpenter.

---

[48] *The Eurymedon* [1975] AC 154. The earlier case of *Shadwell v. Shadwell*, above n. 36 is sometimes taken to have established this exception, but there are difficulties with the decision.
[49] [1991] 1 QB 1.

The decision has been said to stand for the principle that 'where there is a practical conferment of benefit or a practical avoidance of disbenefit, there is a good consideration, and it is no answer [to a claim on a variation of the contract] that the promisor was already bound'.[50]

The effect of this decision, as the court made clear, is that the validity of undertakings of the kind made by the defendants in *Roffey Bros* will now be decided not on the basis of consideration, but according to the doctrine of duress, in particular the new concept of economic duress. This is to be welcomed because it allows courts to openly and flexibly address the real—and difficult—issues raised by variation cases. But it must be stressed that not all voluntarily agreed-upon variations will satisfy the practical benefit test. The rule in *Pinnel's case*[51]—that an agreement to accept part payment of a debt in satisfaction of the whole debt is not enforceable for lack of consideration, the debtor having merely done or agreed to do what she was already legally bound to do—is still good law. Although this rule is effectively an application of the pre-existing legal duty rule, and as such is vulnerable to the same criticisms, the Court of Appeal in *Re Selectmove*[52] refused to overturn it, essentially on the grounds of precedent (*Pinnel's case* being a decision approved by the House of Lords and *Roffey Bros* a decision of the Court of Appeal). In addition, a practical benefit will not be found in cases where the undertaking is made from altruistic or sympathetic motives, or where parties agree to vary a contract out of a concern for their reputation. Here the party performing the undertaking obtains a practical benefit as a consequence, but this benefit will not have been obtained in *exchange* for the undertaking and so the consideration requirement is not strictly satisfied. The reputational benefit is merely a consequence of the arrangement. None of these results is easy to justify.

(3) Compromise agreements

Closely related to agreements to perform pre-existing legal duties are agreements not to pursue a threatened legal action, as where I agree to drop a lawsuit against you if you will pay me £200. The courts have long enforced such agreements, even when the litigation might have ultimately shown the original claim to be baseless.[53] This may be seen as an early example of the courts (wisely) assessing consideration in terms of subjective practical benefits, rather than objective legal benefits. But the interesting feature of the law in this area is that consideration will not be found where the original claim was frivolous or vexatious. The original claim must be bona fide, that is to say the claimant must believe it to be valid. In terms of the classical test of

---

[50] *Anangel v. Hill* [1990] 2 Lloyd's Rep 526.   [51] Above n. 46.
[52] [1995] 1 WLR 474.
[53] See now *Pitt v. PHH Asset Management Ltd* [1993] 4 All FR 961, which shows an even more generous attitude to what is a sufficient consideration for a compromise.

benefit or detriment there is, of course, no difference in principle between giving up a frivolous claim and giving up a bona fide claim. A bona fide claim may be worthless, while the dropping of a frivolous claim may be of significant benefit to a potential defendant who no longer needs to hire a lawyer. But from the perspective of a concern for issues such as duress, extortion, and public policy there is a clear difference between the two cases. The claimant who seeks payment in exchange for giving up a frivolous or vexatious claim is effectively using the legal system as a tool for practicing extortion. The unenforceability of such agreements therefore provides a particularly clear example of the consideration doctrine being used for a purpose that has little to do with benefits or detriments.

(4) Consideration as a formality

We have seen that the consideration doctrine has historically been used to invalidate promises and agreements that were made under duress, in a domestic context, or that were contrary to public policy. But we have not yet explored the most obvious consequence of the doctrine, which is that it renders gratuitous promises prima facie unenforceable. A promise to make a gift or donation to a charity does not satisfy the consideration requirement. The same is true of a promise to keep an offer open for a set period or a promise to vary a contract that is made not in exchange for a counter-promise but for altruistic reasons or to maintain a reputation.

The gratuitousness of gratuitous promises does not in itself explain why such promises are not enforced. An ordinary executory agreement is binding from the moment of formation, before either of the parties receives any benefit. On the other hand, gratuitous promises can be binding if made in a deed or in ostensible exchange for nominal consideration. If there were an objection in principle to enforcing gratuitous promises, then it would seem this objection should apply regardless of the form in which the promise was made. The idea that gratuitous promises are similar to domestic promises, and so are not enforced because they are made in situations in which non-commercial motives dominate and where, therefore, the law should not interfere, is also unpersuasive. This explanation only fits donative gratuitous promises (promises to make a gift) and then only when they are made between relatives or close friends; it does not explain why a donative promise to a charity is prima facie unenforceable. Nor does it explain why a donative promise that is recast for nominal consideration, or put in the form of a deed, is enforceable. Cosmetic changes to the form of a donative promise do not alter its substance.

More generally, the option of using a deed or nominal consideration to make a gratuitous promise enforceable makes it difficult to explain the prima facie unenforceability of such promises on the basis of their being inherently less worthy of enforcement. To the contrary, these options suggest that the

purpose of the consideration doctrine (at least so far as its effect on gratuitous promises is concerned) is essentially formal. There is no question that a
law explicitly stipulating that certain contracts must be supported by nominal
consideration or be made as deeds would be regarded as imposing a formal
requirement of validity. The consideration doctrine is not, of course, typically
described in these terms—in the orthodox account, the doctrine is not presented as a formal requirement for gratuitous contracts, but a substantive
requirement for all contracts—but the *effect* of the doctrine is exactly the
same, namely, to require potential contracting parties to satisfy a formality if
they wish to make a gratuitous promise binding. This leads to the suggestion,
then, that the primary function of the consideration doctrine is to impose
formal requirements of validity on gratuitous contracts.

Support for this interpretation can be found in the fact that there are
good reasons that courts might want to impose just such a requirement on
gratuitous promises. The most important category of gratuitous promises,
promises to make a gift or 'donative' promises, are precisely the kind of
promises for which formalities seem most appropriate. Donative promises are
not generally made in commercial contexts or for commercial motives; thus
there is an increased risk that they may be made hastily or without full
appreciation of the consequences. This is why civil law systems, which do not
have the doctrine of consideration and which regard donative promises as
enforceable in principle, typically require such promises to be made in writing
or to satisfy a different formality.

Admittedly, the consideration doctrine performs the formal role described
above imperfectly: the doctrine applies not just to donative promises, but to
other gratuitous promises, such as a bare promise to keep an offer open or
a promise to compensate the promisee for a past service. Non-donative
gratuitous promises of this kind are arguably more likely to be made hastily
than the standard bargain agreement (if only because they can be made
unilaterally, without negotiation or prior communications), but they do not
seem to be the kinds of arrangements for which formalities are necessary.
But these admissions are consistent with the point made earlier that the
consideration doctrine fulfils roles for which it was not originally intended.

Consideration as a negative requirement: conclusion

In its role as a negative requirement of validity, then, the consideration
doctrine has been used to invalidate agreements made under duress, in
domestic situations, or that are contrary to public policy. In addition, it has
had the effect of imposing a formal requirement of validity on parties who
want to make binding donative promises. All of these functions are useful.
But a strong argument can be made that in each case the relevant function
would be better served by a distinct legal doctrine, one that openly and
directly addresses the relevant issue. To a significant extent, this suggestion

has (as we have seen) already been taken up by the courts: the main exception is the formal function, which in practice can only be overtaken by a legislative enactment.

If such a legislative reform were introduced, it would seem that the consideration doctrine would no longer be needed in order to deny validity to certain kinds of promises and agreements: the doctrine's negative role would be performed by other legal rules. Of course, it might be argued that the doctrine should be maintained as a kind of safety valve or catch-all that courts could use where there is a good reason for non-enforcement but where that reason has not yet been recognized by any other doctrine. But against this suggestion is the argument that safety-valves already exist in the form of the doctrines of public policy and unconscionability. It is difficult to think of a valid reason for non-enforcement that could not be classified under one of these heads. Admittedly, most judges are cautious about extending the defences of public policy and, in particular, unconscionability, but the same judges would be just as cautious about extending consideration, if that were the heading under which public policy and unconscionability arguments were made. In any event, given the modern, highly technical understanding of consideration, it is unlikely that judges could be persuaded to use the doctrine for these purposes except in very rare cases.

Benefits and detriments as (positive) reasons for enforcing certain kinds of agreements and promises

The idea that the consideration doctrine performs a positive function, by identifying certain kinds of promises and agreements that *should* be enforced, is consistent with how the consideration doctrine is actually presented. It also finds support in the common view that the existence of a mere promise or agreement, standing alone, is not and should not be a sufficient basis for legal liability. Promises and agreements, the argument goes, are just words; the failure to perform the actions they describe does not, in itself, cause harm to anyone. If I promise to give you my watch and then change my mind five minutes later, why should I be bound to my undertaking? Prior to making my undertaking, I presumably was under no obligation to give you my watch. And assuming you did nothing in the five minutes before I changed my mind, what harm is caused to you if I withdraw my promise? The suggestion, then, is that something more should be required before a promise or agreement is legally binding—and that that something is consideration.

Those making the above argument typically argue that a promise should be binding only if the promisor has received an unpaid-for benefit from the promisee or if the promisee has detrimentally relied on the promise or both. (The idea is that the same notions that underlie the law of unjust enrichment—that unjust enrichments should be reversed—and that underlie the torts of fraud and negligent misstatement—that reliance-based losses merit compensation—also underlie the consideration doctrine.) In this view, the strongest case for imposing liability is one in which all three factors— promise, benefit, and reliance—combine (as they very often do in an ordinary action for breach of contract). Take the example of a simple loan of money which is not repaid, for instance where A lends B £100 which B then fails to repay. In this situation, B has broken a promise—to repay the £100. In addition, A has relied to his detriment—he relied on B's promise by giving £100 to B. Finally, B has received a benefit—the £100. So here the three factors appear simultaneously: there is a broken promise by B, an act of detrimental reliance by A, and a benefit to B.

This is a compelling suggestion, but as an explanation of how the consideration doctrine *generally* operates it faces an obvious objection: it cannot account for the fact that a mere promise or agreement is sufficient to satisfy the consideration doctrine. Executory agreements are binding at formation. Admittedly, contracting parties typically act in reliance on such promises and agreements, but they do not always do this, and they certainly do not always rely immediately. Moreover, the explanation is inconsistent with the fact that (with certain exceptions that are discussed below) a gratuitous promise does not satisfy the consideration doctrine even when relied upon. A promise to give £100,000 to charity is not binding even if the charity spends the money in advance, say by contracting for the construction of a new building.

The consideration doctrine cannot, then, realistically be said to generally require proof of a benefit or reliance as a pre-condition to contractual validity. But it is not difficult to show that certain of the doctrine's important features and applications are motivated by this idea. One aspect of the doctrine that we have already touched upon is the courts' willingness to find or invent consideration for apparently gratuitous promises. This happens most often in cases where the promisor has received a benefit or the promisee has detrimentally relied. Of greater significance are situations in which the courts explicitly look for benefit or reliance when determining if such a promise is legally enforceable. Three such situations are examined below. In none of them can the parties be said to have made a bargain or exchange— the only undertaking is *a* (mere) promise by one party—but in each case the promise is either binding or can become legally binding, and in each case the triggering factor appears to be that the promisor received a benefit from the promisee or that the promisee relied on the promisor.

(1) Past consideration

In the nineteenth-century case of *Lee v. Muggeridge*,[54] Lord Mansfield stated that the existence of a previous moral obligation was sufficient consideration

---

[54] (1813) 5 Tuant. 36, 46.

for a gratuitous promise. This idea is clearly linked to notions of benefit and reliance since the typical reason for finding a previous moral obligation is that the promisee had conferred a benefit on the promisor or that the promisor had detrimentally relied on something said by the promisor. A famous example of the former category is the American case[55] in which A saved the life of B (A's employer) in an incident which caused A severe personal injury. B's later promise to A to pay him a pension was enforced by the courts despite being entirely gratuitous. In the United Kingdom, however, Lord Mansfield's concept of moral consideration was rejected by later courts,[56] and replaced by the (now) orthodox idea that past consideration is no consideration. It is well-established in current law that if X renders Y some service, and thereafter Y promises to pay X £100 in consideration of this service, this promise is not enforceable as a contract.[57]

But vestiges of Lord Mansfield's heresy, and so of the importance of benefit and reliance in assessing contractual validity, can be seen in three exceptions to the past consideration rule. The first is found in the law governing negotiable instruments, of which a cheque is the most familiar example. By commercial custom, now embodied in the Bills of Exchange Act 1882, 'an antecedent debt or liability', that is to say, a benefit, is sufficient consideration for the drawing or endorsing of a bill of exchange.

The second exception is found in section 29(5) of the Limitation Act 1980, which provides that a promise to pay an existing debt extends the limitation period for the debt, even where the creditor did not promise to forbear from suing. The Act has the effect, therefore, of enforcing a promise to pay where the only consideration for the promise is a past debt.

The third exception is where goods or services are supplied by X to Y at Y's request. In such cases, a subsequent promise by Y to pay for the goods or services is enforceable.[58] It is sometimes said that this is not strictly an instance of past consideration because the contract is made when the earlier request was acted upon. As was pointed out in the last chapter, the absence of a price term does not preclude the formation of a contract, the law often being prepared to imply an obligation to pay a reasonable price. On this basis, the suggestion is that the contract is formed when the request (now interpreted as a conditional promise) is acted upon, with the subsequent promise merely fixing the amount of the reasonable sum that the promisor must pay. This interpretation is supported by the decision in *Pao On v. Lau Yiu*,[59] where the Privy Council stated that such consideration was sufficient only where it was understood that the requested act would be remunerated and where that understanding would have been legally enforceable even without the later

---

[55] *Webb v. McGowin* 168 So 196 (1935).
[56] *Eastwood v. Kenyon* (1840) 11 A & E 438.   [57] *Roscorla v. Thomas* (1842) 3 QB 234.
[58] *Lampleigh v. Brathwait* (1615) Hob 105.   [59] [1980] AC 614.

promise. But in the case itself these qualifications were not followed: the court held that a benefit rendered by A to B was sufficient to support a subsequent promise by B to indemnify A against any loss arising from A's undertaking. If not for the second promise, A could never have obtained from B the indemnity, which B in fact gave. The case cannot really be understood unless it is appreciated that the first agreement contained what was, in a commercial sense, a mistake, since A ought reasonably to have received the indemnity which B later gave him in that first agreement. Clearly the Privy Council thought that A was, in the end, only getting what he was really, morally and commercially, entitled to anyhow.

A further difficulty with supposing that in cases of this kind the courts are merely enforcing an earlier agreement with a missing price is that if this were the case then (as was noted in the previous chapter), the court should simply impose a reasonable price. Instead, the courts impose the price (or term) that is specified in the later promise. The better explanation of such cases would therefore appear to be that they are true exceptions to the consideration doctrine, motivated by the fact that the promisor has benefited from the promisee's past reliance.

(2) Conditional promises (unilateral contracts)

A conditional promise, such as a promise of a reward for anyone who finds a missing dog or a promise to pay a real estate agent a commission if she finds a buyer for a house, may be enforced once the specified condition is fulfilled. According to the orthodox account, the consideration for such promises lies in the performance of the requested act. But it is apparent that consideration means something quite different in such cases than it does in the ordinary contractual agreement. The difference is not merely that it consists of an act rather than a promise; the more important difference is that the act is not given *in exchange for* the promise. As was already noted, a conditional promise cannot, by definition, be given in exchange for the specified act because the act happens later, if at all. In *Carlill*, using the smoke ball and catching influenza were the conditions that Mrs Carlill had to satisfy to claim the promised reward, but it would be an odd use of language to suggest that these were exchanged for the price of the promise.[60] Similarly, it is implausible to suppose that in *The Eurymedon* the stevedores' act of unloading goods was done in exchange for an exemption clause. It was simply the condition on which the stevedores were prepared to unload the goods.

Conditional promises thus seem better understood as a special kind of gratuitous promise. They are enforced, despite being gratuitous, because the

---

[60] There was, of course, a bargain between Mrs Carlill and the retailer from whom she actually bought the smoke ball, but the promise was made by the manufacturer, and the action was brought against them and not against the retailer.

person who performs the specified condition has detrimentally relied on the promise and, in most cases anyway, conferred a benefit on the promisor. Consideration in the sense of something that is given in exchange for the promise does not exist, but it does in the broader sense of a compelling reason to enforce the promise. The importance of reliance in explaining the enforceability of conditional promises is further underscored by the fact that (as was discussed in Chapter 3) such promises often cannot be revoked once performance of the relevant act has commenced. A promise of a prize to anyone swimming the English Channel cannot be revoked once the swimmer is nine-tenths of the way across. Yet the swimmer's part-performance is clearly not 'given' in exchange for the promise; it does not even fulfil the condition specified in the promise. The most plausible explanation for why such promises cannot be revoked is that the courts wish to protect individuals who detrimentally rely on them.

(3) Promissory estoppel

Closely related to the rules regarding conditional promises is the important doctrine of promissory estoppel. According to this doctrine, a promise may be enforced in certain circumstances if it is relied upon by the promisee. The main difference between an estoppel and an enforceable conditional promise, so far as reliance in concerned, is that for an estoppel the reliance need not be specified by the promisor as a condition of the promise. It is enough that the promisee relies on the promise. For example, if a person makes a conditional promise to waive a debt due from his nephew on the nephew's marriage, then the marriage would be a good consideration, and the promise would become enforceable as a contract. But if the promise were simply to waive the debt with no reference (express or implied) to the possibility of marriage, and the nephew were to marry in reliance on the promise, then the act of marriage would not be a good consideration, but it might be sufficient as the basis of a promissory estoppel.

The law on estoppel thus adopts a broader notion of reliance than the law on conditional promises. In other ways, though, estoppel is more limited in scope. First, it has for some years been insisted that promissory estoppel is 'a shield and not a sword': the promisee can set up such a promise as a *defence* to an action, but cannot sue upon it. So the principle applies to a promise to waive a debt or to not insist on strict performance of a service contract, but not to a promise to make a gift or to keep an offer open for a period of time.[61] There is no doubt that this is the law in some cases, and it was so laid down as

---

[61] As a result of the decision in *Williams v. Roffey Bros*, above n. 49, waivers of this kind will now often also be binding as ordinary contracts, the promisor having received a practical benefit in return for the promise.

a general rule in *Combe v. Combe*,[62] though there may have been special reasons for the decision in that case. But, there are signs of impatience with this limitation on the use of promissory estoppel.[63] The United States long ago abandoned the limitation[64] and Australia has recently followed suit.[65] In the United Kingdom, the courts have hived off one group of estoppel cases, now called cases of 'proprietary estoppel', in which it is accepted that estoppel does create a cause of action.[66] For instance, in *Crabb v. Arun District Council*,[67] the defendants told the claimant he could have a right of entry to his land from some land belonging to them, and in reliance on that promise the claimant sold the only part of his land that had direct access to a road. When the defendants then went back on their promise, the court enforced the promise even though the defendants had neither requested that the claimant sell the relevant part of his land nor made reference to any such action at all. Proprietary estoppel cases were once said to be confined to circumstances in which a promise is made with reference to a particular piece of property, but recently this dyke, too, has been breached; it is now said that a promise with reference to the promisor's property generally can be enforced by way of proprietary estoppel.[68]

Secondly, unlike in the case of unilateral contracts, a bare act of detrimental reliance on a promise may not always suffice to establish a case of promissory estoppel. In particular, it has been said that it must also be 'inequitable' for promisors to go back on their word. For this reason, conduct in reliance may not suffice to establish a case of promissory estoppel if the conduct is easily reversible.[69] This focus on the promisor's behaviour may also underlie the idea sometimes raised that promissory estoppel cannot be made out if the promisor did not encourage the belief that she would not change her mind.[70]

A third respect in which promissory estoppel is limited in scope is that, at least in some cases, promissory estoppel operates only to suspend and not extinguish rights. A landlord, for instance, promises to reduce the rent

---

[62] [1951] 2 KB 215; followed in *Syros Shipping Co. v. Elaghill Trading Co.* [1981] 3 All ER 189.

[63] See *Re Wyvern* [1974] 1 WLR 1097; *Crabb v. Arun DC* [1976] Ch. 179; *Taylor Fashions v. Liverpool Victoria Friendly Society* [1981]1 QB 13 (where yet another kind of estoppel was invoked).

[64] *Hoffman v. Red Owl Stores* 133 NW 2d 267 (1965).

[65] *Walton's Stores (Interstate) v. Maher* (1988) 164 CLR 387

[66] See, e.g., *Western Fish Products Ltd v. Penwith DC* [1981] 2 All ER 204; *Salvation Army v. West Yorks Met. CC* (1981) 41 P & CR 179. *Brewer Street Investments v. Barclays Woollen Co. Ltd* [1954] QB 428 should arguably be included in this group.

[67] [1976] Ch 179.

[68] See *Re Basham* [1986] 1 WLR 1498.

[69] *Société Italo-Belge pour le Commerce et l'Industrie SA v. Palm & Vegetable Oils (The Post Chaser)* [1982] 1 All ER 19.

[70] *A-G for Hong Kong v. Humphrey's Estate (Queen's Gardens)* [1987] AC 114.

payable by the tenant; if there is no consideration for this, the promise may indeed be binding (assuming the tenant acts upon it), but it was held in the leading case of *Central London Properties Ltd v. High Trees House Ltd*[71] that the landlord may, on reasonable notice, demand that the tenant resume paying at the full rent again in the future. Precisely when promissory estoppel operates in this way is, however, still controversial.

A final difference between the law on promissory estoppel and that regarding conditional promises relates not to the scope of the doctrines but to their legal classification: in the orthodox view, promissory estoppel is not strictly regarded as a part of the law of contract. This is why estoppel is frequently used to give effect not just to arrangements that are unsupported by consideration, but also to arrangements that cannot be enforced as a contract for other reasons, such as that a necessary formality was not satisfied.[72] Proprietary estoppel in particular is frequently invoked in order to give effect to a promise or agreement that fails to satisfy the writing requirements of the Law of Property (Miscellaneous Provisions) Act 1989. It is also sometimes invoked when an arrangement is deemed to have failed to satisfy the mirror image rule in offer and acceptance.

The usual argument for classifying estoppel as extra-contractual is that the doctrine's underlying purpose is not to give effect to promises and agreements, relied-upon or otherwise, but to protect individuals who detrimentally rely on others. More specifically, the aim of estoppel in this view is not to enforce relied-upon promises, but to enforce relied-upon representations generally, whether or not those representations are promises.[73] If this is correct, then estoppel is indeed more closely related to the tort of negligent misstatement, and to so-called equitable torts such as breach of confidence, than to contractual obligations. In this view, it also follows that the name 'promissory' estoppel is a misnomer; accordingly, advocates of this interpretation usually prefer the name 'equitable' estoppel.

A number of features of the estoppel doctrine may be thought to lend support to the extra-contractual interpretation. The very definition of estoppel is often given in terms not of promises or undertakings, but of 'conduct' or 'representations' that induce reliance. In addition, the idea that estoppel is suspensive and the requirement that the estopped party must have acted inequitably may be thought to show that a promise is not essential.

---

[71] [1947] KB 130.

[72] But note that courts sometimes refuse to use estoppel to avoid formalities where this would render the formal requirement meaningless: *Actionstrength Ltd v. International Glass Engineering*, above n. 3. This refusal may be criticized on the ground that estoppel provides weaker protection than ordinary contract law, and that this difference in protection would be a practical consequence of a failure to respect a formal requirement.

[73] As suggested in the Australian case of *Walton Stores (Interstate) Ltd v. Maher*, above n. 65.

Finally, in jurisdictions such as Australia and the United States that permit estoppel to be used as a cause of action, and so to found an action for damages, damages are sometimes awarded on the basis of the claimant's reliance loss.[74] By contrast, in a standard breach of contract claim, the claimant is entitled to the value of the promise, which may exceed her reliance loss.

But strong arguments can also be made that promissory estoppel[75] should be regarded as part of the law dealing with voluntary obligations, that is to say, the law of contract. Although courts talk about estoppels that involve mere representations, it is difficult to find cases where an estoppel was found in lieu of a contract and where it is clear that no promise or agreement was made. This is why the label 'promissory' estoppel has stuck to this doctrine. The extra-contractual interpretation also cannot easily explain why it appears (though the matter remains controversial) that mere reliance, as opposed to detrimental reliance, may be sufficient to found a defence of promissory estoppel. In *High Trees*, for example, no evidence was introduced that the tenants had incurred any detriment in reliance on the landlord's promise.[76] A further difficulty is that, while reliance damages are sometimes awarded for estoppel (in jurisdictions that allow such claims), it is more common to award relief on the same (more generous) basis that is standard in contract cases.

But probably the main difficulty with the non-contractual interpretation is that, as was noted in Chapter 2,[77] the very concept of a 'reliance-based' obligation is something of a moral and legal puzzle. More specifically, it has been argued—though more by philosophers than lawyers—that it is difficult to identify the moral basis upon which a purely reliance-based claim could bind a non-promisor to an obligation, making it unclear why courts should worry about induced reliance other than when it has been induced by a promise or an agreement.[78] The very reason for making a promise is to assure the promisee that the promisor will not change her mind if she later regrets the promise. It follows, in this view, that a person who refrains from making a promise is thereby indicating that she is reserving the right to change her mind. Cases involving misrepresentation aside, if the listener then chooses to rely on the speaker's statement, the conclusion is that he does so at his own risk.

---

[74] Restatement of Contracts (2d) s. 90. But in the Australian case of *Walton Stores (Interstate) Ltd v. Maher*, ibid, damages appear to have been assessed on a normal contractual basis. See also *Giumelli v. Giumelli* (1999) 196 CLR 101.

[75] The term 'estoppel' is used in other contexts, such as in the rules of evidence. The comments above apply only to cases involving what is commonly called promissory estoppel.

[76] Note also that under the doctrine of 'waiver' courts have sometimes enforced a downward variation of a contract that was unsupported either by consideration or reliance, detrimental or otherwise; see, e.g., *Leather Cloth Co. v. Hieronimus* (1875) LR 10 QB 140.

[77] Above 90–91.

[78] See, e.g., C. Fried, *Contract as Promise* (Cambridge MA, 1981), 10–11.

The debate between these opposing interpretations of estoppel seems unlikely to be resolved anytime soon. As we have seen, the different views are based not just on different interpretations of the case-law, but, more fundamentally, on different interpretations of morality. But before leaving this topic, it is useful to briefly describe the main implications of adopting the alternative 'contractual' interpretation of estoppel. The main implication, of course, is that the current legal classification of estoppel as extra-contractual must be regarded as yet another example of the common law's tendency of allowing in through the back door what is not allowed through the front door. More specifically, it is an example of an attempt to give legal effect to promises that cannot be enforced as contracts for what are essentially technical reasons, such as lack of consideration or the failure to satisfy a formality. As for the current limitations on the scope and force of estoppel claims, they are explained in this alternative view as an imperfect recognition of the fact that the full measure and panoply of contractual protections are not appropriate for all promises. The idea is that the courts are recognizing that arrangements that, for instance, fail to satisfy formal requirements, are made in domestic settings, or fail to perfectly satisfy the mirror image rule sometimes merit a weaker form of protection. This particular suggestion seems sensible; indeed, a strong case can be made for formally recognizing a principle to the effect that certain kinds of voluntary obligations merit less than full contractual protection.

Conclusion: the future of consideration

The doctrine of consideration has served and continues to serve many useful functions, but a strong argument can be made that most, if not all, of these functions would be better served by other legal doctrines. This has already happened in significant measure with the doctrine's traditional function of *denying* contractual enforcement to certain kinds of promises and agreements: the doctrine is now rarely used to invalidate agreements made under duress or in a domestic setting, or that contravene public policy objectives such as the policy against bribing public officials. The few situations where the consideration doctrine is still used for this purpose could be taken over, it would seem, by other doctrines, including those of 'unconscionability' and 'public policy'. This approach would have the advantage that cases raising such issues would be treated alongside others involving similar problems. In particular, reclassifying certain consideration cases as cases raising questions of unconscionability or public policy would force lawyers to address the real issues in these cases more directly, for example, by discussing more openly which kinds of pressure *should* be regarded as unfair and unacceptable.

It also seems clear that the doctrine's other main function—that of imposing formal requirements of validity on donative promises—could be fulfilled more effectively by a legislated solution. A simple rule to the effect that donative promises must be in writing to be binding or in a deed would be more transparent than the current rule and, importantly, would apply only to those promises for which formalities are really needed. A side-benefit of acknowledging that gratuitous promises are in principle enforceable is this would put pressure on English law to consider in a more general way the relationship of such promises to other types of contracts. On the whole, English contract law seems to be shaped by the supposition that most contracts are bargains; a consequence of this is that its rules are not always appropriate for gratuitous promises, especially donative gratuitous promises. For instance, excuses for non-performance (as we shall see later) are very narrowly confined in the present law, and it is not clear this approach could be maintained if it were recognized that gratuitous promises are binding in principle. It is also a serious question whether a gratuitous promise should rank equally with commercial promises in the event of the death or bankruptcy of the promisor. Indeed, it is not clear that a donative gratuitous promise should generally bind the promisor's heirs at all. A donative promise is an act of personal generosity, but should a promisor be entitled to be generous at someone else's expense? These and other questions have been openly addressed in systems in which gratuitous promises are in principle enforced, but thus far they have largely been ignored in English law. This is a problem even under the current law because, as we have seen, many gratuitous promises are in practice enforceable.

The status of conditional promises following any reform of the consideration doctrine would need careful study. Simply eliminating the consideration requirement would mean that conditional promises would continue to be binding once the condition has been satisfied. This seems uncontroversial. But eliminating the requirement would also mean that, unlike under the present law, such promises could not be revoked once made, regardless of whether they had been relied upon (except insofar as the possibility of revocation was itself an express or implied term of the promise). This may not always be desirable. Two types of cases need to be distinguished. The first is where the conditional promise is made to a specific individual or individuals, as for example, if I promise a real estate agent a commission if she finds a buyer for my house. It is not clear what purpose is served by allowing conditional promises of this kind to be revoked at will. Of course, if the promisor expressly or impliedly allowed such revocation (which may in fact be the case in many real estate dealings), there is no problem. As well, a conditional promise cannot be binding for perpetuity. As with ordinary offers, the presumption must be that if no time period is specified the conditional promise is understood to lapse after a reasonable period of time. But these qualifications aside, there is no obvious reason that such promises should be revocable at will (assuming, of course, that they are seriously made, certain, etc.).

The second category of conditional promises involves promises that are made to the world, that is to say 'offers' of rewards or prizes. Here the situation may be different. It was already noted that offers of rewards or prizes seem closer to vows or declarations than to ordinary promises. One consequence of this difference is that revoking the offer of a reward or a prize does not appear to involve the same breach of trust or wrongdoing (for lack of a better word) normally associated with a breach of promise. This does not mean, of course, that revoking a reward or a prize should never attract liability. The swimmer who attempts to cross the English Channel in order to obtain a prize has a valid complaint if the prize is withdrawn when she is nine-tenths of the way across. But it is not necessary to make such offers 'irrevocable' in order to provide relief. The doctrine of estoppel would appear to be the appropriate vehicle for protecting individuals who have relied upon a prize or reward. Whether interpreted as a contractual or extra-contractual form of liability, estoppel can properly be used to provide a measure of relief for individuals who have relied on an undertaking that, for any of a number of reasons (it was made in a domestic setting, it does not satisfy a formal test of validity, it was made 'to the world', etc.), merits less than the full panoply of rights normally associated with an ordinary contract. Even in a legal system without consideration, a doctrine along the lines of estoppel is needed to perform this rule.

Part II

The Content of the Contract

5

Express Terms

HAVING established the steps necessary to create a contract, it falls next to consider the content of a contract. How do courts establish what it is that contracting parties are contractually obliged to do? Part of the answer to this question is found in the law of offer and acceptance: a contract's content is established in the first instance by whatever terms the parties promised or agreed to. But while it may be clear that the parties have reached an agreement, it may not be clear which of their various communications are included in that agreement. In addition, the *meaning* of a contractual term or phrase is also often a matter of dispute. There are also a great many contractual duties that are implied into contracts, either on the basis that they are thought to go without saying or because this is regarded as fair, economically efficient, or otherwise desirable from the standpoint of the general law. Finally, there are certain kinds of contracts or kinds of terms in contracts that, as a matter of general policy, the courts will refuse to enforce. This and the following three chapters examine the courts' approach to these issues.

The legal rules used to determine the content of a contract are practically important; most contractual disputes turn, in the end, on the contract's terms. But they also raise important issues of policy, in particular, the proper scope of the principle of freedom of contract in the modern law. This issue is raised because insofar as contractual obligations are not determined by the parties, freedom of contract in the traditional sense has been impinged. Related to this is a second policy issue: on what grounds (other than the parties' intentions) are contractual duties imposed by the courts? As we shall see, the very different notions of fairness and (economic) efficiency are the usual suggestions.

The discussion of the law in this area is divided as follows: (1) express terms (Chapter 5); (2) implied terms (Chapter 6); (3) the rules that determine the force and scope of contractual obligations (i.e. the rules dealing with standards of care, mistake, frustration, breach, and notice) (Chapter 7); and (4) unenforceable terms and contracts (Chapter 8).

1. TERMS AND REPRESENTATIONS

Contracts are sometimes made in writing, and sometimes orally; they may also be made partly in writing and partly orally, and sometimes (as we have seen), they may even be made partly by conduct. Many contracts today are also made using electronic communications. Written contracts may be made in formal documents, signed by both parties, or in informal writings such as letters, fax messages, emails, and so on. At the same time, the mere presence of a document discussing the matter of a contract does not make it part of the contract, and the same is true of oral and electronic communications. The question to be discussed in this first section concerns the tests for identifying the terms of the contract.

It might be thought that identifying the terms would be simple enough for written contracts, but even written contracts will usually be preceded or accompanied by oral or written communications, which may or may not qualify as contractual statements. According to the traditional approach, the distinction between a term of the contract and a 'mere' (non-contractual) representation depends on the intention of the parties. Once this intention has been ascertained, the courts apply the rules relating to contractual terms or to representations, depending on the case. If the statement is a contractual term, the breach of it always gives a right to claim damages, and may, if the term is sufficiently important, give a right to terminate the contract. On the other hand, if the statement is a mere representation, and so not incorporated into the contract, its legal effect will depend on whether it is a statement of *intention* or a statement of *fact*. A statement of intention that is not incorporated into the contract has practically no legal effect, although, as we have seen, it may sometimes give rise to the defence of promissory estoppel. By contrast, a statement of fact which is not incorporated into the contract normally gives the right to rescind the contract if it is untrue and, in addition, a right to damages in tort. Tortious liabilities are discussed in Chapter 10.

Traditionally, then, the enquiry simply becomes whether or not the parties intended a particular statement to be contractual. This approach has some validity where the parties have signed a formal written contract, in which case it seems reasonable to presume that they did not intend oral statements or even written statements which are not incorporated in the written document to have contractual effect, although even then this starting point can be rebutted. But in many cases, it is much more difficult to separate out the terms of the contract from mere representations, and in these cases the traditional approach has weaknesses, for—as is so often true in the law of contract—the phrase 'the intention of the parties' does not really mean what it says. In the first place, it is highly unlikely that the parties had any intention at all on the matter, for such an intention would virtually require an appreciation of the legal distinction between a term of the contract and a mere representation. In the second place, it is almost certain that the parties will claim that they had different intentions, for if they did not, the case would probably not be in court at all. Thus, we rarely find a court making any real attempt to examine the actual or 'inner' intentions of the particular parties in order to solve this particular type of question. What we find the courts saying is something like this:

The question is whether this statement is a term of the contract or a mere representation. This depends on the intention of the parties. In this case we think that the parties must have intended this statement to be a term of the contract because it is only reasonable to conclude that the party making the statement intended to accept responsibility for it.

We are then likely to find the court explaining the purely objective reasons for which it thinks that the party making the statement accepted responsibility for it, for example, that he was a dealer in the goods in question, or that he, as owner of the land being sold, had better opportunities for discovering the truth of his statement. Alternatively, we may find the court saying that the statement in question was not 'intended' to be a term of the contract because it was made (perhaps) casually, or because the parties had shown that they 'intended' their legal relations to be governed exclusively by a formal written document, and so on.

In short, the same objective approach that courts adopt to determine the *meaning* of contractual terms (as is discussed in more detail below) is adopted when determining if a particular statement was intended to be part of a contractual agreement or promise. This seems appropriate, and for the same reason in each case: communicated words mean what they appear to the reasonable listener to mean. This is not to say that courts always apply the objective approach in a purely neutral fashion; in many cases they clearly base their classification of statements not on how the statement would reasonably be understood, but on the legal consequences that follow from such classifications. In older cases, such reasoning was particularly common. Until 1964, the consequence of classifying a statement as non-contractual was that, except in cases involving a deliberate misstatement, that is to say fraud, the speaker would incur no liability. Moreover, the listener's only remedy would be to seek rescission of (that is, the right to withdraw from) the contract, which might be too harsh, particularly if the misrepresentation concerned a minor matter and was not carelessly made. Then again, even when such a remedy would not be too harsh, it might not be available if the falsity of the statement was discovered too late. The introduction of the tort of negligent misstatement and other developments that are discussed below have made these classificatory questions less important in practice, and so reduced the pressure on courts to engage in result-oriented reasoning. But there is no doubt that courts are still influenced by the fact that, for instance, classifying a statement as contractual means that the speaker is strictly liable for the truth and that any damages awarded will be assessed according to the (usually more generous) contractual measure.

A clear example of this kind of result-oriented reasoning is found in a recent legislative development. Under the Package Travel, Package Holidays and Package Tours Regulations 1992, information in documents detailing travel holidays, package tours, etc., constitutes an implied term in any resulting contract; a retailer or organiser who gives any misleading information is liable to compensate a consumer for any loss suffered thereby. It is perfectly plain that the object of the legislation was to ensure that consumers should be entitled to contractual damages for misleading statements in travel brochures; whatever the common law status of such statements, the law has decisively converted them into contractual terms. It has done so not to give effect to any supposed intentions of the parties, but to give better protection to consumers of package holidays.

2. WRITTEN CONTRACTS

In the case of a written document purporting to contain a part or the entirety of a contract, two questions arise: first, whether the document is a part of the contract at all and, second, if it is, whether it alone constitutes the whole contract.

Is the document part of the contract?: Signed documents

Where a contractual document is signed by one or both of the parties, the rule is that this signature binds the signing party and precludes him from pleading that he had no knowledge of the terms of the contract, save where he can prove fraud, misrepresentation, duress, undue influence, or a mistake of such a fundamental kind as to show that there has been no valid offer or acceptance. Fraud and misrepresentation are dealt with in more detail in Chapter 10; here it is enough to state the essentials.

If the signature is obtained by fraud, then, in accordance with normal principles, the innocent party may take steps to repudiate the contract, but unless and until he does so, the document will be binding, and if it comes into the hands of an innocent third party before then, the signer of the document may be liable on it. If the signature is obtained by pre-contractual misrepresentation short of fraud, then, once again, the innocent party is entitled to rescission provided that no innocent third parties have become involved and it is not too late to rescind. In addition, if the misrepresentation relates to a term of the contract, the innocent party may be entitled to insist that the term should be treated as it was represented to him, and not as it was actually written down. So a misrepresentation as to the scope of an exemption clause may disentitle a party from relying on the clause as a defence to suit for breach of contract.

Duress and undue influence are dealt with in Chapter 11 and they are only mentioned here because cases in which a person signs a document while suffering from a basic misapprehension as to its contents often involve duress or undue influence. If legal duress or undue influence is proved, then (as in the case of fraud or misrepresentation) the contract can be set aside by the innocent party, though subject to the usual restrictions applicable to those doctrines.

The third defence that may be pleaded to a document signed by the defendant is that she was fundamentally mistaken as to the transaction into which she appears to have entered by her signature. It is at this point that the theory of the law of contract comes up against some fundamental questions of practical convenience. In theory, contractual obligations depend on the intention of the parties, but in practical terms it would often be very trouble-some, if not impossible, to prove that parties intended to make every promise or undertaking which may be involved in a complex relationship. So, for a long time it has been customary to record contracts in written documents and to obtain the signatures of the parties to these documents. Although it is not *necessary* for a contract to be made in this way—thousands of contracts are made daily in which the terms are not written down—there is a very strong legal presumption that signed contracts embody the intention of the parties. It is unnecessary to show that the party signing a contract understood or even read it; indeed, the presumption that she is bound is not rebutted even by proof that she is blind or illiterate, or does not speak the language in which the document was written. Nor is it even rebutted by showing that the other party to the transaction *knew* that the first party had not read the document. It is, after all, an everyday affair for consumers to be presented with a con-tractual document to sign, containing pages of small print that they do not read, and *are not even expected to read*. Frequently the other party to the transaction is aware that the consumer has not read the document—it would often take considerable time to read it. And this raises a problem for the theory of the law, because it is generally held (as we saw earlier) that a party is only entitled to rely on the *appearance* of consent where he thinks that the appearance is also the reality. Although the courts have never actually attempted to reconcile the rules with the theory of the law on this point, they might do so by suggesting that a signature shows that the party signing intends to accept whatever is in the document signed, even though she has not read it. But this might only apply on the assumption that the document contains usual or standard terms for a transaction of that kind.

The reality—not yet acknowledged by the theory of the law—is perhaps that signatures are treated as formal grounds of legal liability, rather than as proof of contractual intention. For if they were treated merely as proof of intention, one would expect that a person would be permitted to deny his intention despite his signature in a much wider variety of circumstances than are, in fact, recognised by the law. Treating signatures as a formal ground for imposing legal liability is a very convenient rule of everyday practical application. It is, moreover, a rule that is widely understood—everybody knows that when they are asked to sign a document, important legal consequences may follow. But while the present rule may well be highly desirable, it makes it necessary to bear in mind that liability arising from signed documents is often *not* the result of a conscious intention to assume that specific liability. It also makes it dangerous to argue that the imposition of legal liability in contract can always be justified on the ground that the defendant had promised or undertaken to accept that liability.

Of course, there are limits to the present rule. As explained in Chapter 3, cases occasionally occur in which a person signs a document under a complete misapprehension as to what he is signing. For example, a person may be induced to sign a promissory note, thinking that he is merely signing a document as a witness; or he may be induced to sign a cheque in the belief that it is a guarantee. Such a signature might in principle be valid and binding on the ground that the defendant's intentions must be judged objectively, but, in practice, where the signature is obtained in these circumstances, it will almost always be found that there has been fraud. In this case, the transaction will be 'voidable', meaning that the mistaken party has the right to rescind the contract as against the fraudulent party (but that third parties may rely on the document until rescission).

In addition, we saw in Chapter 3 that there are two other instances where a party under a complete misapprehension will not be bound by their signature (or by any other indication of consent). One is where the other party to the transaction is aware of the mistake. The second instance is where the requirements for the defence of *non est factum* are established. The principles, laid down in the leading case *Saunders v. Anglia Building Society*,[1] may be summarized as follows. First, the plea of mistake in this kind of case can only rarely be relied upon by a person of full age and capacity. Secondly, in exceptional cases, a person who has signed a document under a fundamental mistake as to the *nature* or *effect* of the document can plead the defence of *non est factum*; the plea is more readily admissible if the party signing was blind or illiterate, but it is not absolutely confined to these cases, nor is it automatically applicable in every case of a blind or illiterate person. Thirdly, the plea will be rebutted if the party signing fails to take ordinary care; in particular, if he signs the document without taking reasonable precautions to inform himself of the contents, the defence will probably fail.

Finally, in the case of consumer contracts, the above law is also now subject to an important provision in the Unfair Terms in Consumer Contracts Regulations 1999. Schedule 2 of Regulation 5(5) states that a term may be unfair if, among other things, it irrevocably binds the consumer to terms

---

[1] Also known as *Gallie v. Lee* [1971] AC 1004.

with which he had no real opportunity of becoming acquainted before the conclusion of the contract. Of course, offering a document for signature to the consumer will, in most cases, satisfy this clause, since this is the best way of giving the consumer an opportunity to become acquainted with the document's terms, so the main application of this provision will probably lie in its effect on cases where there is no signature. But some cases of signed documents may be covered, especially cases where it is apparent to the other party that the consumer does not know the language in which the document is written or completely fails to understand the meaning of its terms. The general effects of the Regulations are dealt with later; here it is enough to say that unfair terms as defined by the Regulations are not binding on consumers in their dealings with suppliers and sellers.

Is the document part of the contract?: Unsigned documents

Where a written document is relied upon by one party as representing the contract, but this document has not been signed by the defendant, it is more difficult to determine whether its contents should be treated as embodying contractual terms. In principle, it must be shown that the document has been accepted by both parties as the basis of the contract. This test can be difficult to apply in a variety of contexts. One common type of case—the 'battle of the forms'—has already been considered in Chapter 3. Another group of cases are the so-called 'ticket cases', where one party offers to contract upon certain written terms, often contained, or referred to, in a ticket of some kind, and there is no doubt that a contract has been concluded, but there is doubt as to whether the terms contained in the ticket have been accepted by the other party. The main principles to be applied to such cases were settled in 1877 in the Court of Appeal's decision in *Parker v. South Eastern Railway*,[2] although there has been a certain amount of embellishment and gloss added to them since then.

Before examining these rules, one point of fundamental principle should be stressed. It is elementary that one party cannot alter the terms of the contract unilaterally after it has been finally concluded by the offer and acceptance of the two parties (unless the original terms themselves envisage and permit such unilateral alteration). As a result, where the contract has been completed in this way, the subsequent delivery by one party to the other of a document purporting to contain contractual terms is entirely ineffective. This applies similarly to a notice that is only brought to the attention of the other party after the contract is concluded.[3] On the other hand, a different result may be reached where it is known at the time the agreement is made that a document containing other terms may be brought into existence later. So, for instance, an agreement for the carriage of goods by sea is almost

---

[2] (1877) 2 CPD 416. [3] *Olley v. Marlborough Court* [1949] 1 KB 532.

invariably recorded in a bill of lading that contains standardized, inter-
nationally agreed terms. But in practice, an oral agreement for the carriage of
particular goods on a particular ship will usually be made in advance, often
by telephone, and the bill of lading is not usually issued till after the goods
have been loaded. But because it is known that the bill of lading will be
issued, the oral contract is governed by the carrier's normal bill of lading
terms even before the bill is issued or even if it is never issued.[4]

To return to the ticket cases, the principle of *Parker v. South East Railway*
is simple. According to this case, a person relying on a ticket as a contractual
document must show that she gave sufficient notice to the other party that the
document or ticket incorporated contractual terms. If the party receiving the
ticket reasonably assumes it to be just a ticket or receipt, and nothing more,
and simply puts it into his pocket without reading it, then it will have no
contractual effect. For instance, in *Chapelton v. Barry UDC*,[5] the claimant
hired a deck-chair from the defendants for use at a beach. He bought a ticket
from the attendant that contained a clause excluding all liability for injury or
damage, but which he did not read as he had simply pocketed the ticket. It
was held that this formed no part of the contract as no reasonable person
would have assumed the ticket to be anything but a receipt.

On the other hand, it is well established that, where a person buys a ticket
for a railway or air journey, he should, as a reasonable person, know that the
ticket is bound to contain certain conditions. To the question whether 'notice
of the conditions' means notice of their existence or notice of their contents,
the majority of the court in *Parker* held that mere notice of existence is
sufficient. Thus it has been held that a reference on the front of a ticket to the
back, and an indication on the back that the ticket is issued subject to terms
set out in other documents which might be obtained at the railway station,
is sufficient notice of the terms.[6] This sort of 'incorporation by reference' is
quite common in business transactions of various kinds—some organizations simply print at the foot of their order forms or quotations, 'All goods
supplied [*or* all work done] according to our usual terms', or words to that
effect.

Where the terms are fair and reasonable or (what typically amounts to the
same thing) standard or customary, the *Parker* rule is unobjectionable. It
would be impractical to require contracting parties to give notice of the
contents of each and every term in a contractual document. But where the
terms in a document are not fair or reasonable, and particularly where,
in addition, they are unusual, it seems clear that, assuming no other relief is

---

[4] *Pyrene v. Sciodia Navigation* [1954] 2 QB 402; but compare *Burke (Raymond) Motors v.
Mersey Docks* [1986] 1 Lloyd's Rep. 155, where not even an oral contract had been concluded, so
a bill of lading exemption clause could not be applied.

[5] [1940] 1 KB 532.

[6] *Thompson v. L. M & S. Rly Co.* [1930] 1 KB 41.

available, the *Parker* rule may lead to unfair surprises. The courts' response to this problem has been to hold that what counts as sufficient notice depends on how severe or unusual is the clause in question. At first this was done implicitly, but later the practice was made explicit. In *Thornton v. Shoe Lane Parking Ltd*,[7] for instance, Lord Denning held that insufficient notice had been given of an unusually wide exemption clause in a car-parking ticket issued by an automatic machine; the ticket, he said, was 'so wide and destructive of rights that . . . it would need to be printed in red ink with a red hand pointing to it, or something equally startling'. Another case in which the court found that insufficient notice was given of terms that it regarded as unfair is *Interfoto Picture Library Ltd v. Stiletto Visual Programmes Ltd*[8] The claimants supplied to the defendants, as the result of a telephone order, 47 photographic transparencies in an envelope together with a document containing printed conditions. These conditions required the hirer to return them within 14 days or to pay a 'holding fee' of £5 per transparency per day overdue. The defendants returned the transparencies 15 days late and the claimants sought to charge them in accordance with their conditions—a sum totalling £3,783. According to the evidence, these charges were far higher than those generally applicable in the business—a normal charge was about £3.50 per transparency *per week* rather than the £5 *per day* which the claimants sought to charge. The Court of Appeal held that such unreasonable conditions had to be more clearly brought home to the other party before they could be relied upon as being incorporated in the contract. On the other hand, where the terms are fair and reasonable, and especially where the parties are commercial parties and terms are standard in the industry, they will usually be regarded as properly incorporated even in extreme cases where a bare notice of incorporation by reference is given. Indeed, such standard terms will sometimes be held to be incorporated even without any notice, as where an oral contract is concluded but it is assumed by both parties that some written agreement or document will subsequently be brought into existence,[9] or where it can be shown by proof of a 'course of dealings' that the parties had implicitly agreed to terms that they had used in previous contracts.[10]

It must be admitted that some of these cases look artificial. The object of giving notice of the terms on a ticket or other document must, after all, be to warn the parties of what they are letting themselves in for, and to give them an opportunity to withdraw if they wish. In practice, however, there is often no question of withdrawal because the person requires the facilities offered and must take them on the terms offered, there being no practical alternative.

---

[7] [1971] 2 QB 163.   [8] [1988] 1 All ER 345.
[9] *British Crane Hire v. Ipswich Plant Hire* [1975] QB 303.
[10] *McCutcheon v. David MacBrayne Ltd* [1964] 1 WLR 125.

In short, the real problem with many of the terms that courts have found not to be incorporated is not that insufficient notice was given, but that in the circumstances the terms were unfair and would have been so even if notice had been given. It is important to remember, therefore, that the law now has other means available for dealing with the most common instances of unfair terms. The majority of the incorporation cases deal with exemption clauses, which are subject, under the Unfair Contract Terms Act 1977, to a general standard of reasonableness. In addition, all the terms in consumer contracts (except price terms and those defining the primary obligations) are subject to similarly direct scrutiny under the Unfair Terms in Consumer Contracts Regulations 1999. As already noted, Schedule 2 of the Regulations specifically mentions as an example of a term that may be unfair one which the consumer had no real opportunity of becoming acquainted with prior to concluding the contract. The details of these legislative enactments are discussed in Chapter 12. For the present, it is sufficient to note that they provide courts with a more direct and explicit method of controlling terms they regard as unfair. As such, they should make the incorporation rules less important than they were in the past. Admittedly, neither of these pieces of legislation would apply to clauses such as those in the *Interfoto* case discussed above—despite its title, the Unfair Contract Terms Act 1977 does not deal with all unfair contract terms. But given that the litigants were both commercial parties and that there was no evidence of fraud, duress, or lack of choice in the relevant market, it may be questioned whether the defendant was as deserving of relief as the court appeared to believe.

Is the document exclusive evidence of the contract?

Assuming that the relevant document is held to be a contractual document, the next question is whether it is exclusive evidence of the transaction. The answer, once again, is said to depend on the intention of the parties, but it is at least settled that in two classes of cases the writing will not be considered exclusive. First, where the parties have entered into a definite and clear contract and the contract has been reduced to writing, but owing to some mistake the written contract does not exactly conform with what the parties had agreed, the court has the power to order the contract to be rectified. Naturally, a person who impugns a written contract on this ground undertakes a heavy burden of proof, but if the claimant can satisfy the court of the mistake, the court will rightly be willing to rectify the contract. So, for instance, where A agreed to let certain premises to B at a rent of £230 per annum, but the lease by mistake stated the rent to be £130, and both parties signed the lease without noticing the mistake, it was held that the tenant could not take advantage of the slip and insist on having the premises at the lower figure.

Rectification will only be ordered where it is clear that the document departs from the intention of *both* parties. In *Riverlate Properties Ltd v. Paul*,[11] a lease was granted that failed to impose on the tenant any obligation to contribute to the cost of external repairs. The landlord had intended to require such a contribution, so from his point of view there was a mistake. But the tenant knew nothing of the landlord's intention or mistake, and it was therefore held that she could enforce the written lease as it stood.

When it is said that a contract may be rectified if the writing does not represent the parties' real intentions, it must be understood that we are again referring to the apparent and outward intention of the parties. A written contract can be rectified if, but only if, it is not a correct record of a prior oral agreement, objectively understood.[12] Thus, where A made a contract to buy horse-beans from B, both parties being under the erroneous impression that 'horse-beans' was just another name for feveroles, it was held that the contract could not be rectified by substituting feveroles for horse-beans. The parties had, in fact, made a contract for horse-beans and, although they were mistaken as to the nature of this article, the written contract was a correct record of their oral agreement.[13]

Finally, it should be remembered that, while it is often convenient and advisable to have a written contract rectified by a formal order of the court, especially if it has anything to do with rights in land, as a matter of strict legal principle rectification is superfluous. In law, the contract itself (it must always be remembered) is not a piece of paper, but a set of rights and duties. The court does not alter these rights and duties with a decree of rectification; it only rectifies written documents so that they are a correct record of the parties' rights and duties.

The second type of case in which written documents may be supplemented with other evidence of intention is where it can be shown that either the parties did not intend the written document to be the entire record of their agreement or (what in practice amounts to the same thing) that it did not exclusively represent their intentions because of a 'collateral' contract made during the negotiations. The normal presumption—often called the 'parol evidence rule'—is that the written document is the exclusive evidence of the parties' intentions. According to this rule, evidence is not admissible to contradict or qualify a complete written contract, but the rule has so many exceptions that in practice it is now almost obsolete; in particular the rule will not apply where the court finds that the parties did not intend the document to be the exclusive evidence of their intention.

---

[11] [1975] Ch 133.

[12] It has been held that it is not necessary that this oral agreement should itself have been a binding oral contract: see *Joscelyne v. Nissen* [1970] 2 QB 86.

[13] *F. E. Rose v. Wm. H. Pim* [1953] 2 QB 450.

In cases where (as is common) the written document says 'this is the entire contract and supersedes all previous contracts', or words to that effect, this test of intention is relatively easy to apply. But where the document is silent on such matters, the intention test is elusive. All that can be said by way of general guidance is that 'the person who claims that the written agreement was not intended to be exhaustive must in practice, if not in law, be able to point to something said or done by the other party at the time the agreement was concluded'.[14] For instance, if at the time the agreement is being negotiated one party gives the other oral assurances that a reasonable person would rely upon, it is nowadays accepted almost without question that such assurances override the written contract. This is particularly so in consumer transactions, but it is often also applied to commercial contracts. So where forwarding agents orally undertook to ship the claimant's goods under deck, it was held that this overrode a printed bill of lading clause which permitted shipment on deck.[15] Similarly, where leases were entered into which required the tenants to contribute to the cost of external repairs it was held that the tenants were entitled to rely on the oral assurances of the landlord's agent that the landlords would repair the roof at their own expense.[16]

Finally, it should be remembered that even if the parol evidence rule is applied strictly, such that an oral assurance or other representation is found not to have contractual effect, a party who has relied on such a statement will frequently have a remedy in tort for negligent misstatement. The representation must be a statement of fact as opposed to mere intention, but, as was noted earlier,[17] this test is usually not difficult to meet. It is also true that the written document can attempt to exclude such liability, but courts will require extremely clear language before they will give effect to such an exclusion.[18]

3. ORAL CONTRACTS

If the problem of isolating the terms of the contract from other statements is difficult in the case of written contracts, it is even more so where the contract is purely oral. In the former case, the writing is at least a useful starting point, whereas in the latter case there is no real starting point at all. There is first the purely factual difficulty in establishing what was said; it must then be decided which words used by the parties during (potentially very long) negotiations

---

[14] R. Cross, *Evidence* (3rd edn, London, 1967), 508–9. This passage does not appear in later editions but the general gist remains unchanged.

[15] *J. Evans & Sons (Portsmouth) v. Andrea Merzario* [1976] 1 WLR 1098.

[16] *Brikom Investments v. Carr* [1979] QB 467, where varying reasons for the decision were given by the three judges of the Court of Appeal; *Rigby v. Ferodo* [1987] ICR 457.

[17] Above, 86.

[18] See, e.g., *Thomas Witter Ltd v. TBP Industries Ltd* [1996] 2 All ER 575.

are to be treated as contractual terms or promises. Once again the distinction is said to depend on the intention of the parties, but even more than in the case of written documents (which sometimes contain 'entire agreement' clauses), this test is of little assistance.

In *Schawel v. Reade*[19] the claimant required a stallion for stud purposes, and was examining a horse in the defendant's stables. While he was doing this, the defendant entered and said: 'You need not look for anything; the horse is perfectly sound.' The claimant thereupon ceased his examination, and eventually (though not for several weeks) bought the horse. The House of Lords affirmed the jury's decision that the seller's statement was a term of the contract of sale. Lord Moulton said:

> It would be impossible, in my mind, to have a clearer example of an express warranty where the word 'warranty' was not used. The essence of such a warranty is that it becomes plain by the words and the action of the parties that it is intended that in the purchase the responsibility of the soundness shall rest upon the vendor; and how in the world could a vendor more clearly indicate that he is prepared to and intends to take upon himself the responsibility of the soundness than by saying 'You need not look at the horse because he is perfectly sound', and sees that the purchaser thereupon desists from his immediate independent examination?

As described by Lord Moulton, the question is whether the person making the statement has assumed the responsibility for the truth of what he has said. In general, this will be found when the person making the statement is in a better position to know its truth than the other party, but even this is by no means always the case. Thus, in *Oscar Chess v. Williams*[20] a majority of the Court of Appeal laid it down as a very rough guide that a person is not usually to be assumed to be accepting responsibility for the truth of a statement as to which he had no personal knowledge. In this case the claimants, who were car-dealers, bought a car from the defendant which was believed by both parties, and was stated by the defendant, to be a 1946 model. In fact, the seller had no means of knowing the true age of the car, and was merely passing on the information contained in the log book, which, as it turned out, was wrong. It was held that this statement was a mere representation. But where the role of the parties is reversed the position will normally be different, because a dealer who states that a certain car dates from a particular year should know whether this is true, and if he does not know he can discover the truth by application to the manufacturers. Certainly a statement made by a dealer as to the quality of goods being sold will rarely be held a mere representation. This is borne out by the decision in *Dick Bentley Ltd v. Harold Smith (Motors) Ltd,*[21] where a dealer supplied a car to the claimant as a '20,000 mile Bentley'. In fact, the car had done considerably more than

---

[19] [1913] 2 IR 81.   [20] [1957] 1 WLR 370.   [21] [1965] 1 WLR 623.

20,000 miles and the claimant obtained damages for breach of warranty. This case illustrates the point that the courts tend to place the responsibility on the person who they think reasonably ought to bear the responsibility, rather than on the person who has agreed to bear it, for the simple reason that it is often not apparent whether anybody has agreed to bear it.

These cases do not provide a clear formula for distinguishing terms from mere statements. But the reasoning in these and other older cases is, in any event, of limited relevance because they predate the introduction of the tort of negligent misstatement and the Misrepresentation Act 1967. As already noted, the former gave the courts an additional means (aside from finding that a statement was a contractual term) to protect a negotiating party who relied on a false statement. The latter effectively lowered the burden of proof of negligence, and also gave the courts the discretion to substitute an award of damages for an order of rescission in cases where a contract was entered on the basis of innocent (non-negligent) misstatement. Prior to this, the only remedy for a non-fraudulent misstatement was rescission, which was sometimes too harsh (e.g. if the misstatement concerned a trivial matter) and sometimes too weak (e.g. if it was too late to rescind the contract). The result of these developments was to reduce the pressure on courts to find that statements made during negotiations are contractual terms. In many cases, the only difference between classifying a statement as contractual as opposed to non-contractual will be whether the claimant receives damages on the contractual measure or the tort measure—which in many cases is no difference at all (as we will see later).[22] This is illustrated by a final case[23] in which a company hired two ocean-going barges to dump some excavated waste matter at sea. The claimant's manager had mistakenly told the defendant's manager that the barges had a capacity of 850 cubic metres each. In fact, they did not, and they proved inadequate for the job. The Court of Appeal held (by a majority) that no contractual warranty had been given. But the court then immediately mitigated the effect of this decision by finding that the defendants were entitled to damages under the Misrepresentation Act, on the basis that the claimants could not satisfy section 2(1) of the act, which would excuse them only if they had 'reasonable grounds to believe . . . that the facts represented were true'.

4. THE INTERPRETATION OF EXPRESS TERMS

Thus far we have been examining how courts identify a contract's express terms. When this job has been performed, the court's task is to interpret these terms and, assuming they are neither contrary to public policy (see Chapters

---

[22] Below 404–05.
[23] *Howard Manne & Dredging Co. v. A. Ogden & Sons* [1978] QB 574.

8 and 12) nor altered or overridden by an implied term (see Chapter 6), give effect to them. This interpretative exercise is neither formal nor mechanical. On the contrary, it is one of the most difficult tasks that a court has to face.

Until recently, the approach of English courts to matters of interpretation was, in theory anyway, narrow and technical. Various 'rules of construction' were articulated, usually of a fairly self-evident kind (e.g., where two meanings are possible, that which fits best with the remainder of the document should be adopted), but in the main the courts' task was understood as that of simply giving effect to contractual terms as they appeared on the page. In particular, it was held that external evidence regarding the meaning of a word or phrase in a contract was inadmissible except in cases of clear ambiguity. The only 'evidence' of meaning the court required was the contractual document itself. This approach was sometimes defended on the grounds that words have a 'plain', 'natural', or 'ordinary' meaning, and that the function of the judge is simply to act as a kind of legal dictionary. The fallacies in this argument have been exposed many times, first by modern philosophers and second by lawyers, with particular reference to the problems of legal interpretation. It is now well-recognised that words and phrases typically have a wide range of possible meanings, and that determining which of these meanings is the proper one cannot be done without taking into account the full context in which the word was used. The better justification for the traditional approach, therefore, is that, in most cases anyway, the context in which contract drafters use words is one in which words *are meant to be* understood narrowly and literally. In other words, judges should pay close attention to the actual words of a contractual document, including subtle linguistic distinctions that might be ignored in everyday speech, because this is what those who make and use such documents do themselves. A further justification for the traditional approach is that it encourages parties to write contracts so that they can be understood without using external sources. The argument here is that the courts should discourage parties from drafting contracts in a way that might require lengthy—and costly—adjudication if a dispute arises. Interpreting contracts narrowly and literally encourages contracting parties to write narrowly and literally.

These arguments are compelling, but they do not fully justify the traditional approach. It is true that lawyers typically use words carefully and in their literal senses, but a quick glance at the cases on interpretation show that this is not always the case. In addition, while there are obvious advantages to writing contracts in a way that makes them as self-interpreting as possible, these advantages can be exaggerated. For one thing, it is impossible, even in theory, to make a contract entirely self-interpreting—it is always necessary to take into account at least some facts about the context in which words are used. In addition, the time and cost of trying to make every part of a contract as self-interpreting as possible will often outweigh the benefits. After all, most contracts are performed without any questions arising as to their meaning.

These counter-arguments have long influenced the actual practice of the courts, but it is only in the last 30 or so years, culminating in the landmark case of *Investors Compensation Scheme Ltd v. West Bromwich Building Society*,[24] that courts have openly accepted a more contextual approach to interpretation. In *Investors*, Lord Hoffmann stated that 'almost all the old intellectual baggage of "legal interpretation" has been discarded' and that contractual documents are now to be interpreted according to 'the common sense principles by which any serious utterance would be interpreted in ordinary life.' The result, Lord Hoffmann continued, is that meaning should be ascertained on the basis of 'absolutely anything which would have affected the way in which the language of the document would have been understood by a reasonable man'. The only external evidence that remains inadmissible as a matter of principle is that pertaining to prior negotiations (e.g. prior drafts), though even this may eventually be admissible if Lord Hoffman's approach is given full effect.

Critics of Lord Hoffman's approach have argued that allowing courts to consider evidence that a word should not be understood in its ordinary or natural sense will make contractual interpretation unpredictable. But the old approach was itself unpredictable: while judges claimed to be restricting themselves to the ordinary or literal meaning of a document's words, they were in practice often deciding which of several possible meanings should be adopted on the basis of context. A second criticism of Hoffman's reform is that making external evidence of any kind admissible in principle will make litigation longer and more costly. This is perhaps a more serious objection, but it is best addressed not by artificially restricting evidence, but by subjecting evidence to the ordinary standards of relevance. To say that any kind of evidence is in principle admissible is not to say that any kind of evidence is relevant. At any rate, the contextual approach will yield the same result as the traditional approach in most cases, since in most case the context in question is one in which words and phrases are meant to be understood without significant reliance on external evidence. As was already emphasised, lawyers drafting and reading formal legal documents typically operate in a context in which documents are meant to be relatively self-interpreting. Indeed, one of the reasons for hiring a lawyer to draft a contract is that lawyers are meant to be skilled at putting into words the precise needs and wishes of their clients.

Finally, it should be noted that Lord Hoffmann did not suggest that the meaning of a word or phrase should be determined on the basis of one party's understanding of what that word or phrase was intended to mean. In

---

[24] [1998] 1 WLR 896. The first important case was *Prenn v. Simmonds* [1971] 1 WLR 1580.

this respect, the modern and traditional approaches to interpretation are alike: each supposes that meaning is determined 'objectively', that is to say on the basis of how a contract would have been understood by a reasonable reader.[25] This is clearly correct: the *meaning* of a word or phrase is an 'objective' question, to be determined on the basis of shared or publicly available understandings. As has already been stressed, words are used for communication, and communication is by definition interpersonal. This is not to say, of course, that subjective intentions about meanings must be entirely irrelevant to the law: in some circumstances it might be appropriate to give relief to parties who communicate meanings that they did not intend to communicate. But if this is the case, the reason is not that the meaning of the contract is established on the basis of subjective understandings, but rather that the parties either did not reach agreement or reached an unfair agreement. These possibilities are discussed in Chapters 3 and 12 respectively.

5. THE INTERPRETATION OF EXEMPTION CLAUSES

One aspect of interpretation that requires more extended examination is the treatment of exemption clauses. An exemption clause may take many forms, but all such clauses have in common that they exempt parties from liabilities that they would otherwise have borne. In some cases, an exemption clause merely relieves a party from certain purely contractual obligations, for example, the duties of a seller in a contract of sale regarding the quality and fitness of the goods. In other cases exemption clauses go further and protect the party from liability that would otherwise have arisen in tort. For example, a shipping company's bill of lading may exempt the company from liability for damage to the goods being carried, however caused. In yet other cases, exemption clauses may be only partial in their operation, for example, by restricting the time during which a claim may be made, or by limiting the amount of damages recoverable. Clauses of this latter kind are sometimes called 'limitation clauses' and are occasionally distinguished from exemption clauses.

Over the last half-century, both courts and legislatures have shown a marked hostility toward exemption clauses. Before turning to an examination of the ways in which this hostility has been expressed, it is useful to spend a few moments considering why it exists at all. One possible justification for scrutinizing exemption clauses is that it is wrong in principle to take away or

---

[25] The (continued) inadmissibility of evidence of prior negotiations is sometimes explained on this basis, but this seems mistaken: such evidence is evidence not of what the parties *thought* they were agreeing to, but of what they appeared ('objectively') to be agreeing to. The only basis for excluding such evidence would again seem to be that it is usually irrelevant, since, by definition, prior negotiations do not represent the parties' final agreement. But since relevancy is a question of fact and degree, it is difficult to support a blanket exclusionary rule on this ground.

reduce a person's legal rights. If the law grants certain rights, for example a right to compensatory damages for damage to property, this must be for a good reason, and so any attempt to reduce such rights must be undesirable. Two objections to this suggestion may be made. First, it ignores the possibility that the standard set of legal rights are designed as 'default' terms that, like the standard settings in computer software, are meant to work well for *most* cases, but which 'users' are expected to modify in those cases where they work poorly. Secondly, and more importantly, there are very often good substantive reasons that parties may wish to incorporate exemption clauses in their contracts. In many situations, an exemption clause is effectively an agreement about the allocation of responsibility for insuring against certain risks. For example, a company whose business is the carriage of goods by road may incorporate clauses in its contracts under which it excludes all liability for loss of, or damage to, the goods. In this kind of case the exemption clause is merely an indication that the responsibility for insuring the goods against loss or damage is intended to rest on the owner and not on the carrier. There is nothing necessarily unreasonable or undesirable about this. No doubt the carrier could insure the goods, though he would then have to increase his charges to cover the cost of insurance; but it may well be better for the consignor of the goods to insure them herself. In particular, she would know more about the nature and value of the goods, the way they have been packed, and their vulnerability to damage—all factors that would be relevant to the question of insurance. There are also some situations (of which the above may be an example) in which the relevant property is already insured by the owner in the ordinary course of events. For example, many car owners carry comprehensive policies which cover them against the risk of loss or damage from any cause. If a car owner takes her car to a garage for repairs, therefore, it may be desirable for the garage to exclude its normal liability for causing damage by negligence. If the garage company is unable to do this it will have to insure against the risk and charge the customer accordingly. This would simply mean that the owner would pay twice over for insurance protection.

A second, more common suggestion is that exemption clauses are deserving of special scrutiny because they are frequently forced on unwilling parties. The fact that most standard-form 'take-it-or-leave-it' contracts contain exemption clauses is usually thought to support this view. This suggestion is more persuasive than the previous one: a contracting party with the ability to dictate terms would not hesitate to impose an unreasonable exemption clause. This suggestion is also consistent with the historical fact that unreasonable exemption clauses are commonly found in contracts made in non-competitive markets, such as markets dominated by monopolies and cartels. But the 'monopoly power' explanation fails to explain why exemption clauses *in particular* are subject to judicial hostility, that is to say, why such clauses are more likely to be unreasonable than other kinds of clauses. After all, if a contracting party has the ability to dictate whatever terms he wants, then it is surely the contract price on which he will first focus his attentions. Why bother drafting complex exemption clauses if you can simply set the contract price at whatever amount you like? Even if, as is usually the case, a monopolist does not have complete freedom to set the contract's terms (say because of the threat of regulation or because the consumer may simply choose to do without the product if its cost is too high) the question remains: why would a monopolist focus in particular on exemption clauses? Finally, this suggestion does not explain why unreasonable exemption clauses are also frequently found in contracts made in perfectly competitive markets.

This leads to a more compelling suggestion, which is that exemption clauses are treated in a special way because contracting parties, especially less-experienced contracting parties, frequently fail to understand the full significance of such clauses. The argument is that exemption clauses are usually drafted in highly complex lawyer's language, and they are often buried deep in the small print of standard-form contracts. Moreover, it is difficult for legally unsophisticated parties to understand their significance, even when they are clearly drafted, since this requires first understanding what rights one would otherwise have under the law. A clause exempting liability for 'consequential' damages is meaningless unless one knows what 'consequential' means in law—a point on which even experienced lawyers may disagree.[26] Finally, because contracting parties typically anticipate performance rather than breach, there is a higher-than-average risk that they will underestimate the significance of exemption clauses. Unlike, say, a price term, exemption clauses deal with the legal consequences of far-off and unlikely events.[27]

The most persuasive explanation of the special rules that apply to unreasonable exemption clauses would seem to be that, for essentially 'cognitive' reasons, contracting parties are more likely to 'agree' to unreasonable exemption clauses than to other kinds of unreasonable clauses. This is not to suggest, of course, that all exemption clauses are unreasonable, nor that this explanation fully justifies the (sometimes quite severe) approach that courts have taken to such clauses. Sophisticated commercial parties are

---

[26] See *BHP Petroleum Ltd v. British Steel Plc* [1999] 2 Lloyd's Rep 583.

[27] This explanation is consistent with the fact that unreasonable exemption clauses would appear to be most common in contracts made in non-competitive markets. As noted above, monopolists rarely have complete freedom to set the terms of a contract. Thus even monopolists would prefer to 'hide' the true cost of their products. The main difference between a monopoly and a normal market in this regard is that in the latter competitors may decide to compete on the basis of guarantees, etc. For the reasons described above, 'price' competition is generally more effective, but there may be an incentive to compete on the basis of ancillary terms of a contract if a competitor is able to inform consumers of the significance of these terms (e.g. by an advertising campaign). Competition of this kind is in fact not uncommon today, particularly in markets for high-priced consumer goods (e.g. automobiles).

usually fully aware of what they are doing when they agree to exemption clauses, and as noted earlier, there are often good commercial reasons for such parties to make such agreements (in particular, that they can get a better contract price in return). It should also be stressed that consumers today are sometimes quite sophisticated about exemption clauses. Even an unsophisticated consumer will typically be aware that when he buys something at a cut-rate price he is not likely to receive the same rights and guarantees as if he paid the ordinary price. The point is merely that there are special reasons for scrutinizing such clauses.

As we shall see in Chapter 12, the common law does not contain a general principle against 'unfair surprises' (or against 'unfair terms' generally) and until very recently statute afforded no protection either. Not surprisingly, therefore, judges traditionally resorted to other techniques in order to deny effect to exemption clauses that they regarded as unreasonable. We have already discussed one of those methods, which was to hold that insufficient notice had been given of the incorporation of an exemption clause in an oral contract. Another device was to permit the aggrieved party to sue in tort someone other than the contracting party, such as an employee or contractor employed by the contracting party. The third party was generally held to be unable to protect himself by invoking the exemption clause, although the recently enacted Contracts (Rights of Third Parties) Act 1999 makes it easier for third parties to invoke such clauses.[28]

But the most important procedure by which the courts modified or nullified the effect of exemption clauses was by interpretation. Words have to be interpreted, and if the words appear to produce a result that seems unreasonable, it is often possible to give a strained interpretation to the words to avoid that result. Scores of cases from the 1950s onwards illustrated how judicial ingenuity was able to cut down the effects of drastic exemption clauses by strained interpretation. In the leading case, a lease specifying that the lessee shall 'not have any claim against the lessor for damage to goods' was held by the Privy Council to exclude only a claim for breach of contract and not a claim in tort for negligence[29]—though the words of the clause, read literally, were clearly wide enough to do just this.

Increasingly, though, it came to be felt that all these devices, and especially the methods of interpretation used in dealing with exemption clauses, were somewhat unsatisfactory. Although no doubt much justice was done by these means, they tended to go too far in some ways and not far enough in others. On the one hand, they did not distinguish between reasonable and unreasonable exemption clauses. As we have seen above, it is too simple to condemn all such clauses as unreasonable or unfair: most of them are

---

[28] See below, 359ff. [Ch 13].
[29] *Canada Steamship Lines Ltd v. The King* [1952] AC 292.

positively desirable in the interests of the parties or in the public interest. But strict interpretation and other devices mentioned above were used by the courts quite indiscriminately against all sorts of exemption clauses. On the other hand, these devices did not seem to go far enough in the other direction: if it was accepted that the courts ultimately had to give effect to clear language, the draftsmen of exemption clauses only had to go on wording their clauses more carefully, and in the end the courts would have had to give them effect.

What appeared to be needed was a substantive power to override unreasonable exemption clauses expressly on the grounds that they were unreasonable, and during the past half-century these powers have been increasingly forthcoming from Parliament. In 1964, the Hire-Purchase Act of that year first gave a substantial measure of protection to those who bought goods on hire-purchase; in 1973, similar protection was extended to purchasers of goods who paid cash, or who financed their purchases with loans from banks or other sources. More significantly, in 1977, the Unfair Contract Terms Act enacted a fairly comprehensive code on the subject of exemption clauses generally, and in 1994, the Unfair Terms in Consumer Contracts Regulations gave courts the power to invalidate unfair clauses, including unfair exemption clauses, in consumer contracts generally.

The 1977 Act and the 1999 Regulations are considered further in Chapter 12. Here it is sufficient to make two observations. First, the powers these legislative enactments gave judges to directly and openly invalidate exemption clauses thought to be unfair quite properly led courts to modify the way they approach the interpretation of exemption clauses. It has now been stressed by the House of Lords[30] that courts should no longer strain to interpret an exemption clause narrowly in order to avoid injustice, but should instead interpret the clause according to its ordinary meaning in the usual way. The clause can then be tested against any applicable criteria in the Unfair Contract Terms Act (or, now, the Unfair Terms in Consumer Contracts Regulations) and, if necessary, struck down. Unfortunately, it must also be added that the House of Lords appears also to have endorsed an old distinction between exemption clauses and limitation clauses,[31] which seems to imply that the former are still to be construed in a stricter manner than the latter. It is likely, however, that this will prove a temporary aberration: in the recent case of *Bank of Credit and Commerce International SA v. Ali*,[32] Lord Hoffmann made clear that his reference, in the *Investors Compensation* case discussed earlier, to the 'old intellectual baggage of legal interpretation' that

---

[30] *Photo Productions Ltd v. Securicor Transport Ltd* [1980] AC 827; *George Mitchell (Chesterhall) Ltd v. Finney Lock Seeds* [1983] 2 AC 803.

[31] *Ailsa Craig Fishing Co. v. Malvern Fishing Co.* [1983] 1 All ER 101.

[32] [2001] WLR 735.

has now been discarded, includes the old rules relating to the interpretation of exemption clauses.

The second point is that the problems thought to be raised by exemption clauses are undoubtedly less severe now than they were in the decades following the Second World War. Not only has British industry generally become far more competitive (with the result that consumers today are frequently offered a bewildering choice of guarantees, insurance, and other protection by vendors), but, as has already been noted, consumers (and consumer groups) are far more sophisticated, knowledgeable, and powerful than previously. The sometimes highly paternalist arguments and attitudes displayed in many of the earlier cases in this area should therefore be treated with caution today. Consumers and contracting parties generally are less in need of protection now than when the landmark cases in this area were decided.

6

Implied Terms

In the previous chapter we saw that contracting parties may themselves determine their contractual duties with great precision, in which event the function of the court is (in theory) merely to give effect to these self-imposed obligations. But even if it is assumed that the court will choose to enforce these obligations (see Chapters 9–12), there are several reasons why in practice its function is rarely thus restricted. First, the court must interpret the language used by the parties, a matter referred to in the last chapter. Secondly, legislation implies terms into certain categories of contracts as a matter of course. Thirdly, and finally, even the most carefully drafted contracts contain gaps. It is not possible to deal with all possible contingencies in a contract, and even if it were, it would be too costly to do so. In practice, therefore, no contract is complete, and many cover only the bare essentials. Of course, in some cases, the gaps that remain will be so large as to render the apparent contract unenforceable for uncertainty, as was explained in Chapter 3. Other times, the courts will decide that an apparent gap is not actually a gap, and that the contract should be enforced as it was written.[1] But in many cases, the courts will fill the gap by implying a term into the contract.

I. THE NATURE OF IMPLIED TERMS

Before exploring when and how courts imply terms into contracts, it may be helpful to describe briefly two of the more important issues in this area of the law. The first concerns the scope of the 'law' of implied terms. In the conventional understanding, the law of implied terms deals with those aspects of contracting parties' basic or primary obligations that cannot be directly explained by the contract's express terms. Thus, a vendor's obligation to provide goods of 'satisfactory' quality is explained on the ground that section 14(2) of the Sale of Goods Act 1979 implies such a term into all contracts of sale. Similarly, the reciprocal duty of 'trust and confidence' that employers and employees owe to each other arises because a term to this effect is implied as a matter of precedent into all employment contracts.[2] But the concept of implied terms is sometimes used to explain a much larger

[1] For example, if a contract to renovate a house is silent as to the builder's obligations to clean the site afterwards, the court might decide that the builder has no such obligation.
[2] *Mahmud v. Bank of Credit and Commerce International SA* [1998] AC 20.

group of legal rules. In particular, it is often argued that the rules on mistake, frustration, and discharge for breach are part of the law of implied terms; these rules, it is said, imply terms to the effect that one or both of the parties' obligations may be set aside under certain conditions. Some commentators go further still, arguing that the rules on remedies are part of the law of implied terms. The idea underlying these extensions of the concept is that the rules in question deal with situations that ordinarily do not arise in the life of a contract—for example, that the parties contracted on the basis of a fundamental misapprehension or that one party refused to perform her side of the contract—and for which the parties will therefore normally not have made explicit provision in their contract. In this view, the rules on, for example, remedies imply terms to fill these gaps.

This broader understanding of the law of implied terms will be discussed primarily in later chapters: the examples discussed in this chapter all fit within the conventional understanding of the concept. But it may be useful to mention now that the analysis of mistake, frustration, and discharge for breach in the next chapter effectively adopts an implied term explanation of these areas of the law.

The other main issue raised by implied terms concerns the extent to which implied terms are consistent with the classical view that it is the parties, not the courts, who determine the content of a contract. This issue focuses on the distinction between terms that are *implied-in-fact* and terms that are *implied-in-law*. The former are grounded in the parties' agreement and as such fit easily with the classical view. An example would be an implied term in a contract of sale that goods are to be delivered during ordinary business hours, even if the contractual document merely says that delivery should occur on a particular day. In such a case, the implied term follows as a matter of simple interpretation of what the parties actually said and agreed: it 'goes without saying'.

By contrast, implied-in-law terms are based not on the parties' agreement, but on a general policy that it is fair, (economically) efficient, or otherwise desirable that such a term be included. These kinds of implied terms are not easily reconciled with classical freedom of contract principles; they resemble tort duties more than contractual duties, at least as the latter are classically understood. The clearest examples of implied-in-law terms are mandatory terms, such as an employer's statutory obligation to pay female employees equal wages to those of male employees doing similar work.[3] Of course, many employers are perfectly willing to make such a promise, but the statutory requirement does more than just give effect to such intentions since it applies even if the employer specifically refuses to do so and the employee agrees to

---

[3] Section 1, Equal Pay Act 1970.

this refusal. The term is clearly based on a broader public policy—in this case, a policy against discrimination in the workplace. Implied-in-law terms thus challenge the classical idea that the content of a contract is set by the parties.

2. INDIVIDUALIZED IMPLIED TERMS

An individualized implied term is a 'one-off' term. Such terms are implied into specific contracts on the basis of considerations that, in theory anyway, are unique to those contracts. The general principle governing individualized implied terms is that they should be implied only when this is necessary to give 'business efficacy' to the agreement (the 'business efficacy' test) or if the matter is so obvious that it goes without saying (the 'officious bystander' test). A modern example of an implication of this kind is found in the decision of the House of Lords in *Harvela Investment Ltd v. Royal Trust Co. of Canada Ltd*[4] A trustee was negotiating for the sale of shares to two bidders. In order to ensure that the best price was obtained, the trustee invited the two bidders to make sealed bids stating the highest prices they were prepared to pay and undertook to sell to the highest bidder. One bidder offered £2,175,000, while the other bidder offered '£2,100,000 *or* £101,000 higher than the other bidder'. The question was whether this last bid was valid, or whether a referential bid was by ruled out by an implied term. The House of Lords held that it was implied in the original invitation that such bids could not be made—the whole point of asking for sealed bids was that each bidder had to state an amount.

In cases of this kind, it is generally assumed that the courts are implying terms in-fact, that is, that they are implying terms on the basis that they were tacitly agreed upon by the parties, rather than merely because they are fair, reasonable, or otherwise desirable. This seems broadly correct. The business efficacy test is explicitly described as a test for determining which terms are *necessary* to give business efficacy to an agreement, which is another way of saying 'necessarily following from what the parties did say'; the test is not satisfied merely by showing that a particular term is reasonable or fair in the circumstances. This is not to say that terms implied on the basis of the business efficacy or officious bystander tests are actually before the parties' minds in any conscious sense when they made their agreement. They might be, but this is not required in order that a term be classified as implied-in-fact. All communications rely on complex webs of assumptions and beliefs, most of which are not directly before speakers' minds. The philosopher Ludwig Wittgenstein made this point with a famous example:

---

[4] [1986] AC 207.

Someone says to me, 'Show the children a game.' I teach them gaming with dice, and the other says, 'I didn't mean that sort of game.' Must the exclusion of the game with dice have come before his mind when he gave the order?[5]

The answer to Wittgenstein's question, it seems clear, is 'no'. It is equally clear that similar questions, and answers, could be given in respect of the meaning of a contract. If the parties to a sale agreement stipulate that delivery will take place on a certain day, it just goes without saying—or thinking—that delivery should take place during normal working hours. Such a term is properly understood as flowing from the contract rather than from external standards of fairness or efficiency.

At the same time, it should not be assumed that courts are entirely unconcerned with external values when they imply individualised terms. The business efficacy and officious bystander tests are far from mechanical. In the very case that gave birth to the business efficacy test, *The Moorcock*,[6] a divided Court of Appeal's decision to imply a term relating to the condition of the sea-bed under the defendant's wharf was affirmed by only a bare majority in the House of Lords. And in *Harvela*, discussed above, the Court of Appeal had earlier concluded that business efficacy did *not* require an implication that referential bids were forbidden.

It is not a simple matter, however, to determine when and to what extent the courts' use of these tests has been influenced by their view of what terms would be reasonable (and not just necessary or obvious) in the circumstances. Judges do not usually explain what they are doing when applying these tests, and even when they do, their explanations cannot be accepted uncritically: judges sometimes adopt the (mistaken) view that any term which was not before the parties' minds or did not follow as a matter of strict logic from the express terms qualifies as implied-in-law. More generally, the line between interpretation and creation (or 'addition') is so fine that even experienced judges can have difficulty accurately describing what they are doing. Substantively, what is 'reasonable' (fair, efficient, etc.) is typically the same as what is necessary for 'business efficacy' or what 'goes without saying'. In *Staffs. Area Health Authority v. South Staffordshire Waterworks*[7] the court construed an agreement to supply water at a fixed price 'at all times hereafter' to mean 'at all times hereafter during the subsistence of the agreement'. These words entitled the suppliers to give notice to terminate the agreement, and then offer to enter into a new one at a much higher price. The term implied by the courts radically altered the apparent or literal meaning of the agreement, and did so in a way that appeared to provide for a much fairer agreement. It might seem natural to conclude, therefore, that the implied term was based not on the parties' intentions, but on the basis of external

---

[5] L. Wittgenstein, *Philosophical Investigations* (Oxford, 1972), 33.
[6] (1889) 14 PD 64.   [7] [1979] 1 WLR 203.

considerations. But the very fact that the agreement would have been patently unreasonable if such a term was not implied also supports the argument that the term went without saying. What goes without saying depends (as was noted earlier) on a broad network of assumptions and beliefs, including ordinary notions of what is reasonable; the very unfairness of a contract's literal terms may mean that it should be obvious to any reasonable listener that those terms were not meant to be understood literally.

3. STANDARDIZED IMPLIED TERMS

Standardized implied terms are implied on the basis that the contract in question falls into one of a number of well-recognized categories, such as sale of goods, hire-purchase, agency, employment, partnership, insurance, and so forth. The number and importance of such terms have increased dramatically over the last hundred years. Indeed, their number and importance is the main reason certain categories of contracts, such as employment, landlord and tenant, and even sale, are now regarded for most purposes as governed by distinct legal regimes, separate from the general law of contract. To a significant extent, each of these contracts has its own 'law', which is comprised primarily of implied terms.

Some standardized terms are mandatory, meaning that they cannot be excluded, even if both parties expressly agree. The obligations regarding quality and description imposed on vendors by the Sale of Goods Act 1979, for example, are mandatory for consumer contracts. Most terms implied into employment contracts, such as the employer's obligation to provide a safe workplace, also fall into this category. Standardized terms of this kind provide perhaps the clearest examples of implied-in-law terms. The courts impose them not in an attempt to give effect to the parties' intentions, but because they are directed by statute to do this. Nor does the relevant statute claim to give effect to the parties' intentions—if this were the case then parties would be able to exclude the terms by agreement. Such statutes give effect to broader public policy objectives, such as that of protecting perceived weaker parties.

But most standardized terms are non-mandatory. Such terms can, therefore, be excluded by the parties should they wish to do so; for example, commercial parties can (and often do) exclude the entire set of obligations imposed by the Sale of Goods Act 1979. But these terms are also conventionally described as implied-in-law terms. Indeed, this conclusion is often thought to be true almost by definition: non-mandatory standardised terms are implied not because of what the contracting parties specifically said or implied, but because of the general category of agreement that they entered. It is acknowledged, of course, that sophisticated parties are often aware in advance of such terms, and in this sense might be said to have consented to them, but it is rightly pointed out that such knowledge is not the *reason* such terms are implied: they are implied because the courts or legislature decided that in this kind of contract these terms should be implied unless the parties specify otherwise.

The conventional understanding of non-mandatory standardised terms is clearly correct in one important sense: a court's decision to imply such a term is based on a rule of law, rather than an interpretive inquiry. But this is not the end of the story: it must also be asked *why* the rule in question exists. Is it to give effect to the law's view of what is reasonable? Or is it to give effect to the parties' intentions? The answer is not obvious. This can be seen by examining the main grounds on which standardized terms are implied: judicial decision, custom, and legislation.

Judicial decision

Some non-mandatory standardized terms are implied as a matter of common law, that is to say, on the basis of previous judicial decisions (or 'precedents') which held that such terms should be implied into the relevant category of contract. Historically, this was the most important source of standardized terms, though today that position is taken by legislation.

In deciding whether to set such a precedent, the test is usually described in the same terms as the test for individualized terms: the relevant term must be *necessary* in order to make sense of the contract. The main difference, on the surface anyway, is that the test is applied to entire classes of contracts. But as was true with respect to individualized terms, it may be queried whether the courts are doing what they say they are doing when they apply this test. The leading case is *Liverpool City Council v. Irwin*[8] which concerned the contractual obligations of a local authority to tenants in a block of flats. The flats were the notorious 'piggeries' in Liverpool, which were eventually made uninhabitable by vandals, though at the time of the proceedings the flats were still fully used. The claimant's main complaint was that although the flats were ten storeys high the lifts were constantly out of order, and that even on the stairs lights were frequently broken or missing. The defendants replied that repairs could not keep pace with the vandals. The legal question was the extent of any obligation the defendants had with respect to the lifts and lights on the stairs. The claimant argued that an implied term should be read into a contract of lease requiring the landlord to maintain them, while the defendants contended that their only obligation was to enable the tenants to use the lifts and stairs without unnecessary risk of danger. In the Court of Appeal, Lord Denning said that a term could be implied whenever it was reasonable to do so, and on this basis held that the landlords were under an

---

[8] [1977] AC 239.

obligation to do what was reasonable to keep the lifts and lights in working order, but that this obligation was not breached on the facts. The House of Lords rejected Lord Denning's reasonableness standard, holding that a term could be implied only if it were strictly necessary to do so, but then went on to hold that this test was satisfied and that a term identical to that implied by Lord Denning could be implied.

The difference between the judges on this point seems somewhat unreal. It is obviously not strictly or literally *necessary* to have lifts in blocks of flats ten storeys high, though it would no doubt be exceedingly inconvenient not to have them. So 'necessary' really seems to mean 'reasonably necessary', and that must mean 'reasonably necessary having regard to the context and the price'.

This observation is borne out by the House of Lords decision in *Scally v. Southern Health and Social Services Board*.[9] The claimant was a National Health Service doctor who argued that there was an implied term in his contract of employment that his employers would notify him of some of the complex legal rights to acquire pension entitlements that he had under the statutory regulations governing his employment. Lord Bridge insisted that even in such a case of a standardised contract, a term of the kind sought could only be implied if it were *necessary* to the contract, but he held (and all the Law Lords concurred with him) that the test was satisfied on these facts. It is hard to take the finding seriously. The claimant *could* have found out his legal rights in other ways—he could have employed a solicitor, for instance, or at least consulted a trade union. Clearly, what Lord Bridge meant was that it was 'reasonably necessary' to imply the term in question, not that it was absolutely necessary. Indeed, Lord Bridge came close to admitting this when he wrote that there is a difference 'between the search for an implied term necessary to give business efficacy to a particular contract and the search, based on wider considerations, for a term which the law will imply as a necessary incident of a definable category of contractual relationship'.

This characterization of the test for implying standardized terms as one of 'reasonable necessity' may be thought clear proof that judges in such cases are attempting to give effect to their sense of what is reasonable as opposed to their views of what the parties' implicitly agreed to. But, as with individualized terms, the fact that a standardized term is reasonable is consistent with the conclusion that it 'goes without saying' in the agreement. This suggestion is not refuted by the fact that the terms now under consideration are implied on a category-by-category basis, because contracting parties themselves typically understand the meaning of their contracts using categories. The meaning of a contract depends on the context in which it is made, and this

[9] [1992] 1 AC 1004.

context, in turn, depends in large part on the category into which the contract fits. This is not to say that every standardized implied term is a term that goes without saying. But the same objection can be made to the idea that such terms are based on an external standard of reasonableness. The terms implied by the Sale of Goods Act 1979 may be reasonable for the vast majority of sale contracts, but they are not reasonable for *all* sales contracts. Indeed, each of the explanations we have been considering would fit the law better if standardized terms had the status of mere presumptions, as opposed to being excludable only by express words.[10]

Intertwined with this interpretive debate about the extent to which standardized terms are implied-in-fact as opposed to implied-in-law is a normative debate about whether courts are (or would be) *justified* in creating implied-in-law terms. Two arguments are frequently raised in support of intervention. One is that the process of contract formation cannot be relied upon to ensure that contract terms will be fair or efficient, freedom of contract being an ideal that is rarely realized in practice. The difficulty with this suggestion is that even if the premise is assumed, it is primarily an argument for *mandatory* standardized terms. The kinds of standardized terms now being discussed can be excluded by express terms, and so provide only weak protection against superior bargaining power. Their main value, in this regard, is to force stronger parties to be explicit about what they are doing.

A second argument that is frequently made to support the judicial imposition of implied-in-law contractual duties is that courts do so all the time in tort law. Again, however, the argument is easily overstated. The duties to act reasonably imposed by tort law are, for the most part, negative duties not to harm others. Consistent with the 'harm principle'—the idea that, exceptional cases aside, individuals should be left free to live their lives as they please so long as they do not harm others[11]—tort law does not generally impose *positive* duties, such as a duty to assist a neighbour, no matter how reasonable they might be. Standardized implied terms, by contrast, typically impose positive duties; the obligations imposed on vendors by the Sale of Goods Act 1979, for example, are nearly all positive duties. Another reason the comparison is misleading is that the parties to a contract have settled on an agreement; by implying-in-law a duty, a court is effectively changing the parties' bargain—the court is giving one party a legal right at the other's expense. Obviously, this should only be done on compelling grounds. Redistribution of income or wealth is normally an exercise for Parliament. Judges and the law are expected to be neutral as between different classes of the community. The rich are entitled to justice no less than

---

[10] The best explanation for why standardised terms do not have the status of mere presumptions appears to be that the current rule is easier to administer.

[11] Most famously articulated in J. S. Mill, *On Liberty* (repr. London, 1974).

the poor, landlords no less than tenants, employers no less than employees, consumer-credit companies no less than buyers.[12]

These observations are not meant to show, of course, that courts should never imply terms in-law into contracts. Although non-mandatory terms are of little value in cases of gross disparities in bargaining power, they may be useful in cases involving less serious imbalances. As noted above, such terms have the effect of forcing parties who want more advantageous terms to be explicit about what they are doing. Also, the analogy to duties imposed by tort law *does* work where the relevant duty is of the kind that tort law itself would be willing to impose absent a contract—for example, an employer's duty not to injure his employee. Indeed, assuming that the relevant contract does not expressly or impliedly exclude the relevant liability, it would seem more appropriate to treat the issue in such as a case as a matter of pure tort law, as is actually done in cases of the employer's duty not to injure. This would make it clear that the validity of such duties does not depend on showing that they flow from the parties' intentions. Finally, there are cases (as we have seen) where the contract is silent as regards the relevant issue—the contract contains a 'gap'. In such cases, the courts must either imply a term on the basis of external standards or deny enforcement altogether.

Custom

The arguments just discussed help to explain why, even today, many judges are reluctant to imply terms (standardized or otherwise) unless they feel that the parties would or should have expected these terms to be a part of their agreement as a matter of course. An apparent exception is where terms are implied on the basis of custom. Assuming there is no inconsistency with the words or nature of the contract, the custom of a particular trade, industry, or market may be deemed to be incorporated into a contract made in that trade, industry, or market, even where the affected party was unaware of the custom when the contract was made. But this is only an apparent exception because custom is precisely that part of the context of a contract that most commonly

---

[12] But adding an implied term may not be redistributive in the long run, because once the new decision establishes itself as law, prices will be adjusted. This is illustrated by the problems concerning the liability of surveyors for negligent valuations conducted on behalf of building societies and other lenders. When a borrower was first held entitled to sue a surveyor in tort for negligence (*Yianni v. Edwin Evans & Sons* [1982] QB 438), the result was clearly redistributive in that particular case. The borrower had not paid an appropriate charge for the survey, including a 'premium' entitling him to rely upon it. Later, some surveyors' charges were adjusted to reflect this fact, while other surveyors attempted to disclaim their liability. Since then, the House of Lords has decided that such disclaimers are generally invalid under the Unfair Contract Terms Act, a point discussed again in Chapter 12. The end result was to change the way the market works in this sort of case. Borrowers will now have the right to sue surveyors for negligence, but they will also pay a little more for their surveys to cover the insurance cost of this form of liability.

goes without saying. This is the case even where the affected party was not aware of the custom at the time of making the contract. Interpretation, recall, is an objective exercise: the meaning of a contract, including its implied-in-fact terms, depends on what the contract is objectively (publicly, reasonably) understood to mean—and that objective meaning is determined in part by the customs of the relevant trade, industry, or market.

Legislation

The third, and now most important, source of standardized implied terms is legislation. Most of the terms implied in contracts of sale, service, employment, tenancy, and so on derive from statutes. As such, the basis on which such terms are implied might be expected to be more removed from an interpretive enquiry than is true of custom or precedent-based terms. And it is indeed true that much of the recent legislation in this area was drafted with the frank intention of protecting weaker parties. But it must be kept in mind that most of the best-known examples of (non-mandatory) legislated terms—such as those found in the Sale of Goods Act 1979—were first regarded merely as codifications of existing customary terms, in other words, terms that went without saying. At the time the relevant legislation was passed, these terms were already being implied into contracts on the basis of custom or the business efficacy test. Even protective legislation often duplicates terms that many would argue ought to go without saying. In the end, it is unclear whether the law's determination of what is reasonable in a contract is ever divorced entirely from an interpretive enquiry into the meaning of the contract.

4. A DUTY TO ACT IN GOOD FAITH?

It is worth adding a word about an implication which is *not* made as a matter of course in English law—that contractual duties will be performed in good faith. Good faith is, of course, difficult to define or even to summarise, although it is often easy to recognize examples of bad faith. We noted earlier that there is no general duty of good faith in the making of contracts in English law; the law relating to performance falls in place alongside that relating to formation.

The absence of any general duty of good faith can be explained, at least in part, by the commercial context in which the common law developed (as discussed in Chapter 1). One feature of this context is that English judges have long been wary of open-ended legal principles: the ideal of the rule of law is understood to require that individuals (and companies) be able to ascertain in advance, and with reasonable certainty, the extent of their legal duties, and this is thought to be impossible in the case of duties such as one to act in good faith. Related to this is a fear of 'legal moralism'—using the legal system to enforce the full range of a community's moral and ethical standards (as opposed to merely enforcing rules that prohibit harmful behaviour). The broader concept of good faith appeared (at least to nineteenth-century judges) to be equivalent to a general recognition of ideas of moral right and equity in the law, and as such was thought inconsistent with strict commercial dealings.

These fears are probably exaggerated. Many legal systems impose a general duty of good faith in the performance (as well as the making) of contracts and have encountered little difficulty in circumscribing the scope of such a duty. But more importantly, the stability and predictability of the law are primarily determined by a country's broader judicial culture, rather than by the wording of its legal rules, and the same is true of its propensity towards legal moralism. In short, the prevailing sentiment among English judges regarding the rule of law and legal moralism would most likely limit any good faith requirement to a scope commensurate with English traditions.

There are two other aspects of English law and contracting practices that make it unlikely judges would use a good faith doctrine to introduce radical changes into English law. The first is that judges already are able to deal satisfactorily with much of what, in other systems, might be dealt with by a doctrine of good faith by implying terms and applying existing doctrines such as misrepresentation, notice, and fiduciary duties—all of which are broadly defined in English law. A second aspect is that English contracting practices, particularly among commercial parties, operate on the assumption that the parties will negotiate for any protection they desire; this is one reason that English contracts tend to be more detailed than those found in countries with good faith doctrines. It follows that when such protection is not included in the contract, it is reasonable to assume that this was intentional. Of course, this assumption may be questioned where the party needing protection is a consumer or small businessperson—the arguments for a general duty of good faith are much stronger in the consumer context—but in the case of commercial contracts drafted by legally sophisticated parties, English judges would almost certainly find little room for good faith duties.

Finally, there is one broad class of contracts where relief for bad faith performance is routinely available in practice, even if not as a matter of strict law. Disputes arising in connection with contracts entered into by consumers or small businesses for financial 'products', such as mortgages, insurance, pensions, investments, and so on, may now be brought before the Financial Ombudsman. As is discussed in more detail in Chapters 9 and 12, the Ombudsman has wide-ranging powers to make whatever orders are necessary (including ordering payments up to £100,000) to reach a 'fair and equitable result'. Though not usually described in this language, the complaint in many of the large number of cases brought before the Ombudsman (nearly 100,000 in 2004) is essentially that the financial firm performed in bad faith. Typical cases involve complaints that the firm unfairly terminated or refused to make payments under an insurance policy, unfairly varied interest rates in a loan arrangement, or failed to provide consumers with information necessary for them to take advantage of their rights under their contracts. The reports issued by the Ombudsman's office make clear that generous relief is available in cases of this kind. Indeed, the scope of such relief goes beyond that typically available in legal systems that enforce duties to perform contracts in good faith.

7

The Force and Scope of Contractual Obligations: Standards of Care, Mistake, Frustration, Breach, and Notice

IN examining how courts construe the content of a contract, we have focused up until now on determining what the contract obliges the parties to do or not do. For instance, we have discussed the obligation of a vendor to deliver goods of satisfactory quality and of a purchaser to pay the contract price. In practice, however, courts are equally concerned with a second task—identifying the circumstances in which those obligations are not binding. In many sale of goods cases, for example, it will be clear that the vendor did not deliver: the dispute will concern whether, in those particular circumstances, the vendor was still bound to make that delivery. These two issues are, of course, closely related: a complete description of a vendor's contractual obligations will specify the situations in which the goods must be delivered, and so make clear in which situations non-delivery is not a breach of contract. But the courts have long treated this second issue as raising a series of distinct questions, each of which is subject to an apparently unique set of rules.

I. STRICT DUTIES IN THE LAW OF CONTRACT

The first and perhaps most important question that arises in examining the extent of the parties' duties under a contract is whether a party is to be held liable for a breach that occurs through no fault of his own, that is to say neither by wilful wrongdoing nor failure to take reasonable care. But although this question has been extensively discussed in the law of tort, it has been largely ignored in the law of contract. As a matter of strict law, the question is generally thought to have a straightforward answer: contractual obligations are absolute, and absence of fault is no defence.[1] Thus a shopkeeper who sells goods made by a reputable manufacturer may be liable for a breach of the duty to provide goods of satisfactory quality even though she had no possible means of knowing whether the conditions had been complied

---

[1] *Raineri v. Miles* [1981] AC 1050 at 1086 (Lord Edmund-Davies).

with.[2] The apparent exceptions to this rule—such as the presumption that lawyers, doctors, and other professionals are liable only if they fail to use reasonable care—are explained on the basis that the promise (or agreement) in question was in fact a promise merely to use reasonable care. Moreover, the question of whether a regime of strict liability is justified is not generally thought to be difficult or important; it is usually assumed (if the issue is discussed at all) that strict liability flows directly from the fact that contracts are created by promises and agreements.

The justification for strict liability

On closer inspection, the strict liability principle raises a number of difficult questions. The first is essentially moral: *why* does contract law adopt a strict liability standard when in the law of tort defendants are found liable only if they have failed to use 'reasonable care'? Admittedly, some tort duties are strict—for example, employers are strictly liable for their employees' torts—but such duties are considered exceptions in need of special justification, while the general rule is widely regarded as morally justified. Why should a different standard be applied to contractual obligations?

The usual answer is that by making a contract the parties effectively agree to a standard of strict liability. More specifically, by undertaking to bring about a certain result—the delivery of goods, construction of a building—the contracting party accepts the risk of non-performance. Indeed, the allocation of such risks is said to be one of the primary functions of a contract. This explanation is indeed consistent with the ordinary understanding of a promise or agreement. It is widely understood that by making a promise the promisor assumes responsibility for not bringing about the promised result (unless the promise was only to use reasonable care). This fact alone is a sufficient justification for strict liability: if it is part of the ordinary understanding of a promise (or agreement) that the promisor accepts the risk of non-performance, a party who makes a contractual promise can hardly complain when the courts order him to pay compensation for his failure to perform, faultless or not. But it still may be asked in what sense the failure to bring about a contractually specified result is actually a 'wrong' if the failure was not the promisor's fault in any way. To say that the promisor is 'responsible' for the consequences of non-performance does not mean that non-performance is necessarily a wrong: a parent's responsibility for her child's education does not depend on that parent having acted wrongly. Of

---

[2] In *Grant v. Australian Knitting Mills* [1936] AC 85, for instance, a shopkeeper who sold pants containing (unknown to him) an excess of sulphites was held liable for damages of £2,450 to the claimant who contracted dermatitis from wearing the pants. The manufacturers were also held liable (in tort) and it is probable that the shopkeeper would have been entitled to an indemnity from them.

course, the answer may be that breach of contract is a 'wrong' only in a special sense of this term. That is, breach of contract may not be a 'moral' wrong in the sense that an ordinary tort or crime is a moral wrong. This interpretation might be thought consistent with the fact that even a deliberate breach of contract does not attract criminal sanctions or even punitive damages—though it still leaves unanswered the question of *why* this definition is adopted. Strict liability torts, as has already been mentioned, are generally thought to require special justification.

An alternative suggestion is that, despite what courts traditionally say, contractual liability is not actually strict. In case of faultless non-performance, the legal wrong consists not in failing to perform the 'primary' contractual obligation, but rather in the failure to accept *responsibility* for the consequences of non-performance. It is the failure to take responsibility, either by substitute performance or by paying compensation, that justifies an order of damages. In this view, then, an ordinary contractual undertaking is in effect two undertakings: (1) an undertaking to use one's best efforts to bring about the promised result; and (2) an undertaking to make good whatever losses might be suffered if, despite one's best efforts, the promised result is not achieved. It follows that the justification for ordering compensatory damages in a contract claim is either that the defendant was at fault in failing to perform his primary obligation *or, if he was not at fault in this way*, that he was at fault in failing to compensate.[3]

The obvious objection to this interpretation is that it is inconsistent with what judges say they are doing when they award damages for breach: what judges say is that non-performance of the primary obligation is (always) a wrong, and that such non-performance is a sufficient basis on which to award damages. It is true that, in practice, the distinction between a contracting party's primary and secondary obligation will rarely be important. As a matter of general law, bankruptcy is the only basis on which non-payment of a debt is excusable. Thus where a solvent defendant who has failed to perform his primary contractual obligation further fails or refuses to pay compensation, it may be argued that fault is established automatically, without need of proof beyond the fact of non-payment.[4] But if this is the real explanation, it is strange that judges have never acknowledged it.

---

[3] This should not be confused with O. W. Holmes's famous view that contracting parties have a *choice* as to whether to perform or pay damages: 'The Path of the Law' (1897) 10 Harvard LR 462. The explanation above supposes that there is a duty to perform the primary obligations and that the intentional or careless failure to perform is a wrong.

[4] This is not quite right, since a defendant might reasonably—but mistakenly—believe that he had performed the contract. The law's refusal to admit such a defence is explicable either as a consequence of the general rule that ignorance of the law is no defence or on the basis that in such cases an order to pay 'damages' is in reality an order to specifically perform the defendant's secondary obligation.

Exceptions to the normal rule

The second main issue raised by the strict liability rule is how to explain the cases in which courts make an exception, that is, where courts conclude that the relevant obligation is an obligation only to use reasonable care. The exception is most commonly made for contracts in which professionals give advice or perform a service, such as the typical contract with a doctor, lawyer, or architect. These kinds of professionals are not generally treated as 'warranting' the soundness of the advice that they give nor of 'guaranteeing' results, and so will be liable for breach of contract only if they have acted negligently. Moreover, even where they are liable, damages may be reduced because they are subject to a different standard of liability. For instance, a surgeon who is liable for performing an operation negligently will be liable only to the extent that she has made her patient's condition worse; she will not be liable for damages representing the difference between the patient's original condition and the condition he would have been in if the operation had been properly performed.

Contracts with professionals sometimes stipulate expressly that the professional is only promising to use 'best efforts' or 'reasonable care', but a fault-based standard is applied even where the contract is silent. This result is usually explained on the basis that it was understood by the parties that the relevant obligation was to use reasonable care—in other words, that the contract contains an implied in-fact term to this effect. Thus, it is said that anyone purchasing a service or advice from a professional is likely to appreciate that she is purchasing the professional's skills and abilities rather than a particular result. In most cases, this assumption seems plausible. But the application of a fault-based standard to such contracts can also be explained as a term implied *in-law* on the basis that it is fair, efficient, or otherwise desirable from the courts' perspective. For example, it is often said that it is unfair to make doctors or lawyers responsible for results that they cannot control, or that to do so is inefficient as it will induce overly cautious behaviour. Alternatively—and more critically—it is sometimes suggested that the different standard applied to professionals is the product of a class bias: judges sympathize with lawyers and other professionals, and so attempt to protect them from liabilities they happily impose on builders, mechanics, and others employed in the 'trades'. In support of this view it is noted that courts refuse to hold professionals strictly liable even with respect to routine and straightforward services, such as a routine sterilization operation,[5] where clients may reasonably believe that they have been guaranteed a successful result, and not merely competent services. Another suggestion is that the real distinction is between defendants who are individuals (as professionals are)

---

[5] See *Eyre v. Measday* [1986] 1 All ER 488 and *Thake v. Maurice* [1986] QB 644.

and defendants who are companies, the courts being more willing to hold companies to a strict standard.

One reason it is difficult to explain the basis on which such decisions are made is that the courts rarely articulate their reasons. Instead, they explain their decisions in 'conceptual' language: they place the case in a certain legal category and then apply the rules appropriate to that category. The decision appears to be dictated by pure logic, but a choice is actually made in the initial categorization. Thus an anaesthetist in a hospital who injects an anaesthetic which has been contaminated in a manner which could not have been reasonably foreseen is not liable because he is not at fault.[6] But a veterinary surgeon who inoculates cattle with contaminated serum is liable despite all due care and skill on his part.[7] Similarly, an architect is liable only for negligence—so if he tells the builder to use a certain material which turns out to be unfit for use (despite all due care), he will not be liable.[8] If, however, the builder himself selects unsuitable material (despite all due care), he is liable. Indeed, a builder is liable even if he designs and constructs the whole work.

In addition to cases in which the parties' obligations are treated as obligations only to use reasonable care, there are two other classes of cases in which promisors may be absolved from liability where their failure to perform is not due to their fault. First, where the performance of the contract proves impossible, either because of pre-existing facts or because of unforeseeable developments occurring without anybody's fault, the courts have been loath to hold a contracting party liable, especially in the latter case. In other words, the law does not usually treat a person who has contracted to do something as having taken the risk that the whole performance may prove utterly impossible.

But impossibility is too narrow a concept to explain all the decisions which the courts have made in this area. Thus a second category in which performance may be excused is where, although not necessarily impossible, it would seem excessively hard on one of the parties. Sometimes this is the result of pre-existing facts which were unknown to the parties, and sometimes it is the result of subsequent events which were not expected or foreseen. In the former case, the issue is said to be whether the contract is void for 'common mistake'; in the latter case, the issue is whether the contract is 'frustrated'. The treatment of these two issues in the law books typically assumes that they are separable not just from each other but also from the law relating to interpretation and implied terms. The 'doctrines' of common mistake and frustration are usually thought to be concerned with a contract's validity,

---

[6] *Roe v. Minister of Health* [1954] 2 QB 66.   [7] *Dodd v. Wilson* [1946] 2 All ER 691.
[8] But for a rather special case, see *Greaves & Co. (Contractors) v. Baynham, Meikie & Partners* [1975] 1 WLR 1095, where architects were held to have warranted the soundness of a design.

not its content. But as we shall see, these doctrines can also both be understood as implying terms that define the scope and extent of contractual obligations. Hence, these two issues are dealt with in the ensuing sections of this chapter.

2. MISTAKE AND PRE-EXISTING FACTS

The courts' willingness to excuse a mistaken party from his contractual obligation depends on the kind of mistake that he made. In Chapter 3, we discussed the legal significance of mistakes concerning the terms of a contract, the identities of the parties, or the fact that a contract was being entered at all. In this chapter, the focus is mistakes concerning the existence, value, or other characteristics of the subject matter of the contract. If I purchase a painting that I and the vendor believed to be an old master, can I return the painting if it turns out to be a fake? Or suppose that I arrange the hire of a bus to take my friends to a football match only to discover that the match was cancelled an hour before I made the arrangement—am I still obliged to pay for the bus? In general, the courts' answer to such questions has been that the mistake is irrelevant and the contract has full force and effect. But there are exceptions, and these exceptions have attracted considerable attention from courts and commentators alike.

When is a mistake 'fundamental'?

The basic rule is usually stated to be that the contract is void if the mistake is fundamental and is shared by both parties. A number of questions are raised by this statement, but the first is what is meant by 'fundamental'. The mistakes in the above examples are probably not fundamental, though it may be difficult to explain why. Judges have occasionally attempted to define 'fundamental'—for example in *Associated Japanese Bank v. Crédit du Nord SA*,[9] Steyn J. stated that to be fundamental a mistake must 'render the subject matter of the contract essentially and radically different from the subject matter which the parties believed to exist'. But such attempts add little to the basic concept and in practice the term is explained by illustrations. The leading case is *Bell v. Lever Bros*,[10] where the defendant had been the manager of a large company under a contract which still had some years to run. Although the defendant had rendered valuable services to the company, the directors wanted to reorganise their business such that they would have no further use for him. They therefore paid him £30,000 for loss of office though this was substantially more than he would have earned even if he had worked his contract out to the end. It was then discovered that the defendant had been guilty of certain breaches of his contract that would have justified

[9] [1988] 3 All ER 902.   [10] [1932] AC 161.

his dismissal without any compensation. It was nevertheless held that the claimants could not recover the £30,000. The company's mistaken belief that they had no right to terminate the defendant's contract (which belief the defendant was found to have shared) was not sufficiently fundamental to justify setting aside the agreement.

Bell v. Lever Bros. is usually thought to show that mistakes will rarely be regarded as fundamental, since the claimants would have never agreed to the payment had they been aware of the defendant's breach of contract. This interpretation may overlook that the payment appears to have been made partly as a reward for the value of past services rendered by the defendant, which were considerable and which were in no way affected by his technical breaches of contract. But it remains true that successful pleas of mistake are rare. One famous example is usually thought to be *Couturier v. Hastie*,[11] where the seller sold a cargo of corn which the parties believed to be on its way to England, but which had in fact become overheated and then sold by the master of the ship en route. The House of Lords held that the buyer was not liable to pay the price of the cargo, and it is generally assumed that the seller likewise would not have been liable for damages had the buyer suffered some loss from non-delivery. Thus the contract in this case is usually portrayed as having been void and, although the court never mentioned 'mistake', the reason given is that the parties had made a fundamental mistake. This interpretation was subsequently fixed in the law by section 6 of the Sale of Goods Act (now the Act of 1979), which stipulates that a contract for the sale of goods that have perished is void.

This is a dubious interpretation of *Couturier v. Hastie*: the court's decision is perfectly consistent with the conclusion that the contract is valid, and that the buyer could successfully have brought an action for damages. Moreover, even if the orthodox interpretation is correct, section 6 is too broad. In view of the revolution in methods of communication that has taken place since 1856, a seller who sells goods in circumstances similar to those in *Couturier v. Hastie* today would, absent section 6, probably be to blame for not knowing what had happened. The court would likely conclude that, despite the apparent seriousness of the mistake, the relevant risk was assumed by the vendor. Section 6 cases aside, the modern approach is better represented by *McRae v. Commonwealth Disposals Commission*,[12] an Australian case in which the defendant sold the claimant a shipwrecked tanker stated to be on a certain reef. Unknown to either party, the tanker did not actually exist (nor for that matter did the reef), but the court refused to set the contract aside for mistake. On the contrary, they held that the defendant had impliedly accepted responsibility for the existence of the tanker, and so was liable for breaking its

[11] (1856) 5 HLC 673.   [12] (1950) 84 CLR 377.

promise that it existed. The Australian equivalent of section 6 did not apply because the ship did not perish—it never existed at all.

A second, closely related group of cases in which pleas of mistake have been successful involve contracts that are not capable of being performed at all. For instance, in one case a contract was set aside under which a party agreed to lease a salmon fishery that, unknown to both parties, he already owned.[13] It should not be assumed, however, that 'impossible' contracts will always be void for mistake: as the case of *McRae* shows, it will often be found that one party promised, that is to say guaranteed, that performance was possible, in which case the contract is valid and gives rise to damages.

The category of contracts for the sale of non-existent goods and contracts that are impossible to perform nearly exhausts the class of contracts in which mistake has been pleaded successfully. In particular, a mistake regarding the value (or cost) of the object of performance—as occurred in *Bell v. Lever Bros*—is almost never considered fundamental.[14] A rare counter-example is the *Associated Japanese Bank v. Crédit du Nord SA*[15] case. One JB entered into a transaction with the claimants under which he sold four large machines to them for over £1,000,000, which they then leased back to him. Commercially such a transaction is not unusual—it is simply a way of raising money, rather like a mortgage of goods. But what was unusual in this case was that the four machines did not exist at all, and the whole arrangement was a fraud by JB. However (as commonly happens in such cases), the fraudulent party was unable to repay the money when the fraud was discovered, and the claimants sued the defendants who had guaranteed the performance of JB's obligations under the leaseback transaction. The defendants argued that their guarantee was void because they and the claimants had supposed that the whole arrangement was about four specific machines which did not exist and, consequently, the guarantee imposed wholly different risks on the defendants from those they thought they were undertaking. Of course, as between JB and the claimants there could hardly be any doubt that JB was actually warranting the existence of the machines, but the guarantors were not in the same position as JB, and there was no reason to hold that they were expressly warranting the existence of the machines. Was it then reasonable to impose on them the risk that they did not exist? Steyn J. held that it was not, and that the contract was void because of the mistake. The decision may have been influenced by the fact that, while the contract was not actually for the sale or lease of non-existent goods, the relevant mistake appeared to be similar to those made in cases covered by section 6 of the Sale of Goods Act 1979. In

---

[13] *Cooper v. Phibbs* (1867) LR 2 HL 149.

[14] Most of the counter-examples were decided under the now-discredited doctrine of 'mistake in equity' (discussed below, 180–81), and so can no longer be considered good law.

[15] Above n. 9.

more straightforward cases involving mistakes about the cost or value of performance, for instance a mistake regarding the provenance of a painting that is the subject of a contract of sale, the contract will almost certainly not be set aside.[16]

The juridical basis of the law of mistake

Academic discussion of the law in this area usually begins with the question of why pleas of mistake are so rarely successful, but the first question that ought to be asked instead is why such pleas ever succeed at all. Assuming that fraud, duress, or other wrongdoing cannot be proven, why does the existence of a mistake ever justify a court in releasing parties from their obligations? Why, indeed, is there a doctrine of 'mistake' at all?

Once again, this question is not easily answered. According to orthodox doctrine, a fundamental mistake makes a contract void *ab initio*, that is to say, a fundamental mistake is regarded as a defect of formation, something that prevents the apparent contract from even coming into existence. Yet it is unclear how a mistake could have this effect. If contracting parties reach agreement to do or not do certain things, they will have made an agreement: nothing else is required. To be sure, mistakes regarding terms, identity, or the fact that one is undertaking an obligation at all can, as we saw in Chapter 3, prevent a contract from forming. But these are not the kinds of mistakes that are at issue in cases like *Bell v. Lever Bros*. Moreover, it is unnecessary to invoke any doctrine of 'mistake' to explain the results in these cases—they flow, as we saw, from the ordinary rules of offer and acceptance.

The most common suggestion for *why* a fundamental mistake makes a contract void draws on the civilian origins of the doctrine: a fundamental mistake negates consent. This suggestion does not account for common law's refusal to give relief for unilateral mistakes—if consent is the concern, it should be sufficient to show that one party made a mistake. But the more fundamental objection to this suggestion is that, while it may be true that mistake can negate 'consent'—this is why 'informed' consent is required for medical operations—it is not clear that contractual obligations are actually grounded in consent. As we have seen, contracts are typically created by making promises or agreements—not by 'consenting'. The distinction is crucial because it is of the essence of a promise (and an agreement) that it is binding even if the promisor later regrets the promise. Stated differently, by making promises, promisors impliedly accept the risk that they are acting on the basis of imperfect information.

The difficulty of explaining how a mistake could prevent a contract from coming into existence leads to a second explanation of mistake cases. According to the 'implied term' explanation, the effect of an operative

---

[16] *Leaf v. International Galleries* [1950] 2 KB 86.

mistake is not to prevent a contract from forming, but merely to release the parties from their apparent obligations under the (valid) contract. More specifically, the explanation is that the contract contains an implied term— either implied-in-fact or implied-in-law—that the stipulated duties are binding only if the relevant factual assumption is true. Thus the result in the *Japanese Bank* case would be explained on the basis that the contract should be read *as if* it contained an express term to the effect that the parties' obligations were conditional on the existence of the four machines.

The implied-term explanation of mistake is consistent with the general law on implied terms: it is obviously possible for a contract to contain an express term making performance conditional on the truth of a factual assumption, so it must also be possible for a contract to contain an implied term to this effect. It also fits with the widespread view that the underlying issue in mistake cases concerns the allocation of risk—indeed the allocation-of-risk explanation of mistake cases is another name for the implied-term explanation. The main objection to the implied-term explanation is that it cannot explain why an operative mistake should make a contract *void*. To be sure, judges sometimes say that a contract is subject to an 'implied condition' that it will be 'void' if it was entered on the basis of a mistake, but terms, implied or otherwise, can have effect only if they are in valid contracts. The implied-term explanation assumes that when courts give relief in mistake cases they are *enforcing* a valid contract, not setting it aside. Indeed, the implied-term explanation supposes that what is called the doctrine of mistake is merely one part of the law dealing with the interpretation and implication of contractual terms. None of this fits with the orthodox account of mistake cases.

The objection just described may not, however, be as significant as it appears. In most cases, there is no practical difference between concluding that an (apparent) contract is void and concluding that the obligations under a valid contract are not due: in each case, the primary (and usually only) consequence is that the parties are not liable for non-performance or, if they have performed, that they must undo the transaction. In these cases, the above objection seems purely semantic: the implied-term explanation is consistent with what courts are actually doing even if it is not consistent with what they say they are doing.

Admittedly, there are situations in which the orthodox rule that an operative mistake makes a contract void has practical consequences; in particular, where a contract is void for mistake any third party who obtains property that was transferred under the apparent contract will not receive good title, and so must normally return the property (or its value) to the original owner. This result cannot be explained by the implied-term theory. But this may be thought a small defect in comparison given that the current rule seems transparently unjust. The current rule sacrifices the interests of third parties to those of parties who, though also innocent, had the possibility at least of correcting the relevant mistake. As between the original owner and the third party, the third party's claim to the property is therefore normally stronger on the merits.[17] Moreover, the current rule causes other problems, since it seems clear that one reason courts are so reluctant to admit a plea of mistake is precisely because doing so may unfairly harm the interests of third parties.

The implied-term theory of mistake is consistent with regarding the relevant terms as implied in-fact, implied in-law, or a combination of in-fact and in-law. This point must be stressed because when judges discuss the law of mistake they often suppose that insofar as relief is given on the basis of an implied term the courts must be enforcing the parties' actual, if implicit, agreement.[18] As a matter of legal terminology, this is clearly wrong: the non-excludable terms regarding quality and so forth that are imposed into all consumer sale contracts are universally described as 'implied terms' even though no one supposes that they rest on the parties' actual agreement. They are implied-in-law. There is no reason that an implied term to the effect that the obligations in a contract are conditional on certain factual assumptions being true could not be of the same kind.

As it turns out, both versions of the implied-term account of mistake—the implied-in-fact version and the implied-in-law version—are prima facie plausible. Of course, the implied-in-fact explanation looks implausible if it is supposed that the relevant term must have been before the parties' minds when they made their agreement: a mistake is unlikely to be regarded as fundamental if it can be shown that the parties were contemplating its possibility when they formed their contract. But as has already been noted, the task of interpreting a contract, including the implication of in-fact terms, is not the same thing as identifying what was in the parties' minds when they made the contract. The meaning of a contract, including the existence of implied terms, is a matter of determining what the contract publicly or 'objectively' means, including, in particular, the objective meaning of the context in which the contract was formed. Thus, if a particular assumption or norm 'goes without saying' in the relevant industry or community, it will often be appropriate to conclude that the parties agreed to this assumption or norm even if they were not thinking about it when they made their contract. Indeed, this is the reason that (as we have seen in other contexts) both the in-fact and in-law versions of the implied-term theory are prima facie plausible. The situations in which it is reasonable (i.e. 'fair', 'efficient') to excuse the parties from performance, and thus to imply *in-law* a term to this

---

[17] The third party can bring a claim against the apparent purchaser for breach of section 12 of the Sale of Goods Act 1979 (the implied condition regarding title) but in many cases this claim will be worthless.

[18] See, e.g., paras. 73–81 in *Great Peace Shipping Ltd v. Tsavliris Salvage (International) Ltd* [2002] 3 WLR 1617.

effect, are usually the same situations in which it goes without saying that performance should be excused. In the *Japanese Bank* case, for example, the court clearly thought it would be unfair to hold the bank to their guarantee of a loan to purchase equipment which, unknown to them, did not exist and in respect of which they had less knowledge than the creditor. But they also clearly thought that the parties could not reasonably have assumed that their agreement was intended to be performed in such a case. The same is true for most of the cases involving the sale of non-existent goods: the sale of a specific chattel is normally based on the assumption that the chattel exists. It will also often be clear to both parties that the seller is not responsible for this state of facts. So if the parties were asked at the time of contracting whether their contract was binding if the goods did not exist, they would probably both have replied 'of course not'. For similar reasons, the results in such cases can be defended on the basis that they are fair or efficient. Where the buyer is as well-placed as the seller to discover the truth, it is likely that, had the parties been asked to include a term dealing with this issue, they would have specified that their obligations were conditional on the existence of the goods. Such a term will normally minimize the overall cost associated with the risk of the facts turning out differently.

In the end, the best explanation of the law in this area is probably a mixture of the implied-in-fact and the implied-in-law accounts. More specifically, it seems clear that courts typically begin by considering whether the contract's express or implied-in-fact terms allocate the relevant risk to either of the parties. In most cases this is likely to provide an answer—which is why it is rare for pleas of mistake to be discussed in judgments, let alone to succeed. But in some cases it is not possible, even when taking into account all relevant norms, customs, and the like, to determine how the relevant risk was allocated. Even on an expansive understanding of implied-in-fact terms, contracts will contain gaps or at least be vague on the relevant issue. Thus, at some point—though it is usually impossible to say exactly which point— court will need to consider not merely what the parties intended, but also what seems reasonable in the circumstances.

Why is relief for mistake so rare?

Given what has been said above, it is perhaps not surprising that pleas of mistake rarely succeed. The risks associated with most mistakes, fundamental or otherwise, are in fact usually allocated by the contract to one of the parties. Of course, it is relatively rare that a contract states expressly that the parties' obligations are or are not conditional on the truth of a factual assumption. But where the contract is silent, then, consistent with English courts' general approach to interpreting contracts, the usual assumption, particularly in commercial contexts, is that the contract is meant to be read strictly and literally. Thus, if a purchaser of a painting does not make the purchase conditional on, say, the painting's origin, the assumption is that the promise to pay is to be interpreted strictly—free of any exception. Putting the point in another way, courts and drafters assume that if contracting parties want the kind of protection that would be provided by a broader definition of 'fundamental', they will say so in their contracts. Furthermore, even in cases where the contract genuinely contains a gap or ambiguity there is another reason that the courts will typically refuse to imply (in-law) a term affording relief. The courts are naturally hesitant to allow parties to escape liability on the basis of a mistake that they could have discovered had they been more diligent. A strict doctrine of mistake encourages contracting parties to verify their assumptions or to at least to decide themselves who should bear the cost of a mistake.

No doubt these arguments do not justify all the decisions. Less sophisticated contracting parties, in particular, may reasonably understand their agreement as setting out only a bare framework, with the details to be added as required. It may also be unfair and inefficient to assume that such parties ought to have spent more time and effort discovering the truth or writing a more detailed contract. Admittedly, a decision to set aside the contract in such a case is not neutral: it places the cost of the mistake on the party seeking enforcement. If that party has detrimentally relied on the contract, and if, as will sometimes be the case, those costs cannot be recouped through a claim in unjust enrichment (because the party seeking relief did not benefit from the reliance), then setting aside the contract simply shifts the costs of the mistake onto the other party. This is another reason that relief for mistake is rare.

But in cases where such reliance has not occurred or is trivial, the case for relief is obviously much stronger. In *Great Peace Shipping Ltd v. Tsavliris Salvage (International) Ltd*,[19] the defendants owned a ship that had suffered serious structural damage and was in danger of sinking. Reasonably believing that the claimant's ship, the *Great Peace*, was near to their own ship, the defendants quickly arranged for the *Great Peace* to accompany their ship, at a rate of £16,500 per day with a five day minimum charge. Two hours later they attempted to cancel the contract, having received new information that the *Great Peace* was not in fact nearby, and that another of their own ships could reach the endangered vessel more quickly. Clearly, the owners of the *Great Peace* deserved compensation for any costs they incurred prior to the attempted cancellation of the contract. But their claim for the full contract price was much weaker. Had the parties been required at the time of formation to specify what should happen if the contract were to be cancelled two hours later, it seems likely they would have agreed to a provision stipulating a

---

[19] Ibid.

modest payment by the defendants. This would have minimized the overall cost of the contract to both parties. Given that the parties were presumably risk-averse—the claimants were not 'gambling' on the possibility that their ship would not be needed—such a provision would have been attractive. Admittedly, if the point of the five day minimum was to allocate the risk of the mistake that occurred to the hirer, then relief should be refused. But this seems unlikely. The contract was on the standard form for chartering vessels, and was undoubtedly used (in preference to a more individualised contract) because of the urgency of the matter. In the result, the Court of Appeal refused to set the contract aside. On the assumption that the court's only choice was to enforce the contract fully or declare it void *ab initio*, this result is perhaps defensible. If the contract were void, the owners of the *Great Peace* would have no right to any compensation.[20] This aspect of the decision is discussed further below.

As is often the case in English law, the apparent strictness of the test for mistake is mitigated by other forms of relief. A purchaser who enters a contract of sale on the basis of a mistaken belief about the quality or value of the goods is typically protected by the statutory duties implied on vendors by the Sale of Goods Act 1979. Rather than seeking relief for mistake, the purchaser can simply demand that the vendor abide by her obligations to provide goods that are of satisfactory quality and fit for her use. The same protection is provided by the Supply of Goods and Services Act 1982. It should also be kept in mind that a party who enters a contract on the basis of a mistake that was caused by the other party has extensive protection under the law of misrepresentation. As is discussed in Chapter 10, even in cases in which the misrepresentation is trivial and not the fault of the representor, the contract may be set aside or damages awarded in lieu thereof.

Mistake in equity

In *Solle v. Butcher*[21] Lord Denning held that the narrow test of *Bell v. Lever Bros* was concerned solely with the doctrine of 'mistake at law', and that there also existed a different doctrine of 'mistake in equity'. Denning did not set out the exact parameters of mistake in equity, but it was clear that he regarded the doctrine as broader and more flexible than the doctrine enunciated in *Bell v. Lever*. Mistake in equity might offer relief in situations where mistake in law would not This was undoubtedly a bold suggestion—the House of Lords does not usually overlook such a simple matter as the difference between common law and equity. And the idea that there exist two doctrines of mistake operating side-by-side is complex and confusing.

---

[20] A claim in unjust enrichment would be unavailable since the defendants were not enriched by the temporary change of course by the claimant's ship.

[21] [1950] 1 KB 671.

Probably for these reasons, Denning's suggestion received only limited support[22] and was recently rejected decisively in the *Great Peace* case mentioned earlier. But the underlying idea—that relief for mistake, however it is classified, needs to be more flexible—has much to commend it. In particular, Denning's view that an operative mistake may cause a contract merely to be voidable, rather than void, appears (for reasons already discussed) both fairer and more consistent with the juridical basis of relief than the current rule. This is also true of Denning's suggestion that courts should be allowed to set aside a contract 'on terms', such as by requiring the party seeking relief to compensate the other or at least to share the costs of the mistake. In many cases, this is the result the parties themselves would have provided for had they been required to deal with the risk of a mistake when they made their contract. It may also be worth mentioning that courts would be less hesitant to give relief for mistake if these options were available. The all-or-nothing approach of the current law makes decisions like that in the *Great Peace* case inevitable.

Unilateral mistakes

Finally, something must be said about the difficulty of justifying the rule—unique to the common law—that relief for mistake is possible only when the mistake is shared. In most cases in which this rule denies relief, the result seems appropriate. The prospector who purchases mineral-rich land from the unsuspecting farmer and the art expert who purchases an old master from a bin at a flea market are both reaping rewards for investments in training and searching. It would be unfair and inefficient (because it would remove the incentive to prospect or search for old masters) to invalidate such contracts. But these arguments do not apply to cases involving 'overvaluation' mistakes, such as where a person purchases land that turns out to be worth far less to her than she assumed. Suppose a farmer who wants to plant more crops purchases land that, as only the vendor knows, has recently been re-zoned as residential. If the vendor was unaware of the buyer's purpose, the result given by the current rule is unobjectionable. Assuming the vendor cannot be blamed for his ignorance it is both fair and efficient to hold the farmer responsible for failing to inquire about the zoning. But if the vendor knew of the farmer's purpose, it is difficult to see what value is served by enforcing the contract. Admittedly, the farmer could have made enquiries about the zoning, but it would have been even simpler for the vendor to take the few seconds needed to mention the zoning issue. Enforcing the contract merely rewards the vendor for entering a contract

---

[22] See *Magee v. Pennine Insurance Co.* [1969] 2 QB 507; *Grist v. Bailey* [1967] Ch 532, and the *Associated Japanese Bank* case, above n. 9.

that, as he must have been aware, is unfair to the farmer and inefficient generally (since the farmer will now have to turn around and sell the land to someone else). The most that can be said for the current rule is that disappointed purchasers will usually be protected by either the law of misrepresentation or the statutory duty of 'fitness for use' implied under the Sale of Goods Act 1979 and the Supply of Goods and Services Act 1982 (though neither act applies to sales of *land*).

3. FRUSTRATION AND SUBSEQUENT EVENTS

As we saw in the last section, parties are sometimes excused from performing where they have contracted on the basis of assumptions about pre-existing facts that turn out to be unfounded. This can also happen where the relevant assumptions concern subsequent events. According to the orthodox legal view, these situations raise different legal issues: the former concerns the formation of a contract and is dealt with by the doctrine of 'mistake', while the latter concerns the discharge (or 'termination') of a validly created contract and is dealt with by the doctrine of 'frustration'. This distinction seems artificial. We have already seen that mistake cases can be understood as raising questions about the content (rather than the validity) of a contract; the same is true of frustration cases. In both categories of cases, the court must decide who has assumed, or who is to be treated as having assumed, the risk that that relevant assumption is unfounded. In each situation, therefore, a decision to set the contract aside is effectively a decision to imply a term— either in-fact or in-law—to the effect that the parties' obligations are con-ditional on the assumption being well founded. This is why cases involving unfounded assumptions—whether about the past or the future—are often treated as raising straightforward issues of contract interpretation. To take a simple example, the *Staffordshire Area Health Authority v. South Staffordshire Waterworks Co.*[23] case raised the question of whether a contract to supply water was affected by a fifteenfold increase in costs over a fifty-year period. Strictly speaking, all the court decided was that, as a matter of interpretation, the contract was terminable on reasonable notice; but the result was the same as if the court had concluded that the contract was frustrated—namely, to place on the buyers the risk of the cost increase.

The artificiality of the traditional distinction between mistake and frustra-tion is perhaps best illustrated by those cases in which it is not entirely clear whether the relevant facts are pre-existing or subsequent. For instance, in some of the cases which arose out of the postponement of the coronation of Edward VII (the 'coronation cases') the contract was formed shortly before

[23] [1979] WLR 203.

the official announcement that the coronation was to be postponed.[24] In certain of these cases, the contract was made before anyone was aware that the King had a serious illness (though his condition presumably could have been detected by the proper diagnosis), while in others the King's doctors and advisers were aware of the illness—and so of the need to cancel the coronation—though there was no way the parties could have learned this. Some of these cases were dealt with as cases of pre-existing facts, raising the question of common mistake, and some as cases of subsequent facts, raising issues of frustration. Yet it would be strange if the legal results in such cases varied according to whether the relevant risk arose from pre-existing or subsequent facts.

This is not to deny that the courts distinguish between mistake and frustration cases, and that this distinction has certain practical (though dubious) consequences. In the main, these distinctions concern the consequences of setting aside the contract (e.g. third parties' rights, restitutionary rights). The basic tests for when a contract should be set aside for mistake or frustration are, as we shall see, broadly similar in substance, and serve similar functions.

Frustration through impossibility of performance

In the same way that a contract may turn out to be impossible to perform because of some pre-existing facts, it may turn out to be impossible because of an unexpected development in the future. And in each case the law's response has been to treat the relevant issues as falling into a special legal category of 'impossibility', with a further distinction sometimes being made between 'initial' and 'subsequent' impossibility. We have already seen that cases of initial impossibility are not easily distinguished from ordinary mistake cases: the courts' task in each category is to determine how the relevant risk was or should be allocated. Thus courts sometimes refuse to invalidate contracts where the party obliged to perform had effectively guaranteed performance even if performance proves to have been impossible at the time of formation. The same is true of cases involving subsequent impossibility. The result is simply that damages must be paid in lieu of performance.

At one time, impossibility was the only ground on which a plea of frustration would succeed. This is no longer the case, and today the only real justification for separating cases of subsequent impossibility from other cases

---

[24] See, e.g., *Krell v. Henry* [1903] 2 KB 740, which is discussed in more detail below p. 186. A similar situation arose in *Amalgamated Investment & Property Co. v. John Walker & Sons* [1977] 1 WLR 164, where a contract was made to buy a property for redevelopment, and unknown to the parties the authorities were already considering listing the building, which rendered redevelopment impossible. It was unclear when the internal decision of the authorities had effectively been made. The court ultimately held that the operative date was when the decision was communicated, and so treated the case under the heading of frustration (though they went on to hold that the contract was not actually frustrated).

involving changed circumstances is that there is an established body of case law that enables one to say with some confidence that a promisor does not normally assume the risk of total subsequent impossibility. For instance, where a person contracted to let a hall to the claimant for use for some concerts, and the hall was accidentally destroyed by fire before the date of the first concert, it was held that the contract was dissolved.[25] So also, an agreement to sell specific chattels in which the goods are accidentally destroyed before the risk has passed to the buyer will normally be set aside; indeed, this result is expressly provided by section 7 of the Sale of Goods Act 1979. Similarly, where a ship is chartered for a particular voyage but she is unable to arrive at the required port owing to a disaster at sea, the whole contract is usually dissolved.[26]

The position is more difficult where the contract is one of long duration and the performance is merely interrupted and not eternally impossible. In these cases, the contract is prima facie dissolved if the interruption is likely to prove so lengthy that to compel the parties to resume the contract later would, in effect, be to compel them to enter into a new contract. So, for instance, a contract for the construction of a reservoir which was scheduled to take six years was held frustrated when, after less than two years, all further work was temporarily prohibited owing to wartime restrictions. As it was impossible to foresee how long these restrictions might last, it was unreasonable to hold the parties to the contract—especially as it was certain that the conditions would be quite different after the end of the war.

A similar problem occurs when the performance of the contract becomes not impossible, but illegal, after its creation. In these cases, again, the contract will prima facie be dissolved by such a change in the law because 'there cannot be default in not doing what the law forbids to be done'.[27] So, for instance, where a person sold land and covenanted that no buildings would be erected on adjacent lands retained by him, it was held that he could not be sued for breach of the covenant when a railway company, acting under statutory powers, compulsorily acquired the land from him and built a railway station on it.

Frustration of the common venture

The application of the doctrine of frustration becomes more difficult when the actual performance of the contract remains possible but the need for performance has disappeared. The general principle applied to such cases is that for the contract to be frustrated 'the common object has to be frustrated,

---

[25] *Taylor v. Caldwell* (1863) 3 B & S 826.

[26] *Jackson v. Union Marine Insurance Co.* (1874) LR to CP 125.

[27] Per Lord Macmillan in *Denny, Mott & Dickson v. Fraser* [1944] AC 265 at 278. A person may, however, contract in such a way as to take the risk even of supervening illegality if the intent is clear enough.

not merely the individual advantage that one party or the other might have gained from the contract'.[28] So where a person buys something for a specific purpose and subsequent events make this purpose impossible to fulfil, the contract is not affected. A person who contracts to buy machinery for his factory cannot avoid the contract if the factory should happen to be accidentally destroyed before delivery. Similarly, the courts normally hold that it is no concern of a buyer where or how a seller expects to procure the goods. Hence, in a contract for the sale of unascertained goods, for example 100 tons of corn or the like (but not a specific chattel), the fact that the seller is unable to procure the goods does not normally excuse him from non-delivery.

It is more difficult to describe the kinds of events that *will* be held to frustrate the common object of a contract. Few contracts have a genuinely common purpose. Each of the parties will normally have different reasons for entering the contract, since what each party obtains under the contract is different. At most, it might be said that each party has in common the hope of gaining a profit or other advantage through the contract—but if *that* purpose is frustrated the parties will surely agree between themselves not to go through with the contract. In practice, therefore, 'common object' does not mean what it appears to mean, but, instead, something closer to 'common assumption' or 'common foundation'. This idea is often expressed by saying that a contract will only be frustrated where the change in circumstances makes performance 'a thing radically different from that which was undertaken by the contract'.[29] This closely resembles the test for mistake; indeed, it is sometimes explicitly mentioned when courts try to explain what qualifies as a 'fundamental' mistake.[30] The tests are also similar in that their application is typically explained by illustrations rather than further definition. A final similarity is that, impossibility cases aside, successful pleas of frustration are extremely rare.

A number of the most difficult cases in this area have involved contracts of hire or leases. This is perhaps no coincidence, for in such contracts both parties may make persuasive arguments. The owner of the thing hired or leased may say, in effect, 'What you do with the thing (or land) is no concern of mine; all I want is the rent. If you are unable to use it for the purpose for which you wanted it that is your misfortune, not mine.' On the other hand, the hirer may say that, where his object in hiring the thing is well known to the owner, that use is the common foundation of the contract. The attitude of the law to these opposing viewpoints is a compromise. The courts have taken the view that, provided the hirer can use the thing or land for *some* purpose

---

[28] Per Lord Sumner in *Hirji Mulji v. Cheong Yue SS Co.* [1926] AC 497 at 507.
[29] *Davis Contractors Ltd v. Fareham UDC* [1956] AC 696.
[30] See, e.g., Steyn J in *Associated Japanese Bank*, above n. 9.

(or perhaps for some purpose envisaged by the contract), it is immaterial that he cannot use it for the particular purpose that he had in mind. So, for instance, in a case in 1916 it was held that a lease of a flat was not frustrated merely because the tenant was an enemy alien and unable to occupy the flat himself owing to wartime restrictions.[31] The tenant could still use the flat for other purposes, such as subletting; moreover, in a lease alternative uses are, in a sense, always envisaged by the contract precisely because the lessee can use the property how he pleases. In one of the famous 'coronation cases' the defendant had agreed to hire a ship for the purpose of viewing the naval review by King Edward VII and for a day's cruise round the fleet, and it was held that the contract was not frustrated by the cancellation of the naval review owing to the King's illness.[32] The day's cruise round the fleet was still possible, and, indeed, the ship could have been used for many other purposes. By contrast, in *Krell v. Henry*[33] the same Court of Appeal held that a contract for the use of a flat to view the coronation procession on two successive days was frustrated by the cancellation of the coronation. This decision is a borderline one, and it has been said that 'the authority is not one to be extended'.[34] But it may be justified on the ground that where the owner is aware of the purpose for which a person hires something, and where he well knows that the thing would not be hired for any other purpose, and, particularly where (as happened in this case) the price is inflated because of the special use contemplated, then it is reasonable to say that this use is the common foundation of the contract.

Frustration must obviously be distinguished from breach of contract: if the performance of the contract is rendered impossible by the fault of either party, that party will be guilty of breach of contract and have to pay damages to the other party. 'The essence of "frustration" is that it should not be due to the act or election of the party.'[35] But there are cases in which it is difficult to draw the line between genuine frustration and breach because it is not clear what meaning is to be given to 'fault' in this connection. Certainly it includes deliberate action which prevents performance, and equally certainly it will often include the negligent destruction of, or damage to, property without which the contract cannot be performed. It is not, however, settled whether a

---

[31] *London & Northern Estates v. Schlesinger* [1916] 1 KB 20.

[32] *Herne Bay Steamboat Co. v. Hutton* [1903] 2 KB 683.

[33] [1903] 2 KB 740.

[34] Per Lord Wright in *Maritime National Fish Co. v. Ocean Trawlers* [1935] AC 524 at 529. Surprisingly, the argument does not seem to have occurred to counsel or the court (or to many later commentators) that it might seem unjust if the landlord were able to retain the large windfall profit paid by the defendant, and then make a similar windfall when the coronation was eventually held. (But in fact when the coronation was held the procession was much curtailed, and it is not known whether the procession did still pass within view of the landlord's windows.)

[35] Ibid, at 530.

person who, through his own carelessness, becomes ill can plead that a contract requiring his personal services is frustrated.[36]

Hardship

In the cases discussed in the previous section, the party pleading frustration wants the contract to be set aside because the other party's performance is now of little or no value. The opposite situation is raised by cases in which performance, though possible, has become more onerous than expected. For example, a vendor's cost of manufacturing contracted-for goods may rise dramatically because the vendor's suppliers have raised their prices.

The approach of English law to such cases is clear: mere hardship cannot frustrate a contract. So where a seller sold Sudanese groundnuts under a c.i.f. contract for shipment to Hamburg, the contract was not frustrated by the closure of the Suez Canal, even though the seller was forced to ship the goods round the Cape at much greater expense.[37] Similarly, in *Davis Contractors v. Fareham UDC*, where a builder contracted to build a number of houses for some £94,000, but owing to shortages of labour and materials the work cost some £115,000, it was held that the contract was not frustrated: 'In a contract of this kind the contractor undertakes to do the work for a definite sum and he takes the risk of the cost being greater or less than he expected.'[38] As a general rule, this seems appropriate, but it is not clear why the courts are unwilling to make occasional exceptions just as they do in cases where, though the cost remains the same, the value of performance has dropped dramatically. The two categories seem functionally similar. At present, the only situation in which 'hardship' matters is where the change in circumstances makes performance truly impossible, at least for the relevant party. For instance, a manufacturer faced with severe price increases may not have the money or credit to pay for supplies, and so be unable to produce contracted-for goods. In such cases, a kind of relief is provided, but its basis is the law of bankruptcy, not the doctrine of frustration.

Frustration as a risk-allocation procedure

We noted earlier that the law on frustration is similar to the law on mistake in that it deals with the question of who should bear the risk of events turning out differently than anticipated. In many cases, the parties will have explicitly

---

[36] Perhaps illness would be treated as one of the hazards of ordinary life, and not therefore as self-induced frustration; see *The Super Servant 2* [1990] 1 Lloyd's Rep 148 at 156. It has also been held that a party is not entitled to set up his *own* breach of contract, so as to convert a frustrating event into a case of self-induced breach, where on the particular facts this would have been advantageous to him: *F. C. Shepherd & Co. Ltd v. Jerrom* [1986] 3 All ER 589.

[37] *Tsakirogolou v. Noblee and Thorl GmbH* [1962] AC 93.

[38] Per Lord Reid, above n. 29 at 724.

answered this question in their contract, as where a *force majeure* clause stipulates that non-performance is excused in the event of war or if a price index rises above a certain level. But in other cases, the contract is silent, and then it must be decided if the contract should be enforced as written (with the result that non-performance is a breach) or instead *as if* it included an express *force majeure* clause that excused performance. In neither case is it correct to say that the frustrating event invalidates the contract: when a court releases the parties from their obligations what it is actually doing is enforcing an express or implied (in-fact or in-law) term in the contract to this effect. It follows that, strictly speaking, it makes no sense to speak of a distinct 'doctrine' of frustration. The 'law' of frustration, like the 'law' of mistake, seems best understood as one part of a larger body of rules that deals with the content of contracts.

Consistent with this interpretation, the courts' approach to cases involving changed circumstances is similar to that adopted in other cases involving disputes about the content of a contract. The first step is to determine if the contract expressly stipulates what should happen in the relevant circumstances. In some cases, the contract will include a *force majeure* clause, price-escalation clause, or other clause that deals with the event that occurred, and in these cases the courts simply enforce the clause. In other cases, the contract will not include such clauses or, if it does, the clause will not mention the relevant event. But in these cases, courts typically conclude that the contract *has* allocated the relevant risk, and that the parties intended the contract to be interpreted literally or strictly. This conclusion is generally a sensible one. When parties make contracts they are almost certainly aware that, while it may not be possible to predict the future, the future may turn out differently than they expect. They will almost certainly also be aware that they can, with little difficulty, draft or adopt a *force majeure* clause, price escalation clause, or other clause to provide relief in such a case. When such clauses are not used, the usual assumption (as has been discussed in other contexts) is that the parties intended the contract to be interpreted as not subject to exceptions. This conclusion might even be thought to follow from the very idea of a contractual obligation: it is part of the well-understood meaning of a promise (or an agreement)—and so of a contract—that promisors generally assume the risk that subsequent events might lead them to regret their promise. This idea was well-expressed by Lord Sumner:

If a contract is really a speculative contract ... the doctrine of frustration can rarely, if ever, apply to it, for the basis of a speculative contract is to distribute all the risks on one side or on the other and to eliminate any chance of the contract falling to the ground. ... No one can tell how long a spell of commercial depression may last; no suspense can be more harassing than the vagaries of foreign exchanges, but contracts are made for the purpose of fixing the incidence of such risks in advance, and their occurrence only makes it the more necessary to uphold a contract and not to make them the ground for discharging it.[39]

It should also be kept in mind that *force majeure* clauses and the like are only one way of dealing with risks. An alternative is for one party to receive compensation for assuming a risk, typically in the form of a higher or lower contract price. Indeed, part of what the purchaser is purchasing in a typical sale contract is a form of insurance from the vendor against, for example, the vendor's suppliers increasing their prices. This may be the case even if the relevant event was one that that the parties had neither thought about nor had any reason to think about. In the same way that everyone knows the future is uncertain, they also know that the future may be uncertain in ways that cannot be predicted. Travellers normally carry extra cash for unknown 'emergencies'; in the same way vendors normally charge a premium to cover the risk that their performance may become more difficult—for whatever reason. In such a case, allowing the vendor to escape his obligations because circumstances changed would be like allowing an insurance company to avoid paying compensation on the ground that they never anticipated the loss in question.

This is not to say a change of circumstances should never affect contracting parties' obligations except insofar as they have expressly provided for this result. There are at least three cases where the contrary conclusion might legitimately be reached. The first is where the contract contains an implied-in-fact term to this effect. We have seen already that all contracts—even those of great length and detail—contain implied-in-fact terms and, further, that such terms may sometimes stipulate that the parties should be excused from their obligations in the event that an assumption made at the time of contracting turns out to be unfounded. At least in certain cases, one of the things that 'goes without saying' (or thinking—see the previous section) in a contract is that the contract's obligations are conditional on certain things not happening. In *Krell v. Henry*, for example, it arguably went without saying that the rental arrangement was binding only in the event that the coronation went ahead. The high rent charged suggested that the landlord was accepting—in return for the chance of making a high profit—the risk of cancellation. Similar logic may explain the decision in *Tatem v. Gamboa*.[40] The claimants had agreed to charter a ship to the Spanish Republican Government during the civil war at £250 per day, which was about three times the normal rate of freight prevailing at the time, for use in evacuating government supporters. It was manifest that the dangers of the ship being captured must have been appreciated, and the high rate of freight was only

---

[39] Per Lord Sumner in *Larrinaga v. Société-Americaine* (1923) 92 LJKB 455 at 464–5.
[40] [1939] 1 KB 132; [1938] 3 All ER 135.

explicable on the assumption that the owners realised the risk and were prepared to accept it. Hence, when the ship was captured by the rebels, it was held that the contract was frustrated, and that the owners were no longer entitled to recover freight.

A second situation where courts may—indeed must—look beyond the contract's express terms is where the contract contains a gap or is vague as to the legal effect of the relevant events. This might happen where it is unclear whether a *force majeure* clause covers the relevant event. It can also happen in cases where the contract is entirely silent as to the effect of changed circumstances. Of course, in such a case the *literal* meaning of the contract is clear, and in most cases this literal meaning should be enforced. If a vendor promises to 'deliver on Friday', then that promise is binding even if it rains on Friday, and this is the case despite the fact that the vendor did not say 'I promise to deliver on Friday even if it is raining'. But at least sometimes contracting parties can plausibly argue that they did not intend the words of their contract to be taken literally and, furthermore, that they had not agreed, objectively or otherwise, as to what should happen in the circumstances that actually transpired. Putting the point another way, it must sometimes be the case that contracts contain implied-in-fact terms to the effect that performance *may* not be due given the events that transpired. Certainly, the parties could have expressly made such an agreement. Parties negotiating a delivery contract, for example, might consider whether their obligations should be binding in the event of a war, but then decide that it is not worth investing more time in the discussion (given that war is unlikely), and instead simply agree to go ahead without resolving the issue. They might even wish to record that they 'discussed, but did not decide' what should happen in the event of war. The same thing can happen implicitly, without discussion. In such cases, the courts have no choice but to imply a term, on the basis of fairness, efficiency, or some other standard of reasonableness. And in some cases, the term that is implied would stipulate that performance is conditional on the relevant event.

Finally, a third situation in which a court *might* decide to go beyond the contract's literal terms is where the court concludes that the contract's literal terms accurately represent the parties' agreed allocation of the relevant risk, but where they feel the allocation is unreasonable. In such a case, a court might decide to rewrite the contract so as to reach a result that they feel is more reasonable. In such a case, the court is, in effect, giving relief on the ground that the party demanding enforcement is acting in bad faith or unconscionably. The desirability and likelihood of this happening, covertly or otherwise, will be considered in the general discussion of unconscionability in Chapter 12.

There are a number of situations, then, in which courts might decide to give relief for changed circumstances. But it should be evident why in practice courts grant such relief very rarely. Granting relief in either of the first two situations is inconsistent with the usual assumption that promises are understood to be binding except where expressly stipulated otherwise, while granting relief in the third scenario is inconsistent with the basic principle of freedom of contract and, more specifically, with the rule that unconscionability is not a general defence to a claim of breach of contract.

The question that remains is how to classify the (few) cases in which relief have been given. Are the courts interpreting contracts (situation 1), completing incomplete contracts (situation 2), or rewriting contracts (situation 3)? The answer, once again, is that it is difficult to tell. The few cases in which relief has been given can be explained on any of the bases described above. Admittedly, what courts say they are doing (when they say anything) probably fits most closely with the idea that courts are completing incomplete contracts.[41] But it would be dangerous to place much weight on such comments. Courts will naturally hesitate to say that they are rewriting a contract if an alternative explanation is available. We have also seen that courts often reject explanations that refer to implied-in-fact terms because they (mistakenly) assume that implied-in-fact terms are terms that the parties consciously had before their minds when contracting.

Consequences of frustration

It is usual to deal with the consequences of frustration at this point, but in this book detailed discussion of this question is deferred to Chapter 14 so that remedies can all be conveniently considered together. Here two points of general interest will be made. First, the consequences that follow frustration may influence a court in its decision as to whether frustration has indeed occurred. For instance, a party will occasionally claim that a contract was frustrated even though the contract was fully performed. In the *Davis Contractors* case, discussed above, the builder did not throw up the contract when prices rose faster than he had expected—he went ahead and built the houses and then argued that the contract was frustrated. The purpose of claiming that the contract had been frustrated was to escape the contract price, which binds as long as the contract stands, and to justify a claim for payment outside the contract via a restitutionary claim for payment at a 'reasonable' rate—which may well be higher if prices have risen. As we have seen, in the *Davis Contractors* case the claim failed, as will most such claims.

---

[41] *Davis Contractors v. Fareham*, above n. 29. See also *Panalpina International Transport v. Densil Underwear* [1981] 1 Lloyd's Rep 187, and *Pioneer Shipping Ltd v. BTP Tioxide Ltd* [1982] AC 724.

This leads to the second point: remedies for frustration are generally inflexible—the contract is terminated, and the parties' rights must then be worked out on that footing. But what the parties often want is for the contract to be adjusted rather than terminated, and this is a perfectly legitimate commercial need which the law generally fails to meet. This is one reason for the widespread use of *force majeure* clauses, as these clauses often make provision for adjustment of the contract rather than complete termination. For instance, if performance is held up by serious delays, the *force majeure* clause may allow more time for performance, and so on.

4. BREACH

A breach of contract normally gives the victim the right to a remedy such as an order for damages or specific performance. But in addition the victim will sometimes also have the right to refuse to perform her obligations or to bring the contract to an end entirely. Broadly speaking, the first of these non-performance rights arises where the *order* of performance of the contract is such that the victim's obligation(s) are not due until the obligation that was breached is performed, while the second (the so-called right to 'discharge' or 'terminate' the contract) arises where the breach is considered sufficiently *serious* to justify this result.

The rules for determining when a breach will excuse non-performance—for either of the above reasons—are not usually discussed alongside the rules dealing with mistake and frustration, but they are in fact closely related. As was true of the law regarding mistake and frustration, the main issue addressed by the law on 'non-performance for breach' is when may a contracting party refuse to perform because of an event or fact that happened or came to light after the contract was formed—here a failure to perform by the other party. In answering this question, the courts undertake a similar enquiry to that undertaken in mistake and frustration cases. Assuming there is no applicable legislation or common law rule, they begin by asking whether the contract's express terms provide an answer. This is often the end of the enquiry; indeed, where the question is whether the victim's performance was due (the first of the two situations described above), the courts will look no further than the contract's terms. And even where the question is whether the victim had the right to terminate for breach, the contract often provides an explicit answer: in the same way that contracts often contain *force majeure* clauses setting out the parties' options in the case of war, flood, or other unexpected events, they frequently also contain 'termination' clauses that set out the parties' rights to terminate in the event of certain breaches.

But if the contract does not contain such a clause, the court must decide whether the breach is the kind that gives rise to a right to terminate. The basic test is similar to the test for determining which mistakes are operative and which kinds of subsequent events frustrate a contract: termination is allowed only for 'serious' or 'fundamental' breaches. A final similarity is that attempts to explain and classify the law in this area give rise to the same debates as arise in the law on mistake and frustration. Are the rules on termination for breach a free-standing legal doctrine, or are they merely one part of a larger body of rules for determining a contract's content (in particular its implied terms)? And if the latter, is the right to terminate implied *in-fact* or *in-law*? The most plausible *answers* to these questions are also similar: on the one hand, a strong argument can be made that the rules on termination for breach are a part of the law that deals with the content of contracts; on the other, it is often impossible to say whether the application of these rules is a matter merely of interpreting the parties' actual agreement or, instead, of making a new agreement.

Terminological difficulties

The law in this area is riddled with terminological difficulties. The traditional way of explaining which breaches give rise to the right to terminate is to say that this right arises only if the term breached is a 'condition' of the contract as opposed to a (mere) 'warranty'. Unfortunately, the words condition and warranty also have other meanings. As we have already noted, 'warranty' is frequently used to describe any contractual term that 'promises' (or, more accurately, 'guarantees') the truth of certain facts. Warranties in this sense are not always warranties in the condition/warranty sense. For example, contracting parties have full liberty to specify that the breach of a *factual* warranty gives the right to terminate. Legislation may also do this—for example, section 13 of the Sale of Goods Act 1979 specifies that it is an implied condition (in the condition/warranty sense) that goods will correspond to their description.

The word 'condition' is beset by even more ambiguities. In its broadest sense, 'condition' is sometimes used as a synonym for 'clause' or 'term', so that it can refer to any provision in a contract. More narrowly, condition is sometimes used as shorthand for 'contingent condition'. A contingent condition is a clause describing a state of affairs the existence of which is a prerequisite to the contract coming into force (a 'contingent condition *precedent*') or on which the parties' future obligations depend (a 'contingent condition *subsequent*'). A much-quoted example of the former is found in *Pym v. Campbell*,[42] where the defendants agreed to buy from the claimants a share of an invention, provided that the invention was approved by a third party. This proviso was held to be a condition precedent, so that in the absence of the approval specified the contract never came into operation.

---

[42] (1856) 6 E & B 370.

It would be more accurate to say that the failure of this condition merely prevented the parties' obligations from coming due—if the *contract* does not exist, then neither does the condition precedent—but for present purposes the important point is that conditions precedent are not to be confused with conditions in the conditions/warranties sense. When used in the latter sense, a condition refers to a contractual *duty*, the 'failure' of which is a breach of contract that gives rise to a right to damages. A condition *precedent* describes a state of affairs for which neither party is responsible and whose failure (not 'breach') prevents *both* parties' obligations from coming due. An example of a contingent condition *subsequent* would be a clause in an agreement to lease property stipulating that the lease is terminable if the property is required by a third party. Again, although there are similarities between contingent conditions subsequent and conditions in the condition/warranty sense—each describes 'events' whose occurrence or non-occurrence may put an end to the contract—the vital difference is that conditions subsequent do not describe duties, and so their non-occurrence is not a breach of contract. Thus defined, the law on contingent conditions precedent includes the law of mistake (on the assumption that relief for mistake is based on an implied term), and the law on frustration may be regarded as part of the law dealing with contingent conditions subsequent.[43]

Finally, condition in the condition/warranty sense must be distinguished from a promissory condition. A promissory condition is an obligation whose performance is a pre-requisite (in the temporal sense) to one or more of the other party's obligations. For example, the vendor's obligation in a contract of sale to deliver the goods is normally a pre-requisite to the buyer's obligation to pay the price. If the goods do not arrive, payment is not due. By contrast, a landlord's performance of his obligation to make repairs is not a pre-requisite to the tenant's obligation to pay rent: the tenant must pay the rent and then sue for damages. Unlike a contingent condition, the failure of a promissory condition qualifies as a breach of contract. It follows, further, that promissory conditions are sometimes conditions in the condition/warranty sense: an obligation which is a temporal pre-requisite to another obligation may also be an important obligation. Delivery of goods, for example, is clearly important, and so a failure to deliver will give rise—either immediately or after a reasonable passage of time—to a right to terminate the contract. But it is also clear that not all promissory conditions are conditions in the condition/warranty sense. For example, a particular duty may be a

---

[43] The examples given above involve cases in which the contingent condition prevented the coming into force, or put an end to, an entire contract, but it is clear that a contingent condition may have effect merely on specific obligations in a contract. For example, obligations in a building contract may be contingent on the availability of materials.

temporal pre-requisite to another duty, but both duties may pertain to a small and unimportant part of a larger contract.[44]

Interdependent obligations and 'entire contracts'

The classification of an obligation as a temporal pre-requisite to one or more of the contract's other obligations (a 'promissory condition') is often determined by judicial precedent or legislation. In a contract of employment, for example, the general rule is that payment is not due until the work is performed, and in a contract of sale, section 28 of the Sale of Goods Act 1979 provides that payment and delivery are concurrent obligations (meaning that each party must be ready to perform at the relevant time). But where no such rule exists (or where the parties have overridden the rule, which is usually allowed), the court will look to the contract's terms to determine which, if any, obligations qualify as promissory conditions.

In general, the conclusion that a particular obligation is a promissory condition excuses the innocent party from performance unless and until the breaching party performs the promissory condition exactly as specified. The result is that a trivial (and faultless) non-performance can sometimes excuse the other party from what is often his only obligation—payment. In a building contract, for example, unless the parties stipulate otherwise (which they frequently do), the builder's failure to perform even the smallest contractual obligation will excuse the owner from having to pay anything at all. As one judge put it: 'if a shoemaker agrees to make a pair of shoes, he cannot offer you one shoe and ask you to pay half the price.'[45] This result—the so-called 'entire contracts' rule[46]—can often be justified on the basis that the threat of non-payment may be the only tool the innocent party has to induce complete performance. In building cases, for example, it is rarely worth the owner's trouble to sue the builder for a trivial breach. And English law, unlike some legal systems, contains no provisions for ordering contracting parties to reduce a contractual payment in response to the other party's breach (though, again, the parties themselves may provide for this option). But in

---

[44] Further confusion arises because it is often possible to 'imply' an undertaking or promise not to obstruct the workings of the contract, which effectively converts a non-promissory condition into a promissory condition (and at the same time imports a limited duty of good faith into the contract). For example, if the invention in *Pym v. Campbell* was not approved because the defendant had somehow obstructed or failed to assist the third party, the argument might have been made that such action was itself a breach of contract. Note, however, that there is no general implication in all cases that a party will not allow a contract to fail through a condition precedent. Compare on this point *Mackay v. Dick* (1881) 6 App Cas 25 with *Luxor (Eastbourne) v. Cooper* [1941] AC 108.

[45] Sir George Jessel MR in *Re Hal & Barker* (1878) 9 Ch D 538.

[46] The label is misleading because the point of the rule is not that payment is conditional on performance of the entire contract, but on performance of an entire obligation or set of obligations. It will only sometimes be the case that those obligations constitute the entirety of one side's obligations.

cases where the breach was unintentional and, further, where the breach is impossible or very difficult to cure, it can be harsh to allow even innocent parties to escape their obligations to pay entirely. In a famous American case,[47] the defendant invoked the rule in an attempt to avoid paying for a completed house on the basis that the builder had installed 'Reading' pipe rather than 'Cohoes' pipe as specified in the contract.[48] The two types of pipe were of similar quality, but the cost of replacing one for the other would have been huge.

Not surprisingly, the courts have therefore been reluctant to conclude that a contract (or, more properly, an obligation) is 'entire' in this sense. They have also introduced an exception to the entire contracts rule where the breaching party has 'substantially' performed.[49] In such cases, the innocent party cannot refuse to pay because of the breach (though they may claim damages or a setoff if sued for payment). This exception seems generally appropriate. But it must be remembered that a party who is denied a contractual payment by virtue of the entire contracts rule may have other legal recourse. In particular, such a party may be able to claim for the value of work done on the basis of unjust enrichment law. The actual sum awarded may be less than the contract price, but it will usually be close to that price. Unfortunately, because of the historical underdevelopment of English unjust enrichment law, such relief was traditionally not available and even today is subject to restrictions. Given this history, it is understandable that the courts introduced the 'substantial performance' exception, but today the exception looks anomalous. In cases where the parties truly intended to make payment or any other obligation conditional on complete performance, applying the substantial performance exception is inconsistent not only with the general principle of freedom of contract, but also with the courts' upholding of that principle in cases of termination for breach. As we will see shortly, courts generally enforce termination clauses strictly. Yet a clause that allows one party to escape its obligations to pay on the ground of the other's breach can operate just like a termination clause.

Termination for breach

The victim of a breach of contract will sometimes have the right to terminate the contract on account of the breach. This right may derive from legislation, the contract, or the general law. Each is examined below.

Little needs to be said about legislative rights to terminate for breach. The best known and most important examples are found in the Sale of Goods Act

---

[47] *Jacobs & Young v. Kent* (1921) 129 NE 889.
[48] The argument was ultimately rejected on the basis of the 'substantial performance' exception discussed in the next paragraph.
[49] *Dakin (H.) & Co. Ltd v. Lee* [1916] 1 KB 566.

1979 which classifies its various implied terms (e.g. satisfactory quality, fitness for use, compliance with description, etc.) as either warranties or (as in the examples just given) conditions. In the past, these classifications caused problems because unless the parties stipulated otherwise, even the most trivial breach of a statutorily implied condition might give the right to terminate. For example, if goods deviated in even the slightest respect from their description the buyer could reject them, and this was the case even if the buyer's reason for rejecting had nothing to do with the deviation. But under recent reforms, it is now provided (in section 15(a)) that, at least in the case of commercial contracts, if the breach of the implied conditions of quality, fitness for use, or compliance with description is so slight that to permit the buyer to reject the goods would be 'unreasonable', it is to be treated as the breach of a mere warranty. This welcome change followed a similar development in the common law that is discussed later in this section.

The second basis on which it may be concluded that a breach gives the right to terminate is that the parties have stipulated such a right in the contract. Of course, contract terms are not usually described on their face as 'conditions' or 'warranties' and, even if they are, the terminology used by the parties is not decisive, for they may (not surprisingly) have been using the words in a different sense. For instance, in *Wickman v. Schuler AG*[50] a company appointed another as a distributor for its goods, and made it a 'condition' that the distributor should visit six customers every week. It was held that this was not strictly a condition in the legal sense because the result of so holding would be that even a single omitted visit would justify termination of the whole contract. It was (said the House of Lords) improbable that the parties intended such an extreme result. Thus, rather than describing a duty as a condition, what parties will typically do if they wish to ensure that a particular breach will give rise to a termination right is to simply say this explicitly or to state that the particular duty is essential or 'of the essence'.

Termination clauses sometimes appear harsh, since parties can (and often do) demand the right to terminate for even the most trivial breach—and breach, as we have seen, can normally be established without proving fault. But except in the case of contracts governed by the Unfair Terms in Consumer Contracts Regulations 1999 (see Chapter 12), such clauses are in principle perfectly valid. There is no general duty of good faith or principle against unconscionable terms in English law, and the Unfair Contract Terms Act 1977 does not apply to clauses that stipulate the consequences of breach. The most a court can do when faced with an apparently unreasonable termination clause is to interpret it narrowly. This approach has long been used in the case of unreasonable exemption clauses (see Chapter 5) and there

---

[50] [1974] AC 235.

is no doubt it applies to termination clauses as well. In *Wickman v. Schuler*, for example, it seems likely that the court's interpretation of the contract was influenced by the apparent unfairness of allowing termination for such a trivial breach. But such techniques are of little use if a termination clause is carefully worded.

Where neither legislation nor the contract specifies the consequences of the breach, the court has to fall back on general criteria. The basic test, as we have noted, is one of seriousness or importance. The breach of a serious duty is said to amount to a 'repudiation' of the contract, which the other party may then accept (by 'terminating') or not. The terminology of 'repudiation' is well entrenched, but it can mislead: while the ordinary meaning of repudiation involves some element of intention, a repudiation in the context of breach may be found to have taken place even where the breaching party did not wish to repudiate the contract and even where this was clear to the other party. Thus, a breach may amount to a repudiation even if it was apparent that the breaching party thought she was acting in accordance with the contract. To say that a breach amounts to a repudiation is to say that the breaching party will be treated *as if* she had intended to repudiate the contract. As is discussed later, this terminology seems motivated by an attempt to analogize the steps leading to the termination of a contract to the steps leading to a contract's formation.

The seriousness test was originally applied not to breaches, but to contract terms; the question was whether a particular *term* was a condition or a warranty. This was unsatisfactory because terms can often be breached in more than one way, some serious and some trivial. Thus, if a term was classified as a condition, the innocent party could treat the whole contract as discharged even if that term was breached in a trivial way. The potential unfairness of this approach is exacerbated by the fact that in English law (unlike some legal systems) the innocent party is not required to serve notice on the breaching party or to otherwise give a chance to cure the breach (though the contract itself may require this): the right to terminate vests immediately on breach. Of course, the courts could avoid this result by classifying the relevant term as a warranty, but they would usually hesitate to do so because in another case the same term might be breached in a more serious manner. This is why the original Sale of Goods Act classified nearly all of the Act's implied terms as conditions—a breach of any these terms could easily be serious. The court would only treat a term as a warranty if it felt confident that *any* breach of it would have only trivial consequences.

In the 1960s the courts began to depart from this traditional law, introducing what was in effect an 'ex post' test for certain kinds of terms. In a series of important cases it was held that where a term could be breached in different ways, and where only *some* of the breaches would be serious, termination for breach would be permitted only if the *consequences* of the breach that actually happened were serious. An example is provided by the first case to introduce the concept of an 'intermediate' term (as they were called), *Hong Kong Fir Shipping Co. v. Kawasaki Kisen Kaisha*,[51] where the relevant term promised that a ship for charter would be 'seaworthy'. This might seem a rather important term, but in fact a ship can fail to be seaworthy (which is a term of art in the industry) for both serious reasons (e.g. a large hole in the hull) and trivial reasons (e.g. it is missing a particular flag or a bulb in a signal light). The court reasonably decided that a breach of the latter kind, which is easily cured, should not justify throwing up the entire contract.

The decision in *Hong Kong Fir* provided the courts with an opportunity to reject the confusing language of conditions and warranties, and to explain the test for termination entirely in terms of the seriousness of the relevant breach. Instead, the courts have continued to refer to conditions and warranties, merely adding a third category of 'intermediate' or 'innominate' terms. The retention of the old language has perhaps some value in that it makes it easier to say that there are certain terms whose breach will always permit termination—namely conditions—and others which never permit termination—namely warranties. But the same result could also be achieved by recognizing that there are certain categories of breaches that are always serious, and vice versa. In short, a simple statement to the effect that a serious breach permits termination would accurately describe the law in this area.

There remains the question of which kinds of breaches qualify as serious. The test is sometimes expressed by saying that a breach supports termination if it goes directly to the substance of the contract or is so essential to its nature that the non-performance may fairly be considered by the other party to be a substantial failure to perform the contract at all,[52] but as was true of the law on mistake and frustration, elaborations of this kind add little to the basic concept. In practice, the test is explained by illustrations, and in this regard the main point to make is that, especially in comparison to mistake and frustration, it is common for courts to conclude that breaches are serious. The reason for this is probably not that most breaches are in fact serious; rather it is that the law's remedies for a non-serious breach often give little incentive to perform and offer little protection to a victim of breach. As is discussed in Chapter 14, specific performance is rarely ordered, damages sometimes undercompensate, and, most importantly, it is rarely worth pursuing one's rights in court. Litigation is expensive and parties who breach contracts often have few or no assets. Indeed, this is why so many contracts contain termination clauses and why such clauses frequently stipulate that every breach, no matter how trivial, gives the right to termination.

---

[51] [1962] 2 QB 26.
[52] Per Fletcher Moulton LJ, in *Wallis v. Pratt* [1910] 2 KB 1003 at 1012, a judgment approved in the HL [1911] AC 394.

Contracting parties who stipulate their own 'remedies' recognize that in practice termination is the most important remedy—or 'whip'—that they can possess. The courts are naturally influenced by similar considerations.

There is a second reason courts are quick to find that a breach supports termination, which is the importance commercial parties place on being able to make instant decisions when breaches occur. A test that requires contracting parties to assess the consequences of a breach can be costly and time-consuming, especially when it is remembered that if the innocent party makes a mistake, and so terminates prematurely, he will himself be in breach of contract. One way the courts have been attentive (some might say too attentive) to this concern is by holding that certain categories of terms continue to qualify as 'conditions' even though they are capable of being breached in different ways. The most important example concerns stipulations as to time. At first blush, such clauses appear to be clear examples of intermediate terms, since it is plainly possible to breach time stipulations in different ways and with different consequences. Being one minute late is normally not significant, but being a month late is. Nonetheless the House of Lords has held that, at least in mercantile contracts, stipulations as to time are prima facie of the essence.[53] So in contracts of sale of goods, for example, it is a well–established rule that failure to deliver the goods (or documents of title) by the stipulated date is prima facie a breach of a condition which justifies the other in throwing up the whole contract. It does not matter whether the delay is one month or one minute. Thus, a contract for the sale of a flat was validly terminated because the purchaser tendered the price ten minutes late.[54]

Again, this can sometimes be hard law, and it is made all the harder because English law has no general doctrine requiring contracting parties to behave in good faith. So a technical breach of a time stipulation will permit the other party to throw up the contract even though his real reason for wanting to do this may be that the market has moved against him since the contract was made. Courts are aware of these problems, but this is one of the many situations in which they feel that the need for certainty should prevail over other considerations. This is, perhaps, understandable. If time stipulations were regarded as intermediate terms, then in every case the innocent party would have to decide at what point—one hour, a day, a week?—the consequences of delay had become sufficiently serious to justify termination. There are an infinite number of ways that a time stipulation can be breached, each of which has slightly different consequences. Thus, the very

---

[53] *Bunge v. Tradas Ltd* [1981] 1 WLR 711. There are some exceptions to this rule, for example, s. 10(1) of the Sale of Goods Act 1979 stipulates that time of *payment* is not of the essence in a contract for the sale of goods.

[54] *Union Eagle Ltd v. Golden Achievement Ltd* [1997] AC 514.

factor that normally argues in favour of finding an intermediate term—that it can be breached in different ways—in this case argues for the opposite conclusion.

Anticipatory breach

It goes without saying that a contract cannot generally be terminated for breach until the breach has actually happened. But an exception is made for cases where one party indicates by words or conduct that she does not intend to perform some or all of her contractual obligations when they fall due. According to the doctrine of 'anticipatory breach', in cases where the failure to perform the relevant obligation(s) would deprive the innocent party of substantially the whole benefit of the contract[55] she may choose to immediately terminate the contract, and sue for damages, even though the date for actual performance has not passed. This choice arises, it is said, because the other party has repudiated the contract by her actions.

If the innocent party 'chooses' not to accept the repudiation, say by communicating that she is still expecting performance from the other party, then the contract remains in operation. In this case, the innocent party can terminate or sue for damages if and when the breach actually happens, but in the meantime must remain ready to perform as required by the contract. So where charterers of a ship wrongfully repudiated by giving advance notice that they would not be ready to load when the ship arrived, and the owners refused to accept this repudiation, it was held that they had kept the contract alive, and therefore should have brought the vessel into port to await loading.[56] This principle—that the innocent party must remain able and willing to perform if she keeps the contract alive—is, however, qualified by another principle, to the effect that if the guilty party continues to make it quite clear that she will not perform, then the innocent party can eventually abandon her attempts to perform.[57] This can either be seen as an ultimate acceptance by conduct of the repudiation, after its initial rejection, or as an act of induced reliance by the innocent party, which estops the guilty party from complaining about the former's inability to perform.

Permitting innocent parties to treat contracts as alive even when the other party indicates that they have no intention of carrying through with the contract will often lead to an increase in the innocent party's losses, and so to an increase in any damage award that party obtains. A purchaser who learns that a vendor has no intention of delivering contracted-for goods, but then does nothing until the date of delivery will typically incur greater losses than a purchaser who acts on the vendor's information immediately by seeking

---

[55] *Federal Commerce & Navigation Ltd v. Molma Alpha Inc.* [1979] AC 757
[56] *Fercometal SARL v. Mediterranean Shipping Co. SA* [1989] AC 788.
[57] Ibid.

alternative suppliers. As is discussed in Chapter 14, in a normal case of breach victims are encouraged to minimize their losses by the rule that damages will be calculated on the assumption that they have done just this, for example by seeking out alternative contractual opportunities. The rule that the victim of an anticipatory breach may choose to 'ignore' the repudiation has the opposite effect. This is especially clear in cases where the victim of an anticipatory breach has outstanding obligations under the contract, which she then goes ahead and performs. In *White & Carter (Councils) Ltd v. McGregor*[58] the defendants informed the claimants that they no longer wished to go through with a contract under which the claimants would display advertisements for the defendant's garage on litter bins. The claimants refused to accept the repudiation and proceeded to affix and display the advertisements as required under the contract. The House of Lords held that they were entitled to do this and, therefore, were entitled to sue for the contract price (although had they asked for damages they would in any event have been compensated for the costs of making and displaying the advertisements).

The ruling in *White & Carter* does not apply where the innocent party requires the cooperation of the repudiating party in order to perform, as for example where an employee has been wrongly dismissed. It has also been held, picking up on a comment by Lord Reid in *White & Carter*, that the innocent party may not claim in respect of a performance that he has no 'legitimate interest' in doing. It might be asked what legitimate interest the claimants had in *White & Carter*, but this proviso has nonetheless been widely applied in subsequent cases,[59] with the result that *White & Carter* is now the exception rather than the rule. Still, it remains the case that the victim of an anticipatory breach may generally choose to do nothing rather than accept the breach,[60] thereby increasing the damages she is allowed to claim, and in some cases may perform herself even if such performance is no longer desired.

In principle, this result seems difficult to justify: if a contracting party has indicated that he does not intend to perform, it is not clear what value is served by allowing the other party to act as if this never happened. Parties should not generally be allowed to claim for losses that they could have avoided by acting reasonably—and it would seem unreasonable to act as if one expected performance if you have been told that performance is not going to happen. But some justification for the present rule may be found in the fact that in practice it is often hard to tell if a particular action (or

---

[58] [1962] AC 413.

[59] See, e.g., *The Alaskan Trader* [1984] 1 ALL ER 129.

[60] As confirmed in *Ocean Marine Navigation Ltd v. Koch Carbon Inc. (The 'Dynamic')* [2003] EWHC 1936 (Comm); [2003] 2 Lloyd's Rep 693, where Simon J went so far as to say that the victim would lose this choice only in 'extreme' cases.

description of a future action) amounts to a breach and, if it does, if the breach (anticipatory or otherwise) is sufficiently serious to justify termination. A rule that innocent parties must always accept repudiatory breaches could leave some innocent parties with difficult decisions. In addition, in cases of anticipatory breach it is always possible that the guilty party will change his mind and decide to perform. A threat to breach is often just that—a threat. Given the costs of litigation and the likelihood that the guilty party may have insufficient assets to pay any judgment, it is often reasonable for the innocent party to do anything possible to induce performance. These issues are discussed in more detail in the next section. Here it is sufficient to observe that a rule to the effect that anticipatory repudiations must always be accepted would sometimes unfairly penalise the innocent party.

The act of termination

Although the courts do not appear to have explicitly recognized this,[61] certain of the principles governing termination for breach closely parallel those governing the formation of a contract, and with them the principles governing the termination of a contract by agreement. In the first place, we have seen that a person may be held to have repudiated a contract without intending to do so: it is not what a party intends that matters, but the reasonable interpretation that may be (and is) placed upon his words and behaviour by the other party. In the second place, a repudiatory breach is treated very much like a contractual offer in that it has no legal effect until it is *accepted*. The other party is entitled either to accept or to reject the proposed termination, and thus in effect to reaffirm the contract. In the latter case, the innocent party must remain ready and willing to perform himself, subject to the qualifications already discussed. Thirdly, an acceptance may itself be express, or may be inferred from conduct. And fourthly, a party may be bound by an acceptance of a repudiation either because he intended to accept it, or because he has led the other to believe that he intended to do so, and thereby induced him to act to his prejudice. This last possibility may be treated as an illustration of estoppel.

These attempts to treat termination for breach as parallel to the principles governing the formation of contracts and termination by agreement likely reflect the classical tradition. They seem prompted by a desire to see legal rights as deriving from the exercise of choices and intentional behaviour, rather than from conduct. While they may work well enough in most cases, they do give rise to a number of difficulties. First, it must be appreciated that in this field—unlike the case of formation or termination of a contract by express agreement—an 'acceptance' or a 'rejection' by inference from

---

[61] But for one dictum to this effect, see Winn LJ in *Denmark Productions Ltd v. Boscobel Productions Ltd* [1968] 3 All ER 513 at 527.

conduct is more often the rule than the exception. Conduct is more difficult to interpret than language, and thus it is often difficult to say whether a contract has been 'affirmed' so that the innocent party has lost his right to rescind or terminate.

Secondly, the rigid insistence that a contract can never be discharged by the unilateral breach of one party until it has been accepted by the other has caused trouble in certain kinds of contracts. In an employment contract,[62] for example, if the employee simply walks out after an argument and refuses to come to work again, few employers would see any necessity for giving notice to the employee that his breach has been 'accepted' and the contract terminated. Yet unless this is done there is a risk that the employment will be held not to have been terminated because the breach has not been accepted.

A third source of difficulty is that (as we have seen) it is not always clear what qualifies as a breach as opposed to a justified demand and, further, which breaches qualify as repudiatory breaches. This is a problem because, on the one hand, if the innocent party wrongly assumes that a particular action qualifies as a repudiation he may himself be liable for a wrongful termination. On the other hand, if the innocent party plays it safe, and treats the contract as valid, he may lose out on opportunities to enter alternative contracts. In such a case, the innocent party does, of course, retain the right to damages (unless the affirmation is regarded as equivalent to waiving the breach itself— which may happen), but in practice this right may be of little value because of the costs of litigation or because the breaching party has no assets. Where the relevant breach is anticipatory, the difficulties just described are compounded because of the possibility that the repudiating party will change his mind and perform. In this situation, the innocent party must often try to cover both contingencies at once, as may be illustrated by the common case in which a charterer wrongfully repudiates by indicating that he will not be able to load the ship when shipping is due. The ship owner will often be trying to keep the contract alive, and so must be ready to perform if at the last minute the charterer says he will perform after all; and at the same time he is trying to ensure that, if the charterer fails to load, there may still be time to load the ship with another cargo. The innocent party can easily slip up in this situation, and may then be penalised either by reduced damages or even by being told that he cannot sue at all.[63]

The present rules may therefore appear somewhat hard on the innocent party. But the present law is favourable to the innocent party in another respect, perhaps also as a consequence of the close assimilation of these rules with those governing contract formation. The innocent party's right to terminate, as we have seen, is largely a right to be exercised at his discretion,

---

[62] See, e.g., *Gunton v. London Borough of Richmond* [1980] 3 All ER 577.
[63] As happened in *Fercometal SARL v. Mediterranean Shipping Co. SA* [1989] AC 788.

just like the right to decide whether to enter into a contract in the first place. Assuming that the breach is of a 'condition', the innocent party may choose to terminate for breach even if the real reason for the termination has nothing to do with the breach—for example the market has changed and he wants to escape a bad bargain—and even if the consequences of termination on the guilty party are out of proportion to the loss caused to the innocent party should he continue with the contract. Unlike in some systems, the innocent party is not required to exercise the right to terminate in good faith or even to give the guilty party an opportunity to rectify or cure the breach. This situation parallels, of course, the law on formation—there is no duty to negotiate in good faith or to give offerors the opportunity to 'cure' a badly worded offer—but it is less easily defended since in this case good faith would merely require one party to refrain from acting in a way that causes another party undue harm, rather than require him to assist or benefit the other (as with formation).

5. NOTICE

We have seen that a contract may provide for a right of termination contingent on specified events; it may also provide that it will automatically terminate on a certain event. This event may be a serious breach or a radical change in circumstances that might allow for termination under the general law, but it need not be. Aside from certain statutory protections given to consumers[64] and to parties dealing on the other's standard terms[65] there are no limits on how such rights are written or exercised. In addition, the parties may, of course, terminate the contract by agreement regardless of the contract's terms. Such an agreement is itself a contract, and so the principles governing its formation are the same as those that govern formation generally.

But unless specifically provided for in the contract, it is not generally open to one contracting party to terminate the contract unilaterally. Even breach of contract—as we have seen—must be accepted to terminate the contract. There are, however, many contracts of a continuous nature in which the relationship is entered into without specifying any time limit, and yet which are clearly not intended to be permanent. In these contracts it is permissible for one party to give notice to the other of his intention to bring the relationship to an end even if the contract does not stipulate such right.[66] For

---

[64] Unfair Terms in Consumer Contracts Regulations 1999, especially Sch. 2, paras. 19 (F) & (G).

[65] Unfair Contract Terms Act 1977, s. 3(2) (b) (ii).

[66] Of course, it is possible—and common—for parties to stipulate that a right to terminate on the occurrence of a particular breach or event can only be exercised by giving notice to terminate.

instance, a contract of hire, a contract of agency, a contract of employment, a lease, or any other similarly continuous agreement, if entered into for an indefinite time, may be terminated by notice. The length of the notice, if not expressly agreed upon, will vary according to the circumstances of the case, but it must always be 'reasonable' and in certain contracts, like contracts of employment and leases, it has come to be more or less standardised at common law by reference to the method of payment. So an employee paid by the week was normally entitled to at least a week's notice, and one paid by the month to a month's notice, but under modern legislation even an employee employed by the week will often be entitled to longer notice. It is not possible to determine agreements of this kind by unilateral notice where they are entered into for a fixed term, but if the relationship continues after the expiry of the term, it will usually be held to be 'at will', that is to say, terminable on notice by either party.

The easy way in which continuous contracts can be terminated at common law reflects the classical tradition that contracts are a matter of assent, and when either party no longer wants to continue in a relationship with the other, he should be allowed ready escape. The period of notice is, in a sense, a short-term period in which the other party may then go into the market and obtain there some substitute. This means that although the parties to a contract of unspecified duration may reasonably imagine that it will continue for a long period into the future, neither party has a *right* to the protection of his expectation; his only right is to the period of notice. In modern times, however, it has often been felt that this is unfair, and that long-continued and justified expectations are entitled to some legal protection. So, for instance, employees have been given many new statutory rights in recent decades, including especially a right to compensation for 'unfair dismissal' as well as to redundancy payments if their employment is terminated in many ordinary situations. Similarly, tenants have long enjoyed security of tenure under a variety of statutes.

These statutory rights were created during the period when the principle of freedom of contract was at a low ebb, and it may be questioned whether they should be perpetuated in all circumstances. The need for them arises partly because the market in these matters is often imperfect, so that it simply is not possible for one party to get what he needs elsewhere if his contract is terminated. In periods of high unemployment, an employee cannot always get another job when he is given notice, and in periods of great scarcity of rented accommodation, a tenant may not be able to find other premises if he is given notice to quit. On the other hand, the existence of these legally protected expectations is one of the very reasons the market often works badly. During the 1960s and 1970s the British labour market was almost frozen by the inability of employers to shed unnecessary employees (though this likely had more to do with trade union power than legal protection) and the legal protection of tenants of houses (at absurdly low rents) is certainly one of the main reasons there has traditionally been little accommodation available for rent in Britain. There has been some attempt to nibble away at the legal protection of these expectations by modern statutes reducing the right to redundancy payments, and allowing the possibility of letting houses without the protection of the Rent Acts.

Some will argue that there should at least be protection against 'unfair dismissal', whatever the market situation may be. At common law, if an employer gave the requisite notice, it did not matter what his reasons were for wanting to terminate the employment—whether he had good reasons, bad reasons or no reasons. This again followed the classical tradition: once the employer did not *want* to continue the employment, he was entitled to terminate it, whatever the reasons. But since 1971 an employee has been entitled to statutory compensation (from an industrial tribunal) if he is dismissed for reasons which are unfair, *even if the requisite notice is given.*

There is, however, no general requirement that a contracting party should act fairly (or even in good faith) in exercising his right to terminate a long-continued contract that is not an employment contract, and occasionally, the results of an uncontrolled legal right of termination appear harsh.[67] In 'franchise contracts', for instance, where someone invests capital in setting up a business in cooperation with a franchise company (such as a filling station, or a fast food outlet, or a hotel with a famous name), or where a commercial agent invests money and trouble in establishing a network of relationships on behalf of a commercial principal, the relationship is often terminable on (sometimes short) notice and there is often no contractual restriction on the grounds on which notice to terminate can be given. This is another area in which the fundamental principle of freedom of contract appears sometimes to clash with simple justice. Although the economic arguments for freedom of contract may suggest that such contracts should be terminable for good commercial reasons, the law does not generally supervise the validity of the reasons at all, so termination for whim or caprice—the equivalent of the 'unfair dismissal'—here remains perfectly permissible in law.

---

[67] The Unfair Terms in Consumer Contracts Regulations 1999 (see Ch. 12) includes in the list of suspect terms in the Annex a term enabling a seller or supplier to terminate a contract of indefinite duration without reasonable notice except where there are serious grounds; but because the regulations only apply for the benefit of consumers not acting in the course of business, they are not likely to help in most of these cases.

8

Unenforceable Terms and Contracts

GENERALLY speaking, when the requirements for the creation of a valid contract have been satisfied—that is to say, there has been an offer and acceptance of reasonable certainty; the parties have capacity, there is consideration; and any necessary formalities have been complied with—the resulting agreement will be legally enforceable. But sometimes the courts refuse to enforce a transaction (or parts of a transaction) even when these requirements are present because of its 'connection'—the word is deliberately vague—to an activity of which the law disapproves. An agreement to commit a crime, for example, is normally unenforceable. Other examples include gambling agreements and agreements in restraint of trade.

It is often said such agreements are unenforceable because they are contrary to the public interest or to public policy, but this is really just a way of emphasizing that the arrangement is unenforceable despite the fact that the parties (apparently) voluntarily agreed to it. Admittedly, a concern for the broader public interest explains certain rules in this area, such as rules that invalidate cartel agreements. But it is clear that in many cases the rules are based on a concern for the interests of individual members of the public rather than the public at large. For example, an agreement to defraud a third party is unenforceable because it is contrary to the interests of that particular party. And in yet other cases the courts' main concern appears to be the interests of the contracting parties themselves (as the courts understand those interests), as for instance, with rules invalidating gambling agreements.

The law dealing with substantive limitations on enforceability is riddled with terminological and classificatory difficulties. In part, this is because the subject is inherently complex. There are a variety of ways in which an agreement may be connected to an activity regarded as 'undesirable': it may require a party to perform an act that is itself undesirable; it may require acts that facilitate an undesirable activity; it may (merely) be performed using undesirable means, or finally, the very making of the contract may itself be undesirable. In addition, and overlapping with these distinctions, the reasons for classifying particular activities as undesirable and the degree to which an activity is so regarded also vary greatly. Thus, the law's disapproval, which may be expressed either through common law decision or statute, may be based (as was just noted) on a concern for the public, specific third parties, or even the contracting parties themselves, while the degree of disapproval may range from severe (e.g. in the case of murder) to almost trivial (e.g. in the case of a failure to obtain a statutorily required licence).

But probably the main reason for the terminological and classificatory difficulties associated with this area of the law is that the question of the *enforceability* of a contract has not been kept separate from other legal questions. In particular, it has not been separated from the question of whether parties may recover benefits transferred under unenforceable agreements. In many cases in which substantive limitations are an issue, the parties' real concern is not whether the agreement is enforceable (by an order of specific performance or damages), but whether benefits that were transferred under the agreement may be recovered. For instance, if I have invested money in your company in contravention of foreign currency regulations, can I demand that you return the money to me? While the legal unenforceability of our agreement is a necessary but not sufficient condition for restitution, this question is clearly different (and more difficult) from the question of whether, had I simply refused to go through with our agreement, I could have been required to do so or at least required to pay compensatory damages. Unfortunately, the historical underdevelopment of the English law of unjust enrichment—for it is unjust enrichment law that governs these questions—has meant that these two questions have often not been distinguished. As a result, many of the traditional classifications used when discussing the enforceability of agreements focus on the *consequences* of invalidity, in particular the consequences for a claim for restitution. For example, a distinction is often drawn between 'void' and 'illegal' contracts because, although both categories of agreements are equally unenforceable as contracts, the distinction can be significant when considering a claim for restitution.

Our primary concern in this chapter is the enforceability of a contract. The discussion will therefore be organised not around the consequences of unenforceability, but rather around the *reasons* for unenforceability. More specifically, the discussion is organised around three broad categories of such reasons: (a) the agreement requires that one or both parties do something undesirable (e.g. a contract to steal a painting); (b) the agreement unduly restrains the liberty of one or both parties (e.g. a contract in restraint of trade); (c) the agreement, though initially unobjectionable, was performed by, or otherwise associated with, undesirable acts (e.g., a delivery contract performed using stolen vehicles).[1]

---

[1] Strictly speaking, a fourth category of unenforceable agreements is agreements in which the very *making of the agreement* is regarded as undesirable. For example, a contract of sale may infringe a statutory regulation against 'dealing' in certain goods, and so be unenforceable for that reason alone. More generally, many unenforceable agreements qualify as criminal conspiracies. This may be the case even if the actual object of the agreement is not in itself criminal (although the Criminal Law Act 1977 in general now confines the crime of conspiracy to agreements involving the actual commission of an offence). This category is not treated separately because in each case the relevant agreement is an offence either because of what it requires the parties to do (category one above) or not do (category two above).

1. AGREEMENTS THAT REQUIRE ONE OR BOTH PARTIES
TO DO SOMETHING UNDESIRABLE

It has already been mentioned that this area of the law is beset by terminological difficulties. One particular difficulty is that there is no agreed label for the kinds of acts and agreements that are its focus. The most commonly adopted labels—'contrary to public policy', 'illegal', 'unlawful', 'immoral', 'void'—are, as we shall see, really only appropriate for a subset of the relevant acts and agreements. In this chapter, the label 'undesirable' is adopted because it is sufficiently broad as to include any activity (or restraint on activity) of which the law disapproves, for whatever reason. But precisely because of the term's breadth, it is important to stress that it is being used here in a special sense. 'Undesirable activity' is short-hand for 'an activity of which the law disapproves'. As we shall see, there is a relatively well-defined (though highly varied) group of such activities. A contract will not be set aside merely on the ground that it requires an activity that might be thought by most people or even most judges to be 'undesirable'. At the same time, this category includes activities that most people would condemn in the strongest terms possible, such as murder.

Cases in which performance is a crime or other legal wrong

An agreement (or term in an agreement) that *requires* one or both parties to do something of which the law disapproves is generally unenforceable. For example, an agreement to rob a bank is unenforceable. This conclusion is not surprising. As a matter of ordinary morality, a promise or agreement to do something that harms another or that is otherwise immoral is not binding.

For courts to apply the above principle they must, of course, first determine which acts qualify as 'undesirable' in the appropriate sense. In general (the exceptions are discussed below), courts in contract cases answer this question in the way one would expect, namely by looking to *other* parts of the law, that is to say, to the parts of the law that set out individuals' general legal duties. Thus, a contractual obligation to commit a crime or other legal wrong (e.g. a tort) is not enforceable.

This principle applies without difficulty to cases in which the relevant obligation has yet to be performed: it would be absurd for the law to enforce (by specific performance or damages) an obligation to do something that the law also says must not be done. Problems arise, however, where the unlawful performance has already happened and the court is being asked to enforce the *other party's* (lawful) obligation. The general rule in such cases is that enforcement is denied. An obligation to perform an unlawful act is unenforceable at the moment of formation, and so any agreement that includes such an obligation is (subject to the rules on severance discussed later) regarded as similarly unenforceable at the moment of formation. The contract, it is said, is void *ab initio*. This conclusion is uncontroversial where serious illegality is involved, as in the case of an agreement to commit murder. No one would suppose that a murderer should be allowed to enforce a claim to payment for his crime. But in the modern world, most 'crimes' are for the infringement of technical regulations, and involve little or no moral culpability. In these cases, refusing to enforce the remaining lawful part of the agreement may impose a penalty that is out of proportion to the claimant's crime—and give a windfall to the defendant, who may be equally guilty. Admittedly, disappointed claimants are sometimes able to recoup the value of their performance by an action in unjust enrichment, but this is not always possible (as we will see), and even when it is possible, the amount recovered may be less than the contract price.

Insofar as the courts have responded to this problem, it is by developing a distinction between cases in which it is said that the statute (these cases all involve breaches of statutory provisions) expressly or by implication prohibits the very *contract* and cases in which it merely penalises the *activity*. Only in the former case, it is said, is enforcement refused.[2] Thus a company that committed an offence by overloading its ship was not debarred from recovering a promised payment; the purpose of the relevant provision in the Merchant Shipping Act, it was held, was merely to penalise overloading, not to prohibit contracts performed by overloaded ships.

The terminology used in this distinction is confusing because in cases where the contract is unenforceable it is not strictly true that the 'contract' is prohibited: although the contract might sometimes amount to a criminal conspiracy, it is not generally the case that the relevant legislation penalises the actual making of the contract (the few cases where this happens fall within the third category of unenforceable contracts, discussed below). What is really meant by saying that the contract is prohibited by the statute is simply that (in the court's view) the statute makes any contract involving the activity unenforceable. On the other hand, the conclusion that the statute (merely) renders the activity unlawful is really just a way of saying that despite the unlawfulness of the activity, Parliament did not intend to make a contract involving such an activity unenforceable.

Aside from these terminological difficulties, there are also some substantive problems with this distinction. To begin, even where it is only the activity and not the contract which is said to be 'unlawful', it would surely be wrong for a court to enforce an *executory*, that is to say unperformed, obligation involving the unlawful activity. It would be wrong, for example, to order specific performance of an obligation to carry goods if that obligation could

---

[2] *St John Shipping Corp. v. Joseph Rank Ltd* [1957] 1 QB 267. In many of the cases that apply this principle, the agreement's terms could at least theoretically have been fulfilled without breaking the law. But the same principle is applied to both situations.

only be fulfilled by illegally overloading a ship. Yet if the above distinction is applied consistently, this would indeed be required. Another problem is that the disabling rule applies even if the whole purpose of the statute is to protect a class of persons of whom the claimant is a member. So where a statute prohibited the performance of a certain type of insurance contract (without the necessary authorization) it was held that the contract could not be enforced by the insured, even though the whole point of the statute was to protect insured persons from unauthorised insurers.[3] This decision seems to defy commonsense, and has now been reversed by Parliament.[4] Both of these substantive problem are reflections of a more general problem, which is that the distinction between statutes that prohibit the contract and those that merely prohibit the activity is made, in theory anyway, solely on the basis of the statute's wording and regardless of the seriousness of either the illegality or the consequences of a decision not to enforce.

Perhaps the main thing to be said in defence of the current approach is that the 'intent' of Parliament that is invoked to justify the distinction between statutes that prohibit the contract and statutes that merely prohibit the activity is usually a fiction. In reality, the courts in such cases often do exactly as they should, which is to weigh the seriousness of the offence against the seriousness of non-enforcement. A claimant who inadvertently breaches a trivial technical regulation in the course of building a large factory will not be denied the right to claim the contract price. But because this is not done openly, arguments cannot be addressed to the real issues, nor can the decision be evaluated by reference to those issues. This explains why the results some-times seem to be outrageous, as in the insurance case discussed earlier.

Cases in which performance is not otherwise unlawful

There is a small but important group of agreements that the courts refuse to enforce because they require acts that, while not actually crimes or other legal wrongs, are regarded as immoral or otherwise undesirable. A prostitution agreement, for example, is unenforceable, although prostitution is not itself illegal. The invalidity of such agreements again raises difficult questions. In the case of prostitution agreements and most other agreements in this group (e.g. surrogacy agreements,[5] marriage brokerage contracts), the transactions are often exploitative, but this does not explain a rule of blanket invalidity. The courts' approach to such agreements appears to be based on their view that the activities contemplated by such agreements are objectionable, even if

---

[3] *Phoenix General Insurance Co. of Greece v. Halvemon Insurance Co.* [1988] QB 216.
[4] Financial Services Act 1982, s. 132. See also *Fuji Finance Inc. v. Aetna Life Insurance Co. Ltd* [1994] 4 All ER 1025.
[5] Under the Surrogacy Arrangements Act 1985 it is an offence to negotiate a surrogacy agreement or arrangement, but this only affects agents and middle persons, not the parties directly concerned.

they are not actually illegal. More specifically, their approach seems based on the view that the activity in question 'commodifies' something that should not be commodified. Sexual relations are a valuable and important part of life—but not when they are entered into for money.

The idea that there are certain things that should not be commodified is widely held, but it may still be asked whether it justifies refusing to enforce a contract. If the argument is that paying for sexual relations (or surrogacy etc.) is harmful to the persons involved, this is a clear instance of paternalism; moreover, it is a particularly dangerous kind of paternalism since the consequence is to remove (or make less viable) what may be one of the few options for financial gain available to the selling party. On the other hand, if the argument is that commodifying sexual relations harms society generally, say by changing (for the worse) the meaning and value of such relations for everyone, the question is one of evidence. Is it in fact the case that the social meaning and value of sexual relations are changed for the worse if some individuals participate in the activity for money? And even if this does happen, is it not likely that another (uncommodified) activity will take over this social role?

Aside from commodification cases, the most important group of cases in which the courts refuse enforcement because the agreement requires an act that is considered undesirable, though not unlawful, involves wagers or bets. At common law, wagers and bets were valid contracts, but section 18 of the Gaming Act 1845 declared all such agreements to be null and void. There is nothing in the Gaming Act, however, to prevent parties from making and paying bets. Bets, once paid, cannot be recovered and there is, of course, an enormous betting industry which survives perfectly well without the ability to enforce unpaid bets by legal action. Internet betting, in particular, is a booming industry; it survives without the need of contract law by the simple expedient of requiring the punter to pay in advance, usually by credit card.

Some bets are made in circumstances in which the requirement of an intent to create legal relations would not be satisfied, while others are exploitative or at least extremely imprudent. But the blanket prohibition against enforcing such agreements is, again, difficult to explain except on the basis that gambling is itself an objectionable activity, or at least not particularly valuable, and so ought not be supported. This view may also be questioned: even if gambling appears to serve little economic or other practical purpose, the participants presumably gain enjoyment (or money) from it—which is all that can be said of a great many activities supported by contracts. It might also be queried whether the current law is consistent with the fact that Parliament taxes the gambling industry, and, with the introduction of the national lottery, may even be said to condone it.

In view of criticisms just mentioned, it is perhaps useful to mention that it does not seem inappropriate, in principle anyway, for there to exist a category of agreements that are invalidated on the ground that they require acts that, while not unlawful, are (thought to be) undesirable. Refusing to give legal enforcement to an agreement is clearly less serious than prohibiting an activity. When judges refuse to enforce agreements of the kind described above, they are effectively saying 'we will not stop you from doing this activity, but neither will we help you to do it'. This is a perfectly coherent position. Indeed, it is a position many people take in their day-to-day life in regard to activities such as prostitution, paid surrogacy, and gambling. The reason is straightforward: these are activities that are widely regarded (rightly or wrongly) as objectionable or worthless, but which do not directly affect anyone other than consenting participants.

The one important caveat is that just because an activity is *thought* by most people to be objectionable or worthless does not mean that this is actually the case. This caveat supports the long-standing principle that it is not open to a judge to reject a contract merely because she thinks it contrary to public policy. It is only when a contract falls under one of the well-established categories stigmatized as being contrary to public policy that a judge can interfere. Indeed, it was at one time suggested that courts could no longer invent new heads of public policy, although existing heads could be extended by analogy to new situations. This is probably too extreme a view; and in any event the distinction between a wholly new 'head' of public policy and a 'head' analogous to an existing category is likely to be unreal in practice. But this remains an area of the law in which courts (and legislatures) should proceed cautiously.

Cases in which performance facilitates other acts that are undesirable

For the same reason that agreements to perform acts of which the law disapproves are unenforceable, agreements to perform acts that assist or facilitate such acts are also unenforceable. Thus, an agreement to hide a bank robber is unenforceable. In cases where the facilitating act is itself a legal wrong, as in the example just given, this principle is usually easy to apply. Hiding a bank robber is the crime of 'aiding and abetting' and, as we have already seen, there can be no question of enforcing an agreement to do something that the law prohibits. In other cases, the courts' task is much more difficult. Three factors, in particular, complicate this area of the law. First, some undesirable acts are not (as we have already seen) criminal, and so some acts that assist in the commission of undesirable acts do not qualify as crimes. There is no crime of aiding and abetting gambling. Secondly, the definition of 'facilitating' used for determining the enforceability of an agreement is broader than the definition of 'aiding and abetting' that is used in criminal law. This is appropriate—refusing to enforce an agreement is, at most, a minor infringement of liberty—but it requires the courts to make exceedingly difficult judgments. Is an agreement to provide accommodation to a would-be bank robber enforceable? What if the accommodation is needed in part to prepare for the robbery and in part to accommodate the robber's family?

A final complicating factor is that performing an act that assists another to commit an undesirable act is not wrongful unless the performing party was aware that she was assisting the undesirable act. The person who sells explosives to a would-be bank robber has committed no wrong if she reasonably believes the explosives are to be used for demolishing an old building. Three situations, in particular, must be distinguished—keeping in mind that in each the issue is the enforceability of a partly or wholly *unperformed* agreement (by an order of damages or specific performance) rather than the merits of awarding restitution following a fully or partly *performed* agreement. In the first case, both parties to the contract know that the relevant act will assist in the commission of an undesirable act—for example both parties to an agreement to sell explosives know the explosives are to be used for a bank robbery. In this situation, neither party can enforce the agreement. Thus, in a well-known case it was held that a prostitute cannot be sued by a person who has supplied her with goods or premises which he knows are to be used by her for her professional purposes.[6]

The second situation is where the performing party learns that her act will assist in an undesirable act only after the agreement was made (but before she has performed)—for example, a vendor learns subsequent to making an agreement to sell explosives that the explosives are to be used in a robbery. This scenario is unlikely to come up in litigation—the would-be bank robber will not sue if the vendor will then reveal his criminal intentions, nor will the bank robber defend against a claim by the vendor by pleading those intentions—but it is again clear that the agreement is not and should not be enforceable by either party. A promise to perform an act that the promisor subsequently learns is wrongful has no more force than a promise to perform an act that is known from the beginning to be wrongful. This rule may seem harsh on innocent parties—they will lose the expected profits from what they may have reasonably believed was an innocent transaction—but they are able to bring actions for fraud or misrepresentation if, as will often be the case, they were misled by the other party. Indeed, it may be reasonable to assume that there is an implied representation in all such transactions that the subject matter of the contract will not be used for unlawful purposes.

The third situation is where the assisting party learns of the unlawful purpose only after performing the facilitating act (but before the other has performed)—for example, the vendor of explosives sues for non-payment and then learns in court what the other had intended to do with the explosives. This scenario is slightly more likely than the previous one since a would-be

---

[6] *Pearce v. Brooks* (1866) LR 1 Ex 213.

robber who has already been caught has nothing to lose by pleading his own criminal intentions. But in this case, there seems to be no reason not to allow the innocent party to enforce the contract, is she is truly innocent. The obligation to pay that the vendor in our example is seeking to enforce is not itself wrongful or otherwise undesirable. The vendor must, of course, rely on his own performance to claim payment, but this is not a problem since that performance was itself wholly innocent.

2. AGREEMENTS THAT UNDULY RESTRAIN THE LIBERTY OF ONE OR BOTH PARTIES

There are certain agreements (or terms in agreements) that are not enforceable because of what they *prevent* one or both of the parties from doing. Example include agreements that prevent individuals from working within a certain area or that preclude the parties to the agreement from applying to the courts for resolution of their disputes. For contract lawyers, these are interesting cases because they involve situations in which freedom of contract is limited on the seemingly paradoxical basis that the agreements in question themselves limit freedom. A second reason these cases are interesting is that the agreements in question are nearly all (merely) unenforceable as opposed to being unlawful. It is not generally a crime or otherwise unlawful to make such agreements nor to act in accordance with their terms. This is perhaps not surprising because (as was true of prostitution and gambling agreements) the only parties directly affected by contractually imposed limits on freedom are the parties to the contract. But it means that these limitations again raise the question of the proper scope of 'public policy' in the law of contract—the question of how far courts should be able to refuse enforcement simply on the grounds that they disapprove of the contract, even though what the contract is trying to accomplish is not itself unlawful.

Agreements in this category may be distinguished, in broad terms, according to whether the problem is thought to arise primarily because of the *kind* of freedom that is being given up (e.g. agreements that oust the jurisdiction of the courts) or primarily because of the extent or *scope* of freedom that is relinquished (e.g. agreements in restraint of trade). Two groups of cases in each category are discussed below.

Agreements to oust the jurisdiction of the courts

It is, of course, not unlawful to decline to pursue a legal claim before the courts and parties whose rights have been infringed often have good reasons for not going to the courts. But it is an ancient common law principle that any agreement to limit one's freedom in this way, that is to say to 'oust the jurisdiction of the courts', is void. The rather technical language in which this principle is always couched should not disguise its importance. It is a fundamental, indeed a constitutional principle of the highest importance, that civil disputes can only, in the last resort, be settled by the courts, and any attempt to contract out of this principle is against public policy. It is of the highest public importance that this ultimate power should remain available, even though today many other bodies also handle legal disputes at lower levels.

Given the rather high-sounding language of this principle, it may seem contradictory to recognize that contracting parties are today entitled to incorporate arbitration clauses into their contracts, under which they bind themselves not to apply to the courts until the dispute in question has been submitted to an arbitrator. Such a clause often severely limits the court's powers over the dispute, because the arbitrator may be given sole power to decide all questions of fact and even law that arise out of a contract. Generally speaking, however, there can be no objection to this course because an arbitrator is very much in the position of a (private) judge himself, and must follow and apply English law,[7] unless the contract specifically incorporates the law of some other country. Moreover, leave to appeal to the courts on questions of law can be granted although the courts have begun to insist that such leave should only be granted in special cases, in order that appeals should not be used as a matter of course to delay and clog up the arbitration process. Many business contracts, especially international contracts, today incorporate very wide arbitration clauses, because business people often prefer arbitration to litigation. It is usually quicker, cheaper, and more convenient in that parties can agree on hearing dates and places with the arbitrator. Furthermore, in international contracts parties can avoid the invidious problem of deciding which country is to be entrusted with any litigation arising out of the contract. London, in particular, has a high reputation in the commercial world as a centre of international arbitration, and many cases are heard before English arbitrators that have no connection at all with England or English law.

Sometimes, however, arbitration clauses are not so innocuous, especially when they are effectively imposed by one party on the other. For instance, it is notorious that insurance companies insist on arbitration clauses in all their contracts, partly because they prefer to avoid the publicity of court action. An action of this kind might do the insurance company much harm, especially if it is relying on technicalities rather than on the merits of the case. The Arbitration Act 1979 provides some small degree of consumer protection in this respect: the right to appeal to the courts from an arbitrator cannot be excluded in an insurance contract. It can only be excluded in an insurance

---

[7] But it must be admitted that since the passing of the Arbitration Act 1979 this requirement may be somewhat unreal, because there will often be no way of enforcing it.

case if the parties agree to do so after a claim is made. The Unfair Terms in Consumer Contracts Regulations 1999 also includes in its Annex of suspect terms any clause that requires disputes to be referred to arbitration 'not covered by legal provisions' (though the meaning of these last words may be so obscure as to deprive the provision of any real effect).

Agreements not to marry

Another kind of agreement that is unenforceable because it involves giving up a particular *kind* of freedom is an agreement not to marry. The freedom to marry and to choose one's spouse is obviously important and so it is not surprising that agreements *not* to marry have long been unenforceable. On the other hand, agreements to marry were for centuries legally enforceable contracts, although since 1970 they too have not been enforceable as contracts.

We turn now to consider two, closely related kinds of agreements that, it appears, are unenforceable primarily because of the *amount* or *extent* of freedom that they are thought to curtail.

Restraints on personal freedom

Restrictions on personal freedom have traditionally been kept to an absolute minimum in English law, and contractual restrictions on this freedom are generally void. Of course, contracts of employment are valid, even if made for life, but such contracts must not contain servile incidents. Hence a contract which imposes unreasonable restrictions on a person's right to live where he pleases, or to come and go as he chooses, is void. So too, a contract in which one party effectively agrees to act as another's slave, for example by agreeing to vows of 'obedience', are unenforceable.[8] The law also, and obviously, permits parties to consent (whether by contract or otherwise) to conduct which would otherwise constitute the tort of 'false' or wrongful imprisonment. Clearly a person may validly contract to work in a coal mine, and in that event cannot throw up the contract and demand to be taken to the surface at a moment's notice. However, any contractual clause which deprived him of the right to be taken up to the surface *as soon as reasonably practicable* would almost certainly be unenforceable. Similarly, individuals may obviously contract to travel by ship or air even though, in the process, some limits on their personal freedom of movement are involved. It is not clear whether similar restraints on freedom would be legally valid where they are less strictly necessary as, for example, if a theatre company stipulated on its tickets that clients would not be entitled to leave the theatre while a play was in progress.

---

[8] See the Canadian case of *Archer v. Sacred Heart* (1905) 9 OLR 474.

Restraints of trade

Contracts in restraint of trade are one of the most important categories of unenforceable agreements at common law. The modern term would be 'restrictive practices', which is, indeed, somewhat wider than 'agreements in restraint of trade', but the economic and legal problems are the same. Broadly, these are agreements in which one or both parties limit their freedom to work or carry on their profession or business in some way, such as (for instance) by agreeing not to compete with each other in certain places. Like restraints on personal liberty, such agreements are regulated because it is thought that they may unduly restrict the freedom of the concerned individuals. Such regulation is essentially paternalist—unreasonable restraints are thought to harm the interests of the restrained parties—but we have seen that courts do not hesitate to act paternalistically when they believe an important freedom is being curtailed, particularly if there are reasons to think the normal bargaining process may fail to adequately protect this freedom. This latter concern has long been raised in connection with covenants in restraint of trade, especially post-employment covenants, although the explanation nowadays is not so much that the affected party had no choice in the matter but that such covenants are often poorly understood and their impact underestimated. But in addition to the question of the parties' interests, agreements in restraint of trade are also widely thought to be problematic because of their possible effect on the broader public interest. More specifically, restrictive agreements are often attacked on the basis that they unduly restrict the free flow of labour and goods on which a market economy depends.

Contracts in restraint of trade are thus merely one aspect of a large and complex problem with important social and economic implications. From the legal point of view it straddles the laws of contract, tort, and crime, and is now subject to much public law regulation, as well as the law of the EU. Essentially, the question is the extent to which the law should interfere with the freedom of contracting parties to do business in such a way as to limit or restrict competition. Broadly speaking, the traditional attitude of the courts was to leave the parties to use their own methods of conducting business, even if this was likely to lead to the creation of monopolies, unfair competition, or the enforcement of restrictive practices of various kinds. The influence of economic theories, and in particular of *laissez-faire*, can be seen in many important cases.[9] The influence of *laissez-faire* was reinforced by the difficulty the courts faced in taking positive action without getting even more deeply involved in political or economic theories. In modern times, however, courts have taken a more active approach to agreements in restraint of trade.

---

[9] See *Mogul Steamship Co. Ltd v. McGregor, Gow & Co.* (1889) 23 QBD 598, appealed, [1892] AC 25, especially the speech of Lord Bramwell.

In addition, legislation has become increasingly important in handling the wider implications of anti-competitive practices. The role of the common law is now of relatively minor importance in cases involving agreements to form cartels (e.g. a price-fixing ring) and other kinds of 'horizontal' restraints.

In assessing the validity of agreements in restraint of trade, the general principle of the common law is that they are void unless they are 'reasonable' in the interests of the public and of the parties. The meaning of 'reasonable' in each of these contexts will be examined below, but first it is necessary to say something about what kinds of contractual clauses are subject to the doctrine and, further, what kinds of interests such clauses may legitimately attempt to protect.

What kinds of restraints?

There are countless ways in which a person's freedom to trade or work may be curtailed by contract, but until relatively recently little attention has been given to specifying what kinds of restrictions may be scrutinised under the common law principles. Aside from cartels and other horizontal restraints (now dealt with almost exclusively by legislation), the law of restraint of trade was traditionally thought to be applicable solely to contractual clauses that prohibit a person from working in a certain trade or profession, usually subject to limitations of time and space. Clauses of this kind are commonly found in two types of contract. First, they are found in contracts for the sale of the goodwill of a business or professional practice. Manifestly, the buyer of a shop or practice will want to ensure that the seller will not immediately set up a competing business next door and draw back most of his old clients or customers. Hence the buyer will usually want the seller to agree not to enter into competition with him. By definition, a sale of goodwill necessarily involves some degree of limitation on the seller's freedom to compete. Secondly, clauses of this kind are often found in written contracts of employment, the employer requiring his employee to agree that she will not work for a competing employer or set up a competing business of her own after she leaves her present work. Such clauses are also often found in analogous non-employment relationships, such as the relationship between a self-employed pop singer and his music publisher, or a professional boxer and his agent or manager, and in general they are governed by the same principles as apply to employment contracts.[10]

Most restraint-of-trade cases still involve sale-of-business or post-employment covenants, but the modern cases show that the courts are now willing to develop this part of the law after a long period during which legal changes had been left to Parliament. In particular, in *Esso Petroleum Co. Ltd*

---

[10] See, e.g., *A. Schroeder Music Publishing Co. v. Macaulay* [1974] 1 WLR 1308 and *Watson v. Prager* [1991] 3 All ER 487.

v. Harper's Garage,[11] the House of Lords decided that the categories of restraint of trade are not closed, and that other types of contract may be held void as being in restraint of trade, such as contracts relating to 'tied' garages, that is, garages (or filling stations) where only one brand of petrol may be sold. It is not easy to determine, however, which contracts qualify as being restraints of trade. By definition, every contract involves some restriction on liberty, and indeed, most contracts involve restrictions that are of the same general kind, even if not of the same degree, as those found in recognised restraints on trade. For example, an employee is not free to work except for her employer during ordinary working hours, and a buyer who contracts to obtain all the supplies of some commodity which she needs from a particular seller (a common enough form of business agreement) is restricting her freedom to buy from anyone else. At the same time, it would be wrong to conclude that *all* contracts containing restrictions are now open to challenge as contracts in restraint of trade.

Many customary and accepted forms of business agreement are probably still unchallengeable (at any rate under the common law rules), even though they may, strictly speaking, involve a degree of business restraint. In particular, it has been held that a person who buys land (or a building) may validly agree to some restrictions on how the land is to be used without triggering the restraint of trade doctrine—in other words he cannot challenge the validity of the agreement on the ground that it is an unreasonable restraint.[12] This limit on the scope of the doctrine has been justified on the ground that, if a seller could not validly demand from the buyer some restriction of this kind, he might choose not to sell at all, which would be even more restrictive of competition.[13] Of course, this same argument could be made about any agreement whereby a seller of a business takes an unreasonably wide restraint from the buyer. In the end, there does not appear to be any difference *in kind* between the kinds of restraints that are subject to the doctrine and those that are not. Rather, the explanation would appear to be that various kinds of restraints are exempt simply because it is unlikely in practice that they will be found unreasonable. As will be explained below, certain kinds of restraints—sale-of-business and post-employment covenants are the obvious examples—are more likely to be unreasonable than other kinds.

Restraints must protect a 'legitimate interest'

In deciding whether a restraint of trade is reasonable, the courts have long taken the view that regard must be had to the 'interests' which the restraint is

---

[11] [1968] AC 269.
[12] *Alec Lobb (Garages) Ltd v. Total Oil GB Ltd* [1985] 1 WLR 173.
[13] Ibid.

designed to protect. The general principle is that such clauses are valid if, but only if, they are no wider than is reasonably necessary to protect the legitimate interests of the promisee. The nature of these interests differs according to the type of case. Thus, in cases of buyers and sellers of businesses the courts quite naturally think it reasonable for the buyers to protect against competition by the sellers so as to protect the value of the business. It is, indeed, in the sellers' interests that such contracts be upheld because they would not otherwise be able to get as high prices for their businesses. Once the courts had recognized the concept of goodwill as being property with a money value attached to it, this conclusion was inevitable. But it is still true that the restraint must not be wider than is reasonably necessary to protect the buyer's purchase. For instance, the seller cannot be prevented from opening a new business in a town where the old business had no customers, nor may the clause operate for a length of time disproportionate to the type and size of the business.

Generally speaking, as the restraint grows wider in space and longer in time, the interests of the buyer must be correspondingly larger if the restraint is to be justified. In an extreme case, extreme restraints may be justified. For instance, in one leading case, a company that bought an armament business for the huge sum (in 1897) of £287,000 took a covenant from the seller that he would not enter into competition with this business anywhere in the world for a period of 25 years.[14] This was held to be justified because the business was world-wide in its operations and its customers were mainly governments.

In employment cases, the courts have insisted that an employer cannot protect himself against bare competition. Even though, as is commonly the case, the employer has trained the employee, or enabled her to develop into a skilled or professional worker, he cannot demand that these skills should not be used against him.[15] The employer is not permitted to make a contract which prevents the employee using these skills or experience in competition with the employer unless he has a legitimate interest that requires protection. Basically, there are only two such interests that the courts have recognized, though both are somewhat nebulous and ill-defined concepts: trade secrets and business connections. It would obviously be unjust that an employee should work for a rival and impart to him special methods of manufacture which he has learnt while working for a previous employer. Indeed, the law gives limited protection to employers in this regard even in the absence of a special contractual prohibition, though such prohibitions can be used to extend this protection. So, for instance, a restraint was upheld in *Littlewoods v. Harris*,[16] where the defendant had worked as a senior executive for the

---

[14] *Nordenfelt v. Maxim Nordenfelt Gun Co.* [1894] AC 535.
[15] *Faccenda Chicken Ltd v. Fowler* [1987] Ch 117.   [16] [1977] 1 WLR 1472.

claimants, a large mail-order firm, and then left to work for their only serious rivals after having helped prepare the new season's catalogue for the claimants. So, also, where an employee comes into contact with clients or customers, it is generally felt unacceptable that he should later attempt to use his personal influence with these clients in order to draw them away for a new employer, or for himself, if he chooses to set up business on his own account. Thus, a hairdresser's assistant would not be permitted to work for a rival salon in breach of a reasonable restraint.[17] Restraints in cases of this nature must normally be much more limited in time and space if they are to be upheld than in the case of business sellers; in the hairdresser's assistant case, a restraint covering twelve months, but only a half-mile radius of her previous employer's salon, was held reasonable; and in *Littlewoods v. Harris*, referred to above, a ban on working for the one rival employer for twelve months was also upheld.

No magic attaches to the words 'trade secrets'. In particular, it must be remembered that the doctrine of restraint of trade applies to all sorts of professional and business activities, and is not limited to trade in the usual sense. For instance, it applies even to professional sports, many of which impose highly restrictive rules on the players—preventing them from playing for certain teams, or banning them from selection for national teams. Such restrictions have to be reasonable, like all other restrictions, if they are to be legally valid.

Outside the traditional categories of sale-of-business restraints and post-employment restraints, it seems that a variety of 'interests' may qualify as legitimate. For example, in the leading case[18] dealing with 'tied garages' the court held that the simple desire of a business for an orderly and regular marketing of its products was a 'legitimate interest'—though it is not immediately obvious how this differs from an interest in restraining competition per se, which is clearly not legitimate. A similarly broad approach was taken in one of the cases dealing with sports authorities, *Greig v. Insole*,[19] where it was held that the cricket authorities had sufficient interest in the organization of the game at test and county level to justify the imposition of reasonable restraints on the players, though the restraint in question—a test and county ban on any player playing in an unauthorized tour of Australia— was too wide to be justified. Bans on sportsmen who associated with or played cricket in South Africa in the days of apartheid never came before the courts in England, but if challenged, would also have had to be justified in the same way. Probably, sports authorities would be held to have sufficient interest in the general management of their sports to try to prevent players consorting with countries which are the subject of an international boycott

---

[17] *Marion White v. Francis* [1972] 1 WLR 1423.
[18] *Esso Petroleum*, above n. 11.   [19] [1978] 1 WLR 302.

(as South Africa was) though even that is arguable because it is not wholly clear why sporting authorities should have a legitimate interest in such political matters.

Reasonableness in the interests of the parties and of the public

In all these cases, the principle applied by the courts is that the restraint must be shown to be reasonable in the interests of the parties and of the public. Each limb of this test calls for explanation.

There is no doubt that restraints of trade may have a detrimental effect on the public interest—but this is true of nearly all contracts. Any contract under which goods or services are allocated other than to their most valuable use is prima facie inefficient and so against the public interest. So, for instance, a contract under which an important scientist agrees to work full-time in a fast-food outlet would appear to be contrary to the public interest. Indeed, such a contract is similar in kind to a post-employment covenant prohibiting the scientist from working in a similar field. But the courts do not ask if ordinary contracts of this kind are in the public interest. It is assumed without question that the public interest is simply irrelevant when dealing with the private activities of consenting adults or, alternatively, that the public interest is best served by enforcing private agreements since (following Adam Smith) the private interest and the public interest generally overlap (and in any event, the courts are poor judges of the efficiency of private arrangements). The question, then, is why do these same arguments not apply to contracts in restraint of trade? Why, in other words, do we not assume that an employee's interest in obtaining rewarding work in the future, and an employer's interest in not having to pay for unnecessary restraints, will ensure that any agreement regarding future restraints that they reach is also in the public interest?

In considering this question, it is important to distinguish restraints that are used to create cartels or monopolies from other kinds of restraints. The former are, of course, specifically designed to prevent the market from working. These are arrangements in which private interests clash systematic-ally with the public interest—the cartel members benefit, but the public suffers. But this fact does not wholly explain the public interest test because agreements in support of cartels and monopolies have never been a major concern of restraint of trade law, and are now almost exclusively regulated by statutory provisions. In truth, it is difficult to explain why the public interest is thought to be important when enforcing restraints of trade, but not for enforcing other kinds of agreements. It may be that the 'public interest' has been raised in these cases simply to make the courts' willingness to limit freedom of contract in this area appear less anomalous. Certainly, it is difficult to tell from the cases what role the public interest test is meant to play. Although the courts regularly mention this test, in practice they give it almost no independent weight. The conclusion that a restraint is reasonable in the interests of the parties is generally treated as sufficient to show that the restraint is reasonable in the interest of the public. Indeed, the courts have almost never concluded that a restraint that is reasonable in the interests of the parties is contrary to the public interest.

Since the courts seem to emphasise the parties' interests, it is important to examine the questions surrounding the test for reasonableness under this limb. Here again a question of fundamental importance is immediately raised: why is the normal assumption that the parties are the best judges of their own interests not applied to agreements in restraint of trade? The argument that is sometimes made to justify the regulation of agreements involving sexual immorality or gambling—namely that individuals need to be protected from their own base or perverted desires—clearly does not apply. Individuals who agree to unduly restrictive agreements do not do so because they have a taste or desire to be restrained. The most common explanation for why covenants in restraint of trade are regulated is that such covenants are frequently imposed on parties who have no choice but to accept them even when it is clear the restraints are not in their interests. No doubt this happens in many cases, but it does not explain the law's particular focus on covenants in restraint of trade. The first thing that employers or purchasers of businesses who are in a position to dictate terms are likely to do is to demand a favourable wage or purchase price. But wage and price terms are not generally subject to regulation. Moreover, there is little to show that parties subject to unreasonable post-employment or sale-of-business restraints are forced to accept such restraints. To be sure, the employer or buyer's offer may have been on a take-it or leave-it basis, but this proves little if, as is usually the case, the employee or vendor could have contracted with a different party.

A more plausible explanation for why agreements in restraint of trade are subject to special scrutiny is that contracting parties are often poor judges of whether such agreements are in their best interests. Agreements in restraint of trade typically deal with temporally-distant, low-probability events, the significance of which can be difficult to estimate. Potential employees signing employment contracts naturally expect to remain with their employer and rarely spend much time thinking about their rights on termination. Indeed, it might be inappropriate for an employee to raise the issue of consequences of termination as this could be taken as a lack of commitment. And even when potential employees do think about these matters, it is often difficult for them to judge the significance of a restraint that may not be applied until many years in the future, at which time employment opportunities may be very different. In these respects, post-employment covenants are similar to exemption clauses and stipulated damages clauses. Each deals with the consequences of a low-probability, future event—and each is invalid unless 'reasonable'.

This justification—that agreements in restraint of trade must be regulated because contracting parties are unable to properly assess and understand them—is, of course, paternalistic. The argument would be more compelling, therefore, if it were clear that judges were better than contracting parties at determining the reasonableness of such covenants; unfortunately, this is not always the case. The main reason for this is that the reasonableness of a restraint on trade cannot be assessed properly without considering economic arguments of a kind that judges are not well-equipped to understand. In *A. Schroeder Music Publishing Co. Ltd v. Macaulay*,[20] the House of Lords had to examine a restraint in a contract between a songwriter and a music publisher. The contract required the writer to offer all his songs to the publisher for five years, and the publisher had the option to renew the contract for a further five years; but the contract imposed almost no obligations on the publisher except to pay a royalty on songs actually published. It was held that, while the publisher was entitled to impose some reasonable restraint on the songwriter, ten years was too long, particularly as the publisher was not obliged to publish any of the songs. Effectively, what the contract meant was that if the song-writer became (as this one did) highly successful, the publisher would have the benefit of his songs for ten years even if he had not really helped him to 'hit the jackpot'. It is possible that the House of Lords reached the correct result in this case. But what is striking is that the court failed to discuss the kinds of evidence necessary to support its conclusion. The music-publishing business is highly competitive, with the consequence that publishers operate on very thin profit margins. Because there are many people who want to be song-writers, and very few ever achieve success, it is inevitable that contracts with beginners will not be very rewarding, and will contain clauses demanding that, if the writer does become highly successful, some of the profits should be diverted to the publishers. If publishers are not permitted to make contracts like this with would-be song-writers, fewer beginners will have a chance to have their songs published. The judgment in *Schroeder* did not examine any of these considerations; it appeared to be based largely on the fact that the songwriter was unsophisticated and that *ex post* the contract turned out to be a bad deal for this particular songwriter.

Even if we accept that a degree of paternalism is appropriate in this area, it is clearly more justified in respect of certain kinds of restraints than others. Sale-of-business covenants, for example, take effect immediately, and so are usually inspected carefully by vendors who may be thought to have a good idea of their likely impact. More generally, the argument that parties who agree to agreements in restraint of trade often make cognitive errors is less persuasive where the parties in question are sophisticated commercial parties.

---

[20] Above n. 10.

These considerations may help to explain why the courts are more hesitant to strike down sale-of-business covenants than post-employment covenants. They may also explain why certain categories of post-employment covenants are treated more favourably than others, such as covenants in partnership agreements preventing ex-partners from competing. For instance, in *Bridge v. Deacons*[21] the defendant was a solicitor who had formerly been a member of a firm in Hong Kong. The partnership agreement prevented him for five years from dealing with any client of the firm, or anyone who had been a client within the previous three years. The defendant argued that this covenant was unreasonably wide because the firm's business was divided into some ten branches and he had had no effective dealings with about ninety per cent of the firm's clients. Moreover, the covenant greatly limited the defendant's capacity to work as a solicitor in Hong Kong at all. The Privy Council upheld the covenant, but it seems unlikely that it would have reached the same result if the case had involved a former employee rather than a partner.

In conclusion, while the common law rules dealing with agreements in restraint of trade may be less politically charged than those dealing with, say, prostitution agreements, wagers, and the like, from a legal perspective they are equally controversial. In particular, it may be argued that the courts should give more weight in this area to the traditional principle that it is the parties and not the courts that should determine whether an agreement is in the parties' interests.

Statutory developments

The common law rules concerning agreements in restraint of trade worked reasonably well in the case of sale-of-business and post-employment restraints, but they suffered from four weaknesses that caused particular problems in cases involving cartel arrangements and other horizontal restraints. First, an unreasonable restraint is merely unenforceable rather than prohibited. This meant that parties are free to act in accordance with an unreasonable restraint—which they will frequently have an incentive to do in the case of cartel arrangements. In the famous case of *Mogul Steamship Co. Ltd v. McGregor, Gow & Co.*,[22] a number of shipping companies combined to offer discounts off their freight charges for the China tea trade with a view to preventing the claimant, a rival shipping company, from obtaining a foothold in the trade. These discounts, however, were only available to those who used the shipping companies concerned for *all* their trade. Clearly, this was a severe disincentive to any trader to use other ships at all, and therefore

---

[21] [1984] AC 705.
[22] Above n. 9. It is interesting to note that almost contemporaneously with this decision the US Congress passed the Sherman Anti-Trust Act which converted agreements in restraint of trade into *prohibited* agreements.

a highly anti-competitive device, as economists were by then beginning to appreciate. But while the defendants' agreement was clearly in restraint of trade, and probably unreasonably wide, the claimant (who was not a party to the agreement) lost its case.

The second principal weakness of the common law rules was that the public was not represented in litigation. Indeed, evidence of what is in the public interest is strictly inadmissible because the 'public interest' is supposed to be a matter of law, within the knowledge of the judges. Again, this is problematic in the case of cartel arrangements, because it is precisely this kind of restraint that may be contrary to the public interest even though in the parties' interest.

The third weakness was that the practice and procedure of ordinary courts is ill-suited to an inquiry into the effect of a restraint on the public interest. Such an inquiry may raise wide issues of social and economic policy and may require prolonged and careful examination of the likely effect of such agreements on the national economy or important parts of it. Judicial procedures, with their tradition of oral evidence and cross-examination, and their assumption that issues of fact are just matters for ordinary evidence, are not suited to handling issues of this kind.

The fourth weakness of the common law principles was that they were confined to dealing with agreements and contracts. In the seventeenth century there had been signs of a wider set of doctrines dealing with restraints on competition, but very little remained by the nineteenth century except the rules dealing with agreements. This left a huge hole in anti-competition policy. In particular, it did not account for the restrictive effects of monopolies and mergers. A monopoly is obviously more effective as a form of restriction on competition than an agreement between rivals not to compete, but if the rivals merge to form one large monopoly, the common law rules against restraint of trade simply have no operation at all.

The result of these weaknesses in the common law was that restrictive practices flourished between the last decades of the nineteenth century and the Second World War. By 1950, British industry and trade were riddled with a vast network of restrictive practices of every kind. Resale price maintenance, to take one prominent example, was a system whereby manufacturers combined together to agree to compel retailers to abide by the retail prices set by the manufacturers themselves. First the manufacturers agreed on their own prices so as to reduce or eliminate competition among themselves, and then they ensured that every retailer was forced to observe these prices, so there was no price competition between retailers either. The whole system was rigidly enforced by stop-lists so that any retailer who dared to sell an item at a cut price was liable to be 'fined' by private courts or have his supplies cut off, not merely by the supplier whose goods were in question, but by all other suppliers too.

These failures of the common law eventually led to legislative activity in an attempt to restore competition to the British economy. The first significant sign of the new approach was the passing of the Restrictive Trade Practices Act 1956 (replaced by the Restrictive Trade Practices Act 1976) which created a new court—the Restrictive Practices Court—whose members include non-lawyers with experience of economic matters and of trade and industry. Under this Act many restrictive agreements are required to be registered with the Director-General of Fair Trading. These agreements are then brought before the Court, which is charged with the task of deciding if they are in the public interest. The Director-General has the function of representing the public in these proceedings and he is represented by counsel before the Court like an ordinary litigant. If the Court finds the agreement to be contrary to the public interest it then becomes illegal to carry out the agreement or make any other agreement to like effect.

After the Act was passed a number of important decisions by the Court made it clear that a huge number of restrictive agreements would, in all probability, eventually be found to be contrary to the public interest. Consequently, many such agreements were abandoned or modified and the purposes of the original Act were thus to some degree achieved. Later amendments to the original Act extended it to many restrictions relating to the supply of services as well as goods, though in general, professional services still fall outside the jurisdiction of the Court.

Another important development was the passing of the Resale Prices Act 1964 (replaced by Resale Prices Act 1976) which gave the Restrictive Practices Court jurisdiction to deal with resale price maintenance arrangements and to decide if these were in the public interest. Here again, the work of the Court has now resulted in the almost complete collapse of resale price maintenance. A further statutory development was the creation of the Monopolies and Mergers Commission, an administrative body whose only powers are to inquire and report into various questions concerning restrictive agreements and monopoly situations. The appropriate Minister has statutory powers to prohibit arrangements contrary to the public interest on the strength of a report from the Monopolies and Mergers Commission.

Much of the relevant legislation was consolidated in the Fair Trading Act 1973, which established the office of Director-General of Fair Trading who is charged with a general oversight of restrictive and anti-competitive practices. The Act also created an Advisory Committee to which various sorts of trade practices which may be harmful to consumer interests may be referred. A report of the Advisory Committee may lead to the prohibition or regulation of such practices by statutory order; further powers are granted by the Competition Act 1980.

Finally, there are important provisions in Articles 85 and 86 of the EC Treaty which (in very broad language) are designed to limit anti-competitive devices and arrangements so as to prevent the distortion of competition over the whole or any part of the EC. These articles deal not only with restrictive practices, but also with the 'abuse of a dominant position' in the market by a monopoly or dominant firm. As the Treaty is now part of English law, these articles (and the powers conferred under them on the European Commission, the Council, and the Court) are now also part of English law. A considerable body of law now exists on these provisions, including case law of the European Court and rulings of the Commission, but this law is too specialised for treatment here.

There is no doubt that the British economy is today far more competitive than it was forty or fifty years ago as a result of this legislative activity. Alongside the fact that there is now significant price competition, competition on contract terms on offer to consumers has also become available in a very wide range of transactions. This is a matter of some general importance to contract law, because it greatly affects the validity of the argument, still often used with regard to consumer transactions, that consumer contracts are 'imposed' on them by those with superior bargaining power.

3. AGREEMENTS THAT ARE INITIALLY UNOBJECTIONABLE, BUT THAT ARE PERFORMED USING, OR BECOME OTHERWISE ASSOCIATED WITH, UNDESIRABLE ACTS

The third and probably most complex category of substantive limitations on enforceability is comprised of rules that limit enforcement not because of what the agreement requires or prohibited, but because it has been 'tainted' by association with an undesirable activity. In these cases, it is not the contract per se that is the problem, but rather that the person seeking to enforce the contract has committed a wrong *and* the wrong is connected in some way to the contract. For example, if a salesperson were to reach a quota by closing sales at gunpoint, his entitlement to any bonus tied to that quota would certainly be unenforceable. The main principle underlying these limitations is of ancient lineage and applies both to contractual and non-contractual claims: *ex turpi causa non oritur action* (no action is possible on a disreputable cause). But the application in the present context of the idea that the courts should not assist wrongdoers raises special difficulties because there are various ways in which a contract may be connected to a wrongful act, and various acts are wrongful only in a technical sense.

Agreements that are performed using illegal means

One way an agreement that is not otherwise invalid may be associated with wrongdoing is if it is *performed* using illegal means. In such cases, the principle traditionally applied is that a party who performs using illegal means is denied enforcement, but the other party (assuming the illegality involved only one party) may enforce unless she was aware of the illegal means and condoned them. Thus, a shipper who fulfils a shipping contract using a stolen ship would normally not be able to obtain a court order for payment of the contract price, but the owner of the goods, assuming she was unaware of the shipper's plans, could bring an action for, say, late delivery. There are nowadays numerous exceptions to this principle. One exception is where the illegality relates only to a small part of the performance. Thus, if in the previous example it was not the ship, but merely one of the ship's ropes that had been stolen, the court would almost certainly allow the shipper's claim for enforcement.

A second exception is where the illegality arises from infringing a minor or technical statutory requirement. In these cases, the relevant party is often a wrongdoer in only a weak sense, and in this situation it may be highly unjust to refuse enforcement given that the consequences may be far more serious than the penalty associated with the actual infraction. The rule applied in these cases is the same one that is applied in cases in which the contract actually *requires* illegal performance: the breach of the statute disentitles a person from enforcing the agreement only if the statute is found to expressly or by implication 'prohibit' (or, more accurately, make 'unenforceable') this kind of contract.[23] Thus the merchant who commits the statutory offence of selling goods without delivering to the buyer a note containing certain particulars is breaking the law in the very act of performing a 'prohibited' contract, and will accordingly be unable to enforce it. But a truck driver who breaks the speed limit in delivering goods will not be debarred from claiming the contract price. We noted in the earlier discussion of agreements that require unlawful acts that, while this principle properly recognizes that not all kinds of illegality are equivalent, it is a blunt tool that can produce highly unfair results if applied strictly. This observation applies equally where the principle is applied to cases involving illegal performance.

Conditional contracts where the condition is satisfied using illegal means

A second category of agreements that are (merely) associated with wrong-doing are those in which one party's obligations are conditional on a certain event and that event is brought about by the other party's wrongdoing. The principles governing enforcement in these cases are similar to those in the previous category. Thus, there is a well-established rule of insurance law that insured parties cannot claim under a policy if they actually cause the insured event to occur by deliberate criminal conduct. So in *Beresford v.*

---

[23] *St. John Shipping*, above n. 2. As was explained in discussing the first category of unenforceable agreements, the language of this principle is confusing, since the question before the court is not whether the contract is prohibited but whether it is enforceable.

Royal Insurance Co. Ltd,[24] it was held that suicide by an insured (at a time when suicide was a crime) debarred his administrators from claiming the proceeds of a life insurance policy—even though the policy itself did not exclude such a claim. So, too, at common law, a person who killed another so as to be guilty of murder or manslaughter was debarred from recovering any benefit from an insurance policy. The rule did not, however, apply to an accidental or even negligent killing, so that (for instance) individuals whose negligent driving causes death or injury have never been prevented from getting indemnities from their insurers—indeed the whole road traffic insurance system assumes they will do so.

Miscellaneous cases

There are a variety of other ways in which a contract that does not actually require or itself constitute a wrongful act may be associated with wrongdoing. The general principle the courts apply in these cases is that enforcement is denied if it depends on, arises from, or requires the support of the illegal act. Thus, in *Alexander v. Rayson*[25] a landlord was disentitled from enforcing a lease where he had prepared two separate documents for the tenant to sign in order to defraud the rating authorities by making it appear that the rent was lower than it was intended to be. Here the landlord was trying to sue on *both* documents, so his claim was founded upon the very documents that made up the illegality. In other cases, the courts must rely upon finer distinctions, as is illustrated by a pair of cases from the law of insurance. In *Geismar v. Sun Alliance and London Insurance Ltd*[26] the claimant was held not entitled to claim from his burglary insurers for goods stolen from him, because they had been illegally imported without being declared to the customs authorities. Here the claimant had been in the possession of smuggled goods, and his claim to their value included, of course, an element which represented the unpaid customs duty. On the other hand, this case was distinguished in *Euro-Diam Ltd v. Bathurst*[27] where the claimants had dispatched diamonds to German buyers with an invoice understating their value, to assist the buyers in defrauding the German customs authorities. The diamonds were lost or stolen after they reached the buyers but before they had agreed to buy them, and were therefore still covered by the sellers' insurance policy. Here it was held that the attempt to defraud the German authorities (which was treated as on a par with a violation of English law) was only marginally for the benefit of the sellers, and did not taint their claim to the proceeds of the insurance policy. The sellers did not smuggle the goods, they did not make use of the fraudulent invoice, and they did not have possession of the goods at the relevant time.

---

[24] [1938] AC 586.   [25] [1936] I KB 169.   [26] [1978] QB 383.
[27] [1988] 2 All ER 23.

4. THE CONSEQUENCES OF AN UNENFORCEABLE TERM OR AGREEMENT

From the perspective of contract law, the primary consequence of concluding that an obligation is unenforceable for one of the reasons described above is that (as we have seen) the courts will neither order the obligation to be performed nor require a defaulting party to compensate for its non-performance. We have also seen that such a result is sometimes harsh, particularly when the wrongdoing is trivial or involves only one of the parties. It is important to bear in mind, therefore, that the parties to an unenforceable agreement may have other legal rights. Four such rights are examined below.

Severance

In cases in which the offending obligation constitutes just one part of a larger agreement the court may be willing to 'sever' the obligation, leaving the rest of the agreement enforceable. Thus an invalid restraint on trade or an invalid attempt to oust the jurisdiction of the courts will normally not prevent the other terms in the contract from being enforced. Moreover, in some cases, the court is willing to sever just one part of the offending clause (e.g. one term in a covenant in restraint of trade), and declare the rest of the clause binding. It should be said that the principles governing 'severance', which are important mainly in the field of restraint-of-trade clauses, are not easy to state, and in many cases the courts appear to have acted on an unacknowledged discretion rather than fixed rules of law. Thus, where the courts are faced with a covenant in restraint of trade drafted so widely as to appear oppressive, they have generally refused to assist the promisee by removing the offending part of the clause from the rest.[28] On the other hand, and especially in buyer-and-seller cases, where a covenant is only slightly too wide, for example, in that it covers areas where the seller has never done business, the courts have never hesitated to strike out the excess, while enforcing the rest of the clause.

It should be stressed that one thing even a sympathetic court will not do is 'rewrite' an unreasonable covenant. For example, it will not substitute 'five years' for 'ten years' in a covenant that is in restraint of trade. This rule can be harsh where the excessive term was the result of an innocent mistake but some justification may be found in the fact that the rule discourages parties from intentionally or even carelessly attempting to obtain wider protection than the law allows. Without the rule, there would be no disincentive to including an unreasonably wide restraint in a contract, and there might be considerable advantage as the subject party might assume the restraint was valid.

---

[28] *J. A. Mont (UK) Ltd v. Mills* [1993] IRLR 172.

Collateral warranty

The courts will sometimes find that a party to an unenforceable agreement is liable in contract for breaching a 'collateral warranty' to the effect that the agreement would be enforceable. For instance, an architect who promised a builder that he would obtain a licence for some work to be executed by the latter was held liable on this promise to the builder, although the licence was not obtained and the actual contract to do the work was therefore unenforceable.[29] Again, where a carrier agreed to carry goods in a van for which he did not have the requisite licence, it was held that the carrier impliedly warranted that he would carry the goods legally.[30] In these cases, the implication of a warranty of legality enabled damages to be obtained despite the possible illegality; but the courts have refused to imply a warranty of legality so as to *defeat* a claimant's claim. An insured does not implicitly warrant that he will never commit an illegal act in connection with goods being insured,[31] for that would lead to the absurdity of defeating a legitimate claim where (for instance) the owner of the goods had had them carried in a vehicle whose MOT certificate was overdue.

Enforcement by third parties

A substantive limitation that prevents one party from enforcing an agreement against the other will not necessarily prevent an innocent third party from doing so. Thus a road-traffic third-party insurance policy may be enforceable by an accident victim against the insurer even though it might be contrary to public policy for the insured himself to enforce it as, for example, where he has deliberately run down the victim. Even in cases of murder, where it is plain that the murderer cannot enforce an insurance policy on the life of the victim, it seems that third parties (such as mortgagees or co-owners) may be able to do so.[32]

Restitution

Finally, the parties to an unenforceable agreement may have a right to restitution of any benefits that they conveyed to the other party in performance of the agreement. Such rights are often extremely important in practice: as was mentioned earlier, in most disputes involving substantive limitations on enforceability the real issue is not whether the agreement is enforceable, but whether one or both of the parties can get back the value of benefits they conveyed under the agreement. In a book of this nature, however, restitution can be discussed only in brief outline. The rules in this area are highly

---

[29] *Strongman (1945) Ltd v. Sincock* [1955] 2 QB 525.
[30] *Archbolds (Freightage) Ltd v. Spanglett Ltd* [1961] 1 QB 374.
[31] *Euro-Diam Ltd v. Bathurst* [1988] 2 ALL ER 23.
[32] *Davitt v. Titcumb* [1989] 3 All ER 417.

complex, and are, in any event, a part of the law of unjust enrichment rather than the law of contract.

An initial observation is that the mere unenforceability or 'illegality' of an agreement is not itself a basis for ordering restitution. Restitution is normally awarded in order to reverse an unjust enrichment, and the fact that an agreement was unenforceable does not establish that benefits transferred under it led to an unjust enrichment. An ordinary completed sale of illegal narcotics, for example, does not lead to an unjust enrichment: the transaction is voluntary and each party gets what he or she bargains for.

In most cases involving unenforceable agreements, the basis on which it is argued that one party was unjustly enriched is 'failure of consideration'—meaning that the basis on which the benefit was conveyed (namely the counter-performance) 'failed' or did not materialize. The 'failure of con-sideration' principle only applies, of course, in cases involving partly executed contracts: where both parties have performed (as in the above narcotics example) there is no failure of consideration.[33] But even where a prima facie case for restitution exists on this basis, the courts will normally deny restitu-tion for another reason. As has already been discussed in this chapter, there is a general legal principle to the effect that the courts will not assist wrongdoers: *ex turpi causa non oritur action* (no action can be based on a disreputable cause). This principle has traditionally been applied so as to deny claims for restitution brought by any party associated with undesirable activities in any of the ways described in this chapter.

This result is clearly appropriate where the claimant was involved in serious wrongdoing. But in other cases, the blind application of the *ex turpi* principle can (as we have already seen) lead to injustice. A contract may be unenforce-able even if only one of the parties to it was involved in the undesirable activity. More generally, the consequences of denying restitution are often disproportionate to the gravity of the illegality. Refusing to order restitution may have more severe consequences than any penalty the law attaches to the activity—and at the same time may give the other party (who may be more guilty) a wholly undeserved windfall. In response to such concerns, the courts have developed three exceptions to the general rule.

The first exception is that restitution may be allowed where the claimant and defendant are not *in pari delicto* (not equally guilty). For example, if only the defendant was aware of facts that made performance illegal or had fraudulently misrepresented that performance was legal, or if the statute that was infringed was designed to protect the claimant, then the claimant would

---

[33] Restitution is sometimes available in respect of a completed, but unenforceable, agreement, but in such a case a different basis for restitution must be found, such as that the claimant was acting under duress or had made a mistake. In such cases, the 'illegality' defence that is discussed above does not usually apply: a claimant who was forced to enter an illegal transaction will not be denied restitution on the basis that he was involved in an illegal activity.

normally be able to get back any money paid under the agreement. This principle is often applied to cases involving technical illegalities. In *Shelley v. Puddock*[34] a buyer of a house overseas who paid the price in breach of exchange control regulations was permitted to recover it from a fraudulent seller who failed to convey the house. The buyer was found (perhaps generously) not to know anything about the exchange control regulations, and in such circumstances, the technical illegality committed by one party is grossly outweighed by the fraud of the other.

The second exception is that the claimant may be awarded restitution if he 'withdraws' from the transaction before it has been substantially performed. In such a case, restitution is not strictly awarded on the basis of failure of consideration (since it may be ordered even where there is a counter-performance), but rather on the basis of a policy of encouraging parties to withdraw from illegal or otherwise undesirable activities. Perhaps unsurprisingly, both the meaning of 'withdraw' and 'performance' are not easy to define, but it has recently been held that claimants need not genuinely 'repent' of the transaction: it is sufficient that they withdraw from it.[35]

The third exception is where claimants can establish their right to the money or property without 'relying' on the unenforceable agreement. The leading case on this difficult area of the law is the House of Lords' decision in *Tinsley v. Milligan*.[36] The claimant and defendant bought a house together as a joint venture, each contributing to the purchase price. The house was conveyed into the sole name of the defendant to facilitate a fraud on the social security authorities, but it was held that this illegality did not prevent the claimant claiming a share in the house when the parties split up. While it is clear that the court will not enforce an executory contract designed to facilitate such frauds, the court will recognize a transfer of property where the contract is executed, as it was here, and the claimant does not need to rely on the illegality to make good her claim. Here, the claimant was able to make good her claim by relying on the normal equitable rules that a person contributing part of the price of a property is presumed to be entitled to a share in the property.

The exceptions just described undoubtedly allow the courts to take a more nuanced approach to determining whether parties to an unenforceable agreement can obtain restitution. But the law in this area is still far from ideal. The main difficulty is that it is still often the case that the consequences of denying restitution are out of proportion to the nature of the illegality. As we have seen, many agreements are unenforceable for what are essentially

---

[34] [1980] 1 All ER 1009.
[35] *Tribe v. Tribe* [1996] Ch 107.
[36] [1993] 3 All ER 65. See also *Bowmakers v. Barnet Instruments Ltd* [1945] KB 65, which was for long the leading case.

technical breaches of minor regulations. The *in pari delicto* exception is of no help in such cases if, as frequently happens, both parties are ignorant of the regulation, while the third exception applies regardless of relative guilt. In an earlier edition of this book it was suggested that this and other problems in this area of the law are probably best approached by a careful consideration of all the circumstances of a case rather than by a mechanical application of general rules, and there were a number of lower court decisions which favoured this approach. But in *Tinsley v. Milligan*, the House of Lords rejected this approach, and insisted that, at least where proprietary claims are at stake, they must be judged by fixed rules.

Part III

Excuses for Non-performance

9

The Duty to Disclose Material Facts

THIS and the next three chapters examine various situations in which individuals are excused from the duty to perform a prima facie valid contract. In these instances, the duty is obviated even though the procedural and substantive requirements described in Chapters 2–4 are satisfied and there is nothing unlawful or otherwise objectionable about what the parties undertook to do. Examples include situations in which a promise or agreement is induced by duress, fraud, or undue influence. As is often the case, while the black-letter law in this area is reasonably well-settled, its foundations are controversial. As such, a few preliminary comments are in order before proceeding to specific situations.

In a broad sense, the law on excuses deals with situations in which it is thought to be 'unfair' to hold parties to what they undertook to do. More specifically—though only slightly—the law in this area may be said to deal with situations in which enforcement is thought to be unfair for one or more of three reasons: (1) the defendant[1] did not consent to the contract (or to a particular aspect of the contract); (2) the claimant obtained her contractual right(s) by a wrongful act; and (3) the contract is substantively unfair, that is to say, the parties' obligations under the contract are not equal in value.

It will not be surprising to learn that there is considerable controversy about the extent to which the law does—and should—give effect to these ideas. We will explore this debate in this and the following chapters, but it may be useful to say a few words at this stage about why it has proven so difficult to resolve. In theory, the three reasons just described give rise to distinct arguments for refusing to enforce a contract. The 'consent principle' is defendant-based: the defendant did not consent to the agreement. The 'wrongdoing principle' is claimant-based: the claimant obtained his contractual rights through a wrongful act. Finally, the 'substantive fairness principle' has a mixed basis: the value of the claimant's contractual rights is greater than the value of the defendant's rights. In practice, however, it is often difficult to tell which of these principles (if any) best explains particular rules. In part, this is because many of the rules in this area can plausibly be explained on more than one of these grounds. Consider the rule that a

---

[1] Throughout this and the next three chapters the 'defendant' is the party seeking to have the contract set aside, while the 'claimant' is the party seeking to enforce the contract.

contract signed under duress—for instance, a contract signed at gunpoint—is invalid. The defendant in such a case can plausibly argue that she never consented to the contract. But she can also plausibly argue that the claimant obtained his apparent rights by a wrongful threat and (in most cases anyway) that the actual terms of the agreement are unfair. The end result is that there may be more than one good reason for refusing to enforce such a contract. In principle, this is not a problem, but in practice it exacerbates the difficulty of disentangling the relevant concepts, and may help to explain why the law in this area is complex, if not actually inconsistent, in certain respects.

Another reason it is difficult to tell which principle best explains any given rule is that these principles are often subject to overlapping definitions. For example, lack of consent is often defined in terms of wrongdoing (and vice versa); thus it is often said that consent is negated by illegitimate (i.e. wrongful) pressure or, alternatively, that it is wrongful to do something that impairs another's consent. As for substantive unfairness, it is often defined in terms of lack of consent and/or wrongdoing: a contract is substantively fair, it is often said, if it is procedurally fair.

A third reason that commentators disagree about how to explain the rules on excuses is that the answer has implications for a larger debate in contract law regarding the relative significance of procedural as opposed to substantive fairness. According to classical theory, while procedural matters of the kind that are the focus of consent and wrongdoing principles are properly the concern of the law, the *substantive* outcome of a contract is purely a matter for the parties. In this view, the law regulates the way bargains are made in the marketplace, leaving the parties to insert whatever content they choose into those bargains. In short, even if it is possible to define substantive fairness, such a definition is of no concern to the law of contract. But as we have already seen, this classical view is frequently criticized, both as an account of what the courts actually do and as a prescription for what they should do. The law on excuses—particularly the rules on duress, undue influence, and unconscionability—plays a major role in this debate.

The law in this area thus raises difficult issues, some of which are outside the scope of a book of this nature. For the moment, it is sufficient to make the following observations. First, whatever philosophers may say about the meaning of consent, wrongdoing, and substantive fairness, these concepts are regularly employed in ordinary conversation and, indeed, in legal reasoning. Since judges and others appear to ascribe meaning to them, it is a good starting point to assume that these concepts do in fact matter. Secondly, it would be surprising if the courts were not motivated by concerns about consent, wrongdoing, and substantive fairness. In the cases of consent and wrongdoing this proposition is uncontroversial; these are widely recognized as fundamental moral concepts. It is, admittedly, a more debatable proposition to argue that substantive unfairness is in the same category.

Nonetheless, even if it is agreed that judges might hesitate to set a contract aside solely because it is substantively unfair (assuming they had the power to do this), it would be surprising if they disregarded this concept in instances when it was linked (as it typically is) to a claim that the defendant's consent was impaired or that the claimant acted wrongly, even in cases where such impairment or wrongdoing might not alone be sufficient to justify invalidity. The idea that it is wrong to take advantage of another's vulnerability—for that is how these situations would ordinarily be described—is too ingrained to be ignored entirely by the law.

Finally, it should be mentioned that there is an important sense in which the law on excuses is arguably not a part of the law of contract, strictly understood, or at least not uniquely a part of contract law. A contractual obligation that was induced by a wrongful threat or a fraudulent representation may be set aside by a court. But the same is true of a will, a declaration of trust, or a decision to legally change one's name—yet none of these acts are contracts. So too, an ordinary transfer of property will be undone if it was induced by a wrongful threat or fraud. In principle, the kinds of excuses discussed in the following chapters are therefore relevant not just to the validity of a contract, but to the validity of any 'legal act', that is, any act under which an individual purports to change her legal relations with others. This is why discussions of excuses such as duress occupy as much space, if not more space, in textbooks on the law of unjust enrichment as they do in contract textbooks.

We begin our investigation by considering the excuse that the other party failed to disclose information during negotiations.

2. A *GENERAL* DUTY OF DISCLOSURE?

Unlike many other legal systems, English law has traditionally taken the view that parties to a proposed contract have no general duty to supply information to each other. Each party must make up his own mind and exercise his own judgement in deciding whether to contract, and it is not the duty of either party to notify the other of facts which may influence that decision. Thus, a person who is selling his house is under no obligation to disclose that the drains leak, a Borstal is located around the corner, or the timbers are riddled with woodworm. It is up to the buyer to make his own enquiries. Of course, the buyer may make these enquiries by asking the seller about them, and if the seller chooses to answer, then she must do so truthfully; however, she is perfectly entitled to say (as some do) that the buyer must make his inquiries elsewhere.

That English law should take this approach to duties of disclosure is not surprising in light of two other features of English law that we have already discussed. The first is the rule that no relief is available for *unilateral* (as opposed to shared) mistakes. A duty of disclosure is effectively a duty to remedy (or prevent) a unilateral mistake. The second feature is the absence of any general duty to act in good faith. A duty to disclose material facts is perhaps the classic example of the kind of duty that would be required by a good faith principle, if such a principle existed in English law.

But while English courts' approach to duties of disclosure may be consistent with other features of English law, it is not uncontroversial. To the contrary, the law in this area (like the law on unilateral mistake and good faith) has attracted considerable criticism. These criticisms are discussed below, but before this is done it is important to stress that a *general* duty to disclose information, that is, a duty to disclose any information that may reasonably be thought important to the other party in every case, is not easy to justify. From an economic perspective, a general duty of disclosure would be inconsistent with the idea—fundamental in market economies—that individuals should be given incentives to invest in the acquisition and use of knowledge. If an oil company that has engaged the best experts in the world in order to assess the probability of oil being discovered on a particular piece of land is required to divulge this information to the landowner, there would be little incentive to undertake such research. The oil company must be allowed to reap the reward for its investment.

Even where the relevant information has been acquired casually, with no investment, a similar argument can be made on the basis that the decision to *use* information should be rewarded. In the famous American case of *Laidlaw v. Organ*,[2] a tobacco merchant learned, early in the morning, that a peace treaty had been signed between Britain and the US (ending the war of 1812), and he contracted to buy 111 hogsheads of tobacco from the defendant, Laidlaw, before this fact became public knowledge an hour or two later. The price of tobacco rose sharply once this news broke, but the Supreme Court refused to impose a duty of disclosure on Laidlaw. The decision can be defended in economic terms on the ground that it is important to give buyers in Laidlaw's position an incentive to bring their information forward to the market. By offering to buy the tobacco, Laidlaw was effectively sending a valuable signal to the market that tobacco was worth more than the going price. As a result of the information conveyed by Laidlaw, the vendor and others may have taken further actions such as, for example, ordering more tobacco from suppliers—this may have led, in turn, to more tobacco being produced overall, yielding an eventual net benefit to the public. Admittedly, on the facts in the case, such transactions would have taken place in an hour or two regardless of Laidlaw's actions. But this does not detract from the general point that there are economic benefits to giving

---

[2] 15 US (2 Wheat) 178 (1817).

people incentives to act on valuable information that they have acquired, casually or otherwise. The stock market operates in large part on this basis.

The non-economic arguments against imposing a *general* duty of disclosure are equally strong. It is unfair, and not just inefficient, to require oil companies to disclose information that they have gathered at their own expense. As the law recognises in other contexts, information is a kind of property. Forcing an oil company to disclose information about the likelihood of finding oil on a piece of land is not so different from forcing it to give away physical assets. This argument is admittedly weaker in cases where the acquisition or use of the relevant knowledge involved little cost, but it must be remembered that the defendants in the examples here have not actually been harmed by the contract and, as such, they have relatively weak grounds to complain about the fairness of the transaction. The tobacco vendor in *Laidlaw*, for example, was not made worse off as a result of the transaction: he simply did not get the chance to make a larger profit. The vendor ended up in the same position as anyone else in the market who sold before the news broke.

3. PARTICULAR DUTIES OF DISCLOSURE

It appears, therefore, that there are strong economic and fairness-based arguments against enforcing a general duty to disclose information. But as we saw when discussing unilateral mistakes in Chapter 7, these arguments do not apply in all circumstances; to the contrary, there are situations where considerations of both efficiency and fairness would appear to support a duty of disclosure.

In each of the examples discussed above it was the buyer who had the superior information. But where it is the vendor who has the better information, the arguments typically go the other way. Suppose, to take a simple example, an individual purchases a second-hand automobile from a private vendor for £5,000. Shortly afterwards, the purchaser is informed following a routine maintenance check that the vehicle is unsafe (indeed illegal) to drive because of a crack in the suspension, and that the cost of repair is greater than £5,000. The crack occurred prior to the sale, but while the vendor was aware of this fact, he said nothing to the purchaser. It is difficult to see what value, economic or otherwise, is served by refusing to impose a duty on the vendor to disclose the truth about the vehicle's condition in these circumstances. Enforcing the contract does not reward the vendor for a valuable investment or decision: the vendor did nothing but keep quiet. The only behaviour for which the vendor is being rewarded is helping to bring about a transaction that is both inefficient, in that the buyer will have to turn around and buy another automobile, and unfair in that the buyer has been made worse off (because he has ended up with something worth less than what he paid for it). Admittedly, the buyer could have hired a mechanic to inspect the vehicle suspension prior to agreeing to the purchase. But given that it would have taken no effort for the vendor to disclose the relevant information, this hardly justifies the vendor's silence.

These arguments are not limited to sale contracts. They apply to any case in which one party possesses information that would, if disclosed, make clear to the other party that what he will receive under the contract is unsuitable for his purposes or of such value that he would never have entered the contract had he known the truth. In *Turner v. Green*,[3] for example, two parties already engaged in litigation settled their dispute after a preliminary hearing in London before the Chief Clerk. The Chief Clerk had made it evident that he did not think much of the claimant's case, and the claimant's solicitor had telegraphed to his country associate advising settlement. The other party's solicitor, however, had no knowledge of what had transpired at the London hearing. When these facts came to light the defendant protested that the claimant's solicitor had acted dishonestly, but the settlement was upheld, even though the judge clearly suspected that unscrupulous behaviour had occurred.

Perhaps even more striking is a modern case, *Wales v. Wadham*,[4] in which a husband and wife were negotiating a financial settlement while divorce proceedings were pending. The wife did not disclose her intent to remarry a wealthy man as soon as the divorce became absolute; in the meantime, the first husband agreed to a financial settlement that, to him, was predicated upon his wife's financial dependence. Even in the face of this seemingly manifest injustice, no duty to disclose was found to exist. This decision has now been overruled by the House of Lords,[5] but only on the ground that full disclosure is due *to the court* so that it can properly exercise its statutory discretions. As a matter of common law, the decision might have stood even though it seems repugnant to an ordinary sense of fairness.

It is sometimes suggested that imposing a duty of disclosure in these types of situations would be too onerous because vendors (and others in similar situations) are often unaware of the buyer's intentions. But in a case like the example of the second-hard car mentioned earlier, the buyer's intentions are self-evident. Moreover, the law does not hesitate to impose a nearly identical duty in a range of similar situations. Under section 14(3) of the Sale of Goods Act 1979, for example, business sellers are under a duty to make sure that goods are fit for the buyer's purposes, provided that the seller knows or should have known of the buyer's purpose and that it was reasonable for the buyer to rely on the seller. It is not clear why a similarly limited duty of disclosure would not be practical in situations like those discussed above.

---

[3] [1895] 2 Ch 205.   [4] [1977] 1 WLR 199.   [5] *Jenkins v. Livesey* [1985] AC 424.

Indeed, the duty imposed by section 14(3) is, in substance, nearly identical to a duty of disclosure; the claimants described in the preceding paragraphs are essentially arguing (rightly, it seems) for an extension of this duty to analogous situations.

Another situation in which the courts are willing to enforce something that approximates the (limited) duty of disclosure described above is examined in more detail in Chapter 11's discussion of the law on undue influence. There are certain situations in which contracting parties are under a duty to take reasonable steps to ensure that those with whom they contract are not affected by the undue influence or misrepresentations of a third party.[6] For example, if one co-habitee guarantees the debts of another co-habitee, the creditor bank is usually required to take reasonable steps to ensure that the guarantor has acted independently and understands what he or she is doing. Though not usually explained as such, this is very close to a duty of disclosure: the bank has a duty to make sure the guarantor understands what she is doing and that she is able to act independently. In order to fulfil this duty the bank must *inter alia* inform the guarantor (or the guarantor's solicitor) about the financial risks associated with the guarantee. In these cases, the counter-argument (which claims that such a duty is too onerous) is met through limiting the imposition of the duty to cases in which the risk of undue influence or misrepresentation is especially strong. A similar mechanism could be applied to the duty of disclosure described above.

A strong argument can therefore be made that while a general duty of disclosure may be inappropriate, a duty to disclose in one group of situations—what might be called 'overvaluation' cases—is prima facie appropriate. But as will be explained below, English law has not adopted this position. There are in fact only a small number of situations in which a duty of disclosure is imposed.

Insurance contracts and other contracts uberrimae fidei

Notwithstanding English law's general refusal to impose good faith duties, the courts have identified a small group of contracts as being contracts *uberrimae fidei*—contracts of utmost good faith. In such contracts, there is a full duty to disclose all material facts in both the formation and performance of the contract. By far the most important example is the contract of insurance, where many of the relevant circumstances are known exclusively by one party and it would be impossible for insurers to obtain the facts necessary to make a proper calculation of the risks they are asked to assume without this knowledge. This, at least, was the historical justification for assigning special treatment to contracts of insurance; today, however,

---

[6] *Royal Bank of Scotland plc v. Etridge (No 2)* [2001] 3 WLR 1021.

application of the law can give rise to oppressive results. Insurers are generally well able to take care of their own interests by requiring a prospective
insured to complete an application form giving information on a wide range
of matters. The ordinary consumer might be justified in assuming that by
giving the information specifically requested he has complied with his legal
obligations, but this is not so: he must also disclose any other material fact
known to him whether or not he is aware of its significance. The severity of
the law is aggravated because the materiality of the facts is not assessed from
the standpoint of the insured. Any fact which would influence a prudent
insurer and which was in fact an influence is material. This could include facts
that the public might regard as irrelevant. For instance, a householder
insuring his house or belongings has been held obliged to disclose previous
convictions for robbery because many insurers would regard such a person as
a 'moral hazard', susceptible to making bogus claims. Moreover, the duty is
absolute in the sense that it can be breached without intentional wrongdoing
or even negligence. Consequently, the present law is sometimes a source of
grave injustice, and the Law Commission has published some proposals for
change. Although no change in the law has yet materialised, there has
recently been some welcome change in insurance practice—companies now
regularly draw the attention of the insured (on application forms, and when
renewals are requested) to disclosure requirements of which they may be
unaware, and occasionally furnish examples of such information. This is also
an area where the Financial Ombudsman now offers an important alternative
venue for relief, as is discussed in more detail below.

It has been stated that contracts of insurance impose a duty of disclosure
on the insurer as well as on the insured but there are very few cases illustrating
this. The important decision of *La Banque Financière de la Cité SA v. Westgate
Insurance Co. Ltd*[7] is one such case. Here, insurers accepted a proposal to
insure a bank against certain credit risks without disclosing that the
insurance broker, through whom a similar contract had previously been
negotiated, had been guilty of gross frauds in connection with the previous
contract. This fact was important because in English law a broker is deemed
to be the agent of the insured, which means that any fraud by the broker will
make the insurance policy unenforceable. As it turned out, the broker in *La
Banque Financière* had again committed a fraud, with the result that the
claimant bank could not recover on their policy. The bank complained that
the insurer should have disclosed that their broker had a record of fraud, and
the court agreed. However, the court went on to hold that the only remedy
available to the insured for breach of this duty of disclosure was to rescind
the contract of insurance and recover the premium. Such a remedy seems

[7] [1991] 2 AC 249.

hopelessly inadequate. The court refused to hold that this duty of disclosure could found an action for damages on the highly formalistic ground that the duty of disclosure arose from general equitable principles rather than from an implied term at common law, and equitable duties cannot be remedied with damages. Thus, despite the existence of a formal duty, there is no requirement to provide substantive compensation for loss occurring as the result of the insurer's breach. Such reasoning produces another situation where insurers and insured are treated unevenly: the latter are penalized severely for breaches of the duty to disclose, but the insurer can breach this duty at little cost.

Another situation where a duty of disclosure is recognized by the law is the contract of partnership. By its very nature, a partnership requires that the parties involved have the fullest of confidence in one another. But it should not be thought that there is any general principle that a contract is *uberrimae fidei*, and so requires disclosure, merely because a judge thinks that the particular contract requires good faith. The contract must fall within, or be closely analogous to, the very small group of contracts already labelled *uberrimae fidei*.

Fiduciary relationships

Closely analogous to these cases are those involving what Courts of Equity would call a 'fiduciary relationship', such as the one that exists between a trustee and a beneficiary. In these cases, which often involve contractual relationships, the duty not to abuse the fiduciary position includes a requirement to disclose all material facts. The same applies to many 'undue influence' cases which, it is important to emphasise, are not solely concerned with what might be called undue influence in the ordinary sense. However, in both these and other relevant cases, the duty to disclose is obviously subordinate to the general duty to not abuse the position of trust or exploit the relationship between the parties. These cases are discussed in greater detail in Chapter 11.

Statutory duties

There are today numerous examples of statutory duties of disclosure in certain contractual situations, of which only a few need mention here. The responsibility of dealers in financial services to make customers aware of certain information[8] is an example of a statutory duty to disclose facts to one's clients. Some legislation goes so far as to impose such a duty with regard to communications to the public at large. Under the Companies Act 1985, a prospectus issued to the public inviting subscription for shares must contain information on a large number of points, all of which are specified

---

[8] Financial Services Act 1986, Sch. 3, paras 5–8.

in the Act, and which are obviously matters that might influence a person intending to buy shares. A similar duty of disclosure is provided for by section 44(1) of the Consumer Credit Act 1974 in connection with advertisements offering to supply credit or loans to consumers. Such advertisements have to comply with Regulations designed to ensure that the advertisement contains 'a fair and reasonably comprehensive indication of the nature of the credit or hire facilities offered by the advertiser and of their true cost to persons using them'.

Contracts subject to the Financial Ombudsman Service

The general role of the Financial Ombudsman in resolving contractual disputes is discussed in Chapter 12, but a few words on this subject need to be said here because so many of the large number of complaints directed to the Ombudsman (nearly 100,000 in 2004) are essentially complaints that a contract was entered on the basis of inadequate information. The most important category of disputes addressed by the Ombudsman in recent years concerns mortgage endowment policies, where the policy holder's basic complaint is usually that he would not have agreed to the policy if he had fully understood the risk that was involved (namely the risk of the stock market collapsing). These and many of the other contracts within the Financial Ombudsman's jurisdiction are already subject to the disclosure provisions of the Financial Services Act 1986, but both the scope and substance of the Ombudsman's powers in this regard go beyond the 1986 Act and, indeed, beyond that found in any other legislative or common law provision. Although the Ombudsman has the power to make decisions and order 'damages' (to a maximum currently of £100,000), the Ombudsman is not required to decide on the basis of legal principles (nor is his decision open to judicial review); instead, the Ombudsman is directed to make rulings on the basis of what is 'fair and equitable' in the circumstances. A brief glance at the 'technical notes' and 'news' bulletins issued by the Service (the Ombudsman's actual decisions are not reported) makes clear that it is of the view that significant duties of disclosure are appropriate for the wide range of financial transactions that fall within its jurisdiction (which include insurance, mortgages, consumer credit, investments, etc.). Moreover, it is clear that it is not just appropriate information, but appropriate advice that must be given. This is significant because in many cases a finding that a particular financial product was inappropriate for the particular consumer (or business—the Service is not limited to consumer complaints) seems to be taken as near to proof that inadequate advice (or information) was provided. Of course, neither the reports nor the decisions of the Ombudsman are considered to be 'law' in the official sense, but in practice it is difficult to see the difference between an Ombudsman's ruling (or report) and a ruling (or report of that ruling) by a court of law. For the significant number of contractual situations that fall within the Ombudsman's jurisdiction, it therefore seems misleading to say there is no duty of disclosure.

4. ALTERNATIVES TO DUTIES OF DISCLOSURE

The relatively limited number of situations in which English law is willing to impose a duty of disclosure hardly covers the wide range of situations in which (as we have seen) such a duty might prima facie be thought appropriate. But it cannot be stressed too strongly that in many situations where this is the case the aggrieved party has an alternative ground of relief. The existence of these alternatives is undoubtedly part of the reason English courts have not felt compelled to expand the range of situations in which duties of disclosure are required. Two such grounds are especially important.

Implied terms

As we saw in Chapter 6, the courts will often impose responsibility on contracting parties for a state of facts, irrespective of their knowledge of the facts. Thus, in most contracts for the sale of goods, the seller is liable if the goods prove unsatisfactory or unfit for the buyer's known purpose. This makes a duty of disclosure unnecessary: the seller is already under a duty to guarantee against the goods being defective or unsuitable regardless of whether he knows of the defects. To state, therefore, that a seller of goods is not bound to disclose any defects to the buyer remains true on a literal level, but hardly reflects the present state of the law. Similar duties (requiring fitness for use) have now been imposed on parties who provide services.[9] It is important to bear in mind, however, that terms like these are not implied as a matter of course into all contracts: the example given earlier of the private sale of a second-hand automobile does not fall within the ambit of the Sale of Goods Act or any similar legislation.

In addition to standardised implied terms, the courts are sometimes willing to imply terms on a case-by-case basis to similar effect. Thus, in a recent case it was held that when an employee agrees, as part of a settlement package on termination, to release his employer from all present and future claims, the employer will be held to have impliedly represented that he is not aware of any such claims of which the employee may not be aware.[10] In principle, such implications must satisfy a strict test but, as we have seen (in Chapter 6), the courts' approach is quite flexible in practice. A court can always justify a decision to imply a term by stating that it is merely giving effect to the presumed intention of the parties in the case before it, even if no such term has been implied in similar cases.

[9] Supply of Goods and Services Act 1982, s. 9.
[10] *Bank of Credit and Commerce International v. Ali* [2001] 1 All ER 961, 984.

One advantage of the implied-term technique is that it offers a flexible range of remedies. Under the current law, the only remedy for a breach of a duty to disclose information is to rescind the contract.[11] But as was illustrated by the insurance cases discussed earlier, rescission is not always a satisfactory outcome; in many instances an order of damages is more appropriate. This becomes possible where a term is implied. The court may imply an appropriate warranty which would give rise to a right to damages only, or declare that the contract includes a promissory condition which gives the aggrieved party a choice between obtaining damages or rescinding the contract. Alternatively, the court may even, if it sees fit, imply a condition precedent to the operation of the contract which would release both parties from all liability.

Liability in tort

While a person will not be compelled to speak by a duty of disclosure, the law is careful to ensure that the other party is not misled by anything that he might *choose* to say. Any false statement he makes is, of course, a misrepresentation, and the law provides generous relief which will be discussed in the next chapter. But even where a person makes a statement that is not literally false, he may be held to have misled the other party to the contract if it creates an impression contrary to the truth. For instance, in *Curtis v. Chemical Cleaning Co.*,[12] an assistant working for a dry cleaner indicated to a customer leaving a dress that the receipt she had signed exempted the defendants from liability for damage to any beads or sequins on it. This was true, but the assistant did not state that the receipt further exempted the defendants from any liability whatsoever for damage to the dress. Obviously the assistant's statement created an impression quite contrary to the truth. It was held, therefore, that the defendants were not entitled to rely on the exemption clause and the claimant got her damages.

A 'duty to speak' is also effectively imposed by the law of misrepresentation in cases where a person makes a statement during the course of negotiations which, though true when made, ceased to be true before the contract was concluded. For instance, where a doctor truthfully stated the worth of his practice to a prospective buyer, but later omitted to inform him of its subsequent devaluation, the court held that the contract could be rescinded; the seller should have informed the buyer of the change in value.[13] This duty only arises where the relevant party knew of the change in the circumstances; however, even where he did not know of it, it may be possible

---

[11] See *Bank of Nova Scotia v. Hellenic Mutual War Risks Association* [1989] 3 All ER 628, reversed on other grounds, [1991] 3 All ER 1.

[12] [1951] 1 KB 805.

[13] *With v. O'Flanagan* [1936] Ch 575.

for the courts to give appropriate relief by implying a term that the situation has not changed.[14]

A third situation in which a party may be found to have committed a misrepresentation without actually uttering a falsehood is where there is a misrepresentation 'by conduct'. 'Conduct' is defined quite broadly: 'Simple reticence does not amount to legal fraud . . . But a single word, or . . . a nod or a wink, or a shake of the head or a smile from the purchaser intended to induce the vendor to believe the existence of a non-existent fact'[15] may qualify. A recent case[16] involving a contract between a pop band and a promoter illustrates the close links between misrepresentation by conduct and liability for failure to disclose. Three weeks after the promoters agreed to sponsor a tour of the band, a leading member quit the group, which greatly diminished the promotional value of the sponsorship. It subsequently emerged that the decision to quit had been made before the contract was signed and was known by all band members. The promoters argued that, although the band had never actually *said* that they were intending to remain intact for the near future, they had represented this by their conduct, in particular by participating in a photo shoot at considerable cost to the promoters just prior to the signing. The trial judge agreed, and the Court of Appeal concurred (but on slightly wider grounds), even though it seems clear that the promoter's real complaint was that the band had failed to disclose that one member would soon be leaving.

The common law therefore has various tools at its disposal to protect parties who, in other legal systems, might legitimately seek protection under a broader duty of disclosure. This approach has the advantage of removing from judges the sometimes difficult task of determining the circumstances in which such a duty should apply. But the piecemeal and fragmented protection offered by the common law makes it inevitable that some deserving parties will fall through the cracks. Ultimately, the law would be better served if the courts were to apply a duty to disclose in a wider range of circumstances than is presently the case.

[14] See, e.g., *Financings Ltd v. Stimson* [1962] 1 WLR 118.
[15] Per Lord Campbell in *Walters v. Morgan* (1861) 3 De G F & J 718 at 723.
[16] *Spice Girls Ltd v. Aprilla World Service BV* [2002] EWCA Civ 15.

10

Misrepresentation

WHILE there is no general rule allowing for a contract to be set aside should one party fail to disclose material facts during negotiations, it is a strict and universal rule that such a right exists where one party is induced to enter a contract on the basis of the other's false representation. In principle, such relief may be available even where the 'representor' was not at fault and even if the misrepresentation concerned a trivial aspect of the contract. Moreover, a person who has been induced to enter a contract by a misrepresentation will often have the additional right to claim damages in tort for any loss caused by the misrepresentation.

The wide breadth of relief for misrepresentation in English law raises a number of questions. In general, the reason for allowing a contract to be set aside for misrepresentation is that the representor obtained a benefit (whether in the form of a contractual right or actual performance) through wrongdoing. As has already been noted, it is a long-standing principle of English law that the court will not assist a wrongdoer. But this principle does not account for why a contract may be set aside even where the misrepresentation was wholly innocent. This is also true of the suggestion that English misrepresentation law is as generous as it is in order to allow courts to resolve situations that, in other legal systems, would be addressed by broader doctrines of good faith and mistake: while English law's narrow approach to good faith and mistake has clearly influenced the courts' treatment of misrepresentation, even traditions with very expansive doctrines of good faith and mistake tend not to give relief in cases of innocent misrepresentation. Admittedly, legislation now limits some of the common law rights once enjoyed by victims of innocent misrepresentations. But as we will see, this same legislation also significantly extends the rights available generally to misrepresentees, and does so in ways that are again not easy to justify. We will return to these issues below.

A false statement of fact

A misrepresentation is defined as a false statement of fact. The meaning of 'false' is fairly straightforward, but the meaning of 'statement of fact' is not as simple as it might appear. We have already seen (in the previous chapter) that a 'statement' may be made through conduct and that in such cases the defendant's real complaint is often that the claimant failed to disclose material facts. Courts have likewise taken an expansive approach in defining 'fact'; this can be seen by considering their approach to three kinds of communications that are typically contrasted with statements of fact.

The first are promises and statements of intent. Such communications are not statements of fact since they cannot actually be true or false at all. Thus, in theory, a claimant can only sue on promises and statements of intent if they are incorporated in the contract. This is no doubt the main reason courts are generally reluctant to regard such communications—which are usually influential in negotiations—as non-contractual. And today, it would be relatively unusual for a promise or statement of intent made while a contract is being negotiated not to be classified as incorporated in the contract or, at least, as constituting a collateral contract (which legally comes to much the same thing). But for present purposes, the important point is that while promises and statements of intent cannot themselves be treated as statements of fact, they are often treated as involving an implicit representation as to the state of mind of the speaker, and 'the state of a man's mind is as much a fact as the state of his digestion.'[1] Hence, if a promise is made with no intention of carrying it out, this is a misrepresentation of fact. In other words, the state of the promisor's mind becomes a fact that must be disclosed truthfully along with other more tangible facts. This is, of course, quite different from the case of a promise that is honestly made but not carried out. For example, to borrow money without any intention of repaying it is to commit a misrepresentation, whereas to borrow money and simply fail to repay it is merely a breach of contract.

Statements expressing an opinion are often treated the same way. In strict law, a statement of opinion is, again, not a statement of fact, and so cannot give rise to a misrepresentation. For instance, the estate agent's cliché, 'a very desirable residence', is not a statement of fact which could be complained of as a misrepresentation. And more generally, mere 'puffs', as they are sometimes called, are regarded by the law as statements which would not influence any reasonable person. So, for instance, a seller's statement that what he is offering is worth the asking price is not usually regarded as a representation at all. Indeed, even statements that look more like real statements of fact may be disregarded by the law if they turn out, on analysis, to be matters of opinion. So where a person sold some land and gave his view of the sheep-carrying capacity of the land, this was held to be a matter of opinion because (as the buyer knew) the land had never been used for sheep before.

But while strict law does not view statements of opinion as statements of fact, courts are reluctant to entertain a plea to the effect that a statement is

---

[1] *Edgington v. Fitzmaurice* (1885) 29 Ch D 459 at 483, per Bowen LJ—one of the most famous of all legal dicta.

only an opinion, especially if it is based on facts not known to the other party. In particular, it is well settled that a statement of opinion, like a promise, may involve an implied representation of fact. Typically, the representation is said to be that the person stating the opinion knows no facts which would make the opinion untenable. *A fortiori*, a statement of opinion involves an implicit representation that it is honestly believed to be true: 'A representation of fact may be inherent in a statement of opinion, and, at any rate, the existence of the opinion in the person stating it is a question of fact.'[2] In addition, where the opinion was given carelessly, the court may also find that the speaker impliedly represented that he used proper skill and care in forming his view. This conclusion is commonly reached in situations where the speaker had superior skill or knowledge, as where a petrol company offered inaccurate forecasts about the potential sales of a petrol station to the eventual purchaser.[3] Cases of this kind suggest that the real issue might not be whether a statement is one of fact or opinion, but whether it was reasonable to rely upon it in the circumstances. Though reliance on statements of fact is usually easier to justify than reliance on the other party's opinion, both situations can create legitimate grounds for obtaining relief.

Finally, it is often said that a misrepresentation of law, as opposed to one of fact, has no effect on a contract, unless it was made dishonestly. But in practice, it would be rare that a party would enter into a contract with another in reliance on a statement of some abstract proposition of law, and a statement of private rights is generally treated as a representation of fact, not of law.

Causation

It is sometimes said that a misrepresentation must be important or 'material' in order to ground relief.[4] If this was indeed the case it would bring English law closer to the law in civilian systems. But on closer inspection, the so-called materiality requirement is invoked only in cases dealing with the duty of disclosure in insurance contracts that was discussed in the previous chapter,[5] where it gives necessary definition to the duty; one cannot be required to disclose everything one knows.

So far as ordinary claims in misrepresentation are concerned, 'materiality' is significant only insofar as it relates to causation. A representee must prove that the representation was a factor in his decision to enter into the contract in question, a requirement that applies to cases of both non-disclosure and

---

[2] *Bisset v. Wilkinson* [1927] AC 177 at 182, per Lord Merrivale.
[3] *Esso Petroleum v. Mardon* [1976] QB 801.
[4] See, e.g., *Lonrho v. Fayed (No.2)* [1991] 4 All ER 961 at 966.
[5] *Pan Atlantic Insurance Co. Ltd v. Pine Top Insurance Co. Ltd* [1994] 3 All ER 581.

misrepresentation.[6] Hence, even a deliberate ('fraudulent') misrepresentation has no effect where it did not influence the other party's judgment. Crucially, however, it is not necessary to show that the misrepresentation was the *sole* inducement to enter into the contract, and the mere fact that the innocent party has taken independent advice does not mean that he has not relied on the false statement to some extent. If such a case actually comes to court, the result will largely depend on the evidence of the person to whom the representation was made. If he is prepared to swear that he was influenced by the representation, and remains unshaken in cross-examination, it is unlikely the court will conclude that the misrepresentation had no causal effect.

Moreover, it is no defence to a plea of misrepresentation to allege that the other party might have discovered the true facts by reasonable diligence.[7] Provided that the innocent party relied at least in part on the false statements, she is entitled to have the contract rescinded, although she might easily have discovered the falsity of the statements. All the same, an extreme want of due care by the representee might indicate that his reliance was unreasonable. Although the courts have not recognized this as a principle, it seems to be an implicit feature in many cases where relief is denied. Moreover, where the misrepresentation is being used to found a claim in tort for damages, it seems it would today be possible to take account of contributory negligence for the purposes of apportioning damages. Naturally the primary responsibility for a false statement must always lie with the maker of the statement[8] but there are some circumstances in which apportionment would be justified. Of course, in situations where the claimant's claim is for rescission of the contract, this alternative is not possible.

Fault

In principle, a contract may be set aside for misrepresentation even if the representor was not to blame in any way for making the misrepresentation. As was mentioned earlier, the explanation for this feature of misrepresentation law is not immediately obvious. Where a misrepresentation is deliberately or carelessly made, relief can be justified on the principle that wrongdoers

---

[6] *Pan Atlantic Insurance*, ibid. This decision, to some extent, takes away with one hand what it gives (to insurers) with the other, because in cases where it is held that a non-disclosure was barely material, the court may well now go on to hold that it did not in fact have any causal effect.

[7] See *Redgrave v. Hurd* (1881) 20 Ch D 1, an extreme case in which a claim for some apportionment of damages would surely be justified today.

[8] *Gran Gelato Ltd v. Richcliff (Group) Ltd* [1992] Ch 560. But continued reliance in this case on dicta in *Redgrave v. Hurd* (1881) 20 Ch D 1 and other old cases hardly seems justified since, at that time, the alternatives were full damages or none. It has also been held that there can be no apportionment of damages in an action of deceit or for fraud: *Alliance & Leicester Building Society v. Edgestop Ltd* [1994] 2 All ER 38. However, the reasoning here is equally unsatisfactory.

should not be allowed to retain benefits (including contractual rights) that were obtained through their wrongdoing. But this principle does not explain why a contract may be set aside for an innocent misrepresentation. If relief for innocent misrepresentations were available only in cases where the misrepresentation concerned an essential or important aspect of the contract, then it might be argued that the purpose of the law is, in effect, to give relief for unilateral mistakes. As was discussed in Chapter 7, although the common law doctrine of mistake only applies to shared mistakes, there are situations where relief for purely unilateral mistakes seems justified and, indeed, many legal systems offer broad relief in cases involving unilateral mistakes. But this explanation is unpersuasive because the causation test can be satisfied even where a misrepresentation concerns a trivial feature of the contract. No legal system allows relief for trivial mistakes, unilateral or otherwise.

Historically, the explanation may lie in judicial attempts to get around rules (in particular the parole evidence rule) that made it difficult to incorporate oral representations into written contracts. Many of the early cases in this area dealt with the sale of land, and such contracts, as we have seen, are set down in formal written documents. The courts would find it difficult to incorporate an oral representation into such a contract even if they felt that the representation was in reality a part of the contract. Judges would be particularly inclined to allow alternative relief in the form of rescission in cases where (as often happens) a higher price was paid as a result of the representation. Of course, the claimant in such a case ideally ought to have the alternative of obtaining damages, but even if a legal basis could be found for such an order, a further difficulty was that cases involving land were litigated before the Chancery Courts, which were unable to award damages. This explanation is consistent with the fact that today courts have the discretion (by virtue of section 2(2) of the Misrepresentation Act 1967) in cases involving non-fraudulent misrepresentation to substitute damages for rescission if they are of the opinion that rescission would be unfair in the circumstances.

Insofar as it is possible to provide a *substantive* justification for the rule that a contract may be set aside for an innocent misrepresentation, it would seem to lie in the fact that the innocent misrepresentor is not actually made *liable* for his misrepresentation, but merely *denied a benefit* (the benefit of the contract) that he would otherwise have enjoyed. Described in this way, relief for innocent misrepresentation resembles a mild form of strict liability. The representor is made responsible for anything he says, regardless of fault, but only in the limited sense that he may be denied the benefit of a contract. The innocent misrepresentor is not punished or made to pay compensatory damages. This seems a reasonable result, especially in cases where the misrepresentation has influenced the contract price, even if its juridical basis is not easy to explain. This justification also seems consistent with the discretion given to courts to award damages in lieu of rescission. Although this discretion applies both to negligent and innocent misrepresentation, its primary effect has been to allow judges to refuse rescission for innocent misrepresentations in precisely those cases where such an order would operate as a kind of penalty. Thus, courts are most likely to substitute damages where the innocent misrepresentation concerns a trivial feature of the contract and where, in addition, rescission would have serious consequences for the party who made the statement.

2. BARS TO RESCISSION

It was noted above that section 2(2) of the Misrepresentation Act gives courts the discretion to refuse to order rescission in cases involving non-fraudulent misrepresentations. This is just one of a number of ways in which a prima facie right to rescission may be lost. These so-called 'bars to rescission' may be raised in cases where rescission is sought on a basis other than misrepresentation (such as duress or mistake), but they tend to arise primarily in cases involving misrepresentations and so are conveniently discussed at this point.

First, the right to rescind may be lost because the representee has 'affirmed' the contract after learning of the misrepresentation—as, for example, where the purchaser of a lorry continued to use the vehicle after it was clear to him that the vendor's representation that the lorry was 'in excellent condition' was false.[9]

Secondly, the right may be lost by lapse of time. This may be regarded as a version of affirmation, since the time period does not normally begin to run until the representee has knowledge of the misrepresentation. Exceptionally, however, mere passage of time will bar rescission. Thus, in one case,[10] the purchaser of a painting that was innocently misrepresented to be a Constable was barred on the basis of lapse of time, when, five years later, he discovered the truth and sought rescission.

Thirdly, it has traditionally been said that the right to rescind is lost when it is no longer possible to return the parties to their original positions. This bar is related to the rule that, once a contract is rescinded (for whatever reason), the parties normally have the right, on the basis of unjust enrichment law, to restitution of any benefits conveyed under the contract. It would be unjust to allow the parties to keep benefits received under a contract that was induced by a misrepresentation (and which, moreover, may have only been partly executed), but for the same reason, it would often be unjust to allow rescission where restitution is no longer possible. For example, it would be

---

[9] *Long v. Lloyd* [1958] 1 WLR 753.
[10] *Leaf v. International Galleries* [1950] 2 KB 86.

unjust to excuse a homeowner entirely from the duty to pay for a major renovation just because the renovator had committed a minor misrepresentation during negotiations. The homeowner would end up unjustly enriched. Originally, the common law applied this barrier quite strictly, holding that, monetary benefits aside, the possibility of restoring the very things (if any) transferred under the contract was a precondition for rescission. But it is now recognized that this is not necessary where an adequate 'money allowance' can be paid by the party seeking restitution. This is consistent with the principles of unjust enrichment underlying this bar to rescission, since elsewhere in the law unjust enrichments can be, and typically are, reversed by restitution in money rather than restitution *in specie*.

Finally, it should be mentioned that while the right to rescind arises automatically—it is not necessary to apply to a court—the intention to rescind must normally be communicated to the other party in some way.

3. DAMAGES FOR MISREPRESENTATION

In addition to the right to set aside the contract, the victim of a misrepresentation will frequently have a right to claim damages. The rules in this area come primarily from the law of tort, but they are closely intertwined with contract law rules. Before looking at the substantive rules in this area, two preliminary points should be mentioned. First, the right to damages and the right to rescind are not mutually exclusive. Thus, where the requirements for both rescission and damages are satisfied, the representee has the choice of acting on either or both rights. Equally, the rights can stand alone. Thus, where the right to rescind has been lost (by virtue of one of the general bars on rescission discussed above or by the operation of section 2(2) of the Misrepresentation Act 1967), the representee will retain any right he had already had to claim for damages.

The second preliminary observation is that English law, unlike some legal systems, allows for concurrent liability in tort and contract. This means a representation will sometimes be found to be both a term of the contract *and* a wrongful misrepresentation, thereby giving the representee a choice between seeking damages in contract for breach of a term or in tort for a misstatement. This complicates the law but is perfectly justifiable in principle. As we have seen, a single statement can be both an undertaking (giving rise to contractual liability) and a misrepresentation (giving rise to liability in tort), and there is no reason the victim of both a broken promise and a misrepresentation should not be able to choose on which basis he wishes to recover. The only limit on this choice is that the victim cannot choose both to rescind the contract and bring an action for breach of contract. In practice, of course, most parties with a choice will choose to sue in contract because contract damages are usually more generous than those awarded under tort.

Fraudulent, negligent, and innocent misrepresentation

At one time, damages for misrepresentation were available only for mis-representations that were deliberately made, that is to say fraudulent misrepresentations. This limit was significant because fraud is not easily proven. In the famous case of *Derry v. Peek*,[11] the House of Lords held that a statement is fraudulent only if it is made with knowledge of its falsity, or recklessly, without knowing or caring whether it is true or false. The essence of the decision is that mere carelessness or negligence is not to be treated as dishonesty. It is sometimes said that although negligence cannot amount to fraud, gross negligence may be evidence of fraud. But this is misleading: negligence, gross or otherwise, is the very antithesis of fraud—it can no more be evidence of fraud than it can, in and of itself, amount to fraud. What is evidently meant by this somewhat elliptical expression is that courts—recognizing that the facts of a case can be consistent with fraud or with gross negligence but not both—have chosen to impugn the latter explanation because they are sceptical that the defendant could have been as grossly negligent as is alleged. To take a hypothetical example, suppose that a person were to sell his own second-hand car and were to state that the brakes were in good working order. If, in fact, it transpired that the brakes did not work at all, the seller would find it difficult to convince a judge that he had merely been negligent rather than dishonest.

In any event, in modern times misrepresentation is actionable in damages in a much broader range of circumstances. At common law, it was first held in the House of Lords in *Hedley Byrne v. Heller*[12] that, in special circumstances, liability for damages could arise in the case of negligent misrepresentation. Such circumstances will nearly always be found where the misrepresentation had the effect of inducing the representee to enter a contract (although liability for negligent misrepresentation may arise even in the absence of a contract).

Liability for negligent misstatement (whether the misstatement induced a contract or not) is generally understood as a liability in tort, but there are circumstances in which the process used for determining that liability closely resembles the process for establishing a contract. In a number of cases it has been held that liability arose because the representor *voluntarily assumed the obligation*, a formula often used to characterize contractual duties. Although this test does not feature in every instance of tortious misstatement, many of the cases which have employed it could easily have been classified as contractual if English law had adopted a different conceptual approach to contract formation (particularly concerning consideration and third party

---

[11] (1889) 14 App Cas 337.
[12] [1964] AC 465.

rights).[13] In *Hedley Byrne* itself, for example, a bank negligently gave a misleading reference to the claimants, who were clients of a customer who had
requested the reference. The court held that except for an explicit disclaimer
of liability by the bank, this would have been sufficient grounds to find the
bank liable in tort. On the facts, the claimants had no direct contractual
relationship with the bank, yet the bank voluntarily assumed the duty of
giving them information, and by extension the obligation to give reasonably
careful information.[14] Similarly in *Smith v. Bush*,[15] the House of Lords held
that a surveyor commissioned by a building society to value a house for the
purposes of a mortgage could be liable for negligence to an applicant for a
mortgage with the building society. Although the surveyor was, in theory,
dealing only with the building society, the relationship between the surveyor
and the buyer was in reality close to an ordinary contract. On the other hand,
in cases where it would be difficult in any legal system for the representee to
bring an action in contract, English courts have usually refused to order
damages for negligent misrepresentation. Thus in *Caparo Industries plc v.
Dickman*,[16] the House of Lords held that a company's auditors were not
liable to individuals, including existing shareholders, who purchased shares
on the basis of their negligently prepared financial report. At first blush, the
facts appear similar to those in *Smith v. Bush*; although it is the company itself
which employs, contracts with, and pays the auditors, the auditors are, in
commercial reality, the watchdogs of the shareholders, employed and paid
for their benefit. The difference was that the claimant in *Smith v. Bush* was
a specific individual whose reliance was the very purpose of the transaction.
In the leading speech in the House of Lords, Lord Bridge relied on this as the
key distinction:

The situation is entirely different where a statement is put into more or less general
circulation and may foreseeably be relied on by strangers to the maker of the statement for any one of a variety of different purposes which the maker of the statement
had no reason to anticipate.[17]

The common law rules on negligent misstatements are helpful, therefore, in
exploring the boundaries between tort and contract. But in cases of the kind

---

[13] In civilian legal systems, which do not have doctrines of consideration and which typically
recognise broad third party rights, many of the leading cases in this area would be regarded as
contract cases.

[14] The House of Lords has now reasserted the importance of the voluntary assumption
of responsibility for liability in many tort cases of this kind. See, e.g., *Henderson v. Merrett
Syndicates Ltd* [1994] 3 All ER 506.

[15] [1990] 1 AC 831.

[16] [1992] 2 AC 605.

[17] Ibid. at 621. But note how the very similar argument of the defendants in *Carlill v. Carbolic
Smoke Ball Co.* [1893] 1 QB 256 was disposed of a hundred years before *Caparo*. Of
course, *Carlill* involved a *promise* and *Caparo* a statement of fact, which may well be a valid
distinction.

that are the immediate concern of this chapter—where the misrepresentation was made by a co-contractor and induced the representee to enter the contract—its practical significance is now quite small. Shortly after the *Hedley Byrne* decision, the Misrepresentation Act 1967 substantially modified the common law rules on misrepresentation so that it is now often possible to claim damages for negligent misrepresentation under that Act as well as at common law. Section 2(1) provides:

Where a person has entered into a contract after a misrepresentation has been made to him by another party thereto and as a result thereof he has suffered loss, then, if the person making the representation would be liable in damages in respect thereof had the misrepresentation been made fraudulently, that person shall be liable notwithstanding that the misrepresentation was not made fraudulently, unless he proves that he had reasonable ground to believe and did believe up to the time the contract was made that the facts represented were true.

The section is badly worded and uncertainty regarding its relationship with the common law rules has produced a confusing conceptual tangle. However, its overall effect has been to expand significantly on a victim's common law rights. A party seeking damages for misrepresentation is not required to prove negligence; instead, the representor has the onus of proving that he had reasonable grounds for believing in the truth of his representation. The result, in practice, has been that damages are now available for statements that are very close to innocent misrepresentations. In addition, and of greater importance, section 2(1) permits the representee to treat a negligent misrepresentation as though it had been made fraudulently. This means the representee can take advantage of the generous rules regarding remoteness of damages that, under the common law, were available only to victims of fraud. The predictable result is that claimants invariably bring actions under section 2(1) rather than under the general common law.

It is not easy to justify either of these additional rights. On what basis is it proper to treat those who make negligent misrepresentations—which, remember, are broadly defined—on the same footing as those who make fraudulent misrepresentations? The generous remoteness rule in fraud is justified on the ground that the fraudster deserves to be treated harshly. This justification does not apply as easily to cases involving individuals who are merely careless. Indeed, it seems highly unlikely that the Act's drafters actually intended such a result, but their clumsy wording—together with the courts' refusal to go around the Act's literal words—has led to what can only be described as an embarrassment for English law.

There is one respect in which the Misrepresentation Act is less favourable to a victim of misrepresentation than is the common law. Under the common law, the victim has a prima facie right to rescind for any misrepresentation, no matter how trivial and no matter the effects of rescission on the representor.

As mentioned earlier, section 2(2) of the Act gives the court a discretion to refuse rescission for a non-fraudulent misrepresentation, and to award damages instead, if it is of the 'opinion that it would equitable to do so, having regard to the nature of the misrepresentation and the loss that would be caused by it if the contract were upheld, as well as to the loss that rescission would cause to the other party'. The rationale underlying this provision is that in many cases, and particularly those involving innocent misrepresentations, rescission can be too harsh a remedy. If the representor has incurred expenses in reliance on the contract, the consequences of denying enforcement can be much more severe than any damages award that might be made under section 2(1) or the common law. The courts have also used this section to refuse rescission in cases where the representee's real purpose is to avoid a bad bargain.

Unlike section 2(1), therefore, section 2(2) meets a genuine need under the current law. Again, however, the section is badly worded; in particular, there have been controversies regarding the measure of damages under section 2(2). In the leading case[18] it was held that damages should compensate for loss of the right to rescind, not for loss caused by entering the contract, and, moreover, that they should not exceed the amount the claimant could have received if the representation had been a term of the contract. On this basis, the Court of Appeal held that a claimant who purchased land on the basis of a (minor) misrepresentation could not recover for a loss in the market value of property that occurred after the contract was signed. To allow such recovery would mean the claimant would be left as well off, in financial terms, as if he had been allowed rescission—thereby nullifying the purpose of the section.

The measure of damages in tort

The main practical difference between bringing a claim for damages in tort for negligent or fraudulent misrepresentation and bringing a claim for damages in contract for breach of contract concerns the rules for assessing damages. In theory, the contractual rules are more generous. As is explained in Chapter 14, the usual rule in contract is that damages for breach are designed to put the claimant in the position he would have been in had the contract been performed. In tort, however, damages (including damages for pre-contractual misrepresentation) are intended to put the claimant in the position he would have been in if no tort had ever been committed.[19] Thus, in contract, but not in tort, the claimant can claim for whatever profit he would have made through the transaction.

---

[18] *William Sindall plc v. Cambridgeshire CC* [1984] 1 WLR 1016.
[19] *East v. Maurer* [1991] 1 WLR 461.

In practice, however, these two methods of calculating damages often lead to the same result. Suppose, for instance, that A buys a business from B as a result of a fraudulent misrepresentation by B. Had the representation been true, the business would have been worth £10,000, but in fact it is worth nothing. The purchase price was £5,000. If the representation is a term of the contract, and A sues for breach of this term, then A will be awarded damages to put him in the position he would have been in if the representation were true. So A would be awarded the expected value of the business—£10,000. But in an action for fraudulent misrepresentation, A will be awarded damages to put him in the position he would have been in if the representation had not been made, that is to say, he will be awarded a sum equal to the value of his *detrimental reliance* on the representation. In theory, this sum might amount merely to the £5,000 that A spent on purchasing the business, plus an amount to cover A's incidental expenses. If this is the case, the contractual measure is indeed more favourable. But it is likely that A also incurred what might be called 'negative' reliance losses. Specifically, A may be able to argue that, in addition to relying on the statement by purchasing B's business, he also relied by *foregoing* other, similarly lucrative business opportunities. Thus, A might argue that but for the misrepresentation he would not have bought B's business but another business. In this case, A's claim in tort may legitimately include a claim for the expected value of the other business.[20] In many cases, and particularly in competitive markets, the expected value of this alternative opportunity will be roughly equal to the expected value of the business that was actually bought. Where this is the case, the two measures of damages lead to the same result. Of course, it may be difficult in practice to prove in court the value of a lost opportunity. This is one reason claimants prefer to bring actions in contract where they have the choice. But the important point is that while in theory damages for breach of contract are more generous than damages in tort for misrepresentation, in practice the two measures, if assessed accurately, often lead to the same final result.

4. EXCLUSION OF LIABILITY FOR MISREPRESENTATION

Historically, at common law, there were no rules to prevent parties to a contract from attaching terms that served to exclude liability for misrepresentation (only fraud could not be the subject of such exclusions). But under the Unfair Contract Terms Act 1977 attempts to exclude liability for misrepresentation are invalid insofar as they are 'unreasonable'. Thus, where a bidder at an auction bought land in reliance on various false statements as to planning permission, an attempt in the contract to exclude liability for such

---

[20] Ibid.

misrepresentations was held unreasonable and void.[21] And in *Smith v. Bush*[22] (discussed above), where the main issue was whether the Act applied to disclaimers that were attached to surveyors' reports and subsequently passed on to the applicant, it was held that with an ordinary home-purchase transaction it was generally unreasonable for building societies or surveyors to attempt to disclaim their liabilities. This aspect of the case, as well as the significance of the Unfair Terms in Consumer Contracts Regulations 1999 in assessing such exemption clauses, is discussed in more detail in Chapter 12.

5. MISREPRESENTATION IN THE PERFORMANCE OF CONTRACTS

When lawyers talk of 'misrepresentation' in a contractual context, they typically confine themselves to the sort of statements discussed above, which are made before any contract exists between the parties. Because these misrepresentations are made at a time when no contract exists, they cannot be governed by obligations arising out of the contract itself. Entirely different principles, however, govern liability for false statements made *during the performance of contractual duties*, which very often are governed by the contract (though non-contractual remedies are usually also available). A solicitor, for instance, must perform the duties imposed by her contract with her client, and this contract imposes a duty (via an implied term) to be careful in the making of any statements. Hence there has never been any doubt, even prior to the decision in *Hedley Byrne*, that negligence alone would be a sufficient ground of liability in such a case, as this would amount to a breach of contract. Moreover, many of the principles of the law relating to the effect of pre-contractual misrepresentation are clearly irrelevant to cases of negligent advice. For instance, the distinction between a statement of fact and a statement of law or of opinion is clearly immaterial where the liability of a solicitor for negligent advice is concerned. The same is true of advice given by any professional person during the course of his employment.

---

[21] *South Western Property Co. v. Marton* (1983) 2 Tr L 14.
[22] Above. 15.

Duress and Undue Influence

THE law is reluctant to allow a direct plea that a contract should be set aside because one party was in a vulnerable or weak bargaining position. All persons over the age of eighteen and of sound mind are generally treated as of equal capacity for the purposes of contracting. Nevertheless, from time to time the law will step in to redress imbalances between stronger and weaker parties. Occasionally the intervention is indirect as when, for instance, courts invoke special rules that protect parties subject to exemption clauses or that protect consumers against certain types of unfair terms. Rules of this kind are discussed in Chapter 12. For the present, our attention is directed towards the general rules that courts have traditionally employed in order to deal with cases of inequality. These are the doctrines of duress and undue influence.

Like the law relating to misrepresentation and duties of disclosure, these doctrines are concerned with the manner in which a contract has been formed. But they are (as we shall see) by no means irrelevant to the outcome of contracts and to larger issues of substantive justice.

1. DURESS

In the usual case, duress is established by showing that the agreement of the party seeking to have the contract set aside (the 'defendant') was induced by a threat to commit an unlawful act. Typically this threat was made by the party seeking to enforce the contract (the 'claimant') but a contract will also be set aside for duress if a third party made the threat and the claimant was aware of it.

Many perfectly valid contracts arise, of course, from threat-induced acceptances. A contract of sale entered in response to the purchaser's threat to purchase goods from an alternative vendor will not be set aside for duress. In general (exceptions are discussed later) a threat gives grounds to set aside a contract only if the threatened action is itself a legal wrong. Thus, a threat to injure the other contracting party is sufficient to prove duress (assuming the threat was operative in inducing the contract) because intentionally injuring another is a crime.

It is relatively easy to determine if a contract may be set aside for duress where the alleged threat was to injure the defendant's person or property. Assuming such a threat was made, it is usually clear that the threatened action is unlawful and that the threat actually induced the contract.[1] Much more difficult are cases involving threats to commit purely 'economic' harms. At one time there were few instances of purely economic crimes or torts, and so little chance of pleading duress unless the relevant threat involved physical harm of one kind or another. This limitation on the scope of duress was often criticized, though it might be thought that the criticism should have been directed at the definitions of wrongdoing in criminal law and tort law rather than at the law of duress. In any event, various kinds of economic crimes and torts are now recognized, and this development has been reflected, in turn, in the development of a concept of 'economic duress'. For instance, many strikes and threats of strikes are today unlawful in some sense, such as where they are called without a statutory ballot of the workforce or where they involve secondary boycotts that affect parties not directly involved in the dispute. Thus, in one case where a union had demanded payments to a 'slush-fund' as its price for not (unlawfully) impeding a ship attempting to leave port, it was held that the agreement was not valid and the money could be recovered.[2] In another case, where a contracting party was compelled to agree to a variation that increased the price of his contract because of a strike threat by the *other party's* workforce (of which threat the other party was, of course, aware), it was held that the contract variation was invalid, as made under economic duress.[3] This situation differs from that in which an employer yields to demands made by his own workforce, because relations with his workers are at least *his* business, and it is his responsibility to decide either to capitulate or to suffer the consequences. But where the strike threat arises from the *other* party's workers, the victim of the threat has no responsibility for the relations between the workers and their employer.

Threats to breach

One common way of threatening economic harm is by threatening to break an existing contract. Building contractors, for example, sometimes threaten to break their contracts unless the owner agrees to an increase in the contract price. In theory, the victim can simply ignore the threat, and then sue for damages for breach of contract if the contractor carries through with the threat. In practice, this is rarely a satisfactory solution: litigation is expensive; damages regularly undercompensate; and the party threatening to breach often has insufficient assets (or insurance) to satisfy a court order. It might be thought, therefore, that the courts would long ago have recognized that

---

[1] The test for determining whether a threat 'induced' the threatened party to enter the contract is discussed below in connection with threats to breach a contract. A rare case involving a threat of physical harm in which this test was in issue is *Barton v. Armstrong* [1976] AC 104, discussed below, n. 6.

[2] *Universe Tankships of Monrovia v. ITTF* [1983] 1 AC 366.

[3] *B. & S. Contracts & Design Ltd v. Victor Green Publishers Ltd* [1984] ICR 419.

contracts induced by threats of this kind may be set aside. It is a fundamental and long-standing principle of contract law that contracting parties have legal duties to perform, the breach of which is regarded as a legal wrong. This is the basis on which contract breakers may be ordered to pay damages. Yet common law courts have only recently recognised that contracts induced by such threats may be set aside, and even today a threat to breach is treated differently than, say, a threat of physical injury. In particular, the courts have refrained from stating in categorical terms that contracts induced by such threats may always be set aside.

From an historical perspective, there are at least two explanations why threats to breach were treated in this way. First, (as we shall see) it is often difficult to distinguish threats from other kinds of communication and, in addition, to determine if a threat was causally operative. Admitting the defence of 'threatened breach' thus has the potential to raise difficult evidentiary problems—a significant issue in less-sophisticated legal systems. The second, and probably more important, reason is that prior to the decision in *Williams v. Roffey Bros. & Nicholls (Contractors) Ltd*,[4] most contracts induced by threats to breach were in any event invalid on the basis that they lacked consideration. As we saw in Chapter 4, in such cases the threatening party typically demands an 'upward' modification of the existing contract. Until *Roffey Bros.*, courts could invalidate such modifications on the grounds that the party who agreed to pay more received nothing in exchange: there was said to be no 'legal benefit' in a promise to perform an existing contract. The result was that courts did not have to treat a threat to breach as duress in order to invalidate a contract induced by such a threat.

Historical factors aside, the contemporary reluctance to state clearly that threats to breach always qualify as duress probably arises from the fact that there are often good reasons to enforce a contract (or, more typically, a contractual modification) that, on its face, was induced by a threat to break an existing contract. First, threats to breach are sometimes made because the threatened party had unreasonably refused to renegotiate the existing contract. The usual reason a party wants to modify an existing contract is that circumstances changed since the original contract was formed, such that performance became unexpectedly onerous or costly. In some legal systems, the courts would be permitted in such circumstances to set aside the original contract on grounds of frustration or (what amounts to the same thing) to conclude that it is a breach of good faith to demand strict compliance with the contract's terms. As we have seen, English law has a narrow doctrine of frustration and altogether refuses to recognize good faith duties in the performance of a contract. Nonetheless, it would not be surprising to find that, in practice, English courts are disinclined to set aside a contractual

---

[4] [1991] 1 QB 1, discussed above, 116 [Ch 4].

modification because of a threat to breach when they feel that the defendant was unreasonable in refusing to renegotiate.

A second reason that a court might want to enforce a modification (apparently) induced by a threat to breach is that the apparent threat was not actually a threat, but merely a warning. In situations where one party seeks a modification because his costs have risen, it may be impossible for that party to perform if the original contract remains in place. A building contractor, for example, may not have the funds to purchase higher-priced materials or to hire needed extra workers, and his bank may be unwilling to loan him the money without an enforceable promise of higher payment. In such a case, a statement by the contractor to the effect that he will be unable to perform unless he is promised higher payment is (merely) a warning. The contractor is warning that if he does not receive more money he will have no option but to breach. Obviously, there is nothing wrong with communicating a warning of this kind; indeed, warnings are usually appreciated. This is not to deny that there might be other reasons for not enforcing modifications in such circum-stances; some argue that modifications should be set aside in order to penalise parties who carelessly or intentionally end up in positions where they are unable to perform, such as a contractor who intentionally underbids to obtain a contract.[5] The general point, however, is that modifications are sometimes induced by warnings, not threats, and where this happens it may be appropriate to enforce the modification.

Thirdly, and finally, there are cases where it is appropriate for courts to disregard a threat to breach because, although a threat was made, the threat was not operative. It goes without saying that a contract should not be set aside for duress unless the threat actually influenced the formation of the contract. In principle, the relevant test should be easy to satisfy. The courts have made clear that it is sufficient that the threat was *a* factor—even if not a dominant or even necessary factor—in deciding to enter the contract. Thus in *Barton v. Armstrong*[6] it was held that a threat to murder qualified as duress even if it could be proven that the victim might have entered the contract regardless of the threat. But in cases involving threats to break a contract even this test may not be met. There are various reasons, aside from any possible threat to breach, that a party might agree to an upward modification of an existing contract. For instance, a party might agree to a modification for essentially moral reasons. Even in business situations, a contracting party may feel uncomfortable taking advantage of the other party's bad fortune. Or

---

[5] It should be kept in mind that a general rule to the effect that enforcement will be refused in such cases could harm *both* parties. *Ex ante*, parties who are willing to promise to pay more want such promises to be enforceable, since this is the only way they can induce performance. The problem of parties who underbid or are otherwise at fault for not being able to perform is better solved by regulation, for example, by licensing standards and mandatory insurance.

[6] [1976] AC 104.

one party might agree to pay more in order to maintain good relations with the other party and with third parties with whom she may want to contract in the future. In these cases, as the threat was not operative upon the party who accepted the modification, the modification should usually be enforced.

There are often good reasons, therefore, to enforce contracts that were prima facie induced by threats to break existing contracts. Properly understood, none of these reasons are inconsistent with the conclusion that such threats, if operative, always qualify as duress. But perhaps because the law in this area is still in its infancy these reasons have, in practice, led to a judicial refusal to clearly condemn threats to breach.

A few last words should be said about one feature of the law in this area. In cases where a threat to breach is made, the courts often ask whether the promisor made his promise willingly; more specifically, they consider whether the promisor complained or had a reasonable opportunity to enforce the original contract in court. This test may reflect a concern for whether the defendant 'consented' to the modification. Alternatively, as comments in some cases would suggest,[7] it is possible the test is used to discern if a threat was causally operative. Whatever its theoretical basis, it seems reasonable enough to require a party to object to a perceived threat at the time it is made rather than at some indeterminate point in the future. In practice, however, the test may be too stringent. Objecting is usually a waste of time and going to court (as we have already noted) is rarely a reasonable alternative (though it is perhaps understandable that courts are reluctant to acknowledge this). In one modern decision where a shipbuilder had extracted a promise of extra payment from the purchaser as a condition of delivery, it was held that the purchaser could not get the payment back once it was paid.[8] The court stated that, while the purchaser *could* have validly refused to honour the promise on the grounds of economic duress, the fact that he paid the money without protest meant that he could no longer seek a remedy from the court. In such circumstances it may be unrealistic to suggest that the buyer should resist the demand and go to law to enforce his right to the ship without extra payment; the buyer's need for the ship may be urgent.

Blackmail

Aside from certain cases addressed by the law on undue influence (discussed below), blackmail is the only recognized exception to the rule that a threatened action must be unlawful to qualify as duress. The blackmailer often threatens to do something perfectly valid and even commendable—for

---

[7] See the cases cited below, n. 8.

[8] *North Ocean Shipping Co. Ltd v. Hyundai Construction Co. Ltd* [1979] QB 705; see also *Atlas Express Ltd v. Kafco (Importers and Distributors) Ltd* [1989] QB 833. But compare *CTN Cash and Carry Ltd v. Gallagher* [1994] 4 All ER 714.

instance, to report a thief to the police. Of course, there can be no question that blackmail itself is a legal wrong: extortion is a crime irrespective of the lawfulness of the threatened act. This would appear to be sufficient reason for courts in contract cases to recognize the defence of duress by blackmail. Certainly, it would be strange if contract law took a more lenient view of such threats than does the criminal law; if anything, contract law might be expected to have a wider definition of 'wrongful' than criminal law.[9] But it must be acknowledged that it is not easy to explain why blackmail is legally—and morally—condemned. Various attempts have been made, but none are entirely satisfying. Blackmail remains an oddity.

The theoretical basis of relief for duress

Aside from cases involving threats to breach a contract, there is little dispute regarding the legal outcome of most duress cases, especially those involving obvious threats of violence. The explanations of the rules of duress are more controversial. There are two main views. The traditional view says that the law of duress is concerned primarily with the situation of the *defendant* (the party seeking to have the contract set aside). This view supposes that when a contract is set aside for duress, the underlying reason is that the defendant's consent was impaired. The second, more contemporary explanation of duress focuses on the *claimant*'s situation. According to this view, when a contract is set aside for duress it is because the party seeking to enforce the contract (the claimant) is a wrongdoer. More specifically, the contract is set aside because the claimant obtained his contractual rights by exerting unlawful or 'illegitimate' pressure.[10]

Before turning to examine these explanations in more detail, it may be useful to mention two reasons this area of the law has raised difficulties for theorists. The first is that the 'impaired consent' and 'illegitimate pressure' explanations of duress are not mutually exclusive. Assuming that illegitimate pressure and impaired consent are valid reasons for setting aside a contract, it is perfectly sensible (from the perspective of either explanation) to conclude that a particular contract may be set aside *either* because the defendant's

---

[9] It is arguable that further instances of 'lawful threat' duress should be recognized on the basis that duress law can legitimately adopt a broader concept of 'wrongful' than that adopted by the general law. The consequences of declaring an act to be a crime or a tort are usually more serious than concluding that a contract should be set aside for duress. Thus we should welcome the refusal of Steyn LJ in *CTN Cash and Carry Ltd*, ibid, to state explicitly that there could never be a case of 'lawful act duress', even in a commercial context. At the same time, courts should tread carefully in this area, particularly in commercial cases. Common law courts are not experts in the kinds of problems raised by strikes and most other forms of economic pressure, and litigation is usually a poor method of exploring such problems.

[10] The idea of characterizing duress as illegitimate pressure first gained prominence in the UK following the publication of P. Atiyah's 'Economic Duress and the "Overborne Will" ', (1982) 98 Law Q Rev 197.

consent was impaired *or* because the claimant acted wrongly. The second reason is that it is not entirely clear that these explanations are actually different. Part of what makes an illegitimate threat illegitimate is that the threatening party is trying to force the victim to act in accordance with the threatening party's wishes. The victim's autonomy is therefore threatened, and autonomy is closely related to consent. Similarly, consent may be understood, at least in part, through the concept of illegitimate pressure. As we shall see, impaired consent is often defined by reference to unusual or extraordinary pressure—and pressure arising from an illegitimate threat might be thought a clear example of an extraordinary pressure.

A final preliminary observation is that insofar as judges have tried to explain the law in this area, their view (particularly in recent cases) seems to be that wrongdoing and impaired consent are distinct concepts, and that *both* are required for a claim of duress. In *R v. Attorney-General for England and Wales*[11] Lord Hoffmann, writing the majority judgment of the Privy Council, held that there were two elements to the 'wrong of duress': 'pressure amounting to compulsion of the will of the victim and . . . the illegitimacy of the pressure.' One difficulty with this view is that if illegitimate pressure is proven, it is not clear why anything else (aside from causation) must be shown to establish the 'wrong of duress'. Illegitimate pressure is by definition wrongful. But the larger difficulty—and the reason this view has attracted little academic support—is that it is not clear on what basis *both* illegitimate pressure and 'compulsion of the will' might be relevant. Assuming that these are distinct concepts, it would seem that proof of either should be sufficient grounds to set aside a contract. At a minimum, it would seem that proof the contract was induced by wrongdoing should be sufficient reason to refuse the wrongdoer's request to enforce the contract.

Duress as illegitimate or 'wrongful' pressure

The appeal of the claimant-based 'wrongdoing' explanation of duress should be evident. There is wide support for the idea that the courts should not assist a claimant who is seeking to enforce contractual rights obtained by his own wrongdoing. This same principle, as we saw in the last chapter, underlies most of the law on misrepresentation. This explanation also seems consistent with the main features of the law on duress. In this view a contract induced by a threat to commit a wrongful act may be set aside because such threats are themselves clearly wrongful. The claimant has exercised illegitimate pressure. The same is true of threats of blackmail—although the threatened action is not wrongful the blackmailer is undoubtedly using illegitimate pressure.

---

[11] [2003] UKPC 22.

Furthermore, the weak notion of causation that is used to determine if a threat is operative fits with a concern for wrongdoing. As in the equivalent case of fraud, it is appropriate to place a heavy onus on a wrongdoer who seeks to show that his wrongdoing had no effect. The only substantive feature of the law on duress that is not easy to explain on the basis of a concern for wrongdoing is the rule that a contract may be set aside if the defendant was induced to enter the contract by a third party's wrongful threat (and the claimant was aware of the threat). To be sure, the claimant who has knowledge of the threat is not entirely innocent. As between the claimant and the defendant in such cases, the latter is 'more' innocent. It seems rather strong, however, to say that the claimant is a 'wrongdoer' when a third party was the source of the pressure.

Overall, it is difficult to resist the conclusion that the law of duress can be explained by the idea that the courts will not assist wrongdoers. The difficult question is whether this is the only possible explanation, or whether the law can also be explained by the distinct notion of impaired consent. The question is practically important because if the courts care about impaired consent in these kinds of cases it is but a short step (as we shall see) to the conclusion that the principle must be further developed so as to be given full effect in the law.

Duress as impaired consent

The impaired-consent explanation of duress raises a number of complex and sometimes highly theoretical issues. It may be useful to account in advance, then, for the continuing appeal of this view, which rests on three fairly simple grounds. First, the judgments in duress cases are littered with references to consent and voluntariness.[12] While it is possible that the judges in these cases were simply confused, this seems unlikely: this is not a highly technical area of the law, and notions like 'consent' and 'wrongdoing' are not terms of art. Secondly, relief appears to be given in some categories of cases where the defendant acted under 'pressure' but where it is not clear that the claimant acted wrongly. Arguably cases involving third-party threats comprise one such category, but perhaps the best-known cases (though they are not always described as 'duress' cases) involve contracts for salvage and rescue at sea. These cases are discussed below. Third, and finally, the idea that individuals should not be bound to contracts to which they did not consent is generally considered fundamental to the notion of contractual obligation. It might be thought incredible if this idea were not given effect in an area of the law that appears to raise it so directly.

---

[12] See, e.g., *The Atlantic Baron* [1978] 3 All ER 1171 at 1183; *Pau On v. Lau Yiu Long* [1980] AC 614 at 636; *The Alev* [1989] 1 Lloyd's Rep 138 at 145.

The meaning of consent

The first issue that must be addressed in considering the impaired-consent explanation of duress is the meaning of 'impaired consent'. Critics frequently allege that the concept has no meaning, or at least none that bears any resemblance to the rules that are applied in duress cases.

Broadly speaking, two main approaches to defining consent can be identified: the 'mental state' approach and the 'contextual' approach. According to the mental state approach, statements about consent are descriptions of what is going on in someone's head. In this view, to say that a contracting party's consent was impaired because of pressure is to say that the pressure brought about a particular psychological state—'impaired consent'—in that individual. Occasional judicial statements to the effect that duress 'overcomes' the victim's 'will' would seem to support this approach.

The main difficulty with the mental state view—and the reason consent sceptics tend to focus on this view—is that none of the obvious candidates for the mental state corresponding to 'consent' have much relation to the tests actually applied in duress cases. There are three main candidates. The first equates the mental state of consent with voluntary or intentional action. If this were the definition of consent, a plea of impaired consent would almost never succeed. A person who does something under the most severe constraints (such as throwing his cargo overboard to save his ship during a storm or signing a contract at the point of a gun) is nonetheless acting voluntarily: he is choosing between two unpalatable courses, but he is still making a choice. Indeed, the more strongly he feels the pressure, the more willing he is likely to be to agree—but only because it is the lesser of the two evils open to him.

The second candidate equates consent with complete freedom from pressure of any kind. If this test were applied, we would expect pleas of impaired consent to succeed in nearly every case. Contracts are nearly always made under pressure of some sort. We enter contracts to buy food, clothing, and shelter because we need these things in order to survive. The same is true (at any rate for most people) of employment contracts and of contracts to obtain the things necessary to secure and keep employment (e.g. education, transportation, etc.). Indeed, pressure and threats are implicit in the whole concept of exchange, because the offeror is always demanding something in return, which is another way of saying that he is threatening not to supply what you want unless you can give him what he wants in return.

The third possibility is that the mental state corresponding to consent lies somewhere between these two extremes. This interpretation fits better with the ordinary understanding of consent, but it seems no more helpful in explaining the law. One difficulty is that it is not clear how to usefully describe the relevant state of mind. But the main difficulty is that the law seems unconcerned with the defendant's mental state, however it is defined. To determine if a decision to enter a contract was made in the appropriate mental state requires knowledge of human psychology—yet expert testimony about the defendant's mental state is not relevant in considering a plea of duress. More generally, the legal tests for duress are not directed to assessing the defendant's mental state (aside from determining if the relevant pressure was causally operative—a test that is nearly always satisfied).

For these reasons, contemporary advocates of the impaired consent explanation of duress tend to support some version of the 'contextual' approach. This approach focuses on the external conditions—the 'context'— in which the relevant decision has been made. As with the mental state view, it is possible to define the relevant conditions so that the test is always satisfied (by holding that any pressure short of physical pressure is irrelevant) or never satisfied (by holding that any kind of pressure impairs consent). But the more common and plausible interpretation supposes that statements about consent are basically all-things-considered conclusions about the kinds of pressures that individuals should be expected to put up with in life. They are statements, in other words, about which kinds of pressures are among the 'ordinary' vicissitudes of life and which are 'extraordinary'. In this view, conclusions about consent depend significantly on the time and place that the decision was made—what counts as valid consent in wartime, for example, may not so qualify in peacetime. This explains why the sorts of pressures inherent to any exchange do not negate consent. For instance, consent is hardly vitiated when a consumer is forced to choose between paying the price for what is on offer or else suffering the blandishments of the salesman or a failure to 'keep up with the Joneses': these are perfectly ordinary pressures that exist in any competitive society. According to this interpretation, then, a conclusion that consent was negated by a particular kind of pressure is, in effect, a global statement about the world we live in.

Of the various interpretations of consent discussed above, the contextual interpretation seems closest to how the term is actually used in ordinary conversation. When we say of X's apparent agreement to a contract that 'X did not consent', we do not purport to be saying something about X's inner mind, nor are we saying merely that X was subject to some kind of pressure, however trivial or common. The idea is usually that there was something unusual about the relevant pressure. The difficulty is that the test for consent contemplated by this view—i.e. of whether the pressure was 'extra- ordinary'—is extremely vague. A further difficulty is that it bears little apparent resemblance to the tests of validity the courts apply in duress cases. But while these are important objections to using the concept of impaired consent to explain the law on duress, they may not be decisive. It is generally accepted that one of the law's basic tasks is to translate vague or otherwise indeterminate moral principles into concrete legal rules. Various features of the common law are often explained using this idea; for example, it is often said that although the common law refuses to endorse the general (and extremely vague) principle that contracting parties must act in good faith, it nonetheless gives effect to this principle through a variety of specific rules.[13] The same might be true with respect to the general (and extremely vague) principle that a contract may be set aside whenever one (or both) of the parties was induced to enter the contract by 'extraordinary' pressure. This suggestion is explored in more detail in the next two sections of this chapter.

Threats and impaired consent

Whatever the problems in defining 'consent', the willingness of courts to set aside a contract induced by the other party's threat to commit an unlawful act can be explained equally well by a concern for impaired consent or by a refusal to assist wrongdoers. Wrongful threats are almost by definition the kind of extraordinary pressure that individuals should not be expected to put up with as one of the ordinary vicissitudes of life. Indeed, a threat of bodily injury is perhaps the paradigmatic example of extraordinary pressure.[14] One limitation on the scope of relief for duress appears, however, to be inconsistent with the impaired-consent perspective. Although there are few cases directly on point it is generally assumed that in the common law (unlike in the civil law) an unlawful threat made by a *third party* constitutes duress only where the claimant was aware of the threat. If the courts are truly worried about whether the defendant consented to the contract, it should not matter that the threat was made by a third party.

This limitation is sometimes explained on the ground that, questions of consent aside, it would be both unfair and detrimental to commerce to allow contracts to be set aside for reasons the claimant could not have known. As we have seen in other contexts, the common law has long been influenced by the idea that parties should be able to rely on the appearance of consent. Of course, setting aside an apparent contract is not necessarily a problem, even for commercial parties, if the parties can be put back in the positions they were in prior to the transaction. Thus, another suggestion is that the limitation is essentially an historical anachronism: the rule arose in a period when relief for unjust enrichment was narrowly confined. The only way that

---

[13] A good example is the rule (discussed later in this chapter) that banks and other creditors must take reasonable steps to ensure that sureties who guarantee the debts of a co-habitee understand the risks they are undertaking.

[14] This is not to deny that some wrongful threats, such as a threat to break a construction contract unless the price is increased, might sometimes be considered ordinary, even expected, events. But the explanation now being considered need not suppose that impaired consent is the only basis for setting aside a contract induced by a wrongful threat. The invalidity of contracts induced by 'ordinary' unlawful threats (assuming this category exists at all) may be explained on the ground that the courts should not assist wrongdoers.

courts could protect claimants who had conferred benefits on defendants in the reasonable belief that they had binding agreements was to enforce such agreements.

Neither of these suggestions explains why courts refuse relief even in cases where the claimant did not detrimentally rely on the agreement. It is also worth noting that relief for incapacity—perhaps the clearest example of a 'defendant-based' ground of relief—is not limited to cases in which the claimant was aware of the defendant's incapacity. If impaired consent is the concern, it is not obvious why the courts take a different approach in duress cases.

States of necessity, monopolies, and consent

Cases dealing with wrongful threats seem generally (though not perfectly) consistent with the idea that courts care about impaired consent. But the idea of impaired consent does not do any real work explaining the law of duress unless there are some results that *cannot* be explained by the alternative idea that the courts should not assist wrongdoers. The cases most commonly mentioned in this regard involve contracts for salvage (or rescue) at sea. It is a long-standing rule that a contract of this sort will not be enforced unless it is made for a fair price.[15]

This rule is not easy to explain using the idea of illegitimate pressure. The pressure in salvage cases does not emanate from the claimant, but from the circumstances that caused the defendant's ship or cargo to be in danger. The claimant who makes an offer to save the defendant's goods for a certain price is doing just that—making an offer. Were the claimant under a legal duty to assist the defendant, we might construe the withholding of assistance implicit in this offer as a wrongful threat, but no such duty is recognized in English law. On the other hand, the results in these cases seem prima facie consistent with the idea that a contract may be set aside for impaired consent: the risk of losing a ship's cargo at sea seems a clear example of an extraordinary pressure. In the circumstances, the defendant has no real choice but to agree to a contract with the claimant. From the defendant's perspective, it is no different than if the claimant threatened to destroy the cargo unless a sum of money was paid over.

A potential difficulty with the impaired-consent explanation of salvage cases is that even salvage contracts signed under the most extreme pressure are not generally invalid: a salvage contract is liable to be set aside only where the price stipulated for the salvage is 'extortionate'. Salvage contracts for a fair price will be enforced regardless of the circumstances in which they were made. It is for this reason that many commentators explain the law on

---

[15] *Akerblom v. Price* (1885) 7 QBD 129. For historical reasons, this rule is traditionally classified as a part of 'admiralty law' rather than of the general law of contract.

salvage contracts using a 'fairness-based' concept, such as unconscionability (a suggestion explored in Chapter 12).

But like cases involving third-party threats, this limit on relief in salvage cases might be a consequence of the historical underdevelopment of the English law of unjust enrichment. To ensure that worthy salvors were fairly rewarded for their efforts, English courts had no choice but to find a valid contract.[16] Support for this suggestion may be found in the fact that the final result is roughly the same whether a salvage contract at a fair price is enforced or the contract set aside and the salvor awarded compensation for unjust enrichment. A fair contract price will be roughly equivalent to the amount awarded in a claim for restitution based on unjust enrichment.

It seems possible, then, that the rules on salvage and rescue can be explained on the basis of a concern for impaired consent. The 'fair price' exception may be accounted for as courts ensuring that the beneficiaries of their concern were not unjustly enriched. But from a wider perspective, this conclusion might be thought to show that the law does not generally worry much about impaired consent. The rule providing relief for unfair salvage and rescue contracts is confined to salvage and rescue contracts. Yet it seems clear that the kinds of pressures that (according to the impaired-consent explanation) are the courts' concerns in salvage cases can arise in other situations. The distinguishing feature of salvage contracts is that the claimant had an effective monopoly over badly needed services or, in other words that the defendant was in a 'state of necessity'. This situation is not uncommon. The provision of water, electricity, and many other basic necessities of modern life have traditionally been in the control of large-scale monopolies. Similarly, 'micro-monopolies' of the kind exemplified in the salvage cases are common, even if the potential consequences of not getting the relevant goods or services are rarely as serious. Micro-monopolies typically arise out of the constraints of time or place: someone needs something in a hurry, and there is only one person who is able to supply that thing within the time limit. Even the typical corner store has a degree of monopoly: for someone in a hurry, the corner store may have an effective monopoly over the goods that it sells, especially if it is the only store within a reasonable distance.[17]

Other micro-monopolies arise because the relevant parties are locked into a relationship. For instance, where two contracting parties attempt

---

[16] In practice, the parties to a salvage arrangement made today will typically agree to be governed by a standard form Lloyd's salvage contract (which stipulates that the parties agree to arbitration as to the appropriate fee).

[17] A situation that might be fairly close to that of the salvage cases is the homeowner who urgently needs a plumber in the middle of the night (say because her house is in danger of being flooded as a result of a cracked pipe). In practice, there appears to be a 'market' for emergency plumbers in large cities—although the market is not an entirely normal one, as can be seen in the fact that such plumbers typically demand cash in advance.

to negotiate a variation of their contract, the parties are in a situation that economists term a 'bilateral monopoly'. They are, in a sense, *both* monopolists: the contract variation can *only* be negotiated between these parties. If either party is dissatisfied, he cannot go into the market to renegotiate that contract. He can, of course, try to extricate himself from the relationship altogether, and form a new one elsewhere in the market. There are often enormous practical difficulties with such a course, however, and it would frequently be irrelevant to the problem at hand. A trade union and employer are an example of two parties that are almost permanently locked into a bilateral monopoly—realistically, neither party can break off the relationship.

In some cases involving bilateral monopolies, relief can be given on the basis that one party made a wrongful threat to break an existing contract. But in other cases (as we have seen) the promisor will merely have received a warning (rather than a threat) that the contract will be breached. And, in yet other cases involving bilateral monopolies, there is no existing contract at all, and so no possibility of relief on this basis. A *de facto* monopoly of this kind arises, for instance, when a husband and wife negotiate a financial settlement on divorce, or where an accident victim negotiates a settlement in a tort claim against the tortfeasor or his insurer. Each party is forced to contract with the other exclusively; they cannot turn to the market to supply an alternate tortfeasor or philandering spouse. A contemporary case provides another illustration of how, even in the ordinary commercial market, a state of necessity of this kind can arise and be exploited. In *Leyland Daf v. Automotive Products Ltd*[18] a motor manufacturer became insolvent and a receiver was called in who attempted to carry on the business pending a possible sale. The defendants were sole suppliers of spare parts to the manufacturer, and as a condition of continuing to supply the receiver they required him to pay all existing debts due to them from the manufacturer, even though the receiver was not, of course, liable for past debts. There was no dispute that the whole of the manufacturer's business could be halted for lack of this one part; the coercive power which the defendants could exert was plainly enormous. But even in these circumstances the validity of the contract was not (apparently) challenged on grounds of economic duress or any other basis.

Admittedly, if these situations result in contracts that are substantively unfair courts will often find ways to invalidate them. For example, if one party exploited his monopoly power to demand an unfairly higher price in a renegotiation of an existing contract the modification would probably be set aside for duress, even if no actual threat was made. If the subcontractor in *Roffey Bros.* had demanded three times the going rate to complete the work it

---

[18] [1993] BCC 389.

is highly unlikely the modification would been enforced. We have also seen (in Chapter 4) that courts often invalidate such agreements for lack of consideration. Overall, however, the present state of the law is such that there is no general principle to protect parties who enter into contracts of the kinds described above.[19] There is no general defence of 'state of necessity' in English law.

If the courts care about impaired consent it is therefore puzzling that English law does not recognise state of necessity as a defence. States of necessity can arise in various situations, yet English law appears to give relief only in cases involving salvage and rescue contracts. But before concluding that English courts are simply unconcerned about impaired consent (aside, perhaps, from salvage and rescue contracts), various historical and practical explanations for the courts' behaviour must be explored. As is so often the case, English law's refusal to enunciate a general principle may reveal more about the curious growth and development of English law than about its support for the principle. This topic will be examined in some detail because of its general importance for understanding English law's approach to states of necessities and monopolies. Whatever explanation is ultimately adopted for the availability of relief in salvage and rescue cases, the question arises: why is such relief not generally available?

An initial observation is that the limited scope of relief for state of necessity may simply reflect the fact that few cases involving serious states of necessity have come before English courts other than the salvage and rescue cases. A related observation is that many states of necessity involve recurring events, for which legislation normally has or will provide a solution, usually involving expert tribunals. Judges, who are not experts in identifying states of necessity, naturally hesitate to get involved in such cases. This is particularly true in cases involving large-scale monopolies, such as those involved in the provision of water or electricity—which no doubt explains why most large monopolies are subject to statutory regulation, and indeed ought to be. But it is also true of various 'micro' and 'bilateral' monopolies. An example: when a business closes down as a result of insolvency, a receiver or liquidator will arrive at the premises to examine the books, obtain control of the assets, and ascertain the liabilities of the business. Evidently, he will have very great difficulty in doing any of these things if he cannot switch on the lights or use the telephone. It had, for a long period, been the standard practice of the public utilities to cut off supplies and refuse to restore them

---

[19] But there are a few rules that appear grounded in this idea. For example, money-lending contracts are often entered into by very desperate borrowers. Such people are often willing to sign almost anything to lay their hands on the money they need or want. Although such contracts were valid in the Courts of Law, the Courts of Equity would interfere where the results were thought to be grossly unfair. See also the previous discussion about contract modification cases.

unless and until the receiver or liquidator agreed not merely to be responsible for future supplies, but also to pay all past unpaid bills. By using their monopoly powers these public utilities obtained payment of their bills in preference to other creditors. This practice was never challenged at common law, but is now barred by s. 200 of the Insolvency Act 1985. Of course, in the absence of a general defence and where the appropriate legislation is not yet in place there will be harsh results if the courts simply 'wait for Parliament'.

Another reason that courts might hesitate to generalize a state of necessity defence (even if in principle they recognize the need for it) is because they are worried the defence may be abused. Like concepts such as 'bad faith' and 'unconscionability' (which English courts have also refused to adopt as general defences), the concepts of 'state of necessity' and 'monopoly' lack clear boundaries. Even if we restrict our attention to 'micro-monopolies' the existence of such monopolies is a question of degree. As has been mentioned, most vendors possess at least a limited degree of monopoly power, if for no other reason than that they have a monopoly over the space from which they sell goods or the individuals they employ to provide services. Most such instances of monopoly power are, of course, unobjectionable. No one is suggesting that my purchase of eggs from the corner store should be set aside if it can be shown that I needed the eggs for a recipe and the corner store was the only store that could supply them to me in the relevant time frame. This would not qualify as extraordinary. The difficulty, however, is that it is not easy to devise a test for distinguishing between ordinary pressure and a serious state of emergency. Historically, for instance, contracts of employment were often entered into under extreme pressure. The choice was often between the local industry and the work-house. While it seems obvious that this situation is different from a salvage case, it is not easy to explain the distinction. This fact would have been of concern to common law judges who were (and still are) of the view that there is nothing wrong with employment contracts signed in these circumstances.

More generally, it seems likely that in the past judges would have been worried that a general principle that contracts signed in a state of necessity are invalid might be seen as a license to interfere with the very engines that drive a competitive economy. After all, the whole system of private property rests (in a sense) on recognition of the monopoly rights of the property owner—one person alone owns the property and has the right to use it. So a property owner can sell his property (or rights over it) at whatever price he chooses, and he can therefore (tautologically) threaten *not* to sell it unless he is paid whatever price he wishes to ask. The same goes for human labour: every person can sell his labour at whatever price he can get in the market. He is a monopolist owner of his own labour. In a competitive economy, the ability to command higher prices is an incentive offered to those who identify areas where demand outstrips supply. Though it does not hold true of anti-competitive monopolies, small-scale monopolistic prices can be a sort of reward for stepping in to alleviate an unsatisfied need.

It is not suggested that these concerns justify the extremely narrow scope of relief for state of necessity in English law (whether or not such relief is based on a concern for impaired consent). Certainly the risk is small that judicial intervention in state of necessity cases might lead to widespread interference in the basic workings of a market economy. The point, however, is that the refusal of English courts to generalize a defence of state of necessity may say less about their concern for impaired consent than about their worries over potentially vague law.

Conclusion

The theoretical foundations of the law of duress raise a number of difficult issues, especially in relation to the concept of impaired consent. On the one hand, judicial decisions are littered with references to consent; most of the cases in which relief is given for duress can be explained using this concept; and it seems self-evident (to most lawyers) that consent should play a role in this area of the law. On the other hand, various limitations on the scope of relief for 'pressure' present a puzzle. As we have seen, these limitations can be explained on historical and practical grounds, but explanations of this kind are never entirely satisfying. One cannot help but feel that if English courts took the importance of consent seriously this would be reflected more explicitly in this area of law. In the end, then, while it seems fairly clear that the law on duress reflects a concern for wrongdoing, it remains unclear to what extent—if any—it is also concerned with a distinct notion of impaired consent.

2. UNDUE INFLUENCE

The narrow scope of the doctrine of duress has long been supplemented by the equitable doctrine of undue influence. Unique to the common law, the doctrine of undue influence is peculiar, because (as we shall suggest) many of the most important cases falling under its domain appear to have little to do with 'undue influence' in any ordinary sense. Indeed, in other legal systems the issues raised by common law undue influence cases are governed by legal doctrines such as duress, misrepresentation, unconscionability, and incapacity. It is consequently something of an open question whether such a doctrine is needed at all.

There are two classes of cases that fall within the doctrine: first, those in which actual undue influence is proved, and second, those in which there is a 'presumption' of undue influence.

'Actual' undue influence

In the first class of undue influence cases, it must be shown that the defendant came to possess a dominating influence over the claimant, and then used this influence to coerce or pressure him into a contract to which he would not otherwise have agreed. In most such cases, the party exercising the influence has done so in order to take advantage of the other by extracting a highly favourable transaction from him; however, in these cases of 'actual undue influence', it is not necessary that the contract at issue be unfair. Exercising 'actual' undue influence is a legal wrong, akin to fraud or duress, and as in the case of fraud, the innocent party is entitled to have the transaction set aside irrespective of the fairness or unfairness of the contract which resulted.[20]

Most modern cases of actual undue influence involve defendants who (it is alleged) were not wholly rational. Typical cases arise where a senile person, no longer fully able to get about and seek advice, has fallen under the influence of a companion, nurse, or relative who has been taking care of her. Another typical case arises where a person joins a religious organization and falls totally under the domination of a leader of the group, so as to be apparently incapable of exercising any independent judgement of his own. It is, of course, important not to confuse undue influence with eccentricity; a person is perfectly entitled to make strange contracts, gifts, or wills if he so pleases. In practice, though, the cases which feature such eccentric behaviour are often tainted by suspicious circumstance. For instance, a donor may have been secluded from other advisers or relatives, or a long-maintained plan or will has been unexpectedly altered, and so forth.

Occasionally such cases arise even where the defendant has not acted irrationally. For example, in a leading nineteenth-century case it was held that a promise by the defendant to guarantee payment of certain promissory notes was unenforceable because the promise had been extorted under implied threats that the defendant's son would be prosecuted for forging endorsements on the notes.[21] A contract created in such circumstances is particularly objectionable because, should it have been enforced, it would have tacitly condoned the hushing up of a serious crime. Contracts of this kind are often void on public policy grounds even without the complicating factor of illegitimate pressure. This case also makes clear the close historical links between duress and actual undue influence; the essence of the father's complaint was that he had been coerced into signing the guarantee.

---

[20] *CIBC Mortgages plc v. Pitt* [1994] 1 AC 200. In practice, most cases of actual undue influence arise with regard to a gift or will, and the principles governing them are largely the same.

[21] *Williams v. Bayley* (1866) LR 1 HL 200.

Indeed, it may be said that actual undue influence is best understood generally as a species of duress. Relief is given in actual undue influence cases on essentially the same basis that it is given in duress cases: the defendant was induced to contract on the basis of an illegitimate threat. It is clear that many older cases of actual undue influence were decided under this heading only because (as we have seen) the courts at that time adopted a very narrow approach to duress (and misrepresentation). Today those same cases would likely be decided under the law of duress or misrepresentation. Other cases are decided on the basis of actual undue influence only because, even today, the law of duress is cautious to admit that a threat may be wrongful if it is not actually unlawful.

The issue of classification aside, cases of actual undue influence do not, on the whole, raise many difficult questions of law, although they often give rise to prolonged factual disputes.

Presumed undue influence

The second class of cases—those in which there is said to be a 'presumption of undue influence'—are more difficult as a matter of law, and also tend to be more numerous. These cases developed from an ancient equitable jurisdiction over trustees and other persons in what is called a 'fiduciary' relationship. Courts of Equity, with their emphasis on conscience and good faith, developed a valuable and elastic principle to the effect that a person must not abuse a position of trust or confidence. This principle extends far beyond the confines of the law of contract, and finds its main application in the duties of trustees. For instance, it is a well-established rule that trustees must not profit from their position unless expressly empowered to do so.

The law of presumed undue influence extends this principle, but also qualifies it in certain important ways. The general rule is set out in the leading case of *Royal Bank of Scotland v. Etridge (No. 2)*.[22] A transaction will be presumed to have been entered into because of undue influence if the parties were in a relationship of 'trust and confidence' *and* the transaction 'calls for explanation'. The transaction may then be set aside *unless* the presumption is rebutted. Each element of this rule needs to be examined separately before we turn to consider its basis or rationale.

A relationship of trust and confidence

The first requirement—that there be a relationship of trust and confidence— can be satisfied automatically if the relationship falls within a group of common arrangements that have been deemed to be, as a matter of law, based on trust and confidence. Thus, trust and confidence will be presumed to exist (in

---

[22] [2001] 3 WLR 1021.

addition to the case of trustee and beneficiary) between principal and agent, solicitor and client, and religious adviser and disciple. This presumption is also extended to parent and child (provided that the child is unmarried and under the age of majority), but it does not exist between husband and wife.

Even where the arrangement does not fall into one of these standard categories, a relationship of trust and confidence may exist on the facts of the particular case. Thus, the requirement may be met in any situation where one person turns to another for advice or assistance, and the court thinks that the relationship between the parties (based, for example, on their relative ages or experience, or their blood relationship) is such that one placed trust and confidence in the other. Such a relationship has been found in cases involving a husband and a wife,[23] an uncle and nephew,[24] a banker and customer,[25] and even two neighbouring farmers.[26]

A transaction that 'calls for explanation'

It is evident that many transactions between parties in a relationship of trust and confidence are entirely proper. For example, many business persons enter into perfectly regular commercial ventures with their lawyers. For this reason, the presumption of undue influence will only be raised if, in addition to a relationship of trust and confidence, the actual transaction between the parties is one that 'calls for explanation'.[27] Until recently, this requirement was described in different language: the complainant had to show that the transaction was 'manifestly disadvantageous'. The idea underlying the older language is straightforward: the manifest disadvantageousness of a trans-action is strong evidence that the dependant party was in fact unduly influenced. But courts came to recognize that, while this test worked well in ordinary commercial cases, it was too narrow for the kind of non-commercial cases in which undue influence is commonly argued. The effect of undue influence in such cases may cause parties to enter transactions that, although not necessarily unfair, would not have been made but for the undue influence. Examples might include the sale of the family home or the investment of one's entire savings in a risky venture. The new test of 'calling for an explanation', though linguistically awkward, captures the essential issue in such cases.

It is difficult to lay down general principles as to the kinds of transactions that 'call for explanation'. In each case, the question is whether, on the facts

---

[23] *Barclays Bank v. O'Brien* [1994] 1 AC 180.

[24] *Tate v. Williamson* (1866) LR 2 Ch App 55.

[25] *Lloyd's Bank v. Bundy* [1975] QB 326. It must be stressed, however, that the relationship between a banker and a customer does not give rise to an automatic presumption of undue influence (as was once the case).

[26] *Goldsworthy v. Brickell* [1987] 1 All ER 853.

[27] *Etridge*, above n. 22 at para. 24.

of the particular transaction and in light of the parties' relationship, the transaction can be explained by ordinary motives. A small gift between a patient and her long-time doctor is unlikely to call for explanation. But if the patient sells her land to the doctor at a significantly reduced price, the presumption will almost certainly be raised. One situation that has given rise to much litigation in recent years is where a spouse—usually the wife— guarantees the other spouse's business debts. In some of the cases prior to *Etridge* it was held that such a transaction was manifestly disadvantageous. If the necessary relationship of trust and confidence was also proven the trans- action raised a presumption of undue influence. In principle, this result might be thought appropriate. Because the business is in the husband's name, the wife who acts as guarantor is left incurring a liability with no corresponding legal benefit. The reality in these cases, however, is that the couple's income is usually pooled, meaning that the wife benefits from any profit made by the husband's business. This was explicitly recognized in *Etridge*, where it was held that the guarantee by one spouse of the other's business debts does not—in the ordinary case—call for an explanation.

Rebutting the presumption of undue influence

We have seen that the first two requirements in establishing presumed undue influence are a relationship of trust and confidence, and a transaction that 'calls for an explanation'. Should these be met, the requisite presumption arises. But the presumption is a presumption, which means that it may be rebutted. Thus the contract will be enforced if the claimant is able to prove that, despite initial appearances, the complainant was not in fact unduly influenced. In principle, any evidence establishing that the complainant acted independently may be sufficient to rebut the presumption. As described above, the purpose of the law is not to prevent people from disposing of their property in strange or eccentric ways. In practice, though, it is not easy to rebut the presumption other than by proof that the complainant was independently advised by some suitable person—for instance, by a com- petent, informed solicitor who is not also acting for the other party to the transaction. The difficulty in rebutting the presumption is demonstrated in the recent case of *Hammond v. Osborn*,[28] where a sick and elderly man gave nearly the entirety of his considerable wealth to a friend and caregiver. Despite evidence showing the man had on a number of occasions made clear his intent to make the gift, the court held that this was not sufficient to rebut the presumption. The court viewed these declarations with the same suspicion that they viewed the actual transfer, and emphasised that at no point did the donor receive independent advice of any kind.

---

[28] [2002] EWCA Civ 885.

In cases where the defendant does receive independent advice, it is not necessary to show that the defendant actually acted on the advice in order to rebut the presumption. People must be allowed to make unusual or eccentric transactions should they be so inclined, provided that that they are genuinely aware of what they are doing. On the other hand, as was emphasised in *Etridge*, the mere fact that advice was obtained does not guarantee that the contract will be enforced. This is appropriate because in cases involving severe undue influence, independent advice will often be of little or no value in overcoming the undue influence. The wife who feels obliged to do what her husband asks is unlikely to refuse him just because a solicitor has so advised. Indeed, it is the essence of undue influence that the influenced party disregards the reasons that would normally make her hesitate to enter the relevant transaction.

The basis of relief for presumed undue influence

In cases involving presumed undue influence, courts have generally refrained from describing what it actually means to be 'unduly influenced' and why contracts made in these circumstances should be set aside. In *Etridge*, for example, the court expressly declined to provide a comprehensive definition of undue influence. This caution is understandable. Whatever other purposes it might serve, the law of presumed undue influence—like that of actual undue influence—has long been employed to fill perceived gaps in other areas of the law. In particular, it has filled gaps in the common law's doctrines of duress, misrepresentation, and (arguably) unconscionability. It would therefore be surprising if all the cases decided on this basis could be explained by a single principle. Nonetheless, it is necessary to ask what, if anything, might be regarded as distinctive about a claim for relief based upon presumed undue influence. Without an answer to this question (however tentative), it will be impossible to develop the law in this area in a coherent and logical fashion. Three main possibilities present themselves.

The very label 'presumed undue influence' suggests that the basis of the doctrine is the same as the basis of actual undue influence. In this view, presumed undue influence cases are those in which the court does not have direct evidence that the claimant exerted illegitimate pressure against the defendant but nonetheless suspects that this may have happened. More specifically, this view explains relief on the essentially claimant-centred basis that the claimant is a wrongdoer. This suggestion is supported by statements such as those made by Lord Nicholls in *Etridge* to the effect that a situation of undue influence is one in which the complainant's consent was obtained by 'unacceptable means' or 'unacceptable conduct'.[29]

---

[29] *Etridge*, above n. 22 at para. 7. Two post-*Etridge* decisions of the Privy Council explicitly support this interpretation: *R v. Attorney-General for England and Wales* [2003] UKPC 22, *National Commercial Bank (Jamaica) Ltd v. Hew* [2003] UKPC 51.

There is no doubt that many cases of presumed undue influence involve pressure of this kind. But the existence of a wrongful threat or other pressure does not seem to be essential to a claim of presumed undue influence. For one thing, it seems unlikely that the courts would have constructed such a large and elaborate body of law to deal with what is, according to this interpretation, a mere issue of evidence. It has not been thought necessary to construct doctrines of 'presumed duress' or 'presumed misrepresentation', even though there must be many cases in which duress and misrepresentation can only be proven indirectly. These possibilities are dealt with as issues of proof. More to the point, the actual tests applied by the judges (including Lord Nicholls in *Etridge*) make it clear that a contract may be set aside for presumed undue influence without any assumption—or even allegation—that the claimant acted wrongly. In the well-known words of Cotton LJ in *Allcard v. Skinner*,[30] '[t]he court interferes not on the ground that any wrongful act has in fact been committed by the donee, but on the ground of public policy, and to prevent the relations which existed between the parties and influence arising therefrom being abused.' The court in *Allcard* set aside a gift made by a nun to her sisterhood, even though there was no 'proof that any gift made by the claimant was the result of any actual exercise of power or influence on the part of the lady superior'. Rather, the gift was made because of the nun's 'willing submission to [her] vows' and her 'enthusiastic devotion to the life and work of the sisterhood'.[31] Similarly, in *Hammond v. Osborn*, Sir Martin Nourse held that the transaction could be set aside even if it was shown that the caregiver's conduct was 'unimpeachable'.[32]

Lord Denning suggested a second basis for giving relief for undue influence in *Lloyd's Bank v. Bundy*:[33] the principle of 'inequality of bargaining power' or, as it is more commonly described today, 'unconscionability'. As discussed in more detail in the next chapter, this principle is said to apply to situations in which one party has acted 'unconscionably' by taking advantage of the other's weakness or vulnerability so as to obtain a contract on favourable terms. There is no doubt that most cases in which presumed undue influence has been found would satisfy this test. The defendant is vulnerable because of her trust and confidence in the claimant and the claimant takes advantage of this trust by knowingly procuring a contract on favourable terms. This suggestion also finds support in some of the language used by judges when deciding undue influence cases. In *Etridge*, Lord Nicholls described undue influence as arising in relationships 'where one has acquired over another a measure of influence or ascendancy, of which the

---

[30] (1887) 36 Ch D 145 at 171. See also *Hammond v. Osborn*, above n. 27.
[31] *Hammond*, above n. 28 at para. 183.
[32] Ibid., para. 32.
[33] [1975] QB 326.

ascendant person then takes unfair advantage'.[34] Elsewhere he refers to undue influence as involving an 'abuse of influence'.[35]

But, again, if one looks to the actual tests applied by judges, it seems difficult to sustain the idea that the doctrine's general aim is to give effect to a general principle of unconscionability. It is no longer the case (as it was when Lord Denning decided *Lloyd's Bank*) that a defendant alleging undue influence must prove the transaction was manifestly disadvantageous. This requirement was dropped entirely for cases of actual undue influence and, as we have seen, was replaced in cases of presumed undue influence by the requirement that the transaction 'call for explanation'. In addition, it is generally assumed that a defence of unconscionability requires proof that the claimant has done, or failed to do, something that makes him culpable in some way, even if it does not amount to duress or fraud. The claimant must, it is said, have a guilty conscience. Yet a contract may be set aside for presumed undue influence (as we have seen) even if the claimant's conduct was 'unimpeachable'.

The third explanation of presumed undue influence fits neatly with the courts' (apparent) lack of concern for the claimant's culpability. In this view, which is closely related to the defendant-based 'impaired-consent' explanation of duress, the doctrine is concerned entirely with the defendant's situation.[36] More specifically, the doctrine is designed to provide relief in cases where the defendant 'surrendered his judgment' to the claimant.[37] It does not matter whether this surrender is attributed to the fault of the claimant: what matters is that, for whatever reason, the defendant was unable to act independently. In effect, the suggestion is that presumed undue influence is a particular kind of impaired consent. In legal terms, it is most closely related to the defence of incapacity: the defendant suffered a temporary incapacity because of the nature of his relationship with the claimant. We might call this 'relational' incapacity. Such incapacity is 'presumed' because (as in the case of minors and others whom the law deems incapacitated) the relevant condition cannot be proven directly. The court cannot look into the defendant's mind but must instead rely on indirect evidence. In the case of minors, the relevant evidence is the defendant's age; in the case of relational incapacity the indirect evidence is the nature of the relationship, the facts of the transaction, and the existence of independent legal advice or other proof that the defendant acted independently.

---

[34] *Etridge*, above n. 22 at para. 8.

[35] Ibid., para. 10. Statements found in the Privy Council's recent decisions in *R v. Attorney General and National Commercial Bank*, above n. 29, also support this interpretation.

[36] A recent statement of this position is found in Mummery LJ's Court of Appeal decision in *Pesticcio v. Huet* [2004] EWCA Civ 372.

[37] *Hammond*, above n. 28 at para. 59, quoting *Snell's Equity*, (London 30th edn.) at 617.

The first and second of the above explanations appear to fit best with what judges *say* they are doing, particularly in recent cases,[38] though dissenting voices exist.[39] But the third explanation appears to best explain the actual decisions in which relief is given for presumed undue influence. The third explanation is consistent with the fact that the defence can be made out (it appears) without proof that the claimant was at fault in any way. It also explains why a distinct (and elaborate) doctrine of presumed undue influence exists; though related to ordinary incapacity, 'relational incapacity' is a distinct, and complex, notion. Any final conclusion in this regard must, however, also take into account the law governing 'three-party' undue influence cases—a topic that has attracted considerable judicial attention in recent years.

Undue influence by third parties

A troublesome question in the law of undue influence arises in situations where the contracting party was unduly influenced by a third party. The typical case involves the mortgage of a matrimonial home granted to secure the business debts of one of the spouses, usually the husband. If the wife is joint owner of the home, and signs the mortgage as surety or guarantor under the domination or influence of her husband, is the mortgagee affected even if he is not himself guilty in any way of undue influence?

The law on this point has been the subject of extensive litigation in recent years. In 1997, the House of Lords attempted a comprehensive restatement in *Barclays Bank v. O'Brien*,[40] but this has now been eclipsed by their 2001 decision in *Etridge*,[41] where it was explained that there are two questions courts must answer. The first is whether the complainant did in fact act under the undue influence of the third party. This question should be answered in the same way it would be answered in a two-party case (i.e. by determining if there was actual undue influence and, if not, if the presumption of undue influence arises and is not rebutted). The second question is whether, assuming undue influence from the third party is proven, the claimant—a bank or other creditor in the typical case described above—is affected by the defect.

It is this second question that causes difficulties. In general, the answer is that a bank or other contracting party is *not* affected by the undue influence of a third party. But there are two exceptions. The first is where it can be proven that the husband acted as an agent of the bank; this scenario, however, is unlikely and is not a feature of most cases of this sort. The second, and much more common exception is where the bank is said to have 'notice'

---

[38] See cases cited in n. 29, above. [39] e.g., *Pesticcio*, above n. 36.
[40] [1944] 1 AC 180. [41] Above n. 22.

of the husband's undue influence. If the bank is shown to have had actual knowledge of the influence, the contract will be set aside without further inquiry. This is rare as banks are typically unaware of the personal details of the guarantor's relationship with the third party. Thus, it is much more likely that the bank will be said to have 'constructive notice' of the influence. It is at this point that the law on undue influence appears to diverge from that of duress (where, as we saw, a third party's threat is duress only if the claimant was aware of the threat).

'Constructive notice' itself will be found where two requirements are met. First, it must be shown that the bank was or should have been aware that there was a significant risk of the guarantor being unduly influenced by the third party. The relevant factors are similar to those considered in deciding if a presumption of undue influence arises in two-party cases. Thus, the bank will be 'put on inquiry' (to adopt the language of *Etridge*) if the relationship between the guarantor and principal debtor is one that generally raises a suspicion (e.g. lawyer–client). The bank will also be put on inquiry if, on the facts as known by the bank, the particular relationship and the nature of the transaction raise suspicion. This is essentially a factual issue. It is interesting, however, that in *Etridge* the House of Lords held that a bank is put on inquiry in any case in which a spouse guaranteed the other spouse's business debts—even though the same court held that no presumption of undue influence would be found on similar facts. Indeed, the court held that a bank would be put on inquiry in any case in which it was aware that the guarantor was in a 'non-commercial' relationship with the principal debtor.

The second requirement for establishing constructive notice is proof that the bank, having been put on inquiry of the risk of undue influence, failed to take reasonable steps to guard against it materializing. The bank has a duty, in other words, to help a vulnerable guarantor act independently. What counts as 'reasonable steps' in any particular case will depend on the circumstances; the basic principle is that the greater the risk of undue influence, the more that must be done. As described in *Etridge*, reasonable steps typically involve either advising the guarantor personally as to the nature of the transaction, the risks involved, and of the need to obtain legal advice or—what is more common in practice—ensuring that the guarantor actually receives independent legal advice by someone who has knowledge of the transaction and the relevant risks. If the bank fails to take such reasonable steps, it will be fixed with constructive notice of the undue influence and the guarantee will be unenforceable.

Two features of the courts' approach to three-party cases are particularly interesting. The first is their reliance on the concept of 'constructive notice'. Undue influence cases aside, courts typically employ constructive notice in situations where an individual ought to have known of a fact that he did not know—in particular that title to property he had purchased was defective or encumbered in some way (e.g. a third party had a lien on the property). Further, the only way to avoid being 'fixed' with constructive notice of this kind is to show that one did not in fact have reason to know of the defect or encumbrance. The use of constructive notice in three-party undue influence cases is very different. The banks are not receiving property; the knowledge that is attributed to them is only of the *risk* of a defect; and they avoid being fixed with constructive notice, not by showing that they had no reason to know the truth, but by taking certain steps to assist the other contracting party. In reality, it appears the banks are not so much being fixed with notice of a fact as being fixed with a duty—a duty to take reasonable steps to ensure that the guarantor acts independently. Seen in this light, the courts' use of 'constructive notice' appears to be another illustration of common law courts upholding a duty to act in good faith without actually admitting to it. The bank's duty to take reasonable steps resembles the duty to disclose found in legal systems that enforce general duties to act in good faith. It is a court-ordered responsibility to take positive and unsolicited measures to ensure that the guarantor makes an informed choice. The only difference is that the duty is designed to correct a failure of independence rather than a cognitive error.

The second noteworthy feature of the courts' approach to three-party cases is that the rules in this area focus as much on the claimant's situation as the defendant's. It is assumed without question that a contract between a bank and guarantor will only be set aside if the bank had actual knowledge of the third party's influence or if the bank had knowledge of the risk of influence and then failed to act appropriately. In this regard, the rules on undue influence seem close to those on duress. The requirement that the claimant have 'constructive notice' of the influence is not (as we have just seen) identical to the requirement in the law of duress that the claimant have 'knowledge' of a third party's threat, but they are closely related. In neither case is it sufficient to show that the defendant's consent was impaired—the claimant must be responsible or culpable in some respect, however minimal. But the requirement is nonetheless puzzling because in two-party presumed undue influence cases the courts have made it clear that relief is available on the (defendant-based) ground that the defendant failed to act independently. The claimant might be entirely innocent and yet the contract will be invalidated. Why, then, is there a requirement that there be fault (however mild) in three-party cases—why does it matter in three-party cases what the bank knew or did? Why is it not sufficient to show that the guarantor failed to act independently?

The argument can be made (again) that the law regarding three-party cases developed differently because banks and other creditors traditionally faced difficulties in obtaining a satisfactory restitutionary remedy where a guarantee was set aside.[42] It might also be pointed out that despite the apparent differences in treatment of two-party and three-party cases, the actual results will normally be the same. It will be rare that there is a situation of undue influence without a risk of undue influence of which the bank ought to have been aware. But it seems unlikely that the limits on relief in third-party undue influence cases can be explained away entirely on historical or practical grounds, especially in light of the similarities to the courts' treatment of three-party duress cases and state of necessity cases. The rules in this area seem to reflect a deeper ambivalence in the common law about the extent to which purely defendant-based concerns for consent (whether in terms of pressure or independence) are sufficient grounds to set aside a contract.

3. CONCLUSION

The rules on duress and undue influence are reasonably well-settled, but it is no easy matter to explain their foundations. The main difficulty is not so much that the various rules, taken individually, appear especially odd or unjust, but rather that the courts take different approaches to apparently similar problems. In light of the common law's organic development, this kind of pattern is not entirely unexpected. But the fact that these differences persist today calls for some kind of explanation.

Admittedly, the idea that the courts should refuse to assist claimants who obtained their contractual rights through wrongdoing (for example by making an unlawful threat) is not controversial. Nor is it surprising that (with only a few exceptions) contemporary courts are willing to give relief where such wrongdoing is established. But the other possible basis for relief—that the defendant did not fully consent to the transaction (whether by virtue of pressure or lack of independence)—is controversial. It is not easy to define what 'consent' means and even if it can be defined it is not clear that lack of consent alone should be a sufficient basis for setting aside a contract. Courts and theorists proclaim that the reasonable expectations of contracting parties should be protected nearly as often as they proclaim the idea that parties should not be bound by contractual obligations to which they did not consent.

The unresolved tension between these two ideas is reflected most clearly in the courts' approach to cases where duress or undue influence is pleaded but where the claimant was not a wrongdoer. We have seen that an unlawful

---

[42] See, e.g., *Dunbar Bank Plc v. Nadeem* [1998] 3 All ER 876. In most cases involving spousal guarantees, both the husband *and* the wife obtain a benefit from the loan. If the guarantee is set aside, the bank should be able to claim restitution of this benefit and should, in some cases at least, be able to make such a claim against the guarantor spouse. But the fictional legal separation of husband and wife, together with the historical underdevelopment of unjust enrichment law in general, has meant that such claims are not easy to make.

threat by a third party does not qualify as duress unless the claimant was aware of the threat. The same is true of cases where the defendant claims to have been unduly influenced by a third party, though here the law takes a somewhat more defendant-centred position. The law holds that the contract may be set aside even in the absence of knowledge of undue influence if the claimant should have known of the *risk* of such influence and failed to take reasonable steps to prevent the influence. Finally, in cases where the pressure arises without wrongdoing on anyone's part—a 'state of necessity'—the common law generally refuses to grant relief even where the claimant was aware of the state of necessity (although salvage and rescue contracts are an exception and legislation now provides relief in many such circumstances). On the other hand, the rules governing two-party presumed undue influence cases seem to focus almost entirely on the defendant's position. It does not matter, in theory anyway, whether the claimant was a wrongdoer or was even aware of the undue influence that she exerted. It should also be kept in mind (lest the two-party undue influence cases be thought an aberration) that the courts take the same general approach to claims of incapacity. Though not examined in this book, incapacity cases provide perhaps the strongest example of courts adopting a defendant-centred approach in considering a claim for relief. It is immaterial to the success of a defence of incapacity whether the claimant was aware of the incapacity.

The possibility cannot be discounted that these (apparently) different approaches are explicable on essentially historical grounds or—conversely— that they can be explained on the basis of some not-yet discovered general principle. But as was alluded to above, it seems more likely that they reflect the inherent difficulty of the moral, political, and practical issues raised by pleas for relief in cases where the other party is innocent of any wrongdoing. It is not obvious, as a matter of principle, how courts *should* approach such cases; the consequence of this uncertainty is that courts have adopted a variety of approaches.

12

Unfair Contracts

1. FAIRNESS AND CONTRACT LAW

ACCORDING to the classical theory, the role of courts in handling contract cases is very limited. Classical theory makes a fundamental distinction between fairness in the process of forming a contract on the one hand, and fairness in the outcome of the contract on the other. Courts, according to the theory, are to concern themselves exclusively with the former. Making a contract is thus rather like participating in a contest or game: there are rules designed to regulate the way in which the contest is conducted—to outlaw fouls, to decide upon the appropriate penalty for fouls, and so on. The rules must themselves be fair if the contest or game is to be perceived as fair, so (for instance) the rules must apply equally to both sides, and provision must be made for the interpretation of the rules by impartial umpires. But if the game is played according to the rules, there is very limited scope for any concept of a 'fair outcome'.

In the classical theory, it is understood that, as in a game or contest, some participants will do better than others, because some are more skilful or better equipped than others. But this is not thought to be a cause for concern; if the rules are applied properly and only bargains that are freely and voluntarily entered into are enforced, everyone will benefit. Contracting parties are assumed to have weighed the value of what they propose to give against what they expect to get. If each party is satisfied with the exchange, how can it be said that the result is 'unfair'? In economic terms, the exchange produces what are called 'gains from trade' which amounts to a sort of happy surplus—a surplus that will be divided between the parties as a result of their contract. Suppose S sells his house to B for £100,000. Perhaps S would have been willing to take £98,000, so he is £2,000 better off. Perhaps B would have been willing to pay £105,000, so he is £5,000 better off. Both parties are gainers for having made the contract. True, B has fared moderately better than S in this example, perhaps because he was more skilful at bargaining; but whatever the reason, both parties have gained. The same is true, though the gain less measurable, where the price at which the contract is finalised amounts to the least S would accept and the most B would pay. Even here, there are gains to both parties for the simple reason that S prefers to have the money and B prefers to have the house.

From this perspective, it follows that the law should respect the contract that the parties have made without concern for the fairness of the outcome.

In one extreme version of this approach, it is not possible even in principle to say what a fair contract is—all values are purely subjective, and if the two parties are content with their bargain at the time it is made, there is no basis on which it might be said that a contract is unfair. This view resembles a position in political theory held by certain liberal writers which denies that there is such a thing as substantive justice in the abstract; there are merely just procedures.

This classical vision of the proper role of contract law has strongly influenced the law. As we have seen in the preceding chapters, there are long-standing rules prohibiting the use of fraud, misrepresentation, and coercion in the making of contracts; there are rules designed to ensure that parties have the basic capacities necessary to play the game—to make contracts—such as rules protecting minors or persons suffering from mental illness, and the doctrine of undue influence which protects parties whose independence is impaired. In all these ways, the law is concerned with procedural fairness. But there is no rule stating that substantively unfair contracts are unenforceable.

There is no doubt, then, that the distinction between procedural and substantive fairness is a fundamental idea that continues to influence much of contract law, and the application of the law to individual cases.[1] At the same time, it is equally clear that in practice the law and the courts are not entirely unconcerned with the substantive fairness of contractual outcomes. Some of the ways in which this happens have been discussed in previous chapters. In this chapter we gather these and other examples together in an attempt to approach the issue in a more systematic fashion. But before turning to particular rules and doctrines it is necessary first to directly address the questions of what constitutes a substantively unfair contract and why courts should care about substantive fairness.

The meaning of 'substantive fairness'

Most lawyers would say that contracts or particular contractual terms can be unfair in any of a number of ways. A building contract may be unfair if the builder is entitled to demand extra payment for having to redo his own badly done work; a contract for services may be unfair if the supplier of the services excludes his liability for negligence. This approach to defining 'unfair' is mirrored in the Unfair Terms in Consumer Contracts Regulations 1999 which is discussed in more detail later in this chapter. But a simpler approach to the problem of identifying an unfair contract or unfair term is to define an unfair contract as one in which significantly more (or less) than a fair market price is paid. Economists would probably suggest that this is a complete

---

[1] This distinction is to some extent recognised by the Privy Council in *Hart v. O'Connor* [1985] AC 1000 at 1017–18.

answer (if they admit that the question can be answered at all) in that, in theory, every contingency relevant to the contract should be accounted for in the price. In other words, it is possible to use the price in the market as a means of evaluating the worth of any extra burdens, exclusions from liability or contingencies that a contract may create. One need only recognise that what is unfair at one price may be perfectly fair at another in order to appreciate that, in the final analysis, the price will (nearly) always be determinative of ultimate fairness. Provided that the contract price reflects the benefits and burdens of the contract's terms, the contract as a whole may be said to be fair.

It must also be recognised that the common argument that all prices are subjective is fallacious. No doubt there is a subjective element in many prices, such as in the price of a house or a work of art, but even things of this kind have a market price, however difficult to gauge. And many other things available in the market have a very precise market price. The notion that any person who agrees to make a purchase at a price cannot possibly contend that the price is 'unfair' simply fails to recognize that the buyer may have been mistaken. If a buyer later discovers that she has agreed to pay much more than fair market value it would seem absurd to contend that there is no basis on which it can be held that the contract was unfair. This does not mean that all such contracts should be held invalid, but the view that a free and voluntary contract *cannot* be unfair is grossly overstated.

Why should courts care about substantive fairness?

Assuming that substantive fairness is a meaningful concept, it must still be asked why courts should care about it. Why is it not sufficient (as many contend) for courts to concern themselves with procedural fairness? Four possible reasons will be examined. The first two are arguably consistent with the general principles underlying the classical approach, but the third and especially the fourth conflict head-on with those principles.

First, even the staunchest defender of the classical approach will concede that courts should consider substantive unfairness for evidentiary reasons. Evidence that a contract is substantively unfair can provide indirect proof that the contract was entered as a result of duress, misrepresentation, undue influence, or some other procedural defect. In particular, if the court suspects (but is not certain) that such a procedural defect occurred, evidence of substantive unfairness may be sufficient to confirm the suspicion. There is no doubt that courts often care about substantive fairness for this reason; for example, a presumption of undue influence will be raised (as was explained in Chapter 11) where the relationship between the parties is one of confidence and trust *and* where the transaction is manifestly disadvantageous or in some other respect 'calls for explanation'. The latter requirement, it was further explained, appears to have an essentially evidentiary function: given the parties' relationship, evidence of substantive unfairness is sufficient to raise a presumption that the disadvantaged party was in fact subject to undue influence.

A second, closely related reason that substantive fairness may be relevant to the law of contract lies in the fact that the existing law provides only partial protection against certain kinds of procedural defects (even where there are no evidentiary problems). While the classical theory is based on the premiss that contracts are binding only on those who freely and voluntarily assent to their terms, the law has traditionally been reluctant in practice to declare that such assent has not been obtained. Thus we have seen that the doctrines of undue influence and particularly duress have traditionally been defined narrowly or subject to special limitations. There is no defence of 'state of necessity', and legislation to control monopolies does not generally apply to 'micro-' or 'situational' monopolies, such as the case (discussed in the previous chapter) of a ship in distress whose only possible rescuer is a solitary tugboat. Furthermore, the traditional law provides only limited relief in cases involving what might be called 'cognitive' defects or 'information asymmetries'. A contract will not be set aside merely because the defendant did not understand (or even read) its terms; this is the case even when this lack of understanding was, in the circumstances, entirely reasonable and perhaps even expected. Another kind of information asymmetry that we have discussed arises in situations in which one party has superior information about the product or service that is the object of the contract or about the market price of that product or service. In most cases where this happens, the resulting contract is unobjectionable, even if it turns out that the party with superior information made a large profit. The profit can be justified as a reward for past investments (in information) or as an incentive for future investments, but as was explained in Chapter 9, these arguments do not apply to 'overvaluation' errors, such as where a purchaser buys a house that the vendor knows is suffering from dry rot (or is otherwise unsuitable or overpriced). In this and other cases in which there are information asymmetries, it is difficult to maintain that because both parties freely entered into the contract, both will benefit.

One possible response to the kinds of problems just described is to reform the rules on duress, incapacity, etc, and this has occurred to some extent. But such reform will likely always be incomplete in that there will always be cases that fall through the cracks of whatever scheme is devised. An alternative in cases where there is a risk the traditional procedural rules are too narrow is for courts to turn their attention to the substantive outcome of a contract and include this in their assessment of whether or not the contract is valid. Thus, procedural defects that might be ignored in other cases are not ignored where they lead to a substantively unfair contract. Again, there is no doubt that courts sometimes do just this. An example is provided by the Court of Appeal decision in the *Interfoto* case,[2] which was examined in Chapter 3's discussion of the 'ticket' cases. In that case, it is clear that the 'assent' to the detailed terms of the printed document would have been sufficient had the terms themselves been reasonable. But because the terms were unreasonable, the court invoked a procedural defect—that insufficient notice was given. The maritime salvage cases discussed in the last chapter—where the courts refuse to enforce substantively unfair salvage contracts—are arguably another illustration.

A third reason substantive fairness may be important to courts is that it is important in assessing claims for relief based on the concept of 'unconscionability'. Unconscionability does not have a fixed meaning in law, but in contractual contexts it is generally used to describe situations in which it is believed that, although no duress or fraud took place, one contracting party took advantage of or exploited the other. The test for unconscionability is thus partly procedural and partly substantive. It must be shown, first, that the party seeking relief (the defendant) was vulnerable in some respect. This is a procedural test, and is usually thought to be satisfied by proof that the defendant was cognitively impaired (e.g. suffered from a reduced ability to understand or a lack of information) or that she had little real choice but to enter the contract (because she was in a 'state of necessity' or—what amounts to nearly the same thing—because the claimant had a monopoly over an important good or service). Of course, cognitive impairments and monopolies have just been discussed in connection with first and second reasons for caring about substantive fairness, but the distinctive feature of an unconscionability-based treatment of these 'defects' is that they are not regarded as sufficient grounds, even in principle, to set aside a contract. From the perspective of a concern for unconscionability, monopolies and cognitive impairments are only a problem insofar as one party *takes advantage* of them. Thus, the second, equally important element of the test for unconscionability is *substantive*: proof that the contract was substantively unfair. Some of the contracts that have already been mentioned in this chapter would appear to be unconscionable in this sense. The extortionate salvage contract signed between a ship in distress and a solitary tugboat is an example of a monopolist (the tugboat captain) taking advantage of his monopoly power. So too is a 'ticket' case, such as *Interfoto*, in which the ticket contains unreasonable terms. This latter case provides an example of one party with superior information (the issuer of the ticket) taking advantage of another who does not understand the complex terms or legal implications which the ticket represents.

As will be discussed in more detail later in this chapter, there is controversy concerning the extent to which a principle of relief for unconscionability is,

---

[2] *Interfoto Picture Library Ltd v. Stiletto Visual Programmes Ltd* [1989] QB 433.

and should be, a part of the common law. It is not denied that relief is given in many situations that appear to be unconscionable in the sense just described, but it is frequently argued that such relief is and should be given on different grounds—such as one of the grounds described earlier in this chapter. For present purposes it is sufficient to observe that one reason judges might be expected to care about substantive fairness is because of a concern for unconscionable contracts. The idea that it is wrong to take advantage of another's weakness or vulnerability is broadly accepted by most people; it would be highly surprising if judges did not give effect to this idea at least occasionally (if not regularly).

A fourth and final possible reason for caring about substantive fairness is yet more controversial: substantive unfairness is simply bad in and of itself. The idea that a substantively unfair contract should be set aside simply because it is substantively unfair, regardless of how this came about, is in conflict with the foundations of the classical theory of contract law and with widely held views about the role of law in market economies. But like unconscionability, it is an idea that resonates deeply in everyday views of morality. This everyday notion may apply to contract law insofar as it is not immediately obvious what value is served by enforcing a contract in which one party is made worse off[3] than he was prior to entering the contract. From an economic perspective, the basic justification for markets, and for the law of contract that supports them, is that market transactions are mutually beneficial. The procedural rules on duress etc., are intended to ensure that this actually happens. If a transaction is not in fact mutually beneficial, even where the procedural rules appear to have been met, this justification falls away. Again, therefore, it would not be surprising to find that, despite what courts say they are doing, in practice they care about substantive fairness in and of itself.

There are other objections to the classical theory (which we will encounter), but enough has been said to show that its distinction between procedural and substantive fairness is often more theoretical than practical. No doubt it is a good working rule for courts to occupy themselves primarily with securing procedural fairness; however, it is not possible or desirable for courts to ignore the fairness of contractual outcomes entirely.

We must now turn from this theoretical discussion to demonstrate how, in practice, the law may respond to situations of substantive unfairness. Many of contract law's doctrines and rules permit courts to integrate ideas of fairness in appropriate situations. This can be done relatively briefly at this point, as we have called attention throughout the book to the means by which courts attempt to impose fair solutions in contractual disputes.

---

[3] For obvious reasons these observations do not apply to gift contracts, speculative ventures, and the like.

2. CONTRACT LAW AND SUBSTANTIVE FAIRNESS

One of the principal rules responsible for the myth that contract law has little to say about substantive fairness is the rule that adequacy of consideration is immaterial to the validity of a contract. This rule appears to mean that even if a person enters into a contract which is extremely one-sided, so that the consideration he pays is grossly disproportionate to the consideration he receives in return, the contract must be enforced. Nevertheless, it is misleading to proclaim without qualification the traditional dogma that adequacy of consideration is immaterial. Provided that the contract does not concern a gift, a marked imbalance of consideration will create a strong presumption that at least one of the parties did *not* enter into the transaction fully appreciating the circumstances. If the consideration is grossly inadequate there will be a strong suspicion of fraud, misrepresentation, duress, or undue influence which may then justify a court in setting the contract aside—despite the fact that these doctrines purport to deal exclusively with the procedural aspects of contractual fairness.

As we have seen, the fact that the rules about the 'presumption of undue influence' have long been concerned with the outcome of contracts is usually explained on the ground that substantive unfairness is evidence of undue influence. It seems clear, however, that courts have often used the doctrine as a proxy for an unconscionability principle. In most undue influence cases, one party has in fact taken advantage of the other's (cognitive) vulnerability. Indeed, in the famous case of *Lloyd's Bank v. Bundy*,[4] Lord Denning stated explicitly that relief for undue influence was but one example of relief for unconscionability (which he termed 'inequality of bargaining power'). As will be explained below, this statement received little subsequent support, but it no doubt fits well with many of the actual decisions in this area.

Another area where substantive fairness undoubtedly carries significance is in the law regarding incomplete contracts. Courts are constantly called upon to resolve contractual disputes because of something occurring which the terms of the contract have failed to anticipate. Classical theory says the court must 'imply' suitable terms in these cases, and in doing so it must not impose its ideas of fairness on the parties, but instead give effect to what it thinks the parties implied (or would have implied had they put their minds to the task). But here too, as we have seen in Chapter 6, it turns out that the process by which courts imply terms is often concerned with substantive fairness.

Indeed, the whole process of interpreting contracts is suffused with the notion of fairness in exchange. This has not been recognized by traditional books and case law because it conflicts with traditional contract theory and

---

[4] [1975] 2 QB 326.

also because it is not usually done explicitly. But when the cases and doctrines are put together, it is impossible to avoid the conclusion that notions of fairness underlie much of contract law. Of course, this does not mean that, when the consideration is felt to be seriously inadequate, the court will simply interpret the contract in such a way that it may then be declared void. This does happen, but in most cases it is a rather clumsy way of remedying a serious imbalance in the exchange. A simpler remedy lies in upholding the contract, but adjusting the obligations of the parties; this can be done through interpretation, or by fixing damage awards in order to ensure that some sort of fairness in exchange does occur. In a book of this kind, it is not possible to deal with this subject in the detail it deserves, but some examples must be given of cases in which the adequacy of consideration has been a determinative factor in settling the parties' obligations.

First, in many cases concerning the quality of goods where the interpretation of the contract is doubtful, the amount of the consideration may be an important factor in deciding precisely what obligations the parties have assumed. For example, suppose a manufacturer contracts to sell cloth to a buyer, and he supplies cloth of Grade B while the buyer contends that the contract was for the more expensive Grade A. In such a situation the amount of the consideration—the price—would be most material, because if the price paid was substantially more than the usual cost of Grade B cloth this would be a strong indication that the contract was indeed for Grade A cloth. It would not, of course, be conclusive proof of this, as the buyer may have simply made a bad bargain and agreed to pay much more for Grade B cloth than it was worth.

Then there are the standard implied conditions in contracts of sale which are read into all such contracts (subject to some exceptions) under the Sale of Goods Act, 1979. Under this Act, it is normally an implied condition of a contract of sale of goods that the goods be 'satisfactory' in quality. Though this is a somewhat imprecise term, it seems clear that it is not possible to decide what constitutes satisfactory quality without having regard to the price paid, and to some rough corresponding notion of value to which a buyer is entitled. Suppose that a person buys a second-hand car which turns out to be seriously defective. The court does not engage in an explicit examination as to whether the buyer has got value for money[5] or whether he paid far more than the car was worth, but this is very much what the court ultimately does in practice. If the car is not of 'satisfactory' quality— i.e. quality commensurate with the price paid—the buyer is entitled to damages; in effect, he gets some of his money back. Of course, it would be an intolerable and inefficient process for the courts to adjust every trivial

---

[5] But see *Rogers v. Parish (Scarborough) Ltd* [1987] QB 933 at 944, where Mustill LJ actually says 'The buyer was entitled to value for his money.'

imbalance between the value of the goods and the price paid, but where there is a serious imbalance in the contract, it is very likely that the buyer will be able to claim damages.

More generally, courts interpret contracts with a strong bias in favour of the idea that a contract should ensure a degree of substantial reciprocity. Many of the mistake and frustration decisions illustrate how the courts deal with cases where, as a result of unknown or unexpected contingencies, the contract would impose obligations beyond what the price of the contract allowed for.

A striking example of an ordinary interpretation case which does not fall within these traditional categories is *Staffordshire Area Health Authority v. South Staffordshire Waterworks*[6] (referred to several times already) where the court was concerned with a contract made in 1929 whereby a water company contracted to supply water to a hospital at seven old pence per 1,000 gallons 'at all times hereafter'. By 1975, the contract was operating in a very unbalanced fashion—the water authority having to supply water at far less than its true value—but the contract looked to be binding in perpetuity. The Court of Appeal held that the contract could be interpreted so that the price fixed in it was only chargeable 'at all times hereafter during the subsistence of this agreement'. They went on to hold that the water authority could give reasonable notice to bring the contract to an end, after which it would of course be free to offer a new supply at a new price. Traditional contract theory would say that the court was merely giving effect to the intention of the parties, but this seems wildly improbable; it is scarcely possible that the water authority could have terminated the contract within a year or two of its original formation. The truth appears to be that the court was simply offended by the idea that the hospital should be buying water at far below cost, nearly fifty years after the agreement was made.

Another type of case where the amount of the consideration is likely to be highly relevant involves contracts containing exemptions from liability. In *Photo Productions Ltd v. Securicor Transport*[7] the House of Lords was concerned with the liability of the defendants for a fire caused by one of their security guards while engaged in providing security services at the claimants' factory. The factory was wholly destroyed by the fire, and the claimants sought over £600,000 in damages. Under the contract, the security guards provided by the defendants visited the factory four times a night, with extra visits on Saturdays and Sundays, at a charge of £8.75 per week or about 26p per visit. The House of Lords regarded the very small charge for the services in question as highly relevant to the construction of an exemption clause in the contract. It was the main evidence that showed the clause was not in fact

---

[6] [1979] 1 WLR 203.   [7] [1980] AC 827.

unreasonable. Although this case would today be governed by the Unfair Contract Terms Act 1977[8] (discussed later in this chapter), it is unlikely that the outcome would have been any different. The House of Lords made it clear that on the facts of the case the use of an exemption clause was perfectly reasonable.

It is true that there are modern decisions that appear to contradict this emphasis on unfairness of outcome and inadequacy of consideration as a ground for relief. For example, in *Mountford v. Scott*[9] the grant of an option for £1 entitling the grantee to buy the defendant's house (at a price of £10,000) was held binding. No inquiry was permitted into whether this clearly nominal consideration was a reasonable price for the option. So too, in *Multiservice Bookbinding Co. v. Marden*,[10] a loan agreement was upheld by the judge even though he thought it unreasonable. The capital sum in this case was subject to a clause whereby the amount to be repaid was revalued in accordance with the value of the Swiss franc in order to shield it from inflation. Though this provision might not have been unreasonable in and of itself, the loan was also subject to very high interest rates which were only justifiable on the assumption that the capital was at risk from inflation. Thus, *Multiservice* provides a modern example of courts failing to use an imbalance of consideration as pretext for setting aside a contract that appeared substantively unfair.

At the same time, some of these decisions do not turn out to be serious obstacles to the view that consideration *is* a means by which judges seek to ensure substantive fairness. For instance, in *Mountford v. Scott* a careful reading suggests that the seller may well have received some benefit in addition to the nominal consideration, specifically that of finding a buyer: there were several houses concerned, all of which were needed by the buyer for redevelopment; had he not been able to obtain options on all of them before buying any of them, he would probably have been unable to make any purchases. The very possibility of a sale was created by the grant of the option.

But it is true that judges still pay lip service to the principle that inadequacy of consideration is not a matter for the courts, and no doubt it is also true that where parties have entered into a commercial agreement, with legal advice and with a clear understanding of what they are doing (as in the *Multiservice Bookbinding* case), there is a powerful tendency to uphold the contract, however unfair the outcome may appear. Traditional values of free bargaining clearly influence many judicial decisions. What is being suggested here is that nobody can understand how the law of contract works in practice without understanding that judges, like ordinary citizens, dislike contracts in

---

[8] Below, 313ff.   [9] [1975] Ch 255.   [10] [1979] Ch 84.

which the consideration is grossly excessive or inadequate. When judges strongly dislike a result they normally try to use acceptable legal techniques to avoid reaching it.

There are also a considerable number of situations where statute law provides for some adjusting of the consideration for a contract. An obvious example is the system of rent regulation which enables a tenant to apply for a 'fair rent' to be fixed by a rent officer, thereby overriding any contractual agreement with the landlord. Another particularly clear example is to be found in the Consumer Credit Act 1974 which invalidates exorbitant interest rates on loans.

There are other statutory methods of ensuring fair contracts. One common technique is to regulate the persons who are permitted to make certain kinds of contracts through licensing procedures. It is common knowledge that many kinds of work require special qualifications—for instance, being a doctor or a lawyer—and that the authorities responsible for giving or approving these qualifications exercise control over their members. Many commercial types of business, especially those involving dealings with the general public, also come under complex bodies of law designed to protect the public from unfair dealings or from risky financial enterprises—so, for instance, consumer credit suppliers must be licensed by the Director General of Fair Trading and insurance companies likewise by the Department of Trade and Industry. It may be said that this kind of control is designed more to make special provision for the policing in the marketplace of these special sorts of contracts than to ensure fair outcomes: the new procedures regulating stockbrokers and investment advisers do little to interfere directly with contracts between these parties and the general public, and instead seek to ensure that this kind of work is done by responsible and reputable people who can be called to account for fraudulent or unscrupulous behaviour. But at the same time, control over the persons who may enter into certain types of contracts is one way of controlling the outcomes of those contracts. The Law Society's control over solicitors, for instance, extends to cases of overcharging, an oversight power which relates to fairness in outcome rather than the bargaining process.

3. THE STRIKING DOWN OF EXPRESS CONTRACT TERMS AT COMMON LAW

So far in this chapter we have discussed ways in which the law seeks to effect substantial justice within the general parameters of the contract itself, by means of interpretation, supplementation, or minor adjustments. Occasionally, these methods permit the courts to strike down or set aside offensive terms or even complete contracts (as with the doctrine of undue influence), but most of the cases so far discussed do not entail such drastic measures. But if the law is to be seriously concerned with substantive fairness, there will necessarily be occasions in which it will override the actual terms of a contract.

Agreements contrary to public policy

As was explained in Chapter 8, the common law has always been willing to override a contract (or contractual terms) in certain select cases on the ground that they are 'contrary to public policy'. This is in most cases a different matter from overriding contractual terms on grounds of *unfairness*, yet it is clear that in some cases the line between these two purposes has been blurred. Indeed, it sometimes seems as if public policy is invoked merely to overcome the general common law principle prohibiting the courts from interfering on grounds of fairness. Once the element of public policy is admitted, the court roves freely over the question of fairness. Lord Diplock frankly admitted this to be the case in the House of Lords in 1974,[11] where the principles of 'restraint of trade' were called into question.

The principles concerning agreements in restraint of trade were dealt with in Chapter 8; here, it is enough to recall that such covenants have long been contrary to public policy if they are found to be unreasonable in the interests of the parties or the public. One major class of such agreements is an agreement by which a person undertakes not to use his own labour or skill in a certain profession or trade to compete with another. Although such agreements may be valid within reasonable limits, excessive restraints are unenforceable. It is true that as a matter of strict law such agreements may be set aside even if they are perfectly 'fair' in the sense that a fair price was paid for them: a promise by a minimum wage employee not to compete anywhere in the world for 25 years is—in principle—unenforceable even if the employee received millions of pounds in compensation for agreeing to the restraint. But in practice it seems clear that courts are often concerned with the amount of the consideration received in exchange for the covenant. A person who is paid handsomely for a promise not to compete is likely to find it difficult to challenge the agreement.

Stipulated damages and forfeitures

A second major group of cases in which the courts have long been willing to override express contractual terms are those dealing with stipulated damages and forfeitures. Contracts often provide that if one party fails to perform a contractual obligation, the party must pay a stipulated sum in lieu of damages or forfeit some property or money. Such provisions are often void. The oldest example comes from the law of mortgages. Originally, mortgages would typically provide that the property should be forfeited if the borrower

---

[11] See *A. Schroeder Music Publishing Co. Ltd v. Macaulay* [1975] 1 WLR 1308.

failed to pay off the loan and interest on the due date even though the property might be worth much more than the amount due. Centuries ago, the Court of Chancery began to override these forfeiture provisions and permit borrowers to pay off mortgage debts long after the due date, and so reclaim their property. Similarly, it was for a long time common for written contracts to be made in the form of 'penal bonds' in which the debtor would 'acknowledge' that he owed the creditor a stipulated sum, but which added that this debt would be void if the debtor performed such-and-such an act before a certain date. The sum stipulated in these bonds was commonly *twice* the value of the contract itself, so for instance if the debtor borrowed £100, he would grant a bond 'acknowledging' that he owed £200 unless the £100 plus interest was paid at the due date. The penal element in these bonds was also held invalid, first in equity and then at common law, so that the remainder of such a bond had to be enforced as a simple contractual obligation in which the debt or damages had to be claimed and proved in the usual way.

As was true of the law on agreements in restraint of trade, the law dealing with stipulated damage clauses and forfeitures is not strictly concerned with the substantive fairness of the agreement. A stipulated damage clause will be deemed a penalty, and thus unenforceable, if the amount stipulated is substantially greater than whatever losses might reasonably have been expected to flow from the breach in question—regardless of the compensation received in exchange for the clause. Thus a provision in a construction contract stipulating damages of £1,000 per day late could be judged penal even if the contract price had been doubled or tripled to compensate for the provision. But it is clear that in practice penal clauses are rarely paid for in this way. Rather, they are typically accepted without demanding anything in return, usually because the subject party either does not expect to breach the contract, does not expect the provision to be applied if the contract is broken, or does not understand the clause's legal significance. In practice, then, the insertion of a penal clause into an otherwise fair contract will often make the contract unfair. Removing the clause restores the original equality.

Unconscionability and inequality of bargaining power

A third possible basis on which contractual terms may be overridden at common law is both more general and more controversial. This is the idea that a contract (or a contractual clause) may be struck down on the ground that it is 'unconscionable' or, in other words, that (as was explained earlier) one party has extracted an unfair bargain by taking advantage of the other's weakness. It is curious that the existence of so important a potential power should remain uncertain at this late date in the history of contract law; this anomaly stems from the fact that while courts have rarely been willing to apply such a doctrine (outside a limited class of cases), they have also been unwilling to renounce it entirely.

The jurisdiction over 'unconscionable' contracts, whether or not it continues to exist, has a historical foundation. Courts of Equity, in the eighteenth century in particular, often set aside express contractual provisions on grounds of unconscionability, but nearly all these cases fell into certain special classes. There were mortgages and penal bonds, discussed above; there were also all manner of loan cases that resembled the mortgage ones insofar as the security that was provided (in one form or another) was intended to take a form which could be camouflaged from the eye of the Chancellor in equity. These ruses generally failed, and all loan agreements were subject to being opened up and having their terms rewritten so as to require the borrower simply to pay off what he owed, plus interest.

Another common type of case related to these other classes was the sale or mortgage of a reversionary interest. Today this would seem a very odd sort of transaction but it was a great deal more common in past centuries. When the sons of the aristocracy had no real vocation but to await the parental death, and particularly when the line of succession passed outside the immediate family, it was not uncommon for a person to have very little income but large expectations. Such persons were often tempted to raise money on these expectations by borrowing against or selling their interests. Since they often had little income and extravagant tastes, the bargains they struck were sometimes highly disadvantageous although, to be fair to the lenders, they often incurred high risks as well. Contracts of this kind also fell into the jurisdiction of Courts of Equity and were liable to be set aside for unconscionability, leaving the lender entitled to no more than his capital plus reasonable interest. Indeed, this particular jurisdiction was so widely exercised that it came to be a matter of course to reopen all bargains with 'expectant heirs'. This remedy proved over-protective (some have seen signs of class bias in these cases), and by the Sale of Reversions Act 1867 these cases were effectively returned to the general category of cases in which contracts could be set aside provided they were unconscionable.

This equitable jurisdiction was also extended in some odd and isolated cases to grossly unfair contracts entered into by 'poor and ignorant' persons who did not appreciate what they were doing and who acted without independent advice. These decisions did not have much following, probably because they were widely thought to be contrary to fundamental principle, but in the past few decades they have been revived in a small but significant number of cases. Two of these cases concerned wives who were joint owners of the matrimonial home, subject to a mortgage.[12] In both cases, the marriage had broken down, the wife had left the home, and had been persuaded

---

[12] *Cresswell v. Potter* [1978] 1 WLR 225; *Backhouse v. Backhouse* [1978] 1 WLR 243. But cf. *Butlin-Sanders v. Butlin* [1985] Fam Law 126, where the wife was advised, knew exactly what she was doing, and where the transaction was fairly reasonable.

(though with no overt signs of pressure or undue influence) to sign an agreement surrendering her interest in the matrimonial home in return for an indemnity against liabilities on the mortgage. The indemnity was almost valueless as the house was worth more than the mortgage, but it could not be said that the indemnity was no consideration since remote contingencies might have given it some value. Nevertheless, in the first case the contract was set aside, and in the second the judge would have done the same if it had been necessary for the decision. In the first, it was held that, in modern times, a person could be treated as 'poor' if he or she was a member of the 'lower income group', and could be treated as 'ignorant' if 'less highly educated'. In the second case, the same principle was held to be operative even though the wife was found to be 'certainly not wealthy' instead of poor, and not at all 'ignorant', but 'an intelligent woman'.

What was never wholly clear in the older law was whether the doctrines mentioned above were merely illustrations of a broad equitable jurisdiction to deal with *any* unconscionable contract or contractual term, or whether the jurisdiction was confined to those particular classes of cases. Towards the end of the nineteenth century, this whole area of law fell into disuse, partly because the Moneylenders Act of 1900 gave statutory control over some of the activities formerly regulated by this jurisdiction, and partly for the more general reason that the jurisdiction seemed contrary to the fundamental basis of classical contract theory. So the basic question as to the *extent* of the jurisdiction remained largely unanswered.

In modern times there have occasionally been attempts to revive the old equitable jurisdiction.[13] The best known of these was Lord Denning's suggestion, in *Lloyd's Bank v. Bundy*,[14] that there exists a general equitable jurisdiction to set aside contracts where the parties are of 'unequal bargaining power', and one of them uses his superior bargaining power to extract some unfair or unconscionable advantage. Lord Denning also suggested that the rules dealing with presumed undue influence and salvage agreements were illustrations of this principle.[15] These dicta were not approved by the House of Lords in *National Westminster Bank v. Morgan*.[16] At the same time, even that case did not wholly close the door to the possible recognition of a broader equitable jurisdiction over unconscionable contracts, though

[13] In Australia the High Court has several times reasserted the continued existence of a wide jurisdiction over unconscionable contracts in recent years, while also stressing the need to be hesitant in the exercise of this jurisdiction. See *Stern v. McArthur* (1988) 165 CLR 489; *Commercial Bank of Australia v. Amadio* (1983) 151 CLR 447.

[14] Above n. 4.

[15] Some authors have gone further, arguing that the rules dealing with, for example, 'ticket cases' (such as *Interfoto*, above n. 2), penalties and forfeitures, agreements in restraint of trade, exemption clauses, and consumer contracts generally (the last two of which are discussed further below) are also applications of the principle.

[16] [1985] AC 686.

certainly Lord Scarman, who delivered the opinion of the House, 'questioned' whether there was today any need for a general principle affording relief in cases of inequality of bargaining power.

Lord Scarman's doubts stemmed largely from the enactment of the Unfair Contract Terms Act in 1977 (which is dealt with later in this chapter) which gives wide statutory control over unfair contract terms. But neither this Act nor the more recent Unfair Terms in Consumer Contracts Regulations 1999 (also dealt with later) is all-embracing, and so it may be argued that some residual principle remains necessary to deal with unconscionable contracts. Indeed, if the only question is whether every case of unconscionability will be caught by the existing rules, the argument for introducing a general principle seems irrefutable. There are, however, two other important questions that must be addressed before supporting such a principle.

The most fundamental question is essentially moral: is it legitimate for a court to set aside a contract merely because it is unconscionable? As has been explained in previous chapters, the law appears to recognize two general grounds for setting aside a contract that satisfies the requirements of offer and acceptance, etc. The first is that the defendant did not consent. This ground cannot easily explain relief for unconscionability because it cannot explain the core idea of 'taking advantage' of the other party. If unconscionability were concerned only with consent, it could be established merely by showing that the defendant's consent was impaired, say because of cognitive problems or a state of necessity.

The other recognized ground for setting aside a contract is that the contract was obtained by a wrongful act. This ground appears more promising. Indeed, it might be thought self-evident that it is wrong to 'take advantage' of another's weakness. This suggestion is also consistent with judicial statements to the effect that a plea of unconscionability requires proof not just that the bargain was a hard one, but also that the claimant's behaviour was 'characterized by some moral culpability or impropriety'.[17]

The difficulty lies in identifying exactly what it is about the claimant's behaviour in such cases that makes it improper. The impropriety cannot exist (merely) in what the claimant has actually done, because in most cases thought to fall under the unconscionability principle the only thing the claimant has actually done is to make (or accept) an offer—and making an offer cannot be a wrong, even if the terms are outrageous. An alternative suggestion is that the impropriety consists in making (or accepting) a substantively unfair offer *in the knowledge* that one is thereby taking advantage

---

[17] *Lobb (Alec) (Garages) Limited v. Total Oil (Great Britain) Limited* [1983] 1 WLR 87 at 94. The importance of a guilty conscience was affirmed in *Boustang v. Pigott* [1993] NPC 75, another case in which the old principle of relief for 'poor and ignorant' persons was generously applied.

of the other party's weakness or vulnerability. Thus it is said that unconscionability requires proof that the claimant's actions were such as to 'affect his conscience'.[18] Explained in this way, unconscionability is a distinct ground for setting aside a contract, as there is no similar requirement for a plea of duress, misrepresentation, undue influence, or incapacity. But precisely for this reason this explanation raises further questions. The law does not normally ask whether a wrongdoer knew that what he was doing was wrong. We do not say, for instance, that a murderer acts wrongly only if he murders in the knowledge that murder is wrong. The murderer may have no remorse at all—no guilty conscience—but still be guilty of murder. It is not clear why unconscionability should be different in this respect. The requirement of a guilty conscience could also lead to some odd results if it were taken seriously. According to this interpretation, a contracting party who takes gross advantage of the other's party's weakness will not have actually acted unconscionably if it turns out that he was so morally stunted that he did not realize he was taking advantage of the other party.

In the end, it seems impossible to explain unconscionability as either a purely consent-based or purely wrongdoing-based excuse or, more generally, to reduce unconscionability to some other, more familiar, idea. In this respect, unconscionability appears similar to the broader idea of good faith—indeed unconscionability might fairly be described as one aspect of good faith. Two very different conclusions might be drawn from this observation. The first is that cases in which relief appears appropriate on the basis of an unconscionability principle are better explained on other grounds. In this view, relief for 'unconscionability' is just a label given to relief that, in a fully developed legal system, would be ordered on the basis of duress, undue influence, incapacity, or misrepresentation. For example, it may be argued that the cases involving 'poor and ignorant' persons all involve misrepresentations and/or undue influence. A second conclusion is that the difficulty of defining unconscionability merely shows that unconscionability is a 'basic' concept—like consent or fault—that is not capable of further reduction. In this view, attempts to 'explain' the underlying basis of unconscionability are bound to fail: all that can be done is to explain how the term is used and applied, and then to appeal to the listener's basic convictions and beliefs. Each of these conclusions seem prima facie plausible.

Assuming, however, that unconscionability is a valid and distinct ground for relief, there is a second question that must be addressed: should the principle of unconscionability be applied *directly* by the courts or should it instead be applied in a proxy form, through various specific doctrines such as the rules currently governing rescues at sea? A strong case can be made for either approach. On the one hand, a general principle of unconscionability

---

[18] *Multiservice Bookbinding v. Marden* [1979] Ch 84 at 110.

will necessarily be vague and ill-defined, leading to the risk of unpredictable or arbitrary decisions, motivated by sympathy rather than legal principle. On the other hand, giving expression to the unconscionability principle solely by relying on specific doctrines will almost certainly mean that some deserving cases will fall through the cracks. The very difficulty of defining unconscionability makes it difficult to capture every instance of the concept using specific rules.

4. THE UNFAIR CONTRACT TERMS ACT 1977

There are many statutory provisions (probably hundreds, perhaps thousands) which invalidate particular clauses in particular kinds of contracts. For example, provisions in the Consumer Credit Act 1974 give courts the power to invalidate a variety of clauses formerly found in consumer loan agreements and especially in hire-purchase agreements. One of these powers worth noting is that which allows judges to strike down 'extortionate credit bargains', a power reminiscent of the old equitable jurisdiction dealt with in the last section. Provisions in other statutes invalidate what are thought to be unfair clauses in employment contracts, contractual attempts to bargain away rights conferred on tenants by rent-protection legislation, and so on. Mention should also be made of the broad rights to cancel contracts that consumers enjoy with respect to contracts governed by the Consumer Protection Act 1987, the Consumer Protection (Distance Selling) Regulations 2000, and the Consumer Credit Act 1974. Although these rights apply to all contracts governed by these enactments, and not merely to unfair contracts, their clear purpose is to provide consumers with extra protections against certain kinds of allegedly unfair terms or practices.

The Unfair Contract Terms Act 1977 was the first general statute dealing with unfair contracts. There is now a second piece of general legislation—the Unfair Terms in Consumer Contracts Regulations 1999—which covers much of the same territory, and which is likely to eventually supplant the 1977 Act in importance. It also seems likely that the 1977 Act's provisions will eventually be incorporated into the 1999 Regulations or that the two will be combined into a wholly new Act.[19] This would certainly be welcome as the overlapping jurisdiction of these enactments further complicates an already complex area of the law. But for the moment the only thing that needs to be said about the Regulations is that they are virtually untested in the courts. Thus, even if the 1977 Act becomes less important in the future, its judicial implementation provides the best evidence of how courts are likely to approach the 1999 Regulations or any future consolidating legislation.

---

[19] The Department of Trade and Industry recently asked the Law Commission to consider this question; in their report (Report No. 298: Unfair Terms in Contracts) the Commission recommends new legislation that would consolidate these two Acts and, as well, offer certain new protections to 'small businesses'.

The 1977 Act is an intricate piece of legislation, and only the barest summary will be attempted here. It should first be stressed that the Act deals only with exemption clauses as that term is commonly understood; it does not, despite its title, deal with the whole subject of unfair contracts. Contracts can be unfair as a result of one of two causes: either the contract may impose an excessive burden on one party or it may impose too light a burden on the other party—for example by exclusion clauses. The 1977 Act only deals with one of the ways in which too light a burden may be imposed on one of the parties, and does not have anything to say about contracts which impose too onerous a burden on the other party.

The simplest reform carried out by the 1977 Act was to impose a total ban on clauses exempting negligence actions for personal injury or death. Thus, ordinary tort liability for personal injury or fatal accidents are unaffected by contractual exclusion clauses. Likewise, notices that warn persons that they may enter buildings or land 'at their own risk' are of no effect if an actual injury does occur.[20]

Next, the Act continues the effect of previous legislation concerning defective and dangerous goods.[21] Broadly speaking, the Act renders exclusion clauses in contracts of sale and hire-purchase invalid against *consumers*. Consumers buying or acquiring goods on hire-purchase are generally entitled to goods of 'satisfactory' quality and reasonably fit for their purposes, and no exemption clause can exclude the seller's responsibility for defective goods. However, these provisions only apply to sales to which the relevant conditions are implied under the Sale of Goods Act, namely goods purchased from a person selling in the course of business. So a person who buys a second-hand car from a private seller does not get the protection of the implied terms in the Sale of Goods Act. On the other hand, goods (second-hand or otherwise) sold by a dealer fall within the requirements of the Sale of Goods Act; the sale is likewise protected by the Unfair Contract Terms Act. Of course nobody can reasonably expect a second-hand car to be as good as a new one, but the buyer is still entitled to a car of satisfactory quality and one which is reasonably fit for its purpose, having regard to the price and the general circumstances.

Outside the two fields of personal injury, on the one hand, and consumer sale of goods and hire-purchase on the other, the 1977 Act relies heavily on

---

[20] That said, a person who gives another due warning of some danger may be held in some circumstances to have discharged her duty to take care.

[21] The author of previous editions of this text has elsewhere argued that sense cannot be made of the detailed effect of these provisions on the statutory implied terms under the Sale of Goods Act without realizing that the concept of 'reasonable reliance' substantially underpins them: P.S. Atiyah, 'The Move from Agreement to Reliance in English Law and the Exclusion of Liability Relating to Defective Goods', in D. Harris and D. Tallon (eds.), *Contract Law Today* (Oxford, 1989), 21, especially at 30–7.

the standard of reasonableness. Thus, in all other contracts with consumers (as well as in purported disclaimers of tort liability), exemption clauses are generally only valid if they are reasonable. So too, such clauses must be reasonable in contracts with business parties if (but only if) they are contained in 'standard written terms of business', exclude liability for negligence, or protect the seller from liability for defective goods in a contract of sale or hire-purchase. The Act provides no special protection for business parties who fall outside these categories, although some assistance may be found (as we have seen in Chapters 3 and 5) in the common law rules dealing with the incorporation and interpretation of exemption clauses.

The Act provides guidelines on the term 'reasonable' in relation to exclusion clauses; though these are not always helpful, certain relevant factors are clearly spelt out.[22] For instance, the guidelines declare that it is relevant to inquire into the relative bargaining position of the parties. Bargaining power is not defined, but the courts are most likely to consider the competitiveness of the relevant market and the ability of the party subject to the clause to understand and appreciate its significance. Thus, an exclusion clause in a standard contract imposed by a monopoly supplier on a consumer is more likely to be regarded as unreasonable. It is also expressly provided by the Act's guidelines that it is relevant in determining 'reasonable' to consider whether the customer received an incentive to accept the exemption clause: for example, if a customer opts to have goods carried at the owner's risk knowing that he will be charged less than at carrier's risk, he will have received an 'inducement' to agree to have his goods carried at his own risk. This may make the clause reasonable, at least if the customer fully understood the choice being offered to him. A third relevant factor when considering if a term is 'reasonable' concerns the possibility of insurance. Many of the risks that give rise to litigation are insurable risks, and many battles about exemption clauses are effectively battles between one party and an insurance company, or even between two insurance companies. Thus, it is often entirely reasonable for one or both parties to exclude their liability because of the amount of insurance they hold or even the availability of insurance. This is particularly true in instances where only one party has the relevant knowledge to enable insurance to be bought, and in cases where one of the parties can obtain insurance more cheaply or readily.[23]

---

[22] The Act inexplicably limits the application of some of these factors to one portion of the various cases in which reasonableness is relevant. It is likely that the courts will nonetheless tend to regard them as relevant to all cases arising under the Act, if only because they are directed to consider all the circumstances which were known or contemplated when the contract was made.

[23] See *Wright v. British Railways* [1987] CLY §424, where a suitcase was lost by the defendants, but an exclusion clause was upheld as reasonable, largely because the claimant was much better placed to insure than the defendants, having sole knowledge of the contents.

There have been relatively few decisions exploring how the above factors are to be applied. It has also been stressed (perhaps unfortunately) that this is a matter to be decided by the trial court in each individual case. The leading case is *George Mitchell (Chesterhall) Ltd v. Finney Lock Seeds Ltd*[24] where the claimants were farmers who had ordered cabbage seed from the defendants. The defendants supplied an inferior variety seed, and the claimants suffered considerable losses (over £60,000) in planting and clearing the fields where the crop completely failed. The contract contained a term limiting the liability of the defendants to some trivial sum, but it was held that this clause was void as unreasonable under the predecessor to the 1977 Act. The main factor relied upon by the House of Lords in reaching their decision seems to have been that seed merchants often negotiated settlements and paid proper compensation in cases of this kind even where their contracts contained (as they all did) the relevant clause. This practice seemed to demonstrate to the Lords that even those in the trade did not think their own contractual clauses were reasonable.

An earlier case of a similar kind provides an interesting contrast with *George Mitchell*. In this case[25] a farmer bought some seed potatoes which turned out to be defective, and the crop failed. The sale contract contained two exemption clauses, the first of which required the buyer to give notice of any complaints within three days of delivery, and the second of which excluded the seller's liability for any consequential loss (such as loss of expected profit on the crop). The first clause was held unreasonable because it was proved that the disease from which the potatoes suffered was not discoverable until the crop began to grow, and it would therefore have been quite impossible for the buyer to make his complaint within three days of delivery. But the second clause which excluded the seller's liability for consequential loss was upheld as reasonable for a number of reasons: first, the parties were of roughly equal bargaining power, and, secondly, the seed potatoes in question were uncertified and somewhat cheaper than certified potatoes, so the buyer was in a sense agreeing to an inherent risk by choosing an inferior product.

One area that has caused much difficulty concerns disclaimers of liability that are made by surveyors undertaking valuations for the purposes of building society mortgages, as well as disclaimers of building societies themselves. If a surveyor is paid by a building society to value a house and negligently fails to discover serious defects so that his valuation is grossly excessive, a borrower from the building society is prima facie entitled to sue the surveyor for damages in tort. But many surveyors used to attempt to avoid this liability

[24] [1983] 2 AC 807. See also *Stewart Gill Ltd v. Horatio Meyer & Co. Ltd* [1992] 1 QB 600.
[25] *R. W. Green v. Cade Bros Farms* [1978] 1 Lloyd's Rep 602.

by suitable disclaimers, and in 1988 two cases of this kind were taken to the House of Lords.[26] It was there held that, in cases of ordinary 'consumer' house-buyers, these disclaimers were generally unreasonable, and therefore invalid under the 1977 Act. They were unreasonable because it was clear that the great majority of such buyers would rely on the surveyor's report and not commission an independent survey, a fact well known to surveyors and building societies. Furthermore, in the event the clause was upheld, the buyer would be unprotected against a serious risk, whereas surveyors could insure against their liability. Of course, the cost of the insurance would have to be added to the surveyor's charges, but it was not thought that this would greatly affect the cost of surveys. The House of Lords went on to suggest, however, that the result under the 1977 Act might not be the same where the case concerned large commercial property (such as a block of flats) and the buyer was a company which could reasonably be expected to commission its own survey.

5. THE 1999 REGULATIONS ON UNFAIR CONTRACT TERMS

The EU Directive on Unfair Contract Terms[27] was implemented in the UK by the Unfair Terms in Consumer Contracts Regulations 1999. Although many of the Regulations overlap with provisions of the Unfair Contract Terms Act 1977, they are an important development in English law, most obviously for their expansion of the basis for setting aside unfair contracts. A second noteworthy feature is that the Regulations give the Director General of Fair Trading and other named bodies (e.g. local authorities) the power to apply for injunctions to prevent the *future* use of unfair terms (and thus also the power to negotiate terms with firms in lieu of going to court). But what will perhaps prove the most important aspect of the Regulations is that they give a central role to certain ideas and principles—notably good faith—that were traditionally thought to have little or no importance in English law.

The Regulations give courts the power to nullify certain allegedly unfair terms in consumer sales contracts. Each of the relevant concepts is the subject of definition in the Regulations, although the manner in which they will be applied in England is not yet certain as to date only one appellate level case[28] has examined the Regulations. Nevertheless, it is possible to make several observations concerning the Regulations, and to speculate as to their impact on traditional understandings of contract law.

---

[26] See *Smith v. Bush* [1990] 1 AC 831.

[27] [1993] OJ L 95/29.

[28] *Director General of Fair Trading v. First National Bank plc* [2001] 3 WLR 1297. The case concerned the earlier 1994 version of the Regulations, but the basic test for unfair terms is the same in both versions.

Application of the Regulations

The application of the Regulations differs substantially from that of the 1977 Act. First, the Regulations only apply to protect consumers—meaning natural persons (excluding, therefore, all companies) who are acting for purposes outside their business. In addition, consumers are protected only insofar as they contract with sellers or suppliers who are acting in the course of their business. So the Regulations have no application (for instance) to a consumer who buys a second-hand car from a private seller not acting in the course of business. And though the Regulations applies to contracts for the sale of land they only do so where the seller is acting in the course of business, so while a sale by a builder or developer would be within the Regulations, a private sale would not.

Secondly, a term can only be attacked as unfair under the Regulations if it was 'not individually negotiated'. A term is not individually negotiated where it 'has been drafted in advance and the consumer has therefore not been able to influence the substance of the term', although it is also possible for a consumer to claim that a term was not individually negotiated even if it was not drafted in advance. As most consumer contracts are made on standard forms printed in advance, the 'drafted in advance' requirement will rarely be an issue; however, difficult cases are easy to imagine. Suppose that during negotiations for an oral contract for the sale of a second-hand household appliance from a business seller, a consumer inquires as to possible warranties and is told by the seller that the standard warranty is for three months. The consumer asks for a longer term, but the seller refuses. The warranty could be regarded as not individually negotiated on the grounds that the seller had decided in advance that only a three-month warranty would be offered, and stuck to that decision; but what if the seller decided on a three-month warranty only when the consumer raised the issue? Is the term still subject to the Regulations just because the seller refused to budge? Read literally, the Regulations suggest this conclusion, but this is a very narrow definition of 'negotiations'. If the essential test is whether the consumer was able to influence the term, then any term that remains unchanged is 'not negotiated', even if the parties argued over its content at great length. A further consideration is that even if the seller refuses, in negotiations, to budge on the term in question he may change other terms in the contract to appease the consumer. So the consumer in the above example might have agreed to the three-month warranty only because the seller agreed to lower the price in return. In such a case, while the consumer may not have 'influenced' the substance of the term, it seems strange to say the term was not negotiated. Finally, it is unlikely that any of a contract's terms are absolutely fixed. If the consumer in the above example was willing to pay a million pounds in exchange for a longer warranty, it is likely that the seller would have agreed to such an offer, even if the seller's terms were set down in a pre-printed standard form contract.

In cases where the meaning of 'individually negotiated' is difficult to apply, it is important to bear in mind the general aim or purpose of the Regulations. There are two main views on this question. According to the first view, the purpose of the Regulations is to give relief against substantively unfair terms, full stop. However, this interpretation fails to account for why it should matter whether the term in question was negotiated. Lengthy negotiations over a term are no guarantee that the final version of the term will be fair, and there is no reason in principle why parties with superior bargaining power would not use negotiations as an opportunity to press their advantage. The monopolist who wants to extract maximum advantage from a consumer may well negotiate at great length in order to determine just how much the consumer is able and willing to pay or accept.

According to the (more plausible) second view, the Regulations' main purpose is to protect consumers against unfair *surprises*. Under this interpretation, negotiations *are* relevant: if negotiations have occurred with respect to a particular term then presumably the consumer will at least be aware of the term. But it does not matter, in this view, whether the seller actually modifies his offer or is even willing to modify it. The fact that a consumer is unsuccessful in negotiating a change in a term does not change the fact that the term is unlikely to be a surprise. According to this second view, then, the negotiation requirement will be satisfied wherever the relevant term has been discussed in such a way that the consumer has been made fully aware of its content and meaning. Still, even this standard may be difficult to satisfy in the case of complex exemption clauses and the like.

A further limitation on the scope of the Regulations supports the idea that their primary concern is to protect consumers against unfair surprises. The Regulations do not apply to terms that define the main subject matter of the contract or that specify the price, provided these are in plain, intelligible language. This requirement is perhaps the strongest evidence that the Regulations' purpose is not merely to protect against substantively unfair terms—if substantive fairness were the sole concern, it would make no sense to exclude price and subject matter terms, since the most common reason that a contract of sale is unfair is either that the price is unfair or the goods are of inferior quality. It makes perfect sense, however, to exclude terms setting out the price and subject-matter from scrutiny if the purpose is to protect against unfair surprises. These are the contract terms that a consumer is most likely to be aware of and to understand.

It will not always be obvious whether a particular term qualifies as a term that specifies the price or the main subject matter of the contract. In a sense, *everything* in a contract is part of the 'price' or the 'subject-matter'.[29] But, once again, the notion that the Regulations are intended to protect against unfair surprises can help in understanding this issue. In particular, the court's inquiries should not be directed at formalities such as whether the impugned term deals with monetary matters or whether it is placed at the front or the back of the document. Rather, the court should ask whether it is the kind of term that a reasonable consumer should be aware of and should be able to understand. This interpretation was supported in *Director General of Fair Trading v. First National Bank plc*,[30] where it was held that a term specifying the amount of interest to be paid following a judgment for breach of contract was subject to the Regulations. The rationale behind this decision is easy to discern: consumers expect to perform their contracts, and so pay little attention to provisions that deal with what may happen if they fail to perform. Even if they do pay attention, the full significance of such provisions is usually difficult for anyone but a trained lawyer to appreciate.

But even if price terms are formally excluded from scrutiny under the Regulations, they cannot be entirely ignored in practice. Suppose that a court is asked to assess a clause stipulating that, in the event of a late instalment payment, the consumer must pay a sum of money out of all proportion to the harm caused by the late payment. A 'penal' clause of this kind is often regarded as a clear example of an unfair term (and is mentioned in the Regulations' list of 'suspect' terms discussed below), but if compensation in the form of a lower price is given in return for a penal clause, it may well be fair—though it might still be a surprise. Many consumers would be more than happy to accept such a provision in exchange for a significant reduction in price. Indeed, the possibility that a prima facie unfair term may be fair because an 'inducement' is received in exchange is recognised explicitly in the 1977 Act, as we have seen. The Regulations do not contain a similar provision, but, as will be discussed in more detail below, it can be expected that courts will adopt a similar approach.

Finally, the Regulations do not apply to contracts of employment, contracts relating to succession rights, contracts relating to rights under family law, or contracts relating to the incorporation and organization of companies or partnerships. Unlike the 1977 Act, however, the Regulations contain no exclusion for auction sales, so judicial decisions will have to clarify whether the auction of second-hand cars can continue to exclude all implied

---

[29] As illustrated by *Bairstow Eves London Central Ltd v. Smith* [2004] EWHC 263, where the dispute concerned a contract with a real estate agent that stipulated a 'standard' commission rate for 3%, but which also provided for an 'early payment discounted commission rate of 1.5%'. Gross J held that the 3% rate provision fell within the Regulations, emphasizing that negotiations had proceeded on the assumption that the lower rate would be used and, more generally, that the exclusion for 'price' terms should be interpreted narrowly.

[30] Ibid., at para. 34.

conditions and warranties. Another difference from the 1977 Act is that the Regulations apply to insurance contracts, except for terms that define and circumscribe the insured risk and the insurer's liability—for instance, terms that exclude flood damage from a householder's policy, or accidental damage from a motorist's third party, fire, and theft policy. Notably, some of the many conditions of liability which are at present imposed on insured persons may now be found to be unfair. If a householder's policy declares, for instance, that it is a condition of the insurer's liability that the burglar alarm be properly maintained, it might now be possible to contend that this is an unfair term if there was no apparent defect in the alarm. Many conditions in ordinary insurance policies are very harsh, or are at least capable of operating harshly, and this may well prove one of the most significant practical changes made by the Regulations.

The meaning of 'unfair'

Although the wording is not as clear as it might be, regulation 5.1 appears to envision that a term in a consumer contract which has not been individually negotiated is an unfair term only where two separate requirements are satisfied: the term must be 'contrary to the requirements of good faith' and it must lead to a 'significant imbalance in the rights and obligations of the parties'. In theory, both concepts are new to English law. We will begin with the second requirement, as we have already said something about substantive unfairness earlier in this chapter.

Significant imbalance

According to the traditional view, adequacy of consideration is immaterial in English law, but we have already seen that in many circumstances English law embraces the idea that there should be no significant imbalance between the parties' obligations. A declaration by an eminent judge that a buyer is entitled to 'value for his money'[31] is an acknowledgement that the concept of balance between the two sides of the transaction is already known in the law.

We also noted earlier in this chapter that courts tend to make assessments of substantive fairness by comparing the contract in question to one that might ordinarily have been made in a competitive market (taking it for granted that it may be difficult to identify the relevant market with precision). It can be expected that the same general approach will be taken under the Regulations. Such assessments should not be a problem, provided judges are mindful that an imbalance must be 'significant' to be impugned and, more generally, that they are not trained economists and so should tread carefully in this area. A potentially more serious concern regarding

---

[31] Mustill LJ in *Rogers v. Parish (Scarborough) Ltd*, above n. 5 at 944.

substantive fairness is one that we have already mentioned: the Regulations appear to focus on unfair *terms*, but it is not possible to determine if an individual term is unfair in isolation from the rest of the contract. An apparently harsh term may be perfectly fair if counterbalanced by other terms. But there does not appear to be anything preventing courts from following the dictates of common sense and assessing the fairness of a term in the context of the entire contract (as we have seen is required under the 1977 Act), so this problem may well not arise. Indeed, the definition of 'unfair' arguably instructs courts to do just this, referring as it does to the parties' rights and obligations *under the contract*. In addition, Recital 16 of the Preamble to the Directive (though not included in the Regulations) states explicitly that in assessing good faith, account should be taken of whether the consumer had an inducement to accept the term.

Good faith

Good faith is also considered a novel concept for English law, though we have seen that it is used explicitly in certain contexts (e.g. duties of disclosure in insurance contracts) and also arguably underlies various other contract law rules. While good faith is a well-known concept in civilian systems, the meaning of good faith in the Regulations must be understood in the context of the Regulations' other terms and in light of the Regulations' underlying purpose.

Approached in this way, it would seem inappropriate to define good faith as being wholly or even partly concerned with substantive fairness. To be sure, it can be so understood in the abstract, and in practice the conclusion that a particular term was 'in bad faith' usually implies that the term is unfair in some respect. But given that the definition of 'unfair' in regulation 5.1 already requires the courts to ask whether an impugned term causes a significant imbalance in the parties' rights and duties, it would be redundant to ask the same question under the bad faith requirement, even if the concept of good faith is understood to incorporate an element of substantive fairness.[32] Good faith in the Regulations must therefore be understood primarily as a procedural concept.

It has already been contended that the main purpose of the Regulations is to protect against unfair surprises, but something more needs to be said in support of this claim before considering its implications for the meaning of good faith. Two of the main indicia for the 'unfair surprises' motive were mentioned earlier: the 'not individually negotiated' requirement, and the exclusion of terms specifying the price and main subject matter except where they are not in plain, intelligible language. Three further reasons may be

---

[32] This is the position of Lord Steyn in the *First National* case; see below, n. 33.

mentioned at this point: first, and perhaps most obviously, this interpretation is consistent with the basic fact that the Regulations apply only to *consumer* contracts—consumers are particularly vulnerable to the problem of unfair surprises. To be sure, consumers may also be vulnerable to problems associated with monopolies, cartels, and non-competitive markets generally, but such problems are probably even more prevalent in non-consumer contracts. Outside of regulated industries (gas, electricity), most consumer contracts are nowadays made in highly competitive markets, and the competitiveness of these markets pressures sellers and suppliers to offer contracts with fair terms. But problems will sometimes arise, and the particular problem facing most consumers is that they lack the time or expertise to understand each and every term in the contracts they sign.

Another argument in favour of the 'unfair surprises' interpretation is that the 'grey' list of terms that are set out in Schedule 2 (discussed below) and that 'may be regarded as unfair' are, for the most part, terms which contracting parties are likely to ignore or fail to understand. Schedule 2 focuses on provisions, such as exemption clauses, penal clauses, forfeiture clauses, termination clauses, and unilateral variation clauses, that either modify the rights and duties that would otherwise follow on a breach of contract or allow one party to alter the contract in the event of changed circumstances. They deal, in other words, with the effect of temporally distant, low-probability events, the significance of which is often difficult to appreciate for a non-lawyer. Not surprisingly, consumers rarely pay much attention to such clauses, and rarely understand and appreciate their full significance when they do.

Third, and finally, the Regulations were passed in order to implement an EU Directive. EU Directives are passed for different reasons, but a recurring theme is the importance of facilitating trade and business between EU countries. In the case of consumer sales, a major disincentive to cross-border purchases is the fear of being surprised by some aspect of the transaction. Protecting consumers against unfair surprises may therefore be regarded as another means by which the EU has sought to induce and facilitate cross-border trade.

These observations suggest that the good faith requirement in regulation 5.1 should be interpreted so as to give effect to the general aim of protecting consumers against unfair surprises. Of course, some of the ways by which consumers may be unfairly surprised are already caught by the rules against misrepresentation. But there are many other situations that do not qualify as misrepresentation to which the concept of good faith could be applied. Such examples include terms printed in small type, terms placed on the back of a document, confusing language, and the failure to bring a term to the consumer's full attention.

This interpretation of the good faith requirement is broadly consistent with the House of Lords' approach in the *First National* case.[33] In considering the good faith requirement, Lord Bingham began by stating that '[t]he requirement of good faith is one of fair and open dealing.'[34] He then elaborated in language that makes clear that the courts' primary (though perhaps not exclusive) concern is whether the consumer fully understands the terms to which she is apparently assenting:

Openness requires that the terms should be expressed fully, clearly and legibly, containing no concealed pitfalls or traps. Appropriate prominence should be given to terms which might operate disadvantageously to the customer. Fair dealing requires that a supplier should not, whether deliberately or unconsciously, take advantage of the consumer's necessity, indigence, lack of experience, unfamiliarity with the subject matter of the contract, weak bargaining position or any other factor listed in or analogous to those listed in Schedule 2 of the regulations.[35]

Schedule 2—the 'grey' list

Schedule 2 to the Regulations contains an 'indicative and non-exhaustive' list of terms which *may* be considered unfair. How much weight is given to the Schedule remains to be seen, but it seems clear that terms identified within it (or those that are closely analogous to them) are likely to receive special scrutiny. The list also gives a clear idea of the kinds of terms that are thought to cause problems, and thus helps to give some meaning to concepts like good faith and significant imbalance.

Paragraphs (*a*) and (*b*) deal with exclusion clauses, (*a*) being of little importance in England in that it deals with clauses excluding liability for personal injury or death. Any such clause is already void in England under the 1977 Act.

Paragraphs (*d*) and (*e*) deal with penalties and forfeitures. The second largely restates the English rule against penalties (discussed in Chapter 14). But paragraph (*d*) reads strangely to an English lawyer: it states that a term that requires a consumer to forfeit a deposit in the event she cancels the contract may be 'unfair' whenever it is not reciprocated by a term awarding identical compensation in the event the other party cancels the contract. This could have a significant impact on the drafting of package holiday contracts, where the consumer can generally not recover her deposit if she cancels at too

---

[33] Above n. 28. This is true notwithstanding Lord Steyn's statement that any 'purely procedural or even predominantly procedural interpretation of the requirement of good faith must be rejected' (para. 36). As we have seen, reg. 5.1 explicitly requires substantive fairness to be taken into account. It was argued above that this requirement is distinct from the good faith test, but it could also be regarded as a part of the good faith test (the wording of the regulation is not clear in this regard). This appears to be Lord Steyn's understanding. The question then becomes whether good faith should be defined in *exclusively* substantive terms. Lord Steyn does not argue for such an interpretation.

[34] Ibid., at para. 17.
[35] Ibid.

late a date; customarily, there is no mirror provision for the payment of equivalent compensation should the holiday company cancel. Holiday companies will now have to decide between abandoning this custom and running the risk of having the forfeiture of deposits declared unfair.

Paragraphs (*f*) and (*g*) apply to contracts of indefinite duration, restricting the freedom of the supplier to terminate without notice or retain moneys paid in advance of such termination. But suppliers of financial services (banks, for instance) retain the right to terminate such contracts without notice where there is a valid reason, provided the supplier informs the other party at once. The words 'where there is a valid reason' presumably mean that a bank could not rely on a contract term to terminate an account or withdraw a credit card (if issued indefinitely) unless there really is a valid reason which it is prepared to disclose.

Paragraph (*i*) refers to a term which irrevocably binds the consumer to 'terms with which he has had no real opportunity of becoming acquainted before conclusion of the contract'. This paragraph has already been discussed in Chapter 5.

Paragraphs (*j*) and (*k*) deal with terms which allow the seller or supplier to unilaterally alter contract terms or the specification of goods; in the event that terms are altered, the reason must be specified in the contract. There is a limited exception for suppliers of financial services who have the right to alter interest rates payable by or to a consumer 'where there is a valid reason', so long as notice is given immediately and the consumer is then free to dissolve the contract. These paragraphs could have a significant impact on certain types of consumer contracts. For instance, an ordinary building society mortgage commonly gives the building society the right to vary rates of interest unilaterally by giving public notice. Such a clause might now be held unfair because it does not provide for direct notice to be given to consumers; it also fails to give the consumer the right to dissolve the contract. The same is also true of the converse situation where investors in building society accounts may be at risk of their rates of interest being reduced, without then having the right to withdraw their deposits. Building societies have estimated that the annual cost of compliance with the Regulations could be £60 million,[36] presumably because of the notices that they will be required to give in the future. These costs will, of course, have to be borne by the same borrowers and investors who the Regulations are intended to protect.

Prevention of unfair terms

An important and innovative feature of the Regulations is that the Director General of Fair Trading and certain other listed bodies (e.g. local councils,

---

[36] See DTI, A Further Consultation Document, Implementation of the EC Regulations on Unfair Terms in Consumer Contracts (93/13/EEC) (1994), 38.

certain consumer organisations) are given the authority to apply to the courts for injunctions prohibiting the use of particular examples of unfair terms in consumer contracts. The *First National* case, discussed above, is the only judicial decision so far dealing with such an application and it may be that few will arise since it appears that, in practice, the Director General will accept an undertaking to discontinue the use of the offending provision in place of going to court and, further, that firms and trade associations are generally willing to give such undertakings when they have been approached by the Office of Fair Trading. Reports issued by the Office make clear that they have been successful in a large number of cases in persuading firms and trade associations to rewrite contract terms that the Office regards as potentially unfair. This point should be stressed in light of the small number of judicial decisions (to date) dealing with the Regulations. If early experience is any indication, the main significance of the Regulations will lie not in their use as a defence in contract cases, but as a tool that the Office of Fair Trading employs to bring about negotiated changes in contracting practices. The wide range of industries in which the Office of Fair Trading has successfully negotiated changes in contracting practices include those dealing with flights, used cars, mobile phones, home improvements, household items, and package holidays.

When deciding whether a particular provision should be prohibited, the test is necessarily an *ex ante* test—the court (or the Director General) must imagine the possible sets of circumstances in which the provision might be applied. This can be difficult to do at the best of times, but a particular problem in the case of the Regulations is that (as we have seen) it is difficult to determine the fairness of an individual term in isolation from the other terms in the contract. An apparently unfair term might well be fair if sufficient monetary compensation were offered in exchange. A related difficulty is that the fairness of a term will often depend on whether the term is drawn to the consumer's attention and properly explained. Yet in determining whether an injunction should be granted it does not seem possible for the Director General to state *ex ante* that a term may only be used subject to appropriate price reductions, explanations, etc.

Theoretical justification for legislative protection

It is worth concluding this section by adding a few general comments on the possible justifications for the interferences with freedom of contract that are allowed under the Unfair Contract Terms Act 1977 and the Unfair Terms in Consumer Contracts Regulations 1999. It is sometimes supposed that the primary focus of these pieces of legislation is clauses that are just inherently bad or unfair. Exemption clauses, limitation clauses, penalty clauses, forfeiture clauses, termination clauses, and the like are all similar in that they alter the legal rights (or duties) that contracting parties would otherwise enjoy on the basis of the general law. Thus, an exemption clause exempts one party from liabilities that the general law would otherwise impose. Given that the general law presumably enforces these rights and duties for a reason, it may be thought self-evident that it is a bad thing to derogate from them to the detriment of one party.

We have seen, however, that there are often perfectly good reasons why parties might want to derogate from the rights and duties set out in the general law. The general function of the kinds of clauses described above is to shift the risk of certain losses or injuries from the person who caused the loss or injury (or who had control over the relevant property) to the person who actually suffers the injury (e.g. the owner of property that was lost or damaged). Thus, an exemption clause in a shipping contract might allocate the risk of theft to the owner. Such arrangements depend on two facts for their justification. First, the most effective way of dealing with some risks is not to devote more resources to preventing the relevant loss or injury, but to instead purchase insurance against the risk—this is the reason homeowners buy insurance against theft rather than dig moats around their property or hire full-time security guards. Secondly, in many contractual circumstances insurance can be obtained more cheaply or easily by the party who owns the relevant goods or for whom the relevant service is to be performed. An owner who has contracted for goods to be shipped knows their value and will, in any event, often need to obtain insurance covering the goods for other purposes. Thus, it may be cheaper for the owner to insure the goods against loss or injury during shipping than for the shipper to do so. Of course, the shipper could almost certainly obtain insurance if required to do so, but the cost would then be reflected in the contract price. If the owner can obtain similar insurance more cheaply, the effect of outlawing an exemption clause in such a case may simply be to force the owner to pay more than necessary for insurance. The conclusion to this line of reasoning is that the liability rules stipulated by the general law should be regarded as, in effect, 'default terms'. Like the default terms found in computer software, they work well in most situations, but should be alterable by individual users where appropriate.

It follows from the foregoing that it is appropriate that the list of terms in Schedule 2 of the 1999 Regulations is a grey list and not a black list. In contrast, the 1977 Act will under some circumstances ban outright any clause that excludes or restricts the seller's liability for breach of the implied terms relating to quality or fitness in a contract of sale of goods. An illustration of a case in which this could cause practical problems comes from the personal computer industry. It is a common practice of retail sellers of personal computers to restrict their liability for breach of implied conditions by requiring the buyer to return the computer to the seller for repairs. As many computers are quite heavy and bulky items, this could plainly be a costly and troublesome business. At the same time the seller almost always offers the buyer the option of buying what is called an 'on-site warranty' under which the seller undertakes to repair defects at the buyer's own home or place of business. There does not seem to be anything in the least objectionable about this practice, so long as the buyer clearly understands the choice being offered. But the practice almost certainly falls foul of the 1977 Act because it involves a restriction on the seller's liability for breach of the implied terms under the Sale of Goods Act. (Sellers may sometimes recognize this technically by pro-claiming that their conditions of sale are without prejudice to the consumer's 'statutory rights', but a consumer who has not bought an on-site warranty probably faces an uphill battle in ensuring that her statutory rights are fully respected.) If a test case to this effect ever receives widespread publicity the probable result will be that buyers will no longer be given the option *not* to pay extra for an on-site warranty. So an Act designed for the protection of consumers could have the effect of depriving consumers of a right which they currently enjoy. In this situation the free-market arguments against interference are hard to refute.

Alongside the claim that exemption clauses and the like are inherently unfair is a second, more common suggestion that they merit special scrutiny because they tend to be used to extract unfair advantages by monopolists and other parties who are in a position to dictate the terms of their con-tracts. Clearly, the argument here is not that such clauses are *only* used by monopolists and the like—exemption clauses of one kind or another are common in many types of contract—but that they are commonly used by monopolists wishing to exploit their monopoly powers.

This suggestion is consistent with the fact that, historically, the most egre-gious examples of unfair exemption clauses have been found in contracts drawn up by monopolists or at least in highly uncompetitive markets. But this does not fully explain why such clauses in particular are the focus of legisla-tion such as the 1977 Act or the 1999 Regulations. If a contracting party has a true monopoly, and thus the power to dictate terms more favourable than those that might be obtained in a competitive market, it might be thought he would first focus on price terms, as the easiest way to exploit monopoly power is simply to charge an unfair price. And even if a monopolist does focus on things like exemption clauses, prohibiting such clauses will have little effect if the monopolist is free to change other terms in the contract. Of course, few if any monopolists have complete freedom to dictate whatever terms they like; there is almost always some alternative to paying what the monopolist demands, even if it is not particularly attractive. But this still does not explain why monopolists would favour using exemption clauses instead of overcharging.

The most persuasive explanation of why monopolists would focus on exemption clauses, etc.—and of why such clauses are the main focus of the 1997 Act and the 1999 Regulations—is that (as has already been suggested) such clauses are often poorly understood. In theory, any term in a contract can be unreasonable and so cause a contract to be unfair, but in practice the terms most likely to be unreasonable are those that are not well understood. The most effective way to take advantage of contracting parties is do so in a way that ensures they are not aware they are being taken advantage of. This explanation fits both with the emphasis in the 1977 Act and 1999 Regulations on exemption clauses etc., as well as their focus on consumers and standard-form contracts. Few consumers read, let alone understand, exemption clauses contained in standard-form contracts—nor are they required to do so. As we have repeatedly stressed, the general rules of contract law do not require that the parties assent to or understand the terms of their contracts except in the most general and vague sense.[37] This explanation is also consistent with the fact that the most egregious examples of unfair exemption clauses and the like have been found, historically, in contracts with monopolists. Because few monopolists have perfect monopoly power, and because even if they do have such power they need to worry about the government stepping in and regulating them, it is to a monopolist's advantage to disguise the 'true' cost of her products or services. Moreover, monopolists will generally find that they are better able to hide the true costs of their products than vendors in ordinary markets. The absence of competition and thus of competitors' who may try to compete on the basis of ancillary terms makes it less likely that unfair surprises in a monopolist's contract will be brought to consumers' attention. Thus, while difficult-to-understand terms can raise problems in any type of contract, they seem most likely to raise problems in contracts with monopolists.

It should be said that the difficulty inherent in understanding exemption clauses etc., is no guarantee that any particular clause of this kind is unreasonable. As we have seen, such clauses typically serve a useful purpose, and this is the case regardless of whether the contract involves consumers, monopolists, or whomever. Each clause must be evaluated individually, and this must be done (as has already been explained) in the context of the contract in which the clause is found. In this regard, it is important to remember that consumer choice is far more real and widespread than it used to be. When hostility to exemption clauses first surfaced in the middle of the last century, there was little competition with respect to many consumer goods. Moreover, it was nearly always difficult, if not impossible, for consumers to contract without agreeing to broad exemption clauses for the purchase of a very wide range of consumer goods and services—there was no

---

[37] See Ch. 3. And see also *R. & B. Customs Brokers Co. Ltd v. United Dominions Trust* [1988] 1 All ER 847 at 852, where, in discussing the application of an exclusion clause under the 1977 Act, Dillon LJ mentions in passing that the printed terms were brought to the claimant's attention though he did not trouble to read them.

question of buyers or consumers having the choice between two different sets of terms at different prices. But things have changed a great deal in this respect in recent years, so that buyers and consumers now often have a wide (and sometimes bewildering) range of choices. For instance, buyers of cars and consumer durables today can usually buy, as optional extras, an extended period of 'guarantee' cover, so that defects appearing in the goods for periods of up to five years may be repaired free of charge.[38] It remains only to add that the availability of these 'guarantees' (which are often insurance policies sold quite independently of the manufacturer of the goods) is not itself without problems. Many consumer bodies claim these guarantees are often sold at extortionate prices, and that consumers are not told of the differing guarantees which may be available, often at much lower cost. The problems associated with unfair surprises may therefore arise even in highly competitive markets.

6. THE FINANCIAL OMBUDSMAN

No discussion of 'fairness and contract law' in England can ignore the increasingly important role played by the Financial Ombudsman Service. The Ombudsman Service is a government agency that provides a dispute-resolution mechanism for consumers and small businesses who have complaints regarding 'financial products', such as mortgages, loans, pensions, insurance, and credit cards. Created by the Financial Services and Markets Act 2000, the Ombudsman is not a court, but it nonetheless has the court-like power to make decisions, including the ordering of damages (currently to a maximum of £100,000) and—of particular relevance to the present discussion—the power to declare that a contractual term is not binding. If the complainant is not happy with the decision, she can ignore it and go to court, but if she accepts the decision it will be binding on both her and the financial firm.

To date, the majority of the complaints handled by the Ombudsman (a number totalling nearly 100,000 in 2004) have alleged unfair *practices* rather than terms, in particular failures to disclose information and to properly advise consumers choosing financial products (as was discussed in Chapter 9). But it is clear that the Ombudsman has the authority to resolve disputes

---

[38] In today's market, legislation that prevents vendors from including certain kinds of exemption or limitation therefore sometimes has the effect of limiting consumer choice. An example is arguably the 2005 EU Regulation on Denied Boarding and Cancellations or Long Delays that requires airlines to compensate delayed or bumped passengers. This legislation will bear most heavily on the cheaper airlines, causing them to raise their prices and making it more difficult for them to compete with larger airlines. Yet it must be apparent to nearly all customers of such airlines that one reason prices are so low is that passengers bear the risk of getting delayed etc. Most passengers appear happy to put up with this risk in return for a cheaper ticket.

concerning the fairness of terms in contracts for financial products. Thus, in one group of cases, the Ombudsman ruled that limitation-of-liability clauses in contracts for the transfer of money abroad were unfair and so not binding. The Ombudsman does not produce 'decisions', but its 'reports' suggest that its rulings will closely follow the standards in the Unfair Contract Terms Act 1977 and the Unfair Terms in Consumers Contracts Regulations 1999. In its report on the money transfer cases, the Ombudsman stated explicitly that the clauses in question did not satisfy the test for 'reasonableness' in the Regulations; it is important to bear in mind, however, that the Ombudsman is not required to decide on the basis of legal principles—decisions are to be made on the basis of what is 'fair and equitable' in the circumstances. In the discussion of duties of disclosure in Chapter 9, it was noted that the Ombudsman holds firms to duties that are significantly more onerous than those contemplated by the common law. It is possible, therefore, that the Ombudsman will adopt a broader definition of 'unfair' than that found in the 1977 Act or 1999 Regulations. And even if this is not done, the Ombudsman may expand the scope of relief from that contemplated by the Act and Regulations by virtue of the fact that complaints may be brought by small businesses (in addition to consumers) and in respect of *any* kind of contractual term.

The Ombudsman Service is also important when considering the scope of relief for unconscionability in English law. The general idea that arrangements can be set aside if they involve one party 'taking advantage' of another's vulnerability (e.g. cognitive weakness, lack of choice) finds clear support in the rulings of the Ombudsman. Indeed, the rulings regarding firms' duties to disclose information and properly advise consumers (as discussed in Chapter 9) suggest that financial firms must take into account their customers' interests to an extent far beyond that contemplated by any concept of relief for unconscionability. Even very mild forms of 'advantage-taking', such as the selling of a mortgage endowment policy to a consumer who, through no fault of the firm, did not completely understand the risks involved, have led to rulings against financial firms. In the field of contracts for financial products, then, there is no question that broad relief is available for unconscionable terms, even if it is not strictly 'legal' relief.

Part IV

Enforcement of the Contract

13

Third Parties

I. THE DISTINCTION BETWEEN CONTRACT AND PROPERTY

UNTIL very recently, it has been a fundamental principle of English law—known as the doctrine of 'privity of contract'—that only the parties to a contract (the offeror and the offeree) may sue or be sued upon the contract. Indeed, this principle has long been regarded as a distinguishing feature between the law of contract and the law of property. True proprietary rights are 'binding on the world' in the lawyer's traditional phrase. Contractual rights, on the other hand, are (in the traditional law) only binding on, and enforceable by, the immediate parties to the contract.

The passing of the Contracts (Rights of Third Parties) Act 1999 fundamentally changed the law in this area. The 1999 Act makes it possible for third parties to a contract to obtain rights under the contract provided this was the intention of the contracting parties. But it must be stressed that the 1999 Act by no means does away with the entirety of the older law on third parties. In most contractual situations, the contracting parties do not intend to confer rights on third parties, and so the rights of such parties will continue to be governed by the traditional law—and by the common law rules and techniques that have been developed as exceptions to the rule that third parties have no rights or as means of avoiding the rule's effects. Nor does the Act supersede various legislative exceptions to the privity doctrine, many of which provide third parties with more extensive rights than are found in the 1999 Act. More generally, various aspects of the relationship between contractual principles and extra-contractual principles, in particular tort law principles, cannot be properly understood except against the background of the traditional doctrine. Finally, the 1999 Act only modifies that part of the traditional doctrine which states a contract cannot confer *rights* on a third party; it leaves intact the rule that a contract cannot impose duties on a third party. For these reasons, it will be necessary to discuss the general or 'traditional' law in this area in some detail before examining the 1999 Act.

It is, of course, not true, even under the traditional law, that a contract can never have an indirect *effect* on the rights or obligations of third parties. For instance, the obligations of a guarantor are affected by what happens between the creditor and the debtor. If the debtor pays the debt, the guarantor derives a benefit in that he will not have to pay the same debt; if the creditor and debtor vary the debt by a new contract, the guarantor may be discharged from liability. So too, an insurer may be affected by a contract between his insured and a third party; for instance the insurer may have no rights of subrogation if the insured has contracted with a third party in such terms as to exclude that party's liability for damage. Or again, the right of a claimant to sue in tort under the doctrine of vicarious liability may depend on the terms of the contract between the tortfeasor and the defendant. The doctrine of privity is narrower than this: it states that, prima facie, a person cannot enforce a right arising under a contract if he was no party to it, even if it was intended that he should have such a right. Likewise, a person cannot have any obligations enforced against him if the obligations arise under a contract to which he was no party.

Third parties and representatives of a second party

In the modern law, all contracts, save those of a highly personal nature, can be enforced by or against a party's personal representatives, i.e. his executors or administrators, in the event of his death. And in the event of a debtor's insolvency, contractual duties can generally be enforced by a trustee in bankruptcy (or company liquidator) and, to the extent of the assets in his hands, against him. Lawyers are so accustomed to these cases that they are inclined to regard personal representatives and trustees in bankruptcy as not being third parties at all. Their rights are derivative, and they are merely representatives of the second party. Nonetheless, these are examples of cases in which contracts are enforceable against someone who was not literally a party to them.

Third parties and security

It is common for goods to be bought in such a way as to leave a proprietary right in the unpaid seller as security for the price under a 'retention of title' clause; and it is, of course, even more common for mortgages or charges over property to be given by a debtor in such a way as to confer proprietary rights on the creditor. In the event of the debtor becoming insolvent, his ordinary creditors will then find that their rights to the debtor's assets turn upon a detailed examination of the contract between the debtor and the party claiming the proprietary right—a contract to which the other creditors are, of course, not party. In one sense this is simply a result of the law of securities— it has long been recognized that a debtor can grant a mortgage or charge over his assets so that the other party obtains priority over that property in the event of insolvency. What has not always been recognized is that freedom of contract makes it easy to manipulate the rules relating to property rights between a debtor and a creditor so as to give the creditor such priority, even in circumstances where other parties may not have any warning or notice of what has been done. In such a case, the rules of privity are actually evaded in circumstances in which there is a case for their application: third parties are held bound by clauses in contracts to which they are not parties.

Third parties and property law

There are other kinds of contracts that appear to bridge the gulf between contract and property, especially in connection with land law. For example, a contract to buy or rent land has itself become, over the years, something in the nature of a proprietary interest in land. Originally such contracts became enforceable against third parties when they had notice of them, but this requirement has been replaced by a system of registration. If the contract is registered it becomes virtually as good as an actual transfer, that is, a conveyance of the land. More recently mere licences, hitherto always thought to be purely contractual in their nature, were added to the list of interests in land that could be enforced against third parties, and (at least in some cases) thus crossed the bridge between contract and property.

Leases are a striking instance of the interplay between contract and property conceptions. When two parties execute a lease they enter into certain obligations of a contractual nature, such as the obligation to pay rent on the one hand, and the obligation to allow the tenant possession on the other. However, these obligations are of a somewhat impersonal nature since they are intended to be effective, not so much between the particular parties concerned, as between the landlord and tenant for the time being—the individual identities of the parties are immaterial from this perspective. Hence, from a very early date it came to be recognized that obligations of this kind 'run with the land'. If the tenant assigns his lease (but not if he merely sublets) the new tenant can be sued for the rent by the landlord and if the landlord sells the freehold, the new landlord can sue, or be sued by the tenant, whether he is the original party or an assignee. These old principles were reaffirmed and applied by the House of Lords to the case of a guarantor of the rent of a tenancy, the freehold of which was sold to new buyers. It was held that the buyers—the new landlords—were entitled to the benefit of the guarantee, and could sue the guarantor even though they were not strictly parties to the same contract.[1]

While the law of leases seems largely proprietary, it retains a handful of provisions that indicate the contractual origin of many leasehold rights. For instance, a lessee of a long lease who 'sells' her lease is in law 'assigning' the contract; but such an assignation does not discharge her contractual duties, because these duties are thought to be personal matters arising out of the contract. So the result is that although the assignee (or 'buyer') of the lease becomes the person primarily responsible for performing the tenant's duties under the lease (such as paying the rent) the assignor remains liable in the background as a sort of guarantor. If the assignee becomes insolvent the

---

[1] P. & A. Swift Investments v. Combined English Stores Group [1989] AC 643; see too Coronation Street Industrial Properties Ltd v. Ingall Industries plc [1989] 1 All ER 979.

assignor may be sued—and that remains the position even if (as is usually the case) the landlord retains the right to veto an assignment if she is dubious about the assignee's business reputation. Tenants who have assigned long-term leases are sometimes shocked to discover this liability being enforced against them on the insolvency of the assignee.

The general principle of privity

Despite the preceding observations, the general principle remains that a contract can be enforced neither by nor against third parties. In *Tweddle v. Atkinson*,[2] which is generally taken as the starting point of the modern doctrine, the fathers of an engaged couple contracted with each other to pay some money to the son on the marriage taking place, and it was held that the contract could not be enforced by the son. In *Beswick v. Beswick*[3] this principle was reaffirmed in a case of classic simplicity. In this case a man sold his business to his nephew, who agreed in return to pay an annuity of £5 per week to the seller's widow after the seller's death. It was held that the widow could not enforce this contract in her personal capacity because she was no party to it. But, as we shall see shortly, the widow was able to enforce the promise in another capacity.

The privity doctrine has been much criticised, but it has never been suggested that individuals should generally be allowed to enforce contracts to which they are not a party. I may have a keen interest in my neighbour's renovations, but this has never been thought a good reason to allow me to sue the contractor hired by my neighbour if he breaches his contract. It would be intolerable, indeed absurd, if just anyone were allowed to enforce any contract. It would also be inconsistent with the basic nature of promises and agreements. Promises are not made to the world, but to particular persons—promisees. When a promise is made, it creates a special relationship between the promisor and the promisee; the promisee is meant to treat the promisee's interests as 'special' in the sense that they have a superior claim upon him than do the interests of the general public (at least as regards the subject of the promise). By definition, this kind of special relationship cannot be created with just anyone. The promisor's duty to perform is owed to the person to whom it is undertaken, the promisee.

This feature of promises and agreements is well-understood by most people and, indeed, is consistent with the intentions of most contracting parties. There are many complex commercial relationships between groups of business parties where there is never any intention that rights should be conferred across the contractual boundaries. For instance, to take a simple case, manufacturers often sell goods to wholesalers, who in turn resell the goods to retailers, who in turn resell to members of the public. So there may

---

[2] (1861) 1 B & S 393.   [3] [1968] AC 58.

be four parties to the distributional chain (and often a great many more), but there is rarely any intention to afford contractual rights except as between each pair of contracting parties. The privity rule, which ensures that the ultimate buyer (the consumer) has no direct contractual rights against the manufacturer, is thus consistent with the parties' intentions. A similar story could be told of many complex building and engineering contracts. Here there is usually a main contractor who enters into the primary contract with the client or owner. The main contractor then subcontracts parts of the work to many different, often specialized, firms. For instance, the plumbing, electrical, or plastering work may be subcontracted. In complex cases, the owner often nominates the sub-contractors, but for the most part he does not contract directly with them. Here, too, the parties intend, for good business reasons, to ensure there are no rights that cut across the different contracts. Indeed, the arrangements they make often seem deliberately designed to insulate some parties from others, so as to ensure they do *not* enjoy privity of contract between them. Of course there is nothing sacred about these intentions, and statute here, as elsewhere, can tear down a carefully constructed set of business arrangements. For instance, under the Package Travel, Package Holidays and Package Tours Regulations 1992 a holiday tour operator can in certain circumstances be liable to a consumer for the defaults of hotels or airlines, even though the tour operator claims to act solely as agent and disclaims liability for these defaults. But, in general, it would be undesirable for the law to grant contractual rights to third parties where the parties to the contract did not themselves intend this result.

This is not to deny that in many cases in which the privity rule has been applied the result appears unjust. In most of these cases, however, it is not obvious that it is the privity rule that is actually the cause of the problem. One situation in which the privity rule is thought to cause difficulties is where the promise is made with the understanding that a particular third party will rely upon it, and then the third party does indeed rely. This may have been what happened in *Tweddle v. Atkinson*; the promise may have been made in order to induce the son to marry the daughter. In such a case, the son's complaint is essentially that he was induced to rely to his detriment (though on the facts it would have been difficult to establish that the act done in reliance—getting married—was a detriment). This is properly a claim in estoppel or detrimental reliance. Were it not for the (much criticized) rule that estoppel may only be used a defence,[4] many third parties would be able to make claims on this basis. If the law wishes to allow such claims, it should, therefore, introduce reforms to the doctrine of estoppel, not privity.

---

[4] Above, 124ff.

A second problem that arises in many privity cases is that the promisor is unjustly enriched. In *Beswick v. Beswick*,[5] which was referred to above, the price for the business that was sold to the nephew was the nephew's promise to pay the annuity. The nephew's failure to make these payments left him unjustly enriched; he retained ownership of a business that had been transferred to him on the condition that, inter alia, he pay an annuity to the wife. But under the current law a claim in unjust enrichment by the husband's estate would only be allowed if the nephew failed to pay *any* of the price for the business; there must be, it is said, a 'total failure of consideration'. On the facts this condition was not met because Peter Beswick's estate had actually received part of the price promised in exchange for the business. This conclusion seems unfair but the culprit is not the privity doctrine—it is the (much criticised) 'total failure of consideration' limitation on claims in unjust enrichment.

Finally, in a number of privity cases, the problems appear to stem from difficulties in the law of wills and estates and, more generally, in difficulties associated with laws that give effect (or fail to give effect) to individuals' intentions after they die. In *White v. Jones*,[6] solicitors negligently failed to amend a father's will, with the result that, when he died, his daughters did not benefit as he had intended. The privity rule meant that the daughters could not sue the solicitors in contract (though they succeeded on other grounds, as will be explained below). But the underlying cause of the daughters' problem was that, despite their father's expressed intention to change his will, he had not yet complied with the formalities for doing so. As was discussed in Chapter 4, formal requirements of validity frequently lead to just this kind of result. By their nature, they can prevent courts from giving effect to parties' intentions. This is the reason that courts and legislatures often create exceptions to formal requirements. Such an exception might indeed be appropriate for cases like *White v. Jones*—but if this is done the exception will be to the law on wills, not the law of privity.

The difficulties typically associated with the traditional privity doctrine are therefore often, perhaps usually, difficulties that arise not because of the privity doctrine, but because of other (controversial) restrictions on recovery in contract, tort, unjust enrichment, etc. At the same time, it must be acknowledged that third parties and contracting parties alike are often rudely surprised when they discover that a contract that was intended to confer legal rights on a third party is not recognized by the courts as having this effect. Admittedly, whenever contracting parties have such an intention, they can, even under the old law, confer legal rights on the third party by entering into a separate, collateral contract with that party (perhaps in exchange for nominal consideration). Such contracts are nearly always possible. In

---

[5] Above n. 3.   [6] [1993] 3 WLR 730.

practice, however, it can be time-consuming and expensive to draw up additional contracts. The question thus arises: why not allow the contracting parties to do this directly, in the original contract? No one will be harmed, except perhaps the lawyers who will no longer be able collect fees for drawing up additional contracts.

As we will see, the Contract (Rights of Third Parties) Act 1999 allows contracting parties who want to confer legal rights on third parties to do so directly, without entering additional contracts. But before turning to this Act, it is necessary to examine various rules and techniques that courts, legislatures, and contracting parties have developed over the years to protect third parties from the kinds of problems described above. The breadth and variety of these rules and techniques is such that, even before the 1999 Act, there were few circumstances of practical importance in which the privity principle (or any of other doctrines mentioned earlier) was liable to cause serious injustice or inconvenience. Exceptional cases aside, the objections to the old law rested largely on its form, and the lack of uniformity and consistency, rather than on the actual results of the cases.

2. ENFORCEMENT BY THE PROMISEE

Although the principle of privity of contract has traditionally prevented a third party from enforcing in his own name a contract intended for his benefit, there are situations in which the promisee may enforce the contract on behalf of, and for the benefit of, the third party. In particular, the promisee may be able to obtain a decree of specific performance (i.e. a court order directing the promisor to carry out his promise). In *Beswick v. Beswick*,[7] for example, it was held that the administrator of the seller's estate was entitled to sue for specific performance of the nephew's promise. It so happened that the widow herself was the administratrix of her husband's estate, and in that capacity she obtained a decree of specific performance compelling the nephew to perform his contract so as to deliver a benefit to her in a personal capacity. What was particularly striking about this decision was that one of the chief reasons given by the House of Lords for permitting the contract to be enforced by specific performance was that this might be the only way in which the contract could be enforced at all. Generally speaking, as we shall see in the next chapter, specific performance is not available where damages would be an adequate remedy; but it is arguable that in these privity cases damages may never be an adequate remedy because the third party cannot sue at all, and the promisee may not be able to obtain damages—a point considered further below. There are, however, other barriers to the availability

---

[7] Above n. 3.

of specific performance—for instance it is not available in the case of obligations to perform services—that limit its usefulness in this regard.

Even where the third party and the promisee are not represented by one party (as they were in the *Beswick* case), there are many cases in which the promisee can obtain specific performance on his behalf. If the promisee is in a close relationship with the third party (as he often will be) he may be willing to take proceedings on his own initiative. Even if he has no interest in doing this, the third party may still be able to sue in the name of the promisee. Provided that the third party is able to furnish satisfactory security to see that no liability (e.g. for costs) falls on the promisee, there will often be no reason why he should not give permission for his name to be used in litigation. The case may then be brought and conducted by the third party in all but name.

The only type of situation in which the promisee is likely to refuse permission in practice is where he himself has some interest in conflict with that of the third party. In this situation, the only possibility is for the third party to ask the court to compel the promisee to allow his name to be used in an action for specific performance. This approach (which mirrors the method by which assignments first came to be legally recognised) was suggested by Lord Denning in *Beswick*, but it has yet to receive judicial approval.

Whether the promisee can sue for *damages* to enforce a contractual right on behalf of a third party is (as presaged above) more difficult and controversial. The general rule is said to be that a claimant can obtain damages only for losses that he has personally suffered; he cannot recover for a third party's loss or expected profit. But it is almost inconceivable that the courts would deny all remedy to the promisee if the result were that the promisor could retain the benefits of the contract and be free from any sanction for non-performance. It is not surprising to find, therefore, that the courts have developed well recognized exceptions which permit damages to be recovered by a claimant on behalf of a third party in just such circumstances. For instance, an owner of goods who has been paid for damage done to them by an insurance company can sue on behalf of the insurer (and indeed the insurer can sue in the owner's name). Another exception that has been recognized by the House of Lords has the potential to apply to a wide range of situations.[8] In contracts for the sale of property (and perhaps also of services) where it is in the contemplation of the parties that the property or services will be transferred to a third party, if the buyer has resold the

---

[8] *Linden Garden Trust v. Lenesta Sludge Disposals* [1994] 1 AC 85. In *Darlington Borough Council v. Wiltshire Northern Ltd* [1995] 1 WLR 68, the Court of Appeal extended this principle to a case where there was no change in ownership. There are powerful dicta in Lord Griffiths' speech in *Linden Garden* arguing for a much wider exception on the ground that, wherever the promisor fails to perform, the promisee does suffer actual loss in that he does not receive that for which he bargained, even though the direct beneficiary of the performance would have been a third party.

property or services before it is discovered that the seller has been guilty of a breach of contract (e.g. by supplying defective goods), the buyer is still entitled to recover damages from the seller. The promisee's right to damages crystallizes at the moment of the breach and is unaffected by the later sale of the property, even though in strict law he has suffered no damage. Another exception is settled law as well: where a person sues for damages for breach of contract in respect of a 'family holiday', he can recover for his family's disappointment and inconvenience, as well as for his own.[9]

3. ASSIGNMENT

In the modern law there is nothing to prevent a contracting party assigning (transferring) to a third party specific contractual rights which are already in existence. Such assignment is a transfer, not a contract, and so once completed it is valid without the need for reciprocal consideration. Furthermore, the formalities necessary for such an assignment have been kept to a bare minimum. Although a written assignment and a written notification to the debtor (to inform him whom to pay) are necessary to transfer full legal title, even a verbal assignment will suffice to transfer equitable title. In practice this is almost as good as a legal title, the only important difference being that if the assignment is equitable, the assignor may have to be joined as a party to an action by the assignee against the debtor.

It would be unfair if the debtor was prejudiced by an assignment of contractual rights, and this gives rise to two important rules. First (as just noted) a debtor is not generally affected by an assignment of which he has no notice. Secondly, all assignments are subject to 'equities'. This means that the debtor will be entitled to plead against the assignee any defence which he may have against the assignor. For instance, if the debtor has a right of set-off against the original creditor he will be able to plead it against the assignee.

Not all contractual rights are assignable. Rights of an essentially personal nature, for instance, cannot be assigned at all. So an employer cannot assign the right to his employee's work to another. And it is also possible for a contract to declare specifically that any rights arising out of it are not to be assignable.[10] There are, too, some rules of public policy which declare void an assignment of a 'bare right of litigation'. Overall, though, ordinary money debts are usually assignable, for it can make little difference to a debtor to whom he has to pay the money. Indeed, even where it does make a difference, as where the creditor is a friend of the debtor who is likely to be indulgent to him, this does not prevent the debt being assigned.

---

[9] *Jackson v. Horizon Holidays Ltd* [1975] 1 WLR 1468, approved by the HL in *Woodar Investments Ltd v. Wimpey* [1980] 1 WLR 277.
[10] See the *Linden Garden Trust* case, above n. 8.

The law relating to assignment, like the whole law of privity, probably works smoothly enough in practice in the great majority of cases. Indeed, a large industry (known as factoring) has grown up which depends on the law of assignments, under which small traders assign debts to financial institutions, so as to receive cash today (at a discount, of course) instead of payment of the debt tomorrow. But the concepts with which the courts work to resolve assignment issues are exceedingly confused and technical. This is an area in which the notion of 'equitable' rights, distinct from and inferior to 'legal' rights, has survived despite the abolition, over a century ago, of separate rules of 'equity'.[11]

The fact that the law is prepared in principle to accept the simple assignability of contractual rights makes the doctrine of privity seem anomalous. If the law is prepared to allow a contracting party to transfer his rights, once created, to a third party, it is not clear why there is an objection to his creating the rights for the benefit of the third party in the first instance. For example, if A makes a contract with B under which B is to pay A £100 in return for certain services rendered by A, there is nothing to stop A forthwith assigning to C the right to receive the money. Once B has notice of the assignment, he must pay the money to C, and can be sued by him if he fails to do so. There seems, then, no reason why A should not be able to make the contract for the benefit of C in the first place. Of course, B could not be sued in any event, whether by A or by C, if the money has not yet been *earned*, or is not yet *due*; but once it is due, it is difficult to see the objection of principle to allowing C to sue.

The fact that assignments are generally so easily made means that privity can often be evaded by prior planning, though this will often require skilled legal advice—which must moreover be deployed before problems arise. But difficulties are now common as a result of contractual clauses declaring the benefit of the contract to be non-assignable. Suppose that a building is constructed by a builder for client A (who may be a mere developer), who intends to sell the completed building to client B. If defects show up in the building after it has been conveyed to B, does the latter possess any recourse? B cannot sue the builder in contract because of privity and it is now also established that he cannot sue the builder in tort for negligence. How can A and B try to ensure that B obtains some legal protection against the builder when he buys the property? In the absence of a prohibition against assignment of the contract, it is perfectly simple for A to sell the property together with an assignment of the contract. But it is often the case that builders insert prohibitions against assignment for legitimate commercial reasons. B's only

[11] A contemporary case which to some degree turned on a minute analysis of the distinction between a legal and an equitable assignment is *Deposit Protection Board v. Dalia* [1994] 1 All ER 539 (reversed with less reference to these questions [1994] 2 All ER 577).

remedy in this situation is to try to persuade A to bring suit in his own name against the builder (which is now possible as a result of the *Linden Garden Trust* case)[12] or, more realistically, to permit B to bring the action in A's name. To ensure that this will be possible the contract between A and B should therefore give B the right to enforce the contract by suing in A's name, while at the same time protecting A's interests by requiring B to give adequate security for costs. In this way the doctrine of privity can ultimately be overcome in this situation, though only with the aid of skilled legal advice.

4. AGENCY

English law recognizes a wide doctrine of agency, significant parts of which are irreconcilable with any strict application of the privity doctrine. Agency is a large subject in the law, and here we can do no more than make mention of how this idea has intersected with the law of contract.

A contract of agency may create two entirely different relationships. First, there is the relationship between the principal and the agent himself. This is simply a contract like any other contract, and the rights and duties of the parties between themselves are regulated by the express and implied terms of that contract. For instance, there is a term, implied by law, that the principal must reimburse the agent for any expenses incurred by him in the performance of his principal's business and, on the other hand, there is an implied term that the agent must strictly abide by his instructions, and must not exceed his authority.

For present purposes, however, we are concerned with the possibility that the agency may be created for the purpose of establishing a further relationship between the principal and a third party. A principal may, for instance, authorize an agent to do something on his behalf (including making a contract with a third party) without any consideration passing between the principal and the agent. If the agent makes a contract with a third party on behalf of his principal, that contract is regarded as having been made by the principal himself. Hence he can sue on it and be sued on it. So far it may be thought that there is no real breach of the principles of privity of contract, for when the agent avowedly acts on behalf of his principal it would be pedantic to insist that the principal is not really the contracting party.

However, the law does not stop at this point. In the normal case, the principal will have authorized the agent to make a contract (or a class of contracts), but the agent's power to bind his principal frequently extends beyond the authority that was actually delegated to him. In the absence of notice to the contrary, the third party is entitled to assume that the agent has

---

[12] Above n. 8.

the authority that an agent of that class usually has (usual authority). Further, she may assume that he possesses the authority that he 'appears to have' (apparent or ostensible authority), even if in the actual case the agent was specifically prohibited from making the contract in question. In that event, the agent can no doubt be sued by his principal for acting outside his actual authority, but that does not prevent the third party from holding the principal to the contract made by the agent. The underlying rationale in cases of this kind is close to the principle in which it is insisted that apparent intentions (rather than real ones) are the law's usual concern. A person may mislead the other contracting party either by saying or writing something in a misleading way, or he may mislead him by permitting his agent to appear to have authority which he does not have. In both cases, the underlying rationale for holding the principal liable probably depends on the fact that he has induced the reasonable reliance of the third party—it certainly cannot depend on the intentions or consent of the principal which, by hypothesis, do not exist in this situation. However, the principal himself can enforce the contract even if made in excess of the agent's authority provided that he ratifies the agent's action.

English law goes further yet in recognizing the 'undisclosed principal', that is to say it recognizes the right of a principal to enforce a contract in fact made on his behalf by an agent, even though the agent was not known to be acting for a principal. This is even more inconsistent with privity of contract, especially when viewed in light of the law's usually objective approach to questions of intentions. The third party may find that he has made a contract with a person of whom he has never heard, and with whom he never intended to contract. In a sense, the resulting contract is based on the subjective intention of the agent. However, as is the way with English law when it departs from principle, the departure is rarely pushed to inconvenient extremes. Thus the doctrine of the undisclosed principal is hedged about with certain limitations so as to safeguard the interests of the third party.

In the first place, the third party can always enforce the contract against the agent personally if he chooses. In the second place, the principal who seeks enforcement against the third party must prove that the agent had actual (and not merely usual or ostensible) authority to make the contract at the time it was made. Finally, the principal will not be able to enforce the contract if it is of a personal nature. Obviously, for instance, a person cannot agree to paint another's portrait and then explain that he was acting for an undisclosed principal. Less obviously, a person cannot normally make a contract with a third person by using an agent when this is merely a ruse to obtain something with which he knows the third party is not prepared to supply him. However, this will only be the case where the third party was justified in regarding personal considerations as important. But ordinary commercial contracts (for instance, insurance contracts) can usually be enforced by an undisclosed principal provided only that they were made by the agent intending his principal to have the benefit of the contract.[13]

Despite the breadth of the English law of agency, a third party cannot enforce a contract simply on the vague plea that it was made 'on his behalf'. He must prove that he actually authorized the alleged agent to make the contract on his behalf, or else that he ratified the agent's action, and this, as we have said, he cannot do unless the agent disclosed that he was acting for a principal when he made the contract. This means that many people, who in a commercial sense are called 'agents', are not strictly agents in the legal sense unless actual, apparent, or usual authority is proved in relation to some particular transaction. For example, the ordinary car dealer may be called a 'Ford agent' or a 'Toyota agent' but generally such dealers buy and resell cars as principals, not as agents, in the strict legal sense.

5. INSURANCE CONTRACTS

Even before the enactment of the Contracts (Rights of Third Parties) Act 1999, there existed numerous statutory exceptions to the rule that third parties cannot enforce contracts to which they are not parties. Here it will be sufficient to refer to a number of exceptions that are concerned with contracts of insurance. Thus, the Married Women's Property Act 1882 provides that a life insurance policy expressed to be taken out for the benefit of a wife or a husband or a child may be enforced by the beneficiary—indeed the policy in a sense *belongs* to the beneficiary. In such cases, rigid application of the traditional privity doctrine could lead to unfair, indeed absurd, results. But a policy taken out for any other person is still subject to the common-law rule—although its objectives can easily be met by assigning the policy to the beneficiary or by disposing of the proceeds of the policy by will. In this situation, the traditional privity rule may serve a useful purpose, because a person who insures her own life will normally be better advised to dispose of her policy by will than by naming a beneficiary in the policy. The use of a will leaves her as the owner of the policy, and this may be useful if she later wants to borrow on the security of the policy. Furthermore, if she leaves the policy to a named beneficiary in her will, she retains the right, which may be useful later, to revoke or vary the intended beneficiary.

Another case in which statute has intervened is in the field of road-traffic insurance. The scheme of compulsory third-party insurance which has existed in England since 1930 makes it imperative that an ordinary motor insurance policy should be enforceable by every person whom it purports to cover, notwithstanding that the driver may himself be no party to the contract of insurance. For instance, a lorry-driver is normally covered by an insurance policy taken out, not by himself, but by his employers. Obviously,

---

[13] *Siu Yin Kwon v. Eastern Insurance Co. Ltd* [1994] 1 All ER 213.

the intention is to give him a right to an indemnity if he should be held liable to pay damages for injuries caused in an accident; however, even though the policy may purport to cover anyone driving the vehicle with the consent of the owners, he could not enforce it at common law. This situation was met by the Road Traffic Act 1930 (now the Act of 1988), which permits the driver to enforce the contract directly against the insurance company.

The Road Traffic Act 1988 also allows a third party who has been injured in a road traffic accident to sue the driver's insurance company directly. Under the traditional law, the injured party is, of course, a stranger to the contract of insurance (he is the 'third party' after whom third-party insurance is named), and so would normally be debarred from pursuing this course. In the ordinary case, this would not matter very much because the injured person would claim against the driver, and the driver would claim an indemnity from the insurance company. In most cases, the claim would be negotiated and settled directly between the injured person (or her solicitors) on the one hand, and the insurance company on the other hand. If, however, the driver of the vehicle should happen to be insolvent, his creditors might attempt to intervene and claim a share of the damages which would be payable by the insurance company, while leaving the injured person to take a place in the queue, as it were, with the other creditors. This seemed unjust to Parliament, which accordingly enacted that the injured party should have (subject to various conditions) a right to sue the insurance company directly.

It should not be supposed that legislative exceptions of these kinds cover every situation in which it might have been thought desirable that the intended beneficiary of an insurance arrangement should be allowed to enforce the insurance contract directly. For instance, employers often take out insurance designed to provide accident or sickness benefits to their employees, and these cannot be enforced by the employees. A similar situation arises when retailers take out policies to insure against liabilities related to extended guarantees for consumer goods; these too cannot be enforced by the consumer.[14] The Australian High Court decided to abandon the principle of privity of contract in insurance cases, but the basis of the decision is unclear as a result of differences of opinion among the judges.[15] In England, some insurance contracts now fall within the scope of the 1999 Act, as will be explained below.

6. TRUSTS

It has already been mentioned that the law of trusts, being closely associated with the law of property, is not subject to all the restrictions of the privity

---

[14] The Insurance Ombudsman is likewise powerless to take on such cases.
[15] See *Trident General Insurance Co. Ltd v. McNiece Bros Pty Ltd* (1988) 165 CLR 107.

doctrine. So A and B can create a trust for the benefit of C without the participation of C at all. Indeed, it might happen that C is not even in existence when the trust is created, as frequently used to happen with the classic marriage settlement, where the beneficiaries would include the unborn children of the marriage. Nevertheless, such trusts were enforceable, and the doctrine of privity of contract was, and remains, irrelevant. The trust creates proprietary rights, so that the creation of the trust operates to transfer property rights to C, rather than to create merely personal rights in favour of C. Even if the trust is not completely constituted, so that it has to take effect as a contract, and not as an actual transfer of property (e.g. where the settlor merely covenants to transfer future property to the trustees, rather than making an actual transfer then and there), C will be able to enforce the trust if he is a child of the marriage in question. Despite his being a stranger to the contract and supplying no valuable consideration, he is said to be 'within the marriage consideration'. Any other person, however, who attempted to enforce an imperfectly constituted trust would be met by the plea that he was no party to the contract and had supplied no consideration.

Towards the end of the nineteenth century attempts were made to use the device of the trust as a general method to escape the doctrine of privity. Thus it came to be suggested that, whenever a contract purported to confer rights on third parties, the third parties could claim that a trust over such rights (a so-called 'trust of the promise') had been created in their favour, and could enforce their rights by way of trust. This was more or less the process by which assignments first came to be enforceable, for here also the common law at first refused to permit an assignee to sue on the contract because he was no party to it. In equity, the assignor came to be treated as a trustee for the assignee, and, once this result was reached, it became possible for the assignee to enforce the assignment himself. At first this had to be done in the name of the assignor, but after the Judicature Act 1873 even this was usually unnecessary.

For a time it looked as if a third party beneficiary might be treated in a similar way to an assignee. Specifically, there seemed to be a possibility that the third party would be able to enforce a contract by characterizing the promisee as a trustee. But in the twentieth century, the judicial attitude to this method of circumventing privity gradually hardened until it was almost rejected altogether.[16] While it is, of course, still open to a person to enforce a genuine trust of a contractual right without having been a party to its creation, it is no longer possible (unless the circumstances are wholly exceptional) to allege a fictitious trust merely as a device for the enforcement

---

[16] See especially *Re Schebsman* [1944] Ch. 83; *Vandepitte v. Preferred Accident Insurance Corp.* [1993] AC 70; *Green v. Russell* [1959] 2 QB 226. But in *Darlington v. Wiltshire*, above n. 8, the court showed some openness to applying the concept of a constructive trust (see below, 350) to privity cases.

of contractual rights by a third party. Moreover, although it may be possible to find that a genuine trust has been created without the word 'trust' having been used, the cases show that this is an unlikely eventuality.

It is no doubt correct that in most contracts made for the benefit of a third party the contracting parties did not intend to create a trust or (what amounts to the same thing) to create an arrangement with the same legal consequences of a trust. But the validity of the trust in English law shows that English courts are willing to recognize the possibility of individuals obtaining legally enforceable rights by virtue of consensual arrangements to which they were not a party. Indeed, in legal systems that do not recognize trusts, an English trust is generally regarded as a contract for the benefit of a third party.

It should also be noted that there are a number of situations in which the courts are still willing to impose a 'constructive' (or 'fictional') trust on parties who did not intend to make a trust; this is done in order to give the intended beneficiary of the arrangement the same protection she would have had under a genuine trust. For example, where husband and wife make 'mutual wills' under which they agree to leave all their property in an agreed way, it is possible (subject to various limitations) to enforce the arrangements after the death of one of the parties by means of a constructive trust.[17] One reason that courts have refused to take a similar approach in privity cases is that a trust, once constituted, is prima facie irrevocable except with the consent of the beneficiaries; and if some of the beneficiaries are under-age, or still unborn, it may be irrevocable altogether. If a contract between A and B which professes to confer rights on X is treated as creating a trust, it would follow (the courts have reasoned) that the contract was irrevocable as soon as it was made. So, for instance, if a man makes a contract with his employer that the employer will pay the employee's widow a pension if the employee dies in his employment after (say) twenty years' service, the courts have refused to treat the widow's claim to the pension as enforceable by way of trust.[18] The reason given for this is that the employer and the employee might have wanted to vary or rescind the pension arrangements.

Despite the courts' (sensible) concern that implying a trust in these situations would serve to render contractual terms irrevocable, there are at least two ways such a result could have been avoided. First, they could have held that a contract for the benefit of a third party does create a trust, but a revocable trust. The concept of a revocable trust is by no means unknown to the law;[19] and if it is legitimate to 'imply' a trust in order to do justice, there is no greater difficulty in 'implying' a power to revoke the trust for the same

---

[17] *Gray v. Perpetual Trustee Co. Ltd* [1928] AC 391; *Re Dale* [1993] 4 All ER 129.

[18] *Re Schebsman*, above n. 16.

[19] See, e.g., *Wilson v. Darling Island Stevedoring and Lighterage Co.* (1956) 95 CLR 43 at 67.

purpose. Alternatively, the courts could have held that the promisee holds the right of action to enforce the contract on trust for the third party. It is unnecessary to regard the contract itself as creating a trust in its inception; the need to invoke the concept of a trust only arises when enforcement is sought. At that date the third party could be treated as the beneficiary of a trust.

Thus, it can be seen that here, as so often in the law, results which appear to be dictated by the logic of legal principle are not so dictated at all. Legal rules can often be made to yield up a wide variety of results without any violation of fundamental principles; whether they do so or not depends to a large extent on the willingness of the courts to mould the law to new conditions. Sometimes—as in this area—the courts have taken the easy (one is tempted to say 'lazy') way out and refused to modify the law at all. On other occasions, in different areas of the law, the courts have been much more willing to adapt rules to new situations.

7. COMMERCIAL CASES

There are various situations in which, even prior to the 1999 Act, the doctrine of privity was overturned because it conflicts with common and well-accepted commercial practices. Thus one important exception to the privity rule is found in the law relating to negotiable instruments. Bills of exchange, promissory notes, and cheques, for instance, are generally negotiable, that is to say they may be passed from hand to hand (subject sometimes to endorsement) and they may be enforced against the original drawer by any holder in due course. So if A draws a cheque in favour of B, and B endorses the cheque in favour of C, C may sue A on the cheque if it is not met when presented to A's bank. And this is so notwithstanding that C was no party to the original transaction, and supplied no consideration to A. To avoid confusion, it should be added that the payee of an ordinary cheque acquires no rights against the bank on which the cheque is drawn: a cheque is regarded in law as a mandate or instruction by the drawer to his bank to pay the person named on it, or any person to whom it should be endorsed. The payee is not a third party beneficiary of the contract between the bank and the customer, nor is a cheque an assignment of funds held by the drawer in the bank.

Negotiability differs from assignment, with which it has obvious affinities, in at least two respects. In the first place no notice need be given of the transfer of a negotiable instrument and, in the second place, the transfer of such an instrument is not subject to 'equities'. Thus whereas assignors only transfer their rights subject to any defences which could be pleaded against them, the transfer of a negotiable instrument to someone in good faith, that is, without notice that there may be a problem, passes a good title, free from any such defences. For instance a person who receives a cheque in good faith obtains a good title, even though the cheque may have been stolen. It is not, of course, just any document which has the attributes of negotiability. Only those documents recognized by law or the custom of trade to be transferable by delivery (or endorsement) are negotiable. Other documents can only be transferred by assignment.

Another commercial situation in which the traditional privity rules were long ago by-passed concerns the transfer of bills of lading. When goods are consigned by sea, the consignor usually makes a contract with the carrier which is evidenced in a bill of lading. The transfer of the bill of lading to the consignee (and, sometimes, to other transferees such as sub-buyers) is treated as transferring the whole contract of carriage. This result was originally provided for by the Bills of Lading Act 1855, but is now found in the Carriage of Goods by Sea Act 1992.

8. PRIVITY AND THE LAW OF TORT

During the past half century or so, an enormous amount of litigation has centred on the relationship between the doctrine of privity and liability in tort, especially in negligence. In a nutshell, the essential question is whether courts can legitimately impose tort liabilities whose effect is to increase the burdens or obligations created by a contract. The problem is still giving rise to great difficulties, and it is not possible to treat the subject here with the full consideration it really requires. But while the question is usually treated as one for books on the law of tort, it is as much about contract as tort (indeed in some legal systems this question is answered primarily by contract law), so some discussion is desirable here.

The starting-point for this problem was a series of nineteenth-century cases in which actions were brought by claimants injured by goods made or repaired by the defendant, or by services supplied by the defendant under a contract with another party. One typical case was that in which defective goods were sold by A to B, and the defects caused injury to C. Another typical case was that of a railway passenger who bought a ticket from one company that allowed travel over a second company's lines; the traveller, while on the train of the second company, was then injured in an accident caused by their negligence. Did he have recourse in contract against the second company? For a long time the courts grappled uneasily with these cases, sensing that two fundamental principles were in conflict here. On the one hand, the defendant ought not be liable to compensate a claimant who was no party to the contract under which the goods or services in question were made or supplied. On the other hand, injured claimants ought not to be prejudiced in claiming damages by the terms of a contract to which they were not parties.

Eventually, as all lawyers know, this problem was settled (or was at least thought to have been settled) by the seminal decision in *Donoghue v. Steven-son*.[20] The case decided that the unfortunate consumer of the ginger beer with the snail in the bottle was entitled to sue the manufacturer for injuries suffered by her from drinking (and seeing) the unpleasant contents. It was a fallacy, said the House of Lords, to suppose that an inability to sue on a contract was a bar to suing in tort, particularly if the claimant had suffered injury to her person or her property. Furthermore, this analysis seemed supported by the fact that the standard of liability was different in the two cases. In tort, the defendant had to take reasonable care; but in contract her obligations were to do what the contract required, which might be different.

With the 'privity of contract fallacy' apparently disposed of, this branch of the law seemed now to have no connection with contract law at all. The decision in *Donoghue v. Stevenson* was gradually extended to all sorts of analogous situations, so that repairers, builders, professional people and others came to be covered by the rule. A duty to take care in tort even came to be regularly imposed *as between the parties*, in many contractual situations. Thus it came to be said that in many contractual relationships (especially those between professional persons and their clients) parallel duties of care existed in tort and in contract.[21] So the liability of a doctor or solicitor or other professional person was either in contract or in tort. This did not mean that a contractual exemption clause could be disregarded in a claim in tort—this expansion in two-party cases would have certainly been illegitimate—but it did mean, for example, that an action could be brought in tort even if the limitation period for contract was expired.

One consequence of this expansion of tort liability was that it became less imperative to expand contract law so as to accommodate new species of contractual liability. Without the expansion of tort principles, there might have been far more complaints about doctrines such as privity and consideration. For instance in the *Smith v. Eric S. Bush*[22] situation, where a building society client pays a fee for a mortgage survey to be conducted by an independent surveyor, strict application of contractual concepts leads to the conclusion that there is no contract between the client and the surveyor. But in that same case, the House of Lords held that the surveyor owed a duty of care *in tort* to the client.

Privity of contract and exemption clauses

The first real indication that privity issues had not been totally disposed of by *Donoghue v. Stevenson* did not come, perhaps, until the 1950s. A series of cases came before the courts in which attempts were made to bypass

---

[20] [1932] AC 562.
[21] *Henderson v. Merrett Syndicates Ltd* [1995] 2 AC 145.   [22] [1990] 1 AC 831.

contractual exemption clauses by suing third parties in tort. This was (it will be recalled) a time when exemption clauses in standardized contracts were coming to be viewed by courts with hostility. In this climate, many lawyers saw an opportunity to find a 'way round' the use of such clauses by invoking the privity principle. The Unfair Contract Terms Act 1977, which (as we have seen in Chapter 12) gives courts the power to regulate such clauses directly, had not yet been passed.

So, for instance, where a passenger travelling first class on a ship, was given a ticket exempting the company from all liability for personal injuries, even though caused by negligence, it was held that the shipping company's *employees* could still be sued for negligence in tort.[23] In this case, the contract in the ticket did not actually purport to protect the employees from liability, but it soon became clear that, even if it had, the result would have been no different. The same result was arrived at when a passenger with a free pass was injured on a bus by the negligence of the driver; although the pass stated that the holder would not make any claim for negligence against the driver, the court reasoned that the driver could not defend himself by relying on the terms of the pass—he was no party to the contract.[24]

Decisions of this kind may have produced acceptable results because the exemption clauses in question were arguably unfair. And nobody doubted that, notwithstanding that these actions were brought against employees, it would ultimately be the employer (or his insurer) who would pay. But this same approach was then applied, perhaps unthinkingly (or perhaps in the belief that rules must be applied whatever their origin or purpose), in various other circumstances where the result seemed much less acceptable. In particular, they were applied in cases of damage to property consigned by sea, where the bill of lading explicitly extended protection to third parties such as stevedores who load and unload ships.[25] In these circumstances, the use of exemption clauses was (and still is) widely regarded as acceptable. Goods consigned by sea are almost invariably insured, and the relations between carrier and owner are anyhow largely regulated by international conventions. If the stevedore is not entitled to be protected against liability for negligence, stevedore firms will have to insure against that liability, and hence charge more for their services. Quite possibly, this will increase the total insurance bill.

Perhaps as a result of such considerations, a means was found to give effect to exemption clauses in these circumstances. As we have already seen, in *The Eurymedon*[26] the Privy Council allowed a stevedore to rely on an exemption clause in a bill of lading on the basis, inter alia, that the carrier has acted as agent of the stevedore and that a unilateral contract had been created

---

[23] *Adler v. Dickson* [1955] 1 QB 158.   [24] *Gore v. Van der Lann* [1967] 2 QB 31.
[25] *Scruttons v. Midlands Silicones Ltd* [1962] AC 446.   [26] [1975] AC 154, above, 123.

between the stevedore and the owner. The result was welcomed and affirmed in subsequent cases dealing with bills of lading, but the reasoning seems dubious and has not been extended to other categories of cases. It should be stressed, therefore, that there is another, much simpler, basis on which exemption clauses whose terms extend to cover stevedores and similar third parties could be given effect.[27] Such clauses may be given effect, not as *contractual* terms, but as 'facts' that prove that the elements of the cause of action in tort are not satisfied. It is a basic principle of tort law that no action will lie where the claimant voluntarily assumed the risk of the relevant loss or injury. Such an assumption of risk may be proven in various ways, including proof that the claimant had said that he would not sue the claimant in respect of the relevant loss or injury. If I tell you that I will not sue you if you cause damage to my house by playing cricket, then (subject to the provisions of the Unfair Contract Terms Act 1977), I will be precluded from bringing any such action. An exemption of liability clause that purports to extent to third parties should in principle have the same effect as regards claims against such parties. It is in substance a statement, by the claimant, that he will not seek compensation from certain persons with respect to certain kinds of losses or injuries. Presuming that the third party falls within the terms of such a clause, the third party should be able to introduce the clause, in defence to a claim in tort, to prove that claimant voluntarily assumed the relevant risk. Thus, it would seem that the stevedores in *The Eurymedon* should have been able to argue that the owner, by agreeing to an exemption clause that precluded him from suing the stevedores, voluntarily assumed the risk of the stevedores' damaging the goods. It is true that the exemption clause was in a contract that, under the traditional law, the stevedores cannot enforce. But the stevedores would not be trying to enforce the exemption clause *as a contractual term*; they would merely be arguing that the duty of care necessary for a tort action did not exist. As we have seen in other contexts, a statement may have both contractual and extra-contractual effects. For example, a statement can qualify both as a term in a contract and an actionable misrepresentation. Even in two-party cases, the explanation why an exemption clause in a contract is a valid defence to an action in tort by one contracting party against the other must be that the elements of the cause of action in tort are not satisfied.

There will of course be situations where it is felt that the exemption clause is unfair and so should be ignored for this reason. But as we have seen, it is no longer necessary to invoke the privity rule to reach such a result: the Unfair Contract Terms Act 1977 (and now also the Unfair Terms in Consumer Contracts Regulations 1999) gives courts the power to invalidate exemption

----

[27] As first suggested by Lord Denning in *Midlands Silicone*, above n. 25.

clauses directly. It is irrelevant whether the clause is raised as a defence to a contract claim or as a defence to a tort claim.

The idea that exemption clauses can negate a duty of care in tort was effectively adopted by the Court of Appeal in *Norwich City Council v. Harvey.*[28] The claimant council had contracted for an extension of a municipal swimming pool with a builder under a contract which placed on the council the responsibility for fire damage and insurance against such damage. A fire was caused by the negligence of a sub-contractor who had contracted with the main contractor on the basis of the main contract. The council (or more probably, its insurers) sued the sub-contractors in tort for negligently causing the fire. The sub-contractors were not parties to the main contract, and the council was not a party to the second contract. But the Court of Appeal side-stepped the privity issues by holding that there was no duty of care, and hence no liability in negligence. There are also dicta indicating that, if the individual workmen employed by the sub-contractor who were responsible for the fire had been sued, they too would have been held to owe no duty of care in the circumstances. This seems a sensible result—there can be no liability in tort towards a claimant who has assumed the relevant liability— but for reasons that are not entirely clear, this reasoning has only received intermittent support in other cases.[29] In Canada, where the issue was considered by that country's Supreme Court not long ago, the majority preferred to create an explicit exception to the privity doctrine for cases of this kind.[30]

Economic loss and privity of contract

Many modern tort cases have attempted to push the boundaries of tort law forward by claiming damages for economic loss for negligence. A claim for economic loss is often, perhaps usually, a claim based on a lost *expectation*, rather than any other kind of loss or injury to property to person. A person who claims he has suffered economic loss usually means that he has not been able to obtain certain benefits which he expected to obtain. But the protection of expectations is generally the province of contract law; it is because a contracting party has a *right* to the (future) performance of the contract that he generally has a right to have his expected profits protected by the law. Tort claimants do not have such extensive rights; in principle, they are only entitled to protection against their already existing rights to their persons, property, and liberty. This distinction is well established in the law of damages—tort damages seeks to put the claimant in the position he was in *before* the tort—although it has been somewhat obscured by the fact that so

---

[28] [1989] 1 All ER 1180.

[29] See, e.g., *Pacific Associates Inc. v. Baxter* [1990] 1 QB 93. See also *K.H. Enterprise v. Pioneer Container* [1994] 2 AC 324, where somewhat similar reasoning was adopted in a case dealing with bailment.

[30] *London Drugs Ltd v. Kuehne & Nagel International Ltd* (1992) 97 DLR (4th) 261.

many tort claims are personal injury claims in which damages to put the claimant back in the position he was in before he was injured actually include damages for his lost expected earnings

The rules on the recovery of economic loss in tort are by no means consistent, but in broad terms they reflect the above distinction, and with it the traditional privity doctrine.[31] The most important category of negligence in which a claim for pure economic loss is permitted—the tort of negligent misrepresentation—is very close to contractual liability. Of course, many misrepresentations are made between persons whose relationships are not at all close to contractual. But not all misrepresentations are actionable. The law in this area is extremely complex but, in brief, the House of Lords has held that there is only liability where there is sufficient *proximity* between claimant and defendant.[32] 'Proximity', in turn, has been defined in ways that are immediately suggestive of ideas related to the law of contract. Thus, it has been said that there must be an 'assumption of responsibility' or that there must be 'reasonable reliance' by the claimant on the defendant or—more explicitly yet—that the parties' relationship must be 'close to contract'. All of these ideas were introduced in the first and still most important case to have recognised the tort of negligent misrepresentation—*Hedley Byrne & Co. Ltd v. Heller & Partners Ltd*[33]—and they have been repeated, with small variations in emphasis, in nearly every important case since. In *Hedley Byrne* itself, the defendant bank had negligently given a misleading reference to the claimants who were not customers of the bank, at the request of a third party who was a customer. The House of Lords held that the bank would have been liable in tort but for a disclaimer in the reference. Clearly this case is very close to contract; indeed, in many legal systems the claimants would have been entitled to sue in contract.

On the other hand, in various cases dealing with 'chains' of contracts, the courts have, after some uncertainty, denied liability in tort where to do so would unduly intrude into the sphere of contractual relations. In building and engineering contracts, a long-established practice exists under which the owner or client contracts with a main contractor, who in turn enters into contracts with sub-contractors. The latter may, in turn, buy goods for their sub-contracts from suppliers of their own. A single endeavour thus gives rise to a chain of contracts in which each party is contractually paired with another party immediately above or below. Despite the fact that the

---

[31] A notable exception is *White v. Jones*, above n. 6, where the House of Lords permitted the intended beneficiary of a will that failed to take effect because of the negligence of the testator's solicitor to recover against the solicitor in tort. As was explained earlier, this decision is best explained as an essentially ad hoc response to the injustices that can sometimes be caused by the stringent formalities for creating a will.

[32] *Caparo Industries v. Dickman* [1992] 2 AC 605.

[33] [1964] AC 465.

successful execution of the overall project relies upon the successful execution of every individual contract, the law has long held that privity of contract does not exist between one pair of parties and others who are higher or lower on the chain. This established tradition was upset by a decision of the House of Lords, *Junior Books Ltd v. Veitchi Bros*,[34] in which the owner of a building was permitted to sue a sub-contractor directly for the negligent construction of a floor. The floor was not dangerous and there was no damage to property in the ordinary sense—the floor was defective when built, but it did not damage other property of the claimant—so the claim was purely for the economic loss that arose from the cost of re-laying the defective floor. It was very much as though the claimant in *Donoghue v. Stevenson* had not actually drunk the ginger beer, but had sued the makers for the *value* of the (uncontaminated) ginger beer which she had expected to have. This decision, though, was subsequently overruled.[35] As was pointed out by Lord Brandon in his dissenting speech, it is impossible to see by what standard of care the sub-contractor's conduct was to be judged. In laying the floor he was carrying out a contract which may have imposed on him detailed require-ments as to how the floor should be laid. How, then, could he at once be under a contractual duty to his own co-contractor (the main contractor in the case), and also under a tort duty to the owners, the fulfilment of which might have conflicted with his contractual duty?

The current position is illustrated by *Simaan General Contracting Co. v. Pilkington Glass*.[36] Here the defendants supplied glass to a sub-contractor who installed it in a building which the claimants were erecting, as main contractors, in Abu Dhabi. The glass was not dangerous or faulty, but it was the wrong colour, according to the contract, and had to be replaced at considerable cost to the main contractor. The main contractor attempted to sue Pilkington Glass (the suppliers) directly in tort, but their claim failed. The proper procedure, insisted the Court of Appeal, was for the main con-tractor to sue the sub-contractor, who could claim against the supplier. In that way, the liability of each party would be determined by the contractual burdens he had undertaken, subject to any contractual defences available to him.

The same principle is applied to cases in which the claimants are not contracting for the construction of a building, but are buying already con-structed buildings. If the defects attributable to the builder physically injure the buyer (or anyone else), it is clear than an action lies against the builder under *Donoghue v. Stevenson*. But no action will lie against the builder in tort if the occupier is aware of the defect and fails to eliminate it; and certainly no action lies against the builder for the purely economic loss involved in the

---

[34] [1983] 1 AC 520.   [35] *D. & F. Estates Ltd v. Church Commissioners* [1989] AC 177.
[36] [1988] 1 All ER 791.

building being less valuable than was thought, or for the cost of repairs.[37] The explanation, in term of legal principle, is that the 'defect' has not actually caused any damage to the claimant's person or property. Expressed in policy terms, the justification is that allowing tort liability in such cases would encroach on contractual and privity principles. The buyer of a building is prima facie expected to satisfy himself that the building is worth what he pays, and if he has any concerns he should address those to the person selling the building and seek appropriate assurances. Although this result may seem harsh, and somewhat contrary to modern law's expansion of liability for negligence, there nonetheless seems no doubt that its rationale is ultimately based on the sound contractual idea that the price of anything in the market (buildings or goods) should reflect the risk of defects, except in so far as they are expressly or impliedly covered by warranties given by the seller himself.

Finally, the same principle is applied in cases involving the various kinds of contractual chains created between manufacturers, distributors, retailers, and purchasers of goods. Here also, the usual way of proceeding if the goods are defective is for the ultimate buyer or consumer to sue the retailer with whom he has contracted; the retailer may bring third-party proceedings against his supplier and so on, up the distributional chain to the ultimate manufacturer. There can be practical problems with this method of proceeding, especially where one of the intermediaries cannot be found, or is abroad, or is insolvent. But in cases involving claims for pure economic loss, it is now clear that, again, no liability will lie.[38] A person who buys defective goods can only sue the manufacturer for negligence if the defect causes physical damage to the person or property. If the only complaint concerns defects *in* the goods, there is no claim in tort. The claimant in *Donoghue v. Stevenson* could not have sued the manufacturers for the value of the ginger beer.

9. THE CONTRACTS (RIGHTS OF THIRD PARTIES) ACT 1999

The privity doctrine has long been criticized by academics, lawyers, judges, and law reform bodies. As has already been explained, many of these criticisms might more appropriately be directed against other legal doctrines, in particular consideration, offer and acceptance, and estoppel. We have also seen that there are so many exceptions to privity and so many ways of avoiding its effects that in practice the doctrine rarely leads to a serious injustice. Nonetheless, the current law can be confusing and complex, particularly for parties who are not well-advised. And even well-advised parties

---

[37] *Murphy v. Brentwood DC* [1991] 1 AC 398. But there is a limited statutory right against the builder of a *dwelling-house* for negligence under the Defective Premises Act 1972. There are also extra-legal compensation schemes to protect the buyers of relatively new houses (up to 10 years old) where defects subsequently develop.

[38] *D. & F. Estates*, above n. 35 and *Murphy v. Brentwood* DC [1991] 1 AC 398.

often find the law inconvenient because, while it is almost always possible to ensure, by one method or another, that third parties obtain legally enforceable rights, these methods can be costly and time-consuming.[39]

It is perhaps not surprising, therefore, that in 1999 Parliament acted on a Law Commission report[40] recommending reform of the privity doctrine. The basic effect of the Contracts (Rights of Third Parties) Act 1999 is to permit contracting parties who wish to confer enforceable rights on third parties to achieve this without the need to enter a collateral contract, trust, or other arrangement. More specifically, the Act provides that a contract will confer rights on a third party if it expressly provides for this result *or* if it purports to confer a benefit on the third party *and* it cannot be shown, on the proper construction of the contract, that the contracting parties did not intend the third party to have an enforceable right. In each case, the third party must be identified, but this can be done by class or description as an alternative to actually naming the party.

The intent requirement

The first method by which a contract may confer rights on third parties—by express provision—is straightforward, and unlikely to lead to difficulties in practice. In the ordinary case, it will be satisfied by words such as 'Jones [the third party] shall have the right to enforce provisions 8, 9, and 10 of this contract'.

The second method—the 'benefit' test—is more complex, but in essence does no more than to recognize that an intention to confer legal rights may be expressed implicitly as well as explicitly. This test was held satisfied in the first reported case on the 1999 Act, *Nisshin Shipping Co. Ltd* v. *Cleaves & Co. Ltd*,[41] where it was found that the clause commonly found in charter party agreements stipulating that the ship owner would pay the chartering broker's commission was enforceable by the broker despite his being a third party to that agreement.[42] In principle, this second method is entirely appropriate: the courts have long recognised, in a variety of contexts, that contractual intentions may be implicit or 'go without saying' in a document. There is no reason that an intention to confer a legal right on a third party should not be susceptible to proof of a similar nature. Of course, contracting parties who

---

[39] It is interesting to note that to date commercial parties appear to have made little use of the 1999 Act; instead, they have generally inserted boiler-plate clauses excluding any possible application of the Act to the contract.

[40] Law Commission No. 242, Privity of Contract: Contracts for the Benefit of Third Parties (1996).

[41] [2004] 1 Lloyd's Rep 38.

[42] The court further held that the fact that such clauses had previously been enforced by means of a 'trust of the promise', and thus that the parties might be understood to have intended to create such a trust, did not preclude the broker obtaining rights under the 1999 Act.

have taken legal advice and who wish to confer legal rights on a third party will almost always adopt the first method. But not all parties who have such an intention will be legally advised; the benefit test allows their intentions to be given effect even if they fail to spell them out explicitly.

A potential difficulty with the benefit test is that rather than simply stating that an intention to confer legal rights may be expressed explicitly or implicitly, the test introduces what is, in effect, a rebuttable presumption that such an intent exists wherever the contract 'purports' to confer a benefit on a third party. The difficulty is that there are many contracts that are clearly intended to *benefit* third parties, but which are just as clearly not intended to confer legal rights on such beneficiaries. For example, a contract in which a retailer promises a manufacturer to provide certain services to customers who purchase the manufacturer's good (e.g. to instruct customers in the use of the goods or to return goods to the manufacturer when repairs are required) purports to confer on a benefit on the customers, but it is unlikely the parties intended that the customers themselves should be able to enforce the contract. Admittedly, in cases of this kind the presumption will certainly be rebutted. Nonetheless, the presumption would appear to complicate unnecessarily the basic inquiry into whether the parties intended to confer legal rights on the third parties. Unless it is thought that third parties should obtain rights in some cases in which the parties *did not* intend this result, the presumption seems neither necessary nor useful.

Regardless of how the second limb of the intent requirement is interpreted, it is clear that the 1999 Act leaves most third parties with the same rights they had enjoyed under the traditional law. In most contracts that benefit third parties, the contracting parties do not intend to confer rights on those parties in either of the senses described above. As has already been mentioned, in an ordinary contract to build a school or a road there is no intent to grant citizens who would benefit from the school or the road legal rights. So too, the vast majority of cases involving chains of contracts, such as chains between different parties to a building project or to a sales distribution network, will be unaffected by the Act. The manufacturer who sells goods to a distributor does not intend to confer legal rights on the ultimate consumer. Even the result in a case such as *White v. Jones*[43] would be unaffected by the Act. In that case, the solicitor's duty to prepare a new will was for the benefit of the testator, not the intended beneficiaries under the new will. None of these consequences, it may be added, suggest that the Act was too timid in its reforms. Whatever problems such cases may be thought to present, it would be inappropriate to address them by granting contractual rights to third parties in situations where the contracting parties themselves never intended such a result.

[43] Above n. 6.

There are, of course, many situations in which the intent requirement of
the 1999 Act will be satisfied. Aside from cases where the parties expressly
stipulate that a third party has legal rights, perhaps the clearest examples are
cases in which the parties include an exemption or limitation of liability
clause which purports to extend to an identifiable third party. In such a case,
even if the parties do not expressly state that the third party has the right to
rely on such a clause, such an intention is obvious: exemption and limitation
clauses are meaningless except insofar as they have a legal effect. Third parties in cases like *The Eurymedon*,[44] for example, would therefore be protected
under the Act on the straightforward ground that the contracting parties
intended to grant them the legal benefit of the exemption clause. Another
common arrangement to which the Act will typically apply is where a contracting party agrees to indemnify a third party against legal liabilities, as
for instance where an owner promises a builder that he will indemnify the
builder's employees and any sub-contractors against possible claims arising
from a building project. Again, such an indemnity is almost meaningless
unless it is intended to have legal effect. Certain kinds of insurance contracts
would also almost certainly fall under the Act, even without an express
provision. An example would be where an employer obtains medical insurance for its employees. If the employer disappears or goes bankrupt in such a
case, the employees would be able, under the Act, to seek compensation
directly from the insurer. But not all insurance contracts will be interpreted
as intended to give rights to third parties; for example, a standard liability
insurance policy, such as a policy that indemnifies a homeowner against legal
claims, could not be enforced directly against the insurer by a person with a
claim against the homeowner.

Exclusions and limitations to the 1999 Act

The scope and force of the Act are limited in various ways aside from the
basic intent requirement. First, there are various categories of contracts or
terms in such contracts that are excluded in part or entirely from the Act's
provisions. These include contracts dealing with the articles of association
of a company, employment contracts, bills of exchange, promissory instruments, negotiable instruments, and contracts of carriage that are governed by
the Carriage of Goods by Sea Act 1992.

A second manner by which the effects of the Act are limited is with regard
to enforcement. While the third parties' rights to enforce the contract are in
general the same as if the third party were a true party to the contract—the
third party can obtain damages or specific performance according to
the ordinary contractual principles—these rights are subject to any defence

---

[44] Above n. 26.

or set-off that the defendant might have raised against the other party to the contract. Thus, a third party might be met with a defence of fraud, even where (unknown to the third party), the fraud was committed by the other contracting party.

The final, and most important, limitation of the Act is that third parties rights under a contract may be affected by variations to the contract. The Act provides that the contracting parties have the right to modify or terminate the contract, even if this disadvantages the third party, unless the third party has communicated his 'assent' to the contract or has 'relied' on its provisions. It is clear that the legislators were attempting, in this provision, to strike a compromise between preserving the ordinary freedom of contracting parties to vary their contracts and protecting the rights of third parties. Each limb of their solution is unobjectionable in substance, but taken together the assent and reliance 'triggers' suggest that the legislature could not make up their mind as to the underlying nature of the third parties' rights. The rule prohibiting variation after the third party has communicated his assent to the contract's terms suggests that the third parties' rights are essentially contractual. Although it is not entirely clear what 'assent' means in this context—assent is usually a synonym for 'agreement' or 'approval', yet there is nothing that a third party needs to agree to and it goes without saying that he would approve of receiving a benefit—the general idea, it seems clear, is that the third party is like an offeree, who must accept the offer in order for it to become binding. This interpretation is consistent with granting the third party contractual remedies.

But the rule prohibiting variations after the third party has *relied* on the contract suggests that the third party's rights are essentially extra-contractual. As we have seen, contracts are in principle binding regardless of whether they have been relied upon. Reliance is, however, an element in the cause of action for many tort claims, and is an essential requirement for claims of negligent or fraudulent misrepresentation. From this perspective, the purpose of the Act seems not so much to ensure that the contracting parties keep their promises, as that they do not carelessly or intentionally mislead third parties as to their intentions. This would be an entirely understandable objective for the Act: a standard criticism of the old law was that it failed to protect third parties who reasonably relied on the assumption that contracting parties would do what they said they would do. But it seems inconsistent with giving third parties contractual remedies.

A final observation is that the inconsistencies just noted are probably unavoidable in any reform that attempts to eliminate in a single piece of legislation the main problems associated with the privity doctrine. As was suggested earlier, many of these problems are in reality problems not with the privity doctrine, but with other areas of the law. Some of these areas are clearly part of contract law (e.g. problems in the law of consideration and offer and acceptance), and as such are solved by ensuring that third parties are treated as contracting parties. But others, such as the protection of detrimental reliance, seem more a part of tort law or some other extra-contractual basis of liability, and as such are solved by granting third parties what are essentially rights in tort. Any attempt to solve these different problems with a single reform is almost certain to exhibit a tension between contractual and extra-contractual principles.

10. ENFORCING CONTRACTUAL RIGHTS AGAINST THIRD PARTIES

The arguments in favour of allowing contracting parties to confer rights on third parties obviously do not apply to allowing them to impose *liabilities* on third parties. Naturally enough, it is generally speaking impossible for the parties to a contract to impose liabilities on third parties without their consent. However there are circumstances in which even this may be allowed.

Agency

One clear example of the law permitting contractual obligations to be enforced against third parties has already been mentioned in the earlier discussion of agency. As was explained then, the rules of agency provide that a principal may be liable on a contract made by an agent on his behalf, even though the agent has exceeded his actual authority.

Novation

Earlier in this chapter we discussed the assignment of rights, and observed that a relatively simple legal process can be used so as to transfer a contractual benefit or *right* to a third party. But the only way in which it is possible to transfer a contractual burden or *duty* to a third party is by the process of novation, which requires not just the consent of the person assuming the duty, but also the consent of the other party to the contract. Strictly, novation amounts to the extinction of the old obligation and the creation of a new one, rather than to the transfer of the obligation from one person to another. So if B owes A £100, and C owes B the same amount, B cannot transfer to C the legal duty of paying his debt to A without both C's and A's consents. But if A agrees to accept C as a debtor in place of B, and if C agrees to accept A as his creditor in place of B, the three parties may make a tripartite agreement to this effect, known as novation. The effect of this is to extinguish B's liability to A and create a new liability on the part of C. The requisite consents may be implied or inferred (or express), but it is sometimes difficult to decide whether a new debtor has been accepted by the creditor *in place* of the old debtor (which would be a novation) or as an additional source of payment, leaving the original debtor still liable if that source of payment fails to materialize. An assignment of a lease, even though the landlord's consent may be required (as is customary), is not in general treated as a novation; an assignment makes the assignee liable on the lease, but leaves the assignor also liable as a sort of guarantor. Similarly, where a buyer of goods in an international trade transaction agrees to pay the price with a banker's letter of credit, it is generally held that the bank's undertaking to pay does not displace the buyer's liability. If for some reason the bank fails to pay, the seller may still sue the buyer directly. But an interesting modern example of a genuine novation is provided by many credit-card transactions. Where a customer buys goods and pays for them with a credit card, it has been held that the obligation to pay the price is actually replaced by that of the credit-card company, with the implied consent of the seller.[45] So if the credit-card company fails to pay, the seller can no longer claim against the buyer.

The rule that the burden of a contract cannot be transferred except with the other party's consent can cause problems when an entire business changes hands (unless the change is carried through by selling the shares in a limited company). This is because the transaction may entail transferring many existing contracts by which the business is bound to its customers. It might, therefore, be necessary to obtain consent from these customers regarding the transfer. In the United States, such difficulties are largely avoided by the simple expedient of requiring the transferee of the business to promise to honour all existing contracts, and allowing the other parties to these contracts to sue the transferee on this promise. The interests of these other parties are safeguarded by the fact that the transferor of the business remains liable as a sort of guarantor or surety.

In England, it is possible sometimes to 'imply' a novation, as for example where a retiring partner in a firm is replaced by a new partner. Parties who continue to deal with the firm with knowledge of the change in partners may be held to have consented to an 'implied' novation whereby the old partner is replaced by the new one in any continuing contracts. There is also an important statutory exception to the above rule. Under the Transfer of Undertakings (Protection of Employment) Regulations 1981 (which were made to give effect to an EU Directive), contracts of employment are transferred in their entirety when the employer's business is transferred to a new owner. This is generally beneficial to the employee, which is presumably why his consent is dispensed with but, as originally drafted, the Regulations did not make any provision for cases in which the employee was prejudiced by the transfer—as, for instance, where he has no desire to work for the new employer, and yet would be bound by a severely restrictive covenant if he

---

[45] *Re Charge Card Services Ltd* [1989] Ch. 497. In some cases there is no prior obligation to pay in cash at all, because the seller has made it clear that he will accept payment by credit card from the outset.

left.[46] The Regulations have since been amended to make it clear that an employee cannot be transferred to a new employer if he objects, but in that event he is deemed not to have been dismissed by the transferor, and so cannot claim compensation for unfair dismissal.[47]

Obligations running with property

Just as the benefit of certain obligations (e.g. a landlord's right to receive rent) will 'run with the land' and be enforceable by the owner of the property for the time being, so also the burden of certain contracts may run with the property in the same way. In particular, contractual duties relating to land are frequently binding on anybody in possession of the land. This principle was established very early in regard to leases, with the result that landlords' and tenants' duties are generally enforceable against whoever happens to be landlord or tenant for the time being.

It was not until the middle of the nineteenth century that this principle was extended to cases of the sale of freehold land. In the famous case of *Tulk v. Moxhay*[48] it was held that a person who bought land with knowledge that the former owner had entered into a 'restrictive covenant' in respect of it (limiting the uses to which the land could be put) would be bound by the covenant. Since 1925 restrictive covenants can be registered, and registration has taken the place of the requirement of notice. Thus when a person agrees to buy land he, or his solicitor, will search the Register to discover if there are any covenants restricting the use to which the land may be put. An unregistered covenant will not be binding on him, while a registered covenant will be binding, whether he actually has notice or not. But the principle of *Tulk v. Moxhay* has been confined to restrictive or negative covenants. A covenant which imposes a positive obligation (such as a covenant to repair) does not run with freehold property and cannot be enforced against a buyer.[49]

It was perhaps inevitable that attempts should sooner or later be made to extend the principle of *Tulk v. Moxhay* to goods. The system of resale price maintenance provided the testing ground. This system (as we saw in Chapter 8) constituted an attempt on the part of manufacturers to lay down the minimum price at which their goods could be sold to the public. Since in most cases the goods were sold to the public by retailers who themselves bought, not from the manufacturers, but from wholesalers, it was apparent that the doctrine of privity of contract was a stumbling-block to the enforcement of

---

[46] It seems clear that this is indeed the result of the Regulations. See *Morris, Angel & Son Ltd v. Hollande* [1993] 3 All ER 569 where, however, the CA interpreted the covenant so as to restrict the employee from soliciting business from the transferor's customers, and not the transferee's.

[47] So the amendment would presumably not help an employee subject to a restrictive covenant as in the example described in the text.

[48] (1848) 2 Ph 774.

[49] Old law, but reaffirmed by the HL in *Rhone v. Stephens* [1994] 2 All ER 65.

resale price maintenance. Attempts were made, therefore, to persuade the courts to permit the manufacturer to sue the retailer directly, at least in cases where the latter had been notified about the price maintenance scheme. In particular, it was argued that the retailer was liable on the contract made between the manufacturer and the wholesaler on the principle of *Tulk v. Moxhay*. This argument was rejected by the courts,[50] and so the manufacturers resorted to other methods of enforcement, thought these were also eventually outlawed (as explained in Chapter 8).[51] Thus, while a purchaser of land is bound by a lease created by the seller, a purchaser of goods can generally disregard a contract already made between the vendor and a third party for the hire of the purchased goods. However, in 1926 the decision of the Privy Council in *Lord Strathcona SS Co. v. Dominion Coal Co*[52] extended the principle of *Tulk v. Moxhay* to the case of a ship. Here it was held that a person who buys a ship with notice that it has been let to a charterer for a fixed period is bound to respect the charter. The decision was criticised on the ground that the doctrine of *Tulk v. Moxhay* could only apply, for various reasons, to cases of land, but the case does not seem reasonable or unjust, and it is perhaps regrettable that its principle was later discarded by the High Court.[53]

There is no doubt that, even if correct, the *Strathcona* principle should be carefully confined to cases involving goods of exceptional value and importance. One situation in which it might be desirable to extend the principle is to the common arrangements whereby large business concerns hire (or 'lease') plant, equipment, and vehicles on a substantial scale. Serious practical problems can arise if such contracts are treated as creating only 'personal' rather than 'proprietary' rights. If, for example, A hires a fleet of lorries on a long-term basis from B, and then B sells its business to C, it would be absurd if C could demand immediate possession of the lorries from A. Not only is this result unreasonable from A's perspective, it could make it difficult for a business like B's to be sold at all. B may wish to ensure that, after the sale of its business, its old customers' rights to the continued use of their fleets of lorries are respected, and it may insert into the sale contract with C a clause insisting that C will respect those contracts; however, such a clause would make no difference to the relationship between A and C. There is still the privity gap, and A cannot prevent C demanding the return of its lorries. Of course, this might very well be a breach of contract on the part of B (which remains liable to pay damages despite the sale of its business), and B

---

[50] *McGruther v. Pitcher* [1904] 2 Ch 306. For a summary and restatement of the law in this area, see *Swiss Bank Corporation v. Lloyd's Bank Ltd* [1979] Ch 548.

[51] The same result was reached in cases where the goods were hired rather than sold.

[52] [1926] AC 108.

[53] *Port Line Ltd v. Ben Line Steamers* [1958] 2 QB 146. See also *Law Debenture Trust Corp. v. Ural Caspian Oil Corp.* [1993] 1 WLR 138.

may in turn be able to claim an indemnity against that liability in damages from C which has thus violated the specific clause in the contract requiring it to honour existing hire contracts. But to recognise that A has a right to damages from B in this situation might not be an adequate substitute for an enforceable right to retain the lorries themselves. The only way out of this difficulty is for B to require, as a part of its arrangements for the sale of the business to C, that C should enter into direct contractual arrangements with the existing clients, like A, to honour their contracts.

Other ways of enforcing obligations against third parties

We saw earlier in this chapter that efforts have been made in many cases to enable third parties to a contract to sue one of the parties in tort, thereby evading the privity principle that a contract cannot be enforced *by* third parties. It should come as no surprise that similar attempts have been made to overcome the rule that contractual burdens cannot be enforced *against* third parties. These attempts have also generally taken the form of trying to invoke tort law against third parties, though (more successful) attempts have been made to use other branches of the law for this purpose.

One possible way of trying to enforce contractual obligations against third parties is to argue that these obligations must not be interfered with by other people—that there is a general duty, enforceable in tort, not to interfere with the contracts of other parties. In 1853 it was decided for the first time that a person who persuades a party to a contract to break that contract may be sued by the other contracting party for damages in tort.[54] During the last fifty years or so the tort of 'inducing breach of contract' has been developed and elaborated by the courts and its principles may now be stated with reasonable confidence. The vital element in this tort is knowledge by the defendant of the contract when he induced one party to break it. If this is established, the defendant will be liable unless he can set up some reasonable justification for his act.

In one sense there is no doubt that the recognition of this tort creates something akin to a further exception to the doctrine of privity of contract. In particular there seems no reason why it should not be invoked in the cases of hire or charter discussed in the last section. If A makes a contract to charter his ship to B, there is no doubt that C will be liable to B if, knowing of the charter, he persuades A to sell the ship to X who does not intend to honour the charter. Is there any reason, then, why he should not be liable if he buys the ship himself, and proceeds to renounce the charter for his own benefit? There are, in fact, some cases which come very close to deciding just this, and it remains possible that the *Strathcona* case (or one like it) will come to be justified on grounds such as these.

---

[54] *Lumley v. Gye* (1853) 2 E & B 216.

The tort of inducing breach of contract is, of course, only applicable to cases in which there has been an *inducement* to breach a contract. Merely committing an act that makes it impossible or more costly for a contracting party to perform a contract or which diminishes the benefit of a contract does not qualify as the tort of inducing a breach of contract, even if it is done carelessly. This does not mean that the general tort of negligence could not in theory be extended to cover claims where the only loss suffered arises from some harm to the claimant's contract with a third party. Contractual rights could be treated, for the purposes of such claims, like ordinary property rights. But as was noted earlier in this chapter, claims for 'pure economic loss' (of which this is a clear example) are not permitted under English law. As a general rule, the only way in which harm to contractual rights can form the basis for a claim in negligence for damages is where this harm has arisen from a loss or injury to the claimant's person or property. A charterer of a ship cannot sue a third party for damages for negligence which has resulted in damage to the ship.[55] Nor can a lorry driver bring an action against a motorist for negligently causing an accident on the motorway that has caused the driver to be late for a delivery, in breach of his contract. Various possible justifications for this rule have been suggested, but perhaps the most important goes back to the very foundations of the privity doctrine: contracts create personal rights, not property rights. It is the promisor, alone, who has a duty to perform the contractual promise, and it is to the promisor, therefore, that the promisee should first turn if this duty has not been performed. In theory, then, if the promisee wishes to obtain protection against a third party harming his contractual rights he should attempt to obtain such rights either from the promisor or make an agreement with the third party.

There is a second situation in which the law has long allowed obligations to be enforced against third parties, even though those obligations appear to be of a contractual nature. Where information is given in confidence to one person, on the express or implied understanding that it is not to be divulged to anyone else, a third party who obtains the information with knowledge that it is confidential can be restrained by injunction from repeating it, or making use of it.[56] This principle is treated by lawyers as neither contractual, nor tortious, nor proprietary, but as arising from the equitable principles governing breach of confidence. This is, however, mere labelling. In fact, the principles governing these cases are very close to contractual principles, because it is necessary to show that the information was given to someone who expressly or impliedly agreed to keep it confidential. This is not treated

---

[55] *Candlewood Navigation v. Mitsui Lines* [1986] AC 1 is the leading modern case, but there are many others.

[56] The origin of this jurisdiction goes back to *Prince Albert v. Strange* (1849) 1 Mac & G 25. In modern times it has been applied in a wide variety of commercial and non-commercial situations.

as contractual despite the element of agreement or promise involved, because there is no consideration as conventionally understood (though there is action in reliance—the very giving of the information) and also because the information is sometimes given in personal or matrimonial relations[57] which do not resemble contractual situations. None of this alters the substance of the matter, which is that agreements or promises not to divulge confidential information are enforced against third parties who receive the information with notice of its confidentiality.

  [57] See, e.g., *Argyll v. Argyll* [1967] Ch 302; *Stephens v. Avery* [1988] 2 All ER 477.

14

Remedies for Breach of Contract

1. THE NATURE OF CONTRACTUAL REMEDIES

A VARIETY of remedies are made available to the victim of breach of contract. In one sense these remedies are remarkable examples of the willingness of the state to lend its assistance to the enforcement of private arrangements: when a contracting party goes to law, and obtains a judgment against his defaulting partner, he obtains the right to the support of all the forces of the state to enforce that judgment. In the last resort, bailiffs, sheriff's officers, the police, and even the armed forces can be called in to enforce that contract—and all this at the behest of a private citizen.

But in another sense the legal remedies available for breach of contract are very mild. It is (in general) no crime to break a contract, even when this is done deliberately. It is a crime to cheat or defraud someone, but it is not a crime to fail to pay a debt, even when the debtor is perfectly capable of paying it. Moreover, when a claimant comes to the court for assistance in enforcing his contract, it often seems that the court is not disposed to take a very serious view of breaches of contract. Courts have the power to make a decree of specific performance to compel the performance of a contract, but they rarely do so. Nor do courts in contract cases award punitive damages, such as is occasionally done in tort, to express the community's sense of outrage at the injuries inflicted on the victim or at the way he has been treated. Further, the courts almost never require contract breakers to give up profits that they have made through breaking their contracts, even when the breach is deliberate; if the defendant has broken one contract in order to make another, he will usually be allowed to keep whatever profits he made in the second contract.

The chief legal remedy for breach of a contractual duty, aside from rescission or termination (which are not strictly 'remedies'), is an action for damages for the loss occasioned by the breach. This remedy is itself restricted in various ways. The award of damages for non-pecuniary loss, an everyday affair in tort law, is available only in exceptional circumstances. Awards for other kinds of indirect losses are also subject to limits not found in the law of tort. In an ordinary action for debt, for example for the payment of a sum clearly due under an insurance policy, the creditor is entitled to the debt and, sometimes, costs as well as interest on the debt, but she is rarely able to recover compensation for any additional losses or inconvenience caused. The general rules governing the recovery of 'remote' losses are also (in theory) more stringent in contract. The end result of these restrictions is that victims of contractual breaches frequently obtain nothing more than an award of nominal damages (e.g. £1). A seller who fails to deliver goods which are readily available in the market at the same price as the contract price will not face any real legal sanction. The same is true of the breach of many, if not most, executory contracts.

These features of the law on remedies have led some writers to suggest that a breach of contract is not actually an *unlawful* act. The famous American jurist and judge, Oliver Wendell Holmes, used to argue that in law a contracting party was only bound *either* to perform his contract *or* to pay for the loss caused thereby.[1] Hence if he chose to pay for the loss, he did no wrong; he merely chose one of the two ways of performing his obligation. Some economists have gone further, arguing that the law actually *encourages* parties to break certain contracts. According to this argument (which we will examine in more detail later), the courts give contracting parties the 'choice' to perform or to pay damages precisely in order to encourage performance when—but only when—the value of performance is greater than its cost. Where the value of performance is *less than* the cost of performance, the remedial rules encourage parties to pay damages rather than perform—a so-called 'efficient breach'. Victims of contractual breaches, for their part, are compensated by an award of damages for any losses they have suffered in reliance on their contracts, thereby protecting the general practice of making contracts. Of course, such victims receive monetary compensation rather than the promised performance, but in the economic view now being considered the victim's interest in performance can be translated, like any other interest, into monetary terms. So contracting parties who are paid damages representing the difference between the value (to them) of what they were promised and what they actually obtained, are fully protected. No further sanctions are needed.

These arguments, which have never received much support among English jurists and judges, seem exaggerated. They have difficulty accounting for the rule that specific relief is available in certain cases. They also have difficulty explaining the tort of interference with contractual rights, the existence of which presupposes that contracting parties have legal rights to the performance of their contracts. Finally, but most importantly, the idea that there is no legal obligation to perform a contract supposes the legal understanding of a contract is entirely divorced from the ordinary or moral view. In the ordinary view, contracts are promises, and promises are meant to be kept. It is, of course, understood—particularly by business parties—that contracts sometimes need to be revised or even cancelled altogether when circumstances

---

[1] O. W. Holmes, 'The Path of the Law' (1897) 10 Harvard Law Rev 457 at 462.

change; but few, if any, contracting parties suppose that when they enter a contract they are simply agreeing to a disjunctive obligation to perform or pay damages. The economic theory just described supposes that contracting parties are deeply confused as to the nature of the obligations they are undertaking.

Nonetheless, the economic view highlights, in a particularly evocative way, just how mild contract remedies can be in practice. In particular, it highlights what is (as we shall see) arguably the most perplexing feature of the common law's approach to remedies: the rule that deliberate and non-deliberate breaches are, in principle, treated the same.

2. SELF-HELP

Before we turn to judicial remedies for breach of contract, it is advisable to examine the possibilities of redress that do not involve going to court at all. Virtually everybody would prefer to obtain redress, if they could, without having to go to court. Aside from the fact that (as we have just seen) judicial remedies may have little practical value, courts are expensive, slow, and liable to make mistakes. Creditors, especially, are prone to think that courts are over-sympathetic to debtors, so they often seek some way of obtaining redress without having to sue for it, or, if they have to sue for it, of making the outcome of the proceedings as simple and inevitable as possible. For some centuries, indeed, a battle has raged between creditors (using this in a broad sense) who have sought extra-judicial enforcement of their contracts, and debtors, who have tried to force creditors to go to court before they can exercise their remedies. It will be enough to give a few illustrations of this long history.

One of the most effective means of enforcing debts—though not other contractual obligations—was at one time imprisonment for debt. In its full glory, this system was self-help gone mad. The claimant only had to issue a writ claiming the debt (plus costs), and he could then proceed to arrest the debtor and incarcerate him in a debtor's jail. The debtor remained as a prisoner of the creditor (not of the state) until he paid or was released as an act of mercy by Parliament which every now and then emptied the debtors' jail of those who had been there over twelve months. But this form of imprisonment for debt—before a judgment had even been given—was abolished in 1838. It remained possible to imprison a debtor long after that, but only after first suing and obtaining a judgment, so this had ceased to be a self-help remedy.

Another type of self-help remedy was (and still is) to take 'security' from the debtor. Originally, the creditor might demand a conveyance of land, the debtor simply having the right to a re-conveyance if he paid off the debt when due. Initially this was pure self-help: if the debtor failed to pay, the creditor simply retained the land by virtue of his conveyance. But later the courts of equity intervened, allowing debtors to pay off the debt after it was due, so the creditor never knew for sure whether his self-help remedy was secure. In order to prevent the debtor claiming to re-open the transaction beyond a certain point it became possible for the creditor himself to apply to a court of equity for a foreclosure decree, which would shut out the debtor if he still failed to pay after yet further opportunities. But this meant that the creditor was compelled to go to court to realise his security, one of the very things the security was designed to obviate. So the mortgage ceased to be a self-help remedy and foreclosure decrees became rather unpopular.

The next development was the mortgage—a security interest over property that remains in the debtor's possession and control—which granted the creditor the power to sell the mortgaged property. From the creditor's point of view, this type of security was far more satisfactory. Once the property was sold, the debtor could no longer demand further opportunities to pay off the debt and get his property back. Of course, the debtor had to be given the chance to contest a proposed sale, but this threw on to him the onus of taking proceedings. The creditor had no need to sue, and if the debtor failed to take proceedings, as was usually the case, the remedy became a true self-help remedy once again. And so it remains today. Indeed, the mortgage of today often involves a two-stage self-help procedure. It is common for a debtor simply to deposit (say with a bank) documents, like title deeds or land- or share-certificates, as security for a loan together with a short, signed contract. This contract gives the creditor an irrevocable authority to execute a full mortgage as agent for the debtor to itself as creditor. This, again, is done as a matter of pure self-help, and, once executed, the full mortgage can be enforced by the power of sale.

All these are traditional devices to enable creditors to enforce debts by self-help means. But there are many other possibilities of using self-help, some of which can be used for enforcing claims to damages as well as claims to debts. Many of these are extremely simple, such as requiring advance payment; or, conversely, insisting that full payment will not be made until the other party has completely performed, or even (as is common with building and construction contracts) that a part of the contract price will be retained and only paid several months after full performance is complete.

Other methods of self-help may involve some minimal degree of co-operation by third parties. For instance, it is common in certain kinds of transactions to find that contracting parties are required to provide guarantors of unimpeachable integrity, such as leading banks or insurance companies. But what makes such arrangements virtually a type of self-help remedy is that the guarantor is often required to agree to pay the claim (perhaps up to a specified maximum sum) on the mere demand of the creditor. So if the creditor claims that the other party is guilty of a breach of contract, he may simply write to the guarantor demanding payment and, with guarantors of this class, payment is assured. The guarantor will then claim an indemnity from the other contracting party, and that party may yet have a legal right to challenge the creditor's actions in claiming on the guarantee. But the onus of suing is on him and, in the meantime, the creditor has the money. To commercial parties these are very important considerations indeed.

Many other kinds of self-help exist, though they are not usually identified as such. Rights of termination and of rescission, for instance, are in practice forms of self-help. They do not require the assistance of the courts, although of course (like other forms of self-help) their use can be challenged in the courts by the other party. But this throws the onus of litigation on to that party, and the dislike of litigation is so great that the onus often means that there simply will be no action. At the least, shifting the onus can make a significant difference to the effectiveness of the rights. So, for instance, some modern statutes (of a consumer protection kind) often do shift the onus, by requiring that a court order be obtained before certain rights (otherwise self-help remedies) can be exercised. So, today, a landlord cannot lawfully throw a tenant out of a rented dwelling-house unless he first gets an eviction order from a court, no matter what the lease may say, and no matter how badly the tenant has behaved. So also, under the Consumer Credit Act 1974 a hire-purchase company cannot lawfully retake goods let under a hire-purchase contract after one third of the price has been paid, unless a court order is obtained. Today there is pressure to prevent electricity, gas, and water companies from cutting off supplies (again a form of self-help) without a court order, though at present such orders are not generally required.

These restrictions on contractual self-help remedies raise similar issues to those discussed in Chapter 12 in connection with the Unfair Contract Terms Act 1977 and the Unfair Terms in Consumer Contracts Regulations 1999. Court orders are costly and slow, and they often allow time to pay, during which further debts may be incurred which may never be recovered at all. All these costs must, of course, ultimately be borne by the honest and regular payers of the services in question. Furthermore, if the use of self-help remedies is limited against debtors whose creditworthiness is low, the result may be that they are unable to obtain credit at all, or only on worse terms. As tenants cannot be evicted without court orders, some landlords demand larger deposits from tenants. In the case of gas and electricity supplies, the use of pre-paid slot meters is a far more effective way of ensuring payment by those with low creditworthiness than requiring court orders for disconnections. Thus statutory restrictions on self-help remedies like these need careful examination before they are introduced, as it cannot always be assumed that they are in the real interest of those they appear designed to protect. On the other hand, as we have already seen,[2] the law may at present go too far in leaving contractual rights such as those to rescind or terminate a contract uncontrolled by any requirements to act reasonably or in good faith.

Another kind of self-help remedy which can be of great importance in certain situations is the right of set-off—the right to reduce one's own contractual obligation on the ground that the other party has breached her contractual obligation. In the past, employers were often accused of abusing this right by making unfair and unauthorised deductions from the pay of an employee (for instance, for alleged bad work, or for breakages or losses), but such deductions were eventually subjected to legal control under the Truck Acts and later the Wages Act 1986. One interesting example of the use of the employer's right of set-off as a self-help remedy is provided by the case of local authorities who have deducted pay from teachers involved in 'industrial action'. Of course an employee who goes on strike gets no pay; but an employee who simply refuses to perform a certain part of his duties—a teacher who refuses to teach certain classes, for instance—poses practical problems for an employer. The amounts involved in each case are often small, and the number of cases may be very large, so legal action for breach of contract is hardly practicable. But it has been held that employers are entitled to deduct a proportionate part of the employee's pay as a set-off against such breaches of contract;[3] naturally, the employer will fix the way of calculating the proportion, leaving it to the employee to challenge him in the courts. So here the onus of litigation is left firmly on the employee.

Rights of set-off can also exist the other way round—the debtor may be the person claiming a set-off. A tenant may refuse to pay some or all of the rent on the basis that the landlord was guilty (say) of breach of covenant to repair.[4] In order to prevent this, it is common for certain types of contract (such as leases) to exclude rights of set-off, but very clear words are needed to achieve this result.[5] It has also been held that a clause excluding all rights of set-off may fall afoul of the Unfair Contract Terms Act,[6] and the same conclusion seems likely with respect to contracts governed by the Unfair Terms in Consumer Contracts Regulations 1999.

Another common form of self-help remedy which gives cause for concern in certain situations is the forfeiture of advance payments or deposits. Some businesses (holiday companies, for instance) habitually demand 'deposits' or part payment in advance. If the company then claims a breach of contract

---

[2] Above, 204–05.
[3] See *Sim v. Rotherham Met BC* [1987] Ch 216; *Royle v. Trafford* [1984] IRLR 184.
[4] *Eller v. Grovecrest Investments Ltd* [1994] 4 All ER 845.
[5] *Connaught Restaurants Ltd v. Indoor Leisure Ltd* [1994] 4 All ER 834.
[6] *Stewart Gill Ltd v. Horatio Meyer & Co. Ltd* [1992] 1 QB 600.

by the other party, it may simply claim to 'forfeit' the deposit or advance payment. Here there is some measure of legal control, as we shall see later, in that some types of forfeiture are void, and advance payments (but not deposits) are recoverable. But in practice, because this is a self-help remedy, it is unlikely that many challenges will be made to forfeitures even when there is legal ground to do so.

Finally, there is a sort of half-way house kind of remedy in which legal action to enforce the contractual right may be needed, but the legal action is of a simple type in which procedures are streamlined, defences often shut out, and court orders easily obtained. Cheques and promissory notes and other bills of exchange, for instance, can be enforced by a quick and simple procedure in the courts, which does not usually permit the defendant to raise any defence, except an allegation as to the very validity of the document in question. So a contracting party may demand bills of exchange or cheques in advance as a kind of half-way self-help remedy in certain kinds of transactions. Even a buyer of goods who pays by cheque can be sued on the cheque in such a way that he cannot raise ordinary defences, such as claiming that the goods were defective. He can still make such a claim, but not in the proceedings on the cheque. He must pay first and argue afterwards. This may seem odd, and it is perhaps unacceptable in consumer transactions, but it is more justifiable in commercial transactions where the whole point of agreeing to issue a cheque is to give the seller this degree of self-help entitlement.

It is evident that, like the remedies of rescission and termination, all self-help remedies give rise to the risk that they may be used in cases where they would cause more loss to the defendant than gain to the claimant. Indeed, they are often wanted precisely for this deterrence value. A hire-purchase company which retakes a few pieces of cheap furniture or a battered television set from the hirer is unlikely to get much from reselling them, after payment of its costs. But the threatened loss to the hirer may be great enough to induce him to pay up. In such a case, the remedy may not be unjustified. But there may be other cases where, as with rescission and termination, the threat of using a self-help remedy may be made in order to extract compensation at a level higher than could be obtained in damages. Allowing this to happen is arguably inconsistent with other legal principles. As will be explained below, the law does not generally allow contracting parties to specify the payment of a sum of money by way of damages for breach that is greater than the actual loss caused by the breach.

3. SPECIFIC PERFORMANCE AND INJUNCTION

In English law, a person who complains of a breach of contract cannot, as a general principle, compel the actual performance of the contract by the other party, but must rest content with monetary compensation.[7] In certain circumstances, however, it has long been traditional to say that mere damages would be an inadequate remedy, and in these cases the court may grant a decree of specific performance or injunction ordering the defendant to do (in the case of specific performance) or abstain from doing (in the case of an injunction) the very thing agreed upon. The main sanction behind these decrees is the threat of imprisonment for contempt of court, but in certain cases it is possible for the court to order the contract to be executed by its officials in the event of the defendant proving contumacious. This, of course, is only possible where the defendant's personal assistance is not required.

Specific performance and injunctions were originally granted only by courts of equity, not law, and as a consequence even today they are said to be discretionary in the sense that they cannot be claimed as of 'right' (as damages can) and also in the sense that the court can refuse them on the basis of 'equitable bars', such as that the decree would cause undue hardship or that the claimant, though not actually a wrongdoer, did not have 'clean hands'. On the other hand, as in the case of most judicial discretions, the broad principles on which the courts act are well settled, and there are cases where it is well known that specific performance will issue more or less as a matter of course, while there are other cases where it is perfectly well known that specific performance will never be granted. For instance, specific performance is granted virtually as a matter of course for the enforcement of contracts for the purchase and sale (or lease) of land and buildings (though one modern case[8] shows that the old discretion to refuse specific performance on grounds of personal hardship remains alive). Similarly, injunctions to enforce negative covenants, such as post-employment non-competition covenants, are regularly awarded, though here too the equitable bars may be raised in an appropriate case.[9] On the other hand, specific performance is never granted to enforce performance of a contract for the sale of 'fungible' goods—goods that are readily obtainable elsewhere.

Aside from the equitable bars, the availability of these remedies is governed by three main principles: (1) they will only be granted when damages are

---

[7] Unlike some civilian legal systems, English law has not traditionally permitted the victim of a contract breach to choose, by way of remedy, to pay a reduced price for defective goods or services: the victim's choices are limited to damages, specific performance, or (if the breach is serious) to refusing the goods or performance and demanding the return of the entire price (if it is has already been paid). Under Part 5A of the Sale of Goods Act 1979 (implementing Directive 19994/44 of the European Parliament), however, a consumer is now given the choice of requiring a seller of defective good to reduce the price by an appropriate amount.

[8] *Patel v. Ali* [1984] 1 All ER 978.

[9] In *Shell v. Lostock Garage* [1976] 1 WLR 1187 the Court of Appeal refused an injunction to restrain the defendant from buying petrol from other suppliers in breach of its contract with Shell. The reason for the refusal was that Shell was supplying other rival petrol stations with petrol at much lower prices, with the consequence that the defendant was unable to resell the petrol Shell sold him.

inadequate; (2) they will not be granted for contracts involving personal service; and (3) they will not be granted unless the court is in a position to see that they are executed.[10]

When damages are inadequate

The standard case in which damages are said to be inadequate is a contract for the sale of something unique. Thus, specific performance would be granted of a contract to sell a unique or very unusual chattel such as a painting, an antique, or even a ship if it had some special features rendering it uniquely suitable for the claimant's uses. Specific performance is also granted more or less automatically for a contract for the purchase or sale of land (or a house), the theory being that no two pieces of land are quite the same—which is not entirely convincing in modern times, especially where the claimant is the seller. On the other hand, as was already noted, the court will never decree specific performance of a contract for the sale of goods that are obtainable elsewhere. Specific performance was even refused in the case of a contract for the purchase of a large machine, weighing over 220 tons, at a cost of some £270,000, and which could only be bought elsewhere with a nine to twelve months' delivery date.[11]

The most natural explanation of why specific performance is granted in cases involving unique goods is that the claimant has a right to what was promised under the contract, which in cases involving unique goods can only be realised by the defendant actually performing the contract as promised. This seems perfectly reasonable, but it bears noting that it presumes the purpose of 'damages' in the ordinary case is not in fact to compensate the claimant but instead to give her a kind of 'substitute' specific performance. Some legal systems explicitly provide for monetary awards based on the idea of substitute specific performance, and (as we shall see below) it may well be that the common law does this also, even if it does not admit to it, but in principle, the only monetary award generally available in the common law for an ordinary breach of contract is an award of 'damages',[12] the purpose of which is said to be to *compensate* the claimant.

---

[10] The new Part 5A of the Sale of Goods Act 1979 (discussed above n. 7) appears to change this traditional rule in the case of consumer sales. Under s. 48B the consumer has the right to demand the repair or replacement of defective goods, and under s. 48E the court 'may make an order requiring specific performance' to enforce this right. The court's discretion to refuse such an order appears limited to cases in which one of the other remedies provided under 5A, i.e. recission or reduction in price, is more appropriate. It does not appear the court can refuse specific performance of an order to repair or replace on the basis that damages are adequate or for any of the other traditional common law grounds for refusing specific relief.

[11] *Société des Industries Métallurgiques SA v. Bronx Engineering Co. Ltd* [1975] 1 Lloyd's Rep 465.

[12] Except in claims for 'debt', where a monetary order for the amount owing is available. Such orders are usually described as a form of specific relief.

Perhaps for this reason, the availability of specific performance in cases involving unique goods is sometimes explained on alternative grounds. One suggestion is that specific performance is awarded because no amount of money will suffice to fully compensate the claimant for the loss of a unique good. By definition, such goods do not have a 'market value' (and even if they did, the claimant might not share that value). The difficulty with this suggestion is that except for very rare cases, such as a contract for a family heirloom, there is nearly always a sum of money that would in fact fully compensate the claimant for failing to receive a promised good or piece of property. An individual who contracts to purchase a 'unique' house for £250,000 would almost certainly be more than happy to receive, say, £2,000,000 in lieu of receiving the house. A somewhat more plausible suggestion is therefore that damages are 'inadequate' in cases involving unique goods because it is impossible in such cases to determine the appropriate amount of damages. Without looking into the claimant's head or using a very reliable lie-detector, it is not possible to know the value that a claimant who contracted to purchase a house places on the house. Of course, there is a sense in which this is also true for cases involving fungible goods: different purchasers have different reasons for purchasing the relevant goods and so may place different values on those goods—a bicycle courier contracting to buy a bicycle has greater need for it than does the ordinary purchaser. But in the ordinary case this is not an issue because full compensation is guaranteed if the purchaser is awarded sufficient funds to purchase identical goods elsewhere. By definition, giving the victim funds to enter an identical contract with someone else (plus an amount to cover incidental expenses) ensures that she is left as well-off at the end of the day as if the original contract had been performed.

The idea that what is special about unique goods is that their value to the claimant is difficult to assess is consistent with the rare decisions in which courts have granted specific performance for contracts involving fungible goods. In *Sky Petroleum v. VIP Petroleum Ltd*,[13] the courts granted a decree of specific performance of a contract to supply petroleum. The dispute arose during an oil crisis, and the court suggested that an order of specific performance was appropriate as it was not clear that the claimant could obtain alternative supplies at any price. But it seems clear that anyone willing to pay £1,000,000 a barrel would have had no difficulty obtaining all the oil he wanted. The real difficulty, it appears, was that oil prices were rising and falling so dramatically and unpredictably that it was impossible for the court to determine the appropriate level of compensation.

Whatever the theory underlying the concept of 'adequacy', there has been in modern times a slight movement towards expanding the range of cases in

---

[13] [1974] 1 WLR 576.

which damages are held to be inadequate. For instance, in *Beswick v. Beswick*[14] the House of Lords permitted a promisee to obtain a decree of specific performance of a contractual obligation to pay an annuity, mainly because the doctrine of privity prevented the promisee (in her capacity as beneficiary) from enforcing the contract directly. This was something of an innovation, because there was nothing unique about the promised performance nor was there any difficulty in measuring its value to the claimant. As a matter of strict law, damages were not in fact *inadequate*—the claimant in her position as administrator of the estate could be fully compensated for her loss. The difficulty was that, in the circumstances, specific performance simply appeared to be a more *appropriate* remedy. Following on *Beswick*, some courts have adopted just this idea, holding that specific performance may be granted where it is the more appropriate remedy,[15] but this approach has yet to gain general acceptance.[16]

Personal service contracts

The second principle governing specific relief is that it will not be awarded to enforce a contract of personal service. A contract to paint a portrait or a contract of employment, for example, will not be enforced by orders of specific performance, and this is the case no matter how unique or difficult-to-value the service. But while contracts 'to do' are not specifically enforced, contracts (or contractual terms) 'not to do', such as a covenant prohibiting the defendant from engaging in employment or performing some kind of service, are frequently enforced by means of injunctions.[17] The exception is where an injunction would force the defendant to work or perform a service for the claimant. Thus, the injunction cannot impose on the defendant the choice of either working for the claimant or starving or even of remaining unemployed for any significant period of time.[18] And even where there is no risk of the employee starving (because, for example, the employer is still paying his salary while he is on leave after notice to terminate) the courts are reluctant to grant an injunction unless there is good evidence that the employer will be significantly damaged or affected by what the employee

---

[14] [1968] AC 58, discussed above, 340.

[15] *Tito v. Waddell (No. 2)* [1977] Ch 106 at 322, *Rainbow Estates Ltd v. Tokenhold Ltd* [1998] 2 All ER 860 at 868.

[16] Earlier in this chapter, we saw that a party may be able to use self-help remedies like rescission and termination even when this would inflict loss out of all proportion to their value to the claimant. Thus, unlike in the case of specific relief, there is no rule holding that rescission or termination cannot be invoked where damages would be adequate, even though these measures are tantamount to a form of specific relief. Indeed, they are even more potent than decrees of specific relief, as the claimant simply helps himself to what he claims to be entitled.

[17] For one modern example see *Evening Standard Co. v. Henderson* [1987] ICR 588.

[18] *Marsh v. National Autistic Society* [1993] ICR 453

wants to do.[19] Further, the courts are also unwilling to grant such injunctions where the relationship between the parties involves a high degree of mutual trust which has been destroyed, and where the injunction would almost certainly drive the employee to return to the employer. Indeed, a decree will not be granted if the practical result, looking at matters realistically, will be that the employee is forced to return to work for the claimants.[20]

The usual justification for refusing to specifically enforce personal service contracts (or for granting injunctions where this would have a similar effect) is that such orders are too intrusive of personal liberty. Admittedly, the aim of such orders is merely to get the defendant to do what he had already agreed to do. But for reasons that lie deep in the roots of the Western political tradition, orders by the state to engage in a particular job or to perform specified services—backed up, it will be remembered, by threats of imprisonment—have acquired a symbolic meaning that goes far beyond their practical significance: they carry with them the pall of servitude.

This is a valid concern, but it may be asked whether it fully justifies a general prohibition against specific enforcement of personal service contracts.[21] In particular, it may be asked whether it justifies refusing to specifically enforce an *employer*'s contractual obligation to employ an employee. Where the defendant is a large company, such an obligation may have little, if any, personal element. The order is directed at the company, not a particular individual. Moreover, from the employee's perspective, it is often apparent that damages are an inadequate remedy. In many cases, an employee's self-esteem and integrity are intimately tied up with her employment in a way that an award of damages could never hope to fully reflect. These are cases where it might indeed be said that no sum of money could fully compensate the claimant for her loss.

Difficulty of supervision

The third principle governing specific relief is that it will not be ordered in cases where enforcing the order would require constant supervision by the courts. The underlying concern, as was explained by Lord Hoffmann in *Co-op Insurance Society Ltd v. Argyll Stores (Holdings) Ltd,*[22] is not that courts might have to send their officers on-site to supervise a contract. The concern, rather, is for 'the possibility of the court having to give an indefinite series of rulings in order to ensure the execution of its order'.

---

[19] *Provident Financial Group plc v. Hayward* [1993] 3 All ER 298. In this connection note the dictum of Dillon LJ at 304: 'It is very common for employers to have somewhat exaggerated views of what will or may affect their business.'

[20] *Warren v. Mendy* [1989] 1 WLR 853.

[21] Chapter II of Part X of the Employment Rights Act 1996 provides that an Employment Tribunal may order the re-instatement of a wrongfully dismissed employee, but such orders are rarely made in practice.

[22] [1998] AC 1.

The problem identified by Lord Hoffmann is most likely to arise in cases in which the relevant obligation is to perform a service. A contract of employment, for example, might potentially be breached in innumerable ways that are difficult to specify in advance. But the principle that the courts will not order specific performance of difficult-to-supervise contracts is not identical to the principle that they will not order specific performance of personal service contracts. The latter is primarily concerned with the *personal* element in a contact, while the former with what might be called the *specificity* of the obligation. The distinction is illustrated by the *Argyll Stores* case, in which the owner of a shopping centre was unsuccessful in obtaining specific performance of a grocery chain's obligation to keep open a store as a condition of its lease in the shopping centre. Although the court gave some attention to the 'personal' nature of the obligation, the main reason for refusing specific performance was difficulty of supervision. The judgment adopted a rather traditional view of the latter bar, but in principle the reasoning seems correct. The personal service issues were minimal as the claimant was not seeking an order that any particular person or persons work in the store, but merely that the company keep the store open by some means. On the other hand, there was a serious risk that the parties might get into future disputes over the meaning of 'staying open'. For example, the store might decide to remain technically open, but to have only one employee on site and to leave the shelves bare of goods. What the court was saying, in effect, was that a contract of this sort can only really work if both parties are committed to it; if one party performs under compulsion, innumerable problems may arise that will eventually make their way to the court. This is the same reason specific performance is rarely awarded in connection with building contracts.

Should specific relief be more widely available?

In modern times there has been considerable academic debate over the limited availability of decrees of specific relief. The principle that specific performance is a secondary remedy available only where the primary remedy of damages is inadequate seems in obvious need of explanation. If contracting parties have duties to perform their contractual obligations, as the courts proclaim, then it would seem that victims of contractual breaches should in principle be entitled to demand that defendants perform those duties (as they are in civil law regimes). Of course, in most cases where the parties are before the courts, it is too late to contemplate specific performance, and in other cases the claimant has anyhow lost confidence in the defendant, and does not want him to perform further. But where performance is possible and desired, why is it not presumptively available?

One answer that has attracted considerable attention, particularly among North American academics, justifies the current rule on grounds of economic efficiency. According to the theory of 'efficient breach' alluded to earlier, specific performance is not routinely available because there are cases in which it is efficient for contracting parties *not* to perform their contract. The current rules, it is said, allow and even encourage contracting parties not to perform in just such cases. Suppose that S agrees to sell a machine to B1 for £100. B1 values the machine at £110; that is, he expects to make £10 profit from it. Suppose then that B2 appears on the scene and thinks he can use the machine much more profitably than B1, so he offers S £150 for it. S can afford to sell the machine to B2, break his contract with B1, and pay B1 damages of £10. All three parties appear to be happy with this outcome. S gets more profit, B2 is happy, and even B1 gets the value of his contract, if not the performance of the contract. This is also said to be an economically efficient result because B2, being willing to pay more than B1, is presumed to be able to use the machine more efficiently than B1. And because it is more efficient, it is presumptively in the public interest, as well as in the interests of the parties. On the other hand, if B1 were entitled to a decree of specific per-formance, then he would get the machine, and the more profitable use contemplated by B2 would never be achieved, leading to an inefficient result.

In the example just given, performance was said to be inefficient because a third party valued the promised good or service more than the original promisee. In other cases, performance is said to be inefficient because either the cost of performance to the promisor or the value of performance to the promisee changed since the contract was made. The facts of *Tito v. Waddell (No. 2)*[23] fall into the latter category. The defendants were liable under some contracts which required them to restore the condition of the claimants' land (on an island in the Pacific Ocean) after it had been exploited for phosphates. In fact they left the land in a deplorable state, but it was proved that the cost of actual restoration would have been enormous—it would have involved shipping loads of soil from Australia—and would have far exceeded the value of the land after restoration. For reasons unrelated to the mining, the island had become uninhabitable—the islanders were forced to relocate—with the result that replanting would have been of little value to them or anyone else. In these circumstances, the court refused to award specific performance. The result appears to support the arguments of the efficient breach theory. Assuming the court had the facts correct, restoring the island to its original state would have been hugely wasteful. Had the islanders simply been given a sum of money equivalent to the cost of restoration (which did not happen, for reasons explained below), it seems clear that they would not have used it for this purpose. They would have used the money for something on which they placed a higher value.

Of course, it may be questioned to what extent courts are, or should be, concerned with economic considerations of this kind. But even if it assumed

---

[23] Above n. 13.

that economic considerations should matter, cases such as *Tito v. Waddell* can also be used to illustrate the weaknesses in the efficient breach theory. As economists themselves have pointed out, it is not clear that ordering specific performance would in fact have led to an inefficient result in *Tito*. Certainly it would be inefficient if the work was actually done—it is inefficient to force somebody to use valuable resources in a wasteful manner—but it is not at all certain that granting the decree would actually lead to this result. What probably would have happened is that the parties, or their lawyers, would have discussed the matter and then reached an agreement whereby the specific performance order would be waived in exchange for a payment to the islanders. If the cost of performance was indeed greater than its value, then an agreement in which the sum to be paid was fixed somewhere between the cost and the value of performance would have benefited both parties. Of course, the costs of negotiating such an arrangement will be avoided if the court simply orders damages in the first place. Such costs—termed 'transactions costs' by economists—are real costs, and so must be taken into account in determining the efficiency of a legal rule. But there are also costs associated with an order of damages. If the court is required to assess damages, the litigation will be more complex and expensive than if the court simply orders specific performance. Considerations of this kind are relevant even if the matter does not go to court, since contracting parties' settlement negotiations will be conducted against the background of *their* estimations of what a court would decide. Furthermore, there is always a danger that an order of damages will underestimate the claimant's true loss (indeed, this seems likely given certain restrictions on damages awards, as discussed below).

Other cases in which it appears prima facie efficient to refuse to order specific performance may be analysed in a similar fashion. Thus, in the sale of goods example mentioned earlier where there was a second buyer who valued the goods more than the original buyer, an order of specific performance might not lead to an inefficient result if the original buyer could herself resell the goods to the second buyer. Alternatively, the original seller could pay the original buyer a sum of money in exchange for agreeing to rescind the contract. If the second buyer really is willing to pay more for the goods than the original buyer, then, as in the *Tito* case, there is space for a mutually beneficial bargain of this kind. The end result, once all the relevant factors are taken into consideration, is that it is difficult to say whether the current rule is or is not economically efficient.

The traditional explanation of the common law's approach to specific performance is an historical one: originally, only courts of equity had the jurisdiction to order specific relief, and not courts of law. But this does not explain why even today specific performance remains a secondary remedy in the common law. Courts of law and equity have been joined for well over a century in England, and in any event the common law rules are not static. There is, however, another historical factor: we have seen in connection with personal service contracts that there is a reluctance to embrace measures that evoke the ties of servitude. The principle underlying this limitation—that the state should not generally be able to order one individual to perform a service or work for another individual—applies, even if only weakly, to all contracts. An obligation to deliver an ordinary chattel, for example, has a personal element—the person subject to the obligation must either deliver the chattel herself or arrange for someone else to do this. At a time when most contracts were made by individuals or small businesses, the personal element in such contracts would have been greater than it is today. Moreover, the link between specific performance and ideas of servitude would probably have been felt more strongly in a period when many individuals would have had first hand knowledge of slavery and other forms of servitude. In this context, a concern for personal liberty might reasonably have been thought sufficient grounds for a general requirement to the effect that claimants seeking specific performance must show *some* reason why an 'impersonal' monetary remedy would not be sufficient—such as that damages are inadequate. The only cases where this concern seems entirely irrelevant are those involving purely monetary obligations, because in such cases specific performance and damages are equally impersonal. As is explained in the next section, specific relief has in fact long been available in just such cases.

According to this explanation, then, the common law's position that specific performance is a 'secondary' remedy should be interpreted not so much as a statement of first principle, but as a practical recognition of the fact that *in practice* there are usually good reasons to refuse specific performance. Further support for this conclusion may be found in the fact that legal systems that regard specific performance as a primary remedy (such as France) in practice grant such orders in about the same range of cases as do English courts. This is not to say, of course, that the present law is beyond criticism; in the contemporary world, where most contractual obligations of a non-monetary character are performed by large companies, few contractual obligations have a significant personal element. The common law's view that specific performance is presumptively a secondary remedy arguably makes it too easy for courts to refuse such orders. At present, the party seeking specific performance has the burden of proving that damages are inadequate. Thus, even if it accepted that in practice specific performance should rarely be ordered, it would seem useful for the courts to acknowledge, if only in principle, that specific relief is equally as appropriate as monetary relief.

Recognizing that specific performance is in principle a primary remedy for breach of contract arguably has further benefits. As will be discussed when we turn to monetary remedies, English courts are frequently criticised for failing to ensure that claimants are fully compensated for their non-pecuniary (or subjective) losses and, in addition, for allowing contract breakers to keep the benefits they gain from breaching a contract, even when that gain was paid for in the contract price. It is often suggested that relaxing the rules governing specific relief may provide a solution to these problems. The case of *Tito v. Waddell* provides a good illustration. As a matter of principle, the court's decision not to award specific performance of the obligation to replant the island seems correct: the islander claimants (who no longer lived on the island) were not genuinely interested in specific relief (they made only a few arguments on this point) and the replanting obligation involved a significant personal element. But the court's decision to then award the islanders only nominal monetary damages may be criticised on the ground that the islanders probably placed some non-pecuniary value on the condition of their traditional homeland and, perhaps more importantly, that the mining company was allowed to keep the 'price' that the islanders paid (by accepting a lower fee in exchange for granting mining rights) for the replanting clause. With an order of specific performance in hand, the islanders could demand that the mining company pay them a sum sufficient to cover their subjective losses and the amount that they paid for the replanting clause in exchange for them agreeing to waive the order.

This suggestion needs to be examined carefully. One difficulty is that ordering specific performance provides no guarantee that the victim will in fact receive full compensation and restitution. On the facts of *Tito*, for example, it is unlikely that the mining company would have agreed to pay back everything they had received in exchange for the replanting clause. If the islanders insisted on full repayment, the mining company would probably threaten to go through with the performance—which the islanders did not actually want. It seems likely, then, that they would have agreed on a sum somewhere in between the cost of performance (which was enormous) and the value of performance (which was probably not significant, even taking the islanders' subjective preferences into account). A further difficulty with awarding specific performance in cases of this kind is that there is a risk the victim will be able to demand—and obtain—a sum that is *more* than either the value of performance or the price paid for the relevant obligation. This could happen, for example, if the cost of performance had risen since the contract was signed. Suppose that in *Tito* the cost of performance had doubled since the contract was signed (say because the cost of transport increased as a result of the islanders vacating the island). On these facts, the islanders would have been in a position to demand from the mining company a sum equal or close to the cost of performance, even though that sum would have been greater than the value of replanting or the amount that the islanders paid for the replanting clause.

For these reasons, the problems associated with obtaining compensation for subjective losses and restitution for contractual payments would seem better addressed, in principle anyway, not by changing the rules on specific performance but by reforming the rules governing damages and restitutionary awards. To some extent, this has already happened, as we shall see. But the availability in cases such as *Tito v. Waddell* of restitutionary relief is still severely limited. So long as this is the case, there are strong practical justice arguments for making specific performance more widely available in these situations.

4. THE ACTION FOR AN AGREED SUM

It was noted above that there is a strong argument for allowing claimants to obtain orders of specific performance where they are suing for the breach of a monetary obligation. As it turns out, the courts have effectively accepted this argument. The victim of the breach of a monetary obligation, for instance an ordinary debt, may bring what is called an 'action for an agreed sum'.[24] Such actions are in many ways more like a claim for specific performance than an action for damages. The claimant who brings an action for an agreed sum is asking the court to order the defendant to do precisely what he has contracted to do—that is, to pay over the contractually-specified sum of money. Of course, in both an action for damages and an action for an agreed sum the claimant is asking the court for a monetary order. But the actions are not equivalent because in the case of damages the claimant must prove that the failure to pay caused a loss and, further, that the losses satisfied the rules on remoteness of loss. In an action for an agreed sum, the claimant need only prove that the sum was due and not paid. There are also procedural differences between the two actions. The procedure for recovering an agreed sum is simpler and, especially in uncontested cases, quicker than the ordinary action for damages. Where a defendant fails to appear in answer to a claim, for instance, judgment can immediately be given for the claimant if his claim is for an agreed sum; if his claim is for damages, judgment can only be given for damages to be assessed, and even where the claim is uncontested, the claimant must produce some evidence to support his claim to the losses for which he seeks damages.

Unlike ordinary claims to specific performance, however, the action for an agreed sum is not subject to judicial discretion—it is available as of right and not merely in cases in which damages are an inadequate remedy. This seems entirely appropriate, given that none of the usual reasons for not awarding specific performance apply to such cases. Monetary obligations have no personal element (or at least no more of a personal element than damages) and there are no difficulties of supervision.

---

[24] This action is sometimes just called an 'action in debt'.

Part performance

In order to maintain an action for an agreed sum, the sum must be due, which means that the claimant must himself have performed his duties under the contract.[25] Even if he has been prevented from doing so by the wrongful actions of the other party, he will not generally be permitted to bring an action for an agreed sum. 'You cannot claim remuneration under a contract if you have not earned it; if you are prevented from earning it, your only remedy is in damages.'[26] Thus, in a contract of sale of goods the seller cannot normally sue the buyer for the whole price if the latter refuses to take the goods, unless the ownership has already passed to him.

It has already been mentioned (in Chapter 7) that this rule can sometimes operate harshly, particularly in cases where the claimant's non-performance is trivial and unintentional. It is perhaps for this reason that in certain types of contracts an exception will be made if the claimant has 'substantially performed' his obligations. In building and construction contracts, for instance, the builder can maintain an action for an agreed sum even if his obligations are not absolutely and finally completed, subject to a possible counter-claim for damages by the other party. On the other hand, mere part performance does not give rise to a right to part payment, except in the relatively unusual cases in which the contract is divisible. For instance, if a builder contracts to build a house and leaves the work half-finished he is not (in the absence of express provision) entitled to any payment whatever for the work he has already done,[27] although in practice any substantial building contract will usually contain provisions for stage payments as the work proceeds. Similarly, a builder may be unable to claim any payment at all if he contracts to install central heating in a house but makes such a bad job of it that the buyer has to pay several hundred pounds to have the work put right.[28]

In cases of part performance, the claimant may have the possibility of bringing an action in unjust enrichment for restitution of any benefit that he has conferred on the defendant through his partial performance. But this is generally only allowed where the defendant has received a benefit under the contract which he is not prepared to disgorge, despite being in a position to do so. For instance, if a seller delivers part of a consignment of goods for which payment is to be made in one sum, but fails to deliver the rest, the buyer cannot keep what has been delivered and refuse to pay for the value of the goods. He must choose between returning what has been delivered and

---

[25] On the other hand, it is, in principle, no defence to an action for an agreed sum that the claimant completed his performance *after* the defendant had attempted to repudiate the contract, at any rate in cases where the claimant had a 'legitimate interest' in performance: see the discussion of *White & Carter (Councils) Ltd v. McGregor* [1962] AC 413, above, 202.

[26] Per Lloyd J in *The Alaskan Trader* [1984] 1 All ER 129 at 134.

[27] *Sumpter v. Hedges* [1898] 1 QB 673.

[28] *Bolton v. Mahadeva* [1972] 1 WLR 1009 (the figure has been adjusted for inflation).

claiming damages in respect of the whole contract, or keeping what has been delivered and paying for it, subject to his claim for damages in respect of the balance. But this principle would not apply to the case of the builder who leaves a half-completed house on the other party's land or a defective central heating installation in the other's house. In these cases, the innocent party is perfectly free to have the work completed by someone else without incurring any liability, in contract or unjust enrichment, to the original builder. In situations where this result seems intolerably harsh it may be possible to avoid it by implying a term requiring interim payments under the contract.[29]

The possibility of bringing a restitutionary claim for the value of benefits conferred under an incomplete contract also exists where the reason for non-performance is that the contract was frustrated. In such cases, the Law Reform (Frustrated Contracts) Act 1943 enables the court, in its discretion, to order parties to pay for the value of any benefits they may have received before the frustrating event. Thus, to revert to the example of the uncompleted house, if the reason the work is not finished is a frustrating event, as opposed to a breach of contract by the builder, the builder may be able to recover a sum representing the value to the other party of the building as it stands. This, of course, may not be as much as the cost to the builder of what he has done. In *BP Exploration v. Hunt*[30] a complex contract for the exploitation of an oil concession was entered into by the parties. The defendant received substantial benefits under the contract, while BP received very little in the early stages, the intention of the parties being that BP would be recompensed in the later stages when large-scale production was under way. But the concession was abrogated by the Libyan Government, thus frustrating the contract. BP then sought—and obtained—a large award from the defendant under the 1943 Act, for benefits conferred on it prior to the frustration of the contract.

The 1943 Act does not, however, permit the court to assist a party who has spent money on the performance of the contract without actually benefiting the other party, unless (as we shall see shortly) something has been paid in advance. Thus if a person contracts to make machinery for another, and the contract is frustrated before any of it is delivered, no part of the agreed price can be recovered, notwithstanding that money and work may have been laid out already on the machinery.

Damages for failure to pay an agreed sum?

According to traditional law, in cases where the only obligation breached by the defendant is an obligation to pay money, the claimant *must* bring an

---

[29] As was done by the County Court judge in *Williams v. Roffey Bros* [1991] 1 QB 5, where this was not challenged on appeal. See above, 116.

[30] [1979] 1 WLR 783, affirmed [1982] 2 WLR 253 and (on one point only) [1983] 2 AC 352.

action for an agreed sum, and so cannot recover anything in compensation for losses suffered as a result of the failure to pay.[31] This rule was difficult to justify: even if claimants might generally prefer to bring an action for an agreed sum, it would seem that they ought to have had the option of seeking ordinary compensatory damages. But while this rule has never been cleanly overturned, it now appears to be of little effect, as section 35A of the Supreme Court Act 1981 permits courts to award interest on sums due.[32] Further, the Court of Appeal in *Wadsworth v. Lydall*[33] held that although 'general' damages may not be available for breach of a monetary obligation, 'special damages' can be awarded. The matter is not free from doubt, but the latter category would appear to cover any losses that are not covered by an award of interest, assuming they satisfy the ordinary tests for remoteness of loss etc.

Agreed damages clauses

It sometimes happens that the parties to a contract have themselves provided for what is to happen in the event of a breach by one or both of them. They may, for instance, expressly agree that if one of them breaks the contract she shall pay £100 damages to the other party. An agreement of this sort is in principle valid and unobjectionable, and its enforcement is, in effect, an action on an agreed sum. But the courts have long held that it is essential that the sum payable should really be intended as compensation ('liquidated damages'), and not as a threat or penalty held over the other party's head to compel performance. If the court thinks that the sum is a penalty, it is not recoverable. The innocent party is then left an ordinary claim for damages to be assessed by the court in the usual way.[34]

The general principle is that an agreed damages clause will be classified as liquidated damages, and thus enforceable, only if it is a genuine pre-estimate of the expected loss. The test, it should be emphasized, is in principle *ex ante*; the court compares the agreed sum to the *anticipated* losses as opposed to the actual loss, although in practice it seems clear that courts are influenced by the severity of the actual loss. If the actual loss is greater than the agreed sum, it is unlikely that it will be declared a penalty even if the anticipated loss was much less. It should also be stressed that the test only invalidates clauses that specify a sum *greater* than the anticipated loss. Clauses that specify sums *less than* anticipated losses are regulated by the rules dealing with limitation clauses.[35]

---

[31] *London, Chatham and Dover Rly Co. v. South Eastern Rly* [1893] AC 429.

[32] See also the Late Payment of Commercial Debts (Interest) Act 1988, which prescribes a rate of interest for the late payment of certain 'commercial debts'.

[33] [1981] 1 WLR 598.

[34] Penal clauses are also found in the list of prima facie suspect clauses in Schedule 2 of the Unfair Terms in Consumer Contracts Regulations 1999; see above, 317–326.

[35] Above, 149–154, 326.

The courts have laid down certain common-sense principles to aid in determining if a clause is a penalty or liquidated damages.[36] First, if the sum payable is far in excess of the probable damage on breach, it is almost certainly a penalty. Secondly, if the same sum is expressed to be payable on any one of a number of different breaches of varying importance, it is again probably a penalty, because it is extremely unlikely that the same damage would be caused by these varying breaches. Thirdly, where a sum is expressed to be payable on a certain date, and a further sum in the event of default being made, this latter sum is prima facie a penalty, because a very short delay in payment is unlikely to cause significant damage. Fourthly, the mere fact that the damages for a breach would be difficult to assess does not mean that the agreed sum cannot be liquidated damages—on the contrary, this is precisely the situation in which the parties may reasonably wish to agree on the sum payable for breach. So, for instance, in contracts with public bodies (for the construction of roadworks or defence supplies or the like) where it would often be impossible to quantify the loss caused by delay or non-performance, liquidated damages clauses are almost universally used. Finally, the mere use of the words 'liquidated damages' is not decisive, for it is the task of the court and not of the parties to decide the true nature of the sum payable.

The rule against penalties is an old equitable principle which was absorbed into the common law long before the classical period, and it survived that period although it manifestly involves a rare judicial power to override the express terms of a contract. But attitudes to the use of this power have fluctuated over the centuries and courts have used the power more sparingly in recent decades than in the past. It has been emphasised, in particular, that the courts should hesitate to second-guess commercial parties as to the reasonableness of an agreed damages clause.[37] This seems appropriate. The general arguments in favour of freedom of contract apply to stipulated damages clauses as much as to other clauses. The main reason such clauses would appear to deserve special scrutiny is that they are less likely to be noticed and fully understood than, say, clauses specifying the price or the main subject-matter of the contract. In this respect, they appear similar to exemption clauses in that (as was explained in Chapter 12) they deal with events that the parties do not expect to happen (i.e. breach) and whose consequences are hard to predict. Moreover, it is often difficult for anyone but a trained lawyer to appreciate their true significance. But while these considerations weigh heavily in the consumer context, they are of limited force in cases involving contracts made by sophisticated commercial parties. For such parties, the ordinary assumption that the parties know better than the courts what is in their best interests seems reasonable. Even a manifestly penal clause

---

[36] See in particular *Dunlop v. New Garage* [1915] AC 79.
[37] *Philips Hong Kong Ltd v. Attorney General of Hong Kong* (1993) 61 BLR 41.

may be inserted for good business reasons. For example, the party subject to such a clause may have suggested the clause in order to reassure the other party of his trustworthiness. The common practice whereby pizza-delivery companies promise a free pizza if delivery is even one minute late is an illustration.

Considerations of this kind may lie behind the courts' reluctance to extend the rules on agreed damages clauses to analogous clauses. In *ECGD v. Universal Oil Products Co.*[38] the House of Lords insisted that the penalty rule is only applicable to a sum of money payable on a breach of contract, and has no application to a contractual clause which provides for an agreed sum to be paid on any other contingency. In this case the claimants only sought to recover their actual losses, so the actual claim was unobjectionable; but the defendants argued that, if the clauses in question were enforceable, there might be other circumstances in which sums vastly in excess of the claimants' losses could be recovered. Further, although the event on which the agreed sums were payable here was not a breach of contract between the parties, it did involve a breach of contract with other parties, and the various contracts were all interrelated and interlocking.

On the surface, the House of Lords decision in *ECGD* appears highly formalistic. If the reasoning is followed strictly in other cases, it means that the penalty rules can easily be avoided by careful drafting. For instance, a building contract might contain two clauses, (1) requiring the works to be completed by 1 January, and (2) providing for an agreed sum of £100 per day as compensation in the event of breach. The second clause would clearly be subject to the penalty rules (though whether it actually would be a penalty would depend on the criteria listed above). But the contract could be redrafted to avoid any suggestion that it would be a breach if the works were not completed by 1 January. So the contract could provide that the total price payable should be £X, but in the event of the works being completed after 1 January, the price would be reduced by £100 per day. According to the *ECGD* case, that would evade the application of the penalty rules altogether. There is nothing fanciful about this example. In certain kinds of mortgages it has long been the practice to provide that the interest rate should be X per cent, but if the interest is paid punctually on the due date it should instead be X minus ½ per cent.

While the distinction drawn between agreed damages clauses and agreed sums in *ECGD* seems artificial, it may draw some legitimacy from the complaint that (as we haves seen) the rules applied to agreed damages clauses are themselves not easily justified. Whatever role such clauses may have played in the past,[39] agreed damages clauses (and analogous clauses) are

---

[38] [1983] 1 WLR 399.   [39] See the discussion of 'penal bonds', above, 392.

today regularly employed by business parties for good commercial reasons. This is not to deny that consumers and small businesses may often be unfairly surprised by such clauses. But in the case of consumers, at least, relief is now available against unfair surprises by virtue of the Unfair Terms in Consumer Contracts Regulations 1999. The Regulations have the further advantage of directing the courts to look at all the circumstances surrounding the clause.

These observations may also help to explain a whole series of decisions in which courts have pre-empted some less developed rules of a closely parallel character. These rules concern contractual forfeitures, which enable one party to retain property or money as a result of a breach by the other party, even though the result is out of all proportion to the loss sustained. Although these cases do not involve an action for an agreed sum, they are closely analogous to such cases, and it is convenient to deal with them in conjunction with the rule against penalties.

Historically, there was much support for a judicial power to override contractual forfeiture clauses, parallel to the power to deal with penalties. Penalties and forfeiture often serve the same function, the only difference between them being that the roles of the claimant and the defendant are reversed. In the case of penalties, one party is seeking to recover money from the other without having to prove the loss he has actually suffered; in the case of forfeiture, he already has the money or other property (in substance as security) and is seeking to keep it. The earliest examples of these rules in fact concerned forfeiture, rather than penalty clauses. As we have already seen, in mortgages, the property was usually declared to be forfeited if the debtor failed to repay the debt on the due date, even though the property might be worth much more than the debt itself. The jurisdiction to relieve against these results is several centuries old. It was only later that this jurisdiction was extended to penal bonds, and eventually to all forms of penalty clauses.

Even in relation to forfeiture (in the widest sense) there are some cases where the judicial power to grant relief is well established and often now statutory. For instance, a landlord cannot forfeit a lease, whatever the lease may say, because of a breach of covenant by the tenant,[40] and there is even statutory jurisdiction to order repayment of the customary 10 per cent deposit paid on an exchange of contracts for the sale of land if the seller resells the land without loss, following breach by the buyer.[41] And more

---

[40] Law of Property Act 1925, s. 146. For a modern extension, see *Abbey National Building Society v. Maybeech Ltd* [1985] Ch. 190.

[41] *Universal Corp. v. Five Ways Properties Ltd* [1979] 1 All ER 552. But in practice the customary 10% deposit is so well entrenched that it is hard to imagine a court holding that it is a penalty or ordering any of it to be refunded under the statutory jurisdiction. Contracts for the sale of land requiring forfeitable deposits of more than 10% must be justified by special circumstances, and normally such deposits will be reclaimable as a penalty subject to deduction for the seller's actual loss: *Workers Trust & Merchant Bank Ltd v. Dojap Investments Ltd* [1993] AC 573 (PC).

generally, it is accepted that a contract which provides for the forfeiture of possessory or proprietary rights may be challenged under the penalty rules. In Australia it has been held by the High Court that (even aside from the usual penalty rules) there is a wider equitable jurisdiction to relieve against forfeiture of property where the forfeiture would be unconscionable.[42]

But the House of Lords has several times refused to extend this jurisdiction to other cases at common law. Thus a charterer of a ship (who does not usually have possessory or proprietary rights, but is a mere hirer in law) may find that the owner is entitled to withdraw the vessel under the charterparty if the rent is not promptly paid, even though this may cause huge loss to the charterer.[43] As with other examples of rescission or termination, these forfeiture clauses may enable a renegotiation of the contract under which the innocent party obtains compensation far in excess of the damages (if any) which could be recovered for the breach. Similarly, the House of Lords has refused all relief to a contracting party whose failure to pay an instalment under a settlement of a previous dispute gave the other party the right to sever all ties immediately, and withdraw a licence to use a trade name which the guilty party had been exploiting.[44] Yet in a very similar case the Court of Appeal later granted relief where a contract provided for forfeiture of a share in patent rights which were jointly owned by the parties, on non-payment of some relatively trivial sum by the guilty party.[45] Patent rights are a form of property, so a highly technical distinction now exists here between patent rights and mere licensing agreements which commercially are often almost indistinguishable from property rights.

So also the Court of Appeal has held that there is no jurisdiction to relieve against loss of a deposit payable under a contract which was agreed to be irrecoverable in the event of breach. So where a buyer of a ship contracted to pay a deposit of 10 per cent of the price of £ 2.36 million, and the contract expressly provided that the deposit would be irrecoverable in the event that the buyer failed to pay in full, it was held that the deposit was forfeitable even though the seller had resold the ship for a loss much less than the amount of the deposit.[46] Indeed, in this case, because the buyer had not actually paid

---

[42] *Stern v. McArthur* (1988) 165 CLR 489.

[43] *The Laconia* [1977] AC 850; *Scandinavian Trading Tanker Co. v. Flota Petrolera Ecuatoriana (The Scaptrade)* [1983] 2 AC 694. But the losses alleged in these cases were pure 'expectation' losses, and in one sense there was no 'forfeiture' at all here—they were simply cases of termination causing severe losses of expected profits. The result is more offensive where the sums being 'forfeited' have already been paid over.

[44] *Sport International Bussum v. Inter-Footwear* [1984] 1 WLR 776.

[45] *BICC v. Burndy* [1985] Ch 232.

[46] *Damon Cia Naviera v. Hapag-Lloyd* [1985] 1 All ER 475.

the deposit, it was the seller who was suing for the recovery of the deposit, and yet this manifestly penal claim was upheld.[47]

Nevertheless, a 'part-payment' is generally recoverable because it is assumed that, the rule against forfeitures aside, the parties did not intend such a payment to be forfeited in the event of breach. The distinction depends on whether the payment was intended to be a security for the performance of the contract, in which case it is a 'deposit' and not recoverable, or merely an advance payment against the price, in which case it is recoverable if the contract does not go ahead. In practice, the actual amount is likely to be significant: small payments (such as 10 per cent of the price) are likely to be treated as forfeitable deposits, while larger payments are more likely to be treated as part-payments.

As with the rules on penalties, there has been considerable academic discussion of the rules regarding forfeitures, deposits, and the like. The arguments are by and large similar in both cases, but two points are worth noting. First, the relatively generous relief that is afforded in cases of forfeiture may be justified in part on the ground that the parties seeking relief in such cases are typically consumers rather than commercial parties. As has already been discussed, the cognitive problems associated with clauses of this kind are more serious in consumer contracts. Secondly, the courts' unwillingness to extend relief against penalties to cases involving 'penal' deposits may be partly explicable on the ground that the victims in such cases are often commercial parties and, further, that the cognitive problems associated with penalties are generally less serious when the 'penalty' is in the more visible form of a deposit. The handing over of a deposit makes it very clear to the depositor that there is a risk of losing the deposit if the remaining payment is not made.

5. THE ACTION FOR DAMAGES

The action for damages is the most general remedy recognized by the common law. Its primary purpose is to compensate the innocent party for the guilty party's breach of contract so far as money can do so. Thus, exemplary or punitive damages which may sometimes be awarded in the law of tort as a sort of punishment are almost unknown in the law of contract. Only in the single case of breach of promise of marriage were such damages permissible, and this is the exception which proves the rule, for this resembles an action in tort more than an action in contract. It has, in any case, now been abolished. So too, gain-based remedies, such as the action known as 'waiver of tort', under which a tort victim may (for certain torts) demand that the tortfeasor

---

[47] This extreme decision seems inconsistent both with the *Workers Trust* case, above n. 39 and also with *Rover International v. Cannon Film Sales (No. 3)* [1989] 1 WLR 912.

hand over any profits made as a result of the tort, are almost (though not quite) unknown in the law of contract. Furthermore, awards for certain kinds of losses or injuries, such as pain and suffering and, more generally, remote or consequential losses, have traditionally been harder to obtain in cases involving contractual claims.

These apparent differences between tort and contract damages give rise to a number of questions. In theory, breach of contract is a wrong, that is to say a 'tort', and so it would seem that the law's response to a breach of contract should be broadly similar to its response to other torts. This does not mean that the actual amount of damages awarded for a breach of contract should be identical to that awarded for, say, a tortious misrepresentation, even in a case where the claimant has the choice of suing in contract or tort in respect of the same statement. The amount of damages that is awarded depends on the duty that is breached, and the duty to keep a promise is not the same as the duty to tell the truth. The point, however, is that one might expect that the courts' general approaches to issues such as punitive damages, restitutionary awards, and the kinds of losses recoverable would be broadly similar in contract and tort.

Many commentators have explained the (apparently) special way that claims for contractual damages are assessed on the basis of the economic view (described earlier) according to which the law encourages contracting parties to commit 'efficient' breaches of contract and, more generally, treats contracts as entirely economic affairs in which moral concerns have no place. An alternative explanation is that, despite appearances, the courts' approaches are in fact similar, at least at the level of general principle. This view explains the apparent differences on the basis that the kind of harm typically caused by a breach of contract is different than that caused by other kinds of wrongdoing. We will return to these issues later.

Broadly speaking, the action for damages for breach of contract lies for non-performance and for defective performance. Contract damages cannot generally be recovered for breach of a 'duty' arising independently of the contract, such as duress, misrepresentation, breach of a fiduciary duty, or breach of a duty of disclosure, although in many (not all) cases in which such duties are broken the victim is able to claim damages in tort. In particular, damages in tort may be available for losses caused by negligent, fraudulent, and even innocent misrepresentations.

The principles governing awards for misrepresentation were discussed in Chapter 10; here it is sufficient to recall briefly two respects in which these awards are similar to those given for breach of contract. First, while in theory the victim of a misrepresentation who was induced to enter a contract is entitled only to compensation for losses suffered in *reliance* on the misrepresentation, and not, as would be the case in a contract claim, for whatever gains she would have obtained had the representation been true, in practice these measures are often the same. This is because one common way of 'relying', particularly in commercial cases, is to forgo the opportunity to enter another contract as lucrative as the one entered. Secondly, the Misrepresentation Act 1967 permits courts to award damages in cases involving innocent misrepresentations (in lieu of ordering rescission). Under the traditional law, an innocent misrepresentation gave rise to a claim for damages only if it was found to be incorporated into the contract; courts often reached this conclusion out of a reluctance to rescind the contract, which was otherwise the only available option. Indeed, prior to the decision in *Hedley Byrne & Co. Ltd v. Heller & Partners Ltd*[48] this was also the case with respect to negligent misrepresentations. An important consequence of the Misrepresentation Act 1967 and the *Hedley Byrne* decision is that damage awards that in the past were justified on the basis that a contractual term was breached can now be justified on the basis that an innocent or negligent non-contractual misrepresentation was made.

Contributory negligence

The defence of contributory negligence, commonly raised in tort cases, has traditionally not been allowed in actions for breach of contract (although similar results could sometimes be reached by using the 'mitigation principle', as discussed below, or by invoking causation and holding that the claimant was the sole cause of his own loss). The traditional rule seems appropriate for the large number of contract cases where the defendant's obligation was to bring about a certain result, as for example in an ordinary contract of sale, but it is difficult to defend in cases where the defendant's duty was to take reasonable care, as in the case of a typical contract for the professional services of a doctor or lawyer. In these cases, where the relevant duty is identical to a tort duty, it seems plain that any loss or injury caused by the defendant's failure to use due care is sometimes also partly the fault of the claimant.

This anomaly was partly remedied by the Law Reform (Contributory Negligence) Act 1945, which can be invoked to apportion the damages in a claim based on breach of contract where there is liability both in contract and in tort (as is the case of the typical contract for services).[49] But it has been held that the Act cannot be invoked where the liability exists solely as a matter of contract,[50] even if the liability is based on the breach of a contractual obligation to use due care.[51] This limitation remains

---

[48] [1964] AC 465.
[49] *Forsikringsaktieselskapet Vesta v. Butcher* [1988] 2 All ER 43; affirmed [1989] AC 852.
[50] *Barclays Bank Plc v. Fairclough Building Ltd* [1994] 3 WLR 1057.
[51] *Bank of Nova Scotia v. Hellenic Mutual War Risks Association (Bermuda) Ltd* [1989] 3 All ER 628, reversed on different grounds [1992] 1 AC 233.

an anomaly, and the Law Commission has proposed that it should be eliminated.[52]

6. THE MEASURE OF DAMAGES

Expectation damages

The general principle of contract law is that the innocent party is entitled to damages that compensate for his 'loss', but losses are of various kinds. In particular, there is an important distinction between loss of an expectation, that is to say, the loss associated with not receiving what one was promised, and an actual loss that has resulted from action in reliance on the contract. The general rule in English law is that, prima facie, the innocent party is entitled to damages for his lost expectations; he is entitled, in other words, to be placed in the position in which he would have been if the contract had been fully performed, so far as money can do this, as opposed (merely) to the position he would have been in had the contract not been made at all.

The 'expectation' damages principle is sometimes criticized on the ground that it is too favourable to claimants. The basic argument is that expectation damages compensate claimants for 'losses' that they never actually suffer. The rule enables a contractor to recover damages for his lost profit on a building contract even if the other party repudiates the contract before the contractor lifts a finger to perform, buys materials, or relies on the contract in any other way. Similarly, if a person contracts to buy a new car, and then changes his mind overnight and cancels the contract, the seller is in principle entitled to recover his anticipated profit on the transaction even though he has not, at the time of the cancellation, done anything whatever in pursuance of the contract.

The traditional response to this argument is that the loss of an expectation is indeed a true loss, because a contractual promise creates an entitlement—a right to performance—where none existed before. In this view, failing to perform a contractual promise harms the promisee's existing rights, just as if the promisor damaged her property or person. This response takes us back to the debate, examined in Chapter 3, about the general desirability of enforcing promises, agreements, and other voluntary undertakings *qua* promises, agreements, and voluntary undertakings. The objection to expectation damages is essentially an objection to the idea that the law should enforce promises *qua* promises (as opposed to, for example, relied-upon promises). This is not the place to revisit this (complex) debate, but three observations may be pertinent. First, the expectation damages rule is consistent with the orthodox view that contractual parties have a duty to do what they said they

---

[52] Law Com Report No. 219 (London, 1993).

would do. Any lesser measure of damages would effectively leave contracting parties free to provide a lesser measure of performance. Secondly, even if it is accepted that it is generally appropriate to award expectation damages, it may be queried whether such damages are appropriate for all claims of breach of contract. It has been stressed throughout this book that contracting parties are often liable for the breach of contractual duties to which they gave only minimal assent—as when the contract's terms were not fully read or understood, a mistake was made, the defendant's liability was based on having induced reliance rather than having made a promise, or the defendant's liability arose from breach of an implied-in-law term. In situations of these kinds the usual justification for expectation damages, namely that the defendant is only being asked to hand over the monetary value of what he voluntarily agreed to do, has limited force. To give one example, if a seller of goods is held liable for breach of an implied condition of fitness for purpose under the Sale of Goods Act (an everyday legal problem), he will prima facie be liable for damages to put the claimant in the position in which he would have been had the goods been fit for their purpose. But it may happen that the only goods fit for this purpose would actually have cost far more than the goods sold.[53] So if the buyer is entitled to damages to put him in the position he would have been in if the implied condition had been performed, he will, in the result, obtain the goods he wants at a fraction of their true price. If the seller really intended to assume this liability—if he had directed his mind to the possibility that the goods might be unfit, and had assured the buyer that they would be fit—it may be assumed that the contractual price would have reflected this risk, and included some sort of insurance premium to cover it. But in most such cases the seller does not direct his mind to the risk at all, the contract price probably does not reflect it, and the implied term is anyhow implied under the Sale of Goods Act rather than from the intentions of the parties. In such a case it seems very questionable whether the seller should be liable for the expectation damages of the buyer. The reason he is, nevertheless, is that lawyers have persuaded themselves that contractual liability is always assent-based; as this example shows, this is an elusive and treacherous idea which can easily be misapplied.

A similar approach may be appropriate for certain agreements made between parties in close relationships, such as friends and family members. As was discussed in Chapter 4, enforcing such agreements with the full force of law may be inconsistent with the ideas of trust and confidence on which the relationships are grounded. At present, the courts' only option, if they have this concern, is invoke the 'intent to create legal relations' doctrine and then refuse to give any relief at all. In some cases (as was explained in Chapter 4)

---

[53] See the Canadian case, *Sealand of the Pacific v. MacHaffie* (1974) 51 DLR (3d) 702 on which this example is based.

this seems too harsh; a compromise would be to give relief to the extent—but no more—that the parties relied on the agreement.

The final observation is that whatever the theory of the law, reliance damages are in fact often awarded. We will examine when this happens and the extent to which it is consistent with the traditional theory later in this chapter.

Compensation for what? Diminution in value versus cost of cure

We have seen that contractual damages are intended to compensate the claimant, so far as money is able, for the value of the defendant's contractual undertaking. Where performance is still possible this is generally done by awarding the claimant a sum of money equal to the cost of obtaining substitute goods or performance, plus an amount to cover incidental expenses, etc. This approach, if it is done accurately, should ensure the claimant is fully compensated: in the typical case the claimant values performance at least as much as what performance costs—this is why she entered the contract in the first place. Even if the claimant values the relevant goods or services at more than the market price, she can simply use the award to purchase a substitute, thereby obtaining the full value of the original performance.

But there are cases in which the cost of obtaining a substitute (the so-called 'cost of cure') is greater than the value that the claimant places on performance (the so-called 'diminution in value' resulting from the breach). This may happen because the claimant made a mistake when he entered the contract, because circumstances changed since the contract was entered, or because 'curing' the breach may require costly undoing or redoing work already done. The case of *Tito v. Waddell*,[54] where the defendant mining company breached a contractual obligation to replant mined lands, again provides an illustration. On the facts, although the cost of replanting was enormous, it was of little value to the claimant islanders because they had moved (for other reasons) to another island. A second, more recent illustration is provided by *Ruxley Electronics v. Forsyth*,[55] where the defendant had breached a building contract by constructing a pool that was a few inches shallower than the contractually specified depth. To rebuild the pool to the correct depth would have involved redoing most of the work, at a cost of well over £20,000, but (the court held) would have no effect on the pool's financial value or on the activities for which it could be used. Even accepting (as the court did) that the claimant placed a personal ('subjective') value on the extra inches of depth, the measure of this value (which the court assessed at £2,500) was nowhere near the cost of rebuilding the pool.

The general rule in cases of this kind is that cost of cure is awarded only where it is equal to the actual value placed on performance by the claimant.

---

[54] Above n. 13.   [55] [1996] AC 344.

This is typically proven by evidence of a genuine intent to do the work, not motivated by malice or a desire to punish the defendant or to obtain future bargaining chips. Where a lesser sum of money would fully compensate the claimant, in the sense that it would leave the claimant with no preference between performance and having the money, then it is that sum which will awarded. Applying this rule to the facts of *Tito*, the court awarded the islanders only nominal damages, while in *Ruxley* the homeowner received £2,500 for his loss of pleasure in owning a pool shallower than the specified depth.

The basic purpose of an award of damages, we have said, is to *compensate* the claimant for the lost value of performance; this is why such awards are called 'damages'—they are a response to the damage or injury suffered by the claimant. So far as achieving this purpose is concerned, the decisions in *Tito* and *Ruxley* seem broadly correct. Admittedly, it is difficult to be certain that the courts assessed the actual value of performance accurately. In each case, the claimants could (and in *Ruxley* did) claim that they placed a non-pecuniary or subjective value on performance, and it may be questioned whether the awards provided full compensated for such values. But in broad terms, the conclusion that it was possible to compensate the claimants for their losses by awarding a sum of money substantially less than the cost of cure seems correct. Indeed, so far as the goal of compensation is concerned, the cost of cure would seem strictly irrelevant, except as indirect evidence of the monetary value of performance.

However, even if it is accepted that the awards in *Tito* and *Ruxley* fully compensated the claimants for their losses, there would appear to be two other grounds on which a *monetary* award (even if not strictly an award of *damages*) set at or near to the level of cost of cure might be justified in such cases. For reasons explained below, neither of these grounds is formally recognized in the common law, and so neither was considered by the courts in *Tito* or *Ruxley*. But their intuitive appeal helps to explain the controversies surrounding this area of the law.

A monetary award set at the level of cost of cure might be justified, first, on the ground that it is intended not to compensate the claimant, but to give him a kind of substitute specific performance. We noted earlier in this chapter that a strong argument can be made that in principle, if not always in practice, the victim of a breach of contract should presumptively have the right to demand specific performance in cases where it is still possible. If this is correct, it would appear to follow that in cases where specific performance is inappropriate because it involves a personal element, is too difficult to super-vise, or simply because the claimant wants nothing further to do with the defendant, the courts should be willing to award the claimant a sum of money sufficient to obtain *substitute* specific performance. Indeed, although England (unlike some legal systems) does not officially recognise the concept of substitute specific performance, this might be thought the most natural reason for awarding claimants the cost of cure, even in an ordinary claim for 'damages': if the claimant has the right to performance that the courts proclaim, then the claimant should have the right to a remedy that ensures he is in fact able to obtain such performance, even if not from the defendant.

At the same time, neither ordinary specific performance nor substitute performance would seem justified in a case where the claimant seeks such an award merely in order to punish the claimant or as part of a bargaining strategy.[56] When this factor is taken into account, it appears that English courts actually award cost of cure in more or less those situations in which substitute specific performance seems justified, namely cases where the claimant genuinely intends to do the work.[57] In *Tito*, it appears that the court felt there was little evidence that the claimants were genuinely interested in having their uninhabited island replanted. *Ruxley* is more difficult to analyze from this perspective. The claimant *said* that he wanted a deeper pool and that if he were given the money he would use it for this purpose. Moreover, the court's reason for refusing cost of cure appeared to focus primarily on their assessment of the loss he would suffer if his pool was not rebuilt—something that should be relevant only to questions of compensation. But reading between the lines, it seemed that the trial judge did not actually believe that the claimant was as interested in getting his pool rebuilt as he was in punishing the defendant, and so the result may be justified on this basis. The broader point, however, is that cost of cure awards seem better understood as substitute specific performance than as compensatory damages. Interpreted in this way, it seems possible such awards might become marginally more available than in the past.

A second reason that a monetary award assessed at (or near to) the cost of cure might sometimes be justified in cases like *Tito* or *Ruxley* is that this sum represents the amount by which the defendant was unjustly enriched by his breach. As was mentioned earlier, the mining company in *Tito v. Waddell* presumably demanded compensation in the form of a lower contract price for agreeing, in their contract, to replant the mined lands. In principle, therefore, it would seem that the claimants should have been able to demand restitution of the price 'paid' for the replanting clause. This would be a claim not for

---

[56] Because an order of 'substitute specific performance' is a monetary award there is little risk that a claimant will seek it in order to obtain a bargaining chip for use in settlement negotiations (as may be the case with an order of actual specific performance). But the *possibility* that such an order may be made can be used in this way, since the claimant may demand a large sum of money in exchange for not going to the court and asking for substitute specific performance. This explains why even an undertaking by the claimant to the court that the money will be used for substitute specific performance is not proof that the claimant genuinely wants the work done. If the courts award cost-of-cure damages whenever such undertakings are given, claimants will be able to demand large sums in exchange for not going to court.

[57] As, for example, in *Radford v. De Froberville* [1977] 1 WLR 1262.

damages, nor for substitute performance, but a claim to reverse an unjust enrichment. In *Tito* itself, the actual sum awarded on such a basis would be close to the cost of cure, since the price charged by the mining company for replanting was presumably close to the actual cost of replanting. But this would not always be the case. In *Ruxley*, for example, the cost of rebuilding the pool was much greater than either the contractual price of the extra inches or the amount that the builder saved by his breach.

But while the argument for a restitutionary award seems strong in cases such as *Tito*, under the present law courts cannot actually make such awards because of certain technical, and much criticized (see below), restrictions on the availability of 'partial restitution'. Restitution of benefits conferred under a breached contract can generally only be obtained where the claimant did not receive *any* of what was due under the contract (which was not the case in *Tito*— the mining company paid the mining fee). The result is that there is a strong incentive towards trying to achieve the same result indirectly, by awarding the claimant 'cost of cure' damages. As a matter of principle, this is awkward: cost of cure is not strictly a measure of benefit, and damages are not restitution. But given the difficulty of making ordinary restitutionary awards in such cases, it is perfectly understandable that many writers might support a cost of cure award in such cases.

Reliance damages

It has already been mentioned that some writers have argued that the case for awarding *reliance* damages is stronger in principle than the case for expectation damages. Certain of these writers have also argued that the law is largely consistent with this view despite appearances. Their argument is not that the law explicitly endorses the idea that contract damages are meant to compensate for reliance losses. Admittedly there are situations (as we shall see) where the courts openly award damages on a reliance-based measure, but these are relatively rare and can, in any event, be explained using the orthodox theory. The argument here is based on the much broader and more radical proposition that the expectation damages measure is itself designed to compensate for reliance-based losses. In this view, the expectation measure of damages is effectively a proxy for a reliance-based measure of damages, and is adopted only because it is easier to apply and administer than an explicitly reliance-based measure.

The idea underlying this argument is that one of the main ways contracting parties typically rely on each other's promises is by forgoing opportunities to enter other contracts. In a typical contract of sale, for example, if the purchaser had not agreed to order goods from vendor A, she presumably would have ordered them from vendor B or C. Thus, the true measure of the purchaser's reliance loss, if vendor A fails to deliver, must take into account the value of the alternative contract that the purchaser declined to enter in reliance on A's promise. Furthermore, in an ordinary competitive market the expected value of the best alternative will typically be equal or at least close to the expected value of the contract that was actually made—because in a competitive market prices are roughly equal. The reliance measure and the expectation measure will therefore usually give the same figure. But—and this is a key step in the argument—proving the existence and value of such alternative contractual opportunities in court can be difficult and costly. It is much simpler, the argument goes, for courts to assess the expected value of the contract that was actually made and then to accept this as a proxy for the measure of the claimant's reliance losses. The argument concludes that the orthodox expectations damages rule can therefore be explained on the basis that it provides courts with an easy-to-apply method of ensuring that claimants' reliance losses are compensated.

The idea that the reliance and expectation measures of damages lead, in practice, to similar awards in most cases seems incontrovertible. But there are certain difficulties with the idea that the main *purpose* of contractual damages is to compensate for reliance losses. First, judges do not say that such awards are made in order to compensate claimants for their reliance losses: they say they are made in order to compensate the claimant for the value of the contractual promise. They continue to say this today, a time when the argument now being considered has been well known by lawyers and judges for over half a century.[58]

Secondly, the idea that the courts are primarily interested in protecting against reliance losses seems inconsistent with the existence of specific relief. Specific relief may sometimes prevent reliance losses from occurring, but its justification, it seems plain, is to ensure that claimants receive the very thing they were promised. Defendants are ordered to do what they promised to do, not to do whatever is necessary to ensure that the claimant is not harmed by relying on the promise. Moreover, the reliance theory cannot easily explain the *kinds* of cases where specific performance is ordered. In the typical case of a contract for the sale of land or a unique good there is strong likelihood that the value of the promise will be greater than the value of the claimant's reliance on that promise.

A third difficulty with the claim that contract damages are designed to compensate for reliance losses is that expectations damages are available for all claims for breach of contract, not just claims where the reliance and expectation measures are likely to overlap. If a contract for the rental of a holiday cottage is cancelled by the tenant ten minutes after it is made and thus before the owner has done anything in reliance on the booking, the owner

---

[58] The argument was first developed in what is probably the most famous law review article ever written on the common law of contract: L. Fuller and W. Purdue, 'The Reliance Interest in Contract Damages' (1936) 46 Yale LJ 53.

may, according to the orthodox doctrine, claim for the profit he would have made from the booking if he can show that he was unable to make a new booking. Yet in a case of this kind, it is not difficult to prove that the expectation measure is a poor proxy for the reliance measure. Admittedly, in practice, courts deciding non-commercial cases (such as the example just given) often reach results that are consistent with the reliance theory. This happens in various ways. For example, the court might decide that the contract had not been concluded because negotiations were still ongoing, or because there was no intent to create legal relations, or because the agreement was too uncertain. The court may also interpret an apparent bilateral contract as a unilateral contract, so that the agreement takes effect only when the claimant does an act in reliance (such as giving the tenant a key). Or the court may interpret the contract as subject to a condition precedent that is not fulfilled.[59] Finally, the court might dispute the factual basis on which an award of profits is made; in the above example, the court might conclude that despite the landlord's evidence to the contrary, it would indeed have been possible to rent the cottage to someone else after the cancellation.[60] But notwithstanding such examples, it seems clear that in ordinary commercial cases the courts regularly make awards of expectation damages in situations where the claimant's reliance losses, both positive and negative, are less than the value of the contract. When we examine the remoteness rules later in this chapter, we will see that the law expressly provides for the possibility that claimants may claim the value of an especially or extraordinarily lucrative contract.

It remains to consider two situations where courts are openly willing to award reliance-based damages. First, the courts are generally willing to award reliance damages if the claimant makes a claim on this basis. Such claims are typically made in cases where it is difficult for the claimant to prove the expected value of the contractual obligation in court; indeed, in such cases the claimant may have no choice but to claim reliance-based damages. An illustration is provided by *McRae v. Commonwealth Disposals Commission*,[61] which has already been discussed in a different context. The defendants had sold a shipwrecked tanker which they advertised as lying on a certain reef in the Pacific, and the claimants spent a substantial sum of money equipping a salvage expedition to go in search of the tanker. It turned out that the shipwrecked tanker did not exist, and the claimants were held entitled to damages. Here it was clear that the claimants had incurred substantial expenses—real losses—in reliance on the contract, and the Australian High

---

[59] For a striking example see the Canadian case of *Custom Motors v. Dinwell* (1975) 6 DLR (3d) 342.

[60] As will be explained below when we examine the 'mitigation principle', claimants cannot claim for losses (including lost profits) that they could reasonably have avoided incurring.

[61] (1950) 84 CLR 377; discussed above, 173.

Court awarded these reliance damages to the claimants. Their expectation losses were quite different: their lost expectations consisted of the total expected value of the salvaged tanker *minus* the cost of the salvage expedition, but it was impossible to quantify these losses as there was no basis for putting any sort of real figure on the expected value of the tanker.[62] In such cases, an award of reliance damages can be reconciled with the orthodox theory of contract damages on the evidentiary ground that reliance damages are a good approximation of the profit that the claimants' reasonably expected to make (but which they would have had difficulty proving). This interpretation finds support in the rule that claimants cannot choose to obtain reliance damages where they would have made a loss on their contract.[63]

The second group of cases where reliance damages are openly awarded is where the contractual obligation that was breached was an obligation to use reasonable care. In *Watts v. Morrow*,[64] the claimants bought a house for £177,500 on the strength of a surveyor's (negligent) report stating that the house was in good condition. In fact, major repairs were required at a cost of £33,961. But it was also found that the house in its actual condition was worth £162,500, that is, only £15,000 less than the claimants had paid for it. In an action against the surveyors it was held that the claimants could only recover this sum of £15,000. The reason given for this is that a surveyor's duty in these cases is only to give reasonably careful and competent advice. The surveyor does not promise or *warrant* the accuracy of his advice. If a seller sold a house in a case like this and *warranted* that the house was in sound condition the buyer would be entitled to damages to put him in the position he expected to be in if the contract were fully performed. But the surveyor's duty is more limited than this: the buyer who relies on his report is only entitled to be put in the position he would have been in if the advice had been carefully and competently given. In that case he would presumably not have bought the house at all, or would have paid £15,000 less for it. Similar results are found where a doctor is held liable for negligent treatment or misdiagnosis or the like. A doctor who carelessly lets a patient think that a sterilization operation will be fool-proof does not (it is said) *warrant* that it will be fool-proof. If the doctor had not been negligent the patient might not have had the operation, but if she would have gone ahead anyhow, then she has suffered no loss at all from the doctor's negligence. In no circumstances can

---

[62] See also *Anglia TV v. Reed* [1972] 1 QB 60, where it was held that *pre-contractual expenditure* could also be recovered in such an action, although such expenditure is not, of course, incurred in reliance on the contract.

[63] *C. & P. Haulage v. Middleton* [1983] 3 All ER 94. See also *CCC Films v. Impact Quadrant Films* [1985] QB 316.

[64] [1991] 4 All ER 937.

she recover damages for the full cost of bearing and maintaining a child after the operation.[65]

7. RESTITUTIONARY CLAIMS

There is another sort of monetary claim which is sometimes called a claim to restitution 'damages', though it is not strictly a claim for damages at all. A claim of this kind can arise if the defendant obtained a benefit as a result of the breach of the contract that he ought to return or hand over to the claimant. In such a case, the claimant is not asking for *compensation* for an injury or loss that he suffered (though he may have suffered an injury or loss), but, instead, that the defendant simply return or hand over the benefit he obtained from the breach. The basis of such a claim is therefore that the defendant was unjustly enriched, while the remedy that is sought is that the enrichment be undone. Historically, such claims were closely intertwined with the law of contract—until recently some of them were called claims in 'quasi-contract'—but it is now recognized that they are based on the distinct legal ground of unjust enrichment.[66] It is important, nonetheless, to examine such claims in some detail in this chapter. Although arguably undeveloped in certain respects, they play an important role in filling what might otherwise be considered large gaps in the scheme of remedies available to contracting parties.

There are two distinct ways in which a defendant who has broken a contract may have been enriched, and the law distinguishes sharply between them. First, the defendant may have been enriched by receiving or taking something from the claimant himself. And secondly, he may have been benefited by receiving or taking some benefit from a different source altogether.

Restitution on grounds of failure of consideration

The first situation is very common and is illustrated by the ordinary case of a claimant who has paid something under a contract where the defendant subsequently fails to perform at all, that is to say, where there has been a 'total failure of consideration'.[67] In cases of this kind, it has long been recognized that the claimant has a right to recover his payment, not as damages for breach of contract, but in a quasi-contractual action or, as it would today be called, a claim for restitution. This action is not confined to cases of contract,

---

[65] *Thake v. Maurice* [1986] QB 644.

[66] *Lipkin Gorman v. Karpnale Ltd* [1991] 2 AC 548.

[67] Confusingly, 'consideration' here means something slightly different than in the rules on contract formation. In a formation context, consideration may exist in a mere promise to do something. But to determine if there has been a 'failure of consideration' in the restitution context, the question is whether the defendant actually did what he promised to do under the contract. 'Consideration' in this second sense is closer to 'condition'.

although it finds its most frequent application in this field. It is, in many cases, an alternative remedy for the complete non-performance of a contract. Where money has been paid in advance by one party and the other party fails to perform, the innocent party may simply bring an action for general damages, which will include what he has paid, or he may bring an action to recover what he has paid, without making any further claim for damages. Thus, if a buyer pays for goods which are not delivered, he may sue for damages *or* he may claim the return of his price on the ground of total failure of consideration.[68]

In some cases, this remedy is available where no action can be brought for breach of contract, either because there has been no contract, no breach of contract, or no loss from the breach. For example, an alleged contract may prove to be void owing to lack of a proper offer or acceptance, or a valid contract may fail to become operative owing to the failure of a condition precedent. In these cases, there is a right of recovery of money on a total failure of consideration, although there is no question of a breach of contract. Another illustration is a frustrated contract. If a person pays money under a contract which is subsequently frustrated before he has received any benefit from it, he cannot sue the other party for breach, because there is no breach, but he can recover what he has paid on the ground that there has been a total failure of consideration.

It is therefore frequently advantageous for a person who is content to recover his money to claim it on the ground of total failure of consideration rather than to sue for damages. If he takes the former course he establishes a good prima facie case simply by showing that he has received nothing for his money, whereas if he chooses the latter course he must actually prove that there has been a contract and a breach and some loss flowing from the breach. The restitutionary route is particularly advantageous where the value of performance is less than the contract price. This can happen when the claimant made a mistake in entering the contract or because circumstances subsequently changed. For example, if a defendant contracts to build a store for the claimant at a cost of £100,000 (which is actually paid), and the defendant then breaches the contract, it may be found that the value of the store, if built, would not be anything close to £100,000. Obviously, it would be outrageous to allow the defendant to retain the advance payment on the basis that he had thereby saved the claimant some wasted expenditure. In such a case, the money can again be recovered on a total failure of consideration.

---

[68] It is even possible for the party in *breach* to recover benefits that she transferred before the breach, for example money that was pre-paid (subject to the rules on recovery of deposits and other forms of security for performance): *Dies v. British and International Mining and Finance Corporation Ltd* [1939] 1 KB 724.

The concept of total failure of consideration is somewhat technical. There may be a total failure of consideration even though the defendant has actually done some work or expended some money in the performance of the contract, provided that what he has done has not benefited the other party. For example, if a person orders machinery to be specially constructed for him, there will be a total failure of consideration if none of the machinery is delivered to him, although work may have been commenced and money expended on it.[69]

On the other hand, if some benefit has been received under the contract, no matter how trifling, there is no total failure of consideration. Just as there is generally no right to part payment for part performance, so also there is generally no right to part recovery for partial failure of consideration. Very often, this does not matter because the claimant will have an ordinary action for damages for breach, which will enable him to recover the value of the partial failure of consideration. But in some cases the total failure rule leads to results that appear highly unjust. The American case of *City of New Orleans v. Firemen's Charitable Association*[70] provides a good illustration. A contract was entered into between the claimant city authorities and the defendants for the supply of fire-fighting services. The defendants contracted to keep 124 men, a specified number of horses, and a quantity of hoses available for the fighting of fires. The claimant city claimed that the defendants had in fact maintained fewer men, horses, and equipment than the contract required, and thereby saved themselves some $38,000, but the claimants did not allege, and presumably could not prove, that the defendants had failed to put out any fires as a result of this deficiency. It was held by the Louisiana court that the claimants had no redress for this breach of contract because they had not proved any 'loss' resulting from it, a decision which is entirely in accordance with English law. No separate claim was made for a restitutionary award, but under English law (and American law as well) such a claim would have been denied on the basis that there was no total failure of consideration, as the claimant city had received some of the benefit of the contract.

The refusal to make a restitutionary award in such circumstances seems difficult to justify. In *City of New Orleans* the claimants paid a certain sum of money on the condition that the defendants have ready a certain number of men, etc. to fight fires. If the defendants had not agreed to supply this number of men, the contract price would have been different. Thus, the claimants paid for something they did not get, and the defendants were able to keep something they did not deserve. These are, or at least should be,

---

[69] See *Fibrosa Spolka Akeyjna v. Fairbairn Lawson Combe Barbour Ltd* [1943] AC 32.
[70] (1819) 9 So 486.

compelling grounds for ordering restitution of the price that was paid for the extra men. The same reasoning applies to the case of *Tito v. Waddell* that was discussed earlier.[71] In this case, recall, the defendant mining company was paid (through a reduction in the price that they had to pay for mining rights) to replant mined lands, which obligation they deliberately breached. But the court awarded the claimant islanders only nominal damages, on the basis that the breach had not in fact harmed them (as they had moved to another island). In terms of *compensating* the claimants for the harm caused by the breach, this result (as we saw earlier) may be justified. But issues of compensation aside, it seems clear that the mining company was unjustly enriched— they had retained a payment that was given to them on the condition that they do something which they failed to do. If the replanting obligation had been contained in a separate contract, the claimants clearly could have recovered their payment on the basis of failure of consideration. But because the obligation was included within a larger, partly performed contract, such recovery was not possible; the necessary 'total' failure of consideration could not be proven. Fortunately, the courts have given some indication in recent years that they recognise the rule needs to be revisited.[72]

Paradoxically, the modern law will provide a remedy to a claimant for a partial failure of consideration in certain cases where there has been no breach of contract at all. Where the contract is frustrated, the Law Reform (Frustrated Contracts) Act 1943 enables the court to order part payment in the event of a partial failure of consideration. Thus if a house-holder pays a painter £500 to decorate his house, and the contract is frustrated after one room has been painted (e.g. by the destruction of the house by fire) a proportionate part of the £500 can be recovered. So if a contract like that in *City of New Orleans* was frustrated instead of being breached, the claimants might have been able to recover a proportionate part of the price they had paid.

The 1943 Act also modifies the nature of the right to recover for failure of consideration, whether partial or total. If the contract is not performed owing to frustration as distinct from breach, it seems particularly unfair to permit recovery of all the money paid on the ground of total failure of consideration if work has been done and money expended on the contract, even if the other party is left with no benefit from the work and money. In such cases, the Act of 1943 enables the court to permit some or all of the money to be set off against the cost of what has been done. The same applies to the right to recover for partial failure of consideration.

---

[71] Above n. 13.
[72] *D.O. Ferguson v. Sohl* (1992) 62 Build LR 92, *White Arrow Express Ltd v. Lamey's Distribution Ltd* (1995) 15 Tr LR 69, *Goss v. Chilcott* [1996] AC 798.

Gain-based restitution: restitution for 'wrongs'

The second type of restitutionary claim—where the defendant's enrichment has come from some other source—is much more restricted. Here we come up against a fundamental principle of the law, which some see as a further illustration of the relative weakness of contractual sanctions. If the defendant simply breaches his contract and proceeds to devote his time and resources elsewhere, any gains he makes from that other source are, in general, his, and the claimant has no claim to them. Similarly, he is not required to account for any gains that he makes in the form of saved expenses.

There are two long-standing exceptions to this principle. First, if the defendant's gain comes from exploiting the claimant's property, then a restitutionary claim will be available, even if there is no loss and hence no claim to ordinary damages. For instance, if, in breach of contract, a chauffeur uses his employer's Rolls to take a party of friends for a day's outing, any payment he receives for this breach of contract will be recoverable by the employer.[73] Secondly, a contracting party who owes fiduciary obligations by reason of the nature of the contract or the relationship between the parties, and who obtains gains from some outside source by breaching these obligations, will be liable to pay these gains over in a restitutionary claim. The agent who accepts a bribe from a third party, for instance, is liable to the employer in a restitutionary action even though no loss can be proved.

Neither of these traditional exceptions makes much of a dent in the general principle that gain-based awards are not available for breach of contract. Indeed, each may be explained not so much as responses to breaches of contract per se, but as responses to other kinds of wrongdoing, in particular the wrongs of unlawfully using another's property (the tort of conversion or trespass) and breach of fiduciary duty (an equitable wrong). Two more recent exceptions to the traditional approach are potentially more far-reaching. In *Wrotham Park Estate Co Ltd v. Parkside Homes Ltd*,[74] the defendant built a number of homes in breach of a restrictive covenant that had been included in the contract for the land on which the houses were built. The development caused no loss or injury to the claimant, so a claim for ordinary compensatory damages was not possible. The Court of Appeal nonetheless awarded the claimant 5 per cent of the developer's expected profits, which they held was a reasonable estimate of the amount the claimant would have demanded to relax the covenant. The decision is intuitively appealing, but it raises a number of questions. Clearly, the claimant in *Wrotham could* have sought an injunction preventing the development, and it *could* have then waived this injunction for a fee, but given that it did neither of these things—and given,

---

[73] The leading case is *Reading v. Attorney-General* [1951] AC 507, where a soldier used his uniform to assist in some illegal activities in Egypt.

[74] [1974] 1 WLR 798.

further, that it might have refused to relax the covenant for *any* price—it is somewhat artificial to make an award on this basis. More generally, the decision seems to mix compensatory and restitutionary aims: the award supposedly seeks to give the claimant what it would have received by way of payment for relaxing the covenant (a kind of compensation), but then appears to calculate this amount according to the defendant's profits (a kind of partial restitution—though no formulae has emerged from determining how much of the profits must be returned; the courts have awarded anywhere from 5 per cent to 50 per cent). But notwithstanding these questions the basic idea that a contracting party should not be able to breach clauses of this kind with impunity is compelling, and so it is not surprising that the courts have subsequently applied the *Wrotham* principle to a number of cases involving breaches of restrictive covenants. The Court of Appeal has also recently applied the principle to a case dealing with intellectual property rights. In *Experience Hendrix LLC v. PPX Enterprises Inc*[75] the claimant was awarded a percentage of the profits the defendant had made through awarding recording licenses in breach of the contract by which it had obtained master recordings of the musician Jimi Hendrix. Despite one Court of Appeal to the contrary,[76] it now appears that a *Wrotham*-style award is in principle available in any case where the defendant gained from the breach of a (valid) contractual covenant not to use property or property rights in certain ways.

Even where it is successfully invoked, the *Wrotham* principle only supports awarding the claimant a percentage of the profits earned by the defendant.[77] The second exception to the rule against gain-based awards is potentially more far-reaching because where it is successfully invoked it permits the court to award the full measure of the defendant's profit. In *Attorney-General v. Blake*[78] the defendant was a former member of the intelligence services who published an autobiography in breach of a contractual covenant not to divulge information obtained during his employment. In a clear break with past jurisprudence, the House of Lords held that the Crown was entitled to an award calculated as the amount of the defendant's royalties from the book.

The scope of the exception introduced in *Blake* is unclear. The court stressed that a gain-based award of this kind should only be made in exceptional circumstances,[79] but, unfortunately, they said little more except

---

[75] [2003] All ER (D) 328 (Mar).

[76] *Surrey County Council v. Bredero Homes Ltd* [1993] 1 WLR 1361.

[77] But note that while in *Wrotham* the award was set at 5% of the anticipated profits, in *Lane v O'Brien Homes* [2004] EWHC 303 (QB) the award was set at about 50% of the defendant's profit (the exact basis on which the award was calculated was not made clear).

[78] [2000] 3 WLR 625.

[79] Thus in *Experience Hendrix*, above n.73, a claim for the entirety of the profits made by the defendant was denied on the basis that, unlike in *Blake*, the circumstances were not exceptional.

that ordinary damages must be inadequate and that all the circumstances must be taken into account. In the Court of Appeal, it was suggested that there were at least two categories of cases where such an award would be appropriate. The first are cases of 'skimped performance' where the defendants fail to provide the full extent of contractually specified services. Examples would include cases such as *City of New Orleans* and *Tito v. Waddell*, mentioned earlier. In these cases, the 'gain' awarded to the claimant would be the savings that the defendant made by failing to perform fully (*not* the amount of the contract price that was paid for the relevant obligation— though in practice these amounts will be very similar). The second category is illustrated by the facts of *Blake* itself. This is where the defendant has profited by doing the very thing that he contractually agreed not to do. *Wrotham Park*, which was mentioned earlier, also fits into this category.

The House of Lords' reasons for refusing to support these categories are not difficult to imagine. In cases such as *City of New Orleans*, the claimant's real complaint (as we have seen) is not that the defendant made an unjust gain from an external source, but that the defendant unjustly held on to some- thing—part of the contract price—that was given to him *by the claimant*. The answer to this complaint, in principle anyway, is not to permit a gain-based award, but to remove the artificial 'total failure of consideration' limitation on ordinary restitutionary claims. The issues raised by the second category of cases, where the defendant makes her gain by 'doing the very thing' she agreed not to do, are more complex. The defining feature of these cases is not merely that the defendant made a gain by breaching a negative covenant, but that the claimant did not (it appears) suffer any loss from the breach. It is this feature, indeed, that seems to support a restitutionary remedy, for otherwise the claimant is left with no apparent remedy for a deliberate breach. But, again, in many of these cases the real culprit appears to be the limits imposed on ordinary restitutionary claims. If the claimant paid for the covenant (as will typically be the case), then, as in cases of skimped performance, the claimant should in principle be able to recover the price paid for the covenant in an ordinary action for restitution. The reason this is not possible is, again, the 'total failure of consideration' rule.

Of course, in some cases the claimant may not have paid anything for the covenant or what he paid may be much less than the defendant's gain from the breach. In such cases, an ordinary action for restitution would leave the defendant with his profits from breach. But in these circumstances it is an open question whether a gain-based remedy is still appropriate. Awarding such a remedy effectively punishes the defendant for breaking a negative covenant that (as it turned out) had no value for the claimant. It will be recalled from Chapter 8, that another name for a negative covenant is a restrictive agreement—a restraint on trade (or liberty). The employee in *Blake* was subject to a restrictive agreement. We also saw in Chapter 8 that the law has long regulated restraints on trade agreements, refusing to enforce them unless they give no more than reasonable protection to a legitimate interest of the covenantee. A covenant that prevents a contracting party from doing something that would cause no harm to the covenantee is, almost by definition, *not* protecting a legitimate interest. It is simply a bare restraint on liberty. From this perspective, enforcing a negative covenant by means of a gain-based award, in cases where breaching the covenant causes no harm, is, in effect, to enforce an unreasonable restraint on trade. *Blake* may be an exceptional case in this regard in that it involved considerations of national security, but the general point is that there are often good reasons for hesitating to give effect to a negative covenant where the covenant appears to serve no valid purpose.

An alternative suggestion is that a gain-based award of the kind made in *Blake* is justified in cases where the obligation that was breached is one the court would have been willing to enforce by means of specific performance or an injunction. From this perspective, the award in *Blake* is justified because the court clearly would have been willing to enforce the Blake's covenant not to publish by means of an injunction. The only reason such an injunction had not been sought was that Blake lived outside the jurisdiction of English courts. This suggestion has an intuitive appeal. A right to specific performance is a kind of property right and, as we have seen, the courts are generally willing to make gain-based awards in cases involving the use of another's property. This suggestion also provides a relatively simple test for determining when gain-based damages should be available: is the relevant obligation the kind that courts are generally willing to enforce through specific performance? The difficulty, however, is that the reasons for granting specific relief seem to have little to do with the reasons for awarding a gain-based remedy. The underlying reason for ordering specific relief is that the claimant has a right to performance of the obligation. This is true of every contractual obligations—every claimant has a prima facie right to performance. Of course, specific relief is not in practice always available. But the reasons that it is refused, such as that performance has a personal element or that supervision would be too difficult, appear to have little relation to the merits of a claim for restitution.

The decision in *Blake* itself seems difficult to criticize. As a matter of principle, it might have been preferable for Blake to be subjected to criminal sanctions; this was not possible on the facts. No doubt other cases will arise in which the ordinary remedies for breaches of contract are also inadequate, and in which, therefore, a gain-based remedy appears to provide a useful solution. To this extent, *Blake* is a welcome development. Nonetheless, it remains difficult to identify in advance a category of contract breaches for which gain-based remedies are, as a matter of principle, generally appropriate. Most cases that appear to fall into this category turn out, on reflection, to be cases in which the injustice arises from the fact that the usual compensatory or restitutionary awards are barred or limited by arbitrary restrictions. More generally, the task for those who support gain-based awards is not so much to explain why the defendant deserves to keep his gain, but why the claimant has a right to that gain. If the gain truly came from an external source, on what ground should the claimant—a private individual—be able to demand that it be handed over to her? Seen from this perspective, the result in *Blake* may be explicable on the ground that the claimant was not in fact a private individual.

8. CONSEQUENTIAL LOSSES AND REMOTENESS OF DAMAGE

One question that frequently enters into the analysis of a damages award in contract is whether the defendant is liable for consequential or indirect losses caused as a result of the defendant's breach. Such losses may, in one sense, be outside the scope of the anticipated contractual performance altogether, and may therefore lead to a liability in damages far exceeding the value of the contract. The simplest illustration is the case of defective goods which cause physical injury or property damage to the purchaser. Damages in such cases may run into thousands of pounds even when the inherent value of the goods may be trifling. This problem is known as remoteness of damage because some kinds of damage are treated as too remote to be attributable to the breach of contract in question.

In the law of tort the subject of remoteness of damage has been bedevilled by theories of causation, but fortunately the law of contract has largely escaped these complications, although difficult questions still arise. The traditional principle in the law of contract is that the defendant is liable for all damage that he could have 'reasonably contemplated' or 'reasonably foreseen' as a consequence of his breach of contract. This principle, usually known as the rule in *Hadley v. Baxendale*,[80] is typically divided into two subrules. First, the defendant is liable for all damage occurring in the normal course of things as a result of the breach. This is just another way of saying that he is liable for reasonably foreseeable damage, for the 'normal' is always reasonably foreseeable. The converse, however, is not true, because in particular circumstances a person may foresee the abnormal. Thus, the second rule in *Hadley v. Baxendale* states that a defendant is liable for damage occurring as a result of special or abnormal circumstances if, at the time of making the contract, he had sufficient notice of facts making the damage foreseeable.

The important case of *Victoria Laundries v. Newman Industries*[81] illustrates both branches of the rule in *Hadley v. Baxendale*. In this case the defendants

---

[80] (1854) 9 Ex 341.   [81] [1949] 2 KB 528.

had contracted to sell a large boiler to the claimant laundry company. The defendants were well aware that there was at the time an acute shortage of laundries, and that the claimants were proposing to put the boiler into use at the earliest possible moment with a view to a rapid expansion of their business. When the defendants damaged the boiler in delivering it, with consequent delay in bringing it into use, it was therefore held that they were liable for the estimated loss of profits which the claimants could have been expected to incur. On the other hand, the claimants were not entitled to damages for the loss of certain highly lucrative dyeing contracts of which the defendants were ignorant.

The rule in *Hadley v. Baxendale* is not just an arbitrary, if convenient, formula. The distinction between the normal and the abnormal—the foreseeable and the unforeseeable—runs right through the law of contract; in particular, it plays a central role (as we have seen) in the closely related areas of interpretation and frustration. Generally speaking, it is the function of insurance contracts to take care of abnormal and unforeseeable risks, while other contracts deal in normal and foreseeable risks. The price which the parties have agreed upon as representing the value of the goods or services being bought is typically calculated in the expectation of things turning out normally and not abnormally, or in accordance with the foreseeable and not the unforeseeable. For instance, the cost of freight for the carriage of goods by sea is typically calculated according to the actual cost (itself, of course, a difficult concept) plus a reasonable margin of profit. Certainly it is unlikely that any allowance would be made, for example, for the possibility that the cargo-owner might incur losses in the event that, following a delay in delivery due to a breach of contract, the warehouse through which the cargo was to have been processed was found to have burned down, and the cargo suffered rain damage while waiting on the pier.

But although there is a sound rational basis for paying due regard to the foreseeable results of a breach of contract, it would be quite wrong to think that there are not other important factors to be taken into account such as (in particular) the nature and purpose of the contract. Some contracts, for instance, may be of a risk-allocation character, and the risks allocated may be of an all-embracing kind; unforeseeable results must then fall within the risks assumed. On the other hand, there are some consequences that, while perfectly foreseeable, are clearly not within the risks assumed by either party to the contract. This is not a part of the law which can be satisfactorily solved by a search for a single verbal formula.

The courts appear to have long recognized this in cases in which the second branch of the *Hadley* test is in issue. For example, in *Kemp v. Intasun Holidays*,[82] a holiday-maker told his travel agent that he needed insurance

---

[82] [1987] 2 FTLR 234.

because he was subject to asthma. While he was on the holiday, some breaches of contract for which the defendants were responsible triggered a bad attack of asthma, and the claimant claimed additional damages for this. But the court held that the mention of asthma to the agent was merely conversational, and not part of the booking arrangement (or, as we have suggested, it did not affect the price) and so did not bring into play the second rule in *Hadley v. Baxendale*. In another case, it was suggested that notice of the special circumstances would trigger the second rule only if it could be said, taking all the circumstances into account, that the defendant had impliedly assumed responsibility for this loss, just as if the contract contained an explicit term to this effect.[83] This may be too stringent a test, but it makes clear that the underlying test is not a mechanical concept of foreseeability, but a broader notion of responsibility.

Unfortunately, in the leading decision dealing with the first branch of *Hadley*, the House of Lords interpreted the test in just such a mechanical fashion. In *The Heron II*,[84] damages were sought by a consignee of goods from a shipping company which was liable for late delivery. The question at issue was whether the shipping company was liable for losses resulting from a fall in the market price of the goods between the date when the ship should have arrived and the date when it did arrive. In this sort of case the conventional approach is not a great deal of help; such consequences may be more or less foreseeable, but it is hardly possible to pin down the requisite degree of foreseeability with mathematical precision. Yet this is just what the House of Lords seems to have tried to do; the speeches in this case betray an excessive—indeed an almost obsessive—anxiety to find a single formula which expresses the degree of foreseeability necessary. Thus phrases such as 'in the contemplation of the parties', 'a real danger', 'a serious possibility', or 'not unlikely' are bandied about in the speeches in this case as though the whole law could be reduced to a single such formula. In the result the House of Lords seems to have settled on 'not unlikely' as expressing most accurately the necessary degree of foreseeability.

With respect, it must be said that this is a very unsatisfactory decision. Foreseeability in the purely technical sense is certainly important because (as we have said) prices are fixed on the basis of a foreseeable outcome; it would therefore generally be unjust to impose liability for unforeseeable consequences. But it does not follow that it is always just to impose liability for foreseeable consequences. Whether this is just often depends on the nature or purpose of the contract and on whether the contract price was likely to have been affected by these foreseeable consequences of breach. In a contract for

---

[83] *Horne v. Midland Ry.* (1873) LR 8 CP 131 at 141.
[84] [1969] 1 AC 350. See also *H. Parsons (Livestock) v. Uttley, Ingham & Co. Ltd* [1978] QB 791.

the sale of goods, for example, the price of the goods will normally reflect the scarcity value of those goods. In the *Victoria Laundry* case the sellers were selling a boiler for laundry use at a time when laundries were in great demand; plainly this fact would have affected the price at which the boiler was sold, and it was therefore reasonable to treat the seller as liable for lost profits arising from his delay in delivering the boiler. But in *The Heron II*, there was no contract for the sale of goods: the defendants were shipowners, and the service they were selling was that of carriage of goods. Freight charges for the carriage of goods would not normally be affected by the value or scarcity of the goods being carried, as these facts do not affect supply and demand of shipping space; therefore a shipowner would not increase his freight charges to cover the additional risk of lost profits arising from fluctuations of market price in the goods which he carries. Nor does it seem desirable that he should do so, as he does not have or profess the knowledge of relevant market conditions to enable him to gauge this additional risk accurately. The decision in *The Heron II* has the result, in effect, of making the shipowner an uncompensated insurer of market prices. If the prices rise, the owner takes the benefit from a late shipment, but if they fall, the shipowner bears the cost.

A more recent decision of the House of Lords shows an appreciation of these issues, although the decision involved parallel claims in contract and tort so its significance for purely contractual claims remains uncertain. In *Banque Bruxelles S.A. v. Eagle Star*,[85] the court decided a series of cases in which the claimants lent money on the basis of the defendants' negligently prepared property valuations. The properties were overvalued and, to make matters worse, they decreased further in value after the loans were made because of a general fall in the property market. The main issue was whether the losses for which the defendants should be liable included losses arising from the general fall in prices in cases where it could be shown that the defendants would not have entered the transaction at all but for the negligent valuation. In a sense, the facts were the same as in the *Heron*. In both cases, the fall in market value of the relevant property (sugar, land) was perfectly foreseeable in the technical sense—these sorts of things happen all the time. It was also clear that the claimants would not have suffered the loss associated with the fall 'but for' the defendants' breaches of duty. But in *Banque Bruxelles* the House of Lords concluded that, despite these factors, the valuer was responsible only for an amount equal to the difference between the actual value of the properties at the time of valuation and assessed value. As Lord Hoffmann explained, it was no part of the valuer's duty to protect the defendant from the falling property values. That is a risk that is inherent in the practice of lending on security.

[85] [1997] AC 191.

The mitigation principle

In calculating the claimant's losses according to the above principles, the courts proceed on the assumption that the claimant cannot recover for losses that he could have avoided, or did avoid, by taking reasonable steps. The claimant, it is said, is expected to 'mitigate' his losses. To take a simple example, suppose a person is dismissed wrongfully from his employment where he has been earning £150 per week. His expectation rights are prima facie to the value of the wages he would have earned while serving out the notice to which he was entitled; if he was entitled to four weeks' notice, it would seem at first sight that he has lost the expectation of earning £600. But before the claimant can recover this (or indeed, any) sum as damages it must be clear that he has done his best to find alternative reasonable employment. If in fact the claimant has obtained a new job at the same (or a higher) wage, without any intervening time, then he will not have suffered any actual loss at all. If he is one week out of work while finding a new job, he has lost one week's wages and no more.

Lawyers sometimes talk of a *duty* to mitigate, but this is misleading. It is not possible to bring an action for failure to mitigate; indeed, the mitigation principle operates regardless of whether the claimant has actually mitigated her damages. The principle states that damages will be calculated *as if* the claimant has mitigated. Described in this way, the mitigation principle appears to be (merely) one aspect of the broader idea that defendants are liable only for 'reasonably foreseeable' losses. As has already been noted, it is reasonably foreseeable that events will proceed in the normal or usual fashion, and it is normal or usual for people to try to mitigate any loss they may suffer. In many legal systems, what the common law calls the mitigation principle is in fact regarded as part of the normal assessment of remoteness and causation. Indeed, the common law itself takes this approach in tort cases. For example, when calculating the losses associated with a personal injury that prevents the claimant from continuing in her present occupation, the court will proceed on the assumption that the claimant will seek alternative employment. In tort cases, this assumption is regarded as part of the broader test for determining the reasonably foreseeable extent of the claimant's losses. But the underlying idea is identical to that expressed in contract cases by the mitigation principle. This is not to say, of course, that the mitigation principle is a mechanical or statistical test of what is likely to happen. Like the (so-called) principle of reasonable foreseeability itself, the mitigation principle expresses a complex notion of responsibility.

The main practical difference between mitigation of damages in contract and in tort is that in contract cases mitigation is more often an issue. If the defendant in a contract case does not or cannot fulfil his contractual obligation, someone else usually can. In an ordinary contract of sale, if the buyer fails to pay the price of goods not yet delivered, the seller will invariably have the possibility of reselling the goods to another buyer. Similarly, where a seller fails to deliver in breach of contract, the buyer will usually have the possibility of purchasing similar goods from an alternative source. In each case, damages will be calculated on the assumption that the claimant has pursued these alternatives. The extra expenses incurred by the claimant in doing this are plainly recoverable as damages, as are any losses arising from delays, etc.—these are actual expenses incurred as a result of the breach. But in most cases this is all or nearly all the claimant can recover, because in most cases a close substitute is available.

A striking example of a breach of contract that left the claimants remediless because of the mitigation rule is provided by *The Solholt*.[86] Here sellers had contracted to sell a ship to the defendants for $5 million, delivery not later than 31 August. In fact they were late in delivering the ship, and it was only offered to the defendants on 3 September. The buyers refused to accept it and, the market-price then having risen to $5.5 million, they claimed damages of half a million dollars. Prima facie this would seem to have been a simple case of lost expectation damages, but actually the buyers recovered nothing from an admitted breach. The reason for this was that the buyers made no attempt to mitigate their loss, which they could easily have done by renegotiating a new delivery date with the sellers.

The mitigation rule sometimes gets raised in cases involving what is called the 'lost-volume' problem. In *Lazenby Garages Ltd v. Wright*[87] the defendant contracted to buy a second-hand car from the claimants, who were car dealers, but then changed his mind and refused to take delivery. The dealers resold the car (without loss) and then sued the defendant for their lost profit on the sale. It was held that there was no loss of profit at all because the same car had been resold to another buyer without a lowering of the price. This result appears to be justified by the mitigation principle, but in reality the case has little to do with mitigation. As the claimants themselves pointed out, if the defendant had taken this car, the claimants would probably have sold a different car to the second buyer, so that they would have made two lots of profit. Hence, the breach caused a loss to the claimant's total 'volume' of sales, and so to their total profit. The Court of Appeal was willing to admit this argument in the case of new cars, but rejected it in this case on the basis that a second-hand car was a unique chattel from which only one lot of profit could be made. This seems unconvincing, as very few second-hand cars are really unique in any relevant sense. It seems likely that the defendant's breach of contract did in fact cost the claimants a loss of profit.

---

[86] [1983] 1 Lloyd's Rep 605.   [87] [1976] WLR 459.

Non-pecuniary and intangible losses

Until relatively recently, it was a general principle of English law that no recovery was possible for pain and suffering, mental distress, loss of pleasure, or any other kind of non-pecuniary losses in a claim for breach of contract. Contract damages, it was said, were concerned only with financial losses.[88]

Of course, it has long been recognized that damages for physical injury (or damage to property) are recoverable in contract as in tort, and this includes also physical discomfort as, for example, where the owner of a house has to put up with having repairs done while he is in occupation as a result of a breach of contract by a seller or builder. It has also been recognized that damages for pain and suffering or mental distress are recoverable in those cases where tort and contract overlap, as with physical injury to an employee. But such cases aside, the general principle was that non-pecuniary losses were not compensable in contract.

This traditional principle was first relaxed in cases where it was said that the whole point of the contract was to protect against mental distress (as where a claimant goes to a solicitor to get an order to prevent her husband molesting her[89]) or to provide especial pleasure, such as a consumer contract with a holiday company.[90] It also became common for judges to award damages for 'inconvenience and vexation' in some other consumer contracts, such as for the purchase of a defective car which breaks down on holiday[91] or for the failure of a tradesman to make a proper job of some household repair. But more recently courts have been willing to grant damages for mental distress or loss of pleasure in cases where avoiding such distress or providing such pleasure was said to be merely one of the contract's 'important' purposes. For instance, in *Ruxley Electronics v. Forsyth*,[92] which has already been mentioned, the court awarded the claimant homeowner £2,500 representing the 'loss of amenity' that he suffered as a result of his pool being a few inches shallower than the depth specified in the contract. A second example is *Farley v. Skinner*,[93] where the claimant had purchased a house partly on the basis of a surveyor's report that stated, in response to a specific request by the claimant, that the house was unlikely to be affected by aircraft noise. As it turned out, the house was greatly affected by noise from Gatwick airport, as the defendant should have known. The claimant, who continued

---

[88] *Addis v. Gramophone Co. Ltd* [1909] AC 488; *Bliss v. SE Thames Health Authority* [1987] ICR 700; *Watts v. Morrow* [1991] 4 All ER 937.

[89] *Heywood v. Wellers* [1976] QB 446.

[90] *Jarvis v. Swan Tours Ltd* [1973] QB 233.

[91] *Jackson v. Chrysler Acceptances* [1978] RTR 474. There are scores of such cases (for relatively small sums) in the County Courts, which are noted in *Current Law* every year. But such damages are not awarded in ordinary commercial transactions: *Watts v. Morrow*, above n. 82; *Bliss v. SE Thames*, above n. 82.

[92] Above n. 53.

[93] [2002] 2 AC 732.

to live in the house rather than sell it, was awarded £10,000 by the House of Lords for the distress caused by the aircraft noise.

These are welcome developments. There seems to be no reason in principle why damages for non-pecuniary losses should not be available in contract, as in tort, in appropriate cases. These developments also make clear that the rule against awarding damages for non-pecuniary losses (insofar as it continues to exist at all) is, like the mitigation principle, part of the broader test for remoteness of damages. The justification for the rule, such as it is, is that mental distress is not a reasonably foreseeable consequence (in the complex sense of 'foreseeable' described above) of the ordinary breach of contract. Most commercial contracts are made for essentially financial reasons; the breach of a purely commercial contract, for example a loan arrangement, may well cause the victim of the breach anguish or pain, but this is not the kind of loss that is understood to occur in the ordinary course of events, nor is it the kind of risk that the debtor would normally be understood to have assumed, and so it should not be compensable on the standard ground that remote losses are not compensable. Consumer contracts are, of course, frequently entered for non-commercial reasons, but so long as the consumer's pecuniary losses are compensated he will typically be able to obtain a substitute that will itself provide equal non-pecuniary benefits. And even where no substitute is available, it is not typically foreseeable that the consumer will suffer mental distress because of not obtaining the contracted-for good or service. In practice, therefore, the traditional rule usually leads to the right result. But it would seem appropriate to recognize that, as a matter of principle, recovery for non-pecuniary losses is governed by the same principles that govern recovery for pecuniary losses. In a legal system that no longer uses juries in contract cases, there seems little risk of the courts being inundated with trivial or vexatious claims, so long as it is made clear that non-pecuniary losses are typically too remote to be recovered.

Index